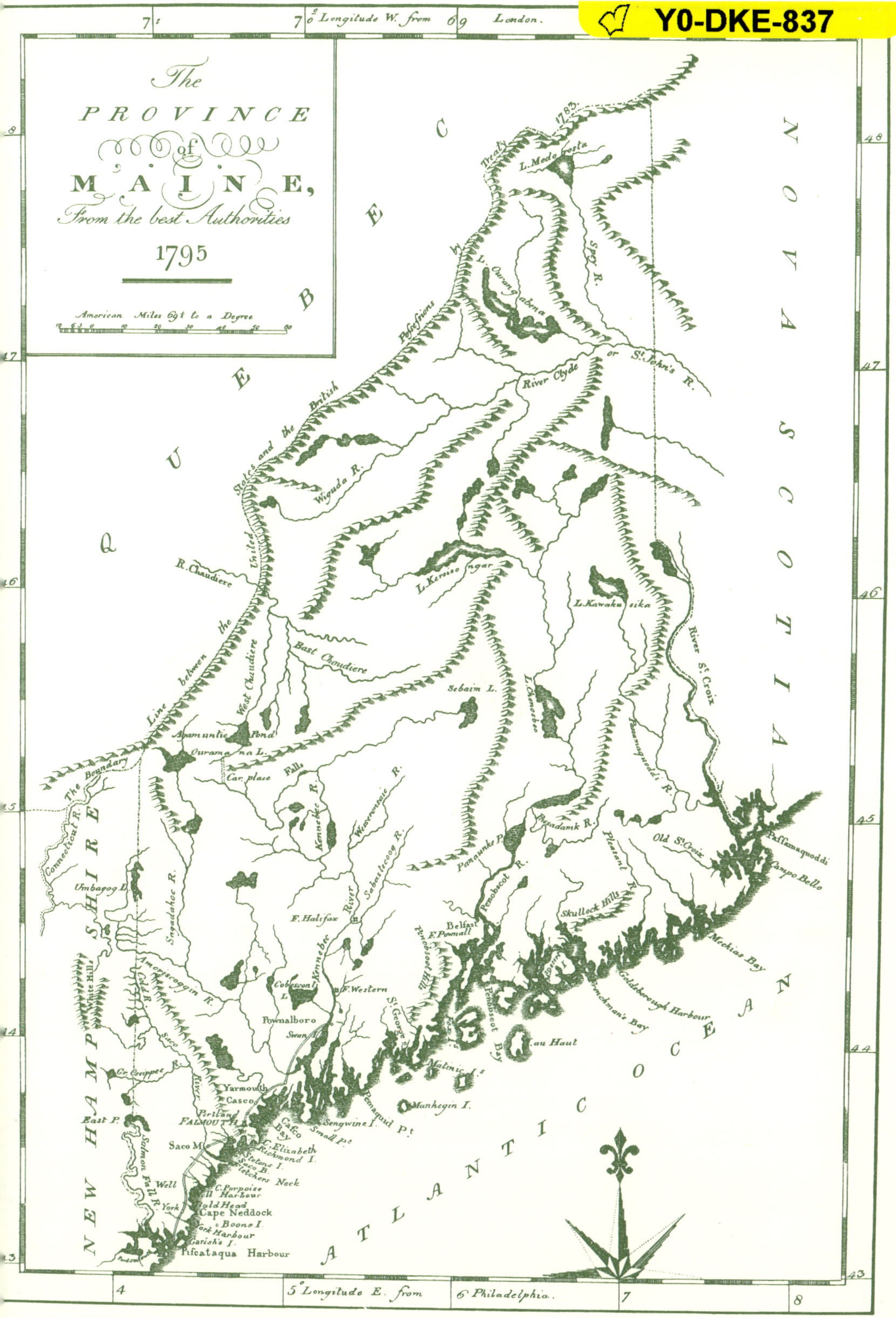
The PROVINCE of MAINE, From the best Authorities
1795
American Miles 69½ to a Degree
70 Longitude W. from 69 London.
5 Longitude E. from 6 Philadelphia.
QUEBEC
NOVA SCOTIA
ATLANTIC OCEAN
NEW HAMPSHIRE
Line between the United States and the British Possessions by Treaty 1783
The Boundary
L. Medoceosta
L. Ouvongabena
Spey R.
River Clyde or St. John's R.
Wiguda R.
R. Chaudiere
L. Kerisiongar
L. Kawakusika
East Chaudiere
West Chaudiere
Sebaim L.
L. Chemobeo
River St. Croix
Passamaquoddi R.
Amamuntic Pond
Ourama na L.
Car. place
Falls
Kennebec R.
Wesseronsaic R.
Sabastecoog R.
Connecticut R.
Umbagog L.
Sagadahoc R.
Passadamk R.
Panaunke P.
Penobscot R.
Pleasant R.
Old St. Croix
Passamaquoddi
Campo Bello
Skullock Hills
F. Halifax
River
Belfast
F. Pownall
Penobscot Hills
Mechias Bay
Goldsborough Harbour
Frenchman's Bay
Penobscot Bay
au Haut
Matinic I.s
White Hills
Amoriscoggin R.
Cold R.
Cobesconte L.
F. Western
St. George
Pownalboro
Swan I.
Saco
Gr. Ossippee R.
River
Yarmouth
Casco
Portland
FALMOUTH
Casco Bay
Manhegin I.
Pemaquid Pt.
Sengwine I.
Small Pt.
East P.
Saco M
C. Elizabeth
Richmond I.
Stetons I.
Saco B.
Fletchers Neck
Salmon Fall R.
Well
C. Porpoise
Well Harbour
York
Bald Head
Cape Neddock
Boone I.
York Harbour
Garish's I.
Piscataqua Harbour

Babcock, Samuel, p. 13-15.
Crowell, Lemuel, p. 62-63.
Mosher, Elisha Jr., 190-192,

Maine Families
in 1790

Vol 4

MAINE FAMILIES
IN 1790

Vol 4

Maine Genealogical Society
Special Publication No. 18

Edited by

Joseph Crook Anderson II
and
Lois Ware Thurston, C.G.

PICTON PRESS
CAMDEN, MAINE

The endpapers in this volume, reproducing a 1795 map of The Province of Maine, give a clear idea of how uninhabited Maine seemed at the time of the 1790 census to many Americans.

All rights reserved
Copyright © 1994 Picton Press
International Standard Book Number 0-89725-126-1
Library of Congress Catalog Card Number 88-62540

No part of this publication may be reproduced, stored in a retrieval system, or transmitted in any form or by any means whatsoever, whether electronic, mechanical, magnetic recording, or photocopying, without the prior written approval of the Copyright holder, excepting brief quotations for inclusion in book reviews.

First Printing December 1994

This book is available from:

Picton Press
PO Box 1111
Camden, ME 04843-1111

Visa/MasterCard orders: (207) 236-6565

Manufactured in the United States of America
Printed on 60# acid-free paper

PREFACE

The goal of *Maine Families in 1790* is to document all of the families living in Maine at the time of the 1790 census. This is a period of genealogical difficulty when vital records were kept inconsistently and families were moving extensively. Our intent is to establish these families through a compilation of accurate and well-documented research and to provide a basis for further research. We are not attempting to present fully-detailed and finished genealogies.

The idea for the *Maine Families in 1790* series was first proposed by Andrew B. W. MacEwen of Stockton Springs, Maine, on October 20, 1983 at a meeting of the Publications Committee of the Maine Genealogical Society. In the eleven years following, this idea has developed into the single most successful project that the Society has undertaken. So enthusiastically has it been received that several other state genealogical societies have started similar programs.

The success of this series owes itself to the skillful leadership of Ruth Gray. As Editor of the first three volumes, Ruth brought the idea to fruition and set the standard for future volumes. The project never would have gotten off the ground without her persistence, hard work, and vision. Upon publication of Volume 3, Ruth took a well-deserved retirement as Editor although she continues to assist as a county researcher. The Society is deeply grateful for all of her efforts.

As the new Editors for Volume 4, we recognize that we have a hard act to follow. To assist us, we assembled a team of county researchers who were both experienced genealogists and physically located near the records:

Penny Brown, Livermore Falls	Frankfort and Oxford Counties
Austin C. Carter, Bar Harbor	Hancock and Washington Counties
Ruth Gray, Old Town	Penobscot and Piscataquis Counties
Constance B. Hutchinson, Winslow	Somerset County
Judith H. Kelley, South Portland	Cumberland County
Barbara Ziegler, Waterville	Somerset County

These dedicated individuals spent hours helping us verify sources, add citations and often expand upon the information submitted. Their work allowed us to finish this volume on schedule while hopefully maintaining the high standard of quality that Ruth established. We extend to them our sincere appreciation.

Joseph C. Anderson II	August 1994	Lois Ware Thurston, C.G.
Dallas, Texas		Chelsea, Maine

INTRODUCTION

The first Federal census of the United States, taken in 1790, covered seventeen of the present fifty states. Each head-of-household was listed by name followed by the number of persons in the household broken down into five categories:

1. The number of free white males of 16 years and upwards including the head-of-household, if male
2. The number of free white males under 16 years
3. The number of free white females including the head-of-household, if female
4. The number of all other free persons
5. The number of slaves

Each family is enumerated under the county and town in Maine in which they lived.

Maine was still a part of Massachusetts in 1790 and consisted of only five counties. It was the only area that was not a state to have a separate census. The non-Indian population was about 96,540 grouped into just over 17,000 households. *Maine Families in 1790*, Volumes 1 through 4, contains sketches on over 1,425 families, or more than 8% of all families in Maine at that time. Considering that these sketches often include not only the nuclear family under discussion but also the head-of household's parents, his spouse's parents, the children's spouses, and the children's spouses' parents, it becomes evident that a much higher percentage of the census population is represented in these volumes—perhaps as high as 30–40% of all individuals in Maine in 1790.

Each family is first listed as it appears in the 1908 printed edition of the 1790 census. For example:

> McCollistor, Richard   32b   1 - 1 - 3 - 0 - 0
> Balltown Town, Lincoln County

This indicates that Richard McAllister is enumerated on page 32, in the second column. His household consisted of 1 white male aged 16 years and upwards, 1 white male aged under 16 years, and 3 white females. There were no other free persons and no slaves. The census taker spelled his name McCollistor. He lived in Balltown, Lincoln County, which is presently either Jefferson or Whitefield. The current names of the towns in 1790 can be found under "Towns of the 1790 Census and their Current Names" which follows beginning on page xi. Please note that three town names were printed incorrectly—Bristol, Nobleborough, and Waldoborough—and these are discussed at the end of the list.

INTRODUCTION

Vital records were not always recorded in the town in which the event took place. In cases where the event and the recording of the event occurred in the same town, the citation (VR) is used. For example:

> m Falmouth 28 Mar 1792 Samuel Allen (VR)

This indicates the marriage, which took place at Falmouth, was also recorded in the Falmouth vital records. In cases where the event occurred in one town, but was recorded in another, the citation includes the town that recorded the information. For example:

> b Taunton MA 9 Jan 1770 (Turner VR)

This indicates that the birth was recorded in the Turner vital records although the place of birth was Taunton, Massachusetts.

All place names are in Maine unless specifically stated otherwise. Readers will notice a scarcity of punctuation marks after dates, abbreviations and sentences. This was done intentionally to make the reading less confusing.

A family sketch may contain references to other families in this same volume or in other volumes. For example, in the Nathaniel Pendleton family, child iii., Cynthia, married Zenas Drinkwater, followed by:

> [see ZENAS DRINKWATER family, *Maine Families*, 3:69]

This indicates that further information will be found in the Zenas Drinkwater family in Volume 3 on page 69.

An Addendum at the back of this book provides corrections to families included in Volumes 1, 2 and 3. Unlike the Addendum sections in Volumes 2 and 3, we made the decision this time to include only corrections. While it is nice to have additional information on these families, additions take up precious room and we felt the space would be better utilized with new families.

We welcome submissions of new families for future volumes and these may be mailed to the address shown below. As more volumes are published, the usefulness of this project for Maine researchers will grow exponentially.

Please send submissions of new families and corrections to:

> Maine Genealogical Society
> P.O. Box 221,
> Farmington, ME 04938

SURNAMES OF HEADS OF HOUSEHOLD
Included in *Maine Families in 1790*, Volume 4

ABBOTT	DORMAN	LEIGH
ALLEN	FARNHAM	LOWELL
ANDREWS	FERNALD	LUCE
ARCHER	FOLLETT	McALLISTER
BABCOCK	GAGE	McCLUER
BACON	GAHAN	MADDOCKS
BANKS	GILLEY	MARROW
BARKER	GINN	MARTIN
BARTLETT	GOODRIDGE	MAXWELL
BENNETT	GOODWIN	MELCHER
BICKFORD	GRANT	MERRIAM
BLAKE	GRAY	MESERVE
BOND	GULLIFER	MILDRAM
BRACKETT	HALL	MILLBANKS
BRADBURY	HAMBLEN	MOODY
BRAGDON	HAMILTON	MOSHER
BROCK	HANSCOM	MURCH
BROOKS	HARRIMAN	NASH
BUFFUM	HEARL	NASON
BUTLER	HEATH	NEAL
CAIN	HIGGINS	NOBLE
CANNELL	HODSDON	NYE
CARLE	HOPKINS	PALMER
CLAY	HOWARD	PARSONS
CLEMENTS	HUNTER	PATTEE
CLOUGH	JELLERSON	PEABODY
COBB	JEPSON	PEASE
COLBURN	JONES	PENDLETON
COLE	JORDAN	PETERSON
COLLINS	JUDKINS	PETTY
CORSON	KEEN	PHILBRICK
CROWELL	KILGORE	PHINNEY
DAGGETT	KILPATRICK	PHIPPS
DAY	KING	PIKE
DECKER	KNIGHT	PITTS
DENNETT	LANE	POTTER
DENNISON	LAPLAIN	PRESCOTT
DOLE	LEEMAN	PULCIFER

SURNAME LIST

RAND	SNOW	TILTON
RANDALL	SNOWMAN	TOMPSON
RANKINS	SOMES	WARDWELL
RICHARDSON	SPURLING	WARREN
ROBBINS	STEVENS	WATSON
RUSSELL	STILLMAN	WEARE
SABINE	STONE	WHARFF
SANBORN	STURTEVANT	WHITMORE
SANDS	SWAN	WHITTIER
SEGAR	TALPEY	WILLIAMS
SIMPSON	THOMAS	YEATON
SKINNER	THOMPSON	YOUNG
SKOLFIELD	THORN	
SMALL	TIBBETTS	

SHORT TITLE CITATIONS

BHM
Bangor Historical Magazine [volume and page numbers cited refer to those of the original magazine, not to the repaginated 4-volume reprint published by the Maine Genealogical Society and Picton Press in 1993.]

DAR Misc Rec
Daughters of the American Revolution, Miscellaneous Records of Maine. Numerous volumes of collected records, at MSL, MHS and other repositories

Dodge's *Bristol*
Christine Huston Dodge, *Vital Records of Old Bristol and Nobleboro in the County of Lincoln, Maine* (1951), 2 volumes

Eaton's *Thomaston*
Cyrus Eaton, *History of Thomaston, Rockland, and South Thomaston, Maine* (1865), 2 volumes

Eaton's *Warren*
Cyrus Eaton, *Annals of the Town of Warren, Maine* (1877), 2 volumes

Fisher's *Soldiers*
Carleton B. and Sue G. Fisher, *Soldiers, Sailors, and Patriots of the Revolutionary War Maine* (1982)

GDMNH
Sibyl Noyes, Charles Thornton Libby and Walter G. Davis, *Genealogical Dictionary of Maine and New Hampshire* (1928-1939)

Greene's *Boothbay*
Francis B. Greene, *History of Boothbay, Southport & Boothbay Harbor* (1906)

SHORT TITLE CITATIONS

IGI LDS
  International Genealogical Index, Church of Jesus Christ of Latter-day Saints
McLellan's *Gorham*
  Hugh D. McLellan, *A History of Gorham, Maine* (1903)
Maine Families
  Maine Families in 1790, Maine Genealogical Society, 4 volumes
MD
  Mayflower Descendant
MHGR
  Maine Historical and Genealogical Recorder
MHS
  Maine Historical Society
MOCA
  Maine Old Cemetery Association
MSA
  Maine State Archives
MSL
  Maine State Library
MS&S
  Massachusetts Soldiers and Sailors of the Revolutionary War (1896-1908), 17 volumes
NEHGR
  New England Historical and Genealogical Register
NEHGS
  New England Historic Genealogical Society
NHGR
  New Hampshire Genealogical Record
TAG
  The American Genealogist
YCGSJ
  York County Genealogical Society Journal

Citations to probate records may include references to the original papers, cited by file number, or to the probate volumes into which the clerks copied selected probate records, cited by volume and page number. Deeds are cited by volume and page number of the county deed books. For example:

York Co Probate #9023 (refers to the original papers in file #9023, York Co Courthouse)
Lin Co Probate 1:76 (refers to probate vol. 1, p. 76, Lin Co Courthouse)
Cum Co deeds 13:242 (refers to deed vol. 13, p. 242, Cum Co Courthouse)

ABBREVIATIONS

abt	about	Plt	Plantation
adm	administration/administrator/administratrix	poss	possibly
		prob	probably
ae	age	pub	publication/published
aft	after	rec	record/recorded
appt	appointed	repr	reprint/reprinted
b	born	res	resident/resided
Bapt	Baptist	Rev	Revolutionary War
bef	before	s/b	should be
betw	between	Sgt	Sergeant
bp	baptized	sic	exactly as original
bro	brother	sis	sister
bur	buried	TR	town record
c	circa/about	TS	typescript
Capt	Captain	Twsp	township
cem	cemetery	unk	unknown
cert	certification	unm	unmarried
Co	county	USC	U.S. census
Col	Colonel	VR	vital record
Coll	Collection(s)	y m d	year, month, day
Cong	Congregational	wid	widow
d	died	**	used for those families believed to be living in Maine in 1790, but not found in the census
dau	daughter		
DAR	Daughters of the American Revolution		
dec	deceased		
Ed	Editor/edition/edited		
ff	following		

MAINE COUNTIES CITED

Gen	General
g.s.	gravestone
ibid.	same as before
info	information
Lieut	Lieutenant
m	married/marriage
m int	marriage intentions
MS	manuscript
n.d.	no date
obit	obituary
op. cit.	previously cited

Cum Co	Cumberland County
Han Co	Hancock County
Ken Co	Kennebec County
Lin Co	Lincoln County
Oxf Co	Oxford County
Pen Co	Penobscot County
Pisc Co	Piscataquis County
Som Co	Somerset County
Wal Co	Waldo County
Wash Co	Washington County
York Co	York County

TOWNS OF THE 1790 CENSUS AND THEIR CURRENT NAMES
Listed by Counties

CUMBERLAND COUNTY

Bakerstown Plantation
   Auburn, Mechanic Falls, Minot, Poland
Bridgton
   Bridgton, part of Naples, part of Harrison
Brunswick
Bucktown Plantation
   Buckfield
Butterfield Plantation
   Sumner
Cape Elizabeth
   Cape Elizabeth, South Portland
Durham
Falmouth
   Falmouth, Falmouth Foreside, Westbrook
Flintstown Plantation
   Baldwin, Sebago
Freeport
   Freeport, Pownal
Gorham and Scarborough
Gray
Harpswell
   Harpswell & offshore islands
New Gloucester
North Yarmouth
   Yarmouth, Cumberland
Otisfield
   Otisfield, part of Naples, part of Harrison
Plantation No. 4
   Paris
Portland
Raymondtown Plantation
   Raymond, Casco, part of Naples
Rusfield Gore (Rustfield)
   part of Norway
Scarborough
Shepardsfield Plantation
   Hebron, Oxford
Standish
Turner
Waterford Plantation
   Waterford
Windham

HANCOCK COUNTY

Barrettstown
   Appleton, Hope
Belfast
   Belfast, part of Searsport
Bluehill (Blue Hill)
Camden
   Camden, Rockport
Canaan
   Lincolnville
Conduskeeg Plantation (Kenduskeag)
   Bangor, Hampden, Hermon, Veazie, Old Town, Orono, Milford, Argyle
Deer Isle
   Deer Isle, Stonington
Ducktrap
   Lincolnville, Northport
Eastern River Township No. 2
   Orland
Eddy Township
   Eddington, Bradley
Frankfort
   Frankfort, Prospect, Stockton, part of Hampden, Searsport, Winterport

TOWNS OF THE 1790 CENSUS

Hancock County, Cont'd
Gouldsborough
   Gouldsboro, Corea, Winter Harbor, Prospect Harbor area
Isleborough (Islesboro)
Mount Desert
   towns on Mt. Desert Island
Orphan Island
   Verona
Orrington
   Orrington, Brewer, Holden
Penobscot
   Penobscot, Castine, part of Brooksville
Sedgwick
   Sedgwick, Brooklin, part of Brooksville
Small Islands not belonging to any town
   Islands out of Penobscot Bay
Sullivan
   Sullivan, Sorrento, Franklin
Trenton (including Township No. 1, East side of Union River)
   Trenton, Lamoine, parts of Hancock and Ellsworth
Township No. 1 (Bucks)
   Bucksport
Township No. 6 (west side of Union River)
   Surry, part of Ellsworth
Vinalhaven
   Vinalhaven, North Haven

LINCOLN COUNTY

Balltown
   Jefferson, Whitefield
Bath
   Bath, West Bath
Boothbay
   Boothbay, Southport, Boothbay Harbor
Bowdoin
   Bowdoin, Lisbon
Bowdoinham
Bristol* (see comment at end of this list)
   Bristol, Bremen, New Harbor
Canaan
   Canaan, Skowhegan
Carratunk
   Bingham, Solon
Carrs Plantation, or Unity
   New Sharon
Chester
   Chesterville
Cushing
   Cushing, St. George
Edgecomb
   Edgecomb, Westport
Fairfield
Georgetown
   Arrowsic, Georgetown, part of Bath, Woolwich, Phippsburg
Great Pond Plantation
   Palermo
Greene
Hallowell
   Hallowell, Augusta, Chelsea, Manchester
Hancock
   Clinton, Benton
Hunts Meadow
   part of Whitefield
Jones Plantation
   China
Lewistown & the Gore Adjoining
   Lewiston
Little River
   Part of Lisbon

TOWNS OF THE 1790 CENSUS

Lincoln County, Cont'd
Littleborough Plantation
    Leeds
Livermore, east side Androscoggin River
    Livermore
Meduncook
    Friendship
New Castle (Newcastle)
New Sandwich
    Wayne
Nobleborough* (see comment at end of this list)
Norridgewock
Norridgewock, settlement east of
Pittston
    Gardiner, West Gardiner, Pittston, Randolph
Pownalborough
    Alna, Dresden, Wiscasset
Prescotts & Whitchers Plantation
    Belgrade
Rockmeeko, east side of river
    Jay
Sandy River, First Township
    Farmington, Wilton
Sandy River, from its mouth to Carrs Plantation
    Starks
Sandy River, Middle Township
    Strong
Sandy River, Upper Township
    Avon
Seven Mile Brook
    Anson, North Anson
Smithtown Plantation
    Litchfield
Starling Plantation
    Fayette

Thomaston
    Thomaston, South Thomaston, Rockland
Titcomb
    Embden
Topsham
Twenty-Five Mile Pond
    Unity, Burnham
Union
Vassalborough
    Vassalborough, Sidney
Waldoborough* (see comment at end of this list)
Wales Plantation
    Wales, Monmouth
Warren
Washington
    Belgrade, Mount Vernon
Winslow, with its adjacents
    Oakland, Waterville, Winslow
Winthrop
    Readfield, Winthrop
Woolwich
Between Norridgewock and Seven Mile Brook
    Madison

WASHINGTON COUNTY

Bucks Harbor Neck
Machias
Plantations East of Machias
    #1   Perry
    #2   Dennysville, Pembroke
    #4   Robbinston
    #5   Calais
    #8   Eastport, Lubec
    #9   Trescott
    #10   Edmunds
    #11   Cutler
    #12   Whiting
    #13   Marion

TOWNS OF THE 1790 CENSUS

Washington County, Cont'd
Plantations West of Machias
- #4   Steuben
- #5   Harrington, Milbridge
- #6   Addison
- #11   Cherryfield
- #12   Columbia
- #13   Columbia Falls
- #22   Jonesboro, Jonesport, Beals, Roque Bluffs

YORK COUNTY

Arundel
    Arundel, Kennebunkport
Berwick
    Berwick, South Berwick and North Berwick
Biddeford
    Biddeford, Saco
Brownfield Township
Brownfield Township—in the gore Adjoining
    East Brownfield
Buxton
Coxhall
    Lyman
Francisborough Plantation
    Cornish
Fryeburgh
Hiram
Kittery
    Kittery, Eliot
Lebanon
Limerick
Little Falls
    Dayton, Hollis
Little Ossipee
    Limington
New Penacook
    Rumford

Parsonsfield
Pepperellborough
    Saco, Old Orchard Beach
Porterfield
    Porter
Sanford
    Sanford, Alfred
Shapleigh
    Shapleigh, Acton
Sudbury-Canada
    Bethel, Hanover
Sudbury-Canada, settlements adjoining
    Newry
Suncook
    Lovell
Washington Plantation
    Newfield
Waterborough
Waterford
Wells
York

---

* The 1908 census publication, upon which the above list is based, transposed three towns in Lincoln County as follows:

"Bristol" should be Nobleborough
"Nobleborough" should be Waldoborough
"Waldoborough" should be Bristol

When working with the published census, these printed town names should be interchanged.

(For a more detailed discussion, see NEHGR 86 [1932]:132.)

Abbot, Benj[a]   55c   2 - 4 - 2 - 0 - 0
Berwick Town, York County

BENJAMIN ABBOTT, bp Berwick 1st Church 26 Dec 1742 son of Thomas & Mary (Legro) Abbott (NEHGR, 82 [1928]:214; Joseph C. Anderson II, "The Family of Thomas and Mery (Legro) Abbott of Berwick, Maine," YCGSJ, 9 [1994]:2:12): prob d Berwick betw 1790 & 1800 (USC): m Berwick 24 Dec 1769 SARAH CHADWICK (John E. Frost & Joseph C. Anderson II, *Vital Records of Berwick, South Berwick and North Berwick, Maine to the Year 1892* [1993], hereafter VR, p. 194), b 12 Dec 1743 dau of William & Abra (Wentworth) Chadwick of Somersworth NH ("The Diary of Master Joseph Tate of Somersworth, N.H.," NEHGR, 74 [1920]:38; John Wentworth, *The Wentworth Genealogy* [1878], 1:282), listed as a widow when she d Berwick 20 Jun 1808 (VR, p. 287). Benjamin was a Rev War soldier and minuteman and served in Capt. Pray's Company (Fisher's *Soldiers*, p. 2). He was on the 1770 Berwick "whole town" list and on the 1773 Berwick tax list for the north parish of town (Wilbur D. Spencer, "Statistics of Berwick, Maine" [TS, 1943, MSA], pp. 19, 26). In 1771, he lived next to his father Thomas Abbott, and brothers Stephen and Thomas Jr. (Bettye H. Pruitt, *The Massachusetts Tax Valuation List of 1771* [1978], p. 746). Neither Benjamin nor Sarah were enumerated as heads of household in the 1800 USC, however their son Edmund's household that year included a woman ae over 45y who was prob Sarah. A deed executed 2 Aug 1810 appears to name all of the heirs of Thomas and Mary (Legro) Abbott alive at that time (York Co deeds 83:101). Among Benjamin's children, only his sons Edmund, Ebenezer and Legro were mentioned suggesting that the other children were deceased.

Children: birth first 4 rec by Master Tate, NEHGR, 74 [1920]:195, last 4 baptized together at the Berwick 1st Church, NEHGR, 82 [1928]:506
  i Esther, b Sunday 15 Jul 1770: d 14 Mar 1771 ("Master Tate," NEHGR, 74 [1920]:195)
  ii Edmund, b Tuesday 23 Aug 1771 and bp Berwick 1st Church 26 Jan 1772 (NEHGR, 82 [1928]:502): d of consumption So. Berwick 14 Jul 1821 (VR, p. 542): m Berwick 28 Nov 1799 Olive Hearl (VR, p. 140), b c1777 dau of John & Martha (Huntress) Hearl of South Berwick (will of John Hearl which names his dau Olive Abbott, York Co Probate #9023), d of "fever" So. Berwick 5 May 1842 ae 65y (VR, p. 550; g.s., Portland St. cem)
  iii Benjamin, b Friday 13 Aug 1773 and bp Berwick 1st Church 14 Nov 1773 (NEHGR, 82 [1928]:503): d bef 18 Mar 1805 when his bro Legro was appt adm of his est (York Co Probate #7). He was described as a joiner and was prob unm
  iv daughter, b 5 May 1778. [Nothing further has been learned about this dau, although it is poss she was the dau Sarah, below, who was bp with 3 siblings in 1791]

v Ebenezer, bp with siblings 20 Feb 1791: d Berwick 11 Jul 1813 (VR, p. 291): m Berwick 2nd Church 29 Apr 1810 Dorcas Spencer (NEHGR, 74 [1920]: 263), b c1779, d So. Berwick 27 Dec 1816 ae 38y (VR, p. 540). The adm of Ebenezer's estate was granted on 14 Feb 1814 to Dudley Hubbard of Berwick (York Co Probate #17), the same person who also acted as the executor for the will of Ebenezer's brother, Legro Abbott. Legro's will left a portion of his personal estate to "my sister Dorcas Abbott wife of my late brother Ebenezer Abbott...for the purpose of supporting her child" (ibid.)

vi Sarah, bp with siblings 20 Feb 1791: prob d bef 1810 (York Co deeds 83:101)

vii Legro, bp with siblings 20 Feb 1791: d Berwick 2 Nov 1813 (VR, p. 292): unm. The will of Legro Abbott, cabinetmaker, dated the day he died, mentioned among others his brother Edmund and his late brother Ebenezer's child (York Co Probate #40)

viii Ichabod, bp with siblings 20 Feb 1791: prob d bef 1810 (York Co deeds 83:101)

Joseph C. Anderson II, 5337 Del Roy Drive, Dallas, TX 75229

Abbot, Dan[l]   56a   1 - 2 - 2 - 0 - 0
Berwick Town, York County

DANIEL ABBOTT, b Berwick 11 Nov 1748 (Rev War pension #W1201) and bp Berwick 1st Church 14 May 1749 son of Aaron & Anna (____) Abbott of Berwick (NEHGR, 82 [1928]:317): d 4 Dec 1834 ae 86y (pension, op. cit.; g.s., Portland St. cem, So. Berwick): m (1) cert Berwick 9 Nov 1782 ABIGAIL LORD (John E. Frost & Joseph C. Anderson II, *Vital Records of Berwick, South Berwick and North Berwick, Maine to the Year 1892* [1993], hereafter VR, p. 20). Her parentage has not been found. She d prior to Nov 1796 when Daniel remarried. [While there were several Abigail Lords baptized at Berwick in the late 1740s, one was bp 14 Feb 1747/8 dau of Aaron Lord (NEHGR, 82 [1928]:314). This Aaron Lord also had a son Ichabod Lord bp in 1750 (ibid., 82:319). In 1790, Daniel Abbott lived 3 households away from an Ichabod Lord]. Daniel m (2) Berwick 3 Nov 1796 HANNAH (HUBBARD) HODSDON (VR, p. 139) dau of Philip & Hannah (____) Hubbard (will of Philip Hubbard naming his dau Hannah Hodsdon, York Co Probate #9868) and wid of Daniel Hodsdon Jr. who had d prior to 13 Oct 1790 when the adm of his estate was granted to his wid Hannah Hodsdon of Berwick with her future husband Daniel Abbott acting as surety (York Co Probate #9539). She was bp Berwick 1st Church 1 Jan 1748/9 (omitted in NEHGR published church recs, but verified from microfilm at MHS) and d bef 1814 when Daniel remarried again. Daniel m (3) 10 Feb 1814 ELIZABETH/BETSEY (HERBERT) (BANKS) WARTMAN (pension, op. cit.) [m cert Berwick 29 Jan 1814 (VR, p. 67)], prob dau of Henry & Catherine (Stevens) Herbert of Kittery (see below). She had m (1) Kittery 21 Jul 1801 David Banks of Kittery (VR) and (2) Kittery 17 Jul 1806 Frederick Wartman (VR). She was b c1782 and d 13 Feb 1857 ae 75y (g.s., Portland St. cem, So. Berwick). Betsey's proposed parentage is based on her and Daniel's association with Catherine Herbert. Catherine Herbert, described on her g.s. as the wife of Henry Herbert, is buried in the Portland St. cemetery in So. Berwick next to Daniel and Betsey. On 18 Jun 1821, Daniel Abbott, Betsey Abbott in her right, and Catherine Herbert sold land in Kittery with a dwelling house to Charles Stimson of Kittery (York Co deeds 107:88). Catherine, also witnessed the will of Daniel Abbott. Daniel was listed at Berwick in 1771 living near his bro Aaron and several cousins (Bettye Hobbs Pruitt, *The Massachusetts Tax Valuation List of 1771* [1978], p. 746). The household next to him in 1790 was headed by "Anney Abbott," perhaps his mother. On 4 Jul 1820, Daniel ae 71y was living with his wife Betsey ae 39y and their dau Abigail ae 4y (pension, op. cit.). Both Daniel and Elizabeth left wills. Daniel's will, dated 2 Aug 1826, mentioned his wife Betsey, his son Edmund and his dau Nabby [i.e. Abigail] (York Co Probate #14). Elizabeth's will, dated 13 Sep 1856, mentioned a dau Eliza Ann Wadleigh (by her 1st husband David Banks) and her dau Abigail L. Mason wife of Albert J. Mason (this dau by Daniel Abbott) (York Co Probate #21).

Children, perhaps others who d young: will of Daniel Abbott, op. cit.
By 1st wife Abigail Lord
  i   Edmund, date of birth unknown. This Edmund apparently did not live at Berwick. [One Edmund Abbott was enumerated at Frankfort in Wal Co in the censuses from 1820 through 1850]
By 3rd wife Elizabeth (Herbert) (Banks) Wartman
  ii Abigail Lord, b c1815-16: d 3 Feb 1823 ae 8y (g.s., Portland St. cem, So. Berwick)
  iii Abigail Lord, m So. Berwick 9 May 1844 Albert J. Mason of So. Berwick (VR, p. 435) who was b 12 Apr 1823 (g.s., Portland St. cem, South Berwick) and d 6 Jul 1891 (ibid.)

Joseph C. Anderson II, 5337 Del Roy Drive, Dallas, TX 75229

Abbott, John   68b   1 - 0 - 1 - 0 - 0
   Sudbury-Canada Town [now Bethel], York County

JOHN ABBOTT 4th, b Andover MA Feb 1718/9 son of John & Hannah (Chubb) Abbott (Maj. Lemuel Abijah Abbott, *Descendants of George Abbott of Rowley,*

Massachusetts [1906]), hereafter *George Abbott*, p. 911): d Andover ME 1803 ae 85y (ibid., p. 914): m Andover MA 17 Jun 1746 HANNAH FARNUM (VR), prob the Hannah b Andover MA 5 Jan 1724/5 dau of Jonathan & Elizabeth (Barker) Farnum (VR), d Andover ME 6 Dec 1808 aged abt 84y (*George Abbott*, p. 914). John was a yeoman and lived at Andover MA until late in life, when he moved to Andover ME (ibid.).

Children: births VR Andover MA
  i Jonathan, b 12 Apr 1748 [note *George Abbott*, p. 915, gives 12 Apr 1747]: d Andover ME 26 Jun 1833 ae 86y (*George Abbott*, p. 919): m Andover MA 10 Nov 1768 Ruth Bragg (VR), b Andover MA 26 Jun 1748 dau of Thomas & Dorothy (Ingalls) Bragg (VR), d Andover ME 25 Jan 1823 (*George Abbott*, p. 919). He was a yeoman and lived in E. Andover ME (ibid.)
  ii Phillip, b 11 Oct 1749: d Andover ME 4 May 1840 ae 90y (*George Abbott*, p. 922): m Andover MA 20 Nov 1771 Elizabeth Frye (VR), b Andover MA 14 Jun 1751 dau of Timothy & Elizabeth (Holton) Frye (VR), d Andover ME 11 Sep 1834 ae 84y (*George Abbott*, p. 922). They moved to E. Andover ME about 1800; he was a cooper and yeoman (ibid.)
  iii Hannah, b 29 Aug 1751: d Andover MA 19 Mar 1785 in her 34th year (VR): m Andover MA 29 Oct 1773 John Johnson Jr. (VR), b Andover MA 28 Jul 1748 son of John & Lydia (Osgood) Johnson (VR)
  iv Susannah, b 20 Dec 1753: m Andover MA 14 Nov 1771 Daniel Stevens Jr. (VR), b Andover MA 28 Mar 1751 son of Daniel & Hannah (Barker) Stevens (VR)
  v Elizabeth/Betsey, b 9 Nov 1758: m Andover MA 20 Sep 1781 Peter Carleton Jr. (VR), b Andover MA 24 Apr 1757 son of Peter & Elizabeth (_____) Carleton (VR)
  vi John Jr. (but called 5th in Andover MA recs), b 24 Jan 1769: d Andover ME 7 Jan 1833 ae abt 64y (*George Abbott*, p. 923): m Andover MA 29 May 1788 Ruth Lovejoy (VR), b c1768, d Andover ME 18 Apr 1834 ae 66y (*George Abbott*, p. 923)

Warren D. Stearns, P.O. Box 35, Hanover, ME 04237

Abbot, Joshua   56a   1 - 0 - 3 - 0 - 0
    Berwick Town, York County

JOSHUA ABBOTT, b prob Berwick aft 1706 (ae under 14y on 19 Apr 1720, guardianship, York Co Probate #46, 3:46) and bef Jan 1716 (when his father remarried) son of John & Abigail (Nason) Abbott: d betw 14 Jan 1795 and 18

Jan 1796 (dates his will was written/probated, York Co Probate #38): m MARY/MOLLY ____ who may have been a Stimpson (see below) and who was not named in Joshua's 1795 will. In Jul 1735, Patience Holmes of Berwick accused Joshua Abbot of fathering her bastard child "lately born" (YCGSJ, 3:4 [1988]:63). Joshua lived at Berwick and appears on the various town lists made during his lifetime. On 22 Nov 1741, Joshua and Mary, his wife, owned the covenant at the Berwick church and he was baptized (NEHGR, 82 [1928]:211). They remained church members in good standing for many years afterward, as all of their later children were baptized there. In his will, Joshua described himself as a bricklayer. He mentioned his son Joshua Jr., his son Theophilus, his dau Mary Abbott, the heirs of his dau Phebe Abbot, his dau Sarah Spencer, his dau Mehitable Goodwin, and his dau Betsey Abbot to whom he left all of his farm, buildings and lands.

[Joshua's association with the Stimpson family leads to the conclusion that his wife was the Mary Stimpson bp at Berwick with siblings 22 Apr 1725 (but prob b several years earlier) dau of Jonathan & Abigail (____) Stimpson (NEHGR, 82 [1928]:86). In 1769, the adm of the estate of Abigail Stimpson, late of Berwick, widow, was granted to Joshua Abbott, bricklayer (York Co Probate 12:59). In 1770, Theophilus Abbott, Joshua's son, was a grantee from Abigail Stimpson's estate (York Co deeds 41:233). Finally, Moses Abbott, Joshua's brother, had a wife named Christian whom he married by 1735 (NEHGR, 82 [1928]:97; York Co deeds 32:85). One Christian Stimpson, singlewoman, owned the covenant at the Berwick church on 14 Dec 1727 (NEHGR 82 [1928]:88). No other candidate for Moses's wife has been found, other than this Christian Stimpson. If she were his wife, then it would seem that the two brothers prob married two sisters.]

Child by Patience Holmes
- i child, b near Jul 1735 (YCGSJ, op. cit.) and bp by Patience at the Berwick 1st Church 3 Feb 1736/7, name and sex not given (NEHGR, 82 [1928]: 206)

Children by his wife Mary/Molly [Stimpson?], bp at the Berwick 1st Church: NEHGR 82 [1928]:209, 213, 215, 315, 318, 324, 329
- ii Amy, bp "at the point of death on ye grandmother's account" 4 Mar 1739/40. [Since Joshua's mother was dead at this time, the grandmother in this case can only be Mary's mother—presumably Abigail Stimpson who was alive and a covenanted member of the Berwick church]
- iii Joshua Jr., bp 17 Oct 1742. As a head-of-household at Berwick in 1790 with 2-2-3-0-0, it seems likely he had a family but none of the members have been identified unless his wife was Mary, wife of Joshua Abbot, who d Berwick 8 Jul 1821 (John E. Frost & Joseph C. Anderson II, *Vital Records of Berwick, South Berwick and North Berwick, Maine to the Year*

1892 [1993], hereafter VR, p. 295). On 3 Jul 1792, Joshua was found guilty of murdering his neighbor Moses Gubtail and the next day was condemned to die, but he received a pardon 2 months later ("Diary of Jeremiah Weare," NEHGR, 55 [1901]:57, 297). On 22 Dec 1794, the selectmen of Berwick assigned him a guardian ruling that he was non compos mentis and "was most of the time strolling the streets from place to place" (York Co Probate 17:10). Joshua is not found in either the 1800 or 1810 USC as a head of household

iv Jeremiah, bp 17 Oct 1742: not named in his father's will

v Mehetable, bp 8 Jan 1743/4: prob d young

vi Theophilus, bp 8 May 1748: m cert Berwick 5 Aug 1776 Mary Wood (VR, p. 13). He was prob the man at Berwick in 1790 and 1800 and at Newfield in 1810, 1820 and 1830 (USC)

vii Phebe, bp 4 Mar 1749/50: d bef 10 Dec 1785 when her husband filed intentions to remarry: m Berwick 29 Apr 1772 Amos Abbot (VR, p. 115), b c1746, d Berwick 14 Feb 1812 ae 66y (VR, p. 290). He m (2) Berwick 21 Mar 1786 Keziah Bragdon (VR, p. 125)

viii Mehitable/Hitty, bp 11 Aug 1754: m cert Berwick 15 Jan 1778 Thomas Goodwin (VR), bp Berwick 2 May 1756 son of Daniel & Martha (Pierce) Goodwin (John H. Goodwin, *Daniel Goodwin of Ancient Kittery, Maine and His Descendants* [1985], p. 48)

ix Mary/Molly, bp 14 Sep 1759: alive Feb 1819 when named in her husband's will: m Berwick 27 Jan 1780 her cousin Isaac Abbott (VR, p. 123) son of Samuel & Elizabeth (Brackett) Abbott (division of Samuel Abbott's estate, York Co Probate #53, 14:9) who d betw Feb and Nov 1819 (dates his will was written/probated, York Co Probate #27)

x Sarah, bp 14 Sep 1759: d Berwick 5 Jan 1820 (VR, p. 294): m Berwick 24 Oct 1775 Freethy Spencer (VR, p. 120), bp Berwick 15 Apr 1753 son of Freethy & Mary (_____) Spencer (NEHGR, 82 [1928]:322), d Berwick 26 Jun 1821 (VR, p. 295)

xi Elizabeth/Betty/Betsey, bp 14 Sep 1759. She was the principal heir and executrix of her father's estate and apparently unm in 1795

Joseph C. Anderson II, 5337 Del Roy Drive, Dallas, TX 75229

Abbott, James [s/b Abbott, Peter]   30a   1-3-4-0-0
   Orphan Island Town, Hancock County

PETER ABBOTT, b prob c1746–47 son of the Moses Abbott who d Sullivan c1793 (Thomas Foss, *A Brief Account of the Early Settlements Along the Shores of Skillings River* [1870]; David C. & Elizabeth K. Young, *Vital Records from Maine*

Newspapers, 1785–1820 [1993], p. 1): d Prospect [the part now Verona] 2 Mar 1812 ae 65y (Young & Young, op. cit., p. 1): m (1) SARAH _____ (birth recs of sons Joshua and Moses in Prospect VR) who d by 1802 when Peter remarried: m (2) Prospect 12 Mar 1802 AMMEY PUMROYE (VR). Peter Abbott "yeoman of Penobscot" was granted rights to land on Orphan Island 24 Nov 1783 by William Lawrence (Lin Co deeds 26:111) and Daniel Lancaster of Frankfort quitclaimed to Peter 1 Jun 1787 100 acres on the westerly side of the island (ibid., 23:95). On 15 Dec 1794, Peter "of Orphan Island" granted 9 acres of his land in 2 tracts on the island to William Wetmore of Boston in satisfaction of a judgment against him (Han Co deeds 3:157). Wetmore was the major landowner on Orphan Island having acquired the rights through his 2nd marriage to Sally Waldo (James C. Wetmore, *The Wetmore Family of America* [1861], pp. 446–51). On 14 Aug 1797, Peter granted to Reuben Abbott 100 acres of land in Sullivan adjacent to Moses Abbott (Han Co deeds 6:182). This deed stated that he had settled on the Sullivan land in 1775. Peter is not found in the 1790 USC of Sullivan, nor in any other location, but is surely the man mistakenly called "James" on Orphan Island in that year. Additionally, the numbers given in "James" Abbott's 1790 census listing match the Peter Abbott family. Peter is found on the 1800 USC of Orphan Island which indicates that he came from Portsmouth NH and he is also on the 1810 USC of Prospect which then included Orphan Island. His will, dated 1 Mar 1812, the day before he died, named his four sons and four daughters and a grandson John Philbrook (Han Co Probate #513). He named his youngest son as executor and required him to support his "mother-in-law, my present wife." The inventory of his estate totaled $2,698.08.

Children by his 1st wife Sarah _____, first 3 prob b Sullivan, rest prob b Orphan Island: Grace Limeburner, "Folks of Orphan Isle," FHL film #859055
- i Samuel, b 27 Sep 1776 (Jonathan Fisher, "Bluehill Family Register" [TS, NEHGS catalogued as MSS/C/3497]): d Etna 6 Oct 1831 (VR) [g.s. in Friends cem, Etna says d 5 Oct 1831 ae 55y]: m Segdwick 8 Mar 1801 Sarah Merrill (Fisher, op. cit.). He res initially in Sedgwick (Han Co deeds 21:204), moved to Blue Hill in 1804 (Fisher, op. cit.), returned to Orphan Island in 1809 (Fisher, op. cit.; 1810 USC) and moved to Etna by 1820 (USC; Pen Co deeds 9:137). He left a will (Pen Co Probate 4:482)
- ii Hannah, b c1778: m int Prospect 5 Jun 1797 John Davis (VR). They res Orphan Island in 1800 (USC) but were prob in Brooksville in 1825 (Han Co deeds 47:172)
- iii Louise/Lovisa, b c1780: called "Luvice" on her m int Prospect 28 Sep 1801 Charles Curtis Jr. of Frankfort (VR). She was prob the "Vice" Abbott who had a child "_____ Filbrooks" b Prospect 10 Dec 1796 (VR). Her father, in his will, named his grandson John Philbrook
- iv Peter, b c Feb 1786: d Verona 28 Dec 1863 ae 77y 10m 16d (g.s., Whitmore cem): m (1) int Prospect 27 Mar 1811 Fanny Clark (VR) who

d by 1823: m (2) int Prospect 16 Oct 1823 Abigail Stover (VR). He res Etna in 1816 (Pen Co deeds 4:235), Orphan Island in 1830 (USC), Etna 1840–1854 (USC; Pen Co deeds 243:2) and Verona in 1860 (USC). His intestate est was probated (Han Co Probate #3865)
v Sally, b c1788: m int Sedgwick 15 Mar 1806 Nathaniel Currier of Sedgwick (VR)
vi Moses, b 17 Mar 1789 (Prospect VR): d Orland bef 24 Oct 1859 when his intestate estate was probated (Han Co Probate #2556): m int Prospect 29 Oct 1810 Jane Fullerton (VR), b 14 Apr 1792 (Fisher, op. cit.), d perhaps Bucksport aft 1860 (USC). They res a short while in Sedgwick but were in Blue Hill by 1820 (Fisher, op. cit.); they returned to Orphan Island by 1830 (USC) and were in Orland by 1837 (Han Co deeds 63:380)
vii Polly, b c Aug 1793: d Orphan Island 12 Mar 1851 ae 57y 7m (g.s., Whitmore cem): m int Prospect 19 Jul 1809 William "Wetmore" [Whitmore] (Sedgwick VR), b Deer Isle 19 Jul 1785 son of Joseph & Abigail (Babbidge) Whitmore [see JOSEPH WHITMORE family], d at sea c1825 (George L. Hosmer, *An Historical Sketch of the Town of Deer Isle, Maine* [1905], p. 129)
viii Joshua, b 17 Sep 1794 (Prospect VR): d Verona 12 Dec 1867 (g.s., Whitmore cem): m c1813 Rachel Bickford (Limeburner, op. cit.), b Sedgwick 19 Feb 1799 dau of Daniel & Hannah (____) Bickford (VR), d Verona 23 Jun 1854 (g.s., Whitmore cem). They res Orphan Island also called Wetmore Isle and Verona. He left a will (Han Co Probate #3090)

Ralph E. Hillman, 4302 James Dr., Midland, MI 48642

Allen, Isaac   14c   2 - 1 - 2 - 0 - 0
Falmouth Town, Cumberland County

ISAAC ALLEN, b prob Phillipstown [Sanford] son of Robert & Catherine (Furbish) Allen of Berwick ("Friends, Society of Falmouth, Maine, Monthly Meeting," compiled from the original records of the Falmouth Monthly Meeting by Dorothy Small [TS, MHS], hereafter Friends Records of Falmouth; Beulah Fogg Maguire, *The Ancestry of Beulah Fogg Maguire of Sanford, Maine*, p. 250; Frederick R. Boyle, *Early Families of Sanford-Springvale, Maine* [1988], pp. 4–5): m 3 Oct 1756 ABIGAIL HALL (Friends Records of Falmouth, op. cit.; Boyle, op. cit.), b Dover NH 12 Feb 1739/40 dau of Hatevil & Sarah (Furbish) Hall (Dover Historical Society, *Vital Records of Dover, New Hampshire 1686–1850* [1977], p. 56) [see HATEVIL HALL family, *Maine Families*, 3:111). Isaac's parents were among the earliest settlers of Sanford, locating there on Oak Hill perhaps as early as 1745–46 (Boyle, op. cit.). [This family also recorded in Rev. Charles N. Sinnett's *Isaac Allen of Falmouth, Maine*.]

Children, b Falmouth: Friends Records of Falmouth, op. cit.
- i Catherine, b 19 10m [Oct] 1757: d 31 Jan 1799 (S. T. Dole, *Windham in the Past* [repr 1974], p. 453): m Lemuel Jones (ibid.), b 26 Feb 1758 son of Lemuel & Wait (Estes) Jones of Brunswick (Friends Records of Falmouth, op. cit.; Everett S. Stackpole, *History of Durham, Maine* [1899], p. 205), d 5 Apr 1845 (Dole, op. cit., p. 453). They settled in Windham (ibid.). He m (2) 9 Oct 1800 Deborah Hawkes dau of Amos & Deborah (Flint) Hawkes of Windham (ibid.; Friends Records of Falmouth, op. cit.)
- ii Robert, b 8 4m [Apr] 1760: d Windham 23 11m [Nov] 1766 (Friends Records of Falmouth, op. cit.)
- iii Sarah, b 8 7m [Jul] 1763: m Falmouth 7 Apr 1781 Elijah Varney of Windham (Friends Records of Falmouth) son of Jonathan & Elizabeth (____) Varney of Wells (ibid.)
- iv Ebenezer, b 7 6m [Jun] 1765: d Windham 23 6m [Jun] 1766 (Friends Records of Falmouth, op. cit.)
- v David, b 20 12m [Dec] 1767: d Falmouth 9 9m [Sep] 1818 (Friends Records of Falmouth, op. cit.): m 31 3m [Mar] 1790 Sarah Hussey (ibid. which gives her parents names), b Somersworth NH 13 11m [Nov] 1766 dau of Daniel & Bethia (Varney) Hussey (ibid.; "Friends Records, Dover New Hampshire Monthly Meeting," NHGR, 4:160), d Falmouth 13 5m [May] 1854 (Friends Records of Falmouth, op. cit.)
- vi Mary, b 7 9m [Sep] 1769: m Falmouth 28 Mar 1792 Samuel Adams (VR), bp 1st Church of Falmouth 19 Mar 1769 son of Benjamin & Miriam (Watson) Adams (Andrew N. Adams, *A Genealogical History of Robert Adams of Newbury* [1900], p. 57) [see BENJAMIN ADAMS family, *Maine Families*, 3:1], d 11 Jan 1853 ae 84y (g.s., Adams cem, Falmouth). He m (2) Gray 30 Dec 1813 Sarah (Staples) Smith (VR) and m (3) bef 1821 Mary Field of Falmouth (Adams, op. cit., p. 57) who d 29 Sep 1850 ae 75y (g.s., Adams cem, Falmouth)
- vii Dorcas, b 27 8m [Aug] 1772: d Falmouth 8 7m [Jul] 1851 (Friends Records of Falmouth, op. cit.): m 3 2m [Feb] 1796 Josiah Dow of Falmouth (ibid.), b 2 9m [Sep] 1776 son of Jedidiah & Dorcas (Neal) Dow of Weare NH (ibid.), d 1 6m [Jun] 1861 (ibid.). They were the parents of Neal Dow (1804–1897), author of "Maine Law," Temperance candidate for the presidency of the U.S. in 1880, and former Mayor of Portland
- viii Isaac, b 6 2m [Feb] 1778: m Jane Hall (Joseph B. Hall, "Hatevil Hall and Descendants," *Portland Monitor*, issue of 8 Jul 1871), b Falmouth 12 Jan 1781 dau of Andrew & Jane (Merrill) Hall [see HATEVIL HALL family, *Maine Families*, 3:111], d Brunswick 15 Apr 1851 (VR). She m (2) Brunswick 21 Jan 1823 James Nelson (VR)

Leroy M. Bailey, 47 Ivy Lane, Wethersfield CT 06109-2516

Andrews, Jeremiah   68b   1 - 3 - 2 - 0 - 0
Sudbury-Canada Town [now Bethel], York County

JEREMIAH ANDREWS, b 6 Apr 1757 (Lapham's *Bethel*, p. 461) and prob he bp Ipswich MA 10 Apr 1757 son of Jeremiah & Lucy (Rust) Andrews (VR): d 25 Feb 1827 ae 69y (g.s., Bartlett cem, East Bethel): m Temple NH 13 Jan 1784 ELIZABETH SAWTELLE (Lapham's *Bethel*, p. 461; William B. Lapham, *History of Rumford, Oxford County, Maine* [1890], p. 300), b Shirley MA 22 Jan 1765 dau of Hezekiah & Margaret (Dodge) Sawtelle (VR), d 2 or 4 Apr 1838 ae 67y [sic] (g.s., Bartlett cem, East Bethel). Jeremiah was a Rev War soldier and pensioner and served in Col. Tupper's regiment (Fisher's *Soldiers*, p. 16; Rev War pension #S36893). He was in the Battle of Bunker Hill and served another term before leaving Temple NH (Lapham's *Bethel*, p. 84). He moved to Bethel soon after his marriage and settled on the south side of the Androscoggin River near the Rumford line (ibid.). He had first come to Bethel in 1780 with a group of men from Dublin NH under the hire of Capt. Joseph Twitchell, the original proprietor of the Bethel mills, to assist in building the first mills (ibid., p. 302). During his years in Bethel, he served several town offices including selectman, surveyor of highways, and treasurer (ibid., pp. 160–63). On 27 Mar 1823, Jeremiah declared that he was "now poor and needing charity" ("Maine Estate Schedules from Revolutionary War Pensions," NEHGR, 145 [1991]:162). He stated he had no real estate and that his personal estate consisted of a cow, a pig and a few ordinary articles of household utensils; he was a farmer who was unable to work due to "age and infirmity"; his wife Elizabeth, ae 58y, was "a feeble old woman" (ibid.).

Children: births of all but last in VR Bethel
    i   Hezekiah, b 4 Oct 1784: d 17 Aug 1868 ae 82y (g.s., Abbott's Mills cem, Rumford): m Phebe Kimball (Lapham's *Bethel*, p. 462), b c1789 dau of Samuel & Hannah (Clark) Kimball (ibid., p. 573), d 13 Feb 1871 ae 82y (g.s., Abbott's Mills cem, Rumford)
    ii Jeremiah Jr., b 28 May 1786: d Rumford 2 Aug 1863 ae 77y (g.s., Rumford Point cem): m 1807 Anna Hodsdon (*History of Rumford*, p. 346), b 1783 dau of Stephen & Anna (Estes) Hodsdon (ibid.), d Rumford 25 May 1866 ae 77y (g.s., Rumford Point cem). They res near Rumford Point
    iii William, b 8 Apr 1788: d 3 Dec 1871 ae 83y (g.s., Beans Corner cem, East Bethel): m Betsey Estes (Lapham's *Bethel*, p. 462), b 28 Dec 1792 dau of Stephen & Relief (Bartlett) Estes (ibid., p. 525), d 14 Nov 1882 ae 90y (g.s., Beans Corner cem, East Bethel). He was a farmer and captain of militia and lived near the foot of Kimball Hill
    iv Elizabeth, b 1 Feb 1790: d 3 Mar 1804 (Lapham's *Bethel*, p. 462)
    v Salome, b 8 Apr 1792: d Hanover 25 Oct 1877 (Lapham's *Bethel*, p. 654): m 8 Apr 1811 Eli Howe (ibid.), b Marlboro MA 19 Mar 1789 son of John

Sr. & Mary (Newton) Howe (ibid.), d Hanover 16 Jun 1870 (ibid.). He lived in Rumford and Brunswick prior to settling in Hanover where he was a miller (*History of Rumford*, p. 350)

vi   Sarah, b 20 Feb 1794: m John Estes (Lapham's *Bethel*, p. 462), b 2 Feb 1795 son of Stephen & Relief (Bartlett) Estes (ibid., p. 525)

vii   Elsie, b 12 Mar 1796: m Otis Howe (*History of Rumford*, pp. 350–51), b Marlboro MA 24 Sep 1794 son of John Sr. & Mary (Newton) Howe (ibid.), d 1863 (ibid.). He m (2) Betsey (_____) Prescott of Chichester NH (ibid.)

viii   Amos, b 15 Jan 1798: m Hannah Bean (Lapham's *Bethel*, p. 462), b 10 Jun 1805 dau of Luther & Lydia (Kimball) Bean (ibid., p. 480). He res in the east part of Bethel on the Rumford–Paris road (ibid., p. 462)

ix   Huldah, b 21 Feb 1801: m Eliphaz Powers (Lapham's *Bethel*, p. 462), b 16 Nov 1796 son of Arnold & Betsey (Lane) Powers (ibid., p. 599)

x   Mary, b 22 Jan 1804: m Hosea Huntress (Lapham's *Bethel*, p. 462)

xi   Eliza, b 27 Jul 1806: m James Estes (Lapham's *Bethel*, p. 462), b 2 Jan 1800 son of Stephen & Relief (Bartlett) Estes (ibid., p. 525). He m (2) Mary York (ibid., p. 527)

xii   Julia, b 18 Jun 1809: d 21 Feb 1884 ae 74y (Alfred F. Howard, *A History of Hanover, Maine 1774–1980* [1980], p. 399): m Bethel 17 Nov 1842 Benjamin Franklin Stearns (Rev. Donald L. McAllister and Lucille E. Naas, *Marriage Returns of Oxford County, Maine* [1993], p. 48; Lapham's *Bethel*, p. 462), b 11 Apr 1821 son of Charles & Thankful (Bartlett) Stearns (ibid., p. 618), d Hanover 7 Jul 1859 ae 38y (*History of Hanover*, p. 399). They res Hanover

xiii   Hannah, b 20 Jul 1812: m 19 May 1833 Jonathan Powers (Lapham's *Bethel*, pp. 462, 602), b 20 Mar 1809 son of Jonathan & Lucy (Bartlett) Powers (ibid., p. 601), d 21 Oct 1862 (ibid., p. 602)

xiv   Stephen, b c1814–15 ("Maine Estate Schedules," op. cit.)

Warren D. Stearns, P.O. Box 35, Hanover, ME 04237

Archer, John   54b   1 - 6 - 4 - 0 - 0
   Plantations West of Machias, No. 13, Washington County

JOHN ARCHER, b Worthen, Salop Co (Shropshire), England, 26 Mar 1752 (Columbia VR; g.s.) and bp Worthen 12 Apr 1752 son of Henry & Mary (_____) Archer (extracted records from Worthen parish register, IGI LDS): d Cherryfield 20 Jan 1830 (Columbia VR; g.s., Archer cem, Cherryfield): m Machias 18 Nov 1778 ELIZABETH TUPPER (Mrs. Beulah G. Jackman, *Earliest Records of Machias, Maine* [1937], p. 37), b Lebanon, Coventry or Stafford CT 3 Apr 1758 dau of William & Margaret (Gates) Tupper (Eleanor Tupper, PhD, *Tupper Genealogy* [1972], hereafter Tupper, p. 71; Columbia VR; g.s.), d 26 May 1830 in her 73rd y (Columbia VR; g.s., Archer Farm cem, Jonesboro). John Archer deserted the British Army and joined the Colonial Army, serving under Col. John Allan (MS&S 1:287; Leroy Archer Campbell, *Descendents of John Archer of Cherryfield, Maine* [1982], pp. 3–5). He was "a man of some education, a land surveyor and a teacher...and at an early date in the settlement of the place [Cherryfield], took up residence on the lot afterwards occupied by his son John, on the Beddington road" (BHM, 7:177). Several of the children were born in the Newburyport/Amesbury MA area because the family moved there for a while when times were difficult in Machias during the war.

[John Archer applied for a Rev War pension in 1818. This pension was quoted by Campbell, op. cit., but was not found in the National Archives and may have been lost. John states in the application that he had a total of 21 children of whom 15 were then alive: 11 sons and 4 daughters. The Columbia vital records list 18 children. Campbell gave the other three as Emily, Charles and an infant, all of whose birthdates are uncertain and who prob d young. No trace of them has been found in the records.]

Children: births VR Columbia which also gives birthplaces
  i Lydia Gates, b Machias 6 Apr 1775, before John and Elizabeth Archer were married: d 9 Dec 1857 ae 83y 8m (g.s., Archer Farm cem, Jonesboro): m int Columbia Aug 1798 George Tenney (BHM, 4:118), b c1764, d 31 Mar 1854 (g.s., Archer Farm cem, Jonesboro; Clarence Drisko & Leonard Tibbetts, *The Tenney (Tinney) Family*, p. 28). He served in the Rev War (Fisher's *Soldiers*, p. 792)
  ii William Gates, b Machias 7 Sep 1779 and bp with his sis Mary at Newburyport MA 6 May 1781 (VR): m Mary Smith (Tupper, p. 71)
  iii Mary, b Newburyport MA 15 Mar 1781 and bp Newburyport MA 6 May 1781 (VR): m Samuel Beale (Tupper, p. 71)
  iv James, b Amesbury MA 6 Aug 1782
  v John Jr., b Amesbury MA 22 Jul 1783: d Cherryfield 20 Mar 1861 (g.s., Archer cem, Cherryfield): m Cherryfield 1 Jan 1805 Lucy W. Colson (*Maine Genealogist*, 15 [1993]:71), b 4 Oct 1785 [1787 per g.s.] dau of Samuel Jr. & Susannah (Willey) Colson (Stanton D. Colson, *The Descendants of Cornielius Cursonwhit of Dover, New Hampshire* [1991], 1:163; Albert E. Myers, *Asa Williams and Direxa Dunn of Great Pond, Maine: Their Ancestors and Descendants*, p. 5), d Cherryfield 6 Mar 1884 (ibid.; g.s., Archer cem; Colson, op. cit.)
  vi Joseph, b Machias 10 Oct 1784: m (1) Dorcas Nickerson (Tupper, p. 71): m (2) Eleanor Durkee (ibid.). He res Nova Scotia

vii   Henry G., b Machias 25 Jan 1786: d Charlotte 21 Mar 1867 (Wash Co Probate, 23:50, 118, 150): m 13 May 1810 Sarah Newcomb (Tupper, p. 71; Bethuel Newcomb, *Andrew Newcomb 1618–1686 and His Descendants* [1923], pp. 102–3), b prob Machias 25 Sep 1791 dau of John & Anne (Chase) Newcomb (ibid.). They res Charlotte (1830 & 1840 USC)

viii Thomas, b Machias 29 Apr 1787: m Cherryfield 2 May 1816 Hannah Tupper (*Maine Genealogist*, 15 [1993]:71; Tupper, p. 71), b 13 Feb 1794 dau of Ansel & Mary/Polly (Seaton) Tupper (ibid., p. 474). They res Cherryfield (1840 USC)

ix   Anna, twin, b Columbia 18 Apr 1789: d Jan 1791 ae 8m [sic] (Columbia VR)

x   Anselm, twin, b Columbia 18 Apr 1789: m 22 Mar 1815 Sally Foster (Reginald Foster, *Foster Genealogy* [1899], p. 252), b 30 Jun 1797 dau of Asael & Lucy (Brackett) Foster (ibid.), d 29 Oct 1865 (ibid.). They res Amherst ME (1840 USC)

xi   Abigail, b Columbia 16 Jun 1791: m Moses Colson (Tupper, p. 72)

xii   Robert Gates, b Columbia 23 Sep 1792: m Deborah Giles (Tupper, p. 72). They res Aurora (ibid.)

xiii Elizabeth, b Columbia 27 Jan 1794: d 9 May 1797 (Columbia VR)

xiv   Eliakim S., b Columbia 8 Apr 1795: d 24 Jan 1872 (g.s., Archer cem, Cherryfield): m 10 Jul 1817 Jane Barfield (1982 letter from Leonard F. Tibbetts, Family Historian, in possession of submitter). They res Cherryfield (1830, 1840 USC)

xv   Allen, b Columbia 19 Nov 1796: m (1) Eliza Small (Tupper, p. 72): m (2) Esther Ingalls (ibid.)

xvi   Ruth, b Columbia 28 Mar 1798: m William Jacques (Tupper, p. 72)

xvii David Cobb, b Columbia 6 Sep 1802: d Jonesboro 15 May 1883 (Leonard F. Tibbetts, op. cit.): m Phoebe Floyd (Tupper, p. 72). They res Jonesboro (1840 USC)

xviii George, b Columbia Mar 1804: m Susan Giles (Tupper, p. 72). They res Aurora (1830, 1840 USC)

Mary Direxa (Haynes) Holmes, 41 Woodmont St., Portland, ME 04102

Badcock, Saml 39a   1 - 0 - 1 - 0 - 0
   Hallowell Town, Lincoln County

SAMUEL BABCOCK, b Boston MA 30 Nov 1720 son of Samuel & Martha (Healey) Babcock (VR): d Augusta 17 Mar 1810 ae 90y (VR), "the Bell was toled for y^e Death of Old mr Babcock, he was 89 years" (Robert R. & Cynthia

M. McCausland, *The Diary of Martha Ballard 1785–1812* [1992], hereafter Ballard Diary, p. 806): m (1) Newton MA 22 Nov 1744 SYBIL PRATT (VR), b Needham MA 19 Jun 1723 dau of Henry & Hannah (____) Pratt (VR), d aft 25 Sep 1763 when her last child was bp and bef 12 Oct 1767 when her mother's estate was divided (Mrs. Charles D. Townsend, Robert S. Wakefield & Margaret H. Stover, *Mayflower Families in Progress, Degory Priest of the Mayflower* [1987], p. 19): m (2) Hallowell 13 Oct 1773 MARY TOLMAN (VR) who d Augusta 23 Jan 1808 (VR) and bur 24 Jan 1808 ("Old Lady BabCock was Baried this day," Ballard Diary, p. 744). On 13 Oct 1763, just after the baptism of his last child at Roxbury MA, Samuel received one of the original grants made by the Plymouth Company at Cushnoc [later Hallowell] on the east side of the Kennebec River (James North, *The History of Augusta* [1870], hereafter North, p. 85). When the town of Hallowell was organized in 1771, he was elected warden (ibid., pp. 105–6). The next year he was elected selectman (ibid., p. 972).

Children by 1st wife, Sybil Pratt
 i Sybil, b Boston MA 28 Feb 1745 (VR): prob d young
 ii Martha, b Boston MA 14 Feb 1747 (VR)
 iii Samuel, b Boston MA 3 Mar 1749 (VR): d Augusta 5 Feb 1830 ae 79y [sic] (VR): m (1) Hallowell 16 Dec 1774 Tabitha Savage (VR), perhaps she b Georgetown 24 Oct 1755 dau of Isaac & Isabella (Allen) Savage (VR), d Augusta 1814 ae 61y [sic] (David C. & Elizabeth K. Young, *Vital Records from Maine Newspapers, 1785–1820* [1993], p. 17, citing obit in *Hallowell Gazette*, issue of 9 Mar 1814): m (2) Augusta 19 Jan 1826 Mrs. Mercy Bickford (VR) who was ae 42y at the time (*Eastern Argus*, issue of 7 Feb 1826)
 iv Henry, b Roxbury MA 20 Dec 1751 (VR): d Augusta 1 Jul 1824 ae 70y [sic] (VR): m (1) Hallowell 11 Jan 1781 Sarah Fish/Fisk (VR), b Providence RI 25 Jan 1761 dau of Asa & Susannah (____) Fisk (Hallowell VR), perhaps she who d Jan 1803 when Martha Ballard, on 16 Jan 1803, recorded that "mrs Badcock was dead" (Ballard Diary, p. 597): poss m (2) int Augusta 10 Jul 1813 Polly Hinkley of Hallowell (Augusta VR): m (3) int Augusta 21 May 1814 Jemima Gould (VR)
 v Sybil, bp Roxbury MA 11 Nov 1753 (VR): prob d young
 vi Jeremiah, bp Roxbury MA 21 Dec 1755 (VR): d Augusta 1 Oct 1821 ae 66y (VR): m int Hallowell 30 Sep 1786 Anna Pettingill (VR), b c1754 dau of Benjamin & Mary (Kingman) Pettingill (North, p. 923), d Augusta 28 Sep 1826 ae 72y (VR)
 vii John, bp Roxbury MA 13 Nov 1757 (VR): d 8 May 1803 (Ballard Diary, p. 606, entry of 9 May 1803 in which Martha Ballard stated "am informd that mr John Badcock Expired lasᵗ night"): m (1) Hallowell 21 Nov 1780 Mary Savage (VR), perhaps she b Woolwich 20 Oct 1762 dau of Isaac and

Isabella (Allen) Savage and sister of Tabitha above (Hallowell VR): m (2) int Hallowell 2 Feb 1797 Tilley/Tily (Ingraham) Perkins (VR) wid of Eliab Perkins of Vassalborough whom she m int Hallowell 25 Nov 1785 (Hallowell VR), b 19 Mar 1766 dau of Jeremiah & Abigail (Hartwell) Ingraham (North, p. 885), d Augusta 1 Apr 1825 ae 59y (VR). She m (3) int Augusta 14 Feb 1807 James Savage (VR)

viii Mercy, bp Roxbury MA 30 Sep 1759 (VR): m Hallowell 28 Jul 1784 Studly Springer (VR), b Dartmouth MA 1755 (Fisher's *Soldiers*, p. 738), d Augusta 23 Apr 1829 ae 73y (VR)

ix Sybil, bp Roxbury MA 25 Sep 1763 (VR)

David C. Young, P.O. Box 152, Danville, ME 04223

Bacon, Thomas 29a 1 - 2 - 1 - 0 - 0
Gouldsborough Town, Hancock County

THOMAS BACON, b Eastham MA 4 Sep 1759 son of Nathaniel & Apphia (Cole) Bacon (MD, 16 [1914]:203, 29 [1931]:16): d bef 30 Dec 1829 when Nathan Shaw of Gouldsborough was requested by Thomas's widow to be appt administrator of Thomas's est (Han Co Probate #874): m MARY ____ (Muriel Sampson Johnson, *Early Families of Gouldsboro, Maine* (1990), hereafter *Gouldsboro*, p. 24). On 19 Apr 1798, Nathan Jones, proprietor in Gouldsborough, deeded to Thomas Bacon 100 acres "for the consideration that the said Thomas Bacon is a settler of Gouldsborough" (Han Co deeds 8:240).

Children: births VR Gouldsboro
  i Thomas, b 20 Jun 1789: m Gouldsboro 8 Oct 1810 Hannah Simons of Gouldsboro (VR), b c1792, d Sullivan 22 Apr 1870 as "the widow of the late Thomas Bacon" ae 78y (*Ellsworth American*, issue of 5 May 1870)
  ii Mary, b 29 Nov 1792 [in York according to *Gouldsboro*, p. 25]: d 7 Mar 1876 (ibid., citing family Bible rec): m int Gouldsboro 24 Jan 1811 John L. Bunker (VR), b Mount Desert Island 11 Mar 1785 son of Isaac & Esther (Ives) Bunker (*Gouldsboro*, pp. 25, 42, 44), d aft 14 Mar 1871 when he filed his War of 1812 pension application (ibid.; Edward C. Moran, Jr., *Bunker Genealogy* [1942], pp. 11, 18) [see ISAAC BUNKER family, *Maine Families*, 1:28–29]

Rev. Charles Austin Joy, The Church of Saint Andrew, 1004 Graydon Ave., Norfolk, VA 23507

Banks, Aaron   30b   3 - 2 - 5 - 0 - 0
Penobscot Town, Hancock County

AARON BANKS Jr., b York 1 Jun 1738 (BHM, 7:25) son of Aaron & Mary (Haines) Banks (Thomas A. Perkins, *Jacob Perkins of Wells, Maine and His Descendants* [1947], p. 9): d Penobscot 9 Aug 1823 ae 85y 2m (BHM, 7:26): m York 6 Jul 1764 MARY PERKINS (VR), bp Wells 1st Church 22 May 1743 dau of John & Elizabeth (Pearce) Perkins (NEHGR, 75 [1921]:120; *Jacob Perkins*, op. cit.), d Penobscot 26 Nov 1833 (ibid.). Aaron served in the French and Indian War and was at Fort Pownal in 1759 and at the capture of Montreal in 1760 (BHM, 7:25). After his marriage, he settled at Bagaduce (now Castine) where in 1779 his house was burned being in the range of the American battery on Nautillus Island and "partly from a spirit of revenge for his supposed sympathy with the enemy" (BHM, 7:26). The family removed after to Penobscot. He was a faithful member of the Orthodox Calvinistic church (ibid.). His will, dated 20 Mar 1823 and probated 20 Oct 1823, names his wife, all 5 daughters and son Aaron (Han Co Probate #1170). He had 4 sons and 5 daughters, "but has no descendants bearing the name Banks" (BHM, 7:26).

Children, order of birth uncertain: BHM, 7:25–26
  i   Elizabeth/Betsy, b Castine 5 Jun 1764 (VR Penobscot; *Jacob Perkins*, op.cit.): m Penobscot 14 Sep 1779 Jeremiah Wardwell [see JEREMIAH WARDWELL family]
  ii Aaron, b Castine c1766 (ae 84y in 1850 USC): reportedly d at ae 80y [sic], the result of a fall (BHM, 7:26): m (1) unknown wife: m (2) Mary Leach (Walter Snow, *Brooksville, Maine: A Town in the Revolution*, p. 58), b c1761 dau of James Leach (ibid.), d Castine 1836 ae 75y as "2nd wife of A. Banks" (ibid.)
  iii Olive, m Castine 1784 William Reidhead/Redhead (BHM, 7:26) whose family were Loyalists and removed to St. Andrews, but returned to Penobscot by 1790 (USC)
  iv Josiah, d prior to 1809 (when his wife remarried), "shipped on board a brig in Portland, bound for Cuba, neither crew nor brig was ever heard from" (BHM, 7:26): m by 1798 Avis Lowder of Bangor (ibid.) who m (2) Castine 21 May 1809 Wilder Taylor (VR)
  v   Mary/Polly, b Castine 17 Apr 1772 (VR Penobscot): d Penobscot 4 Feb 1862 (VR): m Penobscot c1794 Samuel Wardwell (1st child b 1795), b Penobscot 22 Sep 1774 youngest child of Daniel Wardwell (VR) [see DANIEL WARDWELL family, *Maine Families*, 1:280; also see Addendum, *Maine Families*, 3:316 and Addendum, this volume)
  vi Lucy, m 28 Nov 1792 Benjamin Milliken, both of Penobscot (Alice MacDonald Long, *Marriage Records of Hancock County, Maine prior to 1892* [1992], p. 9)

vii Ebenezer, d bef 1823 (not named in father's will), "supposed he was killed and thrown overboard in mid-ocean, first being robbed" (BHM, 7:26). He was a midshipman on a British man-of-war, and became a captain, serving more than 23 years (ibid.)
viii Esther, b Castine c1776: d aft 1850 (ae 74y USC): m (1) David Reidhead (BHM, 7:26): m (2) Penobscot 2 Oct 1817 Joseph Castin (VR): m (3) Penobscot 1 May 1836 Andrew Neally (VR)
ix   James, d bef 1823 (not named in father's will): "was pressed and carried on board a British ship, and in attempting to escape...by swimming, was shot while in the water and devoured by sharks" (BHM, 7:26)

Marjorie Wardwell Otten, 201 4th St. #222, Del Mar, CA 92014

Barker, Dan¹   63c   1 - 3 - 2 - 0 - 0
Limerick Town, York County

DANIEL BARKER, b Exeter NH 22 Apr 1754 son of Josiah & Mary (Heard) Barker (Robert L. Taylor, *Early Families of Limerick, Maine* [1984], hereafter Taylor, p. 26; Elizabeth Frye Barker, *Barker Genealogy* [1927], p. 394): d by suicide as a resident of Exeter ME at Corinna 22 Aug 1820 ae 67y (David C. & Elizabeth K. Young, *Vital Records from Maine Newspapers, 1785–1820* [1993], p. 26): m c1776 ANNA HILL (Taylor, p. 26). Daniel moved to Limerick in 1776 (BHM, 6:77) and moved to Exeter ME by 1802 (Taylor, p. 26). He was a Rev War soldier (Fisher's *Soldiers*, p. 34). His son Josiah was adm of Daniel's estate (Ruth Gray, *Abstracts of Penobscot County Probate Records 1816–1883* [1993], hereafter *Pen Co Abstracts*, p. 10).

Children: Taylor, p. 26
  i   Jonathan, d young
  ii Josiah, b Exeter NH 8 Jan 1779: d Exeter ME 9 Feb 1866 (Taylor, p. 26): m (1) Nancy Pease dau of Joseph & Polly (Clark) Pease (Barker, op. cit., p. 406) who d 22 Jul 1821 (ibid.): m (2) Oct 1831 widow Abiah P. Kenniston (BHM, 6:236)
  iii Nathaniel, b 19 Aug 1784: d Bangor 18 Mar 1823, "killed by a sled running over him" (BHM, 2:180): m 9 May 1807 Sarah/Sally Pease both of "Blaisdelltown Settlement" [Exeter] (BHM, 1:41), b c1789 sis of Nancy above (BHM, 6:77), b c1789, d 6 Jan 1880 ae 91y (ibid.). His probate documents stated he left 10 small children, the oldest ae 16y by Sep 1824 (*Pen Co Abstracts*, p. 10)
  iv Lewis, d Exeter ME 29 Aug 1820, just one week after his father's death (Young & Young, op. cit., p. 26): m (1) int Bangor 5 Dec 1811 Hannah

18   MAINE FAMILIES IN 1790

>   Cowin (BHM, 3:194): m (2) Phebe _____ who was named in Lewis's probate records (*Pen Co Abstracts*, p. 10). His estate was adm in Sep 1820 by one Theophilus Brown (ibid.)
- v   Mary, twin, b 5 Oct 1789: of "Blaisdelltown Settlement" [Exeter] when she m Bangor 23 May 1809 Joseph Pease (BHM, 1:41)
- vi   Nancy, twin, b 5 Oct 1789: m 8 Dec 1809 George Tilson, both of Stetson Settlement (BHM, 1:41)
- vii Sarah, m 1811 Rev. Albana Pease (Taylor, p. 26). He d by Nov 1863 when his will was probated, at which time his widow was an Anna H. Pease (*Pen Co Abstracts*, p. 170)
- viii Tamson
- ix   Elizabeth
- x   Julia, d young (Taylor, p. 26)

Elizabeth (Bette) Barker Taverner, 51 Deaconess Road, Concord, MA 01742-4136

Barker, Jeremiah   14c   1 - 3 - 3 - 0 - 0
    Falmouth Town, Cumberland County

Dr. **JEREMIAH BARKER**, b Scituate MA 31 Mar 1752 son of Samuel & Patience (Howland) Barker (VR) [see discussion below]: d Gorham 3 Oct 1834 ae 84y (McLellan's *Gorham*, p. 398): m (1) 12 Oct 1775 ABIGAIL GORHAM (ibid., p. 396), b 5 Mar 1749 dau of David Esq. & Abigail (Sturgis) Gorham of Barnstable MA (ibid., p. 520) and sister of Judge William Gorham of Gorham [see WILLIAM GORHAM family, *Maine Families*, 3:91]. Abigail d Falmouth 29 Jun 1790 ae 40y (g.s., given in MHGR 2:196): m (2) Gorham 17 Dec 1790 SUSANNA GARRETT (VR, 2nd edition), b c1769 dau of Richard Garrett of Barnstable MA and sister of Judge Gorham's 2nd wife Temperance Garrett. Susanna d 3 Jun 1794 ae 25y (g.s., given in MHGR 2:196): m (3) EUNICE RIGGS, b c1770 dau of Jeremiah Riggs of Capisic (McLellan's *Gorham*, p. 398), d 10 Nov 1799 ae 29y (g.s., given in MHGR 2:196). Dr. Barker's marriage intentions with Mary Williams of Gorham were published 2 Jul 1802 (Gorham VR, 2nd edition), however there is no record that a marriage followed. He m (4) 17 Mar 1808 TEMPERANCE (GARRETT) GORHAM, the sister of his 2nd wife and the widow of Judge William Gorham (McLellan's *Gorham*, p. 398). After Dr. Barker's death, she moved to Providence RI to live with Dr. Barker's daughter, Abigail Gorham (Barker) Johnson, and d there c1840 (ibid.). Dr. Barker studied medicine and surgery with Dr. Lincoln at Cambridge MA and practiced in Barnstable MA. He served during the Revolution as a surgeon and was in the Penobscot Expedition. Following the war, he began construction of a house in Gorham adjacent to his brother-in-law, Judge William Gorham. This house was destroyed by fire. Rebuilt, it was subsequently sold when Dr. Barker removed to Portland prior to 1790. In 1799, he purchased land in Stroudwater where he built a large two-story house. Following his 4th marriage, he returned to Gorham residing in the Judge Gorham homestead until his death.

[Jeremiah's mother was not Deborah (Gorham) Barker as claimed in Samuel Deane's *History of Scituate, Massachusetts* (1831). Deborah, who was Jeremiah's father's first wife, d 11 Dec 1738 "& had been married but 26 days" (Scituate VR).]

Children by 1st wife Abigail Gorham: all info from McLellan's *Gorham*, p. 398
 i Jeremiah C., b c1778: lost at sea 19 Dec 1810 ae 32y
 ii Mary G., b 20 Aug. 1781: m Stroudwater 13 Oct 1800 Daniel Johnson of Portland
 iii David, b 7 Mar 1784: d in Sedgwick: m Deborah Josslyn of Pembrook. He was a physician and lived at Durham and Sedgwick
 iv Elizabeth, b 29 Jan 1787: m Rev. Samuel Clarke
Child possibly by 2nd wife Susanna Garrett: all info from McLellan's *Gorham*, p. 398 [note that McLellan assigned her to the 4th wife, but this could not be true if she married in 1817]
 v Abigail/Abby, m 19 May 1817 John Johnson of Providence RI

Vincent A. Mackesy, 346 Shore Rd., Monument Beach, MA 02553

Bartlett, Enoch   68a   4 - 0 - 4 - 0 - 0
 Sudbury-Canada Town [now Bethel], York County

ENOCH BARTLETT, b Newton MA 27 Sep 1742 son of Ebenezer & Ann (Clark) Bartlett (William B. Lapham, *History of Bethel, Maine* [repr 1981], hereafter Lapham's *Bethel*, p. 466): d Newry 31 Aug 1825 (Martha Fifield Wilkins, *Sunday River Sketches* [1977], hereafter *Sunday River*, p. 167): m (1) Boston MA 23 Jun 1766 ELIZABETH SEGAR (Edward W. McGlenen, *A Volume of Records Relating to the Early History of Boston, Containing Boston Marriages from 1752 to 1809* [1903], p. 361), b Newton MA 20 Dec 1740 dau of Josiah & Thankful (Allen) Segar (Francis Jackson, *A History of the Early Settlement of Newton, County of Middlesex Massachusetts* [1854], p. 404): m (2) int Standish 25 Jul 1794 ANNE HALL (Albert J. Sears, *Early Families of Standish, Maine* [1991], p. 95), b 28 Apr 1769 dau of John & Naoma (York) Hall (ibid.) [note that Lapham's *Bethel* and other secondary sources state that Anna's surname was "House"], d 27 Aug 1868 ae 100y 4m (*Sunday River*, p. 169). Enoch gave patriotic service during the Rev War serving as a teamster (Fisher's *Soldiers*,

p. 39; Lapham's *Bethel*, p. 84). Some time after the birth of his third child in Newton MA in 1769, Enoch moved to Weston MA where he was a taxpayer from 1773 to 1781 (Aldis Everard Hibner, *A Genealogy of the Descendants of Joseph Bartlett of Newton, Massachusetts* [1934], hereafter Hibner, p. 55). He probably moved to Sudbury-Canada about 1780. He had 5 younger half-brothers who also settled in Sudbury-Canada. He lived first on what became the Dr. Carter farm at Middle Intervale, then moved to that part of Bethel which is now Hanover and finally to a farm on Sunday River in Newry (Lapham's *Bethel*, p. 467). He and his second wife are buried in Sunday River Cemetery almost within sight of their home. There were supposedly 10 children by his first wife and 11 by the second (Lapham's *Bethel*, p. 467), although only 19 of these have been identified. A notice of his death in the *Providence (RI) Journal*, dated 23 Oct 1825, stated he had living at the time 17 children, 93 grandchildren and 64 great grandchildren (Hibner, p. 55).

Children, first 3 recorded Newton MA but order and mother of the rest are uncertain: all data from Lapham's *Bethel*, p. 467, unless otherwise cited
  i   Nancy, b Newton MA 4 Nov 1766
  ii Reuben, b Newton MA 17 Apr 1768: m 31 Jul 1792 Lydia Frost ("Sudbury-Canada Marriages," *The Maine Genealogist and Biographer*, 1 [1876]:81). They res on the north side of the Androscoggin River in Bethel (Lapham's *Bethel*, p. 469)
  iii Relief, b Newton MA 2 May 1769: m (1) 24 Oct 1790 Stephen Estes of Bethel (Hibner, p. 116) son of Daniel & Mary (_____) Estes of Shapleigh (Alfred F. Howard, *A History of Hanover, Maine 1774-1980* [1980], p. 446; Lapham's *Bethel*, p. 525): m (2) Abner Foster of Freedom (ibid.). She lived in Bethel and Howard's Gore with her first husband who was a trader. He left on a purchasing trip to NY about 1809 and never returned (ibid.; *History of Hanover*, p. 446)
  iv Submit, m Sudbury-Canada 12 Sep 1790 Silas Powers (Lapham's *Bethel*, p. 600), b Temple NH 2 Sep 1762 son of Gideon & Ruth (Hosmer) Powers (ibid.). He settled in Hanover on part of what has since been known as the Foster farm (ibid.)
  v   Anna, d Newry 2 Jul 1851 (*Sunday River*, p. 216): m 6 May 1790 Asa Foster (*The Maine Genealogist and Biographer*, 1 [1876]: 126); Lapham's *Bethel*, p. 467), b 24 May 1765 son of Abner & Lydia (Nelson) Foster of Newry (*Sunday River*, p. 216), d 29 Sep 1831 ae 66y (ibid.)
  vi Betsey, m 27 May 1792 Richard Estes (Hibner, p. 117), b Berwick 7 Sep 1767 son of Daniel & Mary (_____) Estes (ibid.). He lived in Bethel on the south side of the river near the Rumford line (ibid.)
  vii Burry, m Ephraim Colby of Rumford (Lapham's *Bethel*, p. 467), b 12 Jan 1781 son of Joseph & Molly (_____) Colby of Concord NH (William B. Lapham, *History of Rumford, Oxford County, Maine* [1890], p. 312)

viii Thankful, b 17 May 1776 (Avis Stearns Van Wagenen, *Genealogy & Memoirs of Isaac Stearns and His Descendants* [n.d.], p. 312): d Bethel 3 Feb 1853 (ibid.): m 8 Oct 1792 Charles Stearns (ibid.), bp Watertown MA 8 Jan 1769 son of John & Martha (Harrington) Stearns (ibid.)
ix Jonathan, m (1) ____ Barker (Lapham's *Bethel*, p. 467): m (2) Triphena Horr of Waterford (Hibner, p. 118), b 1795 dau of Isaac & Rebecca (Heald) Horr (ibid.). Jonathan settled in Newry (ibid.)
x Lucy, b c1781 (*History of Hanover*, p. 357): d Howard's Gore [Hanover] 17 Aug 1839 ae 58y (ibid., citing g.s. Hanover cem): m Jonathan Powers (ibid.; Lapham's *Bethel*, p. 467), b Temple NH 3 Aug 1777 son of Gideon & Ruth (Hosmer) Powers (*History of Hanover*, p. 357)
xi Olive, m Nathaniel Frost son of Moses & Sarah (____) Frost of Berwick (Norman Seaver Frost, *Frost Genealogy in Five Families* [1926], p. 292; Hibner, p. 119)
xii Patty, b 4 Feb 1795 (Hibner, p. 119): m 28 Jan 1812 David Sessions (ibid.), b Farby, Orange Co VT 4 Apr 1790 son of David & Rachel (Stevens) Sessions (ibid.). They settled in Newry
xiii Elisha, b c1796–97: d 19 Oct 1874 ae 77y 10m (*Sunday River*, p. 169): m Sarah Barker, b c Jun 1823, d Aug 1877 ae 54y 2m (ibid.)
xiv Enoch Jr., b 5 Jul 1811 (*History of Hanover*, p. 278): m 5 Jul 1835 Sarah G. Hinkson (Hibner, p. 120), b Rumford 29 Apr 1817 prob dau of Robert & Sally (Swain) (Silver) Hinkson (ibid.). He was a blacksmith at Hanover
xv Polly, m (1) Willoughby Russell (Lapham's *Bethel*, p. 607), b 22 Dec 1791 son of Benjamin Jr. & Mehitable (Abbott) Russell of Newry (ibid.): m (2) Urban York (ibid., p. 648), b 10 Nov 1814 son of John & Sally (Kilgore) York (ibid.)
xvi Naomi, m Rev. Tripp (Lapham's *Bethel*, p. 467)
xvii Apphia, m Joseph Chase (Lapham's *Bethel*, p. 467)
xviii Lydia, m Joseph Knapp (Lapham's *Bethel*, p. 467)
xix Lorana, d unm (Lapham's *Bethel*, p. 467)

Warren D. Stearns, P.O. Box 35, Hanover, ME 04237

Bennit, Peter [prob s/b Andrew, see below]   47a   1 - 0 - 2 - 0 - 0
Twenty-Five Mile Pond, Lincoln County

ANDREW BENNETT, b Georgetown 28 May 1757 son of Andrew & Lydia (Brann/Brawn) Bennett (VR): d Troy 1 Nov 1839 (Rev War pension #S36910): m int Hallowell 8 Nov 1788 MARGARET GILLEY (VR), b Hallowell 8 Jul 1770 dau of John & Dorcas (Brawn) Gilley (VR) [see JOHN GILLEY family], d Troy 1 Jan 1853 (VR). Andrew served in the Rev War for three enlistments from 1777 to 1783, as a private at the battle of White Plains NY, at Valley Forge during one winter, and at the surrender of Gen. Burgoyne (pension, op. cit.). In his pension application filed in 1835, he states that he enlisted in Malden MA and at the time was a resident of Mount Desert; that he had resided in Troy for 43y. He wrote his will 6 Oct 1839 in which he mentioned all of his then living children (Wal Co Probate, #515).

[It is believed that the Peter Bennit enumerated in the 1790 census was an error for Andrew Bennett. Andrew Bennet appeared on the 1788 tax list for Hallowell where he was married the same year (James W. North, *The History of Augusta* [1870], p. 216). In the 1800 census, Andrew was enumerated at Twenty-Five Mile Pond. There was no Peter Bennett in the 1800 census, nor has a Peter Bennett been found in other records.]

Children: pension & will
- i Mary/Polly, b c1789 (based on her parents' marriage date and the 1790 USC listing): d bef 1850 (USC): of Bridgton [now Troy] when she m int Winslow 21 Jun 1807 George Brawn/Brann (VR), poss son of Charles & Alice/Elsie (_____) Brawn of Winslow
- ii Isaac, b c1791: d by drowning betw 1830 (USC, Troy) and the 1837 Troy census (Edith & Leola Mitchell, *Troy, Past and Present* [1977], p. 131): m bef 1823 when his 1st son was b (Troy VR), although the name of his wife is unknown
- iii John, b Troy 20 Oct 1793 (VR): d Troy 26 Jun 1850 (VR): m c1819 Bethania Brann (from family papers in possession of submitter)
- iv Andrew, b Troy c1796 (g.s., although he was ae 51y in 1850 USC, ae 64y in 1860 USC, and ae 75y in 1870 USC, Troy): d Troy 1879 (g.s., Rogers cem): of Troy when he m Augusta 5 May 1828 Caroline Page (VR)
- v Margaret, b c1796 (ae 54y in 1850 USC, Troy): d Troy 18 Jan 1853 (VR): m c1820 John Bickmore 3rd as his 2nd wife (John Bickmore family rec in Troy VR; she was apparently not in her father's household in 1820 USC), b c1780 son of John & Margaret (Meserve) Bickmore [see JOHN BICKMORE Jr. family, *Maine Families*, 3:23]
- vi Deborah, b 1801 (g.s.): d Troy 1870 (g.s., Rogers cem): m Orrison Page, b 1803 (g.s.), d 1890 (g.s., Rogers cem, Troy)
- vii Moses, b c1809 (ae 9y in his father's 1818 pension application): d bef 1850 (USC): m int Winslow 23 Oct 1832 his cousin Samantha Brawn (VR), b Winslow 12 Oct 1808 dau of Joseph & Abigail (Gilley) Brawn (VR)
- viii Abigail, b c1812 (ae 6y in her father's 1818 pension application): not in her father's will

Ardell J. Parkman Lynds, 12630 Joy Bell Lane, San Martin, CA 95046

Bickford, Paul   43c   1 - 4 - 1 - 0 - 0
Pownalborough Town, Lincoln County

PAUL BICKFORD, reportedly b 25 Apr 1752 [sic] (Charles E. Allen, *History of Dresden, Maine* [1931], p. 543), although he was under 45 years old in the 1800 USC, prob son of Henry & Abigail (Tibbetts) Bickford who were married at Rochester NH 9 Jan 1755 (NHGR, 4 [1907]:147): d of inflammation of the lungs at Dresden 2 Nov 1838 (VR; *History of Dresden*, p. 544): m Pownalborough 31 May 1781 ELIZABETH KENDALL (VR), b prob 17 Aug 1757 prob dau of Uzziah & Elizabeth (____) Kendall (*History of Dresden*, p. 186), d of cancer 25 Nov 1842 ae 85y (ibid., p. 543). Paul was a volunteer in the Penobscot Expedition at Castine during the Rev War (Fisher's *Soldiers*). After the war, he was a farmer in Dresden (ibid.). [See also *The Bickford Newsletter*, Mahlon C. Bickford, publisher, 230 North Street, B-33, Buffalo, NY, Vol. 3:1[1991], Vol. 4:1[1992].]

Children, b Dresden: births VR Dresden
  i   Henry, b 21 May 1782: "deranged" in 1842 (*History of Dresden*, p. 544)
  ii   George, b 17 Dec 1783: d of erysipelas in Jun 1849 ae 69y [sic] (*History of Dresden*, p. 544): he married but the name of his wife has not been found (ibid.)
  iii Paul, b 12 May 1785: d Salisbury MA in July or Aug 1871 ae 85y (*History of Dresden*, pp. 543, 545): m Salisbury MA 22 Jun 1808 Martha Mansfield (VR), prob b Salisbury MA 25 Sep 1786 dau of John & Anna (Atwood) Mansfield (VR), d Salisbury 2 Oct 1847 ae 61y (VR). Paul went to sea at the age of 12 and later was a sea captain; he took "Lord" Timothy Dexter's warming pans to Cuba and sold them at a good price, the Cubans using them to dip sugar (*History of Dresden*, p. 543)
  iv   John, b 27 Apr 1787: d 11 Mar 1864: m Dresden 25 Dec 1814 Sarah Goubert (NEHGR, 66 [1912]:110), perhaps the Sarah Goubert b Bowdoinham 28 Mar 1792 dau of Nicolas & Dinah (____) Goubert (VR). They res Richmond (*History of Dresden*, p. 544)
  v   Abigail, b 20 Apr 1789: m Dresden 22 Nov 1812 David Meserve (NEHGR, 66 [1912]:110), b 24 Dec 1783 son of Gideon & Elizabeth (Fogg) Meserve [see GIDEON MESERVE family]
  vi   Joanna, b 20 Jul 1791
  vii Hulda, b 23 Sep 1793: d Dresden 6 Nov 1884 (VR): unm. Her journal appears in *History of Dresden*, pp. 544–45
  viii William, b 28 Jan 1796: m cert Dresden Jan 1823 Mehitable Hathorn (VR). Two of their children were named Nathaniel Hathorne Bickford and William Kendall Bickford

Janet S. Seitz, 11521 Upper Sunny Circle, Eagle River, AK 99577-7414

Blake, Caleb   25b   1 - 0 - 0 - 0 - 0
   Turner Town, Cumberland County

CALEB BLAKE, b prob Taunton MA 9 Jan 1770 son of Samuel Sargeant & Abigail (Richard) Blake (VR Turner) [see SAMUEL SARGEANT BLAKE family]: d Turner 5 Nov 1802 (VR) [sic, prob s/b 1801 as his obituary appeared in the *Portland Gazette*, issues of 7 Dec 1801 and 25 Jan 1802, cause of death listed as suicide (David C. & Elizabeth K. Young, *Vital Records from Maine Newspapers, 1785– 1820* [1993], p. 46)]: m Turner 11 Jun 1794 BETSY BRIGGS (VR), b Taunton MA dau of Daniel & Silence (Hart) Briggs (Rev. W. R. French, *A History of Turner, Maine* [1887], p. 32), d Turner 14 Nov 1855 (VR).

Children, b Turner: births VR Turner
- i   John, b Turner 4 Apr 1794: m Turner 1 Aug 1815 Betsey Phillips (VR)
- ii Daniel Briggs, b Turner 18 Jan 1796: d Turner 29 Oct 1841 ae 45y 9m 11d (VR): m Greene 7 Jan 1819 Nancy Libby of Greene (Walter L. Mower, *Sesquicentennial History of the Town of Greene* [1938], p. 144), b Saco 3 Sep 1796 dau of John & Drusilla (Graffam) Libby of Saco and Greene (Charles T. Libby, *The Libby Family in America* [1882], p. 154)
- iii Calvin, b Turner 6 Sep 1798: m int New Gloucester 21 Nov 1825 Louisa Haskell (VR) dau of Eliphalet & Mary (Woodman) Haskell (Ira J. Haskell, *Chronicles of the Haskell Family* [1943], p. 214). They res St. Albans
- iv Jairus, b Turner 7 Jun 1801

Deborah B. Kirwan, 120 Depot Rd. #2, East Kingston, NH 03827

Blake, Nath[l]   50a   1 - 1 - 1 - 0 - 0
   Washington Town [now Belgrade], Lincoln County
[and prob counted again as]
Blake, Nathaniel   50c   1 - 0 - 1 - 0 - 0
   Winslow Town, with its Adjacents, Lincoln County

NATHANIEL BLAKE, b Hallowell 14 May 1767 son of William & Abigail (_____) (Girdy) Blake (VR): d North Belgrade 28 Jan 1859 ae 92y (VR; Carleton E. Blake, *Descendants of Jasper Blake* [1980], hereafter *Jasper Blake*, p. 177; g.s, Old Yard, Belgrade): m c1790 ANNA/ANNIE TAYLOR (*Jasper Blake*, p. 177; date based on birth of 1st child in 1791), b 15 Sep 1767 (Belgrade VR) dau of Elias & Mary (Johnson) Taylor (*Jasper Blake*, p. 177), d Belgrade 15 Apr 1843 ae 75y (VR; g.s., Old Yard, Belgrade). Nathaniel was apparently double-counted in the 1790 census as were several of the heads-of-household listed at the ends of Washington and Winslow towns in the published census on pp. 50a and 50c. He lived in the part of Washington Plantation which became Dearborn in 1812 and which was annexed to Belgrade in 1839. He was a farmer and a soldier in the War of 1812.

Children: births VR Dearborn; all info from *Jasper Blake*, p. 177 unless otherwise cited
  i   John, b 25 Jan 1791: d 25 Dec 1855
  ii Mary, b 27 Aug 1792: d New Richmond WI 2 Sep 1870: m 16 Mar 1817 Henry P. McKenney
  iii Nancy, b 30 Apr 1794: d Lexington 6 Apr 1874: m Sidney 13 Feb 1822 Jesse Savage of Sidney (Dearborn VR). They res Madison, then Lexington (DAR Misc Recs, 2:311)
  iv Avadana, b 19 Aug 1796: d Monroe 15 Feb 1874: m 1834 David Ricker
  v   William, b 26 Feb 1799: d W. Waterville Aug 1841: m 1820 Martha Nelson of Waterville
  vi Nathaniel, b 30 Apr 1801: d 1828: unm
  vii Priscilla, b 5 May 1803: d June 1803 (VR)
  viii David, b 7 Sep 1804: d Jan 1874: m Lucinda Smith of Belgrade, b Belgrade 23 Sep 1805 dau of Capt. Samuel & Chloe (Clark) Smith (VR)
  ix Sarah, b 11 Oct 1806: d Belgrade 26 Apr 1849 (VR): m bef 1834 (when child Joseph was born) Joseph Merchant, b Belgrade 1 Aug 1801 son of Edward & Data (____) Merchant (VR), d Belgrade 5 Jul 1872 (VR)
  x   Jonathan, b 11 Sep 1808: d Holden 4 Apr 1859: m Mary Patterson of Madison, b 16 Sep 1811, d 20 Feb 1894
  xi Samuel, b 8 Mar 1811: m Mary J. ____, b c1816 (1850 USC, Brewer)

Carol F. Nye, RFD 1 Box 388, Belgrade, ME 04917-9722

Blake, Paul   49c   1 - 1 - 2 - 0 - 0
  Washington Town [now Mt. Vernon], Lincoln County

Major **PAUL DEARBORN BLAKE**, b Epping NH 26 Aug 1756 son of Dearborn & Ruth (Dearborn) Blake (Carlton E. Blake, *Descendants of Jasper Blake* [1980], p. 240): d Mt. Vernon 22 Jan 1806 in his 49th year (g.s., West Mt. Vernon cem; Rev War pension #W21676): m Brentwood NH Aug 1783 ABIGAIL GILES (pension, op. cit.), b prob Brentwood NH 17 Aug 1757 (*Jasper Blake*, op. cit.), d Mt. Vernon 22 Nov 1845 ae 88y 3m (g.s., West Mt. Vernon cem). Paul's bro, John Blake of Gardiner, ae 78y in 1838, made an affidavit stating Paul was a resident of Epping NH when he enlisted for Rev War service in 1775 (pension, op. cit.). His Rev War service included many enlistments between 1775 and 1778 which included his participation in the Battle of Bunker Hill (*Jasper Blake*, op. cit.). He was a selectman in Mt. Vernon in 1792 (ibid.). His will, which was dated 1 Oct 1805, named his children Bradbury, John and Nancy (ibid.).

Children, b Mt. Vernon: births VR Mt. Vernon
- i Bradbury, b 24 Apr 1785: d Lee 30 Apr 1870 (*Jasper Blake*, p. 65): m int Mt. Vernon 7 Apr 1806 Abigail Norcross (VR), b Chesterville 12 Apr 1789 dau of Phillip & Joanna (Brackett) Norcross (*Jasper Blake*, p. 65), d Lee 2 Oct 1867 (ibid.). Bradbury was a farmer and a soldier in the War of 1812
- ii Nancy, b 6 May 1787 (Charles C. Whittier et al., *The Descendants of Thomas Whittier & Ruth Green of Salisbury and Haverhill, Massachusetts* [1937], p. 54): d Mt. Vernon 20 Mar 1817 ae 30y (g.s., West Mt. Vernon cem): m Mt. Vernon 16 Apr 1807 Levi Whittier (VR), b Winthrop 13 Aug 1786 son of Nathaniel & Elizabeth (Prescott) Whittier (Everett S. Stackpole, *History of Winthrop, Maine* [1925], p. 672; *Thomas Whittier*, op. cit., p. 54), d New Sharon 24 Feb 1845 (ibid., p. 108). He m (2) May 1819 Polly Gordon (ibid.)
- iii John, b 24 Aug 1791: d Mt. Vernon 19 May 1870 ae 79y (g.s., West Mt. Vernon cem): m 8 Mar 1816 Lovina Blake (*Jasper Blake*, p. 651), b Mt. Vernon 22 Feb 1797 dau Robert & Martha (Dudley) Blake (ibid.) [see ROBERT BLAKE family], d Mt. Vernon 13 Mar 1843 ae 46y 1m (VR; g.s. West Mt. Vernon cem). Paul Blake's Rev War pension application states that John was his 3rd child and was ae 48y in Aug 1839 (pension, op. cit.)

Carol F. Nye, RFD 1 Box 388, Belgrade, ME 04917-9722

Blake, Robert   49c   1 - 2 - 6 - 0 - 0
Washington Town [now Mt. Vernon], Lincoln County

ROBERT BLAKE, b Epping NH 27 Dec 1751 son of Jedediah & Mary/Molly (Rowe) Blake (NHGR 4:137; Carlton E. Blake, *Descendants of Jasper Blake* [1980], p. 65) [Rev War pension #W23635 gives b 27 Dec 1752]: d Fayette 22 Mar 1841 (pension, op. cit.; Fisher's *Soldiers*, p. 63): m Epping NH 4 Feb 1776 MARTHA DUDLEY (pension, op. cit.), b Brentwood NH 14 Mar 1757 dau of Joseph & Hannah (Leavitt) Dudley (ibid.; NHGR 4:137; DAR Lineage Book 150:190, Application #149591), d Mt. Vernon 13 Mar 1844 (*Jasper Blake*, op. cit.). Robert lived at Epping NH when he enlisted in the Rev War (pension, op. cit.). He moved to Mt. Vernon in 1782 and to Fayette in 1825 (ibid.).

Children, 1st four b Epping NH, others b Mt. Vernon: births recorded VR Mt. Vernon
- i Dudley, b 19 Feb 1777: d Bermuda 31 Aug 1819 ae 42y as a resident of Mt. Vernon (VR Mt. Vernon): m c1802 Hannah Page (Everett S. Stackpole, *History of Winthrop, Maine* [1925], p. 533), b Winthrop 10 Feb 1782 dau of Col. Simon & his 3rd wife Mary (Brown) (Clifford) Page (ibid.), d Winthrop 17 Nov 1863 ae 81y 9m (VR; g.s. Robinson Yard cem, Mt. Vernon)
- ii Samuel Ordway, b 14 Jan 1779: d Augusta Jan 1833 (*Jasper Blake*, p. 66): m Epping NH 1804 Mehitable Lyford who d 29 Feb 1836 (ibid.)
- iii Permela, twin, b 25 Dec 1780: d Mt. Vernon 10 Apr 1843 (*Jasper Blake*, p. 66): m Epping NH Sep 1797 David Page (ibid.)
- iv Clymena, twin, b 25 Dec 1780: d Mt. Vernon 2 Oct 1860 ae 80y (g.s., Wells cem): m John Whittier (*Jasper Blake*, p. 65), b Mt. Vernon 25 May 1775 son of William & Elizabeth (____) Whittier (Charles C. Whittier et al., *The Descendants of Thomas Whittier & Ruth Green of Salisbury and Haverhill, Massachusetts* [1937], p. 55), d Mt. Vernon 26 Jan 1842 ae 67y (VR; g.s., Wells cem)
- v Melinda, b 14 May 1784: d Fayette (*Jasper Blake*, p. 66): m Fayette in spring of 1801 Ezra Fiske (ibid.), b Amherst NH 2 Apr 1776 son of Hon. William & Eunice (Nourse) Fiske (Frederick Clifton Pierce, *Fiske and Fisk Family* [1896], pp. 211–12)
- vi Melentha, b 25 Jul 1785: d Farmington 23 Jan 1872 (*Jasper Blake*, p. 66): m Epping NH 22 Jan 1806 Eben Briggs (ibid.). They res Salem ME (ibid.)
- vii Gilman, b 17 Jul 1787: d Mt. Vernon 7 Sep 1788 (VR; pension, op. cit.)
- viii Dorinda, b 8 Aug 1789: d Elk River, Minn. (*Jasper Blake*, p. 67): m Mt. Vernon 14 Jun 1817 or 1818 Ephraim Nickerson (ibid.), b Chatham [MA?] 10 May 1793 son of Thomas & Bethiah (____) Nickerson (Mt. Vernon VR)
- ix Miranda, b 26 Apr 1791: d Farmington 6 Nov 1850 (*Jasper Blake*, p. 67): m 30 Jan 1812 Henry Johnson (Francis G. Butler, *History of Farmington, Maine* [repr 1983], p. 514), b Martha's Vineyard MA 13 Oct 1789 son of Thomas & Thankful (Smith) Johnson (ibid., p. 509–10), d 31 Jul 1861 (ibid., p. 514). He m (2) 26 Mar 1854 Mrs. Millia Sanford of Manchester (ibid.)
- x Robert, b 2 Aug 1793: d Frankfort IN 6 Jul 1875 (*Jasper Blake*, p. 67): m (1) 2 Oct 1816 Hannah Page (ibid.), b Epping NH 26 Feb 1795 dau of William & Sarah (Dudley) Page (ibid.), d Salem ME 9 Apr 1849n (ibid.): m (2) Rachel Emerson (ibid.): m (3) Hannah (Knight) Higgins (ibid.), b 3 Mar 1807, d Frankfort IN 2 Feb 1873 (ibid.)
- xi Lovina, b 22 Feb 1797: d Mt. Vernon 13 Mar 1843 ae 46y 1m (VR; g.s., West Mt. Vernon, cem): m Epping NH 8 Mar 1816 Capt. John Blake

(*Jasper Blake*, p. 65), b 24 Aug 1791 son of Maj. Paul Dearborn & Abigail (Giles) Blake [see PAUL DEARBORN BLAKE family]
xii Gilman, b 15 Apr 1799: d Mt. Vernon 15 Sep 1800 (*Jasper Blake*, p. 65)

Carol F. Nye, RFD 1 Box 388, Belgrade, ME 04917-9722

Blake, Samuel   25b   3 - 4 - 2 - 0 - 0
Turner Town, Cumberland County

SAMUEL SARGEANT BLAKE, reportedly b Taunton MA 3 Apr 1747 son of Grinfill & Desire (Crocker) Blake (research notes of the late Marion Blake, in possession of submitter) [Fisher's *Soldiers*, p. 63, states b Taunton MA 1747]: d Turner 11 Jan 1802 (VR): m Bridgewater MA 30 Nov 1768 ABIGAIL RICHARD (VR), reportedly b Thompson CT 15 Feb 1747 and bp Cong Church of Thompson CT 9 Aug 1747 dau of Joseph & Abigail (____) Richards (research notes of Marion Blake, op. cit.), d Turner 30 Nov 1825 ae 77y (VR). Samuel was a Rev soldier "of Taunton" serving as a sergeant in Capt. Moses Merrill's company, Col. Edmund Phinney's 31st Regiment which was raised from New Gloucester in 1773 (MS&S, 2:135; Fisher's *Soldiers*, p. 63; Nathan Gould, *History of Colonel Edmund Phinney's 31st Regiment of Foot* [1896], p. 43). He was a farmer and a miller. On 25 Oct 1774, the proprietors of "Sylvester Town" [Turner] contracted with Samuel to build a grist and sawmill within one year and to maintain the mill in good repair for 12 years (Rev. W. R. French, *A History of Turner, Maine* [1887], p. 22).

Children, b Turner except as noted: births VR Turner
  i   Caleb, b prob Taunton MA 9 Jan 1770: m Turner 11 Jun 1794 Betsy Briggs (VR) [see CALEB BLAKE family]
  ii Samuel Jr., b prob Taunton MA 16 Sep 1772: d Phillips 20 Dec 1840 ae 67y (g.s, Riverside cem): m (1) Turner 27 Jan 1796 Nabby Bonney (VR), b Pembroke MA 29 Jul 1776 dau of Ichabod & Mary (Turner) Bonney (*History of Turner*, p. 51; Turner VR): m (2) int Turner 30 Aug 1801 Abigail Thomas (VR), b Bowdoinham 4 Nov 1778 dau of George & Susanna (____) Thomas (VR), d Phillips 1 Apr 1854 ae 75y (g.s., Riverside cem)
  iii Thatcher, b New Gloucester 22 Feb 1774: d Foxcroft 29 Oct 1839 ae 65y 8m (g.s., Rural Grove cem): m Turner 11 Nov 1798 Sarah Evans (VR)
  iv Edward, b Turner 25 Oct 1777: "of Hartford" when he m Bowdoinham 20 Oct 1805 Sally Harwood of Bowdoinham (VR)
  v   Abigail "Jr.," b Turner 20 Dec 1779: m Turner 1 Mar 1797 Dr. Michael

Howland of Buckfield (Turner VR) who d Bowdoinham in 1799 (Silas Adams, *The History of the Town of Bowdoinham* [1912], p. 158). He was the first doctor in Bowdoinham (ibid.)

- vi Grinfill, b Turner 27 Jul 1781: d Harrison 9 Aug 1824 ae 43y (Otisfield VR): m Turner 2 Jan 1805 Eunice Cary/Carey (VR), b c1782, d Otisfield 20 Jan 1832 ae 50y (VR)
- vii Dr. Silas, b Turner 20 Apr 1785: d Otisfield 2 Feb 1851 ae abt 66y (VR): of Otisfield when he m Turner 29 Jan 1809 Sophia Cary/Carey (VR) who d Otisfield 1 Dec 1868 (VR)
- viii Joseph, b Turner 8 Jun 1787: d Turner 18 Aug 1813 ae 26y (David C. & Elizabeth K. Young, *Vital Records from Maine Newspapers* [1993], p. 46, citing Portland *Gazette*, issue of 18 Oct 1813)
- ix John, b Turner 23 Mar 1787: d Turner 8 Mar 1790 (VR)
- x Lydia, b Turner 18 Apr 1791: m Turner 7 Apr 1811 Gustavus Newhall (VR)

Deborah B. Kirwan, 120 Depot Rd. #2, East Kingston, NH 03827

Bond, William   24a   1 - 2 - 4 - 1 - 0
Portland Town, Cumberland County

WILLIAM BOND, b Plymouth, Devonshire, England 4 Oct 1754 son of Thomas & Thomazine (Phillips) Bond (St. Andrews Register, Plymouth, Devonshire): d Cambridge MA 22 Feb 1844 ("Annual Report of the Cemetery Department for the Fiscal Year 1904–1905 and a Historical Sketch of the First Burying Ground in Dorchester, Dorchester North Burying Ground," City Document No. 8 [Municipal Printing Office, Boston MA, 1905], copy at NEHGS): m Devonshire, England 23 Sep 1777 HANNAH CRANCH (Devon Record Office), b Kingsbridge, Devonshire, England 14 May 1746 dau of Joseph & Elizabeth (Lidstone) Cranch ("Cranch Family Papers," #429, Boston MA Public Library): d Dorchester MA 13 Sep 1828 ("Index to Deaths in Massachusetts Centinel and Columbian Centinel, 1784–1840" [American Antiquarian Society of Worcester MA, 1952], copy at NEHGS; William Cranch Bond narrative, see below; "Annual Report," op. cit.). In 1786, William emigrated to Maine where he was engaged in the lumber export business until 1792 when business reverses forced his return to his earlier professions of watchmaker and goldsmith. He moved his family to Boston where he founded in 1793 the William Bond & Son company, which was run by him and his son William for many years and which attained international success in inventing and manufacturing extraordinary timepieces and astronomical instruments.

[Much of the information about this family is found in the papers of William's son, William Cranch Bond. The papers are currently housed at the Science Center, Harvard University, Cambridge MA. A personal narrative, written in 1850 in William Cranch Bond's handwriting, covers his family background as it was told to him, his parents' move to America, their stay in Falmouth, his brother's and sisters' marriages, their children, and the family's life in and around Boston. This personal narrative is catalogued under "William Cranch Bond Personal Papers and Bond Family Papers, 1769–1902," Series 1, Box PF, Folder 1 entitled "William Cranch Bond Personal Memoirs."]

Children
- i   Thomazine Elizabeth Fielder, bp Plymouth, Devonshire, England 17 Nov 1778 (IGI LDS, Batter St. Presbyterian Church, Plymouth, Devonshire): d Boston MA 6 Jan 1864 ae 85y 3m (MA VR 176:3): m (1) Dorchester MA 27 Nov 1803 John Minot of Boston (VR): m (2) Dorchester MA 19 Nov 1826 John Hubbard Wilkins ("Dorchester Births, Marriages, and Deaths 1826–1849," City Document No. 54, Vol. 36, at NEHGS)
- ii Thomas, d in infancy (Edward S. Holden, *Memorials of W. C. Bond and G. P. Bond* [1897])
- iii William, d in infancy (ibid.)
- iv Thomas, b 26 Apr 1783, bp Plymouth, Devonshire, England 2 Dec 1783 (IGI LDS, Batter St. Presbyterian Church, Plymouth, Devonshire): bur 3 Dec 1861 (recs of Grand Lodge of Maine, Free and Accepted Masons, Portland): m (1) Shapleigh 10 Mar 1821 Phebe Guptil (VR): m (2) Miranda Towns, b Sep 1811, d 19 Apr 1884 (Edwin Eugene Towne, *The Descendants of William Towne* [1901])
- v   Hannah Cranch, b Falmouth (Portland) 13 Apr 1788 (personal narrative, op. cit.): d Boston MA 7 Mar 1870 (MA VR 231:39): m Dorchester MA 30 Jul 1820 Dr. Noah Fifield of Weymouth MA ("A Report of the Record Commissioners of the City of Boston Containing Dorchester Births, Marriages and Deaths to the end of 1825" [1890], Vol. 21, at NEHGS)
- vi William Cranch, b Falmouth (Portland) 9 Sep 1789 (personal narrative, op. cit.): d Cambridge MA 29 Jan 1859 (VR): m (1) his cousin Selina Cranch, b Kingsbridge, Devonshire, England 4 Apr 1798 (Cambridge MA VR), d 9 Dec 1831 (ibid.): m (2) int 16 Dec 1832 Mary Roop Cranch, sister of his first wife, b Kingsbridge, Devonshire, England 21 Jun 1787 (Cambridge MA VR). William Cranch Bond was the first curator of Harvard University's Astronomical Observatory

Theodore S. Bond, 82 Damon Ave., Melrose, MA 02176

Bracket, Miles   57c   1 - 3 - 3 - 0 - 0
Berwick Town, York County

MILES BRACKETT, b Berwick 6 May 1752 and bp 1st Parish Berwick 10 Nov 1752 son of John & Miriam (Thompson) Brackett (Herbert I. Brackett, *Brackett Genealogy* [1907], p. 253; NEHGR, 82 [1928]:322): d Berwick 4 Mar 1827 ae 75y (John E. Frost & Joseph C. Anderson II, *Vital Records of Berwick, South Berwick and North Berwick, Maine to the Year 1892* [1993], hereafter VR, p. 298): m Berwick 24 Jan 1775 LYDIA KEAY (VR, p. 120), b Berwick 7 Aug 1754 (*Brackett Genealogy*, p. 257) dau of Peter & Hannah (Roberts) Keay ("The Diary of Master Joseph Tate of Somersworth, N.H.," NEHGR, 74 [1920]:190; Joseph C. Anderson II, "The Keay Family of Berwick, Maine," YCGSJ, 7 [1992]:2:10–11), d Berwick 22 Aug 1831 (*Brackett Genealogy*, p. 257). Miles Brackett was a farmer and lived all of his life in Berwick.

Children, b Berwick: births *Brackett Genealogy*, p. 257
  i   Miriam, b 12 Apr 1776: d Oct 1776 (*Brackett Genealogy*, p. 257)
  ii Samuel, b 16 Dec 1777: d Albion 29 Jan 1842 where he is buried (*Brackett Genealogy*, p. 267): m (1) Susan Brown who d 22 Nov 1805 (ibid.): m (2) Berwick 2 May 1811 Jane Fernald (VR, p. 147) who d Berwick 3 Mar 1815 (VR, p. 292): m (3) Berwick 15 Oct 1818 Joanna Hall (VR, p. 153) who d 26 Sep 1844 (*Brackett Genealogy*, p. 267). Samuel was at Berwick in censuses through 1830, but in 1840 was at Albion
  iii Miles Jr., b 26 Sep 1780: d Detroit MI 6 Jun 1834 (*Brackett Genealogy*, p. 268): m Berwick 17 Feb 1803 Sally Heard (VR, p. 201), b 1783 dau of Joseph & Sarah (Wentworth) Heard (John Wentworth, *Wentworth Genealogy* [1878], 1:261), d 1869 (ibid.). He was a farmer
  iv Hannah, b 19 Dec 1783: d No. Berwick 1860 (g.s. in John E. Frost, "North Berwick Record Book" [TS, MHS], p. 16): m Berwick 9 Dec 1802 Joseph Heard (VR, p. 201), b 2 Nov 1779 bro of Sally above (*Wentworth Genealogy*, 1:261), d 5 Feb 1850 (ibid.) and bur No. Berwick with his wife
  v   John, b 28 Jan 1785: d Palmyra 7 Jul 1869 (*Brackett Genealogy*, p. 269): m Berwick 5 Jan 1807 Susannah Heard (VR, p. 143), b 20 Jun 1787 sis of Sally and Joseph above (*Wentworth Genealogy*, 1:262), d 1869 (*Brackett Genealogy*, p. 269). He was a farmer
  vi Jacob, b 15 Mar 1787: d Jun 1789 (*Brackett Genealogy*, p. 257)
  vii Susannah, b 29 Nov 1790: d Chelsea MA 10 Oct 1876 (Chadbourne Family Association, "The Chadbourn(e) Family 1989 Draft Edition," family #54; *Brackett Genealogy*, p. 257): m Berwick 2 Aug 1810 William Chadbourne (*Brackett Genealogy*, p. 257) [m int Berwick 18 May 1810 (VR, p. 61)], b 18 Aug 1787 son of Francis & Olive (Neal) Chadbourne ("Draft Edition," op. cit.), d 12 Dec 1856 ae 70y (*The Great Falls Advertiser*, Somersworth NH, issue of 3 Jan 1857)

viii   David, b 18 Jul 1793: d Wakefield NH 29 Nov 1871 (*Brackett Genealogy*, p. 269): m 12 Feb 1818 Nancy Fernald (ibid.) [m int Berwick 17 Jan 1818 (VR, p. 72)], b 8 Jul 1796 (*Brackett Genealogy*, p. 269), d 2 Mar 1882 (ibid.). He was a farmer

Mary B. Young, P.O. Box 2460, South Portland, ME 04116-2460

Bradbury, Elijah   59a   1 - 3 - 5 - 0 - 0
   Buxton Town, York County

ELIJAH BRADBURY, bp Biddeford 9 Jun 1757 son of Jacob & prob Abigail (Eaton) Bradbury (MHGR, 7:9, see explanation below): d Buxton 1795 (Fisher's *Soldiers*, p. 78): m Buxton 16 Dec 1779 SARAH LANE (Cyrus Woodman, *Records of the Church of Christ in Buxton During the Pastorate of Rev. Paul Coffin* [1989], p. 22), b 28 Nov 1756 dau of Capt. John & Elizabeth (Hancock) Lane (Buxton VR) [see JOHN LANE family], d Buxton Jun 1836 (VR). Elijah served in the Rev War under Gen. Washington on the Hudson and in several other engagements (MS&S 2:394–96; John Merrill Bradbury, *Bradbury Memorial* [1890], p. 98). He settled in Buxton where he was a farmer.

[Elijah's baptismal record gave his mother's name as "Sarah." This would appear to be in error as baptisms for Elijah's siblings, born both before and after the date of Elijah's birth, give Jacob's wife as "Abigail." No other Jacob Bradburys are found in Biddeford at that time and all other authorities agree that Jacob's one wife was Abigail Eaton.]

Children: births VR Buxton
    i   Elizabeth, b 14 Sep 1780: d 26 Mar 1837 ae 57y (g.s., Tory Hill cem, Buxton; Martin H. Jewett & Olive W. Hannaford, *A History of Hollis, Maine, 1660–1976* [1976], p. 182): m Buxton 25 Jul 1802 James Palmer of Phillipsburg [Hollis] (Woodman, op. cit., p. 37), b Buxton 1778 son of Richard & Jane (Hopkinson) Palmer (*History of Hollis*, p. 182) [see RICHARD PALMER family], d 10 Mar 1840 ae 62y (g.s., Tory Hill cem)
   ii   Sarah, b 5 Apr 1782: m 5 Jul 1807 Timothy Ricker (*Bradbury Memorial*, p. 98). They settled in New Portland (ibid.)
   iii   Elijah, b 28 Mar 1784: d Buxton 7 Feb 1869 (*Bradbury Memorial*, p. 144): m (1) 1 Feb 1810 Sallie Gleason Howard (ibid.), b Brownfield 24 Sep 1789 dau of Joseph & Rebecca (Gleason) Howard of Billerica MA and Brownfield (Gideon T. Ridlon, *Saco Valley Settlements and Families* [1895], hereafter Ridlon, pp. 738–39), d 12 Dec 1849 (ibid.): m (2) Ann Pray Hunt who d 26 Jun 1885 (*Bradbury Memorial*, p. 144)

iv	Abigail, b 31 Jul 1785: d 8 Jan 1804 (*Bradbury Memorial*, p. 98)
v	Isaac, b 11 Jun 1787: m 8 Mar 1812 Abigail Small Lane (Ridlon, p. 876), b Hiram dau of William & Alice (Haines) Lane (ibid.) [see JOHN LANE family]. Isaac moved to Hiram where his children were born and afterwards moved to Haynesville, Aroostook Co (*Bradbury Memorial*, p. 145)
vi	Anna, b 2 Jan 1789: d 18 Sep 1807 (*Bradbury Memorial*, p. 99)
vii	Jabez, b 22 Sep 1790: d of smallpox May 1836 ae 43y [sic] (John E. Frost, "Hollis [Maine] Record Book" [TS, MHS, 1967], p. 117; *Bradbury Memorial*, p. 146): m Anna Maria Knight of Calais (ibid., p. 145), b c1806, d 23 Apr 1899 (Frost, op. cit., p. 117). Jabez settled in Hollis soon after his marriage where he was active in town affairs (*Bradbury Memorial*, p. 146)
viii	Joanna Lane, b 28 Aug 1792: d 1845 (*Bradbury Memorial*, p. 99): m 19 Jul 1821 Charles Smith (ibid.)

Phyllis S. Williams, 7468 McKinley St., Mentor, OH 44060

Bragden, Ebenezer   31b   3 - 1 - 3 - 0 - 0
Sullivan Town, Hancock County

EBENEZER BRAGDON, b prob York after 1737 [see discussion below] son of Joseph & Sarah (Stickney) Bragdon (will of Joseph Bragdon in John E. Frost, *Maine Probate Abstracts* [1991], 11/372; GDMNH, p. 106): d Sullivan betw 28 May 1806 when he wrote his will and 25 May 1807 when it was probated (Han Co Probate, 4:65): m York 17 Jan 1765 JANE WILSON (Lester M. Bragdon & John E. Frost, *Vital Records of York, Maine* [1992], hereafter VR, p. 147) who prob predeceased him as she was not named in his will. Ebenezer was in New Bristol [Sullivan] by 1767 when his name was entered in his brother Joseph's ledger (Sullivan-Sorrento Historical Society, *A Bicentennial History of Sullivan, Maine* [1989], p. 116). He was elected to many town offices and was often chosen moderator (TR). He served during the Rev War in Capt. Daniel Sullivan's Co. in the expedition against Majorbagaduce in 1779 (BHM, 6:70) and was granted 200 acres of land in Sullivan because he was a settler prior to 1784 (BHM, 1:147). In his will, Ebenezer Bragdon of Sullivan, Gentleman, named his son James to whom he gave his homestead, his son Ebenezer Jr. and his three daughters Lydia the wife of Edward Pettengill, Mary the wife of Amos Ames, and Jane the wife of Eliphalet Pettengill. James was appointed executor.

[Ebenezer's birth is not recorded on the Joseph Bragdon family listing in the York vital records (York VR, p. 21) although his parentage is proven by Joseph's will. The family listing gives the births of his older siblings down through the year 1736/7 which was likely about the time the information was recorded by the Town Clerk. It is therefore probable that Ebenezer's birth occurred after 1736/7.]

Children, as named in their father's will, order partially speculative
- i Mary/Polly, bp 1st Parish York 23 Feb 1766 (YCGSJ, 4 [1989]:1:10): m Sullivan 9 Dec 1790 Amos Ames (VR)
- ii Jane, b c1767 (ae 83y in 1850 USC, Waltham ME): m Eliphalet Pettengill Jr. son of Eliphalet & Susannah (____) (Chandler) Pettengill [see ELIPHALET PETTENGILL family, *Maine Families*, 3:217–18]
- iii Lydia, m Edward Pettengill (will, op. cit.), b 21 May 1764 bro of Eliphalet Jr. above [see ELIPHALET PETTENGILL family, *Maine Families*, 3:217–18], d Hancock Dec 1849 (ibid.)
- iv Ebenezer Jr., b c1770 (Bragdon family group sheet at Sullivan-Sorrento Hist Soc): d Neville Island, Allegheny Co PA 1849 (ibid.): m int Sullivan 11 Oct 1795 Dorcas Woodbridge (VR), b 1769 (family group sheet, above), d Neville Island, Allegheny Co PA Nov 1839 (ibid.)
- v James, b 1772 (g.s.): d 14 Feb 1839 (g.s., Bragdon/Hall cem, Sorrento): m int Sullivan 6 Dec 1799 Elizabeth Wooster (VR), b 14 Jan 1778 dau of Oliver & Abigail (Clark) Wooster [see OLIVER WOOSTER family, *Maine Families*, 2:316–17], d 28 Dec 1824 (g.s., Bragdon/Hall cem, Sorrento)

Lois Weaver, 24582 Christina Ct., Laguna Hills, CA 92653

Bragden, Jeremiah, jun. 31b 1 - 0 - 2 - 0 - 0
    Sullivan Town, Hancock County

JEREMIAH BRAGDON Jr., b c1768 prob son of Jeremiah & Elizabeth (Wilson) Bragdon who also res Sullivan in 1790 (Rev. Charles A. Bragdon, D.D., "Notes on the Bragdon Family" [MS, MSL, n.d.], hereafter "Bragdon Notes," Vol. 1, Part 2, p. 184): d Franklin 6 May 1844 (Han Co Probate, 22:334): m (1) JOANNA WOOSTER ("Bragdon Notes," 1:2:184), prob she b 26 Oct 1763 dau of Oliver & Abigail (Clark) Wooster (Sarah Alice Worcester, *The Descendants of Rev. William Worcester* [1914], p. 31) [note that Jeremiah and Joanna named a son Oliver Wooster Bragdon]: m (2) Franklin 22 Nov 1825 HANNAH DONNELL (VR): m (3) Franklin 15 Jun 1839 SARAH HOWARD (VR). Jeremiah's parents were married at York in 1760 and their first two children, John and Lydia, were baptized at the York 1st Church in 1761 and 1765, respectively (Lester E. Bragdon and John E. Frost, *Vital Records of York, Maine* [1992], p. 143; YCGSJ, 4 [1989]:1:10). Shortly after Lydia's birth, they prob moved to Sullivan where Jeremiah Jr. was prob born.

Children by 1st wife Joanna Wooster: births VR Franklin
- i   Emma, b 24 Nov 1788: d Oct 1885 ("Bragdon Notes," 1:2:184)
- ii   Oliver Wooster, twin, b 24 Sep 1790 [g.s. gives b 24 Nov 1790]: d Franklin 27 Aug 1885 ae 94y 11m 3d (g.s., Bayview cem; Mrs. Arthur Ward, "Deaths and Marriages as published in the *Ellsworth American* 1884 through 1891" [TS, MSL]), citing issue of 3 Sep 1885): m Franklin Dec 1830 Nancy Hooper (VR), b 24 Jan 1806 (g.s.), d 6 May 1888 (g.s., Bayview cem). [According to her obit, she d Franklin 4 May 1888 ae 82y 4m (Ward, op. cit., citing issue of 10 May 1888)]
- iii   Jeremiah 3rd, twin, b 24 Sep 1790: d Franklin 24 Nov 1790 (VR)
- iv   Samuel, b 23 Sep 1792
- v   Nahum, b 6 May 1795: d Eastbrook 9 Dec 1877 ae 82y 7m 3d ("Bragdon Notes," 1:2:184): m Franklin 12 Jul 1828 Mary/Polly B. Dyer (VR)
- vi   Betsey, b 15 Feb 1798
- vii   Loiza, b 16 Nov 1800
- viii   Theodore, b 16 Jul 1802
- ix   Sarah/Sally H., b 23 May 1805: d 24 Aug 1890 ae 85y 3m (Ward, op. cit., citing issue of 28 Aug 1890): m Franklin 10 Dec 1826 Samuel P. Donnell (VR) who d Franklin 1875 (g.s., Bayview cem)
- x   Arlotty, b 15 Nov 1807: d Waltham 29 Dec 1880 (g.s., Hillside cem): m Hancock 20 Feb 1845 William Mercer of Waltham (Alice MacDonald Long, *Marriage Records of Hancock County, Maine Prior to 1892* [1992], p. 85) who d Waltham 17 Jan 1885 (g.s., Hillside cem)
- xi   Julia, b 22 Jul 1811: d Franklin 13 Dec 1902 (VR)

Danial R. Smith, Box 351 Paddy Lane, Franklin, ME 04634-9728

Bragdon, Jethro   73a   1 - 0 - 7 - 0 - 0
York Town, York County

JETHRO BRAGDON, bp Berwick 1st Church with 2 siblings 13 Jul 1735 son of Thomas & Joanna (____) Bragdon (NEHGR, 82 [1928]:96): d York 1814 (will probated 31 Oct 1814, York Co Probate #1807): m (1) Wells 24 Aug 1759 HANNAH BUSSELL of Wells (VR), bp Wells 23 Mar 1739/40 dau of Isaac & Hannah (Eldridge) Bussell (NEHGR, 75 [1921]:118): of York when he m (2) Wells 8 Apr 1779 MARY (JOHNSON) ADAMS (VR) dau of Jonathan & Sara (Babb) Johnson (will of Jonathan Johnson naming his dau Mary wife of Jethro Bragdon, York Co Probate #10379; Frederick R. Boyle, *Early Families of Sanford-Springvale, Maine* [1988], pp. 173–74) and wid of Richard Adams whom she had m Wells 2 May 1768 (VR). In his will, Jethro called himself a yeoman. He appears to have lived all his life on land he purchased in the part of York which was later annexed to So. Berwick in 1834. In his will, dated 26 Mar 1808, Jethro Bragdon of York, yeoman, named his beloved wife Mary and children Ebenezer Bragdon, Samuel Bragdon, Dominicus Bragdon, Lydia Hatch, Martha Wentworth, Hepzibah Bragdon, Hannah Bragdon, Sarah Sargent, Mercy Jonson, Anne Bragdon and Nahum Bragdon (York Co Probate, 25:169). Upon his death, he devised that the homestead would go to his wife after whose death it would revert to his youngest son, Nahum.

Children, b prob York: baptisms Wells 1st Church (NEHGR, 76 [1922]:103, 104, 106, 109, 181, 183, 186, 187, 188, 247); will, op. cit.

By 1st wife, Hannah Bussell

  i Ebenezer, bp 27 Jul 1760. [One Ebenezer Bragdon m Wells 1 Oct 1783 Phebe Gray (VR)]

  ii Samuel, b York 3 Aug 1762 (DAR Patriot Index) and bp 5 Sep 1762: d Richland NY 22 Nov 1852 (Rev War pension, #W524; g.s., Pulaski Old cem, Pulaski NY): perhaps it was he who m (1) int York 25 Feb 1786 Elizabeth Beedle (VR): m (2) cert Shapleigh 28 May 1791 Mehitable Hanscom of Rochester NH (VR) [Franklin McDuffie's *History of Rochester* (1882), p. 611, states they were married 26 Jul 1791 by Rev. Mr. Haven], b c1771 (ae 49y in 1820, pension, op. cit.) dau of Capt. Thomas & Temperance (Burnham) Hanscom ("The Hanscom Family Newsletter," No. 23 [Feb/Mar 1991]:8), d 18 Jan 1828 ae 55y (g.s., Pulaski Old cem, Pulaski NY): m (3) 10 Nov 1843 Olive Samson (pension, op. cit.), b c1778, ae 75y in 1853 (ibid.)

  iii Lydia, no baptism recorded: m Wells 15 Oct 1800 Jeremiah Hatch both of Wells (VR)

  iv Martha, bp 26 Oct 1766: m _____ Wentworth (will, op. cit.)

  v Dominicus, bp 19 Jun 1768: d Windham bef 22 Feb 1831 when some of his children sold the portions received from his estate (Cum Co deeds, 131:242, 243, 134:1): m (1) Hannah _____ (according to unverified family tradition): m (2) Windham 6 Nov 1827 Betsey Stevens (VR)

  vi Jemima, bp 19 Jul 1772: not named in her father's will

  vii Jeremiah/Jeremy, bp 5 Mar 1775: d in infancy, shot and killed accidentily (according to unverified family tradition)

  viii Hepzibah, no baptism recorded: unm in 1808 (will, op. cit.)

  ix Hannah, bp 7 Dec 1777: unm in 1808 (will, op. cit.)

By 2nd wife, Mary (Johnson) Adams

  x Sarah, bp 2 Jul 1780: m int York 15 Oct 1800 Jotham Sargent (VR) both of York

  xi Mercy, bp 18 Aug 1782: m _____ Johnson (will, op. cit.). [Note that the funeral of one "Mrs. Mercy Johnson" was held at Sanford 4 Feb 1854 (John E. Frost & Joseph C. Anderson II, *Vital Records of Berwick, South Berwick and North Berwick, Maine to the Year 1892* [1993], p. 656) xii Anna, bp 14 Aug 1785: living in 1808 (will, op. cit.) but reportedly d in her 20s (according to unverified family tradition)

xiii Nahum, bp 6 Sep 1789: m int York 15 Jun 1810 Mehitabel Joy both of York (VR), b 8 Jun 1791 dau of Samuel & Lydia (Hamilton) Joy [see SAMUEL JOY family, *Maine Families*, 2:163], d 30 Nov 1846 ae 57y (g.s., small cem on north side of Ogunquit Rd., So. Berwick)

Phyllis S. Williams, 7468 McKinley St., Mentor, OH 44060

Brock, John   63b   3 - 4 - 4 - 0 - 0
Lebanon Town, York County

JOHN BROCK, b Somersworth NH c1740 son of _____ & Damaris (Wentworth) Brock ("The Diary of Master Joseph Tate of Somersworth, N.H.," NEHGR 73 [1919]:312–13; John Wentworth, *The Wentworth Genealogy* [1878], 1:205–6): d prob Lebanon after 18 Jul 1814 when he made his will and before Oct 1814 when the will was recorded (York Co Probate #1917, 24:526): m JANE PRAY (YCGSJ, 7:3 [July 1992]:2–3), bp Berwick 5 Jun 1743 dau of John & Experience (Smith) Pray (ibid.; NEHGR 28 [1928]:214), d Lebanon before 25 May 1830 ae 89y (VR). The given name of John's father has eluded researchers over the years. He apparently died and left his wid to care for their 9 children. Master Tate recorded all of the children in his diary, but only named their mother, the widow Damaris Brock. In his will, John named his wife Jane, his children Nathaniel, Samuel, Simeon, Wentworth, Betsy and Jane, and his grandchildren John, James, Nathaniel and Wentworth, the sons of John Lord late of Buxton, deceased.

Children: all but last bp Berwick 2nd Church, NEHGR 74 [1920]:219, 220, 221, 228, 229, 230, 246

i John, bp 25 Nov 1770: d Sep 1795 (York Co Probate 17:155): m Wells 22 Aug 1793 Hannah Furbush (VR), b c1771, d Wells 29 Apr 1851 ae 80y 1m (g.s., Maxwell Burial Lot). She m (2) Wells 25 Jul 1797 John Shapleigh Maxwell of Wells (Wells VR). John Brock settled in the "Tatnic" part of Wells. His inventory included a 1/8th interest in the schooner SALLY and 42 acres with a dwelling house in Tatnic (York Co Probate #1916). No children

ii Joshua, bp 25 Nov 1770: prob d by 1802 when his wife remarried: m Wells 19 Feb 1789 Huldah Winn (VR) and moved to Wells. She m (2) Wells 3 Jan 1802 James Treadwell (VR). In her will, Huldah named no children and distributed her substantial estate among her nephews and nieces (York Co Probate 21:74)

iii Simeon, bp 25 Nov 1770: "drowned, found off Rye Beach" abt Jun 1839 (John E. Frost & Joseph C. Anderson II, *Vital Records of Berwick, South Berwick and North Berwick, Maine to the Year 1892* [1993], hereafter VR, p. 547): prob m (1) in early 1790s a woman whose name has not been found (dau Sophia b by 1794, see YCGSJ 7:3 [July 1992]:6): m (2) Berwick 7 Jun 1799 Eunice Hodsdon (VR, p. 140): prob m (3) So. Berwick 23 Jun 1830 Mary Shapleigh of York (VR, p. 426). The inventory of Simeon's est included the same house and land originally belonging to his bro John, but no deeds were found to account for Simeon's acquisition (York Co Probate 51:549)

iv Molly, bp 25 Nov 1770: not named in her father's will

v William, bp 29 Dec 1771: not named in his father's will

vi Experience, bp 14 Aug 1774: d Buxton bef 15 Aug 1802 when her mother requested prayers upon the death of her dau who d at Buxton (VR Lebanon): m Lebanon 20 Nov 1794 John Lord (VR) who was dead by 1814 when John Brock wrote his will. Their children were named in John Brock's will

vii Nathaniel, bp 10 Nov 1776: d Lebanon 29 Apr 1835 ae 59y (VR): m Lebanon 28 Jan 1802 Abigail Critchett (VR) who was prob a dau of John & Lydia (____) Critchet, the only Critchet family in Lebanon (VR). Abigail d Lebanon 8 May 1807 ae 25y (VR). Nathaniel m (2) Lebanon 28 Jul 1810 Nancy Kelley (VR): m (3) Lebanon 2 May 1824 Betsey Wallingford (VR). Nathaniel's will names his wife Betsey and children (York Co Probate 46:174)

viii Wentworth, bp 6 Jun 1779: named in his father's will

ix Elizabeth, bp 23 Sep 1781: named in her father's will

x Abraham, bp 9 May 1784: not named in his father's will

xi Jane, bp 15 Apr 1787: "Jane, wife of Thomas Legro" d Lebanon 22 Apr 1858 ae 71y 2m (VR). Jane Brock "of Lebanon" filed intentions at Kittery on 18 Aug 1810 (and at Lebanon on 1 Sep 1810) to marry Caleb Critchet of Fort McClary in Kittery (VR) but no marriage rec was found in either the Kittery or Lebanon VR. Jane "Brock" m Lebanon 23 Sep 1827 Thomas Legro (VR) as his 3rd wife, b Somersworth c1764 son of John & Sarah (Randall) Legro ("Master Tate," NEHGR 73 [1919]:314), d Lebanon 30 Jan 1845 ae 81y 5m (VR)

xii Samuel, bp Lebanon 4 Jul 1790 (VR): m Lebanon 16 Feb 1812 his cousin Elizabeth Libby (VR) dau of Capt Charles & Sarah (Pray) Libby (Charles T. Libby, *The Libby Family in America* [1883], p. 110). They were both in the 1850 USC at Lebanon, ae 60y.

Joseph C. Anderson II, 5337 Del Roy Drive, Dallas, TX 75229

Brock, Simeon 55c 2 - 1 - 4 - 0 - 0
Berwick Town, York County

SIMEON BROCK, b Somersworth NH c1748 son of ____ & Damaris (Wentworth) Brock ("The Diary of Master Joseph Tate of Somersworth, N.H.," NEHGR, 73 [1919]:312–13; John Wentworth, *The Wentworth Genealogy* [1878], 1:205–6): d So. Berwick 25 Mar 1814 ae 66y 14d (g.s., Old Fields cem): m (1) Dover NH 1st Church 2 Dec 1776 JUDITH BUNKER of Dover (*Collections of the Dover, New Hampshire Historical Society* [1894], 1:78, 1:175), b c1754 and bp Dover NH 1st Church 17 Oct 1756 dau of Elijah and Judith (____) Bunker (ibid., 1:159, 1:210), d So. Berwick 17 May 1790 ae 36y (g.s., Old Fields cem). Judith was the sis of Elizabeth (Bunker) Mason who m Simeon's bro William Brock. Simeon m (2) Berwick 23 Apr 1792 JUDITH ROBERTS (John E. Frost & Joseph C. Anderson II, *Vital Records of Berwick, South Berwick and North Berwick, Maine to the Year 1892* [1993], hereafter VR, p. 133), b 7 Jun 1767 dau of Samuel & Judith (Randall) Roberts ("Master Tate," NEHGR, 74 [1920]:55): d So. Berwick 20 Feb 1865 ae 98y 8m (g.s., Old Fields cem). In his will which was undated—but which one Ichabod Butler in Jun 1814 certified "was executed some time in the month of March, 1814" (York Co Probate 24:465)—Simeon named his wife Judith and children [evidently named in their birth order] Love Parsons wife of John Parsons, Betsey Frost wife of James Frost, Nabby Stacpole wife of James Stacpole, John Brock, Polly Brock wife of William Brock, Judith Brock, Sally Brock, Patty Brock, Simeon Brock, Sophy Brock, and Deborah Brock (York Co Probate #1925, 24:465–66).

Children by 1st wife Judith Bunker: will & cited sources
- i Elijah, b Berwick 7 Jun 1777 (VR, p. 221): not in father's will
- ii Love, b 1779 (Henry Parsons, *The Parsons Family* [1912], 1:109): d 22 Feb 1857 ae 77y 10m 25d (g.s., Cong Churchyard, Alfred): m int Lyman 4 Oct 1800 [*Parsons Family* gives m 6 Oct 1800] John Parsons of Coxhall [Lyman] (VR), b So. Berwick 8 Sep 1775 son of William & Abigail Frost (Blunt) Parsons (*Parsons Family*, op. cit.) [see WILLIAM PARSONS family], d 2 Feb 1858 ae 82y 4m 25d (g.s., Cong Churchyard, Alfred)
- iii Elizabeth/Betty/Betsey, bp Berwick 1st Church 24 Jun 1781 (NEHGR, 82 [1928]: 505): m Berwick 15 Mar 1801 James Frost (VR, p. 141) [James Frost "Jr" on m intention]
- iv Abigail/Nabby, m Berwick 13 May 1804 James Stackpole (VR, p. 195)
- v John, b prob bef 1790 (USC): prob d shortly aft 28 Oct 1823 when, from Salisbury VT, he wrote a letter to his family back in So. Berwick (YCGSJ, 7:4 [Oct 1992]:9–10): m int Berwick 29 Jun 1808 Judith Brown (VR, p. 58) [marriage also recorded at Berwick, but only year of 1808 given as the date]. John was of Berlin VT in 1814 when he deeded his interest in his father's est to his bro-in-law William Brock (York Co deeds 90:75). Nine

years later, prob dying of tuberculosis, he wrote a heart-wrenching letter home in which he desired to "make a Present of my Little Baby" daughter to his mother and to "give My Brother Simeon my Boy Simeon"

 vi Mary, bp Berwick 1st Church 18 May 1788 (NEHGR, 82 [1928]:505): d Biddeford 14 Mar 1868 ae 80y (g.s., Greenwood cem): m Berwick 13 Jul 1812 her double cousin [through both the Brocks and the Bunkers] William Brock (VR, p. 149), b 19 Mar 1782 son of William & Elizabeth (Bunker) (Mason) Brock (Lyman VR) [see WILLIAM BROCK family]

 vii Judith, bp Berwick 1st Church 17 May 1790: m So. Berwick 23 Feb 1817 Tristram Fernald of Lyman (So. Berwick VR, p. 420)

Children by 2nd wife Judith Roberts: will & cited sources

 viii Sally, b c1795: d So. Berwick 22 May 1822 ae 27y 6m (g.s., Old Fields cem)

 ix Martha/Patty, b c1797: d So. Berwick 25 Oct 1865 ae 68y (g.s., Old Fields cem): unm

 x Simeon, b c1800: d So. Berwick 15 May 1846 ae 46y (g.s., Old Fields cem): prob unm

 xi Sophia/Sophy, b c1804: d So. Berwick 18 Feb 1864 ae 59y (g.s., Old Fields cem): unm

 xii Deborah, b c1808–9: d So Berwick 14 May 1883 ae 74y (g.s., Old Fields cem): unm

Joseph C. Anderson II, 5337 Del Roy Drive, Dallas, TX 75229

Brock, William 59b 1 - 3 - 3 - 0 - 0
 Coxhall Town [now Lyman], York County

WILLIAM BROCK, b Somersworth NH c1746 son of _____ & Damaris (Wentworth) Brock ("The Diary of Master Joseph Tate of Somersworth, N.H.," NEHGR, 73 [1919]:312–13; John Wentworth, *The Wentworth Genealogy* [1878], 1:205–6): d Lyman 1813 (York Co Probate #1928): m Somersworth NH 15 Jun 1772 Mrs. ELIZABETH (BUNKER) MASON ("Master Tate," NEHGR, 74 [1920]:184), bp at the 1st Church of Dover NH 17 Oct 1756 dau of Elijah and Judith (_____) Bunker and widow of Isaac Mason of Somersworth NH (ibid.; *Collections of the Dover, New Hampshire Historical Society* [1894], 1:159, 1:210). Elizabeth was the sister of Judith Bunker who married William's brother Simeon Brock [see SIMEON BROCK family]. William's probate papers, dated 15 Dec 1815, named his wife Elizabeth and heirs Luke W. Brock, William Brock, Jonathan Hemmenway, Nathan Hanson and John Brock (York Co Probate 25:412).

Children: births recorded in Lyman VR but at least first 4 children prob b NH as they were also recorded (with some apparent errors) in "Master Tate," NEHGR, 74 [1920]:50
  i Sarah/Sally, b 23 May 1773: d Lyman 5 Apr 1867 ae 93y 10m 18d (g.s., Chadbourne cem): m int Lyman 23 Feb 1805 Jonathan Hemmingway (VR), b c1772, d 30 Mar 1855 ae 82y 6m (g.s., Chadbourne cem)
  ii Martha/Patty, b 8 Jul 1776: d Lyman 29 Mar 1858 (g.s., Roberts cem): m int Lyman 1 Sep 1798 Nathan Hanson (VR), b c1777, d Lyman 23 Mar 1834 ae 57y (g.s., Roberts cem)
  iii Luke Wentworth, b 22 Aug 1778: d Lyman 23 Oct 1848 (VR) ae 70y 2m (g.s., Chadbourne cem): m int Lyman 1803 Dorcas Taylor (VR which gives the year of marriage only), b 1786, d Lyman 20 Jun 1877 ae 90y (g.s., Chadbourne cem). [Luke W. Brock's wife is alternately called in the records Dorcas and Jane. She is called Dorcas on the marriage intentions, Dorcas on the recording of the first 3 children's births (Lyman VR), Jane on the recording of later children's births (Lyman VR), Dorcas in the 1850 census at Lyman and Jane on her gravestone. The will of Luke's son John would appear to indicate that Luke had just one wife (York Co Probate 59:11)]
  iv William, b 19 Mar 1782: d Biddeford 8 Sep 1863 ae 81y (g.s., Greenwood cem): m Berwick 13 Jul 1812 his double cousin [through both the Brocks and the Bunkers] Mary Brock (John E. Frost & Joseph C. Anderson II, *Vital Records of Berwick, South Berwick and North Berwick, Maine to the Year 1892* [1993], p. 149), bp Berwick 1st Church 18 May 1788 dau of Simeon & Judith (Bunker) Brock (NEHGR, 82 [1928]:505) [see SIMEON BROCK family], d Biddeford 14 Mar 1868 ae 80y (g.s., Greenwood cem)
  v John, b 29 Sep 1784: d Lyman 3 Sep 1841 ae 57y (g.s., Chadbourne cem): m int Lyman 13 Jun 1807 Lucy Roberts of Lyman (VR), b c1789, d Lyman 27 Mar 1867 ae 78y (g.s., Chadbourne cem)

Joseph C. Anderson II, 5337 Del Roy Drive, Dallas, TX 75229

Brooks, George   30a   1 - 2 - 6 - 0 - 0
    Orrington Town, Hancock County

GEORGE BROOKS, b Bradford, Yorkshire, England 1754 ("Olde Orrington Book," published in Mildred N. Thayer & Mrs. Edward W. Ames, *Brewer, Orrington, Holden, Eddington History and Families* [1962], hereafter OOB, p. xxvii; BHM, 1:154): d Orrington 5 Dec 1807 ae 53y (VR; g.s. Dean Hill cem): m Wellfleet MA 4 Mar 1776 MARY (ATWOOD) THOMPSON (VR; BHM, 1:154), b Eastham MA 16 Aug 1749 dau of Richard & Mary (Atwood) Atwood

(Wellfleet VR), d Castine 2 Sep 1817 ae 68y (g.s., Castine cem). She had m (1) Wellfleet MA 11 Oct 1768 JOHN THOMPSON (VR). She m (3) Orrington 17 Jul 1814 Dea. Mark Hatch of Castine (VR). George Brooks came to Newfoundland in the fishing trade in 1771 at the age of 17. He stayed the winter there and came to Cape Cod the next year to commence whaling and where he was later married. In 1776, he moved to Orrington where he built the first grist mill (OOB, xxvii; BHM, 1:154).

Children (surname THOMPSON) of John & Mary (Atwood) Thompson: OOB; BHM, 1:154
  i   Hannah, m int 29 Apr 1787 William Murch both of New Worcester Plt [now Orrington] (BHM, 5:6) [see WILLIAM MURCH family, *Maine Families*, 3:193], b Gorham 29 Jun 1763 son of John & Anna (Dean) Murch (VR; NEHGR, 71 [1917]:221), d Hampden 1844 (Rev War pension #S18519; g.s., Locust Grove cem, no dates)
  ii Nancy, b c Sep 1770: d Orrington 20 Jul 1854 ae 83y 10m 4d (VR; g.s., Nealey Corner cem, Hampden): m (1) Hampden 19 Oct 1788 Ezekiel Cobb of Hampden (Rev War pension #W22359), b Gorham 9 May 1764 son of Elisha & Elizabeth (Murch) Cobb [see ELISHA COBB family], d Hampden 29 Jun 1816 ae 52y 19d (g.s., Neally Corner cem) [see EZEKIEL COBB family, *Maine Families*, 3:50]: m (2) cert Orrington 13 Jan 1822 as his 2nd wife Shebna Swett of Orrington (VR; pension, op. cit. gives same date as marriage date), b Wellfleet MA 26 Jul 1762 son of Solomon & Jemima (Bickford) Swett (VR Orrington), d 30 Jul 1843 (pension, op. cit.). He had married (1) Joann Nickerson by whom he had several children (VR Orrington)
  iii Mary/Molly, m (1) Wellfleet MA 18 Mar 1793 Levi Young (VR), b Wellfleet MA 21 Dec 1766 son of Barnabas & Anna (Mayo) Young (VR; Clarence Almon Torrey, "John Young of Eastham, Mass. and Some of his Descendants" [TS, NEHGS, 1923]: m (2) Wellfleet MA 24 Jan 1802 Nathaniel Harding (VR)

Children (surname BROOKS) of George & Mary (Atwood) (Thompson) Brooks: first 7 in Orrington VR; last 2 in OOB, p. xxvii
  i   Elizabeth/Betsey, b 11 Nov 1776: d Orrington 12 Mar 1856 ae 79y (g.s., Dean Hill cem): m Orrington 13 Oct 1793 Capt. Daniel Snow (VR), b 21 Mar 1773 son of Capt. Edward & Betsey (Myrick) Snow (Orrington VR), d Orrington 2 Apr 1860 ae 87y (g.s., Dean Hill cem)
  ii John Thompson, b 4 Dec 1778: d c1822 (BHM, 1:155): m 1 Jan 1801 Sally Dean, b 15 Nov 1782 dau of Archeleus & Mary (Higgins) Dean (OOB, p. xxvii; BHM, pp. 1:154–55). They moved to Cincinnati OH in 1814 where both are bur (ibid.; OOB, p. xxvii)

- iii Martha, b 4 Dec 1780: m (1) 30 Dec 1798 Henry Dillingham of Hampden (BHM, 6:181; OOB, p. xxvii): m (2) 14 Nov 1813 Zebulon Young (BHM, 6:247) who was of Hampden 27 Sep 1832 when he wrote his will which was probated in Aug 1837 (Pen Co Probate 5:172)
- iv Joanna, b 3 Mar 1783: d Bangor 12 Mar 1867 ae 84y (OOB, p. xxvii): m 1 Jun 1801 Capt. Jeremiah Simpson of Hampden (ibid.; BHM, 1:154)
- v Abigail, b 14 Mar 1785: d 21 Mar 1864 (OOB, p. lxx): m 10 Mar 1805 Allen Hodges of Orrington but originally from Norton MA, b 29 Sep 1775 son of Tisdale & Naomi (Hodges) Hodges (ibid.), d 4 Jan 1826 (ibid.)
- vi Deborah Atwood, b 16 Apr 1787: m cert Orrington 19 May 1817 Thomas Snow of Hampden (VR; OOB, p. xxvii): res Frankfort 1830
- vii James, b 14 Feb 1789: d Orrington 16 Mar 1868 ae 80y (g.s., Dean Hill cem): m Orrington 18 Aug 1814 Elizabeth Taylor Bartlett (VR), b 24 Nov 1794 dau of Capt. Samuel & Joanna (Taylor) Bartlett (Orrington VR; BHM, 1:155), d 20 Nov 1874 ae 80y (g.s., Dean Hill cem)
- viii Thomas, b Apr 1791: d 1793 (OOB, p. xxvii)
- ix Lucy, b Apr 1793: d Orrington 1794 (OOB, p. xxvii)

T. A. McKay, 615 So. Barton, Arlington, VA 22204

Buffum, Joshua   57a   1 - 0 - 2 - 0 - 0
  Berwick Town, York County

JOSHUA BUFFUM, b Salem MA 15 Oct 1713 son of Caleb & Mary (Gaskill) Buffum (VR): d Berwick 6 Mar 1793 (NHGR, 3:35): m Salem MA 21 May 1741 widow **ELIZABETH (ESTES) OSBORN** (VR) dau of Benjamin & Elizabeth (_____) Estes (Owen A. Perkins, *Buffum Family Volume II* [1983], hereafter *Buffum Family*, p. 32). She was alive on 18 Sep 1788 when Joshua wrote his will (John E. Frost, *Maine Probate Abstracts* [1991], hereafter MPA, 16/290 citing York Co Probate #2161) and was prob alive in 1790 at the time of the census. She had m (1) Salem MA 1 Mar 1737 Isaac Osborn (VR) son of Samuel & Sarah (Clark) Osborn (Sidney Perley, *The History of Salem, Massachusetts* [1924–28], 3:60). Joshua and Elizabeth were Quakers. With his father-in-law, Benjamin Estes, Joshua and family came from Salem MA where Quakers had received a hard time and settled in Berwick about 1743 "without any certificate but conducting orderly were considered as Friends" (NHGR, 3:35; *Buffum Family*, p. 32). They became members of the Dover NH Monthly Meeting and moved to the North Berwick area about 8 years later on a farm near the Friends Meeting House (ibid., p. 33). He was a farmer and cordwainer (ibid., p. 32). His homestead in North Berwick, built in 1765, was a typical colonial farmhouse and was called by Sarah Orne Jewett one of the best examples of its type in York Co (ibid.). In his will, dated 18 Sep 1788 and probated 15 Apr 1793, Joshua Buffum of Berwick, husbandman, "being far advanced in years," named his wife Elizabeth, his sons Samuel, Caleb, Joshua and John, his daus Hannah (described as being under the care of his wife), Elizabeth Cole, and Lydia Buffum, and his grandsons Joshua and Ebenezer Fry. Joshua requested that, upon his wife's death, his son Samuel support Hannah for life.

Children, first 2 b Salem MA, others b Berwick: NHGR, 3:35
- i Mary, b 7 Mar 1742: d 1 Apr 1764 (NHGR, 3:35): m Berwick 4 Nov 1760 Ebenezer Fry (NHGR, 1:61), b 30 Aug 1734 son of William & Abigail (Varney) Fry of Kittery (NHGR, 1:61, 7:8; *Buffum Family*, p. 60). He m (2) Dover NH 2 Oct 1765 Mary Hussey (NHGR, 1:64)
- ii Elizabeth, b 29 Aug 1743: d aft 17 Aug 1798 when named in her husband's will and bef 4 Mar 1802 when called deceased on her son's mar rec (NHGR, 1:163): m Berwick 25 Jan 1768 John Cole (NHGR, 1:66), b Kittery 23 Nov 1735 son of John & Elizabeth (Hill) Cole of Kittery (ibid.; Joseph C. Anderson II & Lois Ware Thurston, *Vital Records of Kittery, Maine to the Year 1892* [1991], pp. 71, 75), d Sanford aft 14 Aug 1798 when he wrote his will and bef 29 Jun 1799 when it was probated (MPA, 18/98 citing York Co Probate #3407)
- iii Caleb, b 5 Apr 1745: d 21 Mar 1826 (NEHGR, 72 [1918]:259): m (1) Berwick 23 Nov 1769 Dorcas Hubbard (NHGR, 1:68) dau of John Heard & Hannah (Neal) Hubbard of Wells (ibid.; Everett S. Stackpole, *Old Kittery and Her Families* [1903], p. 539): m (2) Dover NH 23 Sep 1772 Hannah Varney (NHGR, 1:69), b Somersworth NH 10 Apr 1750 dau of Joseph & Temperance (Smith) Varney of Somersworth NH (NHGR, 4:41), d 24 Feb 1839 (NEHGR, 72 [1918]:259)
- iv Joshua, b 11 Dec 1746: d 29 Sep 1808 (NEHGR, 72 [1918]:261): m (1) Hampton NH 25 Apr 1775 Patience Rogers (NHGR, 5:30; NEHGR, 72 [1918]:261 states they were m at Newbury MA), b 6 Feb 1756 reportedly a dau of Jonathan & Sarah (____) Rogers (ibid.; *Buffum Family*, p. 61), d 20 Dec 1799 (NEHGR, 72 [1918]:261): m (2) Dover NH 3 Feb 1802 Sarah (Hanson) Estes of Dover NH (NHGR, 1:162), b Dover NH 23 Aug 1754 dau of Thomas & Hannah (Sawyer) Hanson of Dover NH (NHGR, 4:42) and wid of Robert Estes (ibid.; NEHGR, 72 [1918]:261). She d 10 (Apr?) 1829 (ibid.; *Buffum Family*, p. 61, gives d 10 Apr 1819)
- v John, b 30 Jul 1749: d 7 Jan 1812 (NEHGR, 72 [1918]:259): m (1) Berwick 30 Dec 1773 Hannah Rogers (NHGR, 1:71), b 1 Feb 1756 dau of Isaac & Lydia (Varney) Rogers of Berwick (NHGR, 4:42), d 11 Apr 1786 (NEHGR, 72 [1918]:259): m (2) Berwick 23 Aug 1787 Mary Dow (NHGR, 1:120), b Berwick 20 Jan 1765 dau of Moses & Hannah (Gove) Dow of Berwick (NHGR, 4:67). She m (2) Berwick 21 Jan 1814 Benjamin Scribner of Sandwich NH (NEHGR, 73 [1919]:45)

- vi Hannah, b 2 Jul 1753: perhaps the Hannah Buffum who d North Berwick 24 Feb 1839 (John E. Frost & Joseph C. Anderson II, *Vital Records of Berwick, South Berwick and North Berwick, Maine to the Year 1892* [1993], p. 652). She was unm and under the care of her mother in 1788 when her father wrote his will
- vii Lydia, b 3 Jul 1759: d Durham 31 Aug 1837 (Everett S. Stackpole, *History of Durham, Maine* [1899], p. 172): m Berwick 23 Jun 1791 Cornelius Douglas as his 2nd wife (NHGR, 1:122), b Middleboro MA 12 Sep 1749 son of Elijah & Phebe (Taylor) Douglas of Durham (NHGR, 1:122; *History of Durham*, p. 172 which mistakenly calls him a son of John Douglas), d Durham 20 Jun 1821 (ibid.). He had m (1) 10 Nov 1767 Ann Estes who d 28 Jan 1790 (ibid.)
- viii Samuel, b 19 Apr 1762: d 31 Oct 1834 ae 72y (John E. Frost, "North Berwick [Maine] Record Book" [TS, MHS, 1964], p. 3 citing g.s., Friends cem, North Berwick): m Berwick 4 Jan 1787 Hannah Varney (NHGR, 1:119), b Dover NH 14 Feb 1765 dau of Timothy & Abigail (Hussey) Varney of Dover NH and Berwick (NHGR, 4:124), d 15 Mar 1851 ae 85y (Frost, "North Berwick Record Book," p. 3, bur with her husband)
- ix Mary, b 7 Jan 1765: d 25 Feb 1779

Joseph C. Anderson II, 5337 Del Roy Drive, Dallas, TX 75229

Butler, Benjamin   44b   1 - 3 - 4 - 0 - 0
Sandy River, First Township [now Farmington], Lincoln County

BENJAMIN BUTLER, b Martha's Vineyard MA 1749 son of Ebenezer & Mehitable (Norton) Butler (Charles E. Banks, *The History of Martha's Vineyard, Dukes County, Massachusetts* [1925]), hereafter Banks, 3:56): d Avon Feb 1828 (Francis G. Butler, *History of Farmington* [repr 1983], p. 400): m abt 1769 AMY DAGGETT, b Edgartown MA 1752 dau of Prince & Sarah (Norton) Daggett (Banks, 3:143– 44), d Feb 1828 (ibid., 3:61). Benjamin removed to Farmington in 1790 and settled on river-lot #23 (*History of Farmington*, p. 400). He was a carpenter by trade and was the contractor for building the first bridge erected in Farmington over the Sandy River (ibid.). He later moved to Avon where he died (ibid.).

Children, first 10 b Martha's Vineyard: births VR Farmington; Banks, 3:61–62; *History of Farmington*, pp. 400–1
- i Nancy, b 2 Feb 1770: m int Farmington 16 Feb 1805 David Paine of Embden (Farmington VR)
- ii Amy, b 10 Feb 1772: d 24 Feb 1772 ae 2 weeks (Farmington VR)

46 MAINE FAMILIES IN 1790

iii Mary, b 1 Mar 1773: d 17 May 1773 ae 11 weeks (Farmington VR)
iv Mary/Polly, b 30 Aug 1774: d 12 Apr 1844 (*History of Farmington*, p. 400): m Farmington 24 Dec 1800 Elisha Bradford of Farmington (VR), b Meduncook 25 Oct 1774 son of Joseph & Abigail (Starling) Bradford (ibid., p. 396) [see JOSEPH BRADFORD family, *Maine Families*, 1:21-22], d 17 Mar 1832 (ibid.). He was a War of 1812 soldier (ibid.)
v Benjamin, b 30 Aug 1776: d New Sharon (*History of Farmington*, p. 400): m (1) Farmington 24 Dec 1800 Hulda Bradford (VR), b 7 Feb 1781 dau of Joseph & Abigail (Starling) Bradford and sis of Elisha above (*History of Farmington*, p. 396): m (2) 1 Nov 1847 Katherine (Luce) Johnson wid of Thomas Johnson (ibid., p. 400)
vi Zimri, b 25 Oct 1778: d 29 Oct 1778 ae 4d (Farmington VR)
vii Ebenezer Cheney/Chancey, b 8 Apr 1780: d Ontario, Canada after 1824 (*History of Farmington*, p. 400): m int Farmington 12 Mar 1802 Betsey Johnson (VR) who was b Farmington (VR)
viii Ralph, b 27 Sep 1782: m int Farmington 26 Sep 1806 Mary Stevens of Strong (Farmington VR). He lived in Farmington, then moved to Avon about 1815 (*History of Farmington*, p. 400)'
ix Melinda, b 5 Feb 1786: m int Farmington 2 Dec 1805 James Paine of Embden (Farmington VR) [*History of Farmington*, p. 400, gives m int 12 Jan 1804 (sic)]
x Lovina, b 28 Dec 1789: d 18 Jan 1790 ae 3 weeks (Farmington VR)
xi Lovina, b 20 Apr 1791: d 25 Apr 1791 ae 5d (Farmington VR)
xii Lovey, b 19 Apr 1792: d 1838 (*History of Farmington*, p. 401): m int Farmington 11 Mar 1809 John Paine of Anson (Farmington VR)
xiii William, b 10 Oct 1795 (Farmington VR): d 13 Sep 1848 (William C. Hatch, *A History of Industry, Maine* [1893], p. 599): m int Farmington 23 Apr 1818 Betsey Davis (*History of Farmington*, p. 401) b 10 Sep 1795 dau of David & Olive (Mayhew) Davis (*History of Industry*, p. 599), d Nov 1858 ae 63y (ibid., p. 599). They moved to Camden Twsp, Kent Co, Ontario, Canada in 1840 (ibid.)

Carol F. Nye, RFD 1, Box 388, Belgrade, ME 04917

Cain, Samuel   31a   1 - 1 - 2 - 0 - 0
    Sedgwick Town, Hancock County

SAMUEL CAIN, b York 30 Nov 1721 son of Nicholas & Mary (Parsons) Cane/Cain (Lester M. Bragdon & John E. Frost, *Vital Records of York, Maine* [1992], p. 30): d prob Sedgwick aft 1790 (USC): m prob Phillipstown [Sanford] c1763 ABIGAIL _____ (Abigail's first name from Samuel Cain family listing in the Sedgwick VR; while not proven, descendants have felt that her surname was Pierce or Pearce), b c1739, d Long Island, Blue Hill Bay aft 1835 when she was listed as ae 96y (Rev. Jonathan Fisher, "Lists of Inhabitants of Bluehill, as they were on 1st Jan 1811," [1835], at Bluehill Town office). Samuel had land dealings in Phillipstown in 1758, 1761, 1764, 1765 and 1770 (York Co deeds). He and Abigail settled in Sedgwick probably about 1770.

Children: births VR Sedgwick
- i Lydia, b prob Phillipstown 24 Jun 1764
- ii Joseph, b prob Phillipstown 11 Apr 1767
- iii Abigail, b Sedgwick 10 May 1771: d Long Island, Blue Hill Bay 16 Dec 1851 ae 81y 7m 6d (g.s., Long Island cem): m Sedgwick 17 Oct 1791 David Carter (VR), b Edgecomb 24 Jul 1768 son of James & Lydia (Day) Carter (BHM, 5:183–84), d Long Island, Blue Hill Bay 14 Mar 1844 ae 74y 8m 10d (ibid.; g.s., Long Island cem)
- iv Mercy, b Sedgwick 10 Nov 1773: d Long Island, Blue Hill Bay 20 Nov 1863 (Bluehill VR; g.s., Carter Point cem, Sedgwick): m prob Sedgwick 12 May 1794 James Carter Jr. as his 2nd wife (BHM, p. 5:183), b 31 Oct 1764 bro of David above (ibid.), d Long Island, Blue Hill Bay 4 Nov 1834 ae 70y (g.s., Carter Point cem, Sedgwick)
- v Mary, b Sedgwick 26 May 1778
- vi Samuel, b Sedgwick 24 Apr 1779: d Brooklin aft 1850 (USC): m (1) Bluehill 26 Dec 1805 Margaret Yeates ("Index to Original J. Fisher Family Register" [MS, MSL]) who d Sedgwick 19 Mar 1815 (VR): m (2) Sedgwick 13 Nov 1815 Joanna Wilson (VR), b 14 Feb 1796 dau of Samuel & Priscilla (____) Wilson (Sedgwick VR)

Paula and Franklin Kane, 3 Josiah Dr., Litchfield, NH 03051

Camel, Phillip   24c   4 - 2 - 5 - 0 - 0
Standish Town, Cumberland County

PHILLIP CANNELL, b Isle of Man, England c1743 (Gideon T. Ridlon, *Saco Valley Settlements and Families* [1895], hereafter Ridlon, p. 127): d 6 Jun 1824 ae 81y (Albert J. Sears, *Early Families of Standish, Maine* [1991], hereafter Sears, p. 44, citing obit in *Christian Mirror*, issue of 11 Jun 1824, which mentioned he was a native of the Isle of Man): m Malew, Isle of Man, England 8 Jan 1763 JANE SHERLOCK (IGI LDS citing parish register), bp Arbory, Isle of Man, England 25 Apr 1742 dau of William & Elinor (Clark or Tyldesley) Sherlock (LDS IGS citing parish register) [note that Phillip and Jane had a grandson named Clark Cannell (Sears, p. 45)], d 1826 ae 81y [sic] (Sears, p. 44). Phillip came to

America with his wife before the Revolution and settled first at Falmouth (McLellan's *Gorham*, p. 422). About 1770, they moved to Pearsontown [Standish] (ibid.). When he bought property in Pearsontown in 1783, he called himself a cooper (Sears, p. 44).

Children: Ridlon, pp. 127–28; Sears, pp. 44–46
- i Ann/Nancy, bp Malew, Isle of Man, England 28 Oct 1763 (IGI LDS citing parish register): d Standish 7 Feb 1835 ae 78y [sic] (Sears, p. 44): m Standish 16 Aug 1789 Joseph West of Raymond (Standish VR), b Falmouth 8 Jul 1768 son of Desper & Mary (Green) West (Sears, p. 299), d c1813 during the War of 1812 (ibid.)
- ii Thomas, b c1768: d Gorham 12 Mar 1854 ae 86y (Sears, p. 45; g.s., No. Gorham cem): m Standish 8 Jul 1797 Margaret Nason (VR), b Gorham c Jul 1778 dau of Uriah & Abigail (Knight) Nason (Marquis S. King, *Records of Gorham, Maine* [2nd Ed. edited by Russell S. Bickford, 1991], p. 151, her parentage, but not her birthdate, given on the record) [see URIAH NASON family], d 28 Dec 1855 ae 77y 5m (Sears, p. 45)
- iii Phillip Jr., b 18 Aug 1771 (Sears, p. 45): d Standish 18 Mar 1849 ae 77y 8m (g.s., Standish Corner cem): m 10 Feb 1802 Rebecca Green (Sears, p. 45), b Gorham 26 May 1782 dau of John & Mary (Stuart) Green (*Records of Gorham*, op. cit., p. 126), d Canton ae abt 92y (McLellan's *Gorham*, p. 526)
- iv Jane, b c1775: d 30 Aug 1855 ae 80y (Sears, p. 45): unm (ibid.)
- v Joseph, reportedly went to sea and d abroad (Ridlon, p. 127)
- vi Ellen/Eleanor, d bef 5 Jul 1835 (Sears, p. 46): m 12 Feb 1821 Daniel Ridlon (ibid.). They settled in Porter

Dorothy K. Lachance, 3 Cedarbrook Drive, Scarborough, ME 04074

Carll, Nathaniel   15a   3 - 1 - 4 - 0 - 0
Falmouth Town, Cumberland County

NATHANIEL CARLE/CARLL, b Dover NH 1 Nov 1713 son of Samuel & Patience (Evans) Carle (VR): d aft 26 Mar 1801 when he deposed (see below): m int Falmouth 9 Aug 1741 ELIZABETH DOUGHTY (VR) dau of James & Mary (Robinson) Doughty (genealogical column in *Portland Evening Express*, dated 15 Oct 1897). Nathaniel deposed 26 Mar 1801, ae 87y, that he came to Falmouth in 1734 and helped to frame a sawmill being built by Thomas Westbrook and Samuel Waldo on the lower falls of the Presumpscot River (Gideon T. Ridlon, *Saco Valley Settlements and Families* [1895, reprinted 1969], p. 556). He appears on the 1748 tax rate of the Falmouth First Parish (*Maine*

Seine, 8:3:72) and he and a Jonathan Carle are listed on the 1766 tax list of Falmouth (Marquis F. King, *Baptisms and Admissions from the Records of the First Church in Falmouth, Now Portland, Maine* [1898], p. 187). Nathaniel listed himself as a resident of Falmouth in 1798 when he deeded to his grandson, Nathaniel Kilpatrick (Cum Co deeds 38:278).

[In *Maine Families* 3:38, this Falmouth man was identified as the Nathaniel Carll, Revolutionary soldier, who lived at Scarborough and Waterborough, Maine. There were two men by this name in Maine. Land records confirm that Nathaniel Carle of Falmouth was the son of Samuel Carle of Scarborough and that Nathaniel was a resident of Falmouth in 1771, 1776, 1782, 1787–89 and 1798 (Cum Co deeds 8:428, 445; 16:142, 369; 38:278). The Nathaniel Carle described in *Maine Families* 3:38 was a nephew of Nathaniel Carle of Falmouth. Although not enumerated at Waterborough in 1790, he was probably a resident there, since he had a daughter born at Waterborough in Sep 1789.]

Children, order unknown, perhaps others
- i Mary, m int Falmouth 13 Jun 1761 Floyd Kilpatrick of Scarborough (Falmouth VR; NEHGR 16 [1862]:319) [see FLOYD KILPATRICK family]. Nathaniel Carle sold his home estate in 1798 to his grandson, Nathaniel Kilpatrick (Cum Co deeds 38:278)
- ii Patience, m Falmouth 19 Jan 1763 Zaccheus Allen ("Book of the Returns of Marriages in the County of Cumberland," Cum Co Commissioners Recs, 2:135; NEHGR 14 [1860]:223). In 1790 they lived at Falmouth near Nathaniel Carle (USC)
- iii Sarah, b c1751, d 8 Apr 1776 "in the 26th year of her age" (g.s., cem at 200 Falmouth Rd., Falmouth): m bef 1770 when their 1st child was born Moses Merrill (Samuel Merrill, *Merrill Memorial* [1917–1928], 2:401), b Falmouth 30 Dec 1743 son of Humphrey & Betty (Merrill) Merrill, d 18 Apr 1834 (ibid.). Sarah's gravestone inscription says she was a dau of Nathaniel Carll.

Clayton R. Adams, 6 Laurel Road, Brunswick, ME 04011

Clay, Rich^d 59b   1 - 0 - 2 - 0 - 0
   Buxton Town, York Town

RICHARD CLAY, son of Richard & Mary (____) Clay of Portsmouth NH (GDMNH, p. 149): d Buxton 27 Sep 1801 "said to be the oldest man in town" (VR): m int Biddeford 18 Mar 1734 RACHEL PENNELL (VR), b Gloucester MA 25 Nov 1721 dau of Thomas & Sarah (Duren/Durrell) Pennell (VR), living on 23 May 1797 when both Richard and Rachel deeded Buxton land to Benjamin Elwell (Sybil Noyes notes on Saco-Biddeford, at MHS, Pennell Family 5/18). Richard settled in Biddeford by 1735 and moved to Narragansett Township No. 1 [now Buxton] in 1755 (Gideon T. Ridlon, *Saco Valley Settlements and Families* [1895], p. 577).

Children: births first 7 VR Biddeford, NEHGR 71 [1917]:132, 211, 212, 214, births last 5 VR Buxton

  i Richard Jr., b Biddeford 3 Jun 1739: d bef 3 Jul 1788 when his wid remarried (MHGR 2:56): m prob Ruth Whitten dau of John & Ruth (Merrill) Whitten of Arundel (Sybil Noyes, "Whidden of Greenland, New Hampshire and Witten of Kennebunkport" [TS, MSL], p. 18). Ruth was called Ruth Clay in her father's will dated 16 Apr 1787 (John E. Frost, *Maine Probate Abstracts*, 14/425). She m (2) Sanford 3 Jul 1788 Samuel Tweed (Noyes, op. cit.)

  ii Sarah, b Biddeford 27 Apr 1743: d Limington 14 Nov 1833 ae 90y (Robert L. Taylor, *Early Families of Limington* [1991], p. 151): m (1) Biddeford 30 Aug 1762 Stephen Safford (MHGR, 6:297), b Newbury MA 18 Feb 1738 son of James & Hepsibah (Hale) Safford (VR): m (2) Buxton 6 Dec 1770 Caleb Hopkinson (Cyrus Woodman, *Records of the Church of Christ in Buxton, Maine During the Pastorate of Rev. Paul Coffin*, [1989], p. 20), b Bradford MA 30 Aug 1749 son of John & Sarah (Morse) Hopkinson (VR), d Limington 19 Feb 1841 (*Limington*, op. cit.)

  iii Daniel, b Biddeford 12 Jul 1745: d Buxton May 1810 (Gideon T. Ridlon, *Saco Valley Settlements and Families* [1895], p. 578): m Pepperellborough [Saco] 7 Sep 1769 Jerusha Elwell (*First Book of Records of the First Church in Pepperrellborough* [1914], p. 110), b 1750, d Buxton 3 May 1810 (VR)

  iv Jonathan, b Biddeford 4 Jun 1747: d Buxton Feb 1839 (VR): m Buxton 25 Sep 1783 Esther Flood (Woodman, *Church of Christ*, p. 24) who d Buxton 9 Nov 1830 (VR)

  v Rachel, b Biddeford 10 May 1748: d an infant (Ridlon, op. cit.)

  vi Thomas, b Biddeford 5 Dec 1750: d Gorham 9 Jan 1846 ae 96y (VR; McLellan's *Gorham*, pp. 429-30): m int Gorham 15 Oct 1781 Ruth Gammon (VR), b Gorham dau of Philip & Joanna (____) Gammon (McLellan, op. cit., pp. 429, 510), d Gorham Apr 1829 (ibid.)

  vii Benjamin, b Biddeford 7 Jun 1753: d Limington 21 Apr 1826 (*Limington*, op. cit., p. 76): m (1) int Gorham 2 Oct 1779 Jane Hunnewell of Pearsontown [now Standish] (VR), b Scarborough 27 May 1752 (*Limington*, op. cit.), d Limington Mar 1825 ae 72y 10m (ibid.): m (2) 2 Nov 1825 Hannah (Presson) (Marriner) (Dunn) Sawyer wid of William Sawyer (ibid.; Robert Taylor, "Early Families of Cornish, Maine" [1985], p. 32), b c1751, d Limington Oct 1835 ae 84y (*Limington*, op. cit.). Benjamin was a Rev War pensioner (pension #S36978)

viii Mary/Molly, b Buxton 1 Jul 1756: d Gorham 11 Aug 1833 (VR): m int Gorham 29 Nov 1777 Samuel Hamblen Jr. (VR), bp Gorham 11 Apr 1753 son of Samuel & Temperance (Lewis) Hamblen (McLellan's *Gorham*, pp. 545–46), d Gorham 24 Dec 1834 (VR)

ix Rachel, b Buxton 5 Jan 1759: m Buxton 13 Dec 1781 James Rounds (Woodman, *Church of Christ*, p. 23) who d Clark Twp OH 3 Jan 1843 (Carl N. Thompson, *Historical Collections of Brown Co OH* [1969], p. 539)

x Jemima, b Buxton 15 Feb 1761: d 1805 (Louise H. Coburn, *Skowhegan on the Kennebec* [1941], 2:998): m Gorham 9 Aug 1787 Butler Lombard (VR), b Barnstable MA 1756 prob son of Nathaniel & Abigail (Lumbert) Lombard (Charles R. Lombard, *Lombard Family: The Progeny of Thomas Lombard in America* [1948], n.p.), d Starks 1826 (ibid.) and bur at Dayton (Fisher's *Soldiers*, p. 483). He was a Rev War soldier (Rev War pension #S37636)

xi Abigail, b Buxton 7 Jul 1763

xii Elizabeth, b Buxton 11 Dec 1765: d Buxton 11 Nov 1852 (VR): m Buxton 16 Mar 1787 Nathaniel Cole (Woodman, *Church of Christ*, p. 25) who d Buxton 7 Jul 1839 (VR)

Dana A. Batchelder, 258 South Sea Avenue, West Yarmouth, MA 02673

Clements, Samuel   57a   3 - 3 - 5 - 0 - 0
Berwick Town, York County

SAMUEL CLEMENTS, b Somersworth NH c1744 son of Samuel & Sarah (Rollins) Clements ("The Diary of Master Joseph Tate of Somersworth, N.H.," NEHGR, 74 [1919]:306; date of birth based on Samuel's Rev War enlistment in 1778 at ae 34y): d Berwick 9 Nov 1805 [sic, prob s/b 1804, see below] (John E. Frost & Joseph C. Anderson II, *Vital Records of Berwick, South Berwick and North Berwick, Maine to the Year 1892* [1993], hereafter VR, p. 247). [While the Berwick VR state Samuel d in Nov 1805, the date was more likely Nov 1804 as the adm of his estate was granted to his wid on 18 Feb 1805, she filing the inventory on 14 Mar 1805 (York Co Probate, 20:27)]. He m (1) (prob abt 1766) SARAH AUSTIN ("Master Tate," NEHGR, 74 [1919]:307) dau of Benjamin & Sarah (Pinkham) Austin (ibid.; Strafford Co NH deeds, 32:356), d 1781 ("Friends Records, Dover, N.H., Monthly Meeting," NHGR, 2:148): m (2) Berwick 10 Apr 1783 JUDITH NOCK/KNOX (VR, p. 127), b Somersworth NH 5 Jan 1754 dau of Ebenezer & Elizabeth (Ricker) Nock (Percival Wood Clement, *Ancestors and Descendants of Robert Clements* [n.d.], hereafter *Robert Clements*, 1:218), d Detroit ME 19 Aug 1840 (ibid.). Samuel was a Rev War soldier in Capt. Hodgdon's 10th Company, 2nd Regiment (MS&S 3:621). When he enlisted on

20 Apr 1778, he was described as being ae 34y, 5'10" in stature, brown complexioned and a resident of Berwick (ibid.). His first wife, Sarah Austin, was a Quaker who left the faith when she married Samuel (NHGR, 2:148). In 1765, Samuel was deeded property in Berwick by his father, from which time forward he prob resided in Berwick (*Robert Clements*, 1:218). He was there in 1771 with a house and real estate with an annual worth of 1£12s (Bettye Hobbs Pruitt, *The Massachusetts Tax Valuation List of 1771* [1978], p. 738).

Children by 1st wife, Sarah Austin: "Master Tate," NEHGR, 73 [1919]:307; all but Lydia named in Strafford Co NH deeds, 32:356, dated 1798, in which they quitclaimed to Joseph Austin of Somersworth NH all their right in the estate of their grandfather, Benjamin Austin
  i Moses, b 1 May 1767: d Berwick 16 Dec 1859 ae 92y 7m 16d (VR, p. 311): m Berwick 23 Jul 1795 Betsey Hanson (VR, p. 198), b c Apr 1776, d Berwick 2 May 1855 ae 79y 10d (Wilbur D. Spencer, *Burial Inscriptions and Other Data of Burials in Berwick, York County, Maine to the Year 1892* [1922], p. 19) [*Robert Clements*, p. 1:363, states Betsey was b Jul 1774 and d 24 May 1855 ae 80y 10m]
  ii Phebe, b 21 Jan 1770: d aft 7 Dec 1816 when she quitclaimed to her half-brother, Ebenezer, her right to her father's estate (York Co deeds, 140:271): m (1) int Lebanon Jan 1801 Jedidiah Ricker (VR), b Lebanon 19 Jan 1777 son of Ezekiel & Mary/Molly (Hanson) Ricker (VR; Berwick VR, p. 198), d Kennebunk 20 or 26 Oct 1801 (Lebanon VR): m (2) int Lebanon 25 Oct 1806 Samuel Ricker (VR). She and Samuel were of Lebanon in 1816
  iii Benjamin, d aft 15 Jun 1846 when he deeded his homestead in Palmyra to his son Oliver (Som Co deeds, 67:17): m Berwick 2 Jun 1796 Mary/Polly Fernald (VR, p. 199) dau of Nathaniel & Mary (Gunnison) Fernald (*Robert Clements*, 1:365). Benjamin, a farmer, left Berwick about 1831 and went to Palmyra (ibid.)
  iv Sarah/Sally, m Berwick 26 Nov 1801 Joshua Grant Jr. (VR, p. 201), bp with 6 siblings at the Berwick 2nd Parish 23 Oct 1782 son of Joshua & Judith (Fall) Grant (NEHGR, 74 [1920]:221; parents' marriage in Berwick VR, p. 198) [see JOSHUA GRANT family]
  v Lydia, prob d young as she was not named in 1798 as an heir of her grandfather, Benjamin Austin (Strafford Co NH deeds, 32:356)
  vi Jeremiah, b 7 Dec 1779 (Berwick VR, p. 247): d Westbrook 2 Jun 1866 ae 86y (*Robert Clements*, 1:366): m Westbrook 21 Apr 1811 Elizabeth/Betsey Conant (ibid.), b Westbrook 15 Feb 1791 dau of Daniel & Anne (Haskell) Conant (ibid.), d Westbrook 1 Nov 1879 ae 88y (ibid.). Jeremiah was of Westbrook on 19 Apr 1819 when he conveyed to Ebenezer Clements all his right to his father's estate (York Co deeds, 140:268)

Children by 2nd wife, Judith Nock/Knox: births recorded at Berwick (VR, p. 247)
- vii Ebenezer, b 14 Sep 1783: d Detroit ME 9 Mar 1856 ae 72y 5m 11d (*Robert Clements*, 1:367): m cert Berwick 13 Jun 1812 Margaret/Peggy Lord of Berwick (VR, p. 64), b Berwick 7 Dec 1789 dau of Jeremiah & Grizzel (Grant) Lord (*Robert Clements*, 1:367), d Detroit ME 13 Oct 1855 ae 66y 10m 6d (ibid.)
- viii Mary/Polly, b 28 Mar 1785: d aft 1850 (*Robert Clements*, 1:220). She never married (ibid.)
- ix Samuel, b 22 Aug 1788: d Perry Feb 1868 (*Robert Clements*, 1:369): m Perry abt 1828 Adaline Frost (ibid.), b Perry 1801 dau of John & Lucinda (White) Frost (ibid.), d Perry Jan 1891 ae 90y (ibid.). Samuel reportedly left Berwick and went to Perry as a result of his fiancee, one Sarah Gowell, marrying another man (ibid.). On 8 Oct 1818, Samuel, of Berwick, quitclaimed his right in his father's estate to his brother Ebenezer (York Co deeds 140:269)
- x Lydia, b 27 Mar 1790: d Berwick 28 Jan 1831 (VR, p. 299). She was described as a singlewoman on 29 Dec 1830 when she quitclaimed her right in her father's estate to her brother Ebenezer (York Co deeds, 140:270)
- xi Abigail, b 17 Aug 1792: d Newton MA 8 Jan 1870 (*Robert Clements*, 1:220): m 1 Apr 1822 William Wiswall (ibid.), b 11 Mar 1796 son of Jeremiah Jr. & Sarah (Craft) Wiswall (ibid.), d 7 May 1867
- xii Lewis, b 10 Mar 1794: d East Corinth 1873 (*Robert Clements*, 1:370): m (1) Berwick 5 Feb 1824 Joanna Goodwin (VR, p. 157), bp Berwick 2nd Parish with 3 sisters 20 Nov 1816 dau of Jonathan & Betsey (Andrews) Goodwin (NEHGR, 74 [1920]:247; *Robert Clements*, 1:370), d 1856 (ibid.): m (2) _____ Hamilton (ibid.)
- xiii James, b 24 Jun 1796: d Somersworth NH 29 Sep 1874 ae 78y 3m (*Robert Clements*, 1:370): m (1) Berwick 19 Jul 1827 Mary Hayes (VR, p. 161), b Berwick 3 Nov 1802 dau of Elijah & Mary (Grant) Hayes (Katharine F. Richmond, *John Hayes of Dover, New Hampshire* [1936], p. 141) [see Hon. ELIJAH HAYES family, *Maine Families*, 3:127; see JOSHUA GRANT family], d Berwick 30 or 31 Oct 1850 ae 48y (Berwick VR, p. 309; *John Hayes*, p. 254): m (2) Somersworth 30 Oct 1851 Olive Hamilton of Somersworth NH (*Robert Clements*, 1:370) [m ints recorded Berwick 26 Sep 1851 (VR, p. 106)], b Waterboro 18 Apr 1816 dau of Adrial & Lovey (Walker) Hamilton (*Robert Clements*, 1:370), d Dover NH 2 Mar 1895 ae 78y 10m 14d (ibid.)

Alice L. Sabin, 2281 Hylaea Road, Tucker, GA 30084-4312

Clough, Asa   26b   1 - 1 - 1 - 0 - 0
Bluehill Town, Hancock County

ASA CLOUGH, b Haverhill MA 25 Aug 1764 son of Daniel Jr. & Abigail (Varnum) Clough (BHM, 5:185; will of Daniel Clough Jr. of Dracut MA, Middlesex Co MA Probate #4623): d Blue Hill 2 Jan 1851 (VR): m 27 Nov 1789 ABIGAIL/NABBY PECKER of Bradford MA (BHM, 5:185, which erroneously gives her surname as "Ricker"), b Haverhill MA 27 Nov 1766 dau of Bartholomew & Hannah (Russell) Pecker (VR), d Blue Hill 16 Mar 1854 ae 87y (VR). Asa owned a farm of more than 100 acres on both sides of the main road in Blue Hill (Rufus Candage, *Historical Sketches of Blue Hill* [1905]). He came to Blue Hill "toward the end of the 18th century" with his brothers John and Benjamin (Eva Clough Speare, *The Story of the Family of John Clough of Salisbury, Massachusetts* [1943]; will of Daniel Clough Jr., op. cit.; BHM, 5:185).

Children: births VR Blue Hill; BHM, 5:185
  i   Daniel, b 11 Apr 1790: d 2 Apr 1867 (BHM, 5:185): m 24 Mar 1818 Polly Tenney (ibid.), b 3 Apr 1797 dau of Dr. Nathan & Mary (Carleton) Tenney of Blue Hill (ibid., 5:212), d 8 Dec 1858 (ibid.)
  ii Cheever Russell, b 22 Jul 1792: d at sea Sep 1815 (Blue Hill VR)
  iii Sally, b 5 Nov 1794: d 10 Jun 1852 (BHM, 5:185): m (1) 24 Feb 1831 Benjamin Clay as his 2nd wife (ibid., 5:184), b 17 Oct 1784 son of Jonathan & Mary (Roundy) Clay (ibid.), d 14 Apr 1836 (ibid.): m (2) John Osgood (ibid., 5:185), b 29 Sep 1793 son of John & Joanna (Obear) Osgood (ibid., 5:185, 203)
  iv John, b 20 Jan 1797: d 14 Sep 1883 (BHM, 5:185): m 5 Dec 1827 Jane Lymburner (ibid.)
  v   Asa Jr., b 8 Jan 1799: d 20 Nov 1861 (BHM, 5:185): m (1) Abigail/Nabby Sinclair (ibid.), b 22 Oct 1794 dau of Edward & Mary (Carleton) Sinclair (ibid., 5:210), d 3 Dec 1827 (ibid.): m (2) 11 Sep 1829 Louisa Ray (ibid.)
  vi Leonard, b 3 Sep 1801: d Blue Hill 10 Jul 1865 ae 63y 10m 7d (VR): m 30 Nov 1837 Mary Jane Wood (BHM, 5:185), b 4 Apr 1816 dau of Samuel & Fanny (Colburn) Wood (ibid., 5:215), living in May 1890 (ibid.)
  vii James, b 3 Sep 1803: m Mary M. Carman of Deer Isle (BHM, 5:185)
  viii Lydia, b 22 Sep 1805: m 21 Oct 1830 Putnam Ingalls (BHM, 5:185)
  ix Zelotes, b 24 Nov 1807: alive 1890 (BHM, 5:185): m 15 Oct 1835 Jane Grover (ibid.)
  x   Louisa, b 27 Sep 1811: d 22 Aug 1847 (BHM, 5:185): m 3 Jan 1832 Isaac Merrill (ibid.), b 5 May 1804 son of Caleb & Betsey (Candage) (Day) Merrill (ibid., 5:199–200), d 18 Dec 1881 (ibid.). He m (2) 11 Jun 1851 Joanna S. Hinckley (ibid.).

Robert Dean Wieser, P.O. Box 6573, Rancho Palos Verdes, CA 90734

Cobb, Elisha 17a 4 - 1 - 3 - 0 - 0
Gorham and Scarborough Towns, Cumberland County

ELISHA COBB, b Eastham MA 6 Jun 1736 son of Elisha & Mary (Harding) Cobb (VR): d Gorham 11 Jun 1794 (VR): m Gorham Nov 1760 ELIZABETH MURCH (VR), b c1735, d Gorham 6 Sep 1798 ae 63y (VR; McClellan's *Gorham*, p. 440). On 1 Sep 1752, Timothy Cole of Eastham MA (an uncle on Elisha's mother's side) was appointed guardian of Elisha Cobb, minor son of Elisha Cobb and grandson of Josiah Harding late of Eastham, yeoman, deceased (Barnstable Co MA Probate 7:258; Marion L. Dunn, "Hardings of Maine and Their Roots" [TS, MSL], pp. 6–7). Elisha came up from Cape Cod to Gorham in the early 1750s with some of his Harding relations (Philip Cobb, *A History of the Cobb Family* [1907]). In 1758 he was in Capt. John Libby's Company, Col. Preble's Regiment, during the French & Indian Wars (McClellan's *Gorham*, p. 440). On 25 Jul 1765 he bought land in Gorham and built his home which burned in 1766 (ibid., pp. 306, 440). He served in the Revolution in 1775 (MS&S 3:669).

Children: births VR Gorham
  i   Elisha Jr, b 10 Jun 1761: d Limington Mar 1809 (Robert L. Taylor, *Early Families of Limington* [1991], p. 82): m int Gorham 4 Sep 1790 Molly Murch of Biddeford (VR), b c1767, d Limerick 31 Aug 1849 ae 82y (Taylor, op. cit.)
  ii Mary A., b 4 Oct 1762: d unm
  iii Ezekiel, b 9 May 1764: d Hampden 29 Jun 1816 ae 52y 19d (g.s. Neally Corner cem): m Hampden 19 Oct 1788 Nancy Thompson of Orrington (Rev War pension #W22359) [see EZEKIEL COBB family, *Maine Families*, 3:50; see also GEORGE BROOKS family in this volume]
  iv Phebe, b 16 Apr 1766: m Gorham 17 Mar 1785 Daniel Eldridge Jr (VR; he "of Buxton" according to McLellan), b c1761, d Buxton 1832 (Fisher's *Soldiers*, p. 233; Rev War pension #W24116)
  v   Reuben, b 9 Mar 1769: d Otisfield 14 Dec 1831 (VR): m Gorham 5 Apr 1801 Betsey Hatch (VR), prob the Elizabeth Hatch b Gorham 13 Sep 1770 dau of Joseph & Sarah (Sawyer) Hatch (VR; McLellan's *Gorham*, p. 567), d Otisfield 21 Oct 1828 ae 58y (VR)
  vi William, b 20 Jul 1771: d Buxton 20 Nov 1843 ae 72y (g.s. Highland cem): m int Gorham 10 Mar 1798 Nancy Poak/Poke (VR; "of Biddeford" according to McLellan) who d Buxton 21 Jan 1875 ae 97y (g.s. Highland cem)
  vii Samuel [C.], b 15 Oct 1773: d 15 Oct 1839 ae 66y (McLellan's *Gorham*, p. 441): m Buxton 9 Dec 1802 Tabitha Elwell of Buxton (Cyrus Woodman, *Records of the Church of Christ in Buxton During the Pastorate of Rev. Paul*

Coffin [1989], p. 37) who d Gorham 18 Oct 1840 (VR)
viii Ebenezer, b 22 Jan 1777: d in Alna (McLellan's *Gorham*, p. 440)
ix Elizabeth, b 22 Jul 1779: d unm at Gorham (McLellan's *Gorham*, p. 440)

T. A. McKay, 615 So. Barton, Arlington, VA 22204

Colburn, Margaret   39b   3 - 0 - 6 - 0 - 0
Hallowell Town, Lincoln County

MARGARET (BURNS) COLBURN (widow of Oliver Colburn), b Medford MA 1743 (Pittston VR; George A. & Silas R. Coburn, *Genealogy of the Descendants of Edward Colburn/Coburn* [1913], p. 89) poss an unrecorded dau of Francis & Margaret (_____) Burns of Medford MA (Medford MA VR lists 3 of their children b 1751–1755): d Pittston 19 Sep 1812 ae 69y (VR): m 13 Jan 1767 OLIVER COLBURN (Hallowell VR), b Dracut MA 20 Mar 1744 son of Jeremiah & Sarah (Jewell) Colburn (*Colburn/Coburn*, op. cit.), d Pittston 10 Jan 1788 ae 44y (VR). On her marriage record to Oliver Colburn, Margaret was called "Mrs. Margaret Burns." However, this would appear to have been a title of respect rather than an indication of a previous marriage, as the marriage record was listed among others in which all the brides were called "Mrs." Oliver Colburn and three brothers and four sisters moved to the Pittston area from Dunstable MA in 1761 (J. W. Hanson, *History of Gardiner, Pittston and West Gardiner, Maine* [1852]). In Jul 1775 Oliver was Captain of a company of Minutemen in Col. Arnold's regiment (MS&S 3:748). His bro Reuben built the batteaux for Arnold's expedition to Quebec (*Colburn/Coburn*, op. cit., p. 89). Oliver was on a list dated 4 Jan 1777 of male inhabitants at Gardinerstown (*Maine Genealogist*, 13 [Aug 1991]:65).

[In the Pittston area were a Robert, James and Joseph Burns, all brickmakers. Joseph, who administered Robert's estate in 1765 (Lin Co Probate 1:76), served in Oliver Colburn's Minuteman Co (MS&S 2:871). James was later of Vassalborough and Anson. He named one of his sons Francis Burns (suggesting James was a son of Francis and Margaret Burns) and witnessed a deed for Oliver Colburn.]

Children: *Colburn/Coburn*, op. cit., p. 89; *History of Gardiner*, pp. 71ff; and cited sources
  i   Rachel, m int Pittston 16 Jun 1804 William Hatch of Berwick (Pittston VR; *History of Gardiner*)
  ii Hannah, b c1769, d Pittston 21 Jul 1861 ae 92y (VR): m Pittston 19 Jun 1796 Joseph Rollins (VR), b c1769 son of Eliphalet & Abigail (Glidden)

Rollins (John R. Rollins, *Record of Families of the Name Rawlins or Rollins in the United States* [1874], pp. 43, 92–93), d Pittston 25 Apr 1828 ae 59y (VR)

iii Rebecca, prob d 27 Oct 1846 (Rev. David Q. Cushman, *The History of Ancient Sheepscot and Newcastle* [1882], p. 406): m Pittston 27 Oct 1793 Robert Murray of Newcastle (VR) son of David & Elizabeth (McLelland) Murray (Cushman, op. cit.). Robert was lost at sea in a hurricane 29 Dec 1800 (ibid.) and Rebecca was prob the widow Rebecca Murray who m (2) 25 Dec 1807 her 1st husband's nephew Robert Cunningham alias Murray (ibid.)

iv Oliver, b Pittston 20 Mar 1774 (VR): d Pittston 3 Jan 1835 ae 60y (VR): m int Pittston 23 Jan 1802 Hannah Smith (VR), b 26 Oct 1782 dau of Henry & Sarah (Colburn) Smith (*History of Gardiner*; *Colburn/Coburn*, op. cit.), d Pittston 15 May 1874 ae 91y 6m (VR)

v Sarah/Sally, m Pittston 30 Nov 1797 Thomas Cutts of Industry (VR), he poss b Pittston 30 Mar 1775 son of Samuel & Sarah (Hill) Cutts (VR)

vi Mary, b 20 Sep 1780: d 22 Oct 1866 (*Colburn/Coburn*, op. cit.): m 10 Mar 1803 Aaron Young of Bangor (ibid.; *History of Gardiner*), b Pittston 12 Mar 1783 son of David & Elizabeth (____) Young (VR) [see DAVID YOUNG family, *Maine Families*, 1:298]. They res Pittston, Wiscasset, Alna and Bangor

vii John, b 1783 (Pittston VR): d Pittston 16 Apr 1850 (VR): m int Pittston Jul 1807 Olive Colburn (VR), b Pittston 20 Nov 1784 dau of Reuben & Elizabeth (Lewis) Colburn (VR), d Pittston 9 Aug 1869 ae 86y (VR)

viii William, b Pittston c1785: m Dresden 19 Jun 1808 Martha Blanchard (NEHGR, 66 [1912]:109) who d in Aug 1863 (*Colburn/Coburn*, op. cit.). They res Richmond

Janet S. Seitz, 11521 Upper Sunny Circle, Eagle River, AK 99577-7414

Cole, Eli   60c   1 - 3 - 4 - 0 - 0
Kittery Town, York County

ELI COLE, b Kittery c1758 of parentage unknown (Rev War pension #S16733 in which he stated he was ae 60y on 14 Apr 1818 and ae 74y on 24 Jul 1832): d Buxton 16 Dec 1832 (VR): m Kittery 19 Feb 1778 OLIVE WILSON (Joseph C. Anderson II & Lois W. Thurston, *Vital Records of Kittery, Maine to the Year 1892* [1991], p. 160), b c1755 dau of Benjamin & Susanna (Staples) Wilson (will of Benjamin Wilson dated 27 May 1783 naming his dau Olive Cole, York Co Probate #20510; Everett S. Stackpole, *Old Kittery and Her Families* [1903], p. 800): d Buxton 19 Jun 1836 (VR). Eli was a Rev War soldier and pensioner serving for almost 3 years (Fisher's *Soldiers*, p. 149 citing pension #S16733; MS&S, 3:761; *New Hampshire State Papers*, 14:664). They lived in the Kittery 3rd parish and moved to Buxton betw 1792–95. Eli lived in Buxton on Lot 4 of Range D of the 3rd Division (William F. Goodwin, *Records of the Proprietors of Narragansett Township, No. 1, now the Town of Buxton, Maine* [1871]). About 1798, he lived in an unfinished 1-story wood house of 1020 square feet with nine windows (Town Valuation of Real Estate, Buxton TR). Eli dated his will 24 Oct 1829 which was in probate in Jun 1833 (York Co Probate #3390, 44:105). In it, he named his wife Olive, his daus Sally, Eunice, Sophia and Charity, his son Benjamin, and grandchildren Abigail Cole and George Cole Jr. The inventory of his estate included 99 acres in Buxton with a one-story dwelling house and barn, a 29-acre wood lot in Standish and a pew in the Central Baptist Meeting House in Buxton (York Co Probate, 44:175).

Children, first 7 b Kittery, last 4 b Buxton: births VR Buxton
  i Sally, b 15 Apr 1778: d Buxton 11 Apr 1799 (VR): m Buxton 13 Dec 1798 Thomas Decker (*The Records of the Church of Christ in Buxton, Maine During the Pastorate of Rev. Paul Coffin* [repr 1989], hereafter Coffin, p. 34), b c1778 son of Joshua & Susanna (Boston) Decker of Buxton (Buxton VR; Gideon T. Ridlon, *Saco Valley Settlements and Families* [1895], pp. 614, 618). He m (2) 16 Apr 1804 Nancy Sweetser (ibid.) and res in Prospect, Clinton and Boothbay (ibid.)
  ii Benjamin Wilson, b 28 May 1780: d 1858 (DAR Lineage 120:186, #119604): of Prospect when he m Buckstown 29 Mar 1805 Maria Burnam of Buckstown (Prospect VR)
  iii Susanna/Sukey, b 7 Apr 1782: d Buxton 7 Aug 1839 (VR): m Buxton 24 Sep 1806 John Smith of Standish (Charles A. Meserve, "Records of Births and Deaths in the Town of Buxton" [TS, MHS, 1891], hereafter Meserve, p. 142)
  iv Charles, b 4 Nov 1784: d 22 Sep 1813 (Buxton VR): m Buckstown 27 Sep 1807 Mary Brown (Prospect VR)
  v Olive, b 21 Aug 1786: d Buxton 6 May 1828 (VR)
  vi Ezra, b 24 Feb 1789: d Buxton 10 May 1816 (VR). He m and had a son George M. Cole b Buxton 3 Oct 1812 (VR), but the name of Ezra's wife was not given on the record
  vii Eunice, b 1 May 1791: alive in 1829 when named in her father's will
  viii Charity, b 25 Mar 1794: m Buxton 18 Jan 1816 Jacob Nutter (Meserve, p. 142), b c1790 son of Lemuel & Sally (Dennett) Nutter (Buxton VR), d 23 Feb 1820 (Stephen E. Nichols, "Buxton Ancient Cemetery Records" [TS, Archives of Buxton Town Hall])
  ix Sophia, b 1 Dec 1797: d 1 May 1838 (g.s., Flanders cem, Buxton): m Buxton 5 Nov 1818 Richard Phenix of Buxton (VR), b c1797, d 27 Aug 1847 (g.s., Flanders cem, Buxton). They were members of the 1st Baptist

Church of Buxton and lived in "Moderation," located 4 miles from the Baptist Church (Cyrus Woodman Collection, MHS Coll. 1589, Series 4, Box 12/14a)
- x Lydia, b 18 Jul 1800: d Buxton 25 Apr 1836 (VR)
- xi Sally, b 26 Sep 1802: m Buxton 2 Aug 1827 Thomas Smith of Buxton (VR). They lived 1½ miles north of the Baptist Church in Buxton on the Standish road (Cyrus Woodman Collection, op. cit.)

Earlene "Kitty" Ahlquist Chadbourne, 1 Fides Drive, N. Saco, ME 04072-9360

Collins, Richard   54a   1 - 1 - 4 - 0 - 0
Plantations West of Machias, No. 5 [now Harrington], Washington County

RICHARD COLLINS, b Cape Elizabeth 1753 (Rev War pension #R2181): d Harrington 31 Aug 1834 (ibid.): m Cape Elizabeth 17 Apr 1777 MARY FICKETT (pension, op. cit.), b Cape Elizabeth c1759 (pension, op. cit.) dau of John & Isabel (Dyer) Fickett (ibid.), d Milbridge 15 Apr 1847 (ibid.). Richard resided in Cape Elizabeth when he first enlisted for Rev War service in 1776 (ibid.). This service included three months as a prisoner on an English guard ship at New York (ibid.). He was one of the early settlers of Harrington who received deeds on 2 Apr 1794 (BHM, 8:222). His lot was No. 35 on the 1794 survey map of Harrington (the part now No. Milbridge).

Children, as found
- i Abigail/Nabby, b prob Cape Elizabeth: d bef 1855 (pension, op. cit.): m Alexander Campbell son of Alexander & Elizabeth (Nickels) Campbell (BHM, 7:167)
- ii Richard Jr., b Cape Elizabeth 1783 (1850 USC): d bef 1855 (pension, op. cit.): m Dolly Ray dau of William & Rachel (Strout) Ray [see WILLIAM RAY family, *Maine Families*, 3:233], d aft 1860 (USC)
- iii Bethia, b prob Cape Elizabeth c1785: d Milbridge 20 Mar 1855 ae 75y (Clarence Day, "Death Notices from the *Machias Union*," Vol. 1, 1853–1873 [TS, MSL], p. 11): m Joseph Ray (pension, op. cit.) bro of Dolly above who d prob Milbridge betw 1860–1870 (USC)
- iv Sophia, b prob Harrington by 1790 (USC; Sophia named as Richard's dau in pension, op. cit.): m William Ray, b c1787 (1850 USC) bro of Dolly and Joseph above, living Harrington 1850 (USC). In 1855, Sophia was described as Richard's only surviving child (pension, op. cit.)

Joyce P. Davis, 2639 Fort Scott Drive, Arlington, VA 22202

Corson, Moses   67c   1 - 7 - 3 - 0 - 0
Shapleigh Town, York County

MOSES CORSON, b Dover NH c1744 son of Zebulon & Mary (Tibbetts) Corson (Stanton D. Colson, *The Descendants of Cornelius Cursonwhit of Dover, New Hampshire* [1991], 1:193; George W. Chamberlain, "Lebanon, Maine Genealogies 1750–1892" [TS, MHS, 1947] 1:#164, 165): d Shapleigh 29 Dec 1802 (Gertrude Ella Hall, "Nathan Goodwin's Book of Remarks, Shapleigh, Maine 1777–1831" [TS, 1950, MHS], hereafter "Nathan Goodwin," p. 4): m Lebanon 15 May 1769 ELIZABETH/BETSY PERKINS (VR), b perhaps Rochester NH c1750, a poss but unproven dau of Gilbert & Charity (Hartford) Perkins of Rochester NH and Lebanon. [Gilbert Perkins came from Rochester NH to Lebanon bef 1766; on 1 Apr 1773 he reportedly deeded to Moses Corson (Chamberlain, op. cit., 3:#143)]. She d Canaan 13 Sep 1827 (VR). Moses served in the Rev War in Capt. Phillip Hubbard's company, Col. Richard Scammon's regiment and was at the Battle of Bunker Hill 17 Jun 1775 (George W. Chamberlain, *Soldiers of the American Revolution of Lebanon, Maine* [1897], p. 14). He sold his place in Lebanon in 1780 and moved to Shapleigh where he had a homestead of 205 acres (Orville Corson, *Three Hundred Years with the Corson Family*, hereafter *Corson Family*, 2:282). The adm of his estate was granted on 21 Feb 1803 to his wid Betsey (York Co Probate 19:177).

Children, order uncertain
 i Isaac, b prob Lebanon c1770: d Canaan 4 Mar 1832 ae 62y (VR; g.s., Old Village cem): m (1) Shapleigh 9 Mar 1789 Esther Nason (John E. Frost & Joseph C. Anderson II, *Marriage Returns of York County, Maine* [1993], p. 8) who prob d Waterville 28 May 1809 (DAR Misc. Records, 11:1941–42): m (2) Canaan c1810 Nancy Tuttle (Corson, op. cit., p. 283) who d Canaan 10 Nov 1863 (VR). She m (2) Canaan 26 Jan 1836 Baxter Crowell (VR). Isaac Corson of Waterville acted as a surety in 1803 on the adm of his father's estate (York Co Probate 19:177)
 ii Tamson/Fanny, d 20 Jul 1822 ("Nathan Goodwin," p. 13): m int Shapleigh 5 Sep 1789 John Quimby (VR; *Corson Family*, 2:282). John Quimby deeded to Moses Corson Jr. his wife's share of Moses Corson Sr.'s estate (York Co deeds, 76:57)
 iii Moses Jr., prob the "Capt. Moses Corson" who d Shapleigh 17 Jun 1816 ("Nathan Goodwin," p. 10): m Roxanna Carpenter (*Corson Family*, 2:282) who was living on 9 Apr 1820 when "widow Rockey courson daughter dec." ("Nathan Goodwin," p. 12). She m (2) Levi Bean of Hartland and in 1833 they gave quitclaim deeds for her share of Moses's estate to her son Alanson Corson of Canaan (*Corson Family*, 2:282). Moses lived in Shapleigh and was a constable in 1815 (TR). His estate was adm in 1817 by his brother-in-law, Andrew Lord (York Co deeds, 102:192)

iv Priscilla, b prob Lebanon c1778: d 28 Jun 1820 ("Nathan Goodwin," p. 12): m 3 Apr 1797 Andrew Lord (*Corson Family*, 2:282) [m int Shapleigh 22 Feb 1797 (VR)], b Lebanon 14 Nov 1775 son of Noah & Keziah (Brackett) Lord (*Corson Family*, 2:282), d Acton 11 May 1850 ae 74y (ibid.; *Boston Evening Transcript*, issue of 22 Jun 1930, query #9569). He acted as a surety in 1803 on the adm of Moses Corson's estate (York Co Probate 19:177) and bought the rights of some of the other heirs (York Co deeds 138:81). He m (2) 21 Dec 1820 Mrs. Hopey (____) Shackley of Shapleigh (VR)

v James, d Canastota NY Jul 1839 (*Boston Evening Transcript*, issue of 17 Jan 1927, query #5038): m (1) Newfield 27 Nov 1800 Theodate Page of Newfield (VR): m (2) Waterville c1813 Sarah/Sally (Evans) Otis, wid of Elwell Otis (*Boston Evening Transcript*, issue of 12 Mar 1930, query #9569; William L. Otis, *Otis Family in America* [1924], p. 133). James acted as a surety in 1803 on the adm of his father's estate (York Co Probate 19:177)

vi Betsy, m Shapleigh 16 Mar 1801 John Wyman Page (VR)

vii Benjamin, b c1785: d Waterville 3 Jul 1854 ae 69y 3m (g.s., Old Cemetery, Oakland). According to descendants of this family, he m (1) Lydia Hussey and m (2) Bathsheba Hussey or Thayer. In 1815, land in Dearborn which included property owned by Benjamin Corson, Robert Hussey and Alvin Thayer, among others, was annexed to Waterville (Henry D. Kingsbury & Simeon L. Deyo, *Illustrated History of Kennebec County, Maine* [1892], pp. 1065–66). Benjamin bought a share of his mother's dower from his brother John (York Co deeds 138:80)

viii John, m Shapleigh 20 Jul 1806 Elizabeth/Betsy Hatch (VR) who d Canaan 6 Oct 1832 (VR). John sold his share in his mother's dower to John & Tamson/Fanny Quimby, Benjamin Corson and Aaron Corson (York Co deeds 138:80). He was a selectman in Canaan in 1818 and 1820 (TR)

ix Love, m int Shapleigh 31 Jan 1808 Edmund Chase of Parsonsfield (VR) who d Parsonsfield 15 Mar 1841 (VR)

x Aaron, d Canaan 4 Jun 1835 (VR): m Keziah ____ who m (2) int Canaan 12 Mar 1839 Robert Murray (VR). Aaron bought a share of his mother's dower from his brother John (York Co deeds 138:80)

xi Seward, b 25 Oct 1793 (Canaan VR): d Canaan 22 Aug 1841 (VR) and bur Old Village cem, Canaan, no dates on gravestone: m 19 Jan 1815 Huldah ____ who was b 19 Nov 1794 (Canaan VR). Seward sold his rights in his father's estate to his brother-in-law, Andrew Lord (York Co deeds 138:81)

Lois M. Griffiths, 338 Norris Hill Road, Monmouth, ME 04259-6925

62   MAINE FAMILIES IN 1790

Crowell, Samuel [s/b Lemuel]   50c   2 - 0 [s/b 1] - 6 - 0 - 0
Winslow Town, with its Adjacents, Lincoln County

[Note: Examination of the original 1790 census sheets on microfilm confirm that the census taker wrote "Lemuel" and not "Samuel" and that there was a male under 16 years of age marked in this household which was not picked up on the printed 1790 census published by the Government Printing Office.]

LEMUEL CROWELL, b Yarmouth MA 16 Mar 1733 son of Thomas [2nd] & Experience (Crowell) Crowell (VR): d prob Waterville [Oakland] prob 1820 (Ken Co deeds 40:159; 1810 and 1820 USC Waterville): m Yarmouth MA 30 Dec 1762 ELIZABETH HAWES (VR), b Yarmouth MA 28 Mar 1742 dau of David & Elizabeth (Cobb) Hawes (VR), d prob Waterville [Oakland] betw 1800 (USC Winslow) and 1810 (USC Waterville). Lemuel and his family came to Winslow bef 1786. On 31 May 1804, Charles Vaughn, agent for the "Proprietors of the Kennebec Purchase from the late Colony of New-Plymouth," granted to Lemuel and his son Moody in quieting deeds the southerly and northerly halves, respectively, of a 191-acre lot No. 1, Plan 8—West Pond Settlement in what is now Oakland (Ken Co grants 2:184, 186). In a deed executed 24 Jan 1821 for $5 each, "we the heirs of Lemuel Crowell," listed in descending order by age, conveyed to Isaiah Crowell of Waterville, the youngest heir, the homestead farm and land that had been granted to Lemuel (Ken Co deeds 40:159, 109:102, 103). The heirs named were Moody Crowell, Judith Mosher, Lucy Wade, Elizabeth Taylor, Experience Burgess, Deborah Rollins and Deliverance Webb.

Children: births first 7 VR Yarmouth MA; Ken Co deed 40:159
  i   Moody, b 7 Aug 1764: d 14 Dec 1838 ae 74y (g.s., Lakeview cem, Oakland): m Winslow 14 Oct 1793 Deborah Webb (VR), b ME c1768 (1850 USC, Waterville), d 9 Oct 1854 ae 86y (g.s., Lakeview cem, Oakland)
  ii son, b 3 Jul 1766: d Yarmouth MA Jul 1766 (VR)
  iii Judith, b 18 Aug 1767: d Belgrade 7 Nov 1832 ae 65y (VR; *Kennebec Journal*, issue of 23 Nov 1832): m Vassalborough 13 Aug 1787 Elisha Mosher (VR), b Dartmouth MA 19 Jun 1765 son of Elisha & Ann (Springer) Mosher (VR), d Belgrade 2 Jan 1847 ae 80y [sic] (VR; *Maine Farmer*, issue of 21 Jan 1847) [see ELISHA MOSHER family]
  iv Lucy, b 16 Jul 1770: d aft 1821 (Ken Co deeds 40:159): m Winslow 17 Jun 1789 Samuel Wade (VR), b MA c1768 (1850 USC, Smithfield), d 28 May 1852 ae 84y (g.s., Old cem, Oakland). Samuel m (2) c1824 Lydia James [see JOHN JAMES Jr. family, *Maine Families*, 2:154–55], b prob Shapleigh c1792 (1850 USC, Smithfield) dau of John Jr. & Lydia (Door) James (DAR Lineage #102307; Lebanon VR)

v Elizabeth, b 10 Jul 1772: d Belgrade 8 Sep 1855 ae 83y 2m (VR; g.s., Quaker cem, Belgrade): m int Winslow 8 Aug 1791 Samuel Taylor (VR), b Hallowell 22 Aug 1769 son of Elias & Mary (Johnson) Taylor (VR; Henry D. Kingsbury and Simeon L. Deyo, *Illustrated History of Kennebec County Maine* [1892], p. 1029), d Belgrade 7 May 1856 ae 86y 8m (VR; g.s., Quaker cem, Belgrade)

vi Experience, b 11 Jul 1774: her husband's 2nd marriage would suggest she d or was divorced by 1818 even though she was listed as an heir and grantor on, but did not sign, Ken Co deed 40:159 dated 4 Jan 1821 (see above): m int Winslow 30 Apr 1798 David Burgess of Harlem [China] (Winslow VR) [Benjamin Burgess, *Memorial of the Family of Thomas and Dorothy Burgess* [1865], p. 59, gives m 21 May 1798], b 28 Aug 1769 son of Benjamin & Rebecca (Parker) Burgess (Burgess, op. cit.), d 23 Mar 1832 ae 63y (ibid.) and bur Stanley Hill cem, China (stone broken, dates missing). David m (2) Vassalborough 3 Dec 1818 Desire Taylor (VR) who is bur next to David and named as his wife. She was b MA c1770 or 1774 (discrepancy betw 1850 USC, China in which she was listed as ae 80y and g.s. giving her age at death as 84), d 18 Mar 1858 (g.s., Stanley Hill cem)

vii Deborah, b 11 Jun 1777: d 29 Apr 1860 ae 83y (g.s., Old Yard, Belgrade): m cert Belgrade 16 May 1796 John Rollins of Belgrade (VR), b Rochester NH c1775 son of Valentine & Mary (Downing) Rollins (g.s.; John R. Rollins, *Records of Families of the Name of Rawlins or Rollins in the United States* [1874], pp. 32, 65), d 11 Nov 1839 ae 64y (g.s., Old Yard, Belgrade)

viii Deliverance, b c1780: d 18 Aug 1834 ae 54y (g.s., Pine Grove cem, Waterville): m 17 May 1798 David Webb Jr. ("The Marriages of Joshua Cushman," *Downeast Ancestry*, 6:11), b c1773 son of David & poss Mary (Carter) Webb (g.s.; Ken Co deeds, 4:200, 5:122–24; Edward W. McGlenen, *A Volume of Records Relating to the Early History of Boston, Containing Boston Marriages from 1752 to 1809* [1903], p. 60), d 30 Sep 1840 ae 67y (g.s., Pine Grove cem, Waterville)

ix Isaiah, b c Apr 1786: d 3 Jan 1830 ae 43y 9m (g.s., Old cem, Oakland): m bef 1810 Olive Greene (1810 USC, Waterville; Kingsbury & Deyo, op. cit., p. 1236), b MA c1785 (1870 USC, Benton), d Benton 29 Jun 1873 ae 88y (g.s., The Old cem, Oakland; *Kennebec Journal*, issue of 9 Jul 1873)

Paul M. Aldrich, P.O. Box 217, Bristol, ME 04539-0217

Daggett, Samuel   47a   1 - 4 - 2 - 0 - 0
Union Town, Lincoln County

SAMUEL DAGGETT, b Tisbury MA 19 May 1753 son of Thomas & Rebecca (Athearn) Daggett (Charles E. Banks, *The History of Martha's Vineyard, Dukes Co, Massachusetts*, [1925], hereafter Banks, 3:136–37; George H. and Sydney B.

Daggett, *A Supplement to the Section Entitled John Doggett-Daggett of Martha's Vineyard from the 1894 Edition of A History of the Doggett-Daggett Family by Samuel Bradlee Doggett* [1974], hereafter *Doggett-Daggett*, p. 23) [see THOMAS DAGGETT Sr. family]: d Union 20 Oct 1835 ae 82y (John L. Sibley, *A History of the Town of Union, Maine* [repr 1987], hereafter Sibley, p. 444): m Tisbury MA 13 Mar 1777 JEDIDAH BUTLER (*Doggett-Daggett*, p. 55), b Tisbury MA 1757 dau of John & Jedidah (Beetle) Butler (Banks, pp. 136–37), d Union 21 Feb 1830 (Sibley, p. 444). Samuel was a privateer during the Rev War, was captured and confined for 4 months on the prison-ship JERSEY at New York (Sibley, p. 329; Banks, 3:136). He was one of 9 men out of 90 who survived (ibid.). After the war, he moved to Union where he became a prominent citizen and served in many town offices.

Children: births in Sibley, p. 444; Banks, 3:137; *Doggett-Daggett*, p. 55
  i   Brotherton, b Tisbury MA 4 Jan 1778: d Union Nov 1866 (*Doggett-Daggett*, p. 118): m (1) int Bristol 30 Dec 1803 Sarah/Sally Campbell of Bristol (Dodge's *Bristol*, 2:61): m (2) Dec 1838 Emily (Chadwick) Marshall of Thomaston (*Doggett-Daggett*, p. 118) who d 14 Oct 1844 (ibid.)
  ii James, b Tisbury MA 9 Sep 1779: d Hodgdon 18 Jun 1858 (*Doggett-Daggett*, p. 119): m Waldoborough 31 Aug 1800 Deborah Upham of Bristol (Sibley, p. 444), b 17 Apr 1785 dau of Jabez & Hannah (Burgess) Upham (Dodge's *Bristol*, 1:700), d Hodgdon 28 Apr 1868 (*Doggett-Daggett*, p. 119)
  iii Polly, b Tisbury MA 12 May 1781: d Union 1835 (*Doggett-Daggett*, p. 55): m Union 5 Sep 1799 Thomas Mitchell (Sibley, p. 474), b No. Yarmouth 21 Sep 1772 son of Thomas & Dinah (_____) Mitchell (VR), d 14 Oct 1843 (Sibley, p. 474)
  iv Jonathan, b Tisbury MA 20 May 1783: d Union 1855 (*Doggett-Daggett*, p. 120): m (1) 1804 Elizabeth/Betsey Martin of St. George (Sibley, p. 444): m (2) bef 1819 Mary Robinson of Belmont (ibid.; *Doggett-Daggett*, p. 120)
  v   William, b Tisbury MA 9 Apr 1785: d Bremen 19 Dec 1876 ae 91y 8m 10d (Dodge's *Bristol*, 1:149 citing g.s., Bremen cem): m Bristol 15 Mar 1813 Silvia Church Weston (Sibley, p. 444–45) [Dodge's *Bristol*, 2:61, gives m int 1 Jan 1813], b 10 Mar 1790 dau of Arunah & Sarah (Martin) Weston [see ARUNAH WESTON family, *Maine Families*, 3:299–300], d 8 Mar 1883 (Dodge's *Bristol*, 1:732 citing g.s., Bremen cem)
  vi Samuel, b Union 15 Oct 1792: d Union 11 Oct 1846 (Sibley, p. 445): m (1) 1817 Priscilla Coggan (ibid.): m (2) Sarah (Wade) Stetson dau of Jacob Wade and wid of Jacob Stetson (ibid.)
  vii Ebenezer, b Union 2 Aug 1797: d Washington 10 Aug 1887 (*Doggett-Daggett*, p. 121): m (1) Union 18 Mar 1819 Margaret Miller of Waldoborough (ibid.; Sibley, p. 445), b 1805 dau of George & Barbara (Hoffs) Miller (*Doggett-Daggett*, p. 121), d 31 May 1830 (Sibley, p. 445): m (2)

Union 9 Jun 1831 Salome Miller (ibid.), b 1805 sis of his 1st wife (ibid.), d Union 9 Jun 1851 (*Doggett-Daggett*, p. 121)
viii Daniel Weston, b Union 19 May 1800: d Union 4 Apr 1833 (Sibley, p. 445): m Union 3 Dec 1827 Lydia Jameson of Warren (ibid.), b Warren 17 Dec 1802 dau of Brice & Priscilla (Bartlett) Jameson of Warren (Eaton's *Warren*, p. 558; *Doggett-Daggett*, p. 122), d 24 Dec 1839 (ibid.). She m (2) Oct 1835 Job Caswell (ibid.; Eaton's *Warren*, p. 558)

Carol F. Nye, R.F.D. 1, Box 388, Belgrade, ME 04917

Daggett, Thomas, Jun.   47a   1 - 1 - 4 - 0 - 0
Union Town, Lincoln County

THOMAS DAGGETT Jr., b Tisbury, Martha's Vineyard MA c1755 son of Thomas & Rebecca (Athearn) Daggett of Tisbury (Charles E. Banks, *The History of Martha's Vineyard, Dukes County, Massachusetts*, 3 [1925]:132–33, hereafter Banks) [see THOMAS DAGGETT Sr. family]: d Union 13 Jan 1822 (VR) ae 67y (John L. Sibley, *A History of the Town of Union, Maine* [repr 1987], p. 445): m Tisbury MA 31 Oct 1782 REBECCA LUCE (VR), b Tisbury MA 18 Mar 1758 dau of Joseph & Jedidah (Claghorn) Luce (VR), d Union 6 Feb 1832 (VR). Thomas went to Union with his father and brothers. He was a Rev War soldier (Fisher's *Soldiers*, p. 182). His will which was dated 20 Dec 1821 was probated 13 May 1822 (Banks, 3:137). He was a deacon in the Baptist Church in Warren (ibid.).

Children, all b Union: births VR Union
  i Hannah, b 14 Apr 1783: d of consumption Union 23 Apr 1826 (VR; Sibley, p. 446): unm
 ii Berintha, b 11 Sep 1786: d Union 5 Jul 1839 (VR): m Union 23 Apr 1809 John Chapman Robbins (VR), b Union 17 Apr 1791 son of David & Elizabeth (Chapman) (Quiggle) Robbins (VR; Sibley, pp. 488–90)
iii Thomas, b 4 Jun 1788: d in NY (Sibley, p. 446): m in NY City Martha Maidman (ibid.), an English lady who d of consumption Union 23 Aug 1818 ae 22y (VR). He was a farmer at Searsmont. After his wife d, he went to NY where her family lived, engaged in business there and d there (Sibley, p. 446)
 iv Sally, b 6 May 1790: m 20 Sep 1818 Samuel Goodwin of Searsmont (Sibley, p. 446 which mistakenly calls him Goodman), b 4 Jun 1798 (Dorothy Albin, *Searsmont: The Old Township of Quantabacook 1764–1976* [n.d.], p. 108), living Searsmont 1850 ae 52y (USC)

v   Edmund, b 23 Aug 1792: m int Union 10 Aug 1818 Deborah Keene of Camden (VR) dau of Josiah Keene of Camden (Sibley, p. 446)
vi Henry, b 3 Aug 1794: d Rushford WI 11 Apr 1881 (George H. and Sydney B. Daggett, *A Supplement to the Section Entitled John Doggett-Daggett of Martha's Vineyard from the 1894 Edition of A History of the Doggett-Daggett Family by Samuel Bradlee Doggett* [1974], hereafter *Doggett-Daggett*, pp. 123–24): m 26 Sep 1816 Meribah Jackson (Sibley, p. 446), b c1793 dau of Isaac Jackson (*Doggett-Daggett*, pp. 123–24), d Rushford WI 21 Jun 1875 (ibid.). He settled in Belmont, then moved to WI (ibid.)
vii Matthew, b 1 Oct 1798: d Union 10 Dec 1798 (VR)

Carol F. Nye, RFD 1, Box 388, Belgrade, ME 04917

Daggett, Thomas   47a   3 - 0 - 1 - 0 - 0
Union Town, Lincoln County

THOMAS DAGGETT Sr., bp Edgartown MA 10 Nov 1728 son of Brotherton & Thankful (Daggett) (Butler) Daggett (George H. and Sydney B. Daggett, *A Supplement to the Section Entitled John Doggett-Daggett of Martha's Vineyard from the 1894 Edition of A History of the Doggett-Daggett Family by Samuel Bradlee Doggett* [1974], hereafter *Doggett-Daggett*, pp. 10, 23; Charles E. Banks, *The History of Martha's Vineyard, Dukes Co, Massachusetts* [1925], 3:130, hereafter Banks): d Union 15 May 1806 (John L. Sibley, *A History of the Town of Union, Maine* [repr 1987], hereafter Sibley, p. 445): m REBECCA ATHEARN (Banks, 3:132), bp Edgartown MA 8 Jun 1729 dau of Solomon & Sarah (Skiff) Athearn (ibid., 3:22), d Union 3 Aug 1805 (Sibley, p. 445). They moved to Union in 1789 (Banks, 3:132). On 24 Jun 1806, his son Samuel was appt adm of his estate (ibid.).

Children, prob all b Tisbury MA: births in *Doggett-Daggett*, p. 23
i   Samuel, b 19 May 1753: d Union 2 Oct 1835 ae 82y (Sibley, p. 444): m Tisbury MA 13 Mar 1777 Jedidah Butler [see SAMUEL DAGGETT family]
ii Thomas, b c1755: d Union 13 Jan 1822 ae 67y (VR; Sibley, p. 445): m Tisbury MA 31 Oct 1782 Rebecca Luce [see THOMAS DAGGETT Jr. family]
iii Andrew, b 1760: d Union of smallpox (*Doggett-Daggett*, p. 25; Sibley, p. 445). Sibley termed him "a foolish son" (ibid.)
iv Hannah, b 1762: d 27 Nov 1838 (Banks, 3:382): m Tisbury MA 26 Dec 1782 William Norton (ibid.; *Doggett-Daggett*, p. 23), b c1759 son of William & Mercy (Osborn) Norton (Banks, 3:377), d 7 Jul 1807 (ibid., 3:382)

v   Aaron, b 1764: d 1813, prob lost at sea (Sibley, p. 443; *Doggett-Daggett*, p. 56): m Rebecca Peabody dau of Stephen Peabody of Warren (Sibley, p. 443). Rebecca was appt adm of his estate 29 Jun 1813 (Banks, 3:137). She m (2) 1815 John Newbit of Waldoborough (Sibley, p. 443)

vi Rebecca, b 1766: d Warren 16 Oct 1848 (*Doggett-Daggett*, p. 57): m 28 Mar 1788 her 1st cousin Matthew Daggett (ibid., p. 23), b 1764 son of Elijah & Jedidah (Chase) Daggett (ibid., pp. 23–24), d Warren 15 Oct 1831 (ibid., p. 57)

vii Jonathan, b 1770: d Jul 1800 of yellow fever in Georgia (*Doggett-Daggett*, p. 23)

Carol F. Nye, R.F.D. 1, Box 388, Belgrade, ME 04917

---

day, benjamin   48a   2 - 3 - 5 - 0 - 0
Waldoborough Town [s/b Bristol], Lincoln County

BENJAMIN DAY, b Ipswich MA 18 Nov 1733 son of John & Eunice (Burnham) Day (VR) [Dodge's *Bristol*, 1:156 gives b 7 Dec 1735]: d 23 Jan 1813 ae 77y 1m 28d (ibid., citing g.s. Old Day cem, Damariscotta): m Ipswich MA 11 Jul 1758 MARTHA KNIGHT of Townsend MA (Ipswich VR), b Gloucester MA 1 Jun 1740 dau of Daniel & Martha (Patishall) Knight (VR), d 15 Nov 1827 ae 86y 6m 11d (Dodge's *Bristol*, 1:158, citing g.s., Old Day cem, Damariscotta). Benjamin came to Damariscotta in 1749 as a teenager to assist in surveying with friends Anthony Chapman of Scituate MA and Stephen Hodgdon (Dodge's *Bristol*, 1:156). He served in the Rev War in Capt. Joseph Jones's Co., 3rd Lin Co regiment, and in Capt. George White's Co, Col. Francis's regiment for a three-year term (MS&S 4:566). In 1779, he was chosen to serve on the Committee of Correspondence, Inspection and Safety for Bristol (John Johnston, *A History of the towns of Bristol and Bremen* [1873], p 350). He owned one mile of shoreline and the lot was two miles in depth in Damariscotta in the area where the old Day shipyard was located.

Children: births Dodge's *Bristol*, 1:156–60
i   John, b 6 Aug 1758: d Strong 8 Aug 1826 (g.s., Conant cem): m int Bristol 1 Jul 1781 Lydia Flint (Dodge's *Bristol*, 2:65), b No. Reading MA 27 Aug 1763 dau of Dr. Thomas & Lydia (Pope) Flint [see THOMAS FLINT family, *Maine Families*, 2:95], d Strong 30 Mar 1839 (g.s., Conant cem)
ii Martha/Patty K., b 5 Oct 1760: d 8 Mar 1832 ae 72y (Dodge's *Bristol*, 1:409 citing g.s., Woodward cem, Damariscotta): m int Bristol 25 Sep 1786 Robert Jones (ibid., 2:65), b 1757 son of Col. William & Margaret (Huston) Jones (ibid., 1:410), d 15 Apr 1845 ae 88y (ibid., citing g.s., Woodward cem, Damariscotta)

iii Eunice, b 20 Nov 1762: m int Bristol 2 Jun 1784 William Hiscock (Dodge's *Bristol*, 2:64), perhaps he b 4 Aug 1763 son of Richard & Jane (McFadden) Hiscock (ibid., 1:353)

iv Benjamin Jr., b 29 Dec 1764: d Bristol 26 Sep 1825 ae 61y (Dodge's *Bristol*, 1:156 citing g.s., Heavner/Day cem, Damariscotta): m Bristol 20 Oct 1796 Ruth Chapman of Nobleboro (ibid., 2:64), b 8 Sep 1775 dau of Dea. Nathaniel & Sarah (Lincoln) Chapman (ibid., 1:94) [see NATHANIEL CHAPMAN family, *Maine Families*, 3:43–44], d 31 Oct 1861 ae 87y (Dodge's *Bristol*, 1:159 citing g.s., Heavner/Day cem, Damariscotta)

v Elizabeth, b 20 Dec 1766: d 14 Jan 1836 ae 69y (Dodge's *Bristol*, 1:349 citing g.s., Bethlehem cem, Damariscotta): m Daniel Hiscock (Dodge's *Bristol*, 1:157), prob he b 18 Nov 1761 son of Richard & Jane (McFadden) Hiscock (ibid., 1:349), d 16 Jun 1844 ae 83y (ibid., 1:349)

vi Nathaniel, b 1 May 1769: d 17 Aug 1840 ae 72y (Dodge's *Bristol*, 1:159 citing g.s., Heavner/Day cem, Damariscotta): m Bristol 30 Oct 1808 Jane Sproul (ibid., 2:65), b c1783, d 19 Mar 1835 ae 52y (ibid., 1:157 citing g.s., Heavner/Day cem, Damariscotta)

vii Sarah, b 9 Oct 1771: d 6 Apr 1849 ae 76y 6m (Dodge's *Bristol*, 1:504 citing g.s., Hillside cem, Damariscotta): m int Bristol 20 Feb 1795 William Metcalf (ibid., 2:65), b c1773, d 19 Feb 1822 ae 49y (ibid., 1:504). He came to Bristol from Newburyport MA and later removed to Damariscotta (ibid.)

viii Susanna, b 24 Oct 1773: d 22 Sep 1819 ae 46y (Dodge's *Bristol*, 1:661 citing g.s., Hillside cem, Damariscotta): m Bristol 4 Oct 1794 Abner Stetson (ibid., 2:65), b Scituate MA 1771 son of Abner & Deborah (Stetson) Stetson (ibid., 1:657), d 20 Sep 1846 ae 75y (ibid., citing g.s. Hillside cem, Damariscotta). He m (2) Susan (Russ) Wiley (ibid.)

ix Daniel, b 24 Mar 1776: d 20 May 1849 ae 73y (Dodge's *Bristol*, 1:156 citing g.s., Hillside cem, Damariscotta): m Bristol 17 Aug 1800 Nancy Milton (ibid., 2:64), b c May 1780, d 7 Nov 1856 ae 76y 6m (ibid., 1:159)

x William, b 20 Jul 1779: d 18 Nov 1857 ae 78y 3m (Dodge's *Bristol*, 1:160): m (1) 1799 Jane Perham (ibid., 1:157): m (2) Bristol 27 Nov 1806 Martha Hatch (ibid., 2:65), b 16 Sep 1785 dau of Elisha & Rebecca (Hilton) Hatch (ibid., 1:321), d East Boston MA 13 May 1864 ae 78y 9m (ibid., 1:158)

xi Robert, b 30 Oct 1781: d 17 Dec 1855 ae 74y (Dodge's *Bristol*, 1:159 citing g.s., Day cem, Damariscotta): m (1) int Bristol 27 Feb 1806 Mary/Polly Sproul (ibid., 2:65), b c1782, d 20 Nov 1828 ae 46y (ibid., 1:158 citing g.s., Day cem, Damariscotta): m (2) int Bristol 12 Apr 1830 Mary Young (ibid., 2:65), b c1795, d 5 May 1856 ae 61y (ibid., 1:158 citing g.s., Day cem, Damariscotta)

xii Mary, b 12 Aug 1785

xiii Abigail, b 2 Oct 1788: d Pittston 25 Oct 1869 ae 81y (VR): m int Bristol 5 Dec 1818 Thomas Fuller of Pittston (Dodge's *Bristol*, 2:64), b 29 Feb 1789 son of Edward & Mary (_____) Fuller (Pittston VR), d Pittston 7 Oct 1869 (VR)

Eunice Calvert, 20 Flower Lane, Marcellus, NY 13108-1326

Dicker, Willm   24b   1 - 2 - 2 - 0 - 0
Rusfield Gore [later Norway], Cumberland County

WILLIAM DECKER/DICKER, b England c1745 (listed as ae 67y in Aug 1812 when the British Aliens census was taken, Kenneth Scott, *British Aliens in the United States During the War of 1812* [1979], p. 3, his name given as William "Dockel"): d Winthrop 2 Apr 1827 ae 84y (VR): m ANN _____, b c1755, d Winthrop 14 Jun 1850 ae 95y (VR, given as wife of William Dicker Sr.). William was enumerated at Monmouth in 1810 (USC). He deposed for the British Aliens census in 1812 that he had resided in the U.S. for 33 years indicating he arrived about 1779 during the Rev War. He also stated that he was a yeoman, a resident of Winthrop and that he had a wife and five children.

Children [one of the 5 mentioned in the British Aliens census has not been found]: Everett S. Stackpole, *History of Winthrop* [1925], p. 351
  i William Jr.: d Winthrop 10 Apr 1876 (VR): m 1808 Sarah Burnham (*History of Winthrop*, p. 351; Sarah's last name of Burnham given in William and Sarah's family record in Winthrop VR, first child b 1809)
  ii Charles: m 2 Jan 1814 Nabby Canwell (*History of Winthrop*, p. 351)
  iii James M., b c1791: d Temple 29 Dec 1867 ae 76y (VR; g.s., Will cem, Avon): m 22 Nov 1814 Mary/Polly Churchill of Wayne (*History of Winthrop*, p. 351), b Buckfield 1 Jun 1788 dau of William & Lydia (Maxim) Churchill (Gardner Asaph Churchill & Nathaniel Wiley Churchill, *The Churchill Family in America* [1904], p. 82), d Feb 1869 ae 82y (Temple VR)
  iv Hannah, b c1792: d Winthrop 24 Mar 1856 ae 64y (VR): unm

Ida Smith Kretschmar, Route #1, Box 155 A52, Paige, TX 78659

Dennet, Saml   65b   2 - 1 - 3 - 0 - 0
Pepperellborough Town [later Saco], York County

SAMUEL DENNETT, b Kittery 19 Mar 1714/5 son of Ebenezer & Abigail (Hill) Dennett (Joseph C. Anderson II & Lois Ware Thurston, *Vital Records of Kittery, Maine to the Year 1892* [1991], hereafter Kittery VR, p. 84; GDMNH, p. 193): d

Saco 27 Oct 1800 (*First Book of Records of the Town of Pepperellborough Now the City of Saco* [1896], hereafter Pepperellborough VR, p. 213): of Biddeford when he m Kittery 14 Oct 1742 SARAH FROST of Kittery (Kittery VR, p. 130), possibly a dau of Bartholomew & Hannah (_____) Frost of Kittery (Everett P. Stackpole, *Old Kittery and Her Families* [1903], pp. 424–25). She was alive in 1795 when Samuel wrote his will and probably survived him, although no death record for her has been found. Samuel came to the Biddeford-Saco area as early as 1738 and lived opposite Spring's island which was later called Dennett's landing (George Folsom, *History of Saco and Biddeford* [repr 1975], p. 262). He was a tanner and described as the first "mechanic" within the limits of the present town of Saco (ibid.). His will, written 9 Jan 1795, was in probate on 1 Nov 1800 (York Co Probate #4335, 18:358). In it, he named his wife Sarah, sons Nicholas, Samuel and Ebenezer, daus Sarah Scammon, Hannah Lord deceased, Abigail Leavit, and Lydia Clark. Sons Nicholas and Samuel were appt executors (ibid.). [Note that the abstract of Samuel's will, in John E. Frost's, *Maine Probate Abstracts* (1991), 18/354, states that Abigail Leavit was his granddaughter. The copy of the will in the probate volumes, from which Frost took his abstracts, clearly names Abigail Leavit as Samuel's daughter, not granddaughter.]

Children, bp 1st Church Biddeford: MHGR, 6:336, 337, 339, 493, 496, 499, 7:14
    i   Sarah, b 13 Jun 1743 ("Early Vital Records of Saco and Biddeford, Maine," NEHGR, 71 [1917]:212) and bp 25 Dec 1743: d Saco 2 Dec 1822 (Pepperellborough VR, p. 228): m Pepperellborough 9 May 1765 Samuel Scammon (*First Book of Records of the First Church in Pepperrellborough, Now Saco, Maine* [1914], hereafter Pepperrellborough Church, p. 37), b c1738 son of Samuel & Mehitable (Hinkley) Scammon (Folsom, op. cit., pp. 240–41), d Saco 10 Dec 1825 ae 87y (Pepperellborough VR, p. 230)
   ii   Nicholas, b Jun 1745 (NEHGR, 71 [1917]:212) and bp 11 Aug 1745: d Saco 24 Sep 1814 (Pepperellborough VR, p. 221): m by 1769 Phebe _____ (Nicholas Dennett family record, Pepperellborough VR, p. 116). Nicholas left a will, dated 28 Jul 1814 and probated Oct 1814, in which he named his wife Phebe and 6 sons (York Co Probate, 24:527)
  iii   Abigail, bp 21 Jun 1747: m Pepperellborough 29 Oct 1765 Daniel Leavit of Narragansett No. 1 [later Buxton] (Pepperrellborough Church, p. 37) as his 2nd wife (Gideon T. Ridlon, *Saco Valley Settlements and Families* [1895], p. 881), b York 27 Apr 1736 son of Joseph & Bethiah (Bragdon) Leavitt (Lester M. Bragdon & John E. Frost, *Vital Records of York, Maine* [1992], p. 41), d Buxton 21 Jun 1829 (Ridlon, op. cit., p. 881). He had m (1) 5 May 1763 Abigail Bradbury (ibid.). He was a deacon of the Congregational Church in Buxton for 48y (ibid.)
  iv   Hannah, bp 20 May 1750: d Limerick 6 Nov 1794 ae 45y (Robert L. Taylor, *Early Families of Limerick, Maine* [1984], p. 88): m Pepperellborough 26 Jul 1770 Ammi Ruhamah Lord of Berwick (Pepperrellborough

Church, p. 39), bp Berwick 1st Church 22 Nov 1747 son of Thomas & Mary (Wise) Lord (NEHGR, 82 [1928]:314; Stackpole, op. cit., p. 596), d Limerick 13 Aug 1824 ae 77y (Taylor, op. cit., p. 88). He m (2) Berwick 30 Jun 1796 Sarah (Nason) Hubbard (John E. Frost & Joseph C. Anderson II, *Vital Records of Berwick, South Berwick and North Berwick, Maine to the Year 1892* [1993], p. 139; Taylor, op. cit., p. 88)

v Lydia, bp 30 Aug 1752: d Limerick 27 Jan 1820 (Taylor, op. cit., p. 37): m Pepperellborough 3 Oct 1773 David Clark (Pepperrellborough Church, p. 39), b Kittery 9 Jul 1750 son of Nathaniel & Abigail (Dennett) Clark (Stackpole, op. cit., p. 322), d Limerick 21 Apr 1828 ae 78y (Taylor, op. cit., p. 37)

vi Samuel, bp 24 May 1755: m (1) Pepperellborough 11 Feb 1779 Abigail Carlile of Biddeford (Pepperrellborough Church, p. 41) who d Saco 17 Jan 1809 (Pepperellborough VR, p. 215): m (2) int Saco 10 May 1810 Hannah Trickey of Adams NH (ibid., p. 30) who d Saco 11 Oct 1816 (ibid., p. 223)

vii Ebenezer, bp 4 Oct 1761: m by 1785 Sophia ____ (Ebenezer Dennett family record, Pepperellborough VR, p. 123) who d Saco 7 Apr 1816 (ibid., p. 222)

Joseph C. Anderson II, 5337 Del Roy Drive, Dallas, TX 75229

Dennison, David   16b   2 - 3 - 5 - 0 - 0
Freeport Town, Cumberland County

DAVID DENNISON, b Gloucester MA 16 Aug 1734 son of George & Abigail (Haraden) Dennison (VR): d prob Freeport 5 Mar 1799 ae 65y (Grace M. Rogers and A. L. Dennison, *The Dennison Family of No. Yarmouth and Freeport, Maine* [1906], hereafter *Dennison Family*, p. 46; David C. & Elizabeth K. Young, *Vital Records From Maine Newspapers, 1785-1820* [1993], p. 160): m int Gloucester MA 19 Nov 1757 JANE/JENNY HARADEN (VR), b Gloucester MA 18 Oct 1741 dau of Joseph & Joanna (Emerson) Haraden (VR), d prob Freeport Oct 1815 ae 75y (g.s., 1st Parish cem, Freeport). They are both buried in the old burying ground on lower Main St., Freeport where the first church was located. David, with his brother Abner, moved from Gloucester MA to the part of No. Yarmouth that later became Freeport (Augustus W. Corliss, *Old Times of North Yarmouth, Maine* (1977), hereafter *Old Times*, p. 989). On 17 Feb 1787, David Dennison was one of the members of a committee requesting the MA General Court to set off the northeasterly part of No. Yarmouth as a separate town (ibid., p. 959–60). The petitioners complained that they had "great and insuperable difficulties of attending Public Worship" living from between "three and...ten miles distance from the First Meeting House" (ibid.). On 17 Feb 1801, the heirs of David Dennison quitclaimed to John and Joseph Dennison all their right to the "real estate of our Father David Dennison" exclusive of the widow's dower and mill privilege belonging to Timothy Dennison (Cum Co deeds 35:225). The heirs named were David & Mehitable Dennison, George and Dorcas Dennison, Barnabas & Jane Soule, Henchman & Esther Sylvester, Timothy & Elizabeth Dennison, Jonathan & Lucretia Cushing, and Abigail Dennison.

Children: births/baptisms first 6 VR Gloucester MA
 i David, b Gloucester MA 4 Nov 175_ (prob 1758): d Gloucester MA 1759 (VR)
 ii David, b Gloucester MA 15 Aug 1760: d Freeport 4 Oct 1843 ae 83y (VR): m (1) No. Yarmouth 1 Aug 1782 Mehetable Soule (VR): m (2) Freeport 18 Nov 1802 Susanna (Haraden) Griffin (VR) [see DAVID DENNISON Jr. family]
 iii George, b Gloucester MA 19 May 1762: d 1844 (Col. Thurlow R. Dunning, "Genealogies of the Soule, Burnham, Dennison Family" [TS, Bartol Library, Freeport, 1984], hereafter "Genealogies," p. 135): m No. Yarmouth 21 Aug 1783 Dorcas Soule (VR) [see GEORGE DENNISON family]
 iv Jane/Jenny, b Gloucester MA 10 Jan 1764: d Freeport 5 Mar 1825 (VR, listed as "widow Jane"): m No. Yarmouth 17 May 1781 Barnabas Soule (VR), b 25 Mar 1758 son of Barnabas & Jane (Bradbury) Soule (*Old Times*, p. 865), d 25 Jan 1823 (*Dennison Family*, p. 89). They res on the Soule family homestead on Cousins River in Freeport; both are bur So. Freeport cem ("Genealogies," p. 142)
 v Joanna, bp Gloucester MA 14 Sep 1765: d Freeport 10 Aug 1794 (VR): m No. Yarmouth 27 Dec 1787 Melatiah Dillingham (VR), b 1762 son of Edward & Martha (Doty) Dillingham ("Genealogies," p. 147), d Dixfield 1833 (ibid.). They moved to Freeport in 1786, then to Dixfield where he died (ibid.)
 vi Esther, b 12 Sep 1767 (*Dennison Family*, p. 100) and bp Gloucester MA 20 Sep 1767: d Freeport 3 Feb 1845 (VR): m No. Yarmouth 24 May 1786 Hinchman Sylvester (VR), bp 18 Jun 1758 son of Caleb & Desire (Stetson) Sylvester (Jedediah Dwelley and John F. Simmons, *History of the Town of Hanover, Massachusetts* [1910], pp. 397–98): d 1829 ("Genealogies," p. 150)
 vii Joseph, bp No. Yarmouth with his brother Timothy 25 Apr 1773 (*Old Times*, p. 802): d 1779 ae 7y (g.s., 1st Parish cem, Freeport)
 viii Timothy, b 28 Aug 1771 (*Dennison Family*, p. 100) and bp No. Yarmouth with his brother Joseph 25 Apr 1773 (*Old Times*, p. 802): d bef 1830 when his wife was enumerated as a head of household at Freeport (USC): of Freeport when he m No. Yarmouth 19 Jul 1799 Betsey Staples of No.

Yarmouth (VR), b No. Yarmouth 27 Mar 1771 dau of Daniel & Lucy (Staples) Staples (VR) [see DANIEL STAPLES family, *Maine Families*, 2:269-70], d Freeport 4 Sep 1830 (VR) and bur Mast Landing cem, Freeport ("Genealogies," p. 150). They were in Freeport in 1800, Dresden in 1810 and Freeport in 1820 (USC)

ix Lucretia, b 20 Jul 1773 (*Dennison Family*, p. 100) and bp No. Yarmouth 23 Aug 1775 (*Old Times*, p. 804): d Freeport 25 Jun 1812 ae 36y [sic] (Young & Young, op. cit., p. 143): m Freeport 29 Jul 1795 Jonathan Cushing (VR), b 1773 son of John & Dorothy (Bagley) Cushing ("Genealogies," p. 150), d 1822 (ibid.). He m (2) No. Yarmouth 5 Nov 1813 Mary Sawyer (VR)

x John, b 12 Sep 1775 (*Dennison Family*, p. 101): d Freeport 25 Dec 1854 (VR): m (1) No. Yarmouth 27 Dec 1798 Hannah Moxey of No. Yarmouth (VR), b No. Yarmouth 2 Jul 1776 dau of Henry & Mercy (_____) Moxey (VR), d Freeport 30 Nov 1844 (VR): m (2) cert Freeport 7 Oct 1846 Louisa Sylvester (VR) who d 1855 and is listed as John's wife on her g.s. in Mast Landing cem, Freeport ("Genealogies," p. 151). John res on Mast Landing Hill, Freeport

xi Abigail, b 19 Feb 1777 (*Dennison Family*, p. 104) and bp No. Yarmouth "sometime ago" [recorded 10 Oct 1779] (*Old Times*, p. 859): m int No. Yarmouth 2 May 1808 Rufus Chandler (VR) as his 2nd wife, b No. Yarmouth 18 Mar 1766 son of Jonathan & Rachel (Mitchell) Chandler (VR), d 1844 and bur Wood Lawn cem, Freeport ("Genealogies," p. 154). She removed to Homewood MS in 1850 (ibid.)

xii Joseph, b 25 Jun 1779 (*Dennison Family*, p. 106): d Freeport 8 Dec 1847 ae 68y (VR): m (1) Freeport 1 Dec 1802 Dorcas Lufkin (VR), b on Cape Ann MA [prob Gloucester] 26 Oct 1784 (*Dennison Family*, p. 106) dau of Capt. Joseph Lufkin (Young & Young, op. cit., p. 160), d 6 Feb 1820 ae 36y (ibid.): m (2) Freeport 16 Jul 1820 Lucinda Townsend (VR) who d 1860 ae 75y and bur Mast Landing cem, Freeport ("Genealogies," p. 154)

xiii Jonathan, b 5 Jun 1781 (*Dennison Family*, p. 46) and bp No. Yarmouth 5 Aug 1781 (*Old Times*, p. 860): d 1 Oct 1787 (*Dennison Family*, p. 46)

xiv Priscilla, bp No. Yarmouth 17 Aug 1785 (*Old Times*, p. 903): d 1 Jun 1858 (*Dennison Family*, p. 46)

Robert D. Griffin, 171 Cedar St., Englewood, NJ 07631

Dennison, David, J^r 16b 1-2-3-0-0
Freeport Town, Cumberland County

DAVID DENNISON Jr., b Gloucester MA 15 Aug 1760 son of David & Jenny (Haraden) Dennison (VR) [see DAVID DENNISON family]: d Freeport 4 Oct 1843 ae 83y (VR; g.s., Burr cem, Freeport; Grace M. Rogers and A. L.

Dennison, *The Dennison Family of No. Yarmouth and Freeport, Maine* [1906], hereafter *Dennison Family*, p. 46): m (1) No. Yarmouth 1 Aug 1782 MEHETABLE SOULE (VR), b No. Yarmouth 12 Apr 1764 dau of John & Betty (Mitchell) Soule (VR; Augustus W. Corliss, *Old Times of North Yarmouth, Maine* (1977), hereafter *Old Times*, p. 971), d 28 Apr 1802 ae 39y (g.s., Burr cem, Freeport): m (2) Freeport 18 Nov 1802 SUSANNA (HARADEN) GRIFFIN (VR), b c1776 niece of Capt. Jonathan Haraden of Salem MA (*Dennison Family*, p. 47) [see discussion below], d 24 Apr 1848 ae 73y (g.s., Burr cem, Freeport). David served as a private in the Continental Army at the age of 15 and was in the engagements at Monmouth and Saratoga, and wintered at Valley Forge under Washington. After three years in the army, he entered the navy as a privateersman, was captured and held prisoner on Antigua Island for a year until peace was declared (*Dennison Family*, p. 46). He later received a pension for his war service (Rev War pension #S29755). He was one of the early members of the Baptist Church in Freeport.

[One Susanna Haraden, dau of Daniel & Susanna (Burnam) Haraden, was b Gloucester MA 16 Oct 1774 (VR), but it has not been proven this was the same person who married David Dennison Jr. David's wife, Susanna, was prob the widow of Benjamin Griffin in whose memory she and David named a son. A Joseph Griffin, b c1797 and d 1810, and named on his gravestone as being a son of Benjamin and Susanna Griffin, is buried in the same plot as David and Susanna Dennison in Burr cem, Freeport. Susanna was not the widow of Daniel Griffin Jr. as some have claimed. That Susanna Haraden and Daniel Griffin Jr. were married at Gloucester MA in 1764 (VR), before this Susanna was born.]

Children: births of all except Joseph VR Freeport
By 1st wife Mehetable Soule
    i Cornelius, b 2 Feb 1783: d near Beardstown IL 15 Apr 1846 (*Dennison Family*, p. 48): unm. He was a farmer and a teacher and graduated from Bowdoin College in 1811
    ii Andrew, b 25 Feb 1786: d Brunswick 3 Jul 1869 (George A. Wheeler & Henry W. Wheeler, *History of Brunswick, Topsham and Harpswell* [1878], p. 728): m (1) Freeport 13 Sep 1807 Lydia Lufkin (VR), b 30 Jun 1788 (*Dennison Family*, p. 48), d 27 Sep 1848 (ibid.): m (2) Mary S. _____ (ibid.), b 1805 (ibid.), d 1879 (ibid.). He served in the War of 1812 and was a shoemaker
    iii David, b 20 Jun 1788: d Freeport 25 Jan 1865 ae 77y (VR) of gangrene of the foot (*Dennison Family*, p. 54): m (1) cert Freeport 29 Nov 1814 Mary Griffin (VR), prob she b Salisbury MA 30 Dec 1795 dau of Benjamin & Susanna (Haraden) Griffin (VR), d 1823 ae 28y (g.s., Burr cem, Freeport): m (2) Freeport 28 Dec 1825 Penthea Stetson Soule (VR),

b 1799 (g.s.), d 1881 (g.s., Burr cem, Freeport). He was a ship carpenter and served in the War of 1812

iv John, b 22 Dec 1790: d Portland 8 Jun 1882 ae 91y (g.s., Eastern cem): m Freeport 9 Feb 1812 Lillis Dennison (VR), b Freeport 6 Apr 1791 dau of Abner & Lillis Turner (Sylvester) Dennison (*Dennison Family*, p. 18) [see ABNER DENNISON family, *Maine Families*, 1:74–75], d Portland 20 Dec 1872 ae 81y (g.s., Eastern cem). He served in the War of 1812

v Clarissa, b 28 Jan 1793: d Turner 14 Jun 1843 (*Dennison Family*, p. 58): m cert Freeport 19 Oct 1815 Andrew H. Bennett (VR), b Freeport 14 Jul 1793 (*Dennison Family*, p. 58), d So. Paris 25 Aug 1872 (ibid.). They res Avon 1819–1835, then moved to Turner (ibid.)

vi Sophronia, b 23 Sep 1794: d 1860 ae 64y (g.s., Burr cem, Freeport): m Freeport 7 Mar 1814 Samuel Soule as his 2nd wife (VR; *Old Times*, p. 1014), b 9 Apr 1791 son of James & Martha (Curtis) Soule of Hanover MA (ibid.), d 1880 ae 89y (g.s., Burr cem, Freeport)

vii Rufus, b 12 May 1797: d Wilton 2 Oct 1885 (*Dennison Family*, p. 61): m (1) cert Freeport 12 Jan 1821 Seba Boston [Baston] of Freeport (VR) who d 3 Jul 1839 (*Dennison Family*, p. 61): m (2) Wilton 1 Jan 1840 Mary Eaton (ibid.), b Goffstown NH 25 Aug 1802 dau of James & Bathsheba (_____) Eaton (ibid.), d Wilton 9 Nov 1892 (ibid.). He was a drummer during the War of 1812. He res Avon, Dixfield, Farmington, Jay, New Sharon and Wilton

viii Joseph, b 1801 (*Dennison Family*, p. 47; birth not recorded in Freeport VR): d 27 Feb 1802 (*Dennison Family*, p. 47)

By 2nd wife Susanna (Haraden) Griffin

ix Joseph Haraden, b 27 Sep 1803: d 14 May 1862 ae 58y (g.s., Burr cem, Freeport): m (1) cert Freeport 1 Dec 1831 Adeline Curtis (VR), b c1810, d 9 Jun 1838 ae 28y (g.s., Burr cem, Freeport): m (2) cert Freeport 29 Sep 1839 Caroline Blackstone (VR), b c1817, d 26 Mar 1888 ae 71y (g.s., Burr cem, Freeport). He res in a house built by his father in 1793 near Beech Hill, Freeport and cared for his parents while they lived

x Mehitable, b 3 Sep 1805: d Freeport 27 Nov 1867 ae 62y (VR; g.s., Burr cem, Freeport): m cert Freeport 7 Dec 1833 Abiel Merrill (VR, which calls her Mehitable "Davis"; Col. Thurlow R. Dunning, "Genealogies of the Soule, Burnham, Dennison Family" [TS, Bartol Library, Freeport, 1984], hereafter "Genealogies," p. 133). She d Freeport 2 Mar 1861 ae 60y (VR; g.s., Burr cem, Freeport)

xi Susan, b 21 Jul 1808: d 1900 (g.s., Burr cem, Freeport): m cert Freeport 2 May 1847 Charles Soule (VR), b 26 Jan 1800 bro of Samuel above (*Old Times*, p. 1014), d 1892 (g.s., Burr cem, Freeport). They lived on the farm owned by their son Benjamin F. Soule

xii Lucy Jane, b 10 May 1810 ["Genealogies," p. 134, calls her Lucy Lane]: d 8 Feb 1852 (*Dennison Family*, p. 70): m cert Freeport 7 Mar 1847

Gershom Mann (VR), b 28 Sep 1805 (*Dennison Family*, p. 70), d 6 Nov 1874 (ibid.)
- xiii Benjamin, b 3 Sep 1812: d Freeport 22 Apr 1814 (*Dennison Family*, p. 47)
- xiv Joanna, b 9 Oct 1815: m Freeport 14 May 1844 Dea. Simeon Pratt as his 2nd wife (VR; *Dennison Family*, p. 71), b 1797 ("Genealogies," p. 134), drowned 1875 aboard a steamer enroute to CA (ibid.)
- xv Benjamin Griffin, b 14 May 1818: d Ocean Springs AL 1878 (*Dennison Family*, p. 72): m cert Freeport 13 Jul 1844 Martha Ann Soule (VR), b 14 Aug 1817 dau of Andrew & Mahala (Porter) Soule (*Old Times*, p. 1013). He was a stevedore in New Orleans (*Dennison Family*, p. 72)

Robert D. Griffin, 171 Cedar St., Englewood, NJ 07631

Dennison, Ame   16a   0 - 1 - 3 - 0 - 0
Freeport Town, Cumberland County

EMMA/AMME (LANE) DENNISON (widow of Abner Dennison), bp Gloucester MA 25 Jan 1735/6 dau of Joseph & Deborah (Haraden) Lane (VR): d 14 Aug 1821 (Grace M. Rogers and A. L. Dennison, *The Dennison Family of No. Yarmouth and Freeport, Maine* [1906], hereafter *Dennison Family*, p. 18) and bur Old Mast Landing cem, Freeport [Emmie on g.s.] (Col. Thurlow R. Dunning, "Genealogies of the Soule, Burnham, Dennison Family" [TS, Bartol Library, Freeport, 1984], hereafter "Genealogies," p. 101): m int Gloucester MA 22 Feb 1755 ABNER DENNISON (VR), b Gloucester MA 2 Oct 1730 son of George & Abigail (Haraden) Dennison (VR): d 18 Oct 1786 in his 57th y and bur Old Mast Landing cem, Freeport (*The Dennison Family*, p. 18; "Genealogies," p. 101). Abner Dennison, with his brother David, moved from Gloucester MA to the part of No. Yarmouth which later became Freeport (Augustus W. Corliss, *Old Times of North Yarmouth, Maine* (1977), hereafter *Old Times*, p. 989). He served in the Rev War from No. Yarmouth in Capt. Roger's Co. (Fisher's *Soldiers*, p. 199).

Children
- i Abigail, b Gloucester MA 17 Jun 1756 (VR): d 19 Jun 1777 (*Dennison Family*, p. 18)
- ii Emma/Amme, b 2 Jun 1758 (*Dennison Family*, p. 18) and bp Gloucester MA 4 Jun 1758 (VR): d 29 Jul 1758 (*Dennison Family*, p. 18)
- iii Abner, b Gloucester MA 2 Sep 1759: d Freeport 16 Apr 1821 (g.s., Mast Landing cem): m (1) No. Yarmouth 30 Nov 1781 Polly Hodgskins (VR): m (2) No. Yarmouth 26 Jul 1786 Lillis Turner Sylvester of Prout's Gore (No. Yarmouth VR) who d Freeport 20 Dec 1844 (VR) [see ABNER DENNISON family, *Maine Families*, 1:74–75]
- iv Gideon, b 5 Aug 1761 (*Dennison Family*, p. 22) and bp Gloucester MA 9 Aug 1761 (VR): m (1) No. Yarmouth 17 Apr 1782 Ruth Curtis (VR): m

(2) Freeport 9 Apr 1809 Amme Sylvester (VR): m (3) Freeport 3 Apr 1823 Rebecca Curtis (VR)
v Emma/Amme, b Gloucester MA 7 Jun 1763 (VR): d 11 May 1765 (*Dennison Family*, p. 18)
vi Elizabeth, b 3 Oct 1765 (*Dennison Family*, p. 25) and bp Gloucester MA 13 Oct 1765 (VR): m No. Yarmouth 30 Aug 1787 John Colquehoun [Calhoun] of No. Yarmouth (VR)
vii Sarah/Sally, b 15 Jan 1768 (No. Yarmouth VR): m No. Yarmouth 2 Mar 1785 Abner Sylvester Jr. of Prout's Gore (No. Yarmouth VR) [m int states Abner was from "Gore bet. No. Yarmouth and Brunswick" (No. Yarmouth VR)], prob son of Abner & Susanna (Stetson) Sylvester
viii Solomon, b 1 Mar 1770 (No. Yarmouth VR) and bp No. Yarmouth in the Fall of 1771 (*Old Times*, p. 802): d 1848 (*Dennison Family*, p. 33): m cert Freeport 2 Nov 1804 Mary Warren (VR) who d Jun 1857 (*Dennison Family*, p. 33). He was a sea captain and was the delegate from Freeport to the Constitutional Convention at Portland in 1819
ix Susanna, b 12 May 1771 (*Dennison Family*, p. 34): d 21 Oct 1856 (ibid.): m No. Yarmouth 27 Aug 1789 Robert Townsend of Freeport (Rev War pension #W22444), b Abington MA 2 Dec 1760 (ibid.), d Freeport 9 Sep 1845 (ibid.). Robert was a Rev War soldier and pensioner
x Martha/Patty, b 23 Apr 1775 (*Dennison Family*, p. 39) and bp No. Yarmouth 23 Aug 1775 (*Old Times*, p. 804): m 18 Dec 1794 John Griffin (VR; he of Newburyport MA on m int) who d 1851 and is bur in Mast Landing cem, Freeport ("Genealogies," p. 119). [The identity of John Griffin, Martha's husband, has presented problems to researchers over the years. While not proven, it has been speculated that he was John Griffin, b Gloucester MA 18 Oct 1771 son of Ambrose & Deborah (Butman) Griffin (VR). John J. Babson's, *Notes and Additions to the History of Gloucester - Second Series* [1891], mentioned on p. 81 that "John arrived in Freeport at about the age of ten with Aaron Lufkin who married his mother's sister." This is the only record found that ties the Gloucester MA John Griffin to Freeport, in spite of the fact that Martha's husband was "of Newbury MA" when they married]
xi Jonathan, b 2 Sep 1777 (*Dennison Family*, p. 18) and bp "sometime ago" No. Yarmouth [recorded 10 Oct 1779] (*Old Times*, p. 859): d 14 Mar 1779 (*Dennison Family*, p. 18)
xii Abigail, b 24 Dec 1779 (*Dennison Family*, p. 42): d 1849 ("Genealogies," p. 122): m Freeport 2 Jan 1803 Charles Stytson [Stetson] of Durham (VR), b 1777 ("Genealogies," p. 122), d 1855 and bur Durham in 3rd cem on left on the road from Freeport to So. West Bend (ibid.)

Robert D. Griffin, 171 Cedar St., Englewood, NJ 07631

Dennison, George   16b   1 - 2 - 2 - 0 - 0
Freeport Town, Cumberland County

GEORGE DENNISON, b Gloucester MA 19 May 1762 son of David & Jenny (Haraden) Dennison (VR) [see DAVID DENNISON family]: d 1844 (Col. Thurlow R. Dunning, "Genealogies of the Soule, Burnham, Dennison Family" [TS, Bartol Library, Freeport, 1984], hereafter "Genealogies," p. 135): m No. Yarmouth 21 Aug 1783 DORCAS SOULE (VR), b No. Yarmouth 11 Mar 1766 dau of John & Betty (Mitchell) Soule (VR), d 1842 ("Genealogies," p. 135).

[Research indicates that George and Dorcas Dennison were perhaps the parents of Esther Dennison, b 1797 (g.s.), d Plum Grove Twsp, Butler Co KS 1886 (g.s., Halderman cem). Esther m Freeport 1 Jul 1816 Andrew Pepperrell Wentworth (VR), b 18 Nov 1792 son of Benning & Phebe (Sawyer) Wentworth (John Wentworth, *The Wentworth Genealogy: English and American* [1878], 2:627), d 30 Jun 1875 (ibid.). They res Plum Grove, Butler Co KS. Two of their children were named George and Dorcas. George Dennison had a sister named Esther.]

Children: births VR Freeport
- i   Emerson, b 19 Feb 1784: d Freeport 12 Sep 1844 (VR): m Freeport 24 Jan 1808 Margaret Hannaford (VR) who d 1857 ("Genealogies," p. 135). He lived near Mast Landing in Freeport and was a tailor by trade (Grace M. Rogers and A. L. Dennison, *The Dennison Family of No. Yarmouth and Freeport, Maine* [1906], hereafter *Dennison Family*, p. 73)
- ii   Betsey, b 2 Dec 1785: d 16 May 1863 (*Dennison Family*, p. 76): m Freeport 28 Jul 1813 Stephen Stetson of Lewiston (Freeport VR), b Durham 28 May 1791 son of Elisha & Rebecca (Curtis) Stetson (Janus G. Elder, *A History of Lewiston, Maine* [repr 1989, ed. by David & Elizabeth K. Young], p. 326), d 15 Jan 1880 (*Dennison Family*, p. 76). He was a soldier in the War of 1812
- iii George, b 15 Oct 1787: d unm (*Dennison Family*, p. 73)
- iv   Washington, b 15 Oct 1789: d Freeport 28 Feb 1860 (VR): unm (*Dennison Family*, p. 73). He was a carpenter by trade
- v   Timothy, b 17 Nov 1791: d 12 Nov 1857 (*Dennison Family*, p. 80): m Milan IN 1821 Alice Hill (ibid.), b 1 Dec 1804 (ibid.), d 15 Mar 1876 (ibid.). They res Milan IN
- vi   Dorcas, b 28 Jan 1794: d 3 Jul 1798 (Freeport VR)
- vii Bradbury, b 28 Jan 1802: d 10 Dec 1866 ae 64y 10m 22d (g.s., Burr cem, Freeport): m cert Freeport 13 Feb 1828 Jane Cushing of Pownal (Freeport VR) dau of Dea. John Jr. & Loammi Betsey (Soule) Cushing (Augustus W. Corliss, *Old Times of North Yarmouth, Maine* (1977), p. 971; "Genealogies," p. 139), d 8 Sep 1874 ae 69y 10m (g.s., Burr cem, Freeport). They res Freeport

viii Jonathan, b 11 Mar 1804: d 9 Jul 1888 (*Dennison Family*, p. 88): m cert Freeport 22 May 1836 Mehitable Coombs (VR), b 24 Jan 1817 (*Dennison Family*, p. 88), d 11 Sep 1864 (ibid.)

ix Dorcas, b 6 Mar 1809: d 1889 ("Genealogies," p. 142): m Leonard Griffin (ibid.), b 1806 (ibid.), d 1884 (ibid.)

Robert D. Griffin, 171 Cedar St., Englewood, NJ 07631
Dorothea Morris Morgan, 327 Rotary St., Morgantown, WV 26505

Dole, John   23c   2 - 2 - 4 - 0 - 0
Portland Town, Cumberland County

JOHN DOLE, b Newbury MA 19 Feb 1747/8 son of John & Sarah (Plumer) Dole (VR): d 13 Jun 1828 (family sampler, copy in possession of submitter, hereafter Dole fam sampler): m (1) 24 Nov 1773 DEBORAH CROCKETT dau of Richard & Elizabeth (Roberts) Crockett (Charles S. Candage, *Crockett Genealogy 1610–1988* [1989], p. 20), d 13 Feb 1775 (Dole fam sampler): m (2) Falmouth 4 Jul 1779 HANNAH THRESHER (Cum Co Commissioners recs, 2:151), b Aug 1750 (Dole fam sampler) dau of Jonathan & Hannah (Dow) Thresher (William Willis, *The History of Portland* [1865], p. 844), d 15 Mar 1792 (Dole fam sampler): m (3) Portland 5 May 1793 ELIZABETH (MORSE) SWEETSER (VR) dau of Jonathan & Experience (Paine) Morse (J. Howard Morse and Emily W. Leavitt, *The Morse Genealogy* [1903], p. 83) and wid of William Sweetser (Cum Co Commissioners recs, 2:227). John was a housewright and lived in his early years at Portland on Hancock Street (Cum Co deeds 32:524, 56:106) and in his latter years at Portland on a large property on outer Washington Avenue, then part of Falmouth, later Westbrook and Portland today (Dole fam sampler). Proof of the identity of this John Dole is contained in the will of his mother, Sarah Dole, who bequeathed to him and two of his children, Deborah Harper and Sarah Harper (Essex Co MA Probate, #8086, 378:511).

Children (Dole fam sampler)
By 1st wife Deborah Crockett
   i Sarah, b 13 Feb 1775 (Dole fam sampler), bp 12 Mar 1775 (Marquis F. King, *Baptisms and Admissions from the Records of First Church in Falmouth, Now Portland, Maine* [repr 1990], hereafter *Falmouth 1st Church*, p. 34): d 7 Jul 1749 (Dole fam sampler): m 30 Apr 1797 Samuel Harper (VR Portland) son of William Harper (Cum Co deeds 159:39)
By 2nd wife Hannah Thresher
   ii Deborah, b 3 Apr 1782 (Dole fam sampler), bp 14 Apr 1782 (*Falmouth 1st Church*, p. 34): d 25 May 1813 ae 31y (g.s., North Deering cem): m bef

23 Nov 1809 (when named as Deborah Harper in her grandmother's will) James Harper (Cum Co deed 56:106)
iii Hannah, b 4 Oct 1784 (Dole fam sampler), bp 10 Oct 1784 (*Falmouth 1st Church*, p. 34): d 3 Mar 1804 (Dole fam sampler)
iv John, b 4 Jul 1786 (Dole fam sampler), bp 9 Jul 1786 (*Falmouth 1st Church*, p. 34: d 31 Oct 1853 (Dole fam sampler): m 23 Sep 1818 Sarah E. Smellage (Isaac Cobb, "Marriages Copied from the Record of the Rev. Caleb Bradley of Westbrook," hereafter "Rev. Bradley," MHGR, 4:282 [but she was incorrectly called Mary in this record]), b 24 Jun 1797 dau of James & Sarah/Sally (Black) Smellage (Family Bible rec; Dole fam sampler), d 22 Oct 1865 (ibid.)
v Mary/Polly, b 1 Jul 1788 (Portland VR): d 4 Oct 1788 (Dole fam sampler)
vi Samuel, b 30 Apr 1791 (Portland VR): d 6 Feb 1793 (Dole fam sampler)
By 3rd wife Elizabeth (Morse) Sweetser
vii Mary/Polly, b 28 Jan 1794 (Portland VR): d Nov 1865 (Dole fam sampler): m 27 Jan 1814 Daniel Knight (Charles S. Tibbetts, "The Knight Family" [TS, 1941, MHS], p. 79), b Falmouth 19 Sep 1786 son of Job & Marrian (Jellison) Knight (ibid.)
viii Eliza, b 13 Dec 1795 (Dole fam sampler): d 28 Jul 1799 (ibid.)
ix Happy M., b 24 May 1799 (Dole fam sampler) [it is not known whether or not in this case "Happy" was a nickname; sometimes Happy was used as a nickname for "Kerenhappuck"—see Kerenhappuck (_____) (Hicks) Brackett in Fabius M. Ray's *Early Westbrook History* (1914), pp. 75–76]: d 12 May 1839 (ibid.): m 16 Nov 1819 John Davis ("Rev. Bradley," MHGR, 4:283) son of Gardner & Dorcas (Goddard) Davis (Cum Co deeds 155:328; DAR TS, MHS, filed at M929.1, D265.15 [1946], pp. 3–4)

Clayton R. Adams, 6 Laurel Road, Brunswick, ME 04011

Dorman, John   54b   1 - 2 - 6 - 0 - 0
    Arundel Town, York County

JOHN DORMAN, b Arundel c1746 (Rev War pension #S35263) son of Jabez & Hannah (Look) Dorman (Charles Bradbury, *History of Kennebunkport* [1837], p. 239) [see JABEZ DORMAN family, *Maine Families*, 3:65–66]: d Kennebunkport 26 Jul 1827 (pension, op. cit.), adm of estate to wid 15 Oct 1827 (York Co Probate 38:14): m c1766 HANNAH HUFF (Bradbury, op. cit.), b c1747 dau of Charles & Priscilla (Burbank) Huff (ibid.; pension, op. cit.), d Kennebunkport 1835 (will, York Co Probate 46:426). John served in the Revolution 10m in 1776 followed by an enlistment of 3y being discharged in May 1780. He res Arundel.

Hannah's will, dated 28 July 1835, mentioned only her son-in-law, Joshua Harris of Kennebunkport, to whom she left all of her real and personal property.

Children: Bradbury, op. cit., & cited sources
- i Charles, b c1767: d Newfield 23 Aug 1857 ae 90y (John E. Frost, "Newfield (Maine) Record Book," [TS, MHS], p. 26): m (1) Pepperellborough 28 Jan 1790 Susanna Boothby (*First Book of Records of the First Church in Pepperellborough, Now Saco, Maine* [1914], p. 46), b Scarboro 31 Mar 1773 dau of Samuel & Molly (Deering) Boothby (VR), d Newfield 17 Apr 1805 (NEHGR, 97 [1943]:366): m (2) Newfield 18 Aug 1805 Abigail Libby (VR), b 30 Nov 1778 dau of Zebulon & Sarah (Milliken) Libby (Charles T. Libby, *The Libby Family in America* [1883], p. 85), d Newfield 26 Apr 1874 (VR) [see CHARLES DORMAN family, *Maine Families*, 3:63–65]
- ii Nathaniel, b c1768: d Arundel 1807 (York Co Probate 20:106): m York 15 Jan 1795 Olive Bradbury (VR), b 3 Jan 1768 dau of Cotton & Ruth (Weare) Bradbury [see COTTON BRADBURY family, *Maine Families*, 3:29–30]. Res Arundel
- iii Priscilla, b 4 Apr 1769 (Gideon T. Ridlon, *Saco Valley Settlements and Families* [1895], p. 764), offered herself for baptism Arundel 8 Apr 1787 (NEHGR 107 [1953]:270): d Pepperellborough 18 Sep 1829 ae 60y 4m (VR): m Arundel 14 Apr 1793 Thomas Jenkins (York Co Marriage Records, 1:16), b 14 Jan 1769 (Thomas Jenkins family record in Saco VR), reportedly lived to be ae 100y (Ridlon, op. cit., p. 764). Res Saco
- iv Hannah, b c1774: d bef 1830 (USC): m Kennebunkport 10 Sep 1794 Joseph Thomas (NEHGR 108 [1954]:188)
- v Mary, b Jan 1781: d Arundel Mar 1873 ae 92y 2m 9d (VR): m Arundel 22 Dec 1804 Daniel Perkins Jr (NEHGR 108 [1954]:191)
- vi Benjamin, b 21 Nov 1787 (E. S. Stackpole, *History of Winthrop, Maine* [1925], p. 351): d Winthrop 26 May 1866 (ibid.): m Bridgton 18 Jul 1820 Hannah Davis (VR). Res Winthrop
- vii Huldah, b c1788 (pension, op. cit.): m (1) 10 May 1806 Jeremiah Fletcher (NEHGR 108 [1954]:191): m (2) 4 Jan 1823 Abel Merrill (MHGR 1:193)
- viii Lucy, b 16 Jun 1789: d 7 May 1864 (g.s.): m Arundel 17 Apr 1814 Edmund Hill (NEHGR 108 [1954]:192)
- ix Sarah, b c1790: m Boston MA 23 Jul 1822 Joshua Harris (VR). Sarah's mother, in her will, referred to Joshua as her "beloved son-in-law"
- x John, b c1792: d bef 1818: m int Wells 5 Oct 1816 Judith Brown

Frank Dorman, 157 Fayerweather St., Cambridge, MA 02138

Farnham, Benj[a]   63a   3 - 3 - 4 - 0 - 0
    Lebanon Town, York County

BENJAMIN FARNHAM, b c1742 son of Matthew & Dorothy (Webber) Farnham (guardian's bond, York Co Probate #21046): m Lebanon 17 Oct 1766 SARAH BLAISDELL (VR), b c1746 dau of Ephraim & Thankful (Webber) Blaisdell (info from Blaisdell Family National Association, hereafter Blaisdell fam assoc; George W. Chamberlain, "Lebanon, Maine Genealogies" [TS, MHS, 1947], 1:#31), d as a result of a miscarriage Lebanon 11 May 1786 (VR). On 16 Oct 1759, Benjamin and three siblings [one of whom was unnamed], termed children & heirs of Matthew Farnam late of York, were placed under the guardianship of Alexander McIntire of York (York Co Probate #21046). No record has been found whether Benjamin married a 2nd wife, although he was in his early 40s when Sarah died. He lived on the east side of the road from South Lebanon to the Center Road, a short distance south of the Town Farm (Chamberlain, op. cit., 1:#294). On 1 Oct 1798, one Benjamin Farham was taxed at Lebanon for one dwelling and 50 acres of land (Chamberlain, op. cit., 1:#294) although it is not clear if this was Benjamin Sr. or Benjamin Jr. In the 1800 census, there was one Benjamin "Varnum" family in Lebanon, however this Benjamin was listed in the aged 26–45 category. Also included was a female in the same age category, a female 16–26, a male 10–16, 2 males 0–10 and 3 females 0–10. This enumeration fits no known Benjamin Farnham family of Lebanon or York, but it could possibly be the household of Benjamin Jr. which included several other relatives. There was no Benjamin Farnham enumerated as a head of household in Lebanon in the 1810 census.

[What happened to Benjamin after the 1790 census is uncertain. In 1795 and 1796, his two eldest sons moved to Belgrade (1800 USC of Belgrade, which gives year of arrival) and several of his other children showed up in Belgrade later. Whether Benjamin also went there is not known, but an unidentified Benjamin Farnham d Belgrade 12 May 1835 (VR). An Elizabeth, wife of Benjamin Farnham, d there 31 Dec 1831 (VR). But no man of Benjamin's age was present in his children's households in the 1800 census listings for Belgrade or Lebanon.]

Tentative children, order and dates of birth speculative: Arthur B. Farnham, "Addenda to Rev. J. M. W. Farnham, Genealogy of the Farnham Family" [1940] which gives names only, no dates of birth
  i   David, b c1767: d Belgrade 16 Feb 1813 ae 46y (g.s., Old Yard): m bef 1790 Lois Lord [see DAVID FARNHAM family]
  ii Matthew, b say 1769: m (1) Lebanon 15 Jan 1795 Catherine Austin (VR) who d Belgrade 24 Aug 1833 (VR): m (2) Rome 3 Aug 1834 Abigail (Fall) Wentworth (VR) who survived him. She was the wid of Mark

Wentworth (John Wentworth, *The Wentworth Genealogy* [1878], 2:409). Matthew left a will dated 10 Apr 1837 (Ken Co Probate, 41:31)

iii Benjamin Jr., b say 1772: d by 1805 when his wid remarried: m Lebanon 13 Jul 1797 Sarah Blaisdell (VR), b Lebanon 8 Jun 1777 dau of Enoch & Sarah (McIntire) Blaisdell (VR; Blaisdell fam assoc; called dau of Enoch Blaisdell on her 2nd m rec; Chamberlain 1:#22), d Lebanon 23 Apr 1859 (VR). She m (2) Lebanon 3 Jan 1805 Richard Horn (VR) and m (3) Lebanon 24 Mar 1822 Eld. John Blaisdell (VR)

iv Gaius, b say 1775: m Lebanon 6 Feb 1800 Polly Gerrish (VR). He was perhaps the "Guss" Farnham enumerated at Lebanon in 1800 and the "Gains" Farnham enumerated at Belgrade in 1810 (USC)

v Mary, b say 1777: reportedly m ____ Trefethen (Farnham Addenda, op. cit.) [note that one otherwise unidentified Polly Farnham m Lebanon 28 Dec 1794 John Dunnel (VR) who was of Berwick on m int in Berwick VR]

vi Sally, b say 1779: prob the unnamed dau of Benjamin Farnham who d 8 May 1808 ae more than 20y "deranged in mind, found dead in ye woods" (Lebanon VR)

vii Samuel, b say 1781: perhaps the Samuel Farnham of Belgrade who m by 1805 Dorcas ____ (Samuel Farnham fam rec in Belgrade VR)

viii Abigail, b say 1783: m int Lebanon Sep 1802 Samuel Varney (VR)

ix John, b c1784: d prob Belgrade 6 Oct 1847 ae 63y (g.s., Old Yard cem): m Belgrade 24 Nov 1808 Betsy Towle of Belgrade (VR), b c1784, d 1 Feb 1860 ae 75y (g.s., Old Yard cem). In 1850, Betsy was enumerated at Rome, ae 66y, living with her dau and son-in-law, Lucretia & Thomas Tracy (USC)

Russell C. Farnham, 678 N. Seton Ave., Lecanto, FL 34461-8786

Farnham, David   63c   1 - 4 - 2 - 0 - 0
   Lebanon Town, York County

DAVID FARNHAM, b c1749 son of Matthew & Dorothy (Webber) Farnham (guardian's bond, York Co Probate #21046) and perhaps the "David Farnam" bp York 22 Oct 1752, no parents given on the record (YCGSJ, 4:2 [1989]:15): d Lebanon 6 Sep 1814 ae 65y (VR; g.s., Camp Hill cem): m (1) Lebanon 26 Mar 1778 ANNA WINGATE (VR), b c1747 dau of Samuel Wingate of Rochester NH (George W. Chamberlain, "Soldiers of the American Revolution of Lebanon, Maine" [Lebanon Hist Soc], p. 43), d Lebanon "newly brought to bed" 9 Mar 1788 ae 41y (VR) [note g.s. gives d 5 Mar 1788 ae 45y 6m]: m (2) int Berwick 8 Nov 1788 ABIGAIL (DUNNELL) SMITH (VR, called "Mrs." Abigail Smith), perhaps the Abigail Donnell b York 7 Jul 1753 dau of Benjamin & Sarah (Kingsbury) Donnell (VR), d Lebanon 30 Sep 1846 ae 92y 3m (VR). She was the wid of Joshua Smith whom she m Berwick 14 Mar 1782 (VR) and by whom she prob had a son Joshua Smith Jr. b 3 Jun 1784 (Lebanon VR). On 16 Oct 1759, David and three siblings [one of whom was unnamed], termed children & heirs of Matthew Farnam late of York, were placed under the guardianship of Alexander McIntire of York (York Co Probate #21046). David enlisted 5 May 1775 in Capt. Ebenezer Sullivan's Co., Col. James Scammon's 13th Regt. of Foot during the Rev War (MS&S 5:514). Based on his service, his wife Abigail received a widow's pension (Rev War pension #W21100). He resided in the western part of Lebanon on the farm that in 1896 was known as the Matthew Farnham farm. His will, which was dated 9 Aug 1814, named his wife Abigail, sons Enoch, Samuel Wingate, Jeremy, David, John, Benjamin and Matthew, and daus Anna, Nabby and Dolly (York Co Probate #5555, 24:563).

Children, b Lebanon: births and baptisms VR Lebanon
By 1st wife Anna Wingate
  i   Enoch, b 20 Jun 1779, bp 22 Oct 1780: m Berwick 7 Aug 1800 Sally Worster (VR), b c1777, d 9 May 1853 ae 76y and bur Berwick (Wilbur D. Spencer, *Burial Inscriptions, Berwick, York County, Maine* [1922], p. 20). According to George W. Chamberlain, "Lebanon, Maine Genealogies 1750–1892" [TS, MHS, 1947], 1:#295, he settled in Lewiston
  ii Samuel Wingate, b 1 Jul 1781, bp 30 Jun 1782: d Belgrade 30 Nov 1827 (VR): m Lebanon 5 Feb 1808 Catherine/Kate Wentworth (VR), b c1787 dau of Reuben & Eleanor (James) Wentworth (ae 63y in 1850 USC Rome; John Wentworth, *The Wentworth Genealogy* [1878], 1:443), d Rome 22 Dec 1867 (ibid.)
  iii Jeremiah/Jeremy, b 25 Jul 1784, bp 28 Jul 1786: m (1) Kittery 18 Sep 1808 Fanny Stacy of Kittery (VR) dau of Ichabod Stacy (York Co Probate #5559). She d prior to Mar 1811 when her will was presented to the probate court (ibid.): m (2) Martha Perkins and settled in Somersworth or Dover NH (Rev. J. M. W. Farnham, *Genealogy of the Farnham Family* [1886], p. 8). On 7 Jun 1810, Jeremiah's first wife, Fanny, wrote a will leaving to her husband Jeremiah Farnham of Eliot all her estate "coming to me in my right as a child and heir of Ichabod Stacy late of Eliot deceased" (York Co Probate #5559, 22:501). [The will was disallowed by the court. Since she was married to Jeremiah at the time she made the will, she was by law not capable of transferring her real estate to him.]
  iv Anna/Nancy, b 24 Feb 1788, bp 20 Sep 1789: d Lebanon 20 Jul 1867 ae 79y 5m (VR): m int Lebanon 10 May 1833 [as Nancy] John Libby (VR), b 1777 son of Capt. Charles & Sarah (Pray) Libby (Charles T. Libby, *The Libby Family in America* [1882], p. 110), d Lebanon 15 Mar 1848 in his 71st year (VR)

By 2nd wife Abigail (Dunnell) Smith
- v David Jr., b 28 Mar 1790: "drowned in crossing the bridge from Lebanon to Milton, N.H." 21 Apr 1824 ae 34y (Lebanon VR): m Lebanon 29 Nov 1810 Elizabeth Burrows (VR), b Lebanon 11 Oct 1789 dau of Lt. Jonathan & Elizabeth (Witherell) Burrows (VR), d Lebanon 28 Feb 1840 ae 51y (VR)
- vi John, b 7 Oct 1792, bp 31 Jul 1793: m (1) 10 Jul 1814 Susan Giles (Everett S. Stackpole and Lucien Thompson, *History of the Town of Durham, New Hampshire* [n.d.], 2:191), b Lee NH 12 Jul 1798 (ibid.), d 28 Jan 1817 (ibid.): m (2) Durham NH 25 Sep 1817 Eliza Hilton (ibid), b Lee NH 10 Jun 1798 (ibid.). They settled in Newmarket NH
- vii Joseph, twin, bp 4 Jul 1795: d "by ye falling of timbers in raising a frame" 16 Nov 1808 ae 13y (Lebanon VR)
- viii Benjamin, twin, bp 4 Jul 1795: d Lebanon 24 Nov 1823 (VR): m int Lebanon 15 Apr 1820 Susan Downs of Milton NH (VR) dau of John Downs (Robert S. Canney, *The Early Marriages of Strafford County, New Hampshire 1630–1850* [1991], p. 163). The adm of the estate of Benjamin Farnham Jr. of Lebanon was granted to his wid Susan 26 Jan 1824 (York Co Probate #5548, 32:19). In settling the estate, Susan sold the reversion of Benjamin's mother's dower in his father's estate to his sister Nabby Farnham (ibid., 34:467)
- ix Matthew, b 7 Aug 1797: d Lebanon 10 Feb 1866 ae 68y 6m (VR): m 1 Aug 1822 Mehitable Keggan of Newton MA, b c1795 [although Chamberlain, op. cit., 1:#298, states she was b 18 Jun 1800], d 5 Jul 1882 ae 87y (Lebanon VR)
- x Abigail/Nabby, bp 8 Jun 1800: m Dover NH 30 Aug 1827 Thomas Wright of Dover (Chamberlain, op. cit., 1:#295; *Collections of the Dover, New Hampshire, Historical Society*, [1894], 1:90). She was unm in 1824 when her brother Benjamin's estate was settled
- xi Dorothy/Dolly, b 10 Dec 1801 or 10 Jan 1802, bp 15 Aug 1802: d Lebanon 7 May 1875 ae 73y 4m (VR): m Lebanon 14 May 1820 Ivory Gerrish (VR), b c Sep 1801, d Lebanon 13 Aug 1863 ae 62y 11m 10d (VR)

Russell C. Farnham, 678 N. Seton Ave., Lecanto, FL 34461-8786

Farnham, David   63a   1 - 0 - 2 - 0 - 0
Lebanon Town, York County

DAVID FARNHAM, b c1767 prob son of Benjamin & Sarah (Blaisdell) Farnham [see BENJAMIN FARNHAM family]: d Belgrade 16 Feb 1813 ae 46y (g.s., Old Yard): m bef 1790 LOIS LORD (Arthur B. Farnham, "Addenda to Rev. J. M.

W. Farnham, Genealogy of the Farnham Family" [1940]), b c Mar 1770, d Belgrade 20 Aug 1868 ae 98y 5m (g.s., Old Yard). In 1790, David was enumerated in Lebanon three households away from his prob father, Benjamin Farnham. Included in his household were two females, prob his wife and an unidentified second female. In 1800, David was enumerated in the census at Belgrade living next to his brother Matthew Farnham. This census stated that David came to Belgrade in 1796 from MA [sic], the year following Matthew's arrival, also from MA [sic]. The naming patterns of David's children would support the proposal that he was a son of Benjamin and Sarah (Blaisdell) Farnham. In addition to his son Benjamin and dau Sally (named for his parents), David also named a dau Dolly (for his paternal grandmother).

[The parentage of David's wife, Lois Lord, has not been discovered although a clue to her identity may be found in the notation that one Elisha Lord reportedly lived during his later years with David and Lois (C. C. and George E. Lord, *A History of the Descendants of Nathan Lord of Ancient Kittery, Maine* [1912], p. 47). Elisha, a son of Elisha & Sarah (Shackley) Lord, was bp at the Berwick 2nd Church 28 Apr 1765 (NEHGR, 74 [1920]:217). However the baptisms of other children of Elisha & Sarah Lord at the Berwick 2nd Church do not include a daughter Lois. Arthur B. Farnham, in his Addenda to the 1889 Farnham Genealogy (op. cit.), stated that Lois was a widow who moved from Lebanon to Belgrade and settled there. The facts do not support this statement as Lois was prob already married to David Farnham when she went to Belgrade. Furthermore, it is not clear if Mr. Farnham was referring to her widowhood after David Farnham's death or to an undocumented claim that she had had a previous husband.]

Children: births VR Belgrade
  i   Dolly, b 26 Oct 1791: m int Belgrade 27 Aug 1808 Frost Littlefield (VR)
  ii Elizabeth, twin, b 4 Aug 1793. She was perhaps the Betsy Farnham of Belgrade who m Belgrade 12 Dec 1810 Asa Turner of Rome (Belgrade VR)
  iii Salley, twin, b 4 Aug 1793: m Belgrade 13 Feb 1812 Ivory Blaisdell of Rome (Belgrade VR)
  iv Jane/Jenney, b 9 Apr 1800: living on 3 Dec 1866 when she was one of the signers of a petition who declared their mother, Lois, to be of "...weak, infirm and unsound mind" (Ken Co Probate, 144:45)
  v   Benjamin, b 1 Apr 1804: d 3 Dec 1893 ae 90y 5m (g.s., Old Yard, Belgrade): m Belgrade 30 Nov 1826 Eliza Kelley (VR), b MA c1807 (1850 USC), d 25 Oct 1875 ae 68y (g.s., Old Yard, Belgrade). Benjamin left a will dated 14 Aug 1884 naming his children and grandchildren (Ken Co Probate #7690)

vi Hannah, b 9 May 1806: d 28 Mar 1880 ae 74y 10m (g.s., Old Yard cem, Belgrade): m perhaps (1) a husband who has not been identified: m (2) Rome 22 Jun 1849 John Farnham (VR) son of Matthew & Catherine (Austin) Farnham [see BENJAMIN FARNHAM family] who d Rome 5 Oct 1852 ae 36y 8m 16d (g.s.): m (3) Rome 13 Mar 1856 Patrick Emmons of Belgrade (Rome VR)

vii David, b 25 Jul 1807: d 18 Sep 1891 ae 84y 1m 24d (g.s., Old Yard, Belgrade): m Belgrade 23 Apr 1830 Sarah Kelley (VR), c Oct 1810, d 23 Feb 1879 ae 68y 4m (g.s., Old Yard, Belgrade)

viii Louise, b 18 Jul 1809: m Rome 26 Feb 1834 William H. Kelley (VR)

ix Eunice, b 22 Jan 1812: m (1) Rome 25 Sep 1842 William Kelley (VR)

Russell C. Farnham, 678 N. Seton Ave., Lecanto, FL 34461-8786

Farnham, Joshua   52b   3 - 1 - 2 - 0 - 0
   Woolwich Town, Lincoln County

Capt. **JOSHUA FARNHAM**, b York prob Nov 1728 son of Daniel & Hannah (Bragdon) Farnham (Lester M. Bragdon & John E. Frost, *Vital Records of York, Maine* [1992], hereafter VR, p. 19) [note that the year of Joshua's birth, 1728 as determined from his age at death, has been torn off on the original York vital records, although the month, November, is clearly written]: d Woolwich 15 Jan 1803 ae 74y (VR): m York 13 Feb 1750 MARY GROW (VR, p. 135), b York 13 Sep 1732 dau of William & Joanna (____) Grow (VR, p. 3), d Woolwich 13 Jan 1820 in her 88th y (VR). Mary was the sister of Joshua's brother-in-law, Col. Edward Grow, who m Joshua's sister Olive. Mary Grow, alias Mary Farnham, was presented at the April 1750 York Co Sessions Court for fornication, the record stating that she had a child born January last [i.e. Samuel] (YCGSJ, 4:1 [1989]:15). Soon afterwards, Joshua and Mary moved to the part of Georgetown which was set off as the town of Woolwich in 1759. They were there by May of 1751 as their son Daniel was born there. All of their children are recorded in the Woolwich records where Joshua later served as Town Clerk. Joshua's heirs are mentioned in Lin Co deed 66:113 in which the heirs of his son Samuel purchased on 21 May 1804 lot #11 in Woolwich from the other heirs, namely: John Curtis and Mary his wife of Woolwich; Zebediah Farnham, mariner, and Jane his wife of Woolwich; John Farnham, yeoman, and Mary his wife of Woolwich; John Perkins, yeoman, and Olive his wife of Dresden; Daniel Farnham, yeoman, and Mary his wife of Balltown; William Chalmers, clothier, and Esther his wife of Fairfax [Albion]; Phineas Farnham, yeoman, and Elizabeth his wife of Fairfax [Albion]; John Cook, yeoman, and Anna his wife of Norridgewock; and Elizabeth Farnham, widow, of Bath [i.e. widow of Thomas].

Children, all but Samuel b Woolwich: births VR Woolwich
  i Samuel, b York 23 Jan 1750: d Woolwich 29 May 1803 ae 53y 4m 7d (VR): m Georgetown 28 Apr 1779 Martha Rowell (VR) who was living 21 Dec 1814 (Lin Co deeds 91:150)
  ii Daniel, b 29 May 1751: m prob (1) Georgetown 13 Jan 1776 Lois Rowell (VR) dau of John & Mary (Reeves) Rowell (ibid.): m prob (2) bef May 1804 Mary ____ (Lin Co deeds 66:113). He lived at Balltown [Jefferson-Whitefield area today] in 1804 (ibid.)
  iii Joshua, b 11 Dec 1753: prob d young as he was not named as an heir of his father in 1804 (Lin Co deeds 66:113)
  iv Mary, b 22 Jul 1754 and bp York 6 Oct 1754 (YCGSJ, 4:2 [1989]:15): m Woolwich 4 May 1775 John Curtis Jr. ("Records of the Rev. Josiah Winship, Woolwich Church," DAR Misc Recs, 13:2:29). They were living in Woolwich in 1804 (Lin Co deeds 66:113)
  v Esther, b 5 Jun 1756: d Albion 9 Aug 1826 (Woolwich VR): m Woolwich 20 Mar 1776 William Chalmers (VR) who d Albion 21 Sep 1838 (VR)
  vi William, b 10 Aug 1758: prob d young as he was not named as an heir of his father in 1804 (Lin Co deeds 66:113)
  vii Hannah, b 1 Jul 1760: d Westport 26 Dec 1800 [two days after the birth of her 6th child] (g.s., Boli-Dunton cem): m 10 Nov 1790 Daniel Dunton as his 2nd wife (VR Edgecomb), b c1755 son of Timothy & Elizabeth (____) Dunton of Westport [see DANIEL DUNTON family, *Maine Families*, 1:88], d Westport 22 Mar 1813 ae 88y (g.s., Boli-Dunton). He left a will dated 12 Feb 1818 (Lin Co Probate 20:155)
  viii Olive, b 12 Feb 1762: d Dresden 4 Feb 1827 (Woolwich VR): m Woolwich 28 Sep 1786 Dea. John Perkins (VR). They were living in Dresden in 1804 (Lin Co deeds 66:113)
  ix Zebediah, b 10 Aug 1765: d aft 1810 (USC Woolwich): m Woolwich 16 Dec 1788 Jane Carlton (VR), prob she bp Woolwich 17 Aug 1766 dau of John & Jane (____) Carlton ("Records of the Rev. Josiah Winship, Woolwich Church," DAR Misc Recs [TS, MSA], 13:2:14), d Woolwich 9 Jun 1831 ae 65y 14d (Zebediah Farnham family record in Woolwich VR). He was a mariner
  x Phinehas, twin, b 1 Apr 1767: d Albion 14 Dec 1837 (VR): m (1) Georgetown 5 Jan 1791 Betsy Stinson (VR), bp Georgetown 6 Dec 1767 dau of James & Mary (Robinson) Stinson (VR), d Woolwich 11 May 1824 (VR; Harry F. Johnston, Ed., *Your Ancestors*, "A National Magazine of Genealogy and Family History," 12 [1958]:3 [at Toledo OH Public Library]): m (2) int Albion 4 Apr 1825 Polly Bessey of Albion (VR)
  xi Joanna, twin, b 1 Apr 1767: d Woolwich 11 Apr 1767 (VR)
  xii Thomas, b 30 Dec 1769: d Bath 20 Jan 1803 ae 32y 21d (Woolwich VR): m int Georgetown 10 Dec 1796 Elizabeth Couillard of Georgetown (VR),

b Georgetown 29 May 1773 dau of Charles & Margaret (Hood) Couillard (VR). Elizabeth was living in Bath in 1804 (Lin Co deeds 66:113)
xiii Anna, b 21 Feb 1771: m Georgetown 1791 John Cook Jr. (VR) [Rev. J. M. W. Farnham, *Genealogy of the Farnham Family* (1888), p. 52, gives m 27 Jan 1791], b Georgetown 11 Dec 1762 son of John & Jerusha (_____) Cook (VR). They were living at Norridgewock in 1804 (Lin Co deeds 66:113)
xiv Lucy, b 26 Aug 1772: d Woolwich 1 Oct 1777 (VR)
xv Joanna, b 10 Jul 1775: d Woolwich 3 Oct 1777 (VR)
xvi John, b 31 Aug 1779: d Woolwich 28 Apr 1862 (VR): m Woolwich 7 Mar 1802 Mary Bagley (VR)

Russell C. Farnham, 678 North Seton Avenue, Lecanto, FL 34461-8786

Farnham, Paul   67b   1 - 0 - 2 - 0 - 0
Shapleigh Town, York County

PAUL FARNHAM, b York 20 Apr 1730 son of Ralph & Elizabeth (Austin) Farnham (Lester M. Bragdon & John E. Frost, *Vital Records of York, Maine* [1992], p. 13): d Acton 12 Apr 1820 (Gertrude Ella Hall, "Nathan Goodwin's Book of Remarks, Shapleigh, Maine 1777–1831" [TS, MHS, 1950], p. 12): m Rochester NH 10 Jun 1753 ELIZABETH DOOR (Franklin McDuffie, *History of Rochester, New Hampshire* [1892], hereafter *History of Rochester*, 1:594), bp Rochester NH 3 Mar 1746 dau of Philip & Lydia (Mason) Door (ibid., 1:589). Her date of death has not been found. Paul was one of the original settlers of Lebanon and prob moved there as early as 1753 when he married at the Rochester NH church. He was certainly there in 1756 when he was termed "of Towow" [i.e., Lebanon] when his son Ralph was baptized. In the division of his father's estate, dated 20 May 1760, Paul was given one-third of his father's rights in the township of Lebanon in addition to money which his brother Joseph was to pay to him (York Co Probate #5570, 10:170). On 20 May 1776, "great fires on lot No. 28 burned through to Mr. Paul Farnhams" (George W. Chamberlain, "Lebanon, Maine Genealogies 1750–1892" [TS, MHS, 1947], 1:#303). Whether the fire was the cause is not known, but he sold his property at Lebanon 27 Jul 1778 and moved on 28 Feb 1779 to the part of Shapleigh that later became Acton (ibid.) and there he lived the remainder of his life.

[In 1790, there were two Paul Farnham families in Shapleigh: one listed on p. 67b with 1-0-2-0-0 and one listed on p. 67c with 1-1-2-0-0. These were prob Paul Sr., the subject of this sketch, and his son Paul Jr. although it is not absolutely certain which listing applied to which man. It is presumed that Paul Sr. was the man on p. 67b because of his proximity to his sons Ralph and Dummer Farnham.]

Children as found, order uncertain
   i Mary, bp Rochester NH 4 Aug 1754 (*History of Rochester*, 1:592): she was prob the Mary Farnham who m Lebanon 22 Apr 1778 Henry Stevens (VR). According to one source, "perhaps they removed to Shapleigh" (Chamberlain, op. cit., 4:#164). In 1790, a Henry Stevens family was enumerated at Shapleigh (with 1-2-3-0-0) located betw Paul Farnham and his son, Ralph Farnham
   ii Ralph, b Lebanon 7 Jul 1756 (Rev War pension #S31018) and bp Rochester NH 5 Sep 1756 (*History of Rochester*, 1:593): d Acton 26 Dec 1860 (Lebanon VR; g.s., Farnham cem): married c1784 Mehitable Bean [see RALPH FARNHAM family]
   iii poss Elizabeth/Betty, described as a singlewoman in 1811 when Paul Farnham deeded to her 12 acres of land, one third part of the house and one third part of the orchard (*150th Anniversary, Acton, Maine 1830–1980*, p. 51). She was perhaps the 2nd female residing with Paul in 1790
   iv Olive, b c Aug 1763: d Lebanon 29 May 1847 (VR) ae 83y 9m (Chamberlain, op. cit.): m 1783 Samuel Runnells of Shapleigh (ibid.)
   v Paul Jr., prob the child of Paul Farnham b Lebanon 15 Jun 1766 (VR): d 7 Jul 1815 (g.s., Farnham cem, Acton): m Berwick 2 Jan 1787 a woman whose name was given as Olley Lord on the intention and Meribah Lord on the marriage record (both in Berwick VR) but who was shown as Olive Lord on her g.s., b c1766, d 16 Apr 1859 ae 93y (g.s., Farnham cem, Acton). [Note, Frost's "Acton Me. Record Book" (TS, MHS) transcribes Paul's age on the g.s. as "79 yrs." This is prob an incorrect reading for 49 yrs as there was no known Paul Farnham b c1736.]
   vi Dummer, prob b in late 1760s: d aft 1830 when he and his son, Dummer Jr., were enumerated in the census at Shapleigh: m Rochester NH 2 Dec 1790 Dorothy Heard of Rochester (*History of Rochester*, 1:610)

Russell C. Farnham, 678 N. Seton Ave., Lecanto, FL 34461-8786

Farnham, Ralf   67b   1 - 2 - 2 - 0 - 0
    Shapleigh Town, York County

RALPH FARNHAM, b Lebanon 7 Jul 1756 (Rev War pension #S31018) and bp Rochester NH 5 Sep 1756 (Franklin McDuffie, *History of Rochester, New Hampshire* [1892], 1:593) son of Paul & Elizabeth (Door) Farnham [see PAUL

FARNHAM family]: d of dropsy Acton 26 Dec 1860 ae 104y 5m 19d (Lebanon VR; g.s., Farnham cem): m c1784 MEHITABLE BEAN (George W. Chamberlain, "Lebanon, Maine Genealogies 1750–1892" [TS, MHS, 1947], 1:#303), b Raymond NH 28 Aug 1765 dau of Lt. Benjamin & Hannah (Smith) Bean (ibid.), d Acton 8 Mar 1842 ae 76y (g.s., Farnham cem). Ralph enlisted 15 May 1775 in Capt. Philip Hubbard's Co., Col. James Scammon's Regiment during the Rev War (*150th Anniversary, Acton, Maine 1830–1980*, pp. 48– 56). They were marched to Boston in May 1775 where they served in the Battle of Bunker Hill (ibid.). He also enlisted in several other companies and saw service in 1777 in Rhode Island, Bennington VT and Saratoga NY (ibid.). In 1779, Ralph, his father Paul and brothers Dummer and Paul Jr., and his maternal grandfather Philip Door moved from Lebanon to Fox's Ridge in the northwest part of Shapleigh [now Acton] (ibid.). In 1847, Ralph was acknowledged as a contributor to Joseph Fullonton's *The History of Acton* [1847], p. iii., and was termed "a living chronicle of the events of the past." Eighty years after arriving in Acton, Ralph was honored in 1860 in Boston MA festivities as being the oldest living survivor of the Battle of Bunker Hill (*150th Anniversary*, op. cit., pp. 52–53).

Children: *150th Anniversary*, op. cit., p. 52
- i Benjamin, b c1785: d Lebanon 14 Oct 1849 ae 64y (VR): m (1) Lebanon 5 Aug 1808 Sally Hill (VR) [he was termed "of Shapleigh" on the m int recorded Shapleigh 14 Apr 1808 (VR)] dau of Jeremiah & Abigail (Stevens) Hill (Chamberlain, op. cit., 2:#194): m (2) Lebanon 26 Jul 1829 Dorcas Frost (VR), b c1779, d Acton 16 Aug 1872 ae 93y (Lebanon VR). Benjamin left a will dated Lebanon, 22 Apr 1844 in which he named his wife Dorcas and 5 children (York Co Probate #5550, 64:246)
- ii Hannah, b 1788 (g.s.): d 1861 (g.s., Runnells cem, Acton): m int Shapleigh 22 Mar 1811 Dea. Samuel Runnels (VR) [note, he was called Samuel "Reynolds" on the m int recorded at Lebanon (VR)], b c1788, d 29 Mar 1854 ae 66y (g.s., Runnells cem, Acton)
- iii Mary, b c Apr 1792: d 7 May 1859 ae 67y 1m 4d (g.s., Maple Grove cem, Acton): m Shapleigh 4 Dec 1814 Job Ricker of Shapleigh (VR), b c Oct 1791, d 16 Apr 1877 ae 85y 7m 16d (g.s., Maple Grove cem, Acton)
- iv Joanna, b c1794–95: d Boston MA 1 Mar 1877 ae 82y (g.s., Farnham cem, Acton): unm
- v John, b c1797: d aft 17 Jan 1878 when he wrote his will (York Co Probate #5561): m Shapleigh 24 Feb 1828 Fanny (Wood) Merrill of Shapleigh (VR), b Acton c Jan 1802 dau of Enoch & Dorothy (Hurd) Wood (from death rec), d Milton Mills NH 4 Jul 1891 ae 89y 6m 2d (NHVR). She had m (1) 1823 Asa Merrill (Shapleigh VR). In 1827, John's father, Ralph, turned over his house, buildings and approximately 83 acres of land to John, stipulating that his sister Joanna always have a home there unless

she married (*150th Anniversary*, op. cit., p. 52). John accompanied his father to the Boston festivities in his father's honor in 1860 (ibid.)
- vi Daniel, b c1800: d 20 May 1852 ae 52y (g.s., Farnham cem, Acton): unm
- vii Ralph Jr., b c1802. He removed to Fairfield ME (*150th Anniversary*, op. cit., p. 52)

Russell C. Farnham, 678 N. Seton Ave., Lecanto, FL 34461-8786

Furnald, Benj[n]   61c   3 - 0 - 2 - 0 - 0
Kittery Town, York County

BENJAMIN FERNALD Jr., b Kittery 27 Jun 1721 son of Benjamin & Catherine (____) Fernald (Joseph C. Anderson II & Lois W. Thurston, *Vital Records of Kittery, Maine to the Year 1892* [1991], hereafter *Kittery VR*, p. 63): d prob Kittery 4 Mar 1798 (Everett S. Stackpole, *Old Kittery and Her Families* [1903], hereafter *Old Kittery*, p. 385): m int Kittery 1 Feb 1745/6 SARAH FERNALD (VR, p. 217) [*Old Kittery*, p. 380, gives m 6 Mar 1746], b 21 Jan 1726 dau of Ebenezer & Patience (Mendum) Fernald (14 Apr 1775 will of Ebenezer Fernald naming his dau Sarah Fernald, York Co Probate #5702; *Old Kittery*, p. 380), d 13 May 1801 (ibid.). Benjamin, describing himself as a ship carpenter, left a will dated 4 Mar 1798, the same day he reportedly died (York Co Probate #5682). In it, he left to his wife one-third of his real estate for life which afterwards would be divided in equal shares by "my three children" whom he named as his dau Miriam Phipps and his sons William and Benjamin Fernald. He also named his grandsons Benjamin Holbrook and Abiah Holbrook and left a cow to one Rebecca Weeks. Benjamin's will and the subsequent division of his estate (York Co Probate 17:558) would appear to indicate that all of his other children were deceased by 1798.

Children: births *Old Kittery*, p. 385; baptisms First Church of Kittery (National Society of the DAR, "Records from the First Church in Kittery, Maine 1715-1797" [TS, MHS, 1979], pp. 62, 65, 67, 69, 70, 72, 74, 76, 78, 82)
- i Lucy, b 25 Mar 1747 and bp 16 Aug 1747: m William Holbrook (*Old Kittery*, p. 385), bp Kittery 1st Church 1 Jun 1746 son of Elisha & Lydia (Dresser) Holbrook, the only Holbrooks living at Kittery ("Records from the First Church," op. cit., p. 60; Victor Channing Sanborn, "Four Boston Families: Holbrook, Yendell, Vail, Witham," NEHGR, 58 [1904]:305). William and Lucy were the parents of the two grandsons named in Benjamin Fernald's will, op. cit.
- ii Josiah, b 13 Jul 1749 and bp 20 July 1749
- iii Joshua, b 11 Nov 1751 and bp 8 Dec 1751

iv   Joseph, b 10 Jan 1753 and bp 24 Jun 1753
v   Alice/Ellis, b 13 Dec [sic] 1754 and bp 7 Dec [sic] 1754
vi   Robert, b 16 Aug 1757 [baptismal records missing for this year]
vii Noah, b 23 Sep 1759 [baptismal records missing for this year]
viii Miriam, b 12 Jul 1762 [sic] and bp 19 July 1761 [sic]: m Kittery 20 Dec 1781 George Phipps (VR, p. 171) who d bef 1790 when Miriam was enumerated in the census at Kittery as "Widdow Phips" [see MIRIAM (FERNALD) PHIPPS family]
ix   Elizabeth, b 25 Sep 1764 [sic] and bp 23 Oct 1763 [sic]
x   Catherine, b Jul 1766 and bp 4 Jan 1767
xi   William, b 6 May 1769 and bp 7 May 1769: d suddenly 17 Apr 1828 ae 59y (YCGSJ, 7:1 [1992]:2): m 14 Apr 1793 Lucy Fernald (*Old Kittery*, p. 393) [m int Kittery 3 Dec 1792 (VR, p. 250)], b Kittery 25 May 1771 dau of Jonathan & Sarah (Weeks) Fernald (VR, p. 164). She was very possibly the "Mrs. Lucy Fernald" who m poss (2) Kittery 21 Jul 1833 Robert Whall of Kittery (VR, p. 283)
xii Benjamin, b 7 Apr 1774 and bp 17 Apr 1774: d 3 Mar 1854 ae 89y (g.s., Fernald plot, south side Whipple Rd. near Kittery Point Bridge): m 2 Dec 1795 Eunice Place (*Old Kittery*, p. 394) [m int Kittery 23 Aug 1795 (VR, p. 252), b Kittery 18 Nov 1773 dau of John & Elizabeth (_____) Place (VR, p. 192), d 4 Feb 1852 ae 78y (g.s., Fernald plot, op. cit.)

Judith H. Kelley, 96 Florence St., So. Portland, ME 04106

Follet, Mercy   61b   0 - 1 - 3 - 0 - 0
Kittery Town, York County

MERCY (MITCHELL) FOLLETT (widow of Robert Follett), bp Kittery 1st Church 16 Oct 1743 dau of Joseph & Isabella (Bragdon) Mitchell of Kittery (National Society of the DAR, "Records From the First Church of Kittery, Maine 1715-1797" [TS, DAR, MSL], p. 54; parents' marriage recorded York, see Lester E. Bragdon & John E. Frost, *Vital Records of York, Maine* [1992], hereafter VR, p. 117): d 24 Dec 1797 ae 54y (g.s., Congregational Churchyard, Kittery Point): m Kittery 16 Jul 1767 Capt. ROBERT FOLLETT (Joseph C. Anderson II & Lois Ware Thurston, *Vital Records of Kittery, Maine to the Year 1892* [1991], hereafter Kittery VR, p. 152), b Kittery 16 Jun 1737 son of John Jr. & Mary (Tripe) Follett (VR, p. 83; parents' marriage int recorded Kittery 16 Sep 1731, p. 97), d 21 Aug 1780 ae 43y (g.s., Congregational Churchyard, Kittery Point). Robert Follett served in the Rev War as captain of an artillery company at Kittery (Fisher's *Soldiers*, p. 263). Both he and his sons were shipbuilders and masters at Kittery Point (Everett S. Stackpole, *Old Kittery and Her Families* [1903], p. 410). On 24 May 1779, Robert Follett of Kittery, mariner, granted freedom to a negro man named William Simmonds who had served him "for 2 yrs from this date & behaving with respect to me" (John E. Frost, *Maine Probate Abstracts* [1991], hereafter MPA, 13/391 citing York Co Probate #6004, 13:202). The inventory of Robert's estate was taken 17 Sep 1781 and included 1 acre of mowing land by the Meeting House, a boat, sail, and oars, a gundalow, some sea books and other items, the sum totaling to just over £587 (MPA, 14/228, citing York Co Probate, 14:280). The division did not occur until 19 Mar 1798 (ibid., 17/449, citing York Co Probate 17:454) at which time the heirs named were sons John and Robert Follett upon whom the bulk of the estate was settled, their sister Mercy, their sister Mary, and their brother Joshua W. Follett. John Follett was called administrator de bonis non as a result of the death of his mother, Mercy, the former administrator. One Nathaniel Sparhawk Jr. acted as agent for Joshua W. Follett who was probably at sea, perhaps on the same voyage from which he never returned.

Children, b Kittery: names of children given in Kittery VR, p. 83; their birthdates given in Stackpole, p. 410
   i   John, b 6 Aug 1768: d 28 Oct 1820 ae 52y (g.s., Congregational Churchyard, Kittery Point): m int Kittery 9 Aug 1806 Lydia Emery of York (Kittery VR, p. 263), b York 24 Feb 1783 dau of John & Mary (Bragdon) Emery of York (her g.s. states she was a dau of John Emery; York VR, p. 84), d 22 May 1861 ae 78y (g.s., Congregational Churchyard, Kittery Point). She m (2) Kittery 5 Oct 1823 John L. Lawrence (as indicated on her g.s. although she is bur next to her 1st husb John Follett; Kittery VR, p. 276)
   ii   Robert, b 19 Sep 1770: d 13 Sep 1815 ae 45y (g.s., Congregational Churchyard, Kittery Point): unm
   iii   Mary, b 1 Apr 1773: d 17 Aug 1839 ae 66y (g.s., Congregational Churchyard, Kittery Point): m Kittery 25 Dec 1814 William T. Gerrish (VR, p. 203), b 11 Feb 1765 son of Col. Joseph & Anna (Thompson) Gerrish (Stackpole, op. cit., p. 447), d 21 Mar 1845 in his 81st y (g.s., Congregational Churchyard, Kittery Point)
   iv   Joshua W., b 19 Oct 1775: Stackpole, op. cit., on p. 410 stated he was lost at sea 15 Nov 1797, however this date most likely should be 15 Nov 1798 as Joshua was alive 19 Mar 1798 when his father's estate was divided. The adm of the estate of Joshua W. Follett, of Kittery, mariner, was granted 20 May 1799 to his bro Robert Follett of Kittery, cooper (MPA 18/74, citing York Co Probate 18:80). Joshua m int Kittery 15 Jul 1797 Dorothy Parsons of Kittery (VR, p. 254). She m (2) Kittery Feb 1803 Samuel W. Seavey of Rye NH (VR, p. 174)

v   Mercy, b 23 Aug 1780 [note that she was born just 2 days after her father's death]: d 21 Jul 1852 in her 72nd y (g.s., Congregational Churchyard, Kittery Point): unm (ibid.). According to Stackpole, at her death the Follett name became extinct in Kittery (*Old Kittery and Her Families*, op. cit., p. 410)

Joseph C. Anderson II, 5337 Del Roy Drive, Dallas, TX 75229

Gage, Amos   68b   1 - 2 - 1 - 0 - 0
Sudbury-Canada Town [now Bethel], York County

AMOS GAGE, b Pelham NH 9 Aug 1758 son of Amos & Mehitable (Kimball) Gage (IGI LDS; Leonard Allison Morrison & Stephen Paschall Sharples, *History of the Kimball Family in America* [repr 1981], p. 85): d Bethel 28 Aug 1833 ae 75y (g.s., Grover Hill cem; Rev War pension #W24271): m Boxford MA 22 Apr 1787 LOIS HOVEY (ibid.), b Boxford MA 14 Jun 1759 dau of Joseph & Rebecca (Stickney) Hovey (IGI LDS), res Waterford 1838 ae 78y (pension, op. cit.). During the Rev War, Amos served in Capt. Eaton's MA company and Col. Stark's NH regiment (Fisher's *Soldiers*, p. 280); he also served on the ship EVOLUTION (ibid.). On one of his enlistments from Boxford MA in 1780, he was described as being ae 21y, 6 feet tall, and light complexioned (MS&S 6:212). He came early to Bethel and was an original member of the Congregational Church (William B. Lapham, *History of Bethel, Maine* [repr 1981], hereafter Lapham's *Bethel*, p. 538).

Children: births VR Bethel
i   Thomas Hovey, b 8 Jun 1789: m Bath 17 Dec 1815 Frances C. Stockbridge of Bath (Lapham's *Bethel*, p. 538; IGI LDS)
ii Leander, b 20 Sep 1791: d 1842 (Henry P. Warren, *The History of Waterford, Oxford County, Maine* [1879], p. 246): m 1820 Anna B. Sargent (Lapham's *Bethel*, p. 538), b 1794 (*History of Waterford*, p. 246). He was a physician and began a practice at Waterford about 1817 (ibid.)
iii William, b 15 Mar 1795: d Bethel 1 Jan 1820 ae 25y (VR; g.s., Grover Hill cem on which he was called the "3rd" son)
iv Amos, b 2 Mar 1797: m Mary Warren (Lapham's *Bethel*, p. 538), b 1797 dau of Major Samuel & Polly (Green) Warren (*History of Waterford*, p. 298)

Warren D. Stearns, P.O. Box 35, Hanover, ME 04237

Gahan, John 37c 1 - 1 - 2 - 0 - 0
Georgetown Town, Lincoln County

JOHN GAHAN, b prob Ireland bef 1755 (ae 45+ years, 1800 USC): d prob aft 1805 when his last child was bp at Georgetown and bef 1810 (USC) and bur Morse Burying Ground, Winnegance: m Woolwich 7 Feb 1787 BATHSHEBA WEBB (VR, he called John "Carnes"), b c1758 dau of Samuel & Sarah (Lincoln) Webb (Georgetown VR, n.d.) [see SAMUEL WEBB family, *Maine Families*, 2:294, and Addendum in this volume], d 1852 ae 94y, bur Morse Burying Ground, Winnegance. Dennis, James and John Gahan were members of "the Irish Volunteers" at the defense of Machias in 1780 (MS&S, 6:224).

Children: births VR Georgetown, baptisms in Phippsburg Congregational Church recs which are included in the published Phippsburg VR
i James, b 1 Feb 1788 and bp 18 May 1796
ii Peggy, b 2 Feb 1790 and bp 18 May 1796
iii John, b 23 Dec 1792 and bp 18 May 1796: d Dresden 17 Jul 1868 (g.s., Maple Grove cem, South Dresden): m int Dresden 17 Apr 1819 Mary Blair (VR), b Dresden 18 Sep 1795 dau of William & Rebecca (Knowles) Blair (VR), d Dresden 14 Dec 1866 (VR)
iv Jeremiah, b 17 Sep 1794 and bp 18 May 1796: m Anson 31 May 1818 Annah Savage (VR)
v Sarah Webb, b 26 Dec 1796 and bp 12 Mar 1797: m Georgetown 26 Nov 1820 Capt. Robert Parker Manson as his 2nd wife (VR). He d 11 Feb 1835 ae 62y (Drummond cem, Phippsburg)
vi William Butler, b 10 Jul 1799: m int Phippsburg 25 Nov 1821 Mary Whaling (VR)
vii Samuel Webb, b 16 Feb 1803 and bp 22 Sep 1805: d Woolwich 9 Mar 1881 ae 78y (Georgetown published VR, citing newspaper; g.s., Laurel Hill cem, Woolwich): m int Dresden 6 Mar 1830 Eleanor Lee Bowker (VR), b Dresden 2 Apr 1813 dau of Jacob & Elizabeth (Williams) Bowker (VR), d Woolwich 5 Jan 1902 ae 89y 2m (g.s., Laurel Hill cem). Their children were rec at Woolwich. [While he was called Samuel "Webb" Gahan on his baptismal rec, his obit called him Samuel "Lincoln" Gahan and other recs called him Samuel L. Gahan. Additionally, he had a son named Lincoln]

Marjorie Gahan Beardsley, 341 Muirfield Dr., Winston-Salem, NC 27104

Gill, John 39a 3 - 4 - 6 - 0 - 0
Hallowell Town, Lincoln County

JOHN GILLEY, b Castle Isles, County Cork, Ireland (James North, *The History of Augusta, Maine* [repr 1981], hereafter North, p. 93): d Augusta 9 Jul 1813 reportedly at the fantastic age of 124y (obits in Hallowell *American Advocate*, issue of 17 Jul 1813, and in the Portland *Eastern Argus*, issue of 22 Jul 1813, given in David C. & Elizabeth K. Young, *Vital Records from Maine Newspapers, 1785–1820* [1993], p. 230): m Hallowell 3 Aug 1769 DORCAS BRAWN (VR), b c1745 a poss but unproven dau of Peter & Elizabeth (Musset/Museet/Muzeet) Brawn of Kittery and Vassalboro (tentative identification based on a process of elimination of other Brawn families), d Augusta Mar 1840 ae 95y (North, p. 94). John arrived in America in 1755 and came to Fort Western where he enlisted for duty in the French and Indian Wars (North, p. 93). Capt. Howard, in command of the fort, tried to determine Gilley's age: by "comparing dates, ages, and various other circumstances, it was conceded that Gilley was seven or eight years older than Howard" (ibid.). From a manuscript account by Judge Cony, made from Gilley's narration, it afterwards appeared that Gilley was 13y older than Howard who d 14 May 1787 at ae 85y (ibid., in footnote). When his wife, Dorcas Gilley, was asked how old her husband was, she claimed not to know—"when she first knew him he was called grandpapa Gilley" (ibid.). He was known as "Little John Gilley," standing only five feet, three inches tall (ibid.). In 1766, he bought from the Howards land on the east side of the Kennebec River (Lin Co deeds at Ken Co Courthouse, 2:210). In 1791, he bought lot #45 on the east side of the river from James Clark (Lin Co deeds at Ken Co Courthouse, 3:468). On 23 Mar 1809, he gave this same lot to his son, James Gilley, in exchange for life support (Ken Co deeds, 19:171). If his age at death was accurate, then he was ae 79y when he married and prob near ae 100y at the birth of his last child. A write-up of Gilley appeared in the 1976 edition of *Ripley's Giant Believe It or Not*.

Children: births first 7 VR Hallowell
- i Margaret/Peggy, b 8 Jul 1770: d Troy 1 Jan 1853 (VR): m int Hallowell 8 Nov 1788 Andrew Bennett (VR) [see ANDREW BENNETT family]
- ii John, b 28 Dec 1771
- iii Robert, b 18 Oct 1773
- iv James, b 27 Jun 1775: d 1843 (Ken Co Probate, File G8): m int Augusta 10 Feb 1808 Elizabeth/Betsey Foster of Woolwich (VR), perhaps the Betty Foster bp Woolwich 5 Nov 1786 dau of Nathaniel & Dolley (____) Foster ("Records of the Rev. Josiah Winship, Woolwich Church," DAR Misc Recs, 13:23)
- v Else/Alice, b 15 Aug 1777: m int Augusta 7 Dec 1799 Benjamin Hussey of Vassalboro (VR)
- vi Dorcas, b 29 May 1779
- vii William, b 28 Nov 1781: m int Augusta 4 Jun 1801 Rebecca Quin (VR)
- viii Dermont, d bef 28 Dec 1840 when his estate was probated (Ken Co Probate, File G3): m (1) int Augusta 26 Feb 1805 Sally Dow of Township No. 4 (Augusta VR): m (2) int Augusta 17 Feb 1839 Naomi Hawes of Sidney (Augusta VR) who survived him

ix prob Isaac F., m Winslow 5 Apr 1809 Catherine Bran (VR)
x   prob Abigail, b c1788: m int Augusta 10 Dec 1807 Joseph Brown/Brann of Vassalboro (Augusta VR). They res Winslow where their children's births are recorded

Ardell J. Parkman Lynds, 12630 Joy Bell Lane, San Martin, CA 95046

Ginn, James   30a   3 - 4 - 6 - 0 - 0
Orrington Town, Hancock County

JAMES GINN, b Virginia 4 Oct 1745 son of Thomas Ginn of Caroline Co, East Shore, MD (Wesley C. Ginn manuscript at NEHGS): d Bucksport 17 Apr 1818 ae 68y (VR; Han Co Probate #643) [BHM, 4:238, says d 1818 ae 71y]: m Gloucester MA 3 Jun 1768 ANN RIGGS (VR), b Gloucester MA 17 Jan 1746/7 dau of Joshua & Experience (Stanwood) Riggs (VR), d Bucksport 19 Sep 1822 (Ginn MS, op. cit.). James first settled at Gloucester where he married and his first four children were born. By 1776, he was in Orrington where he saw Rev War service in Capt. Brewer's Co. (MS&S 6:473). He was one of the petitioners to incorporate Orrington in 1783 and was a grantee of land there in 1786 (H. N. Brooks, "Records of Orrington" [LDS film #11725]). He served as one of two commissioners to examine claims against the estates of Phineas Nevers in 1787 and Silas Hathorn in 1788, both late of Penobscot River (Lin Co Probate 3:250, 2:236). James purchased land in Orland in 1793 and added lots in Buckstown and Orland adjacent to the town line in the same year (Han Co deeds 2:309, 311, 312) where he apparently ran the mill of Robert Treat until 1797 (Mary B. LaRocca, "Early Records of Orland," *Downeast Ancestry*, 8, #4 [Dec 1984]:152–53). He served as Orland Plt clerk during this time (VR). In 1800, he moved to Bucksport and built a wharf and store; in 1803 he built a large house, and in succeeding years he built a number of vessels and was the first importer of foreign goods into Bucksport (Rufus Buck, *History of the Settlement of Bucksport* [1860], pp. 31–35). The 1800 census states that he was from Virginia. By 1818, he had sold his lands in Orland and Bucksport to his children (Han Co deeds 37:29, 537). His intestate estate was probated in 1819 (Han Co Probate #643).

Children, first 4 b Gloucester MA, rest in Orrington: VR Gloucester MA; Ginn manuscript, op. cit.; Brooks, op. cit.
  i James, b 3 Apr 1769: left home due to a disagreement about his marriage (Ginn MS, op. cit.) [although one source claimed he was unm (Mildred N. Thayer & Mrs. Edward W. Ames, "Old Orrington Book," *Brewer, Orrington, Holden, Eddington History and Families* [1962], hereafter OOB, p. 58)]

ii   Ann, b 3 Apr 1771: d Brewer (Brooks, op. cit.): m int Orrington 16 Mar 1793 Josiah Brewer (Brooks, op. cit.), b New Worcester Plt [Orrington] 11 May 1770 son of Col. John & Martha (Graves) Brewer (ibid.), d Brewer 28 Dec 1837 (Brooks, op. cit.)
iii Abraham, b 7 Jan 1773: d aft 1850 (USC): m Bucksport 19 Nov 1794 Hannah Downs (Orland VR), b c1774, d Orland 9 Dec 1831 ae 57y (g.s., Orland Village cem). They res Orland (Ginn MS, op. cit.)
iv   Samuel, b 10 Mar 1775: d Prospect 16 Jul 1816 (g.s., Batchelder cem): m Orland 27 Dec 1798 Hannah Keyes (VR), b c1776 dau of Samuel & Thankful (Hunt) Keyes (Priscilla Jones Collection, Stephen Phillips Memorial Library, Searsport), d Bucksport 31 Jan 1846 ae 70y (*Republican Journal*, issue of 20 Feb 1846). They res Prospect
v   Joshua, b 7 Nov 1776: d Bucksport Jun 1845 ae 68y (VR): m int Bucksport 5 Dec 1804 Susanna Page (VR), b c1772, d Bucksport 14 Nov 1862 ae 90y (VR). They res Bucksport
vi   Daniel, b Aug 1778: d Belmont 18 May 1834 ae 56y (g.s., Hillside cem): m int Prospect 27 Feb 1805 Sally Odom (VR), b c1784 dau of John & Sarah (Haney) Odom of Prospect (Priscilla Jones Collection, op. cit.), d aft 1840 (USC). They res Belmont
vii Susan/Sukey, b 24 Jun 1780: m Bucksport 20 Jan 1801 Samuel Keyes Jr. (VR). They res Orland
viii Polly, b 6 Apr 1782: m int Bucksport 12 Mar 1809 Dudley Parker (VR)
ix   Sally, b 20 Feb 1784: m int Bucksport 25 Feb 1804 Rowland Tyler of Orrington (Bucksport VR) [OOB, p. 58, gives m 10 Mar 1804]
x   William Riggs, b Jun 1786: d Bucksport 20 Apr 1868 ae 82y 3m (g.s., Oak Hill cem): m (1) int Bucksport 5 Jan 1812 Kirty Stewart of Ellsworth (VR), b c1791, d Bucksport 3 Apr 1845 (g.s., Oak Hill cem): m (2) cert Bucksport 20 Dec 1845 Joanna (Swett) Paine (VR), b c1794, d Bucksport 30 Jun 1863 ae 69y (g.s., Oak Hill cem). He res Bucksport
xi   Delia/Peley, b Jan 1788: m int Bucksport 5 Dec 1804 Free Parker (VR)
xii Margaret, b 4 Jul 1791: unm (Brooks, op. cit.)

Ralph E. Hillman, 4302 James Dr., Midland, MI 48642

Goodrige, Danl [s/b Paul]   56c   3 - 2 - 4 - 0 - 0
Berwick Town, York County

[Note: Examination of the original 1790 census sheets on microfilm confirm that the census taker wrote "Paul" and not "Danl."]

PAUL GOODRIDGE, b Berwick 4 Jul 1737 and bp Berwick 1st Church 10 Jul 1737 son of Benjamin & Abigail (Preble) Goodridge (John E. Frost & Joseph C. Anderson II, *Vital Records of Berwick, South Berwick and North Berwick,*

Maine to the Year 1892 [1993], hereafter VR, p. 208; "Records of the First Church of Berwick, Me.," NEHGR, 82 [1928]:206; parents' mar rec in Lester E. Bragdon & John E. Frost, *Vital Records of York, Maine* [1992], p. 116): d Berwick "of a cancer in the left side" 12 May 1815 ae 78y (VR, p. 292): m Berwick 26 Mar 1767 MARY GUBTAIL/GUPTILL (VR, p. 208), prob she bp Berwick 1st Church 14 Mar 1741/2 dau of Benjamin & Elizabeth (____) Gubtail/Guptill (NEHGR, 82 [1928]:212) [see discussion below]. She was prob the "M. Goodrich" who d Berwick 1804 ae 63y who was buried in the same plot as Paul (Wilbur D. Spencer, *Burial Inscriptions and Other Data of Burials in Berwick, York County, Maine to the Year 1922* [1922], hereafter *Berwick Burials*, p. 22, citing a private cem on the south side of Cranberry Meadow Rd.). Paul left a will dated 11 Apr 1815 and probated 3 Jun 1815 (York Co Probate #6906, 25:236). In it, he named his sons Benjamin, Ichabod, James and Paul, and his three unmarried daus Abigail, Molley and Betsey. To the daus, he left one half of his dwelling house while they remain single and the wearing apparel their mother left at the time of her death. Paul lived his entire life at Berwick where he was a farmer (described as a yeoman in his will). While he was not a Rev War soldier, in 1778 he advanced 9s 1p for the use of Capt. Thomas Hodsdon's company (Wilbur D. Spencer, "Statistics of Berwick, Maine" [TS, MSL, 1943], p. 36). His property in Berwick included 70 acres with a dwelling house and other buildings (will).

[The published Berwick 1st Church records give another Mary Gubtail, bp 5 Apr 1741, dau of Nathaniel & Mary Guptail (NEHGR, 82 [1928]:210). However an examination of the original church records on microfilm at MHS showed her name was actually "Marcy" and thus she was prob the Marcy Guptail who m Berwick Oct 1776 Dr. Thomas Chase (Berwick VR, p. 124).]

Children: births VR Berwick, p. 208
  i   Benjamin, b 9 Aug 1767: d Berwick 4 Aug 1828 ae 61y (VR, p. 298): m Berwick 29 Mar 1803 Mary Shorey (VR, p. 201), b c1780, living in 1850 at Berwick ae 70y in the household of her son Benjamin Goodridge Jr. (USC). Benjamin left a will dated 30 Jul 1828 and probated 4 Nov 1828 in which he named his wife Mary and 6 children (York Co Probate #6879, 39:99)
  ii Abigail, b 14 Feb 1769: living in 1850 at Berwick ae 81y with her nephew Hiram Goodridge and sister Betsey (USC): unm (ibid.)
  iii Ichabod, b 17 Apr 1771: d aft 1840 when he was a head of household at Berwick (USC) but bef 1850 when his wid was enumerated in the household of her son at Berwick (USC): m Berwick 15 Aug 1793 Dorcas Guptail (VR, p. 137), b c1774 and bp Berwick 2nd Church with 5 siblings 23 Oct 1782 dau of William & Dorcas (Stone) Guptail ("Records of the Second Church of Berwick, Me.," NEHGR, 74 [1920]:246; ae 76y in 1850 USC, household of Ivory Goodrich), d aft 1860 (USC Berwick, ae 86y)

- iv Mary/Molley, b 18 May 1773: d aft 1815 when named in her father's will and prob bef 1847 (inventory of estate of her brother James, mentioning sisters Abigail and Betsey but not Molley, York Co Probate 61:183)
- v James, b 20 May 1775: d Berwick 14 Oct 1847 ae 72y 4m 24d (*Berwick Burials*, p. 67, citing g.s., Evergreen cem): m int Berwick 15 May 1803 Sally Twambley of Milton NH (Berwick VR, p. 50), b c Mar 1785, d 11 Sep 1846 ae 61y 5m 26d (*Berwick Burials*, p. 67). James left a will dated 9 Jul 1847 and probated Dec 1847 naming 7 children (York Co Probate #6893, 61:72)
- vi Stephen, b 15 Aug 1777: not named in his father's will in 1815
- vii Paul, b 5 Oct 1779: d Berwick 19 Apr 1830 ae 51y (*Berwick Burials*, p. 22): m cert Berwick 30 Jun 1825 Sally Brasbridge (VR, p. 79). Paul left a will dated 23 Oct 1829 and probated 2 Aug 1830 which named his wife Sally and a nephew who lived with him, but no children (York Co Probate #6907, 41:171)
- viii Elizabeth/Betsey, b 28 Jul 1782: living in 1850 at Berwick ae 68y with her nephew Hiram Goodridge and sister Abigail (USC): unm (ibid.)

Joseph C. Anderson II, 5337 Del Roy Drive, Dallas, TX 75229

Goodwin, Elijah   57a   2 - 2 - 2 - 0 - 0
Berwick Town, York County

ELIJAH GOODWIN, bp 1st Church Berwick 23 Mar 1726/7 son of William & Abigail (Stone) Goodwin (NEHGR, 82 [1928]:87; John Hayes Goodwin, *Daniel Goodwin of Ancient Kittery, Maine and His Descendants* [1985], hereafter *Daniel Goodwin*, pp. 16–17, 33): d Berwick 26 ___ 1816 (John E. Frost & Joseph C. Anderson II, *Vital Records of Berwick, South Berwick and North Berwick, Maine to the Year 1892* [1993], hereafter VR, p. 293, month not given on record): m (1) Berwick 21 Dec 1749 ABIGAIL MARTIN (VR, p. 192) [while given in the VR as Martin, Abigail's surname is given as Tarbox in several secondary sources and some propose she may have been a widow when she m Elijah Goodwin]: m (2) Berwick 16 Dec 1782 EUNICE (FOY) HAMMOND (VR, p. 127; *Daniel Goodwin*, p. 33), b c1742, d Berwick 31 Dec 1835 ae 93y (VR). Elijah was a farmer. He resided at Great Falls NH and later at Cranberry Meadow in Berwick (*Daniel Goodwin*, p. 33).

Children by 1st wife Abigail Martin: first 2 bp Berwick 1st Church, NEHGR 82 [1928]:321, 322; rest bp Berwick 2nd Church, NEHGR 74 [1920]:214, 217, 219, 220, 224, 225, 227, 228
- i Abigail, bp 8 Dec 1751: m Berwick 4 Jan 1773 Joseph Holmes (VR, p. 119), reportedly the Joseph Holmes bp Berwick 3 Nov 1726 son of John

& Mary (Abbott) Holmes (*Daniel Goodwin*, p. 33; Everett S. Stackpole, *Old Kittery and Her Families* [1903], hereafter *Old Kittery*, p. 536)

ii Elijah Jr., bp 10 Nov 1752: d Oct 1815 (*Daniel Goodwin*, p. 73): m Berwick 28 Apr 1774 Lucy Avery [see ELIJAH GOODWIN Jr. family]

iii Daniel, bp 8 Jun 1755: d of consumption Lebanon 11 Nov 1790 ae 36y (VR): m Berwick 30 Jan 1781 Mary Downs (VR, p. 122), b Lebanon 27 Jul 1750 dau of Joseph Downs (*Daniel Goodwin*, p. 73), d Middleton NH 21 Aug 1833 (ibid.)

iv Lydia, bp 16 Jan 1757: m Berwick 25 Nov 1779 Simeon Spencer (VR, p. 122), bp Berwick 1st Church 21 Jun 1752 son of Humphrey & Elizabeth [or Sarah] (Early) Spencer (NEHGR, 82 [1928]:320; Berwick VR, p. 192), d Berwick 21 Jan 1840 (g.s., Evergreen cem). He m (2) Berwick 5 Feb 1804 Susanna Hamilton (NEHGR, 74 [1920]:262) [see JONAS HAMILTON family]

v Adam, b 25 Dec 1758 (*Daniel Goodwin*, p. 73) and bp 14 Jan 1759 (this baptism was omitted from the published 2nd Church recs, but was verified in the original records): d 23 Dec 1836 (*Daniel Goodwin*, p. 73): m Berwick 30 Sep 1781 Sarah Goodridge/Goodrich (VR, p. 123), b c1760, d 11 Apr 1834 ae 74y (VR, p. 300; Wilbur D. Spencer, *Burial Inscriptions, Berwick, York County, Maine* [1922], p. 23). He was a Rev War soldier and pensioner (Rev War pension #S19301)

vi Charity, bp 5 Jul 1761: m Joseph Curtis son of Isaac Curtis (*Daniel Goodwin*, p. 33). They res Biddeford and Kennebunkport (ibid.)

vii Simeon, twin (as mentioned in bro Reuben's Rev War pension), bp 17 Jul 1763: d Lebanon 21 Apr 1836 ae 74y (VR): m Berwick 5 Nov 1787 Mary Goodridge/Goodrich (VR, p. 129), b c1765, d Lebanon 15 May 1842 ae 77y (VR). He moved from Berwick to Lebanon in 1792 (*Daniel Goodwin*, p. 74). He was a Rev War soldier and pensioner (Rev War pension #W24293)

viii Reuben, twin (Rev War pension #S18419), bp 17 Jul 1763: d Lebanon 19 Dec 1846 ae 86y (VR): m Berwick 6 Jan 1785 Phebe Downs (VR), b c1758 dau of Daniel & Judith (Canney) Downs (*Daniel Goodwin*, p. 75; George W. Chamberlain, "Lebanon, Maine Genealogies 1750–1892" [TS, MHS, 1976], 1:#247), d Lebanon 20 Dec 1844 ae 86y (VR). He was a Rev War soldier and pensioner (Rev War pension #S18419)

ix Meribah, bp 24 Nov 1765: d Sanbornton NH 2 Apr 1842 ae 75y [sic] (Rev. M. T. Runnels, *History of Sanbornton, New Hampshire* [1881], p. 274): m prob Sanbornton NH 30 Sep 1787 Barachias Farnham of Lebanon & Sanbornton NH as his 2nd wife (Lebanon VR in which date of marriage was given, but not bride's name; *History of Sanbornton*, p. 274), b 10 Nov 1760 (ibid.) prob son of Deacon Joseph Farnham Esqr. of York and Lebanon and his 2nd wife Eunice ____ (see Russell C. Farnham, "The Expanded Family of Joseph[5] Farnham of York and Lebanon, Maine," *The*

Maine Genealogist, 16 [1994]:31–35). Barachias d 27 Mar 1842 ae 81y 4m 17d (*History of Sanbornton*, p. 274)
- x Martha, bp 24 Jul 1768: m (1) Berwick 6 Sep 1790 Davis Varney of Somersworth NH (VR), b Somersworth NH 2 Dec 1768 son of Zaccheus & Margaret (Brock) Varney ("Master Tate's Diary," NEHGR, 73 [1919]:313): m (2) Berwick 1 Dec 1803 Robert Nason (VR), b 1781 son of Caleb & Olive (Andrews) Nason (*Daniel Goodwin*, p. 34; *Old Kittery*, p. 634)
- xi Lemuel, bp 12 Sep 1771: d unm (*Daniel Goodwin*, p. 34)
- xii Jacob, bp 9 Jan 1773: d Lebanon 3 Sep 1841 (VR): m Berwick 3 Oct 1793 Joanna Stanton of Berwick (VR), b 1773 (Lebanon VR) [*Daniel Goodwin*, p. 75, says b 15 Apr 1772], d Lebanon 4 Apr 1856 (VR)
- xiii Charles, bp 24 Aug 1777: d 11 Jan 1817 (*Daniel Goodwin*, p. 75): m Berwick 11 Oct 1801 Experience Pray (VR, p. 200), b 17 Oct 1778 (*Daniel Goodwin*, p. 75), d Jersey Isle Dec 1876 (ibid.)

Child by 2nd wife Eunice (Foy) Hammond
- xiv Simeon, bp Berwick 2nd Church 26 May 1787 (NEHGR, 74 [1920]:222): d in infancy (*Daniel Goodwin*, p. 34)

Mary B. Young, P.O. Box 2460, South Portland, ME 04116-2460

Goodwin, Elijah   57a   1 - 2 - 1 - 0 - 0
Berwick Town, York County

ELIJAH GOODWIN Jr., bp Berwick 1st Church 10 Nov 1752 son of Elijah & Abigail (Martin) Goodwin (NEHGR, 82 [1928]:322) [see ELIJAH GOODWIN family]: d Oct 1815 (John Hayes Goodwin, *Daniel Goodwin of Ancient Kittery, Maine and His Descendants* [1985], hereafter *Daniel Goodwin*, pp. 73): m Berwick 28 Apr 1774 LUCY AVERY (John E. Frost & Joseph C. Anderson II, *Vital Records of Berwick, South Berwick and North Berwick, Maine to the Year 1892* [1993], hereafter VR, p. 198), perhaps the Lucy Avery b York 12 Jun 1748 dau of David & Elizabeth (Allen) Avery (Lester M. Bragdon & John E. Frost, *Vital Records of York, Maine* [1992], pp. 68, 128), d Palmyra Jan 1842 (*Daniel Goodwin*, p. 73).

Children: Berwick VR, p. 232
- i Jonathan, b 13 Jan 1775: d Palmyra 18 Jan 1854 (*Daniel Goodwin*, p. 155; g.s., Goodwin Family cem): m Berwick 2 Nov 1795 Elizabeth Andrews (VR, p. 199), b Berwick 5 Nov 1779 (*Daniel Goodwin*, p. 155) and bp Berwick 2nd Church 26 Dec 1779 dau of Elisha & Joanna (Pray) Andrews

(NEHGR, 74 [1920]:230), d Palmyra 6 Jun 1843 (*Daniel Goodwin*, p. 155). They res Berwick many years before moving to Palmyra (ibid.)
  ii Isaac, b 25 Dec 1776: d 25 Dec 1777 (*Daniel Goodwin*, p. 73)
  iii Isaac, b 28 Nov 1778: d Biddeford 29 Dec 1863 (*Daniel Goodwin*, p. 156): m Mary Moulton (ibid.). They res for many years in Hollis (ibid.)

Mary B. Young, P.O. Box 2460, South Portland, ME 04116-2460

Grant, Joshua   57c   2 - 7 - 5 - 0 - 0
   Berwick Town, York County

JOSHUA GRANT, bp Berwick 1st Church 9 Nov 1748 son of Joshua & Hannah (____) Grant (NEHGR, 82 [1928]:316; Leola Grant Bushman, "Peter Grant Scotch Exile, Kittery and Berwick, Maine, Genealogy" [TS, MHS], Section II, p. 6): d Berwick 22 Nov 1831 ae 84y (John E. Frost & Joseph C. Anderson II, *Vital Records of Berwick, South Berwick & North Berwick, Maine to the Year 1892* [1993], hereafter VR, p. 299; Wilbur D. Spencer, *Burial Inscriptions, Berwick, York County, Maine* [1922], p. 24): m Berwick 2nd Church 25 Apr 1771 JUDITH FALL (NEHGR, 74 [1920]:250), bp Berwick 1st Church 12 May 1749 dau of John Fall (NEHGR, 82 [1928]:317), d Berwick 20 Aug 1825 ae 70y (VR, p. 297; Spencer, op. cit., p. 25). [John Fall, Judith's father, married (1) Lydia Jones and (2) Mary Jones, although it is not known which wife was Judith's mother.] Joshua advanced money in the years 1778 and 1779 to support soldiers going into the service (Wilbur D. Spencer, "Statistics of Berwick, Maine" [TS, MSA, 1943], pp. 36, 43).

Children, all bp Berwick 2nd Church, exact order of birth speculative: NEHGR, 74 [1920]:221, 222, 246
  i   John, bp 23 Oct 1782: m Berwick 13 Apr 1794 Elizabeth Clark (NEHGR, 74 [1920]:260) [he was termed John Grant "3rd" on m int 15 Mar 1794 (Berwick VR, p. 35)]
  ii Mary/Polly, bp 23 Oct 1782: d Berwick 3 Feb 1816 (VR, p. 293): m Berwick 28 Mar 1793 Elijah Hayes (NEHGR, 74 [1920]:259), b Berwick 1 or 5 Jul 1767 son of Elijah & Elizabeth (Chadbourne) Hayes (Katharine F. Richmond, *John Hayes of Dover, New Hampshire* [1936], p. 81) [see Hon. ELIJAH HAYES family, *Maine Families*, 3:127], d Berwick 1 Jun 1832 ae 63y (*Burial Inscriptions*, op. cit., p. 26). He m (2) 3 Nov 1816 Mary Twombly (*John Hayes*, p. 141)
  iii Rachel, b c May 1774 and bp 23 Oct 1782: d Berwick 21 Nov 1827 ae 53½y (VR, p. 298; John E. Frost, "The North Berwick (Maine) Record Book" [TS, MHS, 1964], p. 13): m Berwick 11 Jun 1792 Ebenezer Nowell (NEHGR, 74 [1920]:259), b Berwick 1768 son of Ebenezer & Patience (Hamilton) Nowell (Albert N. Norton, *Some Descendants of Capt. Peter*

Nowell of York, Maine [1947], p. 22), d No. Berwick 14 May 1860 ae 92y 5m 20d ("North Berwick Record Book," op. cit., p. 13)

iv Joshua Jr., bp 23 Oct 1782: m Berwick 26 Nov 1801 Sarah/Sally Clements (NEHGR, 74 [1920]:262) dau of Samuel & Sarah (Austin) Clements (Mary Lovering Holman, *Ancestors and Descendants of Robert Clements* [n.d.], 1:219) [see SAMUEL CLEMENTS family]

v Jonathan, b c May 1777 and bp 23 Oct 1782: d Acton 12 Feb 1840 ae 62y 10m 16d (John E. Frost, "The Acton (Maine) Record Book" [TS, MHS, 1964], p. 36): m Berwick 27 Nov 1800 Mary/Polly Clark (NEHGR, 74 [1920]:262), b c Jan 1776, d Acton 28 Feb 1852 ae 76y 1m 20d ("Acton Record Book," op. cit., p. 36)

vi Peter, bp 23 Oct 1782: m Berwick 8 Sep 1802 Margaret/Peggy Gerrish (NEHGR, 74 [1920]:262), poss she b 25 Mar 1785 dau of Charles & Phebe (Blethen) Gerrish (John J. Gerrish, *Genealogical Record of the Compiler's Branch of the Gerrish Family* [1880], p. 9)

vii David, bp 23 Oct 1782

viii Hannah, b Berwick 10 Jun 1783 (VR, p. 270) and bp 21 Jul 1783: living Berwick 1850 (USC): m Berwick 16 May 1805 James Butler (VR, p. 270), b 17 Jun 1783 son of Moses & Keziah (Mason) Butler (ibid.; George H. Butler, *Thomas Butler and His Descendants* [1886], p. 108), d Berwick 8 Jan 1856 (VR Lebanon)

ix Joseph, b Berwick 17 Apr 1785 (Lebanon VR) and bp 18 Sep 1786: d Lebanon 28 Jan 1866 ae 80y 9m 11d (VR): m Betsey Estes (Lebanon VR)

x Elijah, b Berwick c Jun 1787 and bp 14 Jun 1791: d Acton 22 Aug 1878 ae 91y 2m 15d ("Acton Record Book," op. cit., p. 36): m Shapleigh 8 Sep 1814 Mary Lord (VR), b c May 1795, d Acton 23 Mar 1877 ae 81y 10m 11d ("Acton Record Book," op. cit., p. 36)

xi Humphrey, b Berwick 28 Mar 1790 (VR, p. 274) and bp 14 Jun 1791: d Berwick 23 Aug 1833 ae 44y 5m (ibid.; *Burial Inscriptions*, op. cit., p. 24): m Berwick 20 Aug 1812 Eunice Lord (VR, p. 274), b 10 Dec 1793 [sic] and bp Berwick 2nd Church 11 Aug 1793 dau of Humphrey & Olive (Hill) Lord (VR, p. 274; NEHGR, 74 [1920]:247), d Berwick 17 Jun 1877 ae 84y 6m (VR, p. 313; *Burial Inscriptions*, op. cit., p. 24)

Dana A. Batchelder, 258 South Sea Avenue, West Yarmouth, MA 02673

Gray, Andrew   59c   1 - 1 - 1 - 0 - 0
Coxhall Town [now Lyman], York County

ANDREW GRAY, b c1770 (John E. Frost, "York County, Maine Mortality Schedules" [TS, MHS, 1987], p. 20): d Waterboro 11 Feb 1850 ae 80y (John E. Frost, "Waterboro (Maine) Record Book" [TS, MHS, 1965], p. 83): m Lyman 6 Jun 1790 ELIZABETH/BETTY/BETSEY SANDS ("Early Vital Records of

Lyman, Maine," NEHGR, 95 [1941]:191), b c Aug 1770 dau of James & Mary (Low) Sands (York Co Probate 28:233-34) [see JAMES SANDS family], d Waterboro 16 Oct 1849 ae 79y 2m ("Mortality Schedules," op. cit.; "Waterboro Record Book," op. cit.). Andrew moved from Lyman to Waterboro in 1804 (York Co deeds, 72:253).

[Andrew was perhaps son of Nehemiah & Olive (Goodwin) Gray, the founders of the Waterboro Gray family; but this proposed parentage for Andrew has not been proven.]

Children: first 9 VR Lyman (NEHGR, 95 [1945]:196-97), remaining 3 prob b Waterboro
- i Mary/Polly, b 20 Dec 1790
- ii Samuel, b 2 Aug 1792: d Boston MA 28 Apr 1859 (VR): m int Saco 27 May 1815 Sarah (King) Richards (VR), b Boston MA 13 Nov 1797 dau of Edwin & Sarah (_____) King (VR), d Boston MA 1 Mar 1883 (VR)
- iii Olive, b 23 May 1794: d 13 Nov 1831 (Amos B. Carpenter, *A Genealogical History of the Rehoboth Branch of the Carpenter Family in America* [1898], p. 811): m int Waterboro Sep 1819 James Carpenter (VR), b prob Waterboro son of Thomas & Sally (Wentworth) Carpenter (John Wentworth, *The Wentworth Genealogy* [1878], 1:471; Carpenter, op. cit., p. 811), d 1827 (ibid.)
- iv Rachel, b 12 Aug 1795: d Limerick 18 Jul 1864 ae 68y 11m 6d (Robert L. Taylor, *Early Families of Limerick, Maine* [1984], p. 128): m int Limerick 26 Aug 1820 John Stover (ibid.), b 1793 son of David & Sarah (Boody) Stover (ibid.), d Limerick 8 Sep 1872 ae 78y 10m (ibid.)
- v Elizabeth/Betty, b 14 Apr 1797: living Newfield 1860 (USC): m int Limerick 10 Feb 1827 Joseph Sanborn (Taylor, op. cit.), b 15 Sep 1791 son of Benjamin & Polly (Mason) Sanborn (ibid.), living Newfield 1860 ae 68y (USC)
- vi Ebenezer, b 14 Apr 1799
- vii Sarah/Sally, b 8 Oct 1800: d Limerick 13 Aug 1832 ae 31y (Taylor, op. cit., p. 129): m int Limerick 16 Oct 1831 Henry Stover (ibid.), b 8 Aug 1796 bro of John above (ibid.), d Limerick 20 Oct 1885 ae 89y 2m 11d (ibid.). He m (2) 27 Sep 1852 Mary (Warren) Coffin of Limerick (ibid.)
- viii Martha, b 8 Aug 1802
- ix Lydia, b 3 May 1804: d Waterboro 22 Jul 1839 ae 35y (David C. Young and Robert L. Taylor, *Death Notices from Freewill Baptist Publications 1811-1851* [1985], p. 148, citing obit in *Morning Star*, issue of 21 Aug 1839)
- x poss Ruth S., b c Feb 1806: d 17 Jun 1879 ae 73y 4m and bur in same plot as her putative parents and bro David ("Waterboro Record Book," op. cit., p. 83)

xi   prob John, b c Nov 1807: d Limerick 6 Aug 1866 ae 58y 10m (Taylor, op. cit., p. 93): of Waterboro when he m int Limerick 26 Aug 1832 Hannah McKusick (ibid.), b Jan 1811 dau of William & Mary/Polly (Keen) McKusick (ibid.), d 2 Feb 1861 ae 50y 4d (ibid.)

xii prob Susan, b c1811 ("Mortality Schedules," op. cit.): d Waterboro 30 May 1850 (Carpenter, op. cit., p. 812): m Waterboro 26 Dec 1836 Simon Carpenter (VR), b 2 Apr 1811 son of Nathaniel & Phebe (Shute) (Davis) Carpenter (Carpenter, op. cit., p. 812), d Waterboro 15 Dec 1899 (g.s.). He m (2) Limerick 6 Feb 1851 Dorcas Chadbourne (Carpenter, op. cit., p. 812; Robert Taylor, *Early Families of Limerick, Maine* [1984], p. 35)

xiii David, b c Jul 1814 (York Co deeds, 152:216; g.s.): d Waterboro 7 Mar 1899 ae 84y 8m 5d ("Waterboro Record Book," op. cit., p. 83): m int Waterboro 28 Nov 1835 Lydia B. McKusick (VR), b Limerick c Mar 1817 sis of Hannah above (Taylor, op cit., p. 93), d Waterboro 19 Mar 1883 (Charles E. McKusick, *The Descendants of John McKusick and Mary Barker, 1739–1993* [1993], p. 80)

Dana A. Batchelder, 258 South Sea Avenue, West Yarmouth, MA 02673

Gray, James   56b   1 - 1 - 2 - 0 - 0
   Berwick Town, York County

JAMES GRAY, b Berwick c1723–24 (about 1727 James was described as ae 4y when costs for his and his brothers' care were paid from his father's est, York Co Probate #7678, 4:99) and bp with 5 siblings at the Berwick 1st Church 17 Sep 1727 son of James & Martha (Goodwin) Gray (NEHGR, 82 [1928]:89): d Berwick prob shortly bef 27 Feb 1813 when his obituary notice was published in the Kennebunk *Weekly Visitor* (David C. & Elizabeth K. Young, *Vital Records From Maine Newspapers, 1785–1820* [1993], p. 244): m (1) Berwick Jan 1746/7 MARY HAMILTON (John E. Frost & Joseph C. Anderson II, *Vital Records of Berwick, South Berwick and North Berwick, Maine to the Year 1892* [1993], hereafter VR, p. 192), bp Berwick 1st Church 27 Aug 1724 dau of Gabriel & Judith (Lord) (Meads) Hamilton (NEHGR, 82:85; wills of Gabriel and Judith, York Co Probate #8205, #8221; see also pre-nuptial agreement between Gabriel and Judith, York Co Probate, 4:55)), d by 1767 when James remarried: m (2) Berwick 17 Mar 1767 ELIZABETH (MARR) WORCESTER/WORSTER (VR, p. 113) wid of Simeon Worcester (York Co deeds 40:190). She d 29 Oct 1790 (Everett S. Stackpole, *Old Kittery and Her Families* [1903], p. 807). James m (3) Berwick 13 Jun 1791 HANNAH (AUSTIN) MURREY (VR, p. 134) dau of Joseph Austin and wid of John Murrey (York Co deeds 69:20; will of Joseph Austin, York Co Probate #487). On 4 Mar 1769, James and his 2nd wife Elizabeth sold one-half acre of land in Kittery originally owned by Elizabeth's former father-in-law, William Worcester (York Co deeds, 40:190). After marrying his third wife, Hannah, he and Hannah sold a dwelling house and land in York that Hannah had received from her father's will (York Co deeds, 69:20). In his will dated 23 Dec 1803 and probated Mar 1813, James named his wife Hannah, sons James and Jonathan, and daus Mary Stone, Martha Butler, Margaret Smith and Abigail Brawn (York Co Probate #7681).

Children, all b prob Berwick: will & cited sources
  i   Caleb, bp Berwick 7 Sep 1750 (NEHGR, 82:319)
  ii Mary, bp Berwick 7 Sep 1750 (NEHGR, 82:319): m cert Berwick 29 Dec 1767 William Stone (VR, p. 5) perhaps the son of Skinner and Judith (Meads) (Lord) Stone mentioned as a minor in Skinner's will dated 20 Mar 1764 (York Co Probate #18158)
  iii James, bp Berwick 7 Sep 1750 (NEHGR, 82:319): prob the James Gray who d by 19 Apr 1836 when his will, dated at Whitefield 22 Apr 1830, was probated (unrecorded will, in box labled "Wills 1784–1885," in vault, Lin Co Courthouse, Wiscasset): m Berwick 7 Aug 1770 his prob step-sister Jane Worcester (VR, p. 195) prob dau of Simeon & Elizabeth (Marr) Worcester of Berwick, d Whitefield 17 Feb 1830 (VR). In 1830, James was prob the male aged 70–80 living at Whitefield in the household of his son William (USC)
  iv Jonathan, bp Berwick 15 Apr 1753 (NEHGR, 82:322): m Berwick 7 Sep 1774 Catherine Roberts (VR, p. 116). Jonathan was a Rev War soldier, a large land owner in So. Berwick and a deacon of the church. His biography appears in *Biographical Review of York County* (1896), p. 583.
  v   Martha, bp Berwick 30 May 1755 (NEHGR, 82:325): of Biddeford when she m Biddeford 31 May 1777 Stephen Butler of Biddeford (NEHGR, 71 [1917]:225) who d c Aug 1820. Stephen's estate was adm by widow Martha 4 Sep 1820 who says "he is 30 days dead and leaves only one heir in the State" (York Co Probate 28:503)
  vi Margaret, m Berwick 3 Jan 1781 Daniel Smith (VR, p. 136)
  vii Abigail, m cert Berwick 10 Feb 1802 George Brawn (VR, p. 48)

Myron C. Smith, 2250 64th Avenue, Greeley, CO 80634

Gullison, John   37b   2 - 5 - 4 - 0 - 0
  Fairfield Town, Lincoln County

JOHN GULLIFER, b Middleboro MA 9 May 1745 son of Thomas & Keturah (Samson) Gullifer (Russell L. Warner & Robert S. Wakefield, *Mayflower Families in Progress, Myles Standish of the Mayflower* [1990], p. 50): d Fairfield 30 May

1837 (g.s., Emery Hill cem): m Duxbury MA 31 Aug 1769 BETTY/BETSEY DELANO (VR), b Middleboro MA 30 Apr 1750 dau of David & Deborah (Holmes) Delano (VR), d Fairfield 22 Feb 1842 (g.s., Emery Hill cem). On 4 Apr 1774, John purchased a journal in Boston MA in which are recorded the birth dates of himself, his wife and the names and birthdates of their children (at MHS, Coll. S-1434). According to John's journal, he worked for a Mr. Rose and was residing in Falmouth in 1774 and 1775, and later was in Lewiston, Winslow and in Fairfield by 4 Apr 1789 (ibid.).

Children: journal, op. cit.
- i John, b prob Duxbury MA 2 Sep 1770: d young
- ii Thomas, b prob Duxbury MA 16 Sep 1773: d Old Town 30 Jun 1851 ae 78y 8m (VR; BHM, 6:73): m (1) Fairfield Apr 1797 Hannah Burrill (VR), b Abington MA 31 Dec 1762 dau of Thomas & Grace (Garnett/Gardner) Burrill (VR; George B. Jacobs, "Descendants of John Burrell—1609, 1984" [TS, MSL]), d of "puerperal fever" at Fairfield 20 May 1805 (David C. & Elizabeth K. Young, *Vital Records from Maine Newspapers, 1785- 1820* [1993], p. 251, citing obit in *Kennebec Intelligencer*, issue of 5 Jun 1805): m (2) at the home of her father at Plt No. Four 18 Jan 1808 Abigail Oliver (War of 1812 pension #24327), b c Mar 1789, d Old Town 28 Aug 1885 ae 96y 5m (VR; BHM, 6:73). Thomas served in the War of 1812 participating in the battle at Hampton under command of Capt. T. Sibley's company, Lieut. Col. Grant's regiment (Brig. Genl. Gardner W. Pearson, *Records of the Massachusetts Volunteer Militia* [1913]). Thomas had a dau by his first wife and 12 children by his second wife (death rec of Rhoda Gulliver Lambert, ME VR; War of 1812 Pension #24327)
- iii David, b prob Falmouth ME 25 Jul 1776: d young
- iv Henry, b prob Winslow 3 Sep 1778
- v Betty, twin, b prob Winslow 30 Jan 1781: d Pittsfield 19 Apr 1868 (g.s., Tilton cem): m Waterville 13 Nov 1803 John Hart (Fairfield VR) who d Pittsfield 14 Feb 1857 (g.s., Tilton cem)
- vi David, twin, b prob Winslow 30 Jan 1781: d Fairfield 13 Jul 1860 (VR): m (1) Fairfield 10 Mar 1804 Betsey Page (VR) who d Fairfield 29 May 1829 (g.s., Emery Hill cem): m (2) Winslow 9 Dec 1830 Mrs. Nancy Ann (Dore) Smith (VR)
- vii Abigail, b prob Winslow 18 Aug 1783: m Fairfield 12 Mar 1804 Moses Healy of Anson (VR)
- viii John, b prob Winslow 21 Sep 1785: d Pittsfield 28 Sep 1873 (g.s., Tilton Corner cem): m int Fairfield 9 Apr 1809 Susan Tripp (VR), b New Bedford MA (Fairfield VR) c1791, d Pittsfield 2 Jun 1850 ae 59y (g.s., Tilton Corner cem)
- ix Samson, b prob Winslow 23 Feb 1788: believed to have m a woman named Charlotte

x Lemuel, b prob Fairfield 5 Oct 1790. He served with his bro Thomas in the War of 1812 (Pearson, op. cit.)

Ardell J. Parkman Lynds, 12630 Joy Bell Lane, San Martin, CA 95046

Gullifin, Thomas   50b   1 - 4 - 4 - 0 - 0
Winslow Town, with its Adjacents, Lincoln County

THOMAS GULLIFER, b Duxbury MA 17 Apr 1748 son of Thomas & Keturah (Samson) Gullifer (Russell L. Warner & Robert S. Wakefield, *Mayflower Families in Progress, Myles Standish of the Mayflower* [1990], p. 50): d prob ME betw 1820 and 1830 (USC): m Winslow 18 Jan 1776 PATIENCE TOZIER (VR), b Georgetown 20 Oct 1757 dau of John & Sarah (Pattee) Tozier (VR; NEHGR, 146 [1992]:326). Thomas, then of Vassalboro, purchased land in 1773 from the Kennebec proprietors (Book of Plymouth Grants, Lin Co Courthouse, Wiscasset, p. 261). He was taxed in Winslow in 1780 and 1781 (Winslow Taxpayers, 1780/1, General Court Assessments) and was at Fairfield in 1797. He was described as a bricklayer in 1791 when he sold land to William Kendall (Ken Co deeds 8:2).

Children: Southerd-Gullifer Papers, Vassalboro Historical Society Museum, #82.2, hereafter Southerd-Gullifer Papers
i   Thomas, b 4 Sep 1776: d young
ii John, b 6 Jul 1778: d young
iii Sarah, b 16 Sep 1779: m int Winslow 25 Jul 1799 William Nichols of Fairfield (VR), b Reading MA 31 Aug 1777 (VR). They moved to the midwest
iv Peleg, b 25 Sep 1781: d Bangor 22 Jun 1868 (War of 1812 Pension #8392): m (1) int Winslow 9 Jun 1801 Sarah Stanley (VR): m (2) Hermon Oct 1836 Nancy (Rose) Thurston wid of Nathaniel Thurston of Bangor (pension, op. cit.; Charles T. Libby, *The Libby Family in America* [1882], p. 395). She d 8 Jun 1886 (pension, op. cit.). He served in the War of 1812, from 13 Sep to 24 Sep 1814, in Capt. L. Barrets's company, Lt. Col. E. Sherwin's regiment (Brig. Gen. Gardner W. Pearson, *Records of the Massachusetts Volunteer Militia* [1913])
v   Catherine, b 24 Nov 1783
vi Thomas, b 3 Sep 1785: poss the Thomas who m int Fairfield 23 Nov 1823 Sarah Ann Otis (VR)
vii Joseph, b 4 Sep 1787: m Fairfield 23 Nov 1809 Thankful Tozier (VR). He served in the War of 1812 in 1814 in Capt. D. Bangs company of artillery, under command of Gen. Sewell (Pearson, op. cit.). He res St. Albans

viii Fannie, b 4 Dec 1789: d prob St. Albans 1834 (John Godfrey, *History of Penobscot County, Maine* [1882], p. 255): m Fairfield 25 Dec 1807 John Southeard/Southerd (VR), b Pownalboro 17 May 1786 son of Abraham & Jane (Lambert) Southeard/Southerd (Southerd-Gullifer Papers), d Branford 25 Jun 1880 (Godfrey, op. cit., p. 255). He m (2) abt 1835 Louisa Sampson of Norridgewock (ibid.). He res St. Albans in 1840 (USC)
ix Abigail, b 15 Jul 1792
x Sophie/Sophia, b 1 Sep 1794: d Winslow 26 Jan 1880 (VR): m Winslow 30 Mar 1815 Amos P. Southeard/Southard of Bloomfield (Winslow VR), b 13 Sep 1792 son of Abraham & Susanna (Paris) Southeard and half-brother of John above (Southerd-Gullifer Papers), d Winslow 5 Dec 1874 ae 88y (VR)
xi Relief, b 29 Aug 1796: m Unity Jul 1818 Ebenezer Pattee Farwell (IGI LDS; BHM, 5:36), b Unity 29 Jul 1796 son of Henry & Anna (Pattee) Farwell (VR; NEHGR, 147 [1993]:78), d 1886 (BHM, 5:36)
xii Herbert M., b 24 Apr 1798: d Winslow 6 Aug 1895 ae 98y 3m 8d (VR; g.s. Fort Hill cem): m Winslow 12 Nov 1818 Susanna/Sukey Southeard/Southerd (VR), b Eden 16 Jul 1794 sister of Amos and half-sister of John above (Southerd-Gullifer Papers), d Winslow 2 Apr 1890 ae 96y (VR; g.s., Fort Hill cem)
xiii Amos, b 2 Feb 1800: m (1) Fairfield 2 Feb 1827 Eunice Basset (VR): m (2) Fairfield 18 Jun 1842 Delitha/Elitha/Felitha Noble (VR)

Ardell J. Parkman Lynds, 12630 Joy Bell Lane, San Martin, CA 95046
Stephen J. Chapman, 24 Averill THP, Benton, ME 04901

Hall, Josiah 50a 1 - 0 - 2 - 0 - 0
Washington Town, Lincoln County

JOSIAH HALL, b Wrentham MA 16 May 1743 son of Preserved & Abigail (Whitney) Hall (VR): m Wrentham MA 2 Feb 1764 AMIABLE/AMA ALLEN (VR) who was b 14 Feb 1741 (Everett S. Stackpole, *History of Winthrop, Maine* [1925], p. 408). They removed from Wrentham to Winthrop before the incorporation of the town and settled on lot No. 11 (ibid.). He was prominent in town affairs, selectman and Town Clerk from 1776–78 (ibid., pp. 245, 408). "The Declaration of Independence was spread upon the town records in his full, round and legible hand" (ibid., p. 141). He was one of the Committee of Correspondence, Inspection and Safety in 1778 (ibid.). He was a private in Capt. Oliver Colburn's company of minutemen in Col. Arnold's regiment, enlisting 25 Jul 1775 and serving 20 days (ibid.). About 1782, Josiah moved to Washington Plt, now Mt. Vernon (ibid., p. 408).

112   MAINE FAMILIES IN 1790

Children: births first 2 VR Wrentham MA; births all *History of Winthrop*, p. 408
 i Nathan, b Wrentham MA 21 Jan 1765: d Belgrade 4 Mar 1799 (David C. & Elizabeth K. Young, *Vital Records from Maine Newspapers, 1785–1820* [1993], p. 257, citing obit in the *Kennebec Intelligencer*, issue of 11 Oct 1799): m Levina Lyon (Georgiana Hewins Lilly, "Eliab Lyon and His Descendants" [TS, MSL, 1932], p. 3), b 5 May 1765 dau of Eliab & Meriah (Smith) Lyon (ibid.). She m (2) Joseph Fifield (ibid.) who acted as the administrator of Nathan's estate (Young & Young, op. cit.). In 1790, Nathan was living at Washington next to his father (USC)
 ii Allen, b Wrentham MA 29 Jan 1767: d East Dixfield 19 Apr 1838 (g.s., East Dixfield cem): m 1 Mar 1788 Meriah Lyon (*History of Winthrop*, p. 408; Lilly, op. cit., p. 3), b 10 Mar 1770 dau of Eliab & Meriah (Smith) Lyon and sis of Levina above (ibid.), d 29 Aug 1856 ae 87y 5m (g.s., East Dixfield cem, called "Maria")
 iii Abigail, b 13 Apr 1769: d Farmington 25 Jul 1826 ae 57y (g.s., Center cem; Francis G. Butler, *History of Farmington, Maine* [repr 1983], p. 398): m 16 Apr 1789 Church Brainerd (ibid.), b Haddam Neck CT 8 Feb 1756 son of Benjamin & Mary (Chapman) Brainerd [see CHURCH BRAINERD family, *Maine Families* 1:22], d 27 Aug 1832 ae 72y (*History of Farmington*, p. 398)
 iv Mary, b 27 Aug 1771: d 2 May 1775 (*History of Winthrop*, p. 408)
 v Esther, b 4 Jan 1774

Eleanor W. Townsend, 71 Slab Meadow Rd., Morris CT 06763-1517

Hamblin, Gershom   17c   1 - 5 - 4 - 0 - 0
   Gorham and Scarborough Towns, Cumberland County

GERSHOM HAMBLIN/HAMBLEN, b Barnstable MA 16 Sep 1745 son of Gershom & Hannah (Almony/Almary) Hamblen (VR): d Limington c Jan 1807 ae 66y [sic] (David C. Young & Elizabeth K. Young, *Vital Records from Maine Newspapers, 1785–1820* [1993], p. 258, citing Saco *Freeman's Friend*, issue of 17 Jan 1807): m int Gorham 17 Dec 1774 DEBORAH JENKINS (Marquis F. King, *Records of Gorham, Maine* [2nd Ed., 1991, edited by Russell S. Bickford], hereafter Gorham VR, p. 38), b Barnstable ME 2 Feb 1752 dau of Samuel & Mary (Chipman) Jenkins (McLellan's *Gorham*, p. 591), d Limington 29 Sep 1810 ae 58y (Robert L. Taylor, *Early Families of Limington, Maine* [1991], hereafter Taylor, p. 138; Young & Young, op. cit., p. 258, citing *Eastern Argus*, issue of 4 Oct 1810). Gershom, at about 18 years of age, came with his widowed mother and siblings in 1763 from Barnstable MA to Gorham (McLellan's *Gorham*, p.

539). Gershom settled on a 60 acre farm adjoining Little River (ibid., p. 540). In April 1797, he sold his farm in Gorham to his nephew, Almery Hamblen, and moved to Limington where he purchased land on the west side of the Saco River where he and his wife died (ibid.).

Children: births first 7 in Gorham VR, p. 128; births last 2 in Taylor, pp. 139–40
- i Hannah, b 14 Nov 1775: d Portland 8 Oct 1836 ae 61y (Taylor, p. 138): m 20 Apr 1802 Joab Black both of Limington (ibid.), b 4 Nov 1780 son of Josiah & Marcy (Cookson) Black (ibid., p. 21), d Limington 29 Oct 1821 (ibid.)
- ii Elizabeth, b 12 Mar 1778: d Lincoln 21 Mar 1851 ae 74y 11d (Taylor, p. 138): m int Limington 4 Jan 1801 Daniel Mann of Limington as his 2nd wife (ibid.; McLellan's *Gorham*, p. 646–47), b Wrentham MA 25 Feb 1770 (ibid.), d 10 Dec 1814 in the War of 1812 (Taylor, p. 195). He had m (1) Gorham 22 Aug 1792 Hannah Phinney (VR, p. 87)
- iii Ebenezer, b 9 Jul 1780: d in Canada during the War of 1812 (Taylor, p. 138)
- iv Samuel, twin, b 4 May 1783: m Hannah Whitmore (McLellan's *Gorham*, p. 541), b 6 Dec 1784 dau of William & Ammi-Ruhamah (Knight) Whitmore (Taylor, p. 370)
- v Jacob, twin, b 4 May 1783: d Limington 5 Feb 1866 ae 82y 9m (Taylor, p. 138): m (1) Limington 24 Nov 1808 Jane Small (ibid.), b 28 Feb 1789 dau of Joshua & Mary (Clark) Small (ibid., p. 301), d Limington 24 Mar 1836 (ibid., p. 138): m (2) 18 Mar 1838 Susan (McDonald) Usher of Buxton (ibid.), b c1788, d Cornish 8 Sep 1852 ae 64y (ibid.). She was the wid of Robert Usher (ibid.)
- vi Daniel, b 7 Dec 1785: d Limington 27 Aug 1841 (Taylor, p. 139): m Limington 8 Nov 1812 Mary Clark of Limington (ibid.), b Kittery 1786 dau of Ebenezer & Anna (Hanscom) Clark (ibid., pp. 71–72), d Lovell 27 Mar 1845 ae 59y (ibid., p. 139)
- vii Mary, b 18 Jun 1788: d Buxton 12 Feb 1836 ae 47y 8m (Taylor, p. 139): unm (ibid.)
- viii Ichabod, b 17 Apr 1791: d Lovell 5 Jun 1871 (Taylor, p. 139): m 11 Oct 1815 Lydia Webb Fickett of Gorham (ibid.), b c May 1794, d Lovell 21 Nov 1879 ae 85y 6m (ibid.). They moved to Lovell in 1839 (ibid.)
- ix Statira, b 17 Apr 1795: d Limington 2 Nov 1865 ae 70y 6m 12d (Taylor, p. 140): m 20 May 1821 Rev. Andrew Hobson of Buxton (ibid.), b 10 Sep 1795 (ibid.), d East Cambridge MA 1 May 1877 ae 81y (ibid.)

Elizabeth (Bette) Barker Taverner, 51 Deaconess Road, Concord, MA 01742-4136

Hamilton, Abial   57b   1 - 0 - 0 - 0 - 0
Berwick Town, York County

ABIAL HAMILTON, bp Berwick 1st Church 11 Nov 1722 son of Abial & Abigail (Hodsden) Hamilton (NEHGR, 82 [1928]:84): m Berwick 27 Sep 1749 JOANNA BOLTHOOD/BOLTWOOD (NEHGR, 82 [1928]:510), prob an unrecorded dau of Ebenezer & Mary (Turner) Bolthood/Boltwood of Berwick, the only family of that surname found in Berwick at the time in which Joanna might have been born [Abial's sister, Abigail, married John Turner Bolthood/Boltwood, whose baptism as a son of Ebenezer and Mary was recorded (NEHGR, 82 [1928]:86, 511)]. Abial prob lived at Berwick all of his life. On 17 Jan 1785, Bial [Abial] Hamilton, husbandman, deeded to his nephew, Jonathan Hamilton 3rd, husbandman, his homelot in Berwick including his dwelling house, barn, and all of his personal estate (York Co deeds 75:147). Bial's brother, Solomon, the father of Jonathan 3rd, was a witness to the deed. Ordinarily a deed of this sort would have been made by a father to his son in lieu of a will, but in the absence of living heirs, it would not have been unreasonable for Abial to give his property to a nephew. The proposition that he had no surviving heirs is supported by the 1790 census in which he is found living alone next door to his nephew, Jonathan Hamilton 3rd. He was not a head of household in the 1800 census. There is no will nor administration of his estate in the York County records.

Children: bp Berwick 1st Church, NEHGR 82 [1928]:321, 323
i   David, bp 8 Apr 1752: not seen again in Berwick records
ii Bial, bp 16 Jul 1754: not seen again in Berwick records

Joseph C. Anderson II, 5337 Del Roy Drive, Dallas TX 75229

Hamilton, Jonas   57a   2 - 3 - 4 - 0 - 0
Berwick Town, York County

JONAS HAMILTON, bp Berwick 1st Church 5 Apr 1731 son of Abial & Abigail (Hodsden) Hamilton (NEHGR, 82 [1928]:90): d aft 13 Dec 1801 when he sold property to his son Reuben and bef 3 Mar 1808 when his widow deeded (York Co deeds 68:71, 77:265–66): m Berwick 29 Dec 1757 CHARITY KEAY (John E. Frost & Joseph C. Anderson II, *Vital Records of Berwick, South Berwick and North Berwick, Maine to the Year 1892* [1993], hereafter VR, p. 197), bp Berwick 23 Jun 1737 dau of John & Charity (Hooper) Keay (ibid., 82:206; Everett S. Stackpole *Old Kittery and Her Families* [1903], p. 569). Jonas, termed a husbandman, res Berwick his whole life. He was on the "Roll of the First Troop of Horse," also called the "Blue Troop of Horse," at Berwick in 1757 (John L. M.

Willis, *Old Eliot*, 1:II:28). Jonas was a Rev War soldier serving in Capt. Sullivan's Company & Col. Scammon's 30th Regt in 1775 and in Capt. Waterhouse's Company & Col. Gerrish's Regt of guards in 1778 (MS&S, 7:152). He lived "between Joseph Chicks & John Brewsters Land on the main Road" (York Co deeds, 68:71).

Children, birth order partly speculative: "The Children of Jonas Hamilton...," *Maine Genealogist*, 13:3:59–63
  i Sally, alive on 21 May 1830 and res Strafford Co, NH when she quitclaimed property to her nephew, Abial Emery Hamilton (York Co deeds 136:217): m _____ Brewster (ibid.)
 ii Abigail, b c1763: d Lebanon 25 Feb 1853 ae 89y (VR): m Berwick 2 Oct 1783 David Woodsum (VR, p. 127), bp Berwick 16 May 1762 son of John & Mary (Brackett) Woodsum (ibid., 74:216), d Lebanon 3 Jan 1827 (Rev War pension #W26088) [see DAVID WOODSUM family, *Maine Families*, 2:309–10]
iii Susanna, b bef 1765 (1810 USC Berwick, household of Simeon Spencer, p. 942): d Berwick 5 May 1827 (VR, p. 298; Wilbur D. Spencer, *The Maine Spencers* [1898], pp. 184–85, 189): m Berwick 5 Feb 1804 Simeon Spencer as his 2nd wife (NEHGR, 74 [1920]:262), bp Berwick 1st Church 21 Jun 1752 son of Humphrey Spencer (NEHGR, 82 [1928]:320), d Berwick 21 Jan 1840 (g.s. Evergreen cem Berwick; Spencer, op. cit.). He had m (1) Berwick 25 Nov 1779 Lydia Goodwin (VR, p. 122) [see ELIJAH GOODWIN family]. In the York Co Sessions court held Apr 1791, Susanna Hamilton of Berwick, single, deposed that on 10 Jul 1789 John Brewster of Berwick had "carnal knowledge of her body at the dwelling house of Jonas Hamilton" and begat her with a female child which was delivered on 9 Apr 1790. He was found not guilty. One John Brewster m Berwick 6 Mar 1792 Olive Prime (VR, p. 134)
 iv James, b c1768 (1850 USC): d aft 1850 when enumerated at Conway NH (USC): m Berwick 9 Jun 1791 Mehitable Brackett (VR, p. 134), b 2 Sep 1766 dau of Samuel & Mehitable (Ricker) Brackett (Herbert I. Brackett, *Brackett Genealogy* [1907], pp. 290–92), d Conway NH 26 Jan 1828 (ibid.). They res Francisborough Plt [Cornish] and Conway NH
  v Silas, b c1775: d without heirs 2 Jun 1821 ae 46y (g.s. Stroudwater cem Portland). He was described as a merchant and trader and resident of Falmouth in 1812 and 1813 when he bought property from his brother Abial Hamilton (York Co deeds 89:161–62, 183)
 vi Abial, b 1779 (DAR Lineage #123717): d 1862 (ibid.): m (1) int York 20 Jan 1803 Adah Emery (Lester M. Bragdon & John E. Frost, *Vital Records of York, Maine* [1992], p. 187), b York 4 Dec 1784 dau John & Mary (Bragdon) Emery (ibid., p. 84): m (2) int Berwick 28 Dec 1839 Mary Jane Grandin of Somersworth NH (VR, p. 95)

vii Reuben, b c1783: d 21 Oct 1841 ae 58y (g.s. Pine Hill cem, Somersworth NH): listed as a resident of Lebanon when he m Berwick 29 Nov 1810 Joanna Keay (VR, p. 202), b Berwick 17 Aug 1792 dau of John & Betsy (Wentworth) Keay (VR, p. 253; estate of John Keay, York Co Probate #10737, 50:536) [see JOHN KEAY family, *Maine Families*, 3:159–60], d 17 Nov 1884 ae 89y (g.s. Pine Hill cem, Somersworth NH)

Joseph C. Anderson II, 5337 Del Roy Drive, Dallas, TX 75229

Hamilton, Jon[a]   55c   3 - 5 - 6 - 1 - 0
Berwick Town, York County

Col. **JONATHAN HAMILTON**, bp Berwick 1st Church 25 May 1746 son of Joseph & Elizabeth (____) (Dana) Hamilton (NEHGR, 82 [1928]:217) [see JOSEPH HAMILTON family]: d Suffolk Co MA 26 Sep 1802 ae 57y (York Co Probate 19:227; g.s. Old Fields cem, So. Berwick): m (1) Berwick 8 Feb 1771 MARY MANNING (John E. Frost & Joseph C. Anderson II, *Vital Records of Berwick, South Berwick and North Berwick, Maine to the Year 1892* [1993], hereafter VR, p. 118), bp Berwick 12 Nov 1749 dau of Patrick & Mary (Dyer) Manning (NEHGR, 82 [1928]:319, 55 [1901]:312; York Co Probate #12534, 18:235–36), d 23 Nov 1800 ae 51y (g.s. Old Fields cem, So. Berwick): m (2) 12 Apr 1801 CHARLOTTE (BOURNE) SWETT of Exeter NH (Elisabeth D. & Joseph M. Odiorne, "The Hamiltons of Berwick, Maine" [TS, Androscoggin Historical Society, Auburn], family 4-40), b Marblehead MA 14 Apr 1760 wid of Dr. John Barnard Swett of Newburyport MA and dau of William & Sarah (____) Bourne (ibid.), d Boston MA 1 Oct 1840 ae 80y (Scott Lee Chipman, *New England Vital Records from the* Exeter News-Letter, *1831–1840* [1993], p. 207). She m (3) Gov. John Taylor Gilman of NH (NEHGR, 44 [1890]:362). Jonathan was a self-made merchant, shipowner and West India trader. He became a rich man at a young age and attained the honorary title of Colonel. His large house at South Berwick, built in 1787 at Pipe Stave Landing overlooking the Piscataqua river, is a York Co landmark and a photo of it appears in Everett S. Stackpole's *Old Kittery and Her Families* (1903) on p. 127.

Children prob by 1st wife Mary Manning, order of birth conjectural: bp 1st Church Berwick, NEHGR, 82 [1928]:505–6
 i Joseph, b c1773, bp 12 Jul 1788: d 15 Jul 1788 ae 15y (g.s. Old Fields cem, So. Berwick)
 ii Betsey, bp Berwick 3 Aug 1788, but b yrs earlier: m Berwick 26 Feb 1792 Peter Clark (VR, p. 133), b 25 Nov 1765 son of Rev. Jonas & Lucy (Bowes) Clark of Lexington MA (John Clark, *Records of the Descendants*

of Hugh Clark of Watertown, Massachusetts, 1640–1866 [1866], p. 86). Betsey soon d and Peter m (2) Ann Harris by whom he had 2 children (ibid.). He was imprisoned at Guadaloupe for a time and d in Dec 1798 on the passage home (ibid.)

iii Martha/Patty, bp 3 Aug 1788: not named in her father's probate

iv John, bp 3 Aug 1788, the "eldest [living] son" according to his father's probate (YCGSJ, 1 [1986]:27): d Portsmouth NH ae 28y shortly bef 25 Nov 1805 when his obit was published (Anna C. Kingsbury, "Storer Notes" [TS, MHS], name of paper not given, only the initials "B.C."): he left a widow by name of "M. Hamilton" (York Co Probate 22:213)

v Olive, bp 3 Aug 1788 but b prob several years earlier: m Berwick 12 Sep 1802 Joshua Haven of Portsmouth NH (VR, p. 142), bp 4 Apr 1779 son of Rev. Samuel Haven and his 2nd wife the wid of Capt. Samuel Marshall (William Haven, *Sergeant Richard Haven, 1620–1703* [1927], p. 19). He m (2) Mary Cunningham and lived at Portsmouth NH (ibid.). Joshua acquired Jonathan Hamilton's mansion house at Pipe Stave Landing which he sold in 1815 (York Co deeds 86:108, 91:219–20).

vi Oliver, bp 3 Aug 1788: d by 1815 when his bro-in-law Joshua Haven sold his father's "mansion house" (York Co deeds 86:108, 91:219–20). He was termed a "minor upwards of 14 years" on 15 Nov 1802 when John Lord of Berwick was appt his guardian (York Co Probate 19:154). When his father's final estate papers were processed, he was termed the youngest [living] son (YCGSJ, 1 [1986]:27)

vii George, b c1785, bp 3 Aug 1788: d 24 Nov 1812 ae 27y (YCGSJ, 1 [1986]: 27; VR, p. 291): termed a "minor upwards of 14 years" on 15 Nov 1802 when Joshua Haven, his sister Olive's husband, was appt his guardian (York Co Probate 19:154)

viii Joseph, bp 19 Jul 1789: a Joseph Hamilton ae 22y [sic] reportedly d 10 Apr 1813 (YCGSJ, 1 [1986]:27): termed a "minor under the age of 14 years" on 15 Nov 1802 when Oliver Peabody of Exeter NH was appt his guardian (York Co Probate 19:154)

ix reportedly Mary for whom no birth nor baptismal record has been located who reportedly m John Parker Rowe (YCGSJ, 1 [1986]:27))

Joseph C. Anderson II, 5337 Del Roy Drive, Dallas TX 75229

Hamilton, Joseph   56c   2 - 0 - 3 - 0 - 0
Berwick Town, York County

JOSEPH HAMILTON, b c1709 son of Abel & Deborah (_____) Hamilton of Berwick (obit, see below; York Co deeds 37:133 proves Joseph's parentage): d Berwick shortly bef 8 Mar 1798 ae 88y when his obit was published (Anna C.

Kingsbury, "Storer Notes" [TS, MHS], name of newspaper not given, only its initials "I.C"): m bef 19 May 1737 ELIZABETH (____) DANA, wid of Jonathan Dana of Berwick (York Co Probate #4289). Elizabeth's birth date and parentage is unknown but she was alive when Joseph made his will on 15 May 1792 which was in probate 20 May 1799 (York Co Probate 18:75). Joseph spent his entire life at Berwick where he farmed on land inherited from his father (York Co deeds 37:133). A portion of this, described as "the whole of the land I own on the Western Side of the highway leading Over pine hill so called," he deeded in 1774 to his son, Col. Jonathan Hamilton "Jr." (York Co deeds 48:269).

Children: bp 1st Church Berwick, NEHGR, 82 [1928]:207, 209, 213, 216, 217, 315
- i Abigail, bp 25 Jun 1738: she was termed "Abigail Clark deceased" in her father's will in 1792. She was poss the Abigail wife of James Clark whose 2 children, unnamed, were bp at the Berwick 2nd Church in 1762 (NEHGR 74, [1920]:217, 226)
- ii Sarah, bp 8 Jun 1740: alive in 1792 when named in her father's will: m Berwick 9 Mar 1757 Stephen Perkins (John E. Frost & Joseph C. Anderson II, *Vital Records of Berwick, South Berwick and North Berwick, Maine to the Year 1892* [1993], hereafter VR, p. 196)
- iii Elizabeth, bp 29 Aug 1742: termed "Elizabeth Tibbetts deceased" in her father's will in 1792. She was poss the Elizabeth wife of Moses Tibbetts whose 5 children were bp at the Berwick 2nd Church (NEHGR, 74 [1920]: 220–21, 230)
- iv Deborah, bp 13 Jul 1744: not named in her father's 1792 will and prob d by 1783 when her husband had remarried (John R. Eastman, *History of the Town of Andover New Hampshire 1751-1906* [1910] 2:283, 402-3): m Berwick 8 Oct 1771 James Marston Randall (VR, p. 118), bp Rye NH 17 Mar 1746 son of William & Hannah (Marston) Randall (*History of Andover, New Hampshire*, op. cit.), d Andover NH 11 Apr 1800 ae 53y (ibid.). He m (2) bef 1783 Margaret Fellows by whom his 1st dau was named Deborah Hamilton Randall (ibid.)
- v Col. Jonathan, bp 25 May 1746: d Suffolk Co MA 26 Sep 1802 ae 57y (York Co Probate 19:227; g.s. Old Fields cem, So. Berwick): m (1) Berwick 8 Feb 1771 Mary Manning (VR, p. 118): m (2) 12 Apr 1801 Charlotte (Bourne) Swett of Exeter NH (Elisabeth D. & Joseph M. Odiorne, "The Hamiltons of Berwick, Maine" [TS, Androscoggin Hist. Soc., Auburn], family 4-40), [see Col. JONATHAN HAMILTON family]
- vi Joseph, bp 16 Jul 1748: not named in his father's will in 1792
- vii Mary, no baptism found but named as a living dau in her father's will in 1792: m ____ Rollins (father's will)

Joseph C. Anderson II, 5337 Del Roy Drive, Dallas, TX 75229

Hamilton, Millet   55c   1 - 1 - 2 - 0 - 0
Berwick Town, York County

MILLET HAMILTON, b 1755–1765 (1800 and 1810 USC) son of Jonathan & Hannah (Millet) Hamilton [see JONATHAN HAMILTON family, *Maine Families*, 3:118]: d So. Berwick 20 Sep 1815 (John E. Frost & Joseph C. Anderson II, *Vital Records of Berwick, South Berwick and North Berwick, Maine to the Year 1892* [1993], hereafter VR, p. 539): m (1) int Berwick 25 Jun 1788 BETSEY BODWELL of Somersworth NH (VR, p. 27): m (2) int Berwick 14 Sep 1806 MOLLY ROBERTS of Berwick (VR, p. 55), b Somersworth NH 13 Aug 1769 (Frederick R. Boyle, *Early Families of Sanford-Springvale, Maine* [1988], p. 125, citing family bible) dau of Aaron & Mary (Hanson) Roberts of Somersworth NH ("The Diary of Master Joseph Tate of Somersworth, N.H.," NEHGR, 74 [1920]:49 [which gives Mary's birth date as 13 ___ 1769], d 11 Aug 1840 ae 71y (ibid.). She m (2) Berwick 16 Jun 1816 Stephen Gowen of Sanford (VR, p. 152).

Children, prob by 1st wife Betsey Bodwell
  i Rufus, b Berwick 26 Dec 1789 (VR): d 20 May 1865 (g.s., Portland St. cem, So. Berwick): m (1) Berwick 8 Dec 1814 Margery Gerrish (VR), b 1 Apr 1792, d 2 Jan 1842 (g.s., Portland St. cem, So. Berwick): m (2) int So. Berwick 19 Oct 1850 Mrs. Hannah (___) Wilkinson of So. Berwick (VR, p. 366). [She was perhaps the Hannah Varney of So. Berwick who m John Wilkinson of Sanford at So. Berwick 4 Jul 1824 (VR, p. 438). John, a poss son of Joseph & Dorcas (Nason) Wilkinson of Sanford, had reportedly d by 1849 (Boyle, op. cit., pp. 309–10; m int of Joseph Wilkinson and Dorcas Nason in Berwick VR, p. 20)]
  ii Mary Ann, d 27 Aug 1844 (g.s., Free Baptist cem, So. Berwick): m So. Berwick 22 Jan 1826 her 1st cousin Edmund Haggens Jr (NEHGR, 83 [1929]:14), b Berwick 14 Apr 1796 son of Edmund and Susannah/Sukey (Hamilton) Haggens [see EDMUND HAGGENS family, *Maine Families*, 3:110, and JONATHAN HAMILTON family, *Maine Families*, 3:118]

Joseph C. Anderson II, 5337 Del Roy Drive, Dallas TX 75229

Hunscomb, Jnº   59a   1 - 3 - 3 - 0 - 0
Buxton Town, York County

JOHN HANSCOM, b Saco May 1751 (Rev War pension #S37075) son of Benaiah & Keziah (Rogers) Hanscom (VR Buxton): d Buxton after 1830 (USC), possibly in 1837 (see below): m Saco 7 Apr 1779 ANNA CARLE (VR), b c1761 (pension, op. cit.) dau of Benjamin & Sarah (Berry) Carle (VR Buxton; Sybil Noyes notes of Saco-Biddeford families at MGS), d Buxton 11 Sep 1835 (VR). As a private from Pepperellborough (Saco), John enlisted in the Continental Army in Aug 1775 and served until Jan 1778. He fought in the battles of Trenton, Morristown and Boundbrook, and later marched to the Mohawk (pension, op. cit.). He settled in Buxton in 1779 and lived on a farm adjacent to that of his elder brother William. He applied for a military pension 13 Apr 1818. In 1820, he stated he had no real estate and that his personal estate consisted of a cow, a yearling, an old horse, a calf, 5 sheep, a pig, and a life interest in a small house ("Maine Estate Schedules From Revolutionary War Pensions," NEHGR, 142 [1988]:206). He also stated he had no income and was in debt for $400 (ibid.). He was not able to work due to rheumatism and palsy and his wife, Anna, was described as a feeble woman (ibid.). Living with them were two of their daughters, Priscilla and Anna Sands, and daughter Anna's 3 children (ibid.).

[Erroneous notes in John's pension file indicate that he died in Jan 1827. It was in fact his 1st cousin of the same name, John Hanscom of Litchfield (1764–1827), who died in 1827. Somehow this date made its way into John of Buxton's file. The 1830 census clearly indicates that John Hanscom Sr. was still alive. Records passed down in the Hanscom family indicate that both he and his son, John Jr., died in 1837.]

Children: births VR Buxton
- i Benaiah, b 7 Jul 1779: d Buxton 19 Oct 1859 (VR): m Buxton 29 Mar 1804 Abigail Sands (Cyrus Woodman, *Records of the Church of Christ in Buxton, Maine During the Pastorate of Rev. Paul Coffin*, [1989], p. 38), b Buxton 24 Oct 1778 dau of James & Lydia (Fall) Sands (VR), d Buxton 27 Sep 1860 (VR) [see JAMES SANDS family, *Maine Families*, 3:245]
- ii Sarah, b 6 Jun 1781: d Buxton 17 Mar 1822 (VR): m Buxton 4 Dec 1803 Thomas Sands (Woodman, *Church of Christ*, p. 38), b Buxton 10 Nov 1780 (VR) bro of Abigail above, d Buxton 18 Apr 1860 (VR). He m (2) Sarah's younger sis Abigail
- iii Anna, b 15 Feb 1784: m Buxton 5 Jun 1806 John Sands (Woodman, *Church of Christ*, p. 40), b Buxton 26 Apr 1785 (VR) bro of Abigail and Thomas above, d Boston MA 11 Mar 1850 (VR). By Jun 1820, they had separated and she was living with her parents ("Maine Estate Schedules," op. cit.)
- iv John Jr., b 18 Mar 1786: d Buxton 11 Jan 1837 (VR): m Buxton 29 Sep 1816 Mary/Polly Hill (VR; Woodman, *Church of Christ*, p. 45), b Buxton 9 Jun 1793 dau of Nathaniel & Martha (Crocker) Hill (VR), d Buxton 24 Jun 1825 (VR)
- v Ezra Davis, b 12 May 1788: d prob Chatham NH aft 9 Jun 1863 (Chatham NH land deed in possession of Robert Hanscom, submitter): m int Buxton

10 Jan 1816 Elizabeth/Betsey Smith (VR), b Buxton 26 Jan 1793 dau of John & Elizabeth (McLellan) Smith (VR Buxton; VR Chatham NH), d Chatham NH 19 Mar 1859 (VR)

vi Abigail, b 26 Mar 1790: d Buxton 20 Sep 1857 (VR): m Buxton 17 Nov 1822 Capt. Thomas Sands (VR) widower of her sister Sarah above

vii Martha, b 24 Mar 1792: d Buxton 10 Dec 1871 (VR): m Buxton 22 Apr 1818 Ebenezer Ballard (Woodman, *Church of Christ*, p. 46), b c Nov 1779, d Buxton 28 May 1861 ae 82y 6m (VR)

viii Benjamin Carle, b 14 Jun 1794: d Buxton 10 Dec 1857 (VR): m Buxton 30 Nov 1826 Jane Miller Goldthwaite (VR), b Biddeford 1 Mar 1803 dau of Joseph & Jane (Miller) Goldthwaite (VR), d Buxton 13 Oct 1883 (VR)

ix William, b 18 Jan 1796: d Newfield 30 Dec 1857 ae 59y 11m 15d (g.s., Hanscom cem): m int Buxton 4 Aug 1824 Sarah/Sally Merrow (VR), b c Jan 1797 (g.s.) dau of William & Margaret (Haley) Merrow (Oscar E. Merrow, *Henry Merrow of Reading, Massachusetts and His Descendants* [1954], pp. 380–81), d Newfield 16 Oct 1870 ae 73y 8m 21d (g.s., Hanscom cem)

x Priscilla, b 5 Mar 1798: d Portland 22 Nov 1882 (Artemas C. Harmon, *The Harmon Genealogy* [1920], p. 72): m Buxton 6 Nov 1823 Benjamin Carle Harmon (VR), b Scarborough 14 Nov 1795 son of Benjamin & Elizabeth (Burbank) Harmon (Harmon, op. cit.), d Buxton 2 Mar 1841 (VR)

Dana A. Batchelder, 258 South Sea Avenue, West Yarmouth, MA 02673
Robert Hanscom, 57 Longwood Rd., Reading, MA 01867

Herriman, Simon   41a   2 - 0 - 0 - 0 - 0
New Castle Town, Lincoln County

SIMON HARRIMAN, b Haverhill MA 11 Oct 1761 son of Joel & Mary (Bradstreet) Harriman (VR, 1:157): d Bangor 29 Jul 1837 ae 75y (Rev War Pension #W23188; BHM, 3:46, 7:175): m int Newcastle 30 Nov 1790 ELIZABETH GILMAN of Balltown (VR Newcastle), b c1768, d Bangor 12 Aug 1851 ae 83y (BHM, 7:175). Her son-in-law Henry Head was appointed administrator of her estate Aug 1851 (Ruth Gray, *Abstracts of Penobscot County Maine Probate Records 1816–1866* [1990], p. 95). Simon served in Capt. Joseph Eaton's Co., Col. Samuel Johnson's Regt. in 1777; and in Capt. Jonathan Ayer's Co., Col. Nathaniel Wade's Regt. in 1780 with his brother True Worthy Harriman (MS&S, 7:317). Elizabeth received a pension for Simon's service (pension, op. cit.). Simon came to Newcastle from Haverhill MA with his brother True Worthy who was undoubtedly the other male aged over 16 in his household. Soon after his marriage, Simon moved to Pittston and was enumerated there in 1800 (USC). He was of Balltown in 1801 (Lin Co deeds 59:38) and by 1810 he moved to Bangor, where the family lived on Main St. (USC; BHM, 3:172). He was a member of the First Methodist Society in 1812 (BHM, 3:129). After his house was lost in the great fire of Aug 1825, Simon built the first house (and his blacksmith shop) on Ohio Street (BHM, 3:172). He and his son Simon B. were among those held prisoner in Sep 1814 by the British during the War of 1812 (BHM, 4:177). Simon was among those charged with building a "House for Public Worship" in 1816 (BHM, 7:33). Named in Simon's will, dated 8 Apr 1837 and probated Sep 1837, were his wife Elizabeth and children: Gilman, Simon Bradstreet, James T., Henry Dearborn, Harrison, Mary Reynolds, Eliza Gage, Abigail Head and Caroline Hook (Gray, op. cit., p. 96).

Children, last 4 b Bangor: births in pension, op. cit., citing family bible
i   Gilman, b Pittston (VR Levant) 7 Apr 1791: living 1850 (USC Levant): m (1) prob by 1816 when son William was born (VR Levant) Henrietta B. _____, "consort of Gilman Harriman" who d Bangor 24 Jun 1826 (VR): m (2) St. John, NB Oct 1827 Mary Camilla Anderson (*Kennebec Journal*, issue of 20 Oct 1827), b Frederickton NB 24 Dec 1808 (VR Levant), d 23 Dec 1851 ae 41y [sic] (g.s., Mt. Hope cem, Bangor, Faylene Hutton Coll, Film #37, MSL) [ae 43y on obit published in Mrs. Arthur Ward, Compiler, "Index of Deaths and Marriages as published in the Ellsworth Herald Oct. 24, 1851 through Dec 29, 1865" (TS, MSL)]. Res Frederickton NB 1816 (VR Levant); Bangor 1820; Levant 1827–1850 (USC, Levant VR)
ii   Mary, b prob Pittston 5 Jan 1793: d Bangor 21 Apr 1866 (VR): m 29 Dec 1807 John Reynolds (BHM, 1:40), b prob Dover NH 24 Jun 1783 son of Joseph & Abigail (Pinkham) Reynolds (S. F. Tillman, *Christopher Reynolds And His Descendants* [1959], p. 214), d Bangor 14 Aug 1869 (VR)
iii Simon Bradstreet, b Pittston (VR Levant) 12 Jan 1795: d Kenduskeag 13 Jun 1866 (g.s. Village cem, Kenduskeag): m (1) int Bangor Dec 1816 Mary A. Williams of Concord (BHM, 3:195): m (2) Levant 5 Oct 1834 Eliza Dennett Ladd (VR), b Levant 4 Aug 1805 dau of Daniel & Betsey (Dennett) Ladd (VR; Warren Ladd, *The Ladd Family*..., [1800 (sic)], p. 267), d Kenduskeag 17 Oct 1883 (g.s., Village cem, Kenduskeag). Res Bangor 1820–1830; Levant 1833; Glenburn 1850–1860 (USC, Levant VR). By one Prudence Lovell (sister of the wife of Simon's brother James Thomas), Simon had a son Charles Whiting Harriman, b Bangor 11 Jan 1822 (VR). The undated will of Prudence Lovell, unm of Bangor, was probated Jun 1849 and mentions only her siblings Sarah, Priscilla, & John (Gray, op. cit., p. 135)
iv   Eliza, b 30 Nov 1796: d 3 Jul 1801 ae 4½y (pension, op. cit.)
v   George, b 11 Sep 1798: d ae 3m (pension, op. cit.)

vi   James Thomas, b 6 Nov 1797: living 1850 (USC Searsport): m (1) bef Jan 1822 (when their dau Harriet born) Sarah Lovell (VR Bangor), poss bp Weymouth MA 6 Feb 1791 dau of Enoch & Prudence (Whiting) Lovell and sis of Prudence above (BHM, 6:87), poss divorced bef 1824 when James moved: m (2) Prospect 15 Jul 1824 Olive Porter (VR), b c1805, living Searsport 1850 (USC)

vii Henry Dearborn, b 17 Apr 1802: d Bangor 1 May 1854 ae 52y (Mrs. Arthur Ward, Compiler, "Deaths and Marriages Published in the Eastern Freeman Apr 22, 1853 through July 28, 1854" [TS, MSL])

viii Caroline, b 2 May 1804: living 1850 (USC Castine): m cert Bangor 17 Jul 1831 Benjamin Hook Jr. of Castine (VR Bangor; *Christian Intelligencer and Eastern Chronicle*, issue of 5 Aug 1831, Gardiner Public Library), b c1809, living 1850 (ae 41y in 1850 USC Castine)

ix Eliza, b 6 Jun 1806: living 1870 (USC Bangor): m cert Bangor 14 Oct 1829 Charles C. Gage of Castine (VR Bangor; Grace Maxwell and Georgianna Lilly, "Marriages from American Advocate," issue of 24 Oct 1829 [TS, 1947–1948, MSL]), b c1803, d Bangor 8 Dec 1876 ae 73y and bur Mt. Hope cem (DAR Misc Records, 24:3:181)

x   Dillon, b 11 Jun 1808: d 24 Oct 1833 (pension, op. cit.)

xi "and his mate a girl who was stillborn" (pension, op. cit.)

xii Abigail Hatch, b 10 Feb 1811: d Bangor 7 Feb 1868 ae 57y and bur Mt. Hope cem (DAR Misc Records, 24:3:80): m cert Bangor 17 Jul 1831 Henry A. Head (VR), b c1799 son of John & Margaret (____) Head (DAR Misc Records, 24:3:161; USC 1870 Bangor), d Bangor 18 Apr 1875 and bur Mt. Hope cem (ibid; Gray, op. cit., p. 332)

xiii Harrison, b 10 May 1814: living 1837 when named in father's will

Reference: Alta and Iva Harriman, "Descendants of Leonard Harriman of New England" (1966); Lois Ware Thurston, C.G., *The Harriman Family: Research In Progress* (1992), p. 71.

Berkeley Henley, P.O. Box 102, Norway, ME 04268
Lois Ware Thurston, C.G., 80 Beech Street, Chelsea, ME 04330

Farl (Wid^w)   69a   0 - 3 - 2 - 0 - 0
   Waterborough Town, York County

ANNA (WILKINSON) HEARL/EARL (widow of Samuel Hearl/Earl), b c1755 dau of James & Mary (____) Wilkinson of Berwick (will of James Wilkinson, York Co Probate #20420; "Maine Estate Schedules from Revolutionary War Pensions," NEHGR, 142 [1988]:198): prob d Waterboro betw 1830 and 1840

(USC): m (1) Berwick 4 Mar 1779 SAMUEL HEARL/EARL as his 2nd wife (John E. Frost and Joseph C. Anderson II, *Vital Records of Berwick, South Berwick, and North Berwick, Maine to the Year 1892* [1993], hereafter VR, p. 122), bp Berwick 1st Church 11 Jan 1753 son of Thomas & Dorothy (_____) Hearl (NEHGR, 82 [1928]:322), d prob Waterboro prob just bef the 1790 USC (based on the birth dates of his children). He had m (1) Kittery 30 Nov 1774 Rachel Nason (Joseph C. Anderson II and Lois Ware Thurston, C.G., *Vital Records of Kittery, Maine to the Year 1892* [1991], p. 155). Anna m (2) int Waterboro 6 May 1796 JAMES URAN (VR). He was perhaps the James Uran b Berwick 1 Aug 1756 son of James & Anna (_____) Uran (VR), although James Uran of Waterboro gave his age as 66 years on 7 Jun 1820 implying a birth date c1754 (NEHGR, 142 [1988]:198). He d aft 1823 (Rev War pension #S35685) and prob bef 1830 when Anna was listed as a head of household at Waterboro (USC). Anna, with her 1st husband Samuel Hearl/Earl, moved to Waterboro from Berwick prob about 1780 when he was replaced as guardian of his younger bro Moses Hearl (York Co Probate #9013). Samuel was shown on the 1785 Waterboro proprietor's map as owning lot #89. Anna Earl, widow, resided on this same lot in 1791 (York Co deeds 60:238). In 1820, James Uran stated his property included "30 acres of land in Waterborough, a quarter acre of which is very poor, a house and barn so poor that it is not taxed to me" (NEHGR, 142 [1988]:198). His personal estate was comprised of "2 cows, a small yoke of oxen, 4 sheep, 4 swine, a few mean articles of furniture, pots, kettles, etc."; he claimed he had "no income" and was "considerably in debt"; Anna, his wife, aged 65y, was described as "a sickly woman, having numb palsy and under the care of physicians"; son Samuel Earl, ae 30y, was "a cripple and helpless, his wife and children unable to support themselves" (ibid.).

Children (surname HEARL/EARL), order of birth partially speculative
  i Thomas, b c1781 (1860 USC, Waterboro): d betw 4 Jul 1863 and Oct 1863 (dates his will was written, probated, York Co Probate #4932): m Waterboro 24 Nov 1808 Olive Junkins (VR) who was b c1786 (1860 USC) and who outlived her husband
  ii James, b c1784: d betw 17 Dec 1852 and 7 Nov 1853 (dates his will was written, probated, York Co Probate #4923): m Waterboro 1816 Eleanor Junkins (VR, which gives year of marriage, but not exact date), b 1781–1784 (discrepancy betw 1850 and 1860 USC), living at Waterboro in 1860 with James's nephew, Ivory Earl (USC). James's will mentioned no children and made the statement that it was not his "intention to make any bequest to my brother or sister or to the children of any deceased brother or sister"
  iii Frances/Fanny, b Waterboro 15 Aug 1786 (Robert L. Taylor, *Early Families of Limerick, Maine* [1984], p. 43): d Limerick 23 Apr 1861 ae 74y 8m 8d (ibid.): m Waterboro 21 Nov 1811 Abijah Dearborn (ibid.), b Apr

1787 son of Richard & Mary (Whitten) Dearborn of Limerick (ibid.), d Limerick 4 Oct 1869 ae 82y 6m (ibid.)
iv Samuel, b c1788 (1850 USC, Waterboro): d prob betw 1850 and 1860 (USC): m (1) Waterboro 29 Dec 1810 Nancy Wentworth (VR), b 1787 dau of Silas & Mary (Bickford) Wentworth of Shapleigh (John Wentworth, *The Wentworth Genealogy* [1878]), 2:229-30), d 1832 (ibid.): m (2) Waterboro 5 Mar 1847 Sarah Rann of Buxton (VR) who was not enumerated with him in the 1850 USC at Waterboro
v Hannah, m int Waterboro 21 Jan 1809 Jonathan Goodwin (VR). They had a dau Mary who was ae 13y in 1823 and living in the household of her grandmother and step-grandfather, James and Anna Uran (Rev War pension #S35685). There was no Jonathan Goodwin family at Waterboro in the 1820 USC and this combined with the will of Hannah's bro James would make it seem likely that both Jonathan and Hannah had d by 1820

Joseph C. Anderson II, 5337 Del Roy Drive, Dallas, TX 75229

Heath, Eldad   30b   1 - 3 - 5 - 0 - 0
Penobscot Town, Hancock County

ELDAD HEATH, b Plaistow NH 26 Sep 1751 (Penobscot VR): d Penobscot betw 1820–1830 (USC): m c1772 LYDIA BOWDEN, b York 2 Jul 1755 (Penobscot VR) [but perhaps the Lydia Bowden bp York 14 May 1755 (sic) dau of Paul & Prudence (Provinder) Bowden who were in Penobscot by 1759 ("Bowden Family Research," *The Maine Seine*, 9 [1987]:20)]: d betw 1820–1830 (USC). The 1800 USC states he was from Haverhill MA from which Plaistow NH was taken in 1749. In 1805, he and Joshua Woodman as co-owners were awarded 100 acres of Lot #1 in Penobscot as settlers' rights from the Committee on Eastern Lands (Han Co deeds 16:265) which required his settlement by 1784. He had purchased 50 acres on the Eastern River in Penobscot from Samuel Bowden in 1794 (Han Co deeds 2:353) whose relation, if any, to his wife has not been determined. He purchased Woodman's half of Lot #1 in 1806 and sold his half to his son Merrill (Han Co deeds 22:87, 88). In 1810, he sold the other half of Lot #1 to his son Zebediah (Han Co deeds 29:268) and in 1813 he sold his original 50-acre plot to his son Josiah (Han Co deeds 33:468). He and Lydia were probably living with his son Isaac in the 1820 USC.

Children, all b Penobscot: births VR Penobscot
i Isaac, b 17 Jan 1773: d bef 1850 (USC): m by 1796 Hannah ____, b York 12 Oct 1771 (Penobscot VR). [Because of his proximity to several Bowden and Stover families in Penobscot, and the fact that 2 of Isaac's sisters

married Bowdens, it has been speculated that Hannah might have been a Bowden or a Stover. One Hannah Stover was b York 28 Nov 1771 dau of John & Patience (Young) Stover (VR)]
- ii Prudence, b 11 Sep 1774: m Penobscot 15 Dec 1796 Josiah Colson (VR), b c1772 son of Josiah & Elizabeth (_____) Colson [see JOSIAH COLSON family, *Maine Families*, 2:52]. They res Monroe in 1830 (USC)
- iii Polly, b 28 May 1777: perhaps the Molly Heath who m int Penobscot 2 Mar 1800 John Bowden of Penobscot (VR)
- iv Susanna, b 10 Feb 1779: m int Penobscot 28 Nov 1802 Ebenezer Bowden (VR)
- v Merrill, b 5 Nov 1781: d 21 Aug 1861 (Bertha Bowden, "Cemetery Inscriptions of Penobscot, Maine" [1964–1971], #66): m int Penobscot 5 Apr 1804 Lucy Douglass of Castine (Penobscot VR), b c Aug 1786 prob dau of James & Lydia (Avery) Douglass, blacksmith, of Castine (BHM, 9:100). She d 7 Jan 1862 ae 75y 5m 6d (Bowden, op. cit.). Merrill's est was probated 13 Nov 1861 (Han Co Probate #2656)
- vi Tryphena, b 1 May 1784: d Great Wass Island 26 Nov 1872 (Leonard F. Tibbetts & Darryl B. Lamson, *Early Families of Jonesport, Maine* [1985]): m Penobscot 27 Jun 1804 John Alley of Penobscot (VR), b Boothbay 22 Jan 1782 son of Joshua & Hannah (Brown) Alley (Philip Howard Gray, *Penobscot Pioneers*, Vol. 1 [1992], pp. 2–3). They moved to Great Wass Island in the town of Beals (ibid.) where one of their daus married into the Beal family [see JEREMIAH BEAL family, *Maine Families*, 2:18–19]
- vii Zebediah, b 18 Oct 1788: m Castine 24 Dec 1809 Lydia Douglass of Castine (VR) perhaps another dau of James & Lydia (Avery) Douglass above. They res Penobscot in 1830 (USC)
- viii Josiah, b 24 Mar 1791: m int Penobscot 29 Jan 1815 Elmina Colson of Buckstown (Penobscot VR). They res Penobscot in 1820 (USC)

Ralph E. Hillman, 4302 James Dr., Midland, MI 48642

Higgins, Israel 29c 2 - 5 - 2 - 0 - 0
Mount Desert Town, Hancock County

ISRAEL HIGGINS, b Eastham MA c1742 poss son of Zaccheus & Rebecca (Young) Higgins (Katharine S. Higgins, *Richard Higgins and His Descendants* [1918], p. 200ff): d Eden 11 Nov 1818 (ibid.): m Eastham MA 26 Nov 1767 MARY SNOW (VR), b Truro MA 3 Nov 1744 dau of Joshua & Hannah (Paine) Snow (VR; *Richard Higgins*, op. cit.). Israel Higgins served in the Rev War (DAR Lineage 144:17; MS&S 7:844). He came to Mt. Desert in 1772–73 (George F. Street, *Mount Desert, A History* [1905], p. 156).

Children: births VR Eden; *Richard Higgins,* op. cit.; & cited sources
  i   Henry, b Eastham MA 27 Nov 1769: d West Indies 24 Mar 1794 (Eden VR): m 20 Sep 1791 Anna Coggins of Yarmouth MA, b 4 Jul 1772, d Trenton
  ii Stephen, b 10 Nov 1771: d Eden 19 Dec 1852 (VR): m Deborah Wasgatt, b #1 Union River 8 Nov 1771 dau of Thomas Jr. & Eunice (Robbins) Wasgatt/Wescott (VR Mt. Desert) [see THOMAS WESCOTT family, *Maine Families,* 2:297], d 26 Nov 1845 (Eden VR)
  iii Israel, b 12 Apr 1773: d Eden 17 Mar 1776 (VR)
  iv Oliver, b 22 Jan 1776: d Eden 20 Jan 1862 (VR): m Eden 20 Aug 1802 Rhoda Leland, b 1 Jul 1782 dau of Ezra & Sarah/Sally (Hamor) Leland (Eden VR) [see EZRA LELAND family, *Maine Families,* 2:179–80], d 29 Sep 1871 (ibid.)
  v   Israel, b 5 Mar 1778: d at sea 29 Mar 1823 (Eden VR): m (1) Eden 26 Jan 1800 Polly Hull (VR), b 6 Apr 1783 (Eden VR) dau of Samuel & Charlotte (Phelps) Hull of Derby CT and Eden, d Eden 26 Feb 1818 (VR): m (2) Eden 31 Aug 1819 Zena Stanwood (VR) who d Eden 18 Sep 1821 (VR)
  vi Jonathan, b 19 Sep 1780: d Eden 21 Mar 1796 (VR)
  vii Zaccheus, b 13 Dec 1782: d Eden 16 May 1867: m Eden 9 Feb 1809 Sarah Leland (VR), b 19 May 1786 sis of Rhoda above (Eden VR), d 9 Jul 1869 [see EZRA LELAND family, *Maine Families,* 2:180]
  viii Seth, b 13 Jun 1785: m Mt. Desert 20 Nov 1811 Sarah Hadlock (VR)
  ix Marcy, 2 Apr 1787: m cert Mt. Desert 12 Nov 1805 Nathan Clark (VR)
  x   Mary, b 14 Apr 1791: d Bar Harbor 23 Oct 1877: m int Eden 29 Jul 1822 Christopher Havens (VR)

James B. Vickery, 183 Harlow St., Apt. 220, Bangor, ME 04401

Higgins, Philip   33b   2 - 4 - 4 - 0 - 0
Bath Town, Lincoln County

PHILIP HIGGINS, b Eastham MA 28 Jan 1727/8 son of Thomas & Abigail (Paine) Higgins (MD 16:197): d Bath betw 10 Dec 1795 when he wrote his will and 27 May 1796 when it was probated (Lin Co Probate 6:202–3): m Eastham MA 27 Jul 1748 MARY WILEY of Eastham (MD 24:87). Philip moved to that part of Georgetown that became West Bath where he was a resident by 1759 (Henry W. Owen, *History of Bath* [1936], p. 95). He appraised estates in Georgetown in 1760 and 1766; he was executor of the estate of Hannah Goold of Bath in 1774; and was surety for the bond of Joseph Gould in the estate of Moses Gould in Georgetown in 1777 (Lin Co Probate 1:226, 227, 2:35, 42). The

MA Tax Valuation List of 1771 shows him in Georgetown (#339) with three rateable polls, a house with a shop adjacent, 100 feet of wharf, a mill and 85 tons of vessels. He was the member of a Georgetown committee in Mar 1775 to see that the resolves of Congress were obeyed which forbade the importation and use of English goods; he served on the Committee of Correspondence for Georgetown during the Rev War (*History of Bath*, pp. 112, 119). His will named his wife Mary and children (probably named in birth order) Benjamin Higgins, Reuben Higgins, Ruth Marriner, Abigail Williams, Simeon Higgins, Philip Higgins, Mary Mathes, Sarah Holbrook and Thankful Huffe and several grandchildren. His inventory totaled $3,307.67, a sizable estate for the time (Lin Co Probate 7:83–84).

Children, first 6 perhaps b Eastham MA, last 3 perhaps b Georgetown
  i   Benjamin, b c1749: d Camden 9 Oct 1823 (Josephine Watts and Isabel Maresh, *Camden-Rockport B-D-M* [1985], p. 44): of Georgetown when he m Harpswell 27 Sep 1770 Sarah Mathews of Harpswell (VR) who d 21 Sep 1822 (Watts & Maresh, op. cit.). Benjamin moved to Camden in 1793 (Reuel Robinson, *History of Camden and Rockport, Maine* [1907], p. 97)
  ii Reuben, b c1750: d Bath 3 Sep 1829 ae 79y (g.s., Higgins cem, Foster's Pt., W. Bath, Nathan Hale, Compiler, Surname Index Project [MSL], hereafter SIP): m (1) Harpswell 16 May 1776 Marcy/Mercy Hopkins ("Harpswell VR Recorded by Rev. Elisha Eaton, 1754–64, and by his son Samuel Eaton, V.D.M. 1765–1843" [TS, MHS], p. 28), b Truro MA 6 Aug 1756 dau of Simeon & Betty (Cobb) Hopkins of Truro and Harpswell (Katharine S. Higgins, *Richard Higgins and His Descendants* [1918], p. 286), d Bath 4 Aug 1817 ae 62y (g.s., Higgins cem): m (2) Bath 18 Nov 1821 Susanna Philbrook (*Richard Higgins*, op. cit., p. 286), b 11 Sep 1759 dau of Joshua Philbrook of Bath (ibid.), d 3 Dec 1847 ae 85y [sic] (g.s. Maple Grove cem, Bath, SIP, op. cit., which names her father as Dea. Joshua Philbrook). From his father's will, Reuben received "the Farm on which he now lives containing about eighty five Acres situate in said Bath"
  iii Ruth, b c1752, m John Marriner of Brunswick (*Richard Higgins*, op. cit., p. 188), b Falmouth [no date] son of John & Sarah (Roberts) Marriner (Lora Altine Woodbury Underhill, *Descendants of Edward Small of New England...* [1934], 3:1237)
  iv Abigail, b c1754: m int Georgetown 22 May 1774 John Williams of Georgetown (VR)
  v   Simeon, b c1756: d Bath 4 Apr 1830 ae 74y (g.s., 1st Parish cem, W. Bath): m int Georgetown 27 Jan 1781 Elizabeth Macantior [McIntire?] of Georgetown (VR) who d 28 Mar 1837 ae 80y (g.s., 1st Parish cem). From his father's will, Simeon received 80 acres of land on the road leading to Foster's Point

- vi Philip, b "in the part of Georgetown that later became Bath" 13 Sep 1759 (Rev War pension #W23277): d 14 Jun 1837 and bur W. Bath (ibid.; Fisher's *Soldiers*, p. 365): m 5 Oct 1780 Mary Spaulding of Georgetown (pension, op. cit.) who was b c1756 and was living at Bath 3 Oct 1838 ae 82y (ibid.). From his father's will, Philip received the homestead farm
- vii Mary, b c1760: m ____ Mathes [or Mathews]
- viii Sarah, b c1763: m ____ Holbrook [note, an Abizah Holbrook family lived next to Philip Higgins in 1790 (USC)]
- ix Thankful, b c1766: m Moses Huff of Bowdoin by 1795 when a child Samuel was b there (VR). In her father's will, she was called Thankful Huffe of Bowdoin

Ralph E. Hillman, 4302 James Dr., Midland, MI 48642

Hodsdon, W^m 56a   1 - 3 - 2 - 0 - 0
Berwick Town, York County

WILLIAM HODSDON, bp Berwick 1st Church 20 Mar 1746/7 son of Richard & Judith (Fall) Hodsdon (NEHGR, 82 [1928]:313; Everett S. Stackpole, *Old Kittery and Her Families* [1905], p. 532): living So. Berwick 1820 (USC): m Berwick 16 Apr 1772 AMY/ANNA NASON (John E. Frost & Joseph C. Anderson II, *Vital Records of Berwick, South Berwick and North Berwick, Maine to the Year 1892* [1993], hereafter VR, p. 115), bp Berwick 1st Church 4 Aug 1751 dau of William & Keziah (Lord) Nason (NEHGR, 82 [1928]:320 says she was bp 1 Aug, however the original church records at MHS clearly show 4 Aug; Ricker family Bible rec at NEHGS). William served in the Rev War (MS&S 8:55).

Children, b prob Berwick: Stackpole, op. cit., p. 533
- i Richard, b 25 Dec 1774 (Berwick VR, p. 511): d So. Berwick 14 Dec 1851 (VR, p. 555; John E. Frost, "South Berwick (Maine) Record Book" [TS, MHS, 1967], p. 131): m (1) Berwick 21 Jan 1796 Lydia Cooper (VR, p. 139), b 16 Jan 1774 (VR, p. 511) dau of John Cooper (York Co Probate #3550), d So. Berwick 23 Dec 1819 in the 46th y of her age ("South Berwick Record Book," p. 131): m (2) So. Berwick 16 Dec 1822 Eunice Lord (VR, p. 422), b 1 Jan 1790 (VR, p. 511), d So. Berwick 13 May 1862 ae 72y ("South Berwick Record Book," p. 131)
- ii Benjamin, m Berwick 25 Aug 1803 Sally Cooper (VR, p. 142) sis of Lydia above
- iii Robert, d bef 17 Apr 1829 (York Co Probate #9584): m Berwick 19 Sep 1803 Fanny Wadleigh/Wadley (VR, p. 51), b Berwick 27 Aug 1779 dau of John & Elizabeth/Betsey (Thompson) Wadleigh (Mrs. Page I. Thorpe,

"Wadleigh Collection" [TS, NEHGS]) [see JOHN WADLEY family, *Maine Families*, 3:288], living 17 Apr 1827 (York Co Probate #9584)
- iv Keziah, b c Sep 1789: d Lebanon 17 Jan 1862 ae 72y 4m 14d (VR): m int Lebanon 1 May 1809 Moses Ricker Jr. (VR), b Lebanon 20 Jan 1789 son of Ebenezer & Mary (Butler) Ricker (Percy L. Ricker, "Descendants of George and Maturin Ricker" [TS, NEHGS], p. 123), d Lebanon 17 Dec 1873 ae 84y 11m (VR)
- v Judith, b c1795-97: living Jay 1860 (USC): m Lebanon 5 Dec 1824 Amos Pray (VR), b c1799, living Jay 1860 ae 61y (USC)

Dana A. Batchelder, 258 South Sea Avenue, West Yarmouth, MA 02673

Hopkins, Bazilah   29c   1 - 3 - 3 - 0 - 0
Orphan Island Town, Hancock County

BARZILLA HOPKINS, b prob Chatham MA c1735 (g.s.) son of Elisha & Experience (Scudder) Hopkins (General Society of Mayflower Descendants, *Mayflower Families Through Five Generations*, Vol. 6, Stephen Hopkins Family, John D. Austin, Ed. [1992], hereafter Austin, p. 498): d 17 Aug 1819 ae 84y (g.s., Bucks cem, Bucksport): m (1) Chatham MA 12 Jan 1758 LYDIA ELDRIDGE (MD, 9:34), b c1739 prob dau of Jeremiah & Lydia (Hamilton) Eldredge (Austin, p. 498), d Chatham MA 5 Jan 1773 in her 35th y (MD, 8:238): m (2) Chatham MA 19 Aug 1773 MARTHA (GODFREY) HOWES (MD, 16:38), b c1754 (g.s.) dau of George & Mercy (Knowles) Godfrey and wid of Joshua Howes (Austin, p. 498), d 22 May 1824 ae 70y (g.s., Bucks cem, Bucksport). Barzilla and family moved from Chatham MA to Orphan Island after 1781 and later moved to Orrington (Austin, p. 498).

Children: births MD, 15:215-16
By 1st wife, Lydia Eldridge
- i Experience, b Chatham MA 11 Sep 1760: d bef 23 Jan 1792 when her husband remarried: m Chatham MA 9 Mar 1780 Ephraim Doane (*Genealogies of Mayflower Families*, 2:307), b Chatham MA 15 Jul 1759 son of Joseph & Dorcas (Eldridge) Doane (ibid.), d Orrington 2 Feb 1804 (ibid.). He m (2) Chatham MA 23 Jan 1792 Nancy (Buck) Cole wid of Peter Cole (ibid.)
- ii Roxana, b Chatham MA 3 Jul 1762: m Chatham MA 8 Sep 1785 William Nickerson as his 2nd wife (MD, 38:110), b Chatham MA 24 Feb 1736 son of William & Sarah (Covell) Nickerson (ibid.), d Orland bef 5 Oct 1805 (ibid.). He had m (1) Harwich MA 28 Nov 1755 Martha Ellis (ibid.).

iii Barzillah, b Chatham MA 13 Feb 1764: d Bucksport 20 Sep 1837 ae 73y (g.s., Bucks cem): m c1792 Jedida Dexter (Austin, p. 498), b c1770, d Bucksport 18 May 1850 ae 79y 10m 15d (g.s., Bucks cem)
iv Lydia, b Chatham MA 21 Jun 1769: prob d young before her younger sister Lydia was born

By 2nd wife, Martha (Godfrey) Howes
v Joshua, b Chatham MA 12 Nov 1774: d 2 May 1816 ae 41y (g.s., Bucks cem, Bucksport)
vi Lydia, b Chatham MA 30 Nov 1776: d bef 16 Jun 1856 (MD, 38:110): m [perhaps John] Buckley (Austin, p. 499). When her brother John's estate was divided in 1848, his sister Lydia Buckley received one fourth (Han Co Probate #1674)
vii Elisha, b Chatham MA 22 Aug 1779
viii John, b c1783: d 29 Oct 1848 ae 65y 6m 22d (g.s., Bucks cem, Bucksport): unm (Austin, p. 499). His estate papers named his sister Lydia Buckley and several others, prob nephews and nieces (Han Co Probate #1674)

Deborah H. Conley, 191 Fowler Rd., Cape Elizabeth, ME 04107

Howard, Edward   30b   1 - 1 - 6 - 0 - 0
Penobscot Town, Hancock County

EDWARD HOWARD, bp Kittery 1st Church 12 May 1740 son of Edward & Susanna (Mitchell) Howard ("Records from the First Church in Kittery, Maine 1715–1797" [TS, DAR, MSL], p. 45; m int of Edward and Susanna in Joseph C. Anderson II & Lois W. Thurston, *Vital Records of Kittery, Maine to the Year 1892* [1991], p. 95): d Brooksville 18 May 1820 (NEHGR, 104 [1950]:59): m prob (1) c1765 JUDITH EATON dau of Theophilus & Abigail (Fellows) Eaton of Brunswick (George Hosmer, *An Historical Sketch of the Town of Deer Isle* [1886], pp. 72, 180), d 1767 (ibid.): m prob (2) Harpswell 21 Oct 1767 HANNAH BLITFIN/BLITHEN ("Rev. Elisha Eaton and Rev. Samuel Eaton, Records of Harpswell Congregational Church" [TS, MHS]) [he was of Deer Isle on the m int Harpswell 25 Sep 1767 (VR)]. Edward prob accompanied his father when he moved to Scaroborough by 1742 and Brunswick by the mid-1750s (Philip H. Gray, *Penobscot Pioneers*, "Vol. 2: Bray, Closson, Howard" [1992], hereafter *Pioneers*, p. 10). In 1765, he settled jointly with Jeremiah Veazie on 60 acres at Majorbagaduce (BHM, 8:57). He lived on Deer Isle, occupying Saddle Back Island [now Stonington] (Hosmer, op. cit.). He was described as a mariner when he sold land on Bucks Harbor in 1796 (Han Co deeds 4:14). In the tax evaluation list of Castine for 1801, he was shown as having 91 acres of land, real estate valued at $36 and personal estate valued at $18 (*Pioneers*, p. 13).

[Gray, in *Penobscot Pioneers*, disagrees with Hosmer's *Historical Sketch of Deer Isle* stating that the order of Edward's wives given above should be reversed, i.e. he m (1) Hannah who d in 1767 and (2) Judith. If Hannah d in 1767, it had to have been within only a month or two of her marriage in late Oct 1767. Neither theory has been proven.]

Child by 2nd wife, prob others who have not been identified
  i   Susannah, b c1781: d 1858 ae 77y (*Pioneers*, p. 13): m c1800 Joseph Bates of Brooksville (ibid.)

Richard J. Brownell, 52 Pilgrim Rd., Needham, MA 02192

---

hunter, henry   48a   4 - 3 - 3 - 0 - 0
  Waldoborough Town [s/b Bristol], Lincoln County

HENRY HUNTER, b Ballygruba, County Londonderry, Ireland c1725 (Dodge's *Bristol*, 1:375; "In Memóriam, David Hunter, late of Strong, Maine" [1871], in possession of submitter, hereafter "David Hunter Memorial"): d Bristol 11 Jan 1799 "in the 74th year of his age after a long and distressing confinement with Dropsey" (family record as written in the Bible of Henry's son, Henry Jr., in possession of submitter, hereafter Hunter Bible) [g.s., in Old Walpole Meeting House cem states ae 74y; Dodge's *Bristol*, 1:375, states d 11 Jan 1899 (sic)]: m (1) "under the Old Elm tree on Boston Common" 1 Mar 1759 SARAH WIER (Dodge's *Bristol*, 1:375; "David Hunter Memorial"), b prob Londonderry, Ireland (ibid.), d Boston "after four happy years of wedded bliss" and bur in cem on Boston Common near corner of Tremont and Boylston Streets ("David Hunter Memorial") [but she is not listed in *Gravestone Inscriptions and Records of Tomb Burials in the Central Burying Ground, Boston Common*]: m (2) poss Bristol 24 Aug 1764 SARAH WIER/WYER of Londonderry, NH (Hunter Bible; Dodge's *Bristol*, 1:375), b 1737 (from g.s.) reportedly the "daughter of Robert Wyer, also of Ireland, who went to Londonderry, New Hampshire" (L. B. Goodenow, *The Brett Genealogy* [1915], p. 258), d Bristol 17 Feb 1836 ae 99y (Hunter Bible) and bur Old Walpole Meeting House cem. Henry Hunter and his first wife supposedly came to America from Londonderry on the same ship (Dodge's *Bristol*, 1:375). There are no known children of this marriage. The second Sarah Wyer was reportedly a cousin and schoolmate of Henry's first wife of the same name ("David Hunter Memorial"). Henry came to America before the French & Indian Wars. He was in business with his nephew of the same name as the captain of a small schooner which sailed between Boston and Bristol bringing supplies and an occasional passenger. He was a Rev soldier (Dodge's *Bristol*, 1:375). Henry left a will dated 20 Feb 1798 and probated 3 Jun 1799 (William D.

Patterson, *Probate Records of Lincoln County, Maine, 1766–1800* [1895], pp. 331–32). In the will, he named his wife Sarah, his daughters Nancy McClure and Sarah Chamberlain and his sons Henry, John, David, William, James and Thomas.

Children by 2nd wife, Sarah Wier, b Bristol: births in Dodge's *Bristol*, 1:374–76; Hunter Bible
- i Nancy, b 13 Nov 1766: d Bristol 28 May 1800 (Hunter Bible): m Bristol 21 Jan 1787 Thomas McCluer/McClure (Dodge's *Bristol*, 2:140) [see THOMAS McCLUER/McCLURE family]
- ii Henry, b 17 Aug 1768: d Bristol 16 Mar 1846 ae 77y (Hunter Bible): m Bristol 20 Mar 1800 Ruth Robinson (Hunter Bible), b prob Pemaquid 19 Oct 1777 dau of Alexander & Jane/Jenny (Nickels/Nichols) Robinson of Pemaquid (Dodge's *Bristol*, 1:608, 610), d 10 Feb 1873 ae 95y 4m (ibid.). They are bur in the cem next to the old Walpole meeting house in Bristol
- iii John, b 13 Nov 1770: d aft 1840 (USC): m int Bristol 6 Jan 1797 Elizabeth Hanley/Hanly (Dodge's *Bristol*, 2:140), b Bristol 5 May 1778 dau of Roger & Margaret (Erskine) (McMurphy) Hanley (ibid., 1:374, 1:304), d prob bef 1840 when there is no female of her age living in John Hunter's household (USC)
- iv David, b 26 May 1773: d Strong 13 May 1871 ae 98y (Dodge's *Bristol*, 1:374; "David Hunter Memorial") [g.s., David Hunter Family cem states d 7 May 1871]: m Bristol 9 Feb 1797 Eleanor Fossett (Dodge's *Bristol*, 2:140), b Bristol 26 Jul 1778 dau of Henry Jr. & Anna/Annar (Clark) Fossett/Fasset (ibid., 1:219), d Strong 4 Sep 1872 ae 94y (g.s., David Hunter Family cem)
- v Sarah, b 17 Oct 1775: d Bristol 1 May 1837 ae 61y (Hunter Bible; g.s., Chamberlain cem, Round Pond ME): m Bristol 5 Mar 1795 William Chamberlain (Leland E. Peary, Leland Edwin Peary papers, housed at the Cutler Memorial Library, Farmington ME, hereafter Peary papers), b Charlestown MA 8 Feb 1765 son of Wilson & Eliza (Austin) Chamberlain of Charlestown MA (Dodge's *Bristol*, 1:77; Peary papers), d Bristol 18 Dec 1851 ae 86y (Dodge's *Bristol*, 1:77; g.s., Chamberlain cem, Round Pond)
- vi William, b 2 Feb 1778: d Bristol 20 Dec 1876 ae 98y 10m 18d (Dodge's *Bristol*, 1:376): m Bristol 18 Jul 1805 Esther Huston (ibid., 2:140), b Bristol 20 Dec 1784 dau of Robert & Jane (Houston) Huston (ibid., 1:384, 2:140), d Bristol 29 Aug 1871 ae 86y 8m (ibid., 1:374). They are both bur in the Old Walpole Meeting House cem, Bristol
- vii James, b 2 Apr 1782: d Strong 19 Sep 1854 ae 72y 6m (VR): m prob Strong c1806 Rachel Dodge, b Strong 12 Jun 1790 dau of Benjamin & Mary/Polly (Merrow) Dodge (VR), d Strong 28 Jun 1871 ae 81y (Peary papers). They are both bur in Strong Village cem

viii Thomas, b 21 Aug 1784: d Farmington 28 Jan 1865 (Peary papers; g.s., Riverside cem) [his death is confused with that of his nephew, Thomas Hunter Chamberlain, in Dodge's *Bristol*, 1:375]: m Farmington 20 May 1819 Martha Stoyell Belcher (Francis G. Butler, *A History of Farmington, Maine* [repr 1983], p. 504), b Farmington 20 Feb 1795 dau of Supply & Margaret (More) Belcher (Dorothy Wirth, "Farmington, Franklin County, Maine-Marriages-Births-Deaths 1784–1890" [TS, 1961, NEHGS]; g.s.), d Farmington 8 Apr 1876 ae 81y (g.s., Riverside cem)

Chuckie Blaney, 11 Hollis Street, Sherborn, MA 01770-1254

Jeleson, George   69a   1 - 5 - 2 - 0 - 0
   Waterborough Town, York County

GEORGE JELLERSON, b Berwick 24 Jun 1750 son of Alexander & Margaret (Nason) Jellerson (George Jellerson family record in "Early Vital Records of Waterborough, Maine," NEHGR, 91 [1937]:115–16, hereafter Jellerson family rec) and bp Berwick 1st Church with his bro James 24 Sep 1751 (NEHGR, 82 [1928]:320): d 1 Aug 1836 ae 86y (Jellerson family rec): m 12 Oct 1773 ELIZABETH WADLIN (ibid.), b 28 May 1752 (ibid.) a possible but unproven dau of Moses & Jane (Perry) Wadlin of Biddeford, d 30 Nov 1845 ae 93y (ibid.). George and his father were early settlers and proprietors of Waterborough, arriving there about 1770 (Samuel King Hamilton, *The Hamiltons of Waterborough* [1912], p. 3). They settled on the Mast Camp Road which they and others built through a part of town thickly covered with huge pines, hence its name (ibid.). George was listed on 20 Aug 1778 as being among the soldiers in Massebesick [Waterboro] enlisted in Capt. John Smith's Co. (MHGR, 8:84–86). He was a farmer who owned and ran a sawmill.

Children: births in Jellerson family rec
   i James, b 28 Jun 1774: d Waterboro 3 Jun 1843 ae 69y (John E. Frost, "Waterboro (Maine) Record Book" [TS, MHS, 1965], hereafter Frost, p. 2): m int Waterboro 25 Aug 1809 Betsey Wadlin of Biddeford (Waterboro VR), b c1782, d Waterboro 21 Apr 1862 ae 80y (Frost, p. 2)
   ii Moses, b 16 Nov 1776: d 16 Jan 1777 (Jellerson family rec)
   iii Olive, b 18 Sep 1779: d 20 Oct 1783 (Jellerson family rec)
   iv Caleb, b 14 Sep 1781: went to sea in 1801 "& returned no more" (Jellerson family rec)
   v Nahum W., b 17 Aug 1783: d Waterboro 7 Nov 1834 ae 51y (Frost, p. 11): m May 1810 Abigail Carpenter of Waterboro (VR), poss she b Waterboro 26 Jun 1789 dau of Benjamin & Hannah (_____) Carpenter (VR)

vi   Betsey, b 1 May 1785

vii   Abel, b 1 Mar 1790: m Sanford North Parish Church 30 Nov 1815 Mary/Polly Bean of Sanford (Frederick R. Boyle, *Early Families of Sanford-Springvale, Maine* [1988], p. 24), b Sanford 7 Oct 1793 dau of Joseph & Charity (Tebbetts) Bean (ibid.)

viii   Abijah, b 2 Mar 1792: m cert Lyman 30 Aug 1813 Abigail Hill of Lyman (VR), b 23 Apr 1791 dau of John Burley & Sally (Sawyer) Hill of Lyman [see JOHN BURLEY HILL family, *Maine Families*, 1:150]

Earlene "Kitty" Ahlquist Chadbourne, 1 Fides Drive, N. Saco, ME 04072-9360

Jebson, James   57b   1 - 1 - 2 - 0 - 0
Berwick Town, York County

JAMES JEPSON [also Gypson, Jipson, Gibson], b Wells 8 Feb 1752 (Monroe VR; Rev War pension #S35343) prob son of James & Elizabeth (Came) Jepson (Donald Lines Jacobus, "The Gipson or Jepson Family of Maine," TAG, 18 [1941]:180): d Lincoln 27 Jul 1834 (pension) [his obit in the *Morning Star*, issue of 12 Nov 1834, states he d Lincoln 28 Sep 1834 ae 94y (David C. Young and Robert L. Taylor, *Death Notices from Freewill Baptist Publications 1811–1851* [1985], p. 185)]: m (1) Wells 12 Dec 1785 ELIZABETH JEPSON (VR), prob dau of William & Mary (Gould) Jepson [see WILLIAM JEPSON family], d c1790 after the birth of her second son: m (2) cert Berwick 2 Jan 1794 ESTHER FORD (VR), b c1754 (pension, in which she was ae 66y on 5 Jul 1820), d prob Monroe betw 1820 and 1830 (USC). James served in the Rev from Wells enlisting as a private in May 1778 in Capt. Cogswell's company, Col. Wesson's regiment. He served at Fishkill and in the vicinity of West Point and was discharged in Mar or Apr 1779 (MS&S 6:474; pension). He was living in Wiscasset in 1800 and 1810 and was in Lee Plt (Monroe) in 1820. When he applied for his pension in 1818, he was described as a resident of Monroe ae 67y, his wife Esther ae 66y. He was in Lincoln with his son's family in 1830. The final payment papers of his pension list, as his only survivors, two sons Henry and William "Gibson", the same name used in his pension applications.

Children
    i   Henry (spelled name Jipson, descendants spelled name Jepson), b poss Wells c1785 (1850 USC): d Monroe betw 1850 and 1860 (USC): m c1809 Ann Rebecca Brown. He res Monroe his entire life
    ii   poss a dau, listed as a second female in the family in USC of 1790, 1800 and 1810

iii William (spelled name Jipson and Gipson), b Berwick 7 Nov 1790 (Monroe VR) [Burlington VR gives b 1789]: d Burlington 28 Sep 1870 ae 84y [sic] (War of 1812 pension #WC2222; g.s., Jipson family cem, Burlington): m Swanville 11 Mar 1813 Bashaba Booden (pension, op. cit.), b 17 Sep 1792 (Monroe VR) [Burlington VR gives b 18 Sep 1794] prob dau of William Booden, d Burlington 4 Sep 1876 (pension, op. cit.). They moved to Lincoln abt 1828 and to Burlington in 1835. He served in the War of 1812 as a private in Capt. Chamberlain's militia, Col. Ulmer's company for 4½ months, discharged at Eastport 31 Dec 1812 (pension, op. cit.) and as a private in Capt. J. Neally's company, Lt. Col. Andrew Grant's regiment raised at Monroe with service in the Battle of Hampden (*Massachusetts Volunteers in the War of 1812*, p. 215)

See Alan H. Hawkins, *A Genealogy of the Jipson/Jepson/Gipson Family of Maine: The Descendants of William Jepson (ca. 1695–1723) of Moywater, co Mayo, Ireland and Wells, Maine* (1991).

Alan H. Hawkins, 14 Adelbert St., South Portland, Maine 04106-6512

Gipson, Zedediah   70c   1 - 1 - 4 - 0 - 0
   Wells Town, York County

JEDEDIAH JEPSON, b prob Wells 18 Dec 1758 ("Records of the Society of Friends at Harlem (China), Me.," NEHGR, 70 [1916]:320) son of William & Mary (Gould) Jepson ("Friends Records, Dover, N.H., Monthly Meeting," NHGR, 1:116) [see WILLIAM JEPSON family]: d China 9 Apr 1822 (NEHGR, 70 [1916]:320; NHGR, 5:60): m Berwick 1 Nov 1781 MARGARET ROBINSON (NHGR, 1:116), b Berwick 1 Dec 1759 dau of Daniel & Elizabeth (Bean) Robinson (NHGR, 4:69), d China 16 Apr 1822 (NEHGR, 70 [1916]:320). They were Quakers, members of the Dover NH Monthly Meeting, then the Berwick Monthly Meeting, moving to Vassalboro in 1806 (NHGR, 1:116, 5:60; NEHGR, 72:262) and finally settling in Harlem [China]. Jedediah, his wife, their son, daughter-in-law, and three grandchildren all died in 1822. Jedediah left a will and an estate valued at $1800 (Ken Co Probate).

Children: births NEHGR, 70 [1916]:320, 72 [1918]:262; NHGR, 5:60
  i John, b Wells 24 Aug 1782: d China 23 Sep 1822 (NEHGR, 70 [1916]:320): m Vassalboro 23 Oct 1806 Lydia Runnels ("Records of the Society of Friends at Vassalborough, Me.," NEHGR, 68 [1914]:166), b Rochester NH 15 Apr 1789 dau of Benjamin & Rebecca (Wentworth) Runnels (NEHGR, 69 [1915]:177; John Wentworth, *The Wentworth Genealogy* [1878], 2:2), d China 30 Mar 1822 (NEHGR, 70 [1916]:270)

ii Susanna, b Wells 2 May 1784: d China 28 Apr 1822 (NEHGR, 70 [1916]:320): m Harlem [China] 25 Jun 1806 Abel Jones (NEHGR, 68 [1914]:166), b Brunswick 14 Jan 1781 (NEHGR, 70 [1916]:271) son of Caleb & Peace (Goddard) Jones (Donald Lines Jacobus, "The Gipson or Jepson Family of Maine," TAG, 18 [1941]:181), d China 20 Jun 1853 (NEHGR, 70 [1916]:271)

iii Mary, b Wells 6 Apr 1786: d 8 Aug 1855 (NEHGR, 70 [1916]:320): m China 27 Sep 1815 John Caswell son of Job & Mary (____) Caswell of Greene (ibid., 70:331)

iv Lois, b Wells 14 Oct 1788: d 10 May 1879 (NEHGR, 70 [1916]:320): m China 24 Apr 1816 Ebenezer Varney (ibid., 70:331), b Dover NH 27 Sep 1779 son of Hanson & Elizabeth (Jenkins) Varney (ibid., 70:331; NHGR, 5:57)

v Lydia, b Wells 7 Feb 1791: d China 18 May 1830 (NEHGR, 70 [1916]: 320): unm

vi Abner, b Wells 1 May 1794: d China 6 Nov 1841 (NEHGR, 70 [1916]: 320): m Vassalboro 26 Feb 1818 Comfort Frye (NEHGR, 68 [1914]:168), b Kittery 5 Jun 1793 dau of Silas & Mary (Folsom) Frye (NHGR, 5:27–28), d China 2 Dec 1850 (NEHGR, 70 [1916]:277)

vii Judith, b Berwick 7 Jun 1796: d 16 Mar 1864 (NEHGR, 70 [1916]:320): m China 21 Jul 1830 Nathaniel Austin (ibid., 70:332), b 6 Aug 1790 son of Nathaniel & Mary (Hanson) Austin of Dover NH (NHGR, 5:64), d 2 Dec 1873 ae 83y 3m 26d (g.s., Lakeview cem, China). He had m (1) Miriam Hussey (NEHGR, 70 [1916]:277)

viii Oliver, b Berwick 28 Nov 1798: d China 1 May 1856 (NEHGR, 70 [1916]:320): m China 25 Nov 1829 Syrena B. Ricker (ibid., 70:332), b Dover NH 2 Oct 1807 dau of Eliphalet & Mercy (Hanson) Ricker (Marion T. Van Strien, *China, Maine: Bicentennial History* [1975], 2:50), d 18 Jul 1886 ae 78y (g.s., Oak Grove cem, Vassalboro). She m (2) China 25 Aug 1858 Gilbert Aldrich (*Downeast Ancestry*, 6:104)

ix Margaret, b 12 Mar 1801: m China 18 Apr 1854 John Deane of Temple (NEHGR, 70 [1916]:335), b Greene 16 Aug 1796 son of Cyrus & Mary (Winslow) Deane (Davis P. & Mrs. Frances K. Holton, *Winslow Memorial* [1888], 1:438), d West Branch, Cedar Co IA 16 Jun 1872 (ibid.). He had m (1) Wilton 24 Aug 1826 Abigail Baker (ibid.). They res Temple and Solon ME, Johnson Co IA, and West Branch IA (ibid.)

x Elizabeth, b 2 Apr 1803: d China 6 Dec 1828 (NEHGR, 70 [1916]:320)

See Alan H. Hawkins, *A Genealogy of the Jipson/Jepson/Gipson Family of Maine: The Descendants of William Jepson (ca. 1695–1723) of Moywater, co Mayo, Ireland and Wells, Maine* (1991).

Alan H. Hawkins, 14 Adelbert St., South Portland, Maine 04106-6512

Gipson, Willm   70c   1 - 0 - 2 - 0 - 0
Wells Town, York County

WILLIAM JEPSON, bp Wells 3 Jun 1722 son of William & Elizabeth (Boothby) Jepson (NEHGR, 75 [1921]:52; Donald Lines Jacobus, "The Gipson or Jepson Family of Maine," TAG, 18 [1941]:172ff): d aft 3 May 1797 (York Co deeds 73:86) and apparently bef the 1800: m (1) MARY GOULD, b Amesbury MA 15 Feb 1722 (VR) dau of Samuel & Lydia (Dow) Gould (TAG, 18 [1941]:176). She was living in Jun 1770 but probably survived much longer (ibid; York Co deeds 42:24). He m (2) Wells 19 Oct 1785 MERCY (BUTLAND) RINES (TAG, 18 [1941]:176), dau of George Butland (ibid., citing York Co deeds 59:93 in which William and Mercy sold property set off to Mercy out of her father George Butland's estate). Mercy was a widow of uncertain name when she married William Jepson. On the marriage intentions and on the marriage record, both recorded at Wells, she was called Mercy "Burns" and Mary "Barnes," respectively. Citing a 1760 marriage intention at Wells between John Rines and Mercy Butland, Jacobus felt that Burns/Barnes were misreadings and that Rines seemed the most likely name of Mercy's first husband (TAG, 18 [1941]:176). William was a farmer and evidently became a Quaker through his marriage (ibid.).

Children, prob more: TAG, 18 [1941]:179–80 & cited sources
   i Anna, b c1752, described at her marriage as a daughter of William Jepson of Wells and Mary his wife: d 18 Jan 1834 ("Records of the Society of Friends at Berwick (North Berwick), Me.," NEHGR, 72 [1918]:259): m Berwick 26 Oct 1769 Enoch Peasley son of Joseph & Martha (_____) Peasley of Newton NH ("Friends Records, Dover, N.H., Monthly Meeting," NHGR 1:67)
   ii Judith, presumably dau of William but not so described, b c1756: m Berwick 1775 Caleb Hanson (NEHGR, 72 [1918]:261). They res Berwick, Sanford and Vassalboro
   iii Jedediah, b 18 Dec 1758 (NEHGR, 70 [1916]:320): d China 9 Apr 1822 (ibid.): m Margaret Robinson [see JEDEDIAH JEPSON family]
   iv William, b Wells 18 Mar 1761 (NEHGR, 72 [1918]:270): d Wells 26 Feb 1843 ae 81y (NEHGR, 72 [1918]:270, 93 [1939]:337): m Abigail Varney [see WILLIAM JEPSON Jr. family]
   v Elizabeth, placed hypothetically with this family: m James Jepson, presumably her first cousin [see JAMES JEPSON family]

See Alan H. Hawkins, *A Genealogy of the Jipson/Jepson/Gipson Family of Maine: The Descendants of William Jepson (ca. 1695–1723) of Moywater, co Mayo, Ireland and Wells, Maine* (1991).

Alan H. Hawkins, 14 Adelbert St., South Portland, Maine 04106-6512

Gipson, Willm, J^r   70c   1 - 3 - 2 - 0 - 0
Wells Town, York County

WILLIAM JEPSON Jr., b Wells 18 Mar 1761 son of William & Mary (Gould) Jepson ("Records of the Society of Friends at Berwick (North Berwick), Me.," NEHGR, 72 [1918]:270; Donald Lines Jacobus, "The Gipson or Jepson Family of Maine," TAG, 18 [1941]:172ff) [see WILLIAM JEPSON family]: d 26 Feb 1843 ae 81y and bur in Jepson lot, Wells (NEHGR, 72 [1918]:270; "Inscriptions From Gravestones at Wells, Maine," NEHGR, 93 [1939]:337): m Wells 23 Jul 1781 ABIGAIL VARNEY (VR; TAG, 18 [1941]:182), b Berwick 31 May 1765 dau of Jonathan & Elizabeth (Varney) Varney of Dover NH, Berwick and Wells (ibid, citing her father's will, York Co Probate #19339; NEHGR, 72 [1918]:270). She was alive in 1834 when William dated his will. They lived at Wells and were Quakers. He left an estate valued at $1189.73 (ibid; York Co Probate #10293). In his will dated at Wells 28 Jul 1834, William named his wife Abigail, his 2 daughters Sarah Austin and Huldah Lunt, sons Elijah, Samuel, Timothy and William Jr. and granddaughter Cynthia Huntington (York Co Probate 53:430).

Children: births in Berwick Friends records, NEHGR, 72 [1918]:270; TAG, 18 [1941]:186–91; & cited sources
  i   Elijah, b 14 Aug 1781: named in his father's will in 1834: m Sanford 10 Mar 1804 Hannah Hill of Sanford perhaps dau of Joseph & Susanna (Whitcher) Hill (Frederick R. Boyle, *Early Families of Sanford-Springvale, Maine* [1988], p. 155). He married out of meeting and was disowned by the Quakers (NEHGR, 73 [1919]:127). He moved to Windham where he was restored in 1811 to the Windham Monthly Meeting (NEHGR, 75 [1921]:9)
  ii Samuel, b 24 Aug 1784: named in his father's will in 1834: m Wells 27 May 1805 Hannah Roberts (VR), b Cape Elizabeth 21 Nov 1784 dau of Samuel & Hannah (Small) Roberts (TAG, 18 [1941]:188)
  iii Abraham, b 23 Sep 1786: d 17 Jul 1819 (TAG, 18 [1941]:187): m Falmouth 3 Mar 1813 Lydia (Winslow) Morrison (ibid.), b Falmouth 28 Feb 1790 dau of Job & Mary (Robinson) Winslow (ibid.; Davis P. & Mrs. Frances K. Holton, *Winslow Memorial* [1888], 2:855), d 11 Mar 1815 (ibid.). She had m (1) John Morrison (ibid.)
  iv Sarah, b 10 May 1790: d 7 Oct 1866 (NEHGR, 72 [1918]:267): m Berwick 3 Sep 1812 Andrew Austin (ibid.), b 27 Aug 1774 son of Andrew & Mary (Hoag) Austin (ibid., 72:256), d 9 Sep 1850 (ibid.). He had m (1) Lydia Morrel (ibid., 72:266)
  v   Huldah, b 28 Dec 1793: m Westbrook 3 Mar 1817 Bartholomew Lunt (Thomas S. Lunt, *A History of the Lunt Family in America* [1914], pp. 44, 92), b 24 Jan 1796 son of Daniel & Eunice (Covant or Conant) Lunt (ibid.), d 14 Feb 1837 (ibid.). They res Berwick and Farmington (ibid.)

vi   Timothy, b 13 Jun 1797: alive 8 Apr 1861 (TAG, 18 [1941]:187): m Hannah Plaice (Ada Jepson file, Windham Historical Society). She res Lynn MA 19 Feb 1885
vii William Jr., b 28 Jun 1804: d Wells 26 Dec 1887 ae 83y 6m and bur in the Jepson family cem, Wells (NEHGR, 93 [1939]:337): m (1) Berwick 1 Sep 1825 Phebe C. Page (NEHGR, 73 [1919]:47), b 6 Jun 1804 dau of Samuel & Zeruiah (_____) Page (ibid, 72:272, 73:47), d 14 Feb 1836 ae 32y and bur in Jepson family cem, Wells (NEHGR, 93 [1939]:337): m (2) Berwick 13 Mar 1837 Mary Fry (NEHGR, 73 [1919]:50), b c1804 dau of John & Martha (_____) Fry (ibid.), d 9 Dec 1839 ae 35 y and bur in Jepson family cem, Wells (NEHGR, 72 [1918]:272; NEHGR 93 [1939]:337): m (3) int Wells 22 Oct 1840 Dorothy Grant (VR), b c Jul 1814, d Wells 12 Jan 1895 ae 80y 11m 11d (ME VR) and bur in Jepson family plot (NEHGR 93 [1939]:337)
viii Lydia, b recorded in Berwick Friends records, but no date given: not named in her father's will in 1834

See Alan H. Hawkins, *A Genealogy of the Jipson/Jepson/Gipson Family of Maine: The Descendants of William Jepson (ca. 1695–1723) of Moywater, co Mayo, Ireland and Wells, Maine* (1991).

Alan H. Hawkins, 14 Adelbert St., South Portland, Maine 04106-6512

Jones, John   * *
Scarborough Town, Cumberland County

JOHN JONES, b Portsmouth NH 27 Dec 1710 son of John & Joanna (Cotton) Jones (GDMNH, p. 387; workpapers of Charles Thornton Libby, MHS Coll. 1724): d Scarborough 6 Dec 1792 ae 82y (ibid.; g.s., Black Point cem): m int Kittery 31 Oct 1735 MEHITABLE WAKEHAM of Durham NH (Kittery VR), bp Oyster River [now Durham NH] 21 May 1721 dau of Edward & Sarah (Meader) Wakeham (GDMNH, p. 709; Everett S. Stackpole & Lucien Thompson, *History of Durham, New Hampshire* [1913], 2:377), d Scarborough 9 Mar 1759 (g.s., Black Point cem). John was deeded 300 acres in Scarborough by his father (GDMNH, p. 387). He kept a tavern in the Wilbur house in Scarborough. While John was not enumerated in 1790 as a head of household, his advanced age at that time would support the contention that he was probably living with one of his children.

Children: Charles T. Libby workpapers, op. cit., & cited sources
   i   Sarah, b Portsmouth NH 19 Oct 1738: m 2nd Cong Church Scarborough 3 Dec 1761 Robert Huston (MHGR, 4:32), b Falmouth 14 Dec 1737 (Philip Howard Harris, *William Huston of Falmouth, Maine* [1951], p. 8)

ii John, b Portsmouth NH 1740: d Scarborough 7 Oct 1808 ae 68y "a mason by trade" (g.s., Black Point cem; NEHGR, 103 [1949]:192): m (1) Mary Savage, b c1740, d Scarborough 15 Feb 1797 ae 57y (g.s., Black Point cem): m (2) Mary Chase Tappan [see JOHN JONES, Jr. family, *Maine Families*, 2:159]
iii Mehitable, m 1st Church Scarborough 16 Sep 1773 Nathan Lord of Falmouth (MHGR, 3:89)
iv Samuel, bp 1st Church Scarborough 3 Mar 1745 (MHGR, 1:170): d 1786
v Stephen, bp 1st Church Scarborough 22 Jun 1746 (MHGR, 2:29): d 1825

Leroy M. Bailey, 47 Ivy Lane, Wethersfield CT 06109-2516

Jones, Nat   63c   1 - 1 - 2 - 0 - 0
Lebanon Town, York County

NATHANIEL JONES, son of William & Mary (____) Jones (George Walter Chamberlain, *Lebanon, Maine, Genealogies* [1947], 2:#254): d Lebanon bef 14 Feb 1824 (York Co deeds, 125:32): m Lebanon 11 Oct 1781 MARY/MOLLY ROBERTS (VR), b Somersworth NH Dec 1766 dau of Thomas & Elizabeth (Fall) Roberts ("The Diary of Master Joseph Tate of Somersworth, N.H.," NEHGR, 74 [1920]:39), d Lebanon 27 Dec 1837 (VR). Nathaniel's mother, "Mrs. Mary Jones, wife of Mr. William Jones of Berwick," d 29 Apr 1771 and Nathaniel's father, William, m (2) 25 Oct 1773 Nathaniel's future mother-in-law, Elizabeth (Fall) Roberts "widow of Thomas Roberts late of Somersworth" ("Master Tate," NEHGR, 74 [1920]:87, 184). Nathaniel settled in Lebanon a little distance northwest of his father who lived in the northwest part of Lebanon on the road leading to Milton NH (Chamberlain, op. cit.). He was prominent in town affairs and was a captain of militia (ibid.). He fell from a frame and broke his thigh and arm which was later amputated. Within a few years, he died from the injuries (ibid.).

Children, b Lebanon: all except first 3 listed in York Co deeds 125:32
  i child, b c Jan 1782: d of "throat distemper" [diphtheria] Lebanon 14 May 1786 ae 4y 4m (VR)
  ii child, b c Feb 1785: d of "throat distemper" Lebanon 12 May 1786 ae 15m (VR)
  iii child, d Lebanon bef 6 May 1787 (VR)
  iv Nathaniel, b abt 21 Sep 1788 (Chamberlain, op. cit.): d Lebanon 1 Oct 1826 ae 38y (VR): m Lebanon 14 Nov 1811 Susan/Suky Hodgdon (VR), bp Lebanon 1 Nov 1788 dau of Thomas & Molly (Gowell) Hodgdon (VR)

v   Daniel, b abt 10 Jul 1791 (Chamberlain): m Lebanon 1 Jan 1818 Eleanor Chamberlain (VR), b Lebanon 22 Jan 1792 dau of Nathaniel & Sarah (Furbush) Chamberlain (VR)

vi   Relief, m int Lebanon 13 Nov 1818 Ivory Goodwin (VR) son of Samuel & Sarah (Hodgdon) Goodwin (John H. Goodwin, *Daniel Goodwin of Ancient Kittery, Maine* [1985], pp. 50, 112). Ivory d at sea (ibid.)

vii Abigail B./Nabby B., b 24 Jul 1793 (Lebanon VR): d Lebanon 29 Mar 1873 (VR): m Lebanon 16 Apr 1812 Nathaniel Chamberlain (VR), b Lebanon 10 Sep 1789 bro of Eleanor above (VR), d Lebanon 20 Aug 1875 (VR)

viii Mary/Polly, b 15 Mar 1798 (Lebanon VR): d Lebanon 17 Apr 1882 (VR): m Lebanon 19 Jul 1818 Samuel Kenney (VR), b Lebanon 1 Aug 1791 son of Joshua & Molly (Door) Kenney (VR; Chamberlain, op. cit.), d Lebanon 29 Jan 1878 (VR)

ix   Jonathan R., b c Dec 1802: d Lebanon 29 Mar 1866 ae 63y 4m (VR): m (1) int Lebanon 26 Jun 1825 Rebecca Knox/Nock (VR), b Lebanon prob 3 Jun 1804 dau of John Jr. & Sarah/Sally (Dore) Knox/Nock (prob the child for whom Sally was "churched", Lebanon VR; Eugene F. Weeden, "Genealogical Collection of Berwick, Maine and Somersworth, New Hampshire Families" [TS, NEHGS, n.d.]), d Lebanon 14 Nov 1848 ae 43y (VR): m (2) Lebanon 12 Oct 1851 Esther H. Corson (VR), b Lebanon c Nov 1805 dau of John & Tamson (Hodgdon) Corson (Chamberlain, op. cit.), d Lebanon 2 Jul 1883 ae 77y 7m 10d (VR)

Dana A. Batchelder, 258 South Sea Avenue, West Yarmouth, MA 02673

Jones, Samuel   53b   1 - 2 - 4 - 0 - 0
Plantations East of Machias, No. 4 [now Robbinston], Washington County

SAMUEL JONES, b Dorchester MA 8 Feb 1747 son of Samuel & Mercy (Trott) Jones (VR): d Eastport 9 May 1824 ae 76y (g.s., Eastport cem): m Dorchester MA 18 Oct 1770 MARY RICHARDS (Weymouth MA VR), b Weymouth MA 9 Apr 1753 dau of Dr. Benjamin & Abigail (Thayer) Richards (VR; BHM, 7:130), d Eastport 12 Mar 1815 ae 62y (BHM, 7:131; g.s., Eastport cem). Samuel came to the area that became Robbinston on 5 May 1788 as a surveyor employed by Gov. Edward H. Robbins of MA and founder of Robbinston (William H. Kilby, *Eastport and Passamaquoddy* [1888], pp. 66–67). He lived on the south side of Mill Cove in Robbinston (ibid.). He and his son Samuel were original members of the Congregational church in Dennysville in 1805 (BHM, 7:131). In their old age, Samuel and Mary moved to Eastport (ibid.).

Children
- i Samuel, b Brookline MA 29 Apr 1773 (BHM, 7:131): d 27 Dec 1860 (ibid.): m Robbinston 8 May 1795 Joanna Leshur (ibid.), b Charlestown MA 4 Apr 1777 (ibid.), d 13 Jan 1856 (ibid.)
- ii Benjamin Richards, b Milton MA 28 Aug 1776 (VR): d Dennysville 6 Dec 1858 (BHM, 7:133): m Mehitable Lewis Hersey (ibid.), b 19 Mar 1781 dau of Zadock & Abigail (Lewis) Hersey of Pembroke (BHM, 4:160 in footnote; BHM 7:133), d Dennysville 30 Dec 1857 (ibid.). He was Town Clerk in Eastport in 1803 and 1804 and soon moved his family across the river to Dennysville (ibid.)
- iii Ruth Richards, b Milton MA 21 Dec 1778 (VR): d 24 Jan 1838 (BHM, 7:134): m 26 Oct 1800 Aaron Hayden of Eastport (ibid.), b 8 Sep 1775 son of John & Hannah (Claflin) Hayden of Hopkinton MA (ibid.), d 18 Jun 1842 (ibid.). They settled in Eastport
- iv Mary, b Milton MA 18 Apr 1781 (VR): d 1 Jan 1834 (BHM, 7:135): m Edward Johnson (ibid.)
- v Stephen, b Milton MA 24 Feb 1784 (BHM, 7:131): d Eastport 14 Jun 1856 ae 72y 4m (g.s., Eastport cem): m (1) 5 May 1805 Elizabeth Bracket Young of Eastport (BHM, 7:137), b Newmarket NH 4 Nov 1789 (Stephen Jones family rec in Eastport VR), d 17 Apr 1828 ae 39y 2m (g.s., Eastport cem): m (2) 28 Sep 1828 widow Mary Kane Bishop (ibid.), b Horton NH 12 Feb 1802 (Stephen Jones family rec in Eastport VR)
- vi Sarah, b Milton MA 28 Nov 1786 (VR): alive 18 Jan 1850 when she was appt adm of her husband's estate (Wash Co Probate 15:489): m John Leighton (Perley M. Leighton, *A Leighton Genealogy* [1989], p. 49), b Perry 10 Jan 1781 son of Samuel & Elizabeth (Frost) Leighton (ibid.), d c1849 (ibid.)
- vii Lemuel Howe, b prob Robbinston 8 May 1789 (BHM, 7:131): m Margaret NcNeill of St. John, New Brunswick (ibid.)
- viii Sophia, b prob Robbinston 4 May 1792 (BHM, 7:131): d 19 Jun 1872 ae 80y (g.s., Eastport cem): m Jesse Gleason of Eastport (ibid.), b c1791–92, d Eastport 26 Jul 1839 ae 47y (g.s., Eastport cem)

Rosemary Flamion, P.O. Box 6163, Los Osos, CA 96412-6163

Jordon, Abner   35a   1 - 1 - 1 - 0 - 0
   Bowdoin Town, Lincoln County

ABNER JORDAN, b Falmouth (Cape Elizabeth) 10 Aug 1760 son of Nathaniel & Susanna (Hill) Jordan (Tristram Frost Jordan, *The Jordan Memorial* [repr 1982], hereafter *Jordan Memorial*, p. 193; John Wentworth, *The Wentworth*

Genealogy: English and American [1878], hereafter *Wentworth Genealogy*, 1:518): d Lisbon 25 Sep 1820 (VR; Rev War pension #W26688): m Cape Elizabeth 21 May 1786 HANNAH WENTWORTH (VR), b Kittery 5 Jan 1768 dau of Capt. John & Sarah (Bartlett) Wentworth (Joseph C. Anderson II & Lois Ware Thurston, *Vital Records of Kittery, Maine to the Year 1892* [1991], pp. 146, 226), d Lisbon 31 Aug 1849 (VR; pension, op. cit.). She m (2) 10 May 1829 John W. Jordan who d 22 Mar 1838 (ibid.). Abner enlisted in Apr 1782 in Col. H. Jackson's 4th MA Regt and served continually until Jun 1784 when he was discharged at West Point (ibid.). In the spring of 1790, he moved from Cape Elizabeth to a place called Burntmeadows, later Lisbon and now Webster (*Jordan Memorial*, p. 271). There he lived next to his brother Ephraim and made his living as a farmer (ibid.). In 1820, ae 58y, Abner claimed that he had no real estate, that his personal estate consisted of a house and a few articles of very old household furniture and that he was not able to work due to palsy. Living with him were his wife Hannah, 52, and children Sarah, 14, Wentworth, 9, and Lydia, 7 ("Maine Estate Schedules From Revolutionary War Pensions," NEHGR, 142 [1988]:303). Nathan B. Jordan, son, declared on 19 Nov 1850 that the only surviving children of Abner and Hannah at that time were Nathan B. Jordan, John W. Jordan, Nathaniel Jordan, Timothy Jordan, Sarah Stinchfield, Wentworth Jordan and Lydia H. Stinchfield (pension, op. cit.).

Children: births VR Lisbon; *Jordan Memorial*, pp. 271–74
    i   Nathan Bartlett, b Cape Elizabeth 21 Dec 1787 [*Wentworth Genealogy* gives b 2 Nov 1789]: d Auburn 31 May 1876 ae 88y (*Jordan Memorial*, p. 271; g.s., West New Portland cem, New Portland): m Lisbon 13 Mar 1815 Hannah True (*Jordan Memorial*, p. 271) [he of New Portland, she of Lisbon on m int Lisbon dated 7 Jan 1815 (VR)], b 19 Mar 1790 (ibid.), d 28 Feb 1865 ae 75y (g.s., West New Portland cem, New Portland) [*Jordan Memorial* gives d 28 Jul 1865]
    ii   John Wentworth, b Lisbon 6 Jul 1791: d New Portland 10 Jan 1859 ae 67y 6m (g.s., West New Portland cem): m Hillsboro NH 1816 Mehitable Roach (*Jordan Memorial*, p. 272), b 4 Feb 1793 (ibid.), d New Portland 26 Mar 1873 ae 80y (g.s., West New Portland cem)
   iii   Hannah, b Lisbon 19 Sep 1793: d 2 Feb 1848 (*Jordan Memorial*, p. 273): unm (*Wentworth Genealogy*, 1:519)
   iv   Abner, b Lisbon 30 Nov 1796 [*Wentworth Genealogy* gives b Dec 1795]: d Lisbon 4 Jul 1822 (VR)
    v   Nathaniel, b Lisbon 31 Jan 1799 [*Wentworth Genealogy* gives b Jan 1798]: d 11 Sep 1856 (*Jordan Memorial*, p. 273): m Danville 1823 Anna Jordan dau of Ebenezer Jordan (ibid.)
   vi   Timothy, b Lisbon 29 Sep 1801: d Beloit KS 4 Mar 1890 (Walter L. Mower, *Sesquicentennial History of the Town of Greene, 1775–1900* [1938], p. 532): m Monmouth 15 Jan 1827 Climena Augusta Welch (*Jordan*

Memorial, p. 273), b May 1805 (ibid.). In Aug 1856, Timothy and Climena were members of the newly reorganized Free Baptist church in Greene (Mower, op. cit., p. 61). A photograph of Timothy is given in Mower, op. cit., on p. 533

vii   Sarah Bartlett, b Lisbon 20 Sep 1805: m (1) Samuel Dyer Jordan of Danville (*Wentworth Genealogy*, 1:519) son of Ebenezer Jordan (*Jordan Memorial*, p. 275): m (2) John Stinchfield (*Wentworth Genealogy*, 1:519)

viii   Benning Wentworth, b Lisbon 30 Jan 1810 [*Wentworth Genealogy* gives b Jan 1809]: d IA 1869 (*Jordan Memorial*, p. 274): m 1840 Lydia Ann Chase (ibid.) dau of Jonathan & Hannah (Jordan) Chase of Danville (ibid.)

ix   Lydia H., b Lisbon 26 Mar 1813 [*Wentworth Genealogy* gives b Dec 1813]: m William Stinchfield of Auburn (*Jordan Memorial*, p. 274)

Odile Williams, 4 Merrill St., Waterville, ME 04901

Judkins, Jacob   41b   1 - 0 - 3 - 0 - 0
New Sandwich Town [now Wayne], Lincoln County

JACOB JUDKINS, b Deerfield NH c1762 (Rev War pension #S35483) of unknown parentage: d Wayne 11 Jul 1821 (ibid.): m ANNA BLUNT (Everett S. Stackpole, *History of Winthrop, Maine* [1925], p. 456), b Sturbridge MA 8 Apr 1762 dau of Capt. John & Rebecca (Streeter) Blunt (ibid., p. 292; pension, op. cit.). In the Rev War, Jacob was in Capt. Isaac Farwell's Co., Col. Joseph Cilley's Regt. and served near West Point (pension, op. cit.). He was also on the JERSEY at the time Maj. Andre was executed (ibid.). After the war ended, he lived for a while at Winthrop, then moved to New Sandwich [Wayne] (*History of Winthrop*, p. 456). In Feb 1804, his house burned down and destroyed all of his military records (pension. op. cit.). When he applied for his pension in 1820 ae 58y, he resided at Wayne with his wife Anna ae 58y and his daus Eunice ae 23y and Eliza ae 21y. He described himself as "a farmer, but from age and infirmity am able to do very little, having lost the use of my right hand."

Children

i   prob Anna Maria, b prob bef 1790 (USC): of Wayne when she m 16 Dec 1815 William Burgess of Wayne (*History of the Town of Wayne, Kennebec County, Maine* [1898], p. 125)

ii   Clarrissa, b Winthrop 11 Apr 1788 (VR): of Readfield when she m 9 Oct 1817 Alpheus Wing of Wayne (*History of Wayne*, op. cit., p. 126)

iii   Lorain Moody, b Winthrop 4 Feb 1790 (VR): d Augusta 10 Jan 1862 ae 72y (VR; War of 1812 pension #13.404): m (1) Livermore 17 Mar 1811 Anna Morse (VR): m (2) 22 Oct 1815 Mary D. Clark (War of 1812 pension, op. cit.), b Hallowell 16 Feb 1787 [sic, see below] (ibid.), d Readfield 4 Feb 1827 ae 39y 11m 16d (ibid.) [Mary's birth was not recorded in the Hallowell VR, however Hallowell's midwife and diarist, Martha Ballard, delivered on 16 Feb 1785 (not 1787) the daughter of Charles Clark (Robert R. & Cynthia A. McCausland, *The Diary of Martha Ballard 1785-1812* [1992], p. 26)]: m (3) Readfield 19 Aug 1827 Mary Fling (War of 1812 pension, op. cit.), b Cornish NH 28 Jan 1802 (ibid.), d Augusta 23 Dec 1880 ae 77y (VR)

iv   Rebecca, b Winthrop 16 Feb 1792 (VR): m Winthrop 6 Nov 1817 Nathaniel Dailey (VR)

v   Hannah Blunt, twin, b Winthrop 4 Jun 1794 (VR): d Wayne 11 Oct 1830 (VR): m 19 Aug 1815 John Drew (Wayne VR), b 20 Aug 1793 (ibid.), d Bangor 21 Nov 1851 (VR). He m (2) Bangor 3 Aug 1735 Mary T. Austin (VR) who survived him

vi   John Blunt, twin, b Winthrop 4 Jun 1794 (VR)

vii   Eunice, b c1797 (pension, op. cit.)

viii   Eliza, b c1799 (pension, op. cit.). In her father's pension application, she was described in 1820 as having a "bad scrphcilus [sic] tumor"

Kathi Judkins Abendroth, 1538 N.W. 60th Street, Seattle, WA 98107-2328

Judkins, Samuel   36a   4 - 5 - 2 - 0 - 0
Chester Plantation, Lincoln County

SAMUEL JUDKINS, b prob Exeter NH son of Joel & Rebecca (_____) Judkins of Exeter NH and Brentwood NH (will of Joel Judkins of Brentwood NH dated 11 Mar 1758 naming his son Samuel, Rockingham Co NH Probate #2384, 20:520-23; Rockingham Co NH deeds 89:173 in which Samuel Judkins of Brentwood NH on 24 Feb 1762 sells land that was part of the estate of his father Joel Judkins): d Chesterville aft 25 Oct 1804 when he and his wife deeded to their son Benjamin (Ken Co deeds 10:533) and bef 3 Sep 1805 when his estate was probated (Ken Co Probate, 3:138-39, 266): m HANNAH _____ who was appointed administratrix of Samuel's estate (ibid.). Samuel was one of the original lot owners of Unity NH (listed in the TR on 5 Sep 1772 as an owner with original rights). He served several town offices in Unity through the early 1780s. He was reportedly the second settler in the south part of Chester Plantation, called Wyman's Plantation where he probably settled as early as 1786-1787 (Oliver Sewell, *History of Chesterville, Maine* [1912], p. 15). The area later became the town of Chesterville. In a deposition found in Samuel Jr.'s Rev War pension file, it is stated that Samuel Sr. had nine sons and one daughter (Rev. War pension #W1778).

Children: based on land records, court records and the fact that this was the only Judkins family known to have lived in the Chesterville area, order of birth partially speculative

- i Samuel Jr., b Brentwood NH c1758 (Fisher's *Soldiers*, p. 427; Rev War pension #W1778): d Wilton 19 Apr 1838 (ibid.): m Fayette Sep 1794 Elizabeth Knowles (pension, op. cit.), bp Rye NH 29 Nov 1761 dau of Amos & Elizabeth (Libby) Knowles (pension, op. cit.; Kathleen Hosier, *Vital Records of Rye, New Hampshire* [1992], pp. 52, 123), living at Wilton ae 90y [sic] on 7 Dec 1748 (pension, op. cit.). Elizabeth stated she was raised in Candia NH and that she had 5 bros who moved from Candia to Fayette (pension, op. cit.). Samuel Judkins Jr., of Wyman's Plantation, executed several deeds with his father and siblings establishing his connection to this family (Ken Co deeds 2:238, 3:309, 3:309–10, 3:317)
- ii Hannah, d Chesterville Nov 1806 (VR): m Winthrop 12 Mar 1789 Jeremiah Bragdon (VR) who d Chesterville Nov 1812 (VR). They were both of Wyman's Plt on their m int rec at Hallowell 14 Feb 1789 (VR)
- iii Joel, b 25 Feb 1762 (Industry VR): m New Sharon 10 Nov 1816 Anna Chesley (VR), b Industry 26 Jul 1784 (VR). In Jun 1804, Joel of New Sharon posted bond for Jesse Judkins of Chesterville (Supreme Judicial Court, Ken Co, Dec 1804 session)
- iv Jesse, he prob m and had children but the name of his wife has not been learned. In 1790, he was enumerated at Wayne (USC). In Oct 1804, Jesse Judkins of Chesterville and Benjamin Judkins of Chesterville were ordered by the Ken Co Supreme Judicial Court to appear at the May 1805 session to answer a charge for stealing the goods of one Moses Joy (Supreme Judicial Court, Dec 1804 session)
- v Zachariah, b NH c1769 (1850 USC, Katahadin Iron Works, Piscataquis ME): d Katahadin Iron Works, Piscataquis 25 Aug 1851 ae 82y (g.s., located one half mile on highway from entrance to Iron Works): m c1793–94 Mary/Polly Cowen (Ken Co deeds, 40:83), b Hallowell 28 Mar 1769 dau of Ephraim & Susannah (Kilbourne) Cowen (VR), d Westport MN 12 Mar 1867 (g.s., Lake Amelia cem). Zachariah, of Farmington, was appt on 3 Sep 1805 a bondsman of his father's estate
- vi David, b NH c1770 (Erma Lee Judkins Masters et al, *The Judkins Family* [1983]): d Vandeburgh Co IN 18 Sep 1846 (ibid.; Vandeburgh Co IN Probate #657): m c1797 Lydia Glidden (Masters, op. cit.), b NH dau of Jeremiah & Mehitable (____) Glidden (Masters, op. cit.; George W. Chamberlain & Lucia G. Strong, *The Descendants of Charles Glidden of Portsmouth and Exeter, New Hampshire* [1925], pp. 90–92), living in 1850 with her son Lewis at German Twsp, Vandeburgh Co IN (USC). David, of Farmington, was appt 3 Sep 1805 a bondsman of his father's estate
- vii Joseph, b NH 1770–1780 (ae 50–59 in 1830 USC, Chesterville): d Chesterville 13 Jun 1836 (VR): m int Fayette 3 Feb 1801 Betsey Palmer (VR), b

NH c1772–74 (1850 USC, Chesterville), d Chesterville 5 Jan 1864 (VR). On 16 Nov 1802, Joseph sold a lot of land in Farmington to David Judkins of Farmington (Ken Co deeds, 9:391)

viii Benjamin, b Unity NH 6 Jul 1780 (Chesterville VR): prob d bef 1840 (not in USC): m Chesterville 20 Mar 1805 Betsy Gordon (VR). On 25 Oct 1804, Samuel and Hannah Judkins sold a lot of land in Chesterville to Benjamin Judkins of Chesterville (Ken Co deeds, 10:533). The same month, Benjamin and Jesse Judkins of Chesterville were ordered by the Ken Co Supreme Judicial Court to appear at the May 1805 session to answer a charge for stealing the goods of one Moses Joy (Supreme Judicial Court recs, Dec 1804 session)

ix Jonathan, b Unity NH 4 Jun 1783 (Chesterfield VR): m int Fayette 4 Oct 1804 Anna Gay (VR), b Meduncook 20 Jan 1785 dau of Peter & Mary (Payson) Gay (Francis G. Butler, *A History of Farmington, Maine* [1885], p. 472–73). They reportedly moved to Canada (ibid.). On 25 Oct 1805, Jonathan Judkins of Chesterville sold a lot of land to Hannah Judkins relict of Samuel Judkins late of Chesterville (Ken Co deeds, 8:498)

x son, prob not the youngest child, whose identity has not been found

Kathi Judkins Abendroth, 1538 N.W. 60th Street, Seattle, WA 98107-2328

Judkins, Samuel   51b   1 - 2 - 2 - 0 - 0
  Winthrop Town, Lincoln County

SAMUEL JUDKINS, b Kingston NH 8 Jun 1760 son of John & Esther (Swett/Sweat) Judkins (VR; Rockingham Co NH deeds, 154:52): d Readfield 25 Jun 1818 ae 59y (David C. & Elizabeth K. Young, *Vital Records from Maine Newspapers, 1785–1820* [1993], p. 327, citing the Hallowell *American Advocate*, issue of 4 Jul 1818): m (1) ANNE/NANCY HUBBARD (Rockingham Co NH deeds, 128:306), b Kingston NH 25 Feb 1757 dau of John & Joanna (Davice) Hubbard (Harlan Page Hubbard, *One Thousand Years of Hubbard History, 866 to 1895* [1895], p. 91), d by 1806 when Samuel remarried: of Readfield when he m (2) 29 Oct 1808 MEHITABLE/HITTY CARLE of Mt. Vernon (Mt. Vernon VR). She m (2) Readfield 23 Aug 1820 Benjamin Follansbee (Young & Young, op. cit., p. 327). Samuel prob came to Readfield soon after 8 Mar 1806 when he and Anna, Anna's mother, and one Francis Hubbard sold "the undivided three fifths parts" of a parcel of land at Kingston NH containing a house and a barn (Rockingham Co deeds, 128:306). He was a taxpayer in Readfield in 1790 and a member of the Methodist Church (Elizabeth Littlefield Judkins, *Job Judkins of Boston, Massachusetts & His Descendants* [1962], n.p.). On deeds, he was described as a blacksmith.

Children
- i Richard, b 9 Jun 1785 (Readfield VR) prob at Kingston NH (Rockingham Co NH deeds 128:306 in which Samuel and Anne Judkins were "of Kingston" on 8 Mar 1786): d Readfield 15 Jan 1855 (VR): m Readfield 12 Jan 1808 Catherine Adle (VR), b c Dec 1784, d 22 Jul 1870 ae 85y 7m (*Job Judkins*, op. cit.)
- ii Elisha, b 7 May 1787 (Readfield VR): d in Cuba (*Job Judkins*, op. cit.): m Readfield 2 Sep 1816 Sally Whittier (VR), b Readfield 7 May 1791 dau of Moses & Lydia (Taylor) Whittier (*Job Judkins*, op. cit.), d 7 May 1869 (ibid.)
- iii Nancy, b 2 May 1792 (Readfield VR)

Kathi Judkins Abendroth, 1538 N.W. 60th Street, Seattle, WA 98107-2328

Keen, Elezer   38c   1 - 0 - 0 - 0 - 0
Greene Town, Lincoln County

ELEAZER KEEN, b c1768: drowned in the Androscoggin River 6 Aug 1811 ae 43y (Walter L. Mower, *History of the Town of Greene* [1938], p. 541) [Everett S. Stackpole, in his *History of Winthrop, Maine* [1925], p. 495, says he d in the Bay of Fundy]: a resident of Greene when he m 13 Nov 1790 RHODA MARROW (Medway MA VR; *History of Winthrop*, p. 495), b Medway MA 17 Feb 1771 dau of Daniel & Elizabeth (Harding) Marrow (VR; *History of Winthrop*, p. 494–95) [see DANIEL MARROW family]. According to *History of Greene*, Eleazer was a member of the old Keen family of Turner. At the time of Eleazer's drowning, the family was residing in Dexter (*History of Winthrop*, p. 495). In 1820, Rhoda Keene was a head of household at Greene.

Children: *History of Greene*, p. 541
- i Sarah/Sally, b 6 Nov 1791: d 13 May 1819 ae 27y (*History of Winthrop*, p. 660): m 18 Jan 1816 Joel White Jr. (ibid.), b 24 Jul 1790 son of Joel & Amelia (Comings) White (ibid.), d 2 Dec 1877 (ibid.). He m (2) Lucy Keen and (3) Marinda Keen, both sisters of Sarah
- ii Polly, b 22 Jan 1793
- iii Nancy, b 13 Jan 1795: d Dexter 24 Dec 1877 ae 82y (g.s., Elmwood cem): m Greene 11 Jul 1813 Otis Additon of Leeds (Dexter VR), b Leeds 14 Apr 1790 son of Thomas & Bethia (Richmond) Additon (VR) [see THOMAS ADDITON family, *Maine Families*, 3:2], d Dexter 15 Sep 1826 ae 37y (g.s., Elmwood cem)
- iv Lucy, b 29 Aug 1796: d 27 Dec 1835 ae 39y (*History of Winthrop*, p. 660): m Apr 1823 Joel White Jr., widower of her sister Sarah above (ibid.)

v Lydia, b 3 Apr 1798: perhaps the Lydia Keene who m Greene 1 Dec 1820 Samuel Quimby (*History of Greene*, p. 145), b 29 Jun 1797 son of Benjamin & Mary (_____) Quimby (ibid., p. 407)
vi Reuben, b 21 Jan 1800: d 1 Jul 1817 (*History of Greene*, p. 541)
vii Samuel, b 15 Nov 1801: one Samuel Keene of Dexter d 10 Mar 1865 leaving a wife Maria and oldest dau Angeline M. Marsh (Ruth Gray, *Abstracts of Penobscot County, Maine Probate Records 1816–1866* [1990], p. 121)
viii Eleazer Jr., b 8 May 1805
ix Marinda or Malinda, b 26 May 1807: d 5 Jun 1873 ae 66y (*History of Winthrop*, p. 660): m 23 Feb 1848 Joel White Jr., widower of her sisters Sarah and Lucy above (ibid.)
x Christina, b 16 Sep 1809

Eunice Calvert, 20 Flower Lane, Marcellus, NY 13108-1326

Kilgore, John, Junr   68a   1 - 1 - 1 - 0 - 0
Sudbury-Canada Town [now Bethel], York County

JOHN KILGORE Jr., b Kittery 14 Apr 1766 son of John & Elizabeth (Brackett) Kilgore of Berwick, Fryeburg and Bethel (Fisher's *Soldiers*, p. 437; William B. Lapham, *History of Bethel, Maine* [repr 1981], hereafter Lapham's *Bethel*, p. 571): d Newry 10 Apr 1843 (Rev War pension #W7995): m (1) 6 May 1790 ANNA YORK ("Sudbury Canada Marriages," *The Maine Genealogist and Biographer*, 1 [1876]:126), b 11 Feb 1774 dau of Col. John & Abigail (Bean) York (Lapham's *Bethel*, p. 647), d 6 Apr 1825 (Collection of Kilgore family papers, on file at Bethel Historical Society, Bethel, hereafter Kilgore papers): m (2) Paris 30 Apr 1827 ABIGAIL (SOULE) SHURTLEFF (pension, op. cit.; Kilgore papers), b 7 Sep 1775 dau of Ephraim & Rebecca (Whitmarsh) Soule of Plympton MA and widow of Isaac Shurtleff (ibid.), d Dexter 6 Apr 1876 (ibid.). John was a Rev War soldier enlisting at Fryeburg (pension, op. cit.). He lived at Middle Intervale in Bethel where he often served as selectman and was otherwise prominent in town affairs (Lapham's *Bethel*, p. 571). In 1805, he was one of the charter members of the First Baptist Society in Bethel (ibid., p. 219) and for many years served as a delegate to the yearly Baptist associations (ibid., pp. 221–22). In 1820, when he applied for his pension, he was living with his wife Anna ae 46y, his mother Elizabeth ae 81y and children John, Joanna, Nabby [Abigail], Ira, Moses, Phineas, and Julia Anne (pension op. cit.). His wid Abigail was living in Dexter in 1853 ae 77y (pension, op. cit.).

Children by 1st wife Anna York, b Bethel: births VR Bethel for all except Eliphaz Chapman and Julia Anne; all other info from Lapham's *Bethel*, pp. 571–72, unless otherwise cited
- i Urban, b 30 May 1790: d 11 May 1815 in War of 1812 (Kilgore papers)
- ii Elihu, b 30 Jan 1792: d 10 Nov 1863 (Kilgore papers): m 9 Apr 1812 Sally York (Kilgore papers), b 18 May 1793 dau of Job & Sally (Jones) York (Lapham's *Bethel*, p. 647). They lived on the River Road between Bean's Corner and Rumford
- iii Eliphaz Chapman, b 4 Apr 1794 and named for Rev. Eliphaz Chapman, an early preacher in Bethel (Lapham's *Bethel*, pp. 207–10): d Dixfield 24 Jan 1879 (Maj. Lemuel Abijah Abbott, *Descendants of George Abbott of Rowley MA* [1906], p. 920): m 22 Nov 1816 Sarah/Sally Abbott Frost (Kilgore papers), b 1798 dau of Dominicus & Dorcas (Abbott) Frost (*George Abbott*, p. 920; Kilgore papers), d Dixfield 1877 (ibid.). They res Newry and Dixfield
- iv Sally, b 19 Mar 1796: m int Bethel 31 May 1814 John York (Kilgore papers), b 5 Jul 1787 son of Isaac I. & Elizabeth (Thompson) York (Albert J. Sears, *Early Families of Standish, Maine* [1991], p. 331). They res Newry
- v Alvah, b 27 Mar 1798: d 13 Oct 1868 (Kilgore papers): m Polly Powers of S. Newry (ibid.) reportedly a dau of Isaac & Mary (Searle) Powers (papers of Mabel Foster Roys, granddaughter of Alvah Kilgore). They res Newry
- vi Joanna, b 22 Jun 1800: d 1 Aug 1801
- vii John, b 24 Jun 1802: m 29 Nov 1821 Almira Frost (Kilgore papers) dau of Dominicus & Dorcas (Abbott) Frost (Lapham's *Bethel*, p. 535). They res Newry
- viii Joanna, b 25 Sep 1804: m (1) Elijah Searle: m (2) Ephraim McKusick
- ix Abigail/Nabby, b 7 Oct 1806: d 27 Jan 1871 (Kilgore papers): m (1) Luke Reilly Russell, b 6 Apr 1801 son of Benjamin Jr. & Mehitable (Abbott) Russell (Lapham's *Bethel*, p. 607): m (2) Silas Billings of Woodstock (William B. Lapham, *History of Woodstock, Maine* [repr 1983], p. 179), b 24 Mar 1800 son of John & Phebe (Cole) Billings (ibid.)
- x Ira, b 19 Oct 1808: d Augusta 28 Oct 1877 ae 67y (VR): m 25 May 1834 Lydia Russell (ibid.), b 31 Aug 1812 dau of Benjamin Jr. & Mehitable (Abbott) Russell (Lapham's *Bethel*, p. 607), d Augusta (Kilgore papers)
- xi Moses Hadley, b 30 Mar 1811: m 19 Jun 1831 Irene Shurtleff (Kilgore papers)
- xii Phineas F., b 17 Jul 1813: m Jane Severance. They moved early to WI
- xiii Julia Anne, b 24 Jun 1815: m 21 Sep 1834 Peregrine Sessions (Kilgore papers). They moved to Utah

Warren D. Stearns, P.O. Box 35, Hanover, ME 04237

Kilpartrick, Iland   15c   1 - 2 - 3 - 0 - 0
Falmouth Town, Cumberland County

FLOYD KILPATRICK, prob an immigrant from overseas: d prob Falmouth aft 1824 (Cum Co deeds 102:143): he was of Scarborough when he m int Falmouth 13 Jun 1761 MARY CARLE/CARLL (Falmouth VR; NEHGR 16 [1862]:319) dau of Nathaniel & Elizabeth (Doughty) Carle (Cum Co deeds 38:278) [see NATHANIEL CARLE family]. In the Falmouth 1790 USC, the name Iland Kilpartrick immediately follows that of Increase Pote. The relationships noted below between the children of Floyd Kilpatrick and Increase Pote rationalize the conclusion that Iland and Floyd were one and the same person. Examination of the original census sheets confirm that name was written "Iland"—perhaps Floyd was an Americanized version of Iland. Only one other Kilpatrick appears on the Falmouth 1790 USC and he was Daniel, a son of Floyd. The surname in deeds and other records was usually Kilpatrick, sometimes Patrick, seldom Gilpatrick. Floyd was called a cordwainer when he sold land in Scarborough (York Co deeds 36:144) and a miller when he bought land at Falmouth (Cum Co deeds 54:357).

Children, order and number unknown
   i   Nathaniel, b c1760: d Falmouth 21 Feb 1839 ae 79y (Charles S. Tibbetts, "Falmouth, Maine Marriages and Deaths" [TS, MHS]): m (1) Falmouth 26 Jun 1788 Mary Chase ("Book of the Returns of Marriages in the County of Cumberland," hereafter Cum Co Commissioners Recs, A:14), b Falmouth 1 Jan 1768 dau of Dr. William & Mary (Buxton) Chase, d 13 Nov 1809 (John Carroll Chase & George Walter Chamberlain, *Seven Generations of the Descendants of Aquila and Thomas Chase* [1928], p. 188): m (2) wid Apphia (Merrill) Ilsley (Samuel Merrill, *Merrill Memorial* [1917–1928], 2:402), b Falmouth 20 Apr 1779 dau of Humphrey & Hannah (Lunt) Merrill and wid of Joshua Ilsley (ibid.). Nathaniel Carle, his grandfather, sold his entire home estate to him (Cum Co deeds 38:278)
   ii Elizabeth, b c1762: d Falmouth 21 Sep 1839 ae 77y (Tibbetts, op. cit.): m Falmouth 28 Dec 1780 Josiah Locke (Cum Co Commissioners Recs, 2:252), b Falmouth 21 May 1757 son of Nathaniel & Mary (Stubbs) Locke, d Falmouth 12 Apr 1841 (Arthur H. Locke, *A History and Genealogy of Captain John Locke of Portsmouth and Rye, New Hampshire* [1916], pp. 21, 40)
   iii Lydia, b Falmouth 18 Oct 1764 (Merrill, op. cit., 1:355): d Sidney 2 Aug 1842 ae 78y (g.s., Springer cem): m Falmouth 12 Feb 1790 Cutting Merrill (Cum Co Commissioners Recs, A:23), b W. Falmouth 31 Jul 1765 son of Edmond & Jane (Noyes) Merrill (Merrill, op. cit., 1:258), d Sidney 2 Jan 1849 ae 83y (g.s., Springer cem)

iv Mary, b 16 Mar 1769 (Rev War pension #W23334): d Falmouth 13 Jan 1852 ae 83y (Tibbetts, op. cit.): m Falmouth 27 Mar 1788 Josiah Hobbs (Cum Co Commissioners Recs, A:10), b Hampton NH 27 Oct 1762 son of Jonathan Hobbs (pension, op. cit.; Fisher's *Soldiers*, p. 372), d Falmouth 29 Oct 1849 (pension, op. cit.). He was a sgt in the Rev War

v Daniel, m Falmouth 17 Nov 1789 Nancy Wormell (Cum Co Commissioners Recs, A:23)

vi Lucretia, d bet 1810 and 1820 (USC): m abt 1800 William Pote son of Increase & Anna (Bucknam) Pote [see INCREASE POTE family, *Maine Families*, 3:223-24 and Addendum in this volume which corrects the account in Vol. 3]. William d bef 1810 (USC). Josiah Locke and Nathaniel Kilpatrick, Lucretia's bro-in-law and bro, were appt adms of the estate of William Pote (Cum Co deeds, 65:39) and Josiah Locke was appt guardian of William's minor children (Cum Co deeds 87:193)

vii Arethusa/Elathusa, m ___ Roberts. Wid Arethusa Roberts was admitted 22 Aug 1813 to full communion at the Falmouth First Parish (Samuel D. Rumery, "Notes Toward a History of the First Parish of Falmouth, Formerly Known as the Third Parish of Falmouth" [TS, MHS, 1926]). Floyd Kilpatrick sold her land in Falmouth with a house on it (Cum Co deeds 102:243). Anna Pote, dau of William & Lucretia (Kilpatrick) Pote, bequeathed to her aunt Arethusa Roberts who gave a receipt for the bequest as "Elathusa" Roberts (unprobated will of Anna Pote in the Bucknam papers at MHS). The uncommon name of Arethusa appears frequently among the descendants of Nathaniel Carle.

viii prob Lucy, d aft 1850 (USC, New Gloucester): m Elisha Pote, son of Increase & Anna (Bucknam) Pote [see INCREASE POTE family, *Maine Families*, 3:223-24). Lucy is placed as a probable dau of Floyd Kilpatrick because she and Elisha named two of their children Elathusa and Mary Floyd (Cum Co deeds 297:137). They lived at New Gloucester.

Clayton R. Adams, 6 Laurel Road, Brunswick, ME 04011

King, Benjamin 33a 3 - 4 - 2 - 0 - 0
Balltown Town, Lincoln County

BENJAMIN KING, b New Ipswich NH 23 May 1749 son of Benjamin & Sarah (Taylor) King (Harry H. Cochrane, *History of Monmouth and Wales* [1894], hereafter Cochrane, 2:95): d 31 Aug 1801 ae 59y [sic] (g.s., Kings Mills cem, Whitefield) [note Cochrane states he d 30 Jul 1802]: m Pownalborough 8 Apr 1772 RUTH BARTLETT of "Head of the Tide" (Wiscasset VR), b Plaistow NH 26 Dec 1745 dau of Jonathan & Lydia (Chase) Bartlett (VR) [and bp Haverhill

MA No. Parish Church 23 Feb 1745/6 (Haverhill MA VR)] [see JONATHAN BARTLETT family, *Maine Families*, 2:15], d Whitefield 1808 (Henry C. Waters, "Kings Mills, Whitefield, Maine 1772–1982" [TS, MSL, 1983], p. 65) [note Cochrane states she d 23 Sep 1802]. Benjamin served in the Rev War from New Ipswich NH as a private in Capt. James Gray's company, Col. Thomas Marshall's regiment enlisting 5 Jun 1776 for 1 month 26 days (MS&S 9:243; Fisher's *Soldiers*, p. 440). In 1779, he settled on the west side of the Sheepscot River at Balltown (Waters, op. cit., p. 5). The location became known as Kings Mills from the saw and grist mills that he built there (ibid.). His death was caused by a falling beam while he was working in his mill (Waters, op. cit., p. 5).

Children: births VR Whitefield
- i Peter, b 30 Nov 1773: d 30 Sep 1818 ae 45y 10m (g.s., Kings Mills cem, Whitefield): m Mary Glidden (George W. Chamberlain, *The Descendants of Charles Glidden* [1925], p. 119), b Whitefield 6 Apr 1772 (VR) dau of Benjamin & Eunice (Averill) Glidden (ibid.) [see BENJAMIN GLIDDEN family, *Maine Families*, 3:88], d 17 Oct 1848 ae 76y (g.s., Kings Mills cem, Whitefield)
- ii Elijah, b 28 Nov 1775: d Bradford 11 Mar 1845 (Cochrane, 2:96; Dr. Robert E. Philbrick, "Philbrick-Philbrook Families, Sheepscot, Maine to California" [TS, MSL, 1985], p. 6): m Whitefield 25 Jun 1803 Bethiah Philbrick (VR), b 30 Jul 1781 dau of Ebenezer & Mehitable (Bartlett) Philbrick (Philbrick, op. cit., p. 6), d Bradford 28 Sep 1853 (g.s., Bradford cem) [see EBENEZER PHILBRICK family]
- iii Benjamin, b Whitefield 6 Aug 1776 [sic, this birth recorded in the vital records as occurring just over 8 months after the birth of Elijah above]: d 23 Nov 1866 (VR; g.s., Kings Mills cem, Whitefield): m Alna 7 Jun 1802 Ruth Glidden (VR), b Whitefield 21 Oct 1780 sister of Mary above (VR), d Whitefield 16 Dec 1877 (VR; g.s., Kings Mills cem)
- iv Moses, b Whitefield 28 Dec 1777: d Whitefield 12 Aug 1848 (VR; g.s., Kings Mills cem): m Whitefield 8 Mar 1803 Lydia Peaslee (VR), b 22 Jul 1775 dau of Nathan & Lydia (Bartlett) Peaslee (VR Whitefield), d Whitefield 8 Apr 1847 (VR; g.s., Kings Mills cem)
- v John, b c1779: d 27 Oct 1798 ae 19y (g.s., Kings Mills cem, Whitefield)
- vi Rice, b Whitefield 22 Dec 1783: d 7 Jan 1844 (Cochrane, 2:96): m int Whitefield 14 Sep 1811 Levina Hopkins of Winthrop (Whitefield VR), b 16 Jan 1788 (Whitefield VR) dau of Peter & Hannah (Alexander) Hopkins of Monmouth (Cochrane, 2:84), d 27 Dec 1844 (ibid., 2:96)

Thelma Eye Brooks, P.O. Box 136, Waterville, ME 04903

Knight, Daniel   34b   5 - 2 - 6 - 0 - 0
Boothbay Town, Lincoln County

DANIEL KNIGHT Jr., b Gloucester MA 18 Mar 1744 son of Daniel & Martha (Pattishall) Knight (VR; parents' marriage in Manchester MA VR): d 8 Jan 1798 (Greene's *Boothbay*, p. 556): m Bristol 7 Sep 1768 MARY WINSLOW of Bristol (Dodge's *Bristol*, p. 2:162), b c1736, d 17 Mar 1820 ae 84y (Greene's *Boothbay*, p. 556). Daniel's parents moved from Kettle Cove in Gloucester MA to Boothbay about 1750 (Charles S. Tibbetts, "The Knight Family" [TS, NEHGS, 1941], 3:16). They settled on Damariscove Island (Greene's *Boothbay*, p. 223). At the time of the Rev War, the family took refuge on the mainland at Pleasant Cove (Greene's *Boothbay*, p. 556). Daniel returned to Damariscove Island after the war as he had received one-half of the island from his father's will which was probated in 1781 (William D. Patterson, *The Probate Records of Lincoln County, Maine 1760–1800* [repr 1991], p. 103).

Children: Greene's *Boothbay*, p. 556
  i   William, b 1769: d 25 Jun 1821 (Greene's *Boothbay*, p. 557): m int Boothbay 12 Jan 1793 Martha Burnham (ibid., p. 268) who d 14 Jun 1837 ae 60y (ibid., p. 557)
  ii Nicholas T., b 1771: d 12 Feb 1848 (ibid.): m (1) int Boothbay 7 Nov 1791 Rachel Auld (ibid., p. 268), b c1770 dau of John & Mary (McCobb) Auld (ibid., p. 492), d 17 Jun 1813 ae 43y (ibid., p. 557): m (2) int Boothbay 27 Nov 1813 Sarah/Sally Auld (ibid., p. 275), b 3 Dec 1786 dau of James & Frances (McCobb) Auld (ibid., p. 492), d 26 Oct 1872 ae 87y 11m (ibid., p. 557)
  iii Patty, m int Boothbay 15 Nov 1794 John Andrews of Ipswich MA (ibid., p. 269) [called John Andrews Jr. on Ipswich MA intentions dated 18 Oct 1794 (VR)], perhaps the John Andrews bp Ipswich MA in 1767 son of John & Sarah (Kinsman) Andrews (VR). They first settled in No. Yarmouth and moved to Bristol in 1808 (Greene's *Boothbay*, p. 469). He was a fisherman (ibid.)
  iv Betsey, b 1774: d 10 Sep 1807 (ibid., p. 591): m int Boothbay 7 Apr 1800 Nathaniel Montgomery (ibid., p. 271), b 27 Dec 1773 son of John & Lydia (Winslow) Montgomery (ibid., p. 590), d 8 Jul 1858 (ibid., p. 591). He m (2) int Boothbay 6 Oct 1808 Elizabeth Emerson (ibid., p. 273)
  v   Nathaniel, b 12 Jan 1776: m (1) int Boothbay 25 Nov 1798 Elizabeth Barber of Edgecomb (ibid., p. 270): m (2) int Boothbay 23 Mar 1813 Lucy Webster of Edgecomb (ibid., p. 275)
  vi Daniel Jr.
  vii Lydia, m int Boothbay 7 Jan 1799 Alfred Wadsworth of Bristol (ibid., p. 270)

viii Mary, b c1782: d No. Yarmouth 26 Apr 1843 ae 61y (g.s., Walnut Hill cem): m No. Yarmouth 27 Mar 1803 Joseph Hayes of No. Yarmouth (VR), b No. Yarmouth 25 Jul 1780 son of David & Dorcas (Allen) Hayes of No. Yarmouth (VR), d No. Yarmouth 3 Mar 1838 ae 57y (g.s. Walnut Hill cem)

ix Sarah/Sally, b 1784: d 27 Feb 1857 (ibid., p. 492): m int Boothbay 28 Nov 1802 James Auld (ibid., p. 271), b 9 Apr 1778 son of James & Frances (McCobb) Auld (ibid., p. 492), d 7 Nov 1837 (ibid.)

Eunice Calvert, 20 Flower Lane, Marcellus, NY 13108-1326

Lane, John   58c   3 - 1 - 3 - 0 - 0
Brownfield Township, York County

JOHN LANE, b York 4 Jul 1734 son of Capt. John & Mary (Nowell) Lane (Charles A. Meserve, "Records of Births and Deaths in the Town of Buxton" [TS, MHS, 1891], hereafter Meserve, p. 76): d Buxton 14 Jul 1822 ae 88y (ibid.; g.s., Tory Hill cem): m (1) 8 May 1755 ELIZABETH HANCOCK (Rev. Jacob Chapman & Rev. James H. Fitts, *Lane Genealogies* [1891], 1:230, hereafter *Lane Genealogies*) dau of William & Sarah (____) Hancock (Meserve, p. 76; Gideon T. Ridlon, *Saco Valley Settlements and Families* [1895], hereafter Ridlon, p. 723): m (2) 21 Sep 1777 HANNAH (BOYNTON) HAZELTINE (Cyrus Woodman, *Records of the Church of Christ in Buxton During the Pastorate of Rev. Paul Coffin* [1989], hereafter Woodman, p. 22), b Haverhill MA 18 Jun 1742 dau of John & Mary (Hancock) Boynton (VR) and wid of Samuel Haseltine whom she had m Buxton 18 Feb 1768 (Ridlon, p. 519; Woodman, op. cit., p. 19): m (3) Brownfield 14 May 1788 HANNAH BEAN of Exeter NH (*Lane Genealogies*, 1:235; Meserve, p. 16), b c1759, d 11 Mar 1847 ae 88y (g.s., Tory Hill cem, Buxton). At the age of 20, John was commissioned a 2nd Lieutenant under his father at Fort Halifax on the Kennebec during the French and Indian Wars (Ridlon, p. 874). In 1756, he was commissioned a 1st Lieutenant (ibid.). During the Rev War, he was appointed commander of a company in 1775 consisting of 120 men raised by him and subordinate officers (ibid.). After the war, he settled in Hiram and later moved to Brownfield living on Ten Mile Brook where he had a mill (ibid.). Tradition is that he had 22 children by 3 wives, but 19 are recorded.

Children: Meserve, p. 16; *Lane Genealogies*, 1:234–35
By 1st wife, Elizabeth Hancock
  i   Sarah, b 28 Nov 1756: d Buxton Jun 1836 (VR): m Buxton 16 Dec 1779 Elijah Bradbury (Woodman, p. 23) [see ELIJAH BRADBURY family]
  ii Joanna, b 10 Apr 1759: d Buxton 5 Jul 1843 (Meserve, p. 76): unm (Ridlon, p. 876)

iii Abigail, b 28 Mar 1761: d Gardiner 27 Oct 1859 ae 98y 7m (VR): m Buxton 7 Feb 1790 Gibbins Edgecomb of Buxton (Woodman, p. 27, which calls him "Gibeon"), b 13 Apr 1770 son of Gibbins & Rhoda (Elwell) Edgecomb (Ridlon, p. 657), d Plattsburgh NY 7 Jan 1814 ae 46y [sic] (Gardiner VR, which termed him "late of Standish"). They lived at Gardiner

iv John, b 8 Aug 1763: d Buxton during the summer of 1805 (Rev War pension #W24477; g.s., Tory Hill cem, no dates): m Buxton 4 Feb 1786 Elizabeth/Betsey Woodsum of Buxton (Woodman, p. 25), b Buxton Apr 1765 dau of Michael & Elizabeth (Dyer) Woodsum (Joseph C. Anderson II, *The Woodsum Family in America* [1990], p. 45) [see MICHAEL WOODSUM family, *Maine Families*, 2:313-14], d aft 3 Jul 1841 when she applied for a Rev War widow's pension (pension #W24477) [see JOHN LANE Jr. family, *Maine Families*, 2:171]

v Isaac, b 23 May 1765: d 6 Apr 1804 (Meserve, p. 76)

vi Ann/Nancy, b 5 Jul 1767: m 25 May 1790 Joseph Atkinson (Meserve, p. 76) son of Moses & Rebecca (Woodman) Atkinson (Ridlon, p. 448)

vii William, b 19 May 1769: of Hiram when he m Buxton 7 Nov 1793 Alice Haines of Buxton (Woodman, p. 30). He lived at Hiram as a farmer (Ridlon, p. 876)

viii Daniel, twin, b 8 Mar 1771: d Hiram 21 Dec 1858 (VR): m Buxton 30 Nov 1797 Keziah Hanscom of Buxton (Woodman, p. 33), b Buxton 4 Nov 1774 dau of William & Elizabeth (Sands) Hanscom (VR), d Hiram 6 Mar 1817 (Buxton VR). They lived at Hiram (Ridlon, p. 876)

ix Elizabeth, twin, b 8 Mar 1771: d 1773 (Meserve, p. 76)

x Living, b 10 Oct 1773: m Buxton 25 Oct 1801 Love Dunnel of Buxton (Woodman, p. 36)

By 2nd wife, Hannah (Boynton) Hazeltine

xi Elizabeth/Betsey, b 17 Apr 1778: d 1780 (Meserve, p. 76)

xii Samuel, b 19 Aug 1779: d 1856 (*Lane Genealogies*, 1:235): m 8 Sep 1805 Emma Kimball (Meserve, p. 76) [*Lane Genealogies*, 1:235 erroneously called her "Naomi"], bp Buxton 2 Jun 1782 dau of Joshua & Martha (Elden) Kimball (Woodman, pp. 19, 57)

xiii Hannah, b 5 Oct 1783: m 1802 Jonathan Clemons (Meserve, p. 76; Ridlon, p. 582), b Danvers MA 7 May 1770 son of John & Abigail (Southwick/Sudrick) Clemons (ibid., pp. 580, 582), d Hiram 15 Jun 1855 ae 85y (ibid.)

xiv Mary, b 11 Mar 1786: d 10 Mar 1805 (Ridlon, p. 877)

By 3rd wife, Hannah Bean

xv Alcestis, b 20 Jun 1790: d 4 Jan 1873 (*Lane Genealogies*, 1:235; g.s., Tory Hill cem, Buxton gives dates of 1790-1872): m 8 Feb 1822 Stephen Woodman Lane (*Lane Genealogies*, 1:235), b 5 Nov 1786 son of Capt. Jabez & Sarah (Woodman) Lane (Ridlon, p. 880; g.s., Tory Hill cem), d 1855 (ibid.)

xvi Elizabeth/Betsey, b 12 May 1793: m (1) 23 Dec 1810 Thomas Moulton of Scarboro (Woodman, p. 43): m (2) John Dunnell (Meserve, p. 76)
xvii Mary/Polly, b 7 May 1796: d 24 Aug 1883 (*Lane Genealogies*, 1:235): m John Berry (Meserve, p. 76) who d 19 Jan 1832 (*Lane Genealogies*, 1:235)
xviii Nathan, twin, b 8 Aug 1800: m (1) Hannah Merrill (Meserve, p. 76): m (2) May (Digeo) Merrill of Cape Elizabeth dau of Dr. Jean Digeo (Meserve, p. 76; Ridlon, p. 877)
xix Isaac, twin, b 8 Aug 1800: d young (*Lane Genealogies*, 1:235)

Phyllis S. Williams, 7468 McKinley St., Mentor, OH 44060

Laplain, James   42b   1 - 0 - 3 - 0 - 0
Norridgewock Town, Lincoln County

JAMES LAPLAIN, possibly the James Laplain bp in the parish of Wrockwardine, Shropshire, England 30 Jul 1756 son of William & Hannah (Edwards) Laplain (IGI LDS citing parish register; Hannah's maiden name from recs of Brian de laPlain of South Africa): d Pittston 20 Mar 1845 in his 94th y (VR): m poss in England JANE _____, b c1763, d Pittston 22 Oct 1839 in her 76th y (VR). Both James and Jane are bur in the Laplain burial lot, River Rd., Pittston (VR). There is some disagreement as to James's place of origin. His and Jane's gravestones both say they were natives of England and this would appear to be a better source than J. W. Hanson's *History of the Old Towns of Norridgewock and Canaan* [1849] which stated that they were from Scotland. Naming patterns support the assertion that James was the same person baptized at Wrockwardine. In addition to naming two children William and Hannah for his possible parents, James of Maine named two other children Joseph and Salome, names which were also given to two siblings of the Wrockwardine James. Additionally, James's son Joseph of Maine named a son Ormon. James of Wrockwardine had a brother named Armand. According to Hanson, James came to Norridgewock in 1783/4 where he acquired a few small tan-pits in the south part of the town in what was called Fairfield woods (Hanson, p. 227–28). He and Jane had supposedly emigrated because her parents were against the marriage (ibid.). James was "of Pittston" by 1 Oct 1794 (Ken Co deeds 3:536).

Children: births of last 6 VR Pittston
  i Sarah, b c1785: d 22 Mar 1851 ae 66y (g.s., Riverside cem, Pittston): m (1) Pittston 5 Aug 1803 William King of Hallowell (VR): m (2) Pittston 18 Jan 1824 Capt. David Reed of Dresden (Pittston VR). Sarah's g.s. indicates she was a dau of James Laplain, the relict of Capt. David Reed, and the former wife of Capt. William King

ii Elizabeth, b c Jan 1787: d Pittston 18 May 1844 ae 57y 4m (VR): m int Pittston 7 Jul 1807 Tristram Folsom Jr. (VR), b 13 Sep 1787 (VR Pittston), d Pittston 2 or 22 Oct 1868 ae 81y (VR). He m (2) int Pittston 29 Dec 1844 Hannah Lapham (VR). Tristram and Elizabeth named a daughter Jane B. Folsom, perhaps giving the first letter of her mother's maiden name. [Elizabeth K. Folsom, in her *Genealogy of the Folsom Family* (1938), states on p. 358 that Elizabeth was "of Cornwall, England." This would contradict Hanson's contention above that the family was in Norridgewock well before this Elizabeth was born.]

iii Hannah, b 25 May 1792: d Pittston 25 Sep 1843 in her 52nd y (VR)

iv James Jr., b 2 Jun 1795: d Pittston 9 May 1829 ae 34y (VR): m int Pittston 1 Nov 1828 Drucilla Standley (VR) [see Robert below]. She m (2) his bro Robert Laplain

v Salome, b 25 Sep 1797: d Pittston 18 Nov 1876 ae 80y 2m (VR): m int Pittston 18 Jul 1815 Oliver Moulton, b York 9 Jun 1788 son of William & Lucy (Bradbury) Moulton [see WILLIAM MOULTON family, *Maine Families*, 3:192–93], d Pittston 15 Jul 1836 ae 48y (VR)

vi William, b 23 Jul 1800: d Pittston 5 May 1831 in his 32nd y (VR)

vii Joseph, b 1 Mar 1802: d Gardiner 3 Sep 1865 ae 63y 6m (VR): m int Pittston 1 Sep 1838 Belinda Jones (VR), b 30 May 1806 dau of William & Abigail (____) Jones (Hallowell VR; g.s., Hallowell cem, Hallowell which states she was born at Stratford NH), d Gardiner 9 Dec 1890 ae 84y 6m 9d (VR)

viii Robert, b 13 Feb 1804: d 15 Jan 1880 ae 74y 11m 2d (g.s., Allard cem, Richmond): m Pittston 6 Jun 1830 Drucilla (Standley) Laplain (VR) wid of his bro James above, b Nova Scotia c Mar 1804 (1870 USC, Richmond, Robert Laplain family), d 19 Sep 1882 ae 78y 5m 24d (g.s., Allard cem, Richmond). They res Gardiner in 1860 and Richmond in 1870 (USC). Drucilla was listed as a wid in 1880 at Richmond ae 76y (USC).

Janet S. Seitz, 11521 Upper Sunny Circle, Eagle River, AK 99577-7414

Leman, Jacob   44c   1 - 1 - 5 - 0 - 0
Sandy River, from its mouth to Carrs Plantation, Lincoln County

JACOB SMITH LEEMAN, b Edgecomb 22 Apr 1758 son of John & Elizabeth (____) Leeman (VR): d Abbot prob betw the censuses of 1830 and 1840 (Joan Pratt & Alice Stewart, *Ancestors and Descendants of Paul Pratt of New Vineyard, Maine*, [1988], p. 56; USC): m Edgecomb 11 Oct 1778 KEZIAH CHAPMAN of Pownalboro (VR), b Pownalboro 23 Oct 1757 dau of John & Elizabeth (Lambert) Chapman (VR). The deposition of Abiel Wood, Esq. of Wiscasset dated 1792 calls John Chapman's wife a dau of Robert Lambert of Wiscasset Point (Suffolk Court Files #140918). Jacob settled in 1782 at Sandy River [Starks/Mercer] (*Paul Pratt*, op. cit.). He and his son, Jacob Jr., later moved to Abbot (ibid.).

Children: births last 6 VR Mercer
- i   Sally, b c1780 (William C. Hatch, *History of Industry* [1893], p. 670): d Livermore 14 Feb 1867 (ibid.): m int 9 Nov 1797 James Johnson (ibid.), b 16 Mar 1773 son of Thomas & Thankful (Smith) Johnson (ibid.), d 3 Nov 1843 (ibid., p. 672)
- ii Samuel C., b c1782 (*History of Industry*, p. 633): m (1) 4 Sep 1806 Amy Greenleaf (ibid.) [m int Mercer 5 Jul 1806, he of Mercer, she of Industry (VR)], b 12 Aug 1789 dau of Levi & Amy (____) Greenleaf (*History of Industry*, p. 633), d of typhoid fever Jun 1811 (ibid.): m (2) 14 May 1812 Love Daggett (ibid.), b Martha's Vineyard MA dau of Elijah & Margaret (Smith) Daggett (ibid., p. 586)
- iii prob Kesiah, b Starks 1786: d aft 28 Apr 1857 and bef the 1860 census (*Paul Pratt*, op. cit., p. 55): m Paul Pratt, b Middleboro MA 9 Jun 1781 son of Paul & Jael (Bennett) Pratt (ibid.), d Foxcroft prob shortly aft 26 Jul 1856 (ibid.). Both Paul and Kesiah are bur in Lee cem, Foxcroft but the stones are broken and the dates are missing
- iv Betsey, b 24 Jul 1788: d Norridgewock 22 Dec 1809: m Mercer 21 August 1809 Joseph Ulrich of Norridgewock (VR)
- v   Charlotte, b 6 Sep 1792: d 1 Jun 1861 and bur family cem New Sharon: m 22 Apr 1814 Josiah Brainerd son of Church & Abigail (Hall) Brainerd [see CHURCH BRAINERD family, *Maine Families*, 1:22]
- vi Jacob, b 23 Oct 1794: d Abbot c1878 (g.s. Adams cem): m Mary ____, b 1802, d 1869 (ibid.)
- vii Sophie, b 10 Sep 1796
- viii Clarissa, b 12 Dec 1798
- ix Irena, b 8 Jun 1804: d bef 16 May 1841 when her husband remarried: m 1 Mar 1832 Telemecus Ballard (New Sharon VR)

Eleanor W. Townsend, 71 Slab Meadow Road, Morris, CT 06763

Lee, Martha   55c   1 - 1 - 3 - 0 - 0
    Berwick Town, York County

MARTHA (CHADBOURNE) LEIGH (wife of Thomas Leigh), b Berwick 26 Apr 1744 dau of Benjamin & Sarah (Heard) Chadbourne (John E. Frost & Joseph C. Anderson II, *Vital Records of Berwick, South Berwick and North Berwick,*

Maine to the Year 1892 [1993], hereafter VR, p. 212) [see BENJAMIN CHADBOURNE family, *Maine Families*, 1:37]: d So. Berwick 10 Jul 1834 ae 89y (g.s., Old Fields cem): m Berwick 1 Oct 1769 Capt. THOMAS LEIGH of Portsmouth NH (Berwick VR, p. 194). Family tradition claims he was b Stoneleigh, Warwickshire, England in 1735 and d in 1815 however no primary records have been found to verify these assertions. Thomas Leigh was a shipmaster. On 22 June 1761, he sailed for the West Indies on the brigantine MERCURY, owned by Samuel Cutts of Portsmouth. The ship was captured by a French privateer and was only released when two of Leigh's crewmen agreed to be held hostage until Leigh could return with ransom money. In October, Leigh sailed again from Portsmouth in the schooner DOLPHIN with the intent of redeeming his crewmen who were held at St. Martins. For some unknown reason, the ransom money failed to reach the captors. One of the crewmen escaped, but the other, William Bennett, contracted smallpox in December and died within four days (William G. Saltonstall, *Ports of Piscataqua* [1987], pp. 38–39). According to one account, Leigh went insane from grief as a result of Bennett's death (Charles W. Brewster, *Rambles About Portsmouth* [1869], second series, pp. 147–50), but this would not seem possible as Leigh married and had children during the next 20 years following the Bennett incident. But he may have become insane later in life as Brewster reported that Leigh had lived for more than 20 years at the Portsmouth NH almshouse, subject to "violent ravings," when William Vaughan took over the superintendence of the almshouse in the early 1800s (ibid., p. 150). This would explain why his wife, Martha, was a head of household at Berwick in 1790 even though Thomas was reportedly still alive. In 1800, Martha and her eldest dau Mary were prob the two women aged 45+ and 26–45, respectively, in the household of her son Thomas Jr. at So. Berwick (USC). No man of Thomas Sr.'s age was present in the same household.

Children
- i Maj. Thomas, b Portsmouth NH 13 Apr 1773 (Berwick VR, p. 502): d 12 Apr 1831 ae 58y (g.s., Old Fields cem, So. Berwick): m 7 Jan 1813 Nancy Baker (Berwick VR, p. 502) [she "of Limerick" on m int], b Westboro MA 24 Oct 1788 (Berwick VR, p. 502) dau of John & Salome (Drury) Baker (Westboro MA VR), d 22 Oct 1853 ae 65y (g.s., Old Fields cem, So. Berwick)
- ii Polly, bp Portsmouth NH 18 Apr 1773 ("Records of the South Church of Portsmouth, N.H.," NEHGR, 82 [1928]:45). Either she d young before her sister Mary was born or the record of her baptism was an error for that of her brother Thomas who was born 5 days before the baptism attributed to Polly. No baptism is on record for Thomas
- iii Mary, bp Portsmouth NH 30 Oct 1775 (NEHGR, 82 [1928]:45): d 4 Oct 1860 ae 84y and bur in same plot as her mother, brother Thomas and other family members (g.s., Old Fields cem, So. Berwick): unm

iv Benjamin Chadbourne, bp Portsmouth NH 9 Nov 1777 (NEHGR, 82 [1928]:45)

v Martha/Patty, b prob Portsmouth NH c1779–1780 (Rev War pension #S35958) and bp Portsmouth NH 10 Jan 1780 (NEHGR, 82 [1928]:45): d Furnessville, Porter Co IN 1863 (g.s., Furnessville cem): m Berwick 25 Jul 1799 Capt. William Furness (Berwick VR, p. 140), b c1759 (pension, op. cit.) and bp at the Berwick 1st Church 10 Nov 1759 son of Robert & Abigail (____) Furness (NEHGR, 82 [1928]:329), d bef 17 Nov 1826 when his wife was termed a widow on a membership list of the Berwick 1st Church (NEHGR, 83 [1929]:152). Martha was a graduate of Berwick Academy, sent there by her mother. William Furness was a Rev War soldier and served with Capt. John Paul Jones on the ship RANGER (Rev War pension #S35958). He was a mariner and ship captain. He is believed to be the same William Furness of Berwick who was captured by Algerians while sailing the vessel OLIVE BRANCH from Lisbon, Portugal in 1792 (Richard E. Winslow III, *Wealth and Honour, Portsmouth During the Golden Age of Privateering, 1775–1815* [1989], pp. 79–80). During the 4 years he was a prisoner in Algiers, he was forced to work as a slave (ibid.). His release was obtained by the American government on 12 Jul 1796 (ibid.). At the time he applied for his Rev War pension in 1820, he was listed as a resident of Arlington VA

Peter G. Parkhurst, 12143 Hilltop Drive, Los Altos Hills, CA 94024

Lowell, Abner   32a   1 - 2 - 6 - 0 - 0
    Township No. 1 (Bucks), Hancock County

ABNER LOWELL, b perhaps Falmouth c1735 of parents unidentified, but perhaps a son of Samuel Lowell who was granted land at Falmouth betw 1728–1740 (Delmar R. Lowell, *The Historic Genealogy of the Lowells of America* [1899], p. 665): d Bucksport 1802 (petition for adm of his estate dated 11 Sep 1802, Han Co Probate #161): m (1) c1758 POLLY AYER who d c1765 (Lowell, op. cit.): m (2) c1766 SARAH WEBBER who d after 1810 (ibid.). The 1800 USC states he was from Portland. Abner had been granted land near Fort Pownal as early as 1765 (BHM, 8:166, 9:24). His accounts from the trading post at Fort Point were entered 5 Jul and 31 Aug 1773 in a "Wast Book" from Fort Pownal (NEHGR, 90 [1936]:85–87). Abner later settled on Lot #15 in Bucksport according to Jonathan Buck's survey of 1790 (map on roll #17, Han Co deeds). Upon his death, part of the lot was set off to his wife, Sarah, and the remainder was divided into fourteen parcels for each of his children (Han Co Probate

#161). Petitioners to have William Homer appt adm of his estate included Abner's two sons, Benjamin and Nathaniel, and four sons-in-law, Abner Clements, Anson Lanpher, Samuel Crage, and Adam Couillard (ibid.).

Children, prob b Bucksport: Lowell, op. cit., pp. 666–67; Han Co Probate #161 & cited sources

By 1st wife Polly Ayer
- i Benjamin, b 11 Mar 1759: d Bucksport 11 Mar 1834 (g.s., Riverside cem): m c1782 Lydia Anice (Lowell, p. 666), b 15 Mar 1761 (ibid.), d 15 Mar 1836 (g.s., Riverside cem). Benjamin was a Rev War soldier and pensioner (Rev War pension #S37194). He settled on part of Lot #28 in Bucksport (1790 map, op. cit.)
- ii Nathaniel, b 28 May 1761: d bef 1830 when not in USC: m (1) c1785–1787 Lois/Louisa Colson dau of Josiah & Elizabeth (____) Colson [see JOSIAH COLSON family, *Maine Families*, 2:52]: m (2) Bucksport 1 Aug 1810 Sarah Kimball (VR). He settled on Lot #38 in Bucksport (1790 map, op. cit.)
- iii Mary/Polly, b c1763: m bef 1790 Anson Lanpher (USC; division of Abner Lowell's estate, op. cit.)

By 2nd wife Sarah Webber, dates of birth speculative, based on census and marriage records
- iv Esther, b c1766: m bef 1790 Samuel Craig Jr. of Orland. Their children are rec at Orland
- v Jane, b c1768: m bef 1800 William Homer who served as administrator of Abner Lowell's estate (op. cit.)
- vi Sarah, b c1770: d bef 1805 when her husband remarried (Bucksport VR): m Prospect 10 Sep 1790 James Colson (VR), b c1770 bro of Lois/Louisa above, d Bucksport 15 Aug 1858 (VR)
- vii Emma, b c1773: m Bucksport 8 Sep 1793 Abner Clements (VR). Their children are rec at Bucksport
- viii Betsey, b c1775: m bef 1800 Adam Couillard. They res in the back settlement of Frankfort called "Goshen" in 1800 (USC)
- ix Abner, b c1778: d Bucksport 26 Jun 1853 (VR): m int Buckstown 22 Apr 1799 his 1st cousin Polly Lowell (BHM, 5:235), b c1782 dau of Stephen Lowell (Lowell, op. cit., p. 667), d bef 1850 (USC). He purchased the easterly end of Lot #18 in Aug 1802 (Han Co deeds 15:57)
- x Samuel, b c1780: prob d unm bef 1820 when his nephew Samuel, the son of Benjamin Lowell above, was no longer called "Jr." (USC)
- xi Phoebe, b c1782: m Bucksport 10 May 1804 Jeremiah Colson (VR), b c1783 bro of Lois/Louisa and James above, d Bucksport 31 Jul 1861 (VR)
- xii Dorcas, b c1784: m Bucksport 1 Dec 1803 Thomas Ladd (VR). Dorcas was called a minor over the age of 14 when her father's estate was settled

xiii   Lucy, b c1786: d Bucksport 21 May 1845 (VR): m Bucksport 5 Nov 1807 her 1st cousin Robert Lowell (VR) son of Stephen Lowell (Lowell, op. cit., p. 668). Lucy was a minor over the age of 14 when her father's estate was settled

xiv   Rachel, b c1788: m Bucksport 21 Oct 1817 Richard B. Fuller (VR). She was a minor over ae 14y when her father's estate was settled

Ralph E. Hillman, 4302 James Dr., Midland, MI 48642

Luce, Seth   47a   1 - 4 - 3 - 0 - 0
Union Town, Lincoln County

SETH LUCE, b Tisbury, Martha's Vineyard MA 11 Oct 1752 son of Joseph & Jedidah (Claghorn) Luce (Charles E. Banks, *The History of Martha's Vineyard, Dukes County, Massachusetts* [1925], 3:258, hereafter Banks): d Union 5 Mar 1833 (VR; John L. Sibley, *A History of the Town of Union, Maine* [repr 1987], p. 468): m 18 Jan 1776 his cousin SARAH LUCE (Banks, 3:258), b Tisbury MA 1757 dau of George & Remember (Merry) Luce of Tisbury MA (ibid.), d Union 8 Sep 1825 (VR). Seth was a Rev War soldier and pensioner, enlisting at Martha's Vineyard (Rev War pension #S31226). They moved to Union in 1789 and settled in the western part of town (Sibley, pp. 66–67).

Children, first 5 b Martha's Vineyard MA, next 4 b Union: births VR Union

  i   Freeman, b 1778: m Eliza Clark and res Union and Newburgh (Sibley, p. 468)

  ii   Jeremiah, b 1780: d Union (Martha F. McCourt and Thomas R. Luce, *The American Descendants of Henry Luce of Martha's Vineyard 1640–1985* [1985], p. 269): m Union 1 Sep 1806 Susannah Hathorne (VR) and res Appleton (Sibley, p. 468)

  iii   Thaddeus, b 13 Jul 1782: m Union 18 Dec 1806 Lavina Pease of Appleton (Union VR), b c1786 dau of Prince Pease (1850 USC; Sibley, p. 468). They res Union

  iv   Obadiah, b 22 Jan 1784: d Harrisville Twp, Medina Co OH 15 Mar 1852 (McCourt & Luce, op. cit., p. 270): m Union 18 Oct 1804 Mary/Mercy Chaffin (VR), b Littleton MA 23 May 1786 dau of Simon & Mercy (Sanderson) Chaffin (William L. Chaffin, *History of Robert Chaffin and His Descendants*, pp. 21–22), d OH 15 Oct 1870 ae 84y (McCourt & Luce, op. cit., p. 270). They moved to OH by 1812

  v   Sarah/Sally, b 10 Sep 1786: m Union 25 Sep 1808 Gorham Butler (VR), b 9 May 1785 son of Christopher & Lydia (Luce) Butler (Sibley, p. 435), fell down dead in his cowyard 17 Sep 1836 (ibid.; VR)

vi   Remember, b 22 Oct 1789
vii Thankful, b 22 Feb 1793: m int Union 1 Dec 1811 Ebenezer Robbins (VR), b 4 Oct 1783 son of David & Elizabeth (Chapman) (Quiggle) Robbins (Sibley, p. 488; VR Union), d 27 May 1857 or 1854 (Union VR). They res Appleton
viii Betsey, b 31 May 1795: m int Union 10 Sep 1839 Caleb Howard (VR)
ix   Maria, b 4 Aug 1800: d of fever Union 8 Sep 1819 (VR; Sibley, p. 469)

Carol F. Nye, RFD 1, Box 388, Belgrade, ME 04917

McCollistor, Archable   32b   3 - 0 - 1 - 0 - 0
Balltown Town [now Jefferson], Lincoln County

ARCHIBALD McALLISTER, b Scotland or Ireland c1735 son of Richard & Ann (Miller) McAllister (Ethel Stanwood Bolton, *Immigrants to New England, 1700-1775* [1931]): d prob Montville betw 1810–1820 (USC): m prob Bedford NH MARY ANNE BOISE (MOCA Rev. soldiers #3574), b c1733 (aged 87y in son Richard's 1820 pension application), d prob Montville betw 1820–1830 (USC). Archibald settled in Newcastle by 1763 and purchased land in 1766 on Dyer's River, later Balltown and Jefferson (plan in Lin Co deeds 5:256). He was a soldier in the Rev War during which time he was commissioned captain on 10 Jul 1776 (MS&S 10:412–13, 418). He served during the retaking of the GRUELL in 1777, was a member of the Penobscot Expedition in 1779 and was on the Eastward campaign in 1780 (ibid.). He sold land in Balltown to son Richard in 1789 and to son Archibald Jr. in 1788 and 1794 (Lin Co deeds 25:75, 33:7–9). By 1800, he was living in Davistown [Montville] (USC) and the census of that year indicated that he had emigrated from Londonderry [prob NH]. In 1810, Archibald and Mary were prob living at Montville in the household of their son Richard to whom Archibald had sold property in 1805 (Lin Co deeds 55:249). By the time Richard made his Rev War pension application in 1820, Mary, aged 87y, was still alive but Archibald was not mentioned (Rev War pension #W2147). Mary does not appear in the 1830 census and therefore prob died in the interim. Archibald and Mary are prob bur in White's Corner cemetery, Montville, where Archibald's son Richard and other members of the family are buried. A small footstone has the initials "A.M.," this possibly being Archibald McAllister's stone.

Children, poss others
   i Richard, b Bedford NH 25 Aug 1760 (Rev War pension #W2147): d Montville 11 Feb 1848 (ibid.; g.s., White's Corner cem): m (1) Peggy Cunningham: m (2) Sarah Thomas [see RICHARD McALLISTER family]

ii   Mary, bp Newcastle 6 Sept 1763 (*The Essex Institute Collections*, 45 [1909]:88)
iii Rosannah, bp Newcastle 27 July 1766 (VR Phippsburg)
iv   Archibald Jr., b 25 Feb 176_ (VR Jefferson), bp Newcastle 12 Jun 1768 (VR Phippsburg): d bef 1820 when his wife was listed as a wid (USC): m Jefferson 26 Dec 1791 Ruth Cunningham (VR), b 5 Feb 177_ (VR Jefferson). Ruth m (2) Jefferson 27 Jul 1823 John Erskine (VR)

Ref: Mabel McAllister Sanderson, "Our McAllister, Marsh, and Gove Kin" [TS, MSL, 1993]

Mabel (McAllister) Sanderson, 8109 Cawdor Ct., McLean, VA 22102

McCollistor, Richard 32b   1 - 1 - 3 - 0 - 0
Balltown Town [now Jefferson], Lincoln County

RICHARD McALLISTER, b Bedford NH 25 Aug 1760 (Rev War pension #W2147) son of Archibald & Mary Anne (Boise) McAllister [see ARCHIBALD McALLISTER family]: d Montville 11 Feb 1848 (pension, op. cit.; g.s., White's Corner cem): m (1) Jefferson 26 Dec 1785 PEGGY CUNNINGHAM (pension, op. cit.) who d 21 Jul 1798 (ibid.): m (2) Whitefield 24 Jan 1799 SARAH THOMAS (VR), b c Jul 1777, d Montville 15 Sep 1865 ae 88y 1m 20d (VR; g.s., White's Corner cem). Richard was a Rev War soldier during the period 1775–1780 (MS&S, 10:412–13). In 1789, he purchased land in Jefferson from his father (Lin Co deeds 33:7) and was afterwards active there in town affairs (Balltown TR 1797–1803). He purchased his father's property in Montville in 1805 (Lin Co deeds 55:249) where he also engaged in many town offices bet 1806–1837 (Montville TR, vols. 1 & 2).

Children by 1st wife, Peggy Cunningham: births VR Montville; and in family Bible rec included in Rev War pension file #W2147
i   Mary, b Jefferson May 1786: d 10 Sep 1792 (Bible rec)
ii Peggy, b Jefferson 19 Mar 1788: d 7 Sep 1792 (Bible rec)
iii William, b Jefferson 23 Apr 1790: d 1 Sep 1792 (Bible rec)
iv Archibald, b Jefferson 23 Mar 1792: d Burnham 18 Mar 1873 ae 84y [sic] (g.s., Mount cem): m (1) int Montville 22 Jan 1814 Betsey Stevens (VR), b c Jan 1792, d Burnham 24 May 1854 ae 62y 4m (g.s., Mount cem): m (2) Montville 4 Mar 1855 Sarah Jewell of Montville (VR), b c1797, d Burnham 13 Apr 1872 ae 75y (g.s., Mount cem). He served in the War of 1812 (Brig. Gen. Gardner W. Pearson, *Records of the Massachusetts*

Volunteer Militia...during the War of 1812–1814 [1913], p. 181). He res first at Montville and moved to Burnham by 1850 (USC)
- v Richard Jr., b Jefferson 13 Apr 1794: d prob Milford in the 1860s (correspondence dated 1864 in family possession): m int Jefferson 18 Sep 1819 Margaret Cunningham (VR). Richard served in the War of 1812 (Pearson, op. cit., p. 181). He res Liberty in 1830 (USC), thereafter Dover ME (Pisc Co deeds, T:314, 26:454–55)
- vi Polly, b Jefferson 10 Jul 1796
- vii Enoch, b Jefferson 18 Jul 1798: d 24 Dec 1798 (Bible rec)

Children by 2nd wife, Sarah Thomas: births family Bible rec
- viii Guy, b Jefferson 12 Jul 1799: d Freedom 11 Oct 1848 (g.s., Pleasant Hill cem): m Jefferson 29 Dec 1825 Jane Trask (VR), b 12 Jun 1805 (g.s.), d 5 Apr 1873 (g.s, Pleasant Hill cem, Freedom). She m (2) Jefferson 16 Jan 1853 David Merry of Boothbay (Jefferson VR)
- ix Margaret, b Jefferson 28 Jul 1800: d Jefferson 24 Apr 1857 ae 57y (g.s., White's Corner cem): m int Montville 3 May 1823 David Bartlett (VR), b c1775–76, d Jefferson 29 May 1855 ae 79y 6m (g.s., White's Corner cem)
- x Sally, b Jefferson 20 Apr 1802: d 11 Aug 1846 (Bible rec): m Oswell Atkinson, b c Mar 1809, d Montville 16 Oct 1881 ae 72y 7m 11d (VR). He m (2) int Montville 9 Jun 1848 Abby Plummer of Searsmont (Montville VR)
- xi Abiel, b Jefferson 24 Jun 1803: d 1870 (g.s., White's Corner cem, Montville): m (1) Montville 3 Jan 1828 Lucinda Atkinson Nash (VR), b 1801, d 1865 (g.s., White's Corner cem, Montville): m (2) Jefferson 1 Jan 1867 Sarah F. Peaslee (VR). Abiel is bur with his 1st wife and son Cushman
- xii Lydia, b prob Montville 26 Apr 1805: m Montville 15 Oct 1826 John H. Thomas (VR) who d Montville 14 Sep 1857 (g.s., White's Corner cem)
- xiii Cushman, b Montville 9 Oct 1808 [note that a Job Cushman McAllister, b 10 Nov 1807, is rec in the Montville VR]: d Montville 18 Nov 1838 ae 30y 1m (VR) [g.s., in White's Corner cem, states d 10 Nov 1838]: m int Montville 6 Mar 1837 Martha Poland (VR)
- xiv Alfred, b Montville 9 Jan 1810: m int Montville 13 Dec 1834 Waity P. Foster of Freedom (Montville VR), b c1815, d Freedom 25 Oct 1848 ae 33y (g.s., Pleasant Hill cem)
- xv Isaac Case, b Montville 21 Apr 1812: m Montville 29 Mar 1840 Rosanna Atkinson (VR)
- xvi Rosannah, b Montville 29 Dec 1815: d Jefferson 17 Mar 1901 (g.s., Trask-Ford cem): m Montville 6 Jun 1839 Christopher Erskin of Jefferson (Elizabeth M. Mosher & Isabel Morse Maresh, *Marriage Records of Waldo County, Maine Prior to 1892* [1990], p. 38), b c1798, d Jefferson 8 May 1867 ae 69y (g.s., Trask-Ford cem). [Note, a g.s. in Trask-Ford cem, Jefferson, gives him a 1st wife Rosannah who d 9 Dec 1835 ae 51y (sic)]

xvii Thomas, b Montville 2 Sep 1816: d Jefferson 18 Sep 1879 ae 63y (g.s., Trask-Ford cem): m int Montville 7 Jun 1838 Sarah Bachelder of Freedom (Montville VR)

xviii Harriet N., b Montville 5 Feb 1820: d Jefferson 23 Dec 1899 (g.s., Hopkins cem): m int Montville 30 Apr 1842 Benjamin Harris (VR)

Mabel (McAllister) Sanderson, 8109 Cawdor Ct., McLean, VA 22102

M^ccluer, thomas   48a   1 - 1 - 2 - 0 - 0
Waldoborough Town [s/b Bristol], Lincoln County

THOMAS McCLUER/McCLURE, b poss Boston MA c1754–55 (based on his age at death): d of apoplexy Boston MA 3 Jun 1826 "Saturday morning, aged 71" (*Columbian Centinel*, issue of 7 Jun 1826; Suffolk Co MA probate #28016): m (1) Bristol 21 Jan 1787 NANCY HUNTER (Dodge's *Bristol*, 2:140), b Bristol 13 Nov 1766 dau of Henry Hunter & his 2nd wife Sarah Wyer (ibid., 1:375) [see HENRY HUNTER family], d Bristol "in childbed" 28 May 1800 in her 34th y (family record as written in Henry Hunter's Bible, in possession of submitter; Dodge's *Bristol*, 1:375): m (2) at 1st Presbyterian Church, Boston MA 2 Feb 1802 MARY WILSON (*Early History of Boston, Boston Marriages from 1752 to 1809* [1903], hereafter *Boston Marriages*, p. 350), b c1765 dau of "Widow Wilson" (*Columbian Centinel*, issue of 13 Feb 1802), d Boston MA of influenza 11 Dec 1831 ae 66y "consort of the late Thomas McClure, Esq." (VR; *Columbian Centinel*, issue of 17 Dec 1831). Thomas and Mary were bur in Tomb #17, Park St. Church, Boston MA, but were later moved to Forest Hills cem, Boston MA (cem records). When Thomas's real estate in Maine was divided on 7 Sep 1829, his heirs were his daughter Lucretia Peters, his son Charles, two children of his daughter Eliza Thayer, deceased, his son Thomas, his son Alexander and one daughter of his daughter Nancy Murdock, deceased (Lin Co Probate, 31:133–38).

Children by 1st wife, Nancy Hunter
  i Ruth, b prob Bristol c1788–89: d Boston MA 29 May 1807 ae 18y (g.s., Forest Hills cem): unm
  ii Eliza, b prob Bristol c1790–91: d Braintree MA 11 Aug 1818 ae 27y (g.s., Forest Hills cem, Boston MA; *Columbian Centinel*, issue of 19 Aug 1818): m Boston MA 20 Jul 1812 Jechonias Thayer as his 1st wife (*Boston Marriages*), b Braintree MA 24 Jul 1786 son of Solomon A. & Elizabeth (Thayer) Thayer (Bezaleel Thayer, *Memorial of...Richard and Thomas Thayer* [1874], p. 637), d Boston MA 28 Oct 1876 (adm of his estate, Suffolk Co MA probate #59283)

iii Nancy, b prob Bristol c1791–92: d "in Boston, Tuesday last" in childbirth 16 May 1815 ae 22y (VR; *Columbian Centinel*, issue of Saturday, 20 May 1815): m Boston MA 3 Jun 1813 George Murdock as his 1st wife (*Boston Marriages*, 2:79; *Columbian Centinel*, issue of 12 Jun 1813), b c1779, d of consumption at Boston MA 27 Dec 1837 ae 58y (VR). He was a merchant. Nancy is bur in Forest Hills cem, Boston MA. George and his 2nd wife are bur in an adjoining lot

iv Lucretia, b Bristol 26 May 1793 (Edmond Frank Peters and Eleanor Bradley Peters, *Peters of New England* [1903], p. 137): d Forest Hill [Boston MA] 14 Sep 1862 (MA VR): m Boston MA 26 May 1817 Edward Dyer Peters (*Boston Marriages*, 2:182), b Bluehill ME (as stated on the death records of his children) 14 Nov 1785 son of John & Mary (Dyer) Peters (g.s.; Peters, op. cit., p. 137), d Forest Hill [Boston MA] 21 Oct 1856 ae 70y 11m 7d (g.s., Forest Hills cem)

v Thomas Jr., b Bristol Jan 1800 (g.s.): d Bristol 7 Aug 1863 ae 63y 7m, "found dead in bed in his house and was buried at night" (Dodge's *Bristol*, 1:467; g.s., Old Walpole Meeting House cem): m int Bristol 19 Jan 1824 Margaret R. McKown (Dodge's *Bristol*, 2:180), b Bristol c1802, d Bristol 1 Nov 1862 ae 60y (ibid., 1:467)

vi poss Alexander, who d young. [A son Alexander is assigned to this marriage by James Harold Hunter in *John Hunter, A History and Genealogy of his Descendants* [1986], p. 4, and by Leland E. Peary in the "Leland Edwin Peary papers," housed at the Cutler Memorial Library, Farmington ME. The 1790 census entry has one male, under 16, who is unaccounted for.]

Children by 2nd wife, Mary Wilson: based on cemetery and probate records

vii Mary Ann, b prob Boston MA c May–Jun 1803: d Boston MA 13 Sep 1804 ae 15m (VR) and bur Forest Hills cem, Boston MA

viii Charles, alive as late as 7 Sep 1829 when he is included in the distribution of his father's property in Maine (Lin Co Probate, 31:131–38), but prob d by 11 Jan 1830 when he did not sign off with the other heirs (ibid.). He was not included in the division of Thomas McClure's property in Boston MA on 11 May 1835 (Suffolk Co Probate, 41:481)

ix Alexander Wilson, b Boston MA 8 May 1808 (*Amherst College Biographical Record 1963* [1963], p. 7): d Cannonsburg PA 17 Sep 1865 (ibid.): m South Hadley MA 25 Dec 1832 Mary Brewster Gould dau of Rev. Vinson Gould of Southampton MA (ibid.; *Columbia Centinel*, issue of 16 Jan 1833)

Chuckie Blaney, 11 Hollis Street, Sherborn, MA 01770-1254

Maddox, Joshua   32b   4 - 0 - 3 - 0 - 0
Township No. 6 (West Side of Union River), Hancock County

JOSHUA MADDOCKS, b Berwick 1 Apr 1732, bp Berwick 1st Church 20 Aug 1732 son of Caleb & Elizabeth (Smith) Maddocks (H. Freemont Maddocks, "The Maddocks Genealogical Chart" [1907], hereafter "Maddocks Chart," copy at MSA; NEHGR, 82 [1928]:91; 28 Jan 1724/5 marriage of Caleb & Elizabeth in Berwick VR): d Ellsworth aft 1790: m 29 Aug 1754 SUSANNAH AUSTIN (BHM, 3:220), b 20 Sep 1736 (ibid.) prob dau of Ichabod & Elizabeth (Billings) Austin (based on the naming of one of their children Ichabod Austin Maddocks; Susannah was prob one of the children of widow Elizabeth Austin mentioned in John E. Frost, *Maine Probate Abstracts* [1991], 6/208; marriage of Ichabod & Elizabeth in Biddeford VR). Joshua was of Biddeford in 1753 (William MacBeth Pierce, *Old Hancock Families*, p. 72). As early as 1771, he and his family settled at Union River (now Ellsworth) (BHM, 3:220). In 1784 he built the first grist mill on the banks of the Union River (Albert H. Davis, *History of Ellsworth, Maine* [1927], pp. 22, 50). That same year he was one of the inhabitants who sent a petition to the MA General Court asking for a grant of lands (ibid., p. 51).

Children, all but youngest b Saco/Biddeford area: "Maddocks Chart"; BHM, 3:220

  i   Joshua, b 20 Jun 1755: m and had children

  ii Caleb, b 30 Nov 1757: d 1838 (Fisher's *Soldiers*, p. 499): m (1) Sarah Flye dau of Jonathan & Phebe (Tuttle) Flye (Pierce, op. cit., p. 73) [see CALEB MADDOCKS family, *Maine Families*, 2:191]: m (2) Mary _____ (Fisher's *Soldiers*, p. 499). He was a Rev War soldier (ibid.). He resided Union River and later Ellsworth in 1833 (ibid.)

  iii Ichabod Austin, b 1 Mar 1759: d Franklin 1807 (Fisher's *Soldiers*, p. 499): m Dorcas _____ who d Bangor 28 May 1845 ae 89y (ibid.; BHM, 4:40). He was a Rev War soldier, enlisting as a private in Capt. Eleazer Crabtree's Co 24 Aug 1775 and discharged 31 Dec 1775 (Pierce, op. cit., p. 73)

  iv Elizabeth, b 27 Dec 1761: m Nathaniel Jellison of Ellsworth (BHM, 3:220)

  v   Samuel, b 12 Dec 1762: d Ellsworth 5 Nov 1855 ("Maddocks Chart"): m (1) int Wells 16 Oct 1784 Abigail Day both of Wells (VR), bp 13 May 1757 dau of Benjamin & Mary (Taylor) Day (William S. Thompson, "The Records of Kennebunk and Kennebunkport" [TS, MHS], 3:327; will of Benjamin Day in John E. Frost, *Maine Probate Abstracts* [1991], 18/145): m (2) Rebecca Clements ("Maddocks Chart")

  vi William, b 4 Apr 1764: m Hannah Dyer ("Maddocks Chart")

  vii John, b 9 Mar 1766: m Catherine Hilton of Surry ("Maddocks Chart")

  viii Oliver, b 10 May 1768: m Bangor 3 Jun 1801 Betsey Bunker ("Maddocks Chart")

ix Susanna, b 8 Dec 1770: d c1843 (John Wentworth, *The Wentworth Genealogy* [1878], 2:430–31): m as his 2nd wife Moses Wentworth (ibid.), b Somersworth NH 6 Apr 1766 son of Nathaniel & Patience (Abbot) Wentworth (ibid.)

x Rebecca, b Ellsworth 4 Dec 1772: m Abraham Tourtelotte Jr. ("Maddocks Chart"), b RI c1769 son of Abraham and Mallason (Walling) Tourtelotte of Kenduskeag Plt [see ABRAHAM TOURTILOTTE family, *Maine Families*, 3:279], d 27 Jul 1849 ae 80y (g.s., Elmwood cem, No. Ellsworth)

Mrs. Dorothy Moore Tower, 65 Matthew Drive, Brunswick, ME 04011

Marrow, Daniel   51b   1 - 2 - 5 - 0 - 0
   Winthrop Town, Lincoln County

DANIEL MARROW, b Reading MA 1735 (MOCA Rev Soldiers): d Winthrop 3 Apr 1812 (g.s., Lakeview cem): m Medway MA 29 May 1759 ELIZABETH HARDING (VR) [Everett S. Stackpole, in his *History of Winthrop, Maine* [1925], p. 494, states that Daniel was a resident of Holliston MA at the time of his marriage], b Medway MA 14 Feb 1738 dau of Ens. Samuel & Mary (Cutler) Harding (VR), d Winthrop 12 Jan 1827 (g.s., Lakeview cem). Daniel served in the Rev War as a private in Capt. Joshua Partridge's Co. of militia in Col. John Smith's regiment which marched on the alarm of 19 Apr 1775, service of 9 days (MS&S, 10:235). He was also included on the list of men returned by a committee of the town of Medway 13 Apr 1778 as having rendered service at various times subsequent to 19 Apr 1775 (ibid.). He was a proprietor of Lot #1 in Winthrop which he purchased on 7 Apr 1779, at the time listed as a resident of Hopkinton MA (*History of Winthrop*, p. 32). He also purchased Lot #2, paying £490, lawful money of the Continental Currency, for each lot (ibid.). He served on the Committee of Correspondence in Winthrop in 1782 and on the Committee of Safety in 1783 (ibid., p. 119).

Children: births first 9 VR Medway MA; *History of Winthrop*, pp. 494–95
   i Hannah, b 4 Jan 1760
   ii Elizabeth, b 20 Apr 1762: d 9 May 1827 (*History of Winthrop*, pp. 612–13): m 1 Jan 1794 Jonas Stevens as his 2nd wife (ibid., p. 612), b New Ipswich NH 20 Apr 1763 son of Joseph & Elizabeth (Sawtelle) Stevens (ibid., pp. 609–10), d 14 Sep 1830 (ibid., p. 613)
   iii Daniel, b 5 May 1764: d Phillips 3 Jul 1847 ae 83y (g.s., Number Six Rd. cem): m Winthrop 20 Sep 1786 Hannah Chandler (VR), b New Ipswich NH 19 Jan 1768 dau of John & Lydia (Taylor) Chandler (VR) [see JOHN

CHANDLER family, *Maine Families*, 1:42], d Phillips 27 Jun 1856 ae 89y (g.s., Number Six Rd. cem)
iv   Eben, b 27 Sep 1766: d 24 Sep 1844 (*History of Winthrop*, p. 495): m 5 Jan 1792 Abigail Fisher (ibid.), b 16 Jul 1771 dau of William Fisher of Wrentham MA (ibid.), d 16 Jan 1859 (ibid.). Eben lived on his father's homestead at Winthrop (ibid.).
v   Timothy, b 21 Sep 1768: d 17 Sep 1775 (*History of Winthrop*, p. 495)
vi   Rhoda, b 17 Feb 1771: d aft 1820 when she was a head of household at Greene (USC): m Winthrop 13 Nov 1790 Eleazer Keen of Greene [see ELEAZER KEEN family]
vii Sarah, b 22 Jan 1773
viii Catherine, b 20 May 1775 [perhaps she and her sister Celia were one and the same person, see below]
ix   Samuel Harding, b 29 Oct 1777: drowned 21 Dec 1801 while skating on Cobbosseecontee Pond (*History of Winthrop*, p. 496): m 1798 Chloe Titus of Winthrop (ibid.). She m (2) 16 Apr 1807 James Stevens and moved to Strong (ibid.).
x   Celia, m Elijah Norcross of Readfield (*History of Winthrop*, p. 524). [One Elijah Norcross, b Newton MA 16 Feb 1757 son of Samuel & Mary (Wiswall) Norcross, d 1802, reportedly m "Catherine" Marrow and res Readfield—see SAMUEL NORCROSS family, *Maine Families*, 2:207. The Hallowell *Eastern Star* reported on 10 Mar 1795 the marriage of "Katy" Marrow of Winthrop and Elijah Norcross (David C. & Elizabeth K. Young, *Vital Records from Maine Newspapers* [1993], p. 382)]
xi   Reuben, b Winthrop 14 May 1780, m 1801 Sally Stevens of Winthrop (*History of Winthrop*, p. 495). He left Winthrop in 1811 (ibid.)

Eunice Calvert, 20 Flower Lane, Marcellus, NY 13108-1326

---

martin (widow)   48c   1 - 1 - 3 - 0 - 0
   Waldoborough Town [s/b Bristol], Lincoln County

MARY (STUARD) MARTIN (widow of William Martin), b Georgetown 2 Jul 1734 dau of Charles & Mary (_____) Stuard (VR): d Bristol 8 Nov 1828 ae 94y (Dodge's *Bristol*, 1:492): m int Georgetown 30 Dec 1758 WILLIAM MARTIN of Fort Halifax (Georgetown VR), b early 1730s prob son of John & Margaret (_____) Martin of Brunswick (Cum Co deeds 8:307 in which William called John Martin Jr. of Brunswick his brother; while no birth rec for William is found in the Brunswick VR, other children of John and Margaret are recorded including John Jr., above, who m Lettice Wilson—a name given by William and Mary to one of their daus). William d Bristol bef 1790 (USC). The adm of William's estate was granted on 20 Sep 1791 to his wid Mary (William D. Patterson, *The Probate Records of Lincoln County, Maine* [repr 1991], p. 206). William bought and sold land in Brunswick and Bristol before moving permanently to Bristol betw 1765–70. On 8 May 1776, he was commissioned a 2nd Lieut. in Capt. James Hilton's 7th Bristol company, Col. William Jones's 3rd Lin Co regiment during the Rev War (MS&S, 10:292). He was a constable at Bristol during the 1770s.

Children: births VR Bristol
- i Margaret, b Brunswick 11 Apr 1760: m 30 Jul 1789 Joseph Butler of Union (Dodge's *Bristol*, 2:193), b Framingham MA Apr 1764 son of Phinehas & Bathsheba (Graves) Butler (John L. Sibley, *History of the Town of Union* [1851], pp. 436–37)
- ii Mary, b 22 Oct 1762
- iii William, b 24 Nov 1764: d 29 May 1845 ae 80y 7m (g.s. Old Bremen cem, Bremen): m (1) Abigail _____, b c1769, d 24 Dec 1806 ae 37y (g.s., Old Bremen cem, Bremen): m (2) 28 Nov 1810 Lucy Osier (Dodge's *Bristol*, 2:194), b c Feb 1781, d 9 Jun 1868 ae 87y 3m 16d (g.s., Old Bremen cem)
- iv Elizabeth, b 3 Apr 1766: m Samuel Peabody (C. M. Endicott, "The Peabody Family," NEHGR, 3 [1849]:370), b 1773 son of Samuel & Ruth (Trask) Peabody (ibid., 2 [1848]:368, 3 [1849]:370). They settled at Dixmont (ibid.)
- v Lettice Wilson, b 22 May 1769
- vi Charles Stuart, b 17 Oct 1772: poss the same who m Bristol 3 Feb 1793 Lucy Martin (Dodge's *Bristol*, 2:192). The adm of the estate of Charles Martin of Cushing, mariner, was granted on 19 Sep 1797 to his wid, Lucy Martin of Bristol (Patterson, op. cit., p. 298)
- vii John, b 23 Aug 1774: d prob at Appleton 1845–50: m Bristol 23 Dec 1798 Hannah Cudworth (Dodge's *Bristol*, 2:193), b Scituate MA 18 Nov 1773 dau of Joseph & Lydia (Tower) Cudworth of Scituate MA (VR; W. John Calder, *A History of the Ancestors and Descendants of James Cudworth of Scituate, Massachusetts* [1941]), d prob Appleton 1845–49
- viii Sarah, b 12 Sep 1776

Kenneth Alton Clark, 36125 Kilarney Rd., #D208, Willoughby, OH 44094

---

martin, thomas   48b   1 - 0 - 2 - 0 - 0
Waldoborough Town [s/b Bristol], Lincoln County

THOMAS MARTIN, bp 1st Church Marblehead MA 8 Oct 1721 son of Thomas & Eleanor (Knott) Martin (VR): m (1) St. Michael's Episcopal Church, Marblehead MA 20 Nov 1746 MARY GOURDON/GORDON (VR), bp

Marblehead MA 28 Jan 1728 dau of Henry & Tabitha (____) Gordon (VR), bur Marblehead MA 26 Sep 1747 (VR): m (2) Marblehead 27 Feb 1750 SARAH GOODWIN (VR), bp Marblehead MA 10 Jul 1726 dau of William & Joan (Curtis) Goodwin (VR). Thomas settled in the Bremen section of Old Bristol. In 1771, he sold land to Hezekiah Eggleston in return for help in setting up a water mill (Lin Co deeds 8:166, 8:217). In 1797, Thomas sold 100 acres to his son-in-law, Joshua Webber, including the sawmill and a landing at Muscongus Harbor (Lin Co deeds 26:271).

Child by 1st wife, Mary Gordon
- i Richard, bp Marblehead MA 12 Jul 1747 (VR): d Marblehead MA 1 Oct 1747 ae 3m (VR)

Children by 2nd wife, Sarah Goodwin: births/bps VR Marblehead MA
- ii Hannah, bp 3 Feb 1751
- iii Samuel, bp 29 Oct 1752: m Lynn MA 26 Aug 1780 Mary Foot of Lynn MA (Marblehead MA VR)
- iv Mary, bp 18 Aug 1754: m Marblehead MA 11 Dec 1774 James Fuller (VR)
- v   Richard, bp 20 Jun 1756: d St. George 1799 ae 43y (g.s., Ridge cem, Martinsville): m (1) Bristol 4 Aug 1778 Sarah (Le)Ballester of Bristol (Dodge's *Bristol*, 2:7) who d St. George 1790 ae 38y (g.s., Ridge cem, Martinsville): m (2) Mary ____ who d St. George 1805 ae 52y (g.s., Ridge cem, Martinsville)
- vi Sarah, b 23 Apr 1758: d Bristol 24 Jan 1844 ae 85y 9m 7d (Dodge's *Bristol*, 1:731): m Bristol 4 Feb 1777 Arunah Weston (ibid., 2:193), b Duxbury MA 4 Feb 1746 son of Eliphas & Priscilla (____) Weston (VR) [see ARUNAH WESTON family, *Maine Families*, 3:299]
- vii Eleanor, bp 15 Jul 1759: d 12 Feb 1833 ae 73y (Eaton's *Thomaston*, 2:141): m (1) Bristol 15 Jan 1778 Timothy Kimball (Dodge's *Bristol*, 2:192) who d bef 12 Jan 1788 when his wife filed intentions to remarry: m (2) int Bristol 12 Jan 1788 Samuel Bartlett of Thomaston (ibid., 2:161), b 1754 (Eaton's *Thomaston*, 2:141), d 9 Feb 1819 (ibid.). On 16 Jan 1788, Eleanor, widow, was appt adm of the estate of her husband, Timothy Kimball, late of Bristol, mariner (William D. Patterson, *The Probate Records of Lincoln County, Maine* [repr 1991], p. 163). One of the sureties was her bro-in-law, Arunah Weston. In 1791, she, now Eleanor Bartlett, and her 2nd husband, Samuel Bartlett, were listed as joint administrators (ibid.)
- viii Rachel, bp 18 Oct 1761: m Bristol 23 May 1779 Timothy Weston (Dodge's *Bristol*, 2:193)
- ix Elizabeth, bp 15 Jan 1764: d in infancy
- x   Ann, bp 24 Feb 1765

xi   Elizabeth/Betsey, bp 2 Aug 1767: d Bristol 12 Nov 1841 ae 75y (Dodge's *Bristol*, 1:718): m Bristol 26 Jan 1791 Joshua Webber (ibid., 2:292), b c1761, d Bristol 3 Mar 1819 ae 58y (ibid., 1:719)
xii Lucy, bp 15 Jul 1770: m Beverly MA 22 Jul 1787 John Vickery Jr. of Beverly MA (VR)

Kenneth Alton Clark, 36125 Kilarney Rd., #D208, Willoughby, OH 44094

Maxwell, Alexander   70b   1 - 1 - 6 - 0 - 0
Wells Town, York County

ALEXANDER MAXWELL, bp 1st Church Wells 4 Dec 1748 son of David & Abigail (Morrison) Maxwell ("Records of the First Church of Wells, Me.," NEHGR, 75 [1921]:113; parents m int on 12 Jul 1746 in Wells VR): d Wells 13 Mar 1843 ae 94y and bur Walnut Grove cem, Ogunquit ("Incriptions from Gravestones at Wells, Me.," NEHGR, 93 [1939]:239): m Wells 17 Sep 1772 PHILADELPHIA RANKIN (VR), b Wells 14 Nov 1751 dau of James & Philadelphia (Nason) Rankin (VR; parents m int rec at Kittery 19 Dec 1741), d Wells 14 Jun 1821 ae 70y and bur with her husband (NEHGR, 93 [1939]:240). Alexander was a Rev War soldier (Fisher's *Soldiers*, p. 511) and in 1779 served on a committee of correspondence at Wells (Edward E. Bourne, *The History of Wells and Kennebunk* [1875], p. 515). His grandfather, Gershom Maxwell, a tailor of Scottish origin, came to Wells in 1717 and settled on the east side of the Old Post Road [now Rte. 1] (YCGSJ, 3 [1988]:2:33). The stretch of road just north of the Ogunquit village center where his descendants built their homes became known as Scotch Hill (ibid.).

Children, b Wells: births VR Wells
  i   Moses, b 29 May 1774: d Wells 30 May 1774 (VR)
  ii   Aaron, b 6 Aug 1775: d Wells 8 Mar 1781 (VR)
  iii Daniel, b 28 Dec 1777: d Wells 24 Jan 1782 (VR)
  iv   David, b 4 May 1780: d Wells 29 Dec 1874 ae 94y 7m (g.s., Walnut Grove cem, Ogunquit, NEHGR, 93 [1939]:239): m Wells 7 Oct 1802 Mary Staples (VR), bp 1st Church Wells 13 Oct 1782 dau of John & Tabitha (Littlefield) Staples (NEHGR, 72 [1922]:188), d 31 Mar 1867 ae 84y 6m (g.s., Walnut Grove cem, Ogunquit, NEHGR, 93 [1939]:240)
  v   Philadelphia, b 1 Jul 1782: d Wells 1855 (g.s., Oceanview cem, NEHGR, 93 [1939]:57): m Wells 27 Apr 1806 James Winn (VR), bp 1st Church Wells 25 Aug 1782 son of Daniel & Olive (Berry) Winn, d 1861 (g.s., Oceanview cem, NEHGR, 93 [1939]:57)

vi   Sarah, b 31 Dec 1784: d York 26 Feb 1863 ae 78y 2m (Lester M. Bragdon & John E. Frost, *Vital Records of York, Maine* [1992], hereafter VR, p. 637, citing g.s., Swett Lot, Ground Nut Hill Rd.): m Wells 2 Feb 1809 John Swett (VR), b c Jun 1783 (g.s.) and prob he bp 1st Church York 13 Aug 1783 son of Nathaniel & Sarah (Carlile) Swett (YCGSJ, 5 [1990]:1: 18), d 15 Sep 1860 ae 77y 3m (York VR, p. 637, bur with his wife)

vii   Elizabeth, b 11 Jul 1787: m int Wells 3 Aug 1811 Nathaniel Littlefield (VR), bp Wells 1st Church 22 Jul 1788 son of Daniel & Sarah (Perkins) Littlefield (NEHGR, 76 [1922]:114), alive 1860 (USC). He m (2) Mary _____ (1860 USC)

viii Lucy, b 29 Jan 1790: d York 8 Jun 1855 ae 65y (VR, p. 434): m int York 24 Mar 1815 John Trafton of York (VR, p. 202), perhaps he who d York 2 Nov 1830 (VR, p. 463)

ix   Olive, b 13 Oct 1792: m int Wells 16 Dec 1815 Daniel Felch of Newburyport MA (VR)

x   Persis, b 10 Sep 1795: d 3 Apr 1886 ae 90y 6m (g.s., Walnut Grove cem, Ogunquit, NEHGR, 93 [1919]:241): m 1826 Oliver Stevens (YCGSJ, 3 [1988]:2:36), b c May 1796, d Wells 31 Jan 1867 ae 70y 8m (g.s., Walnut Grove cem, Ogunquit, NEHGR, 93 [1919]:241)

Joseph C. Anderson II, 5337 Del Roy Drive, Dallas, TX 75229

Melcher, Joseph   12b   5 - 2 - 4 - 0 - 0
Brunswick Town, Cumberland County

JOSEPH MELCHER, b prob Arundel/Kennebunkport c1733 prob but unproven son of Edward & Elizabeth (Bailey) Melcher (McLellan's *Gorham*, p. 616): d Topsham 21 Aug 1821 in his 86th y (VR): m [Topsham?] 1757 MARY COBB of Gorham (Topsham VR), b c1738 dau of Nathaniel & Bethiah (Harding) Cobb of Gorham (McLellan's *Gorham*, p. 616), d Topsham 18 May 1825 in her 87 y (VR). Joseph settled in Bunganuc in Brunswick and was enumerated there in the 1790, 1800, 1810 and 1820 censuses. He was a private in Capt. George White's company in 1777 (George A. & Henry Wheeler, *History of Brunswick, Topsham & Harpswell, Maine* [1878], p. 881; Fisher's *Soldiers*, p. 530). He was a housewright (Wheeler, p. 843).

Children: births from Joseph Melcher family Bible rec included in Mary Pelham Hill, "Melcher, Family Notes" [TS, MHS, 1931], hereafter "Melcher Notes"
  i   Mary, b 24 Nov 1759: d in infancy
  ii   Joseph, b 2 Dec 1760: d in Rev War service 18 Oct 1777 ae 16y 10m (Topsham VR) while serving in Capt. George White's company

iii Noah, b c1763 and bp 1st Parish Brunswick 29 Apr 1763 ("Records of the First Parish Church, Brunswick, Maine" in "Early Maine Records" [TS, DAR, MSL], 2:49–65): d Topsham 21 Jul 1836 ae 73y (VR): m Brunswick 20 Jan 1789 Susanna Purinton (VR) [see NOAH MELCHER family]

iv Nathaniel, b c1765: d Topsham 20 Jul 1840 ae 75y (VR): m (1) Topsham 31 Jul 1796 Rebeckah Purinton (VR), b 19 May 1772 dau of James & Priscilla (Harding) Purinton (Topsham VR) [see JAMES PURRINGTON family, *Maine Families*, 1:229], d Topsham 22 Nov 1802 ae 30y (VR): m (2) cert Topsham 25 Sep 1805 Lucy (Matthews) Spear (VR; Brunswick VR). Nathaniel res Brunswick

v Mary, b c1766: d 10 May 1839 ae 73y ("Melcher Notes"): m Brunswick 22 Apr 1786 Thomas Merryman (VR), b Harpswell c1765 son of Thomas & Sarah (Bailey) Merryman (Rev. Charles N. Sinnett, "Walter Merryman of Harpswell, Maine and His Descendants" [1905], p. 6)

vi Abner, twin, b 25 Dec 1769: d Topsham 5 May 1858 ae 88y 4m 11d (VR): m (1) Brunswick 25 Dec 1798 Mary Hunt (VR): m (2) int Brunswick 9 Jun 1805 Anne/Nancy Morse/Moss (VR), b Brunswick 8 Nov 1779 dau of Joseph & Hannah (____) Moss (VR; Mrs. Victor L. Warren, "Historical & Genealogical Items Presented to MHS by Maine Chapters D.A.R." [TS, 1931–32], p. 267), d Brunswick 14 Dec 1873 (ibid.; g.s. Growstown cem). Nancy was a sister of Sarah & Benjamin Moss/Morse who m children of Noah Melcher [see NOAH MELCHER family]

vii Josiah, twin, b 25 Dec 1769: d Topsham 11 Dec 1849 ae 79y 11m 16d (VR; "Melcher Notes"): m (1) Brunswick 28 Dec 1797 Peggey Dunning (VR), perhaps the Margaret Dunning b c1776–77 dau of Andrew & Margaret (Miller) Dunning (NEHGR, 74 [1920]:104), "Mrs. Peggy [sic] wife of Josiah" d 13 May 1800 ae 23y (g.s., Old Maquoit cem, Brunswick): m (2) int Brunswick 1 Nov 1802 Nancy Anderson of Freeport (Brunswick VR), b c1781, d Brunswick 2 Apr 1842 ae 61y (Topsham VR; "Melcher Notes")

viii Samuel, d in infancy

ix Samuel 2d, b c1776: d Topsham 15 Oct 1844 ae 68y (VR; "Melcher Notes"): m (1) Harpswell 26 Jan 1804 Elizabeth Melcher ("Rev. Elisha Eaton and Rev. Samuel Eaton, Records of Harpswell Congregational Church" [TS, MHS], hereafter Eaton CR), b c1777, d Feb 1804 ae 27y (g.s., Old Maquoit cem, Brunswick): m (2) Brunswick 2 Feb 1809 Sally Litchfield dau of Samuel & Sarah (Curtis) Litchfield of Freeport (NEHGR, 9 [1855]:218; VR Brunswick which mistakenly gives her name as Sally "Litttlefield")

x Myriam, b 13 May 1777: d Topsham 13 Apr 1866 ae 88y 11m (VR): m Harpswell 28 Jan 1806 James Purinton Jr. (Eaton CR), b 25 Feb 1777 bro of Rebeckah above, d Topsham 8 Aug 1862 ae 85y 6m (VR)

xi Elizabeth, b 28 May 1779: d Topsham Mar 1850 ae 71y (VR): m _____ Miller [the Brunswick VR include the birth of a John Miller Jr. on 19 Sep 1799 to John & Elizabeth Miller]
xii Joseph, b 8 Jul 1782: d 6 Nov 1802 ae 20y 4m, castaway on Ipsage Carr in a gale (Topsham VR)

Thomas P. Doherty, 3321 N. Rockfield Dr., Devonshire, Wilmington, DE 19810-3238

Melcher, Noah   12b   2 - 1 - 1 - 0 - 0
Brunswick Town, Cumberland County

NOAH MELCHER, b c1763 and bp 1st Parish Brunswick 29 Apr 1763 ("Records of the First Parish Church, Brunswick, Maine," in "Early Maine Records" [TS, DAR, MSL], 2:49ff) son of Joseph & Mary (Cobb) Melcher [see JOSEPH MELCHER family]: d Topsham 21 Jul 1836 ae 73y (VR): m (1) Brunswick 20 Jan 1789 SUSANNA PURINTON (VR), b Topsham 26 Jan 1770 dau of James & Priscilla (Harding) Purinton (VR) [see JAMES PURRINGTON family, *Maine Families*, 1:229], d Brunswick 6 May 1819 ae 49y (g.s., Growstown cem): m (2) Topsham 24 Feb 1820 MARGARET (PATTEN) SWETT (VR) dau of Capt. Actor & Jane (McLellan) Patten (Topsham VR) and wid of Joseph Swett (ibid.).

Children: births VR Brunswick
  i Abner, b 16 Oct 1790: m (1) Brunswick 8 Oct 1812 Sarah Morse/Moss (VR), b Brunswick 20 Jul 1790 dau of Joseph & Hannah (Hunt) Moss (VR; George A. & Henry Wheeler, *History of Brunswick, Topsham & Harpswell, Maine* [1878], p. 845): m (2) Jefferson Co IL 1 Jun 1845 Priscilla Meek (Marriage Record Index, IL State Archives), b NC c1802 (1850 USC). He lived at Brunswick and moved to Mt. Vernon IL prob bef 1837 when his dau, Priscilla, married in Jefferson Co IL. He was a soldier in the War of 1812 serving as a private in Capt. Richard Dunlap's company (Wheeler, op. cit., p. 888). In 1850, he was listed as a machinist (USC)
  ii Priscilla, b 22 Jan 1793: m Brunswick 1 Jun 1818 Nathaniel Joss (VR) [he of Scarborough on m ints]
  iii Levinia, b 28 Feb 1795: d Brunswick 12 Feb 1797 (VR)
  iv Levinia, b 29 Jul 1797: m Brunswick 22 Apr 1817 Benjamin R. Morse/Moss (VR), b Brunswick 7 May 1793 bro of Sarah above (VR)
  v Anstress, b 28 Nov 1799: m Brunswick 14 Oct 1819 Abner Coombs (VR), b Brunswick 1 Dec 1794 son of John & Hannah (_____) Coombs (VR)
  vi Rebecka, b 29 Aug 1801

vii Thankful, b 8 Sep 1803. In 1835, she was a member of the Growstown Freewill Baptist Church, Brunswick ("Members of the Growstown Freewill Baptist Church, Brunswick" [TS, MSL])
 viii Gladden, b 11 Mar 1806: m Nancy Soule (Mary Pelham Hill, "Melcher, Family Notes" [TS, MHS, 1931]). In 1840, he res Nobleboro (USC)
 ix Noah, b 6 Oct 1809: m (1) Gallatin Co IL 26 Aug 1841 Lury Ann Gillet (Marriage Record Index, IL State Archives): m (2) Jefferson Co IL 11 Oct 1849 Susan Melissa Wells (ibid.), b OH c1825 (1850 USC). He was a carpenter (ibid.)
 x Zoah, b 19 Jan 1812

Thomas P. Doherty, 3321 N. Rockfield Dr., Devonshire, Wilmington, DE 19810-3238

Melcher, Sam[1] 12a 2 - 2 - 7 - 0 - 0
Brunswick Town, Cumberland County

SAMUEL MELCHER, b prob Arundel/Kennebunkport c1743 prob but unproven son of Edward & Elizabeth (Bailey) Melcher (McLellan's *Gorham*, p. 616): d Brunswick 3 Mar 1834 in his 90th y (George A. & Henry Wheeler, *History of Brunswick, Topsham & Harpswell, Maine* [1878], p. 843) [Brunswick VR give d 3 Mar 1842]: m Brunswick 12 Jan 1768 ISABELLA HINCKLEY (VR), b 27 Apr 1747 dau of Judge Aaron & Mary (Larrabee) Hinckley (Marlene A. H. Groves, *Hinckleys of Maine: The Ancestry and Descendants of Samuel[4] Hinckley of Brunswick, Maine* [1993], p. 39), d Brunswick 17 Aug 1832 in her 86th y (ibid.). Samuel settled on a farm at New Meadows [Brunswick], built a house there in 1767 (Wheeler, op. cit.), and was enumerated there in the 1790, 1800, 1810 and 1820 censuses. He was a housewright (William D. Shipman, *The Early Architecture of Bowdoin College and Brunswick, Maine* [1985], p. 2). Both he and his wife are buried in the Hinckley Cemetery at Hardings in East Brunswick.

Children: births VR Brunswick
 i Reliance, b 15 Nov 1768: d Brunswick 29 Nov 1804 ae 36y (Wheeler, op. cit., p. 843; g.s., Hinckley cem)
 ii Mary, b 1 Aug 1771. [One Mary Melcher m Brunswick 18 May 1800 James Crawford Jr. (VR)]
 iii Aaron, b 23 Feb 1773: d Falmouth 1 Feb 1845 ae 72y (g.s., Pine Grove cem, Falmouth Foreside): m (1) Brunswick 15 Jan 1801 Elizabeth Dunning (VR), b Brunswick 24 Jan 1774 dau of Andrew & Elizabeth (Dunlap) Dunning ("The Dunnings of Maine," NEHGR, 74 [1920]:107; also Brunswick VR), d Brunswick 15 Nov 1802 ae 28y (g.s., Old Maquoit cem): m (2) Brunswick 24 Feb 1805 Jane/Janney Owen (VR), b Brunswick

9 Apr 1776 dau of William & Mary (_____) Owen (VR), d Brunswick 28 Jan 1806 ae 30y (g.s., Old Maquoit cem): m (3) Falmouth 5 Oct 1807 Phebe Bucknam (Ann Theopold Chaplin, *A Bucknam-Buckman Genealogy* [1988], p. 32), b Falmouth 28 May 1778 dau of Jeremiah & Dorothy/Dolly (Pote) Bucknam (ibid.), d Falmouth 2 Feb 1834 ae 52y [sic] (g.s., Pine Grove cem, Falmouth Foreside)

iv   Samuel, b 8 May 1775: d Brunswick 3 Mar 1862 ae 86y (g.s., Pine Grove cem): m as Samuel Jr. at Harpswell 26 May 1803 Lois Dunning ("Rev. Elisha Eaton and Rev. Samuel Eaton, Records of Harpswell Congregational Church" [TS, MHS], hereafter Eaton CR), b Brunswick 30 Sep 1783 sister of Elizabeth above (VR), d Brunswick 3 Jun 1867 ae 88y [sic] (g.s., Pine Grove cem). He was a renowned architect of Brunswick area buildings, including several at Bowdoin College (Shipman, op. cit., pp. 2, 69–76)

v   Elizabeth, b 13 May 1777: m Boston MA 3 Aug 1806 William Hager (*Columbian Centinal*, issue of 9 Aug 1806)

vi   Lois, b 2 Jul 1780: d 2 Jun 1860 ae 80y (g.s., Hinckley cem, Brunswick)

vii   Rebecca, b 6 Mar 1783: m Brunswick 8 Mar 1803 Jonathan S. Donnell (VR). They res West Bath (Wheeler, op. cit.)

viii   John, b 19 May 1785: m Nobleboro 13 Mar 1828 Betsey Dodge both of Newcastle (Dodge's *Bristol*, 2:196)

ix   Noah, b 30 May 1788: d "27 day October following" (Brunswick VR)

x   Rachel, b 23 Feb 1793: d 30 Sep 1863 ae 70y 7m (g.s., Hinckley cem, Brunswick)

Thomas P. Doherty, 3321 N. Rockfield Dr., Devonshire, Wilmington, DE 19810-3238

Merriam, Revd Matthew   58a   1 - 2 - 4 - 0 - 0
   Berwick Town, York County

Rev. **MATTHEW MERRIAM**, b Wallingford CT 25 Jan 1738/9 son of Capt. Nathaniel & Elizabeth (Hull) Merriam (*Sibley's Harvard Graduates*, hereafter *Sibley*, 14:464): d Berwick 18 Jan 1797 (ibid.): m (1) cert Berwick 18 Mar 1766 ELIZABETH THATCHER of Milton [NH? or MA?] (John E. Frost and Joseph C. Anderson II, *Vital Records of Berwick, South Berwick, and North Berwick, Maine to the Year 1892* [1993], hereafter VR, p. 4), b 26 Mar 1744 dau of Oxenbridge & Sarah (Kent) Thatcher of Boston MA (*Sibley*, 10:322, 328), d of dropsy at Berwick 28 Nov 1789 (ibid., 14:465): m (2) cert Berwick 3 Jan 1791 Mrs. BETHIAH (_____) EVANS of Dover NH (Berwick VR, p. 31) [*Sibley*, 14:465, states she was of Boston MA], b c1735, d Eliot 11 Apr 1817 ae 82y (Everett S. Stackpole, *Old Kittery and Her Families* [1905], p. 285). She was of

Dover NH when she m (3) int Kittery 2 Jun 1799 John Heard Bartlett of Kittery (Joseph C. Anderson II and Lois Ware Thurston, *Vital Records of Kittery, Maine to the Year 1892* [1991], hereafter Kittery VR, p. 255) [see JOHN HEARD BARTLETT family, *Maine Families*, 2:14]. Matthew Merriam received an A.B. degree from Yale in 1759 and an A.M. degree from Harvard in 1765 (Charles Henry Pope, *Merriam Genealogy in England and America* [1906], hereafter *Merriam Genealogy*, p. 83; Sibley 14:464). After teaching for a short time, he received a call from the Blackberry Hill parish (2nd Parish) of Berwick where he was ordained on 25 Sep 1765 (ibid.), replacing Blackberry Hill's first minister, Rev. John Morse. He remained pastor at Berwick until his death. In his will, dated 8 Oct 1796 and probated 20 Feb 1797, he named his wife Bethiah, sons Nathaniel, John and Matthew Thatcher, and daus Elizabeth wife of William Mathers, Sarah and Persis (John E. Frost, *Maine Probate Abstracts* [1991], 17/287, citing York Co Probate #13007).

Children, b Berwick: births VR Berwick, p. 225
- i Nathaniel, b 19 May 1767: d Portsmouth NH 4 Dec 1821 (Katharine F. Richmond, *John Hayes of Dover, New Hampshire* [1936], hereafter *John Hayes*, p. 140): m Berwick 5 Aug 1790 Mehitable Hayes of Berwick (VR, p. 133), b Berwick 28 or 29 Nov 1764 dau of Elijah & Elizabeth (Chadbourne) Hayes (*John Hayes*, p. 81) [see Hon. ELIJAH HAYES family, *Maine Families*, 3:127], d Portsmouth NH 28 Oct 1848 ae 84y (Scott Lee Chipman, *New England Vital Records from the* Exeter News-Letter, *1847–1852* [1994], p. 64). He was a house carpenter of Portsmouth NH (*John Hayes*, p. 140)
- ii Elizabeth, b 24 Feb 1770: d 12 Sep 1823 (*Merriam Genealogy*, p. 83): m Berwick 27 Sep 1789 William Mather of Berwick (VR, p. 131), b "in the town of Jedburgh, County of Taviotdale & shire of Roxburgh; in the Kingdom of Great Britton" 20 Aug 1766 (Kittery VR, p. 187)
- iii Sarah, b 5 Mar 1773: m Belfast 12 Apr 1801 John Haskell (VR)
- iv John, b 1 Aug 1776: d Belfast 1 May 1832 ae 55y (VR): m Berwick 25 Oct 1798 Patience Neal (VR, p. 200), b 3 Apr 1781 (*Merriam Genealogy*, p. 117) and bp Berwick 2nd Parish 12 Sep 1781 dau of Johnson & Sarah (Furbush) Neal (NEHGR, 74 [1920]:230; parents' marriage in Kittery VR, p. 140), d Belfast 6 Dec 1826 ae 45y 7m (VR) [her g.s. says d 6 Apr 1826 ae 45y 3m 3d (also in Belfast VR)]. He was a representative to the General Court in 1817, repeatedly a selectman of Belfast, and Chief Justice of the Court of Sessions 1820–26 (*Merriam Genealogy*, p. 117)
- v Matthew Thatcher, b 20 Jul 1782: d Morrill 21 Mar 1857 (Mrs. Theoda Mears Morse and Mr. & Mrs. Charles White, *A Genealogical History of the Families of Morrill, Maine* [1957], p. 247): m Sanbornton NH 1 Dec 1805 Abigail Smith (ibid.; *Merriam Genealogy*, p. 118) [m int Belfast 19 Oct 1805 both of Greene Plt (VR)], b Sanbornton NH 27 Apr 1789 dau of

Benjamin Sr. & Elsie (Woodman) Smith of Sanbornton NH and Greene Plt [now Morrill] (Morse & White, op. cit., p. 247), d Lawrence MA 29 Sep 1877 (ibid.). Matthew Thatcher Merriam was a tanner and a farmer. He lived for at time at Sanbornton NH and came to Greene Plt in 1803 (ibid.)

vi Persis, b 29 Jan 1783 [*Merriam Genealogy*, p. 83, gives b 27 Jan 1784, a date that would seem more probable given the birth date of her brother Matthew Thatcher, above]: d Berwick 3 Mar 1817 (VR, p. 293)

Joseph C. Anderson II, 5337 Del Roy Drive, Dallas, TX 75229

Meserve, Dan¹, Senʳ   18c   1 - 0 - 1 - 0 - 0
Gorham and Scarborough Towns, Cumberland County

Dea. DANIEL MESERVE, b Scarborough abt 1715 son of Clement & Elizabeth (Jones) Meserve (Gideon T. Ridlon, *Saco Valley Settlements & Families* [1895], pp. 948–51): d Scarborough 13 May 1803 ae 88y (ibid.): m Scarborough 1st Church 24 Jan 1737/8 MEHETABEL BRAGDON (MHGR, 3:84), b York 7 Mar 1715 dau of Arthur & Mehitabel (Marston) Bragdon (VR; GDMNH, p. 105), d after 1803. Daniel lived in Scarborough all of his life. When he died, he left a widow with whom he had lived more than 65 years and 8 children, the youngest being 47 years of age (*Saco Valley Settlements*, p. 949).

Children: births first 7 VR Scarborough
  i Daniel, b 5 May 1739: m Scarborough 2nd Church 22 Apr 1760 Susanna Small (MHGR, 4:31)
  ii Elisha, b 19 Jan 1741: m Scarborough 1st Church 16 Jan 1765 Hannah Fogg (MHGR, 3:87), b 24 May 1741 dau of Seth & Mary (Pickernale) Fogg of Kittery and Scarborough (Charles T. Libby, *The Libby Family in America* [1882], p. 46)
  iii Solomon, b 9 Jul 1743: m Scarborough 19 Dec 1769 Isabella Jordan (*Saco Valley Settlements*, p. 950)
  iv Sarah, b 27 Jun 1745: d c1822 (*Libby Family*, p. 92): m Scarborough 1st Church 31 Oct 1765 Joseph Libby (MHGR, 3:87), b Scarborough 6 Jan 1740 son of Lieut. Andrew & Esther (Foster) Libby (*Libby Family*, p. 52), d in the spring of 1816 (ibid., p. 92). They moved to Machias in 1765 (ibid., p. 91)
  v Nathaniel, b 20 Apr 1747: d Limington 18 Jan 1825 ae 78y (Robert L. Taylor, *Early Families of Limington, Maine* [1991], p. 215): m (1) Scarborough 1st Church 25 Feb 1773 Anna Hunnewell (MHGR, 3:88), b Scarboro 27 Jun 1750 dau of Richard & Hannah (Brown) Hunnewell

(MHGR, 5:215; Taylor, op. cit.; *Libby Family*, p. 73): m (2) int Buxton 10 Oct 1789 Sarah Jordan of Limington who d Limerick 1 May 1828 ae 82y (Taylor, op. cit., p. 215). Nathaniel moved to Limington c1782 (ibid.)

vi   Gideon, b 31 Jan 1749: d Dresden 5 Jun 1818 ae 66y (Rev War pension #W23958): m Elizabeth Fogg [see GIDEON MESERVE family]

vii Elizabeth, b 5 Jan 1754: m Scarborough 1st Church 20 Jan 1774 Samuel Smith of Arundel (MHGR, 3:89), b Kittery 29 Mar 1749 son of Charles & Rebecca (Haley) Smith [see CHARLES SMITH family, *Maine Families*, 1:254]

viii Abigail, bp Scarborough 1st Church 25 Apr 1756 (MHGR, 2:35): d 15 Sep 1838 (Phyllis O. Whitten, *Samuel Fogg 1628–1672 His Ancestors and Descendants*, vol. 1, #197): m (1) Scarborough 2nd Church 5 Oct 1775 David Fogg (MHGR, 4:88), b Scarborough 18 Apr 1751 son of Reuben & Margaret (Elder) Fogg (MHGR, 5:215; *Libby Family*, p. 74) and bro of Elizabeth above, d before 1789 (*Samuel Fogg*, op. cit.): m (2) Scarborough 1st Church 6 Oct 1789 James Patten (MHGR, 3:145), b Arundel c1747 (*Samuel Fogg*, op. cit.)

Janet S. Seitz, 11521 Upper Sunny Circle, Eagle River, AK 99577-7414

Meserve, Gideon   18c   1 - 4 - 4 - 0 - 0
Gorham and Scarborough Towns, Cumberland County

GIDEON MESERVE, b Scarborough 31 Jan 1749 son of Daniel & Mehitable (Bragdon) Meserve (MHGR, 5:117, 3:84) [see DANIEL MESERVE family]: d Dresden 5 Jun 1818 ae 66y [sic] (Bible rec contained in Rev War pension #W23958): m Scarborough 31 Dec 1774 ELIZABETH/BETTY FOGG (Bible rec, op. cit.), b Scarborough 22 Apr 1755 dau of Reuben & Margaret (Elder) Fogg (MHGR 5:117; Charles T. Libby, *The Libby Family in America* [1882], p. 74), d 18 Oct 1840 ae 87y [sic] (Bible rec, op. cit.). Gideon's Rev War pension application states that he still lived at Scarboro during the war. He served as an adjutant in Col. Nathan Mitchell's Cum Co regiment. He moved to Dresden prob in the early 1800s. His wid, Elizabeth, was described as having lived with her son Reuben during the last 26y of her life (pension, op. cit.).

Children, b Scarborough: births MHGR, 6:402–3
   i   Margaret, b 30 Nov 1775 [Bible gives 31 Dec 1775]: d Sep 1838 ae 63y (Bible) [Robert L. Taylor's *Early Families of Limington, Maine* (1991), p. 174 gives her death at Limington 20 Sep 1841; *Libby Family*, p. 116, gives 27 Sep 1841]: m Scarborough Mar 1794 Henry Libby (MHGR, 3:146), b

14 Apr 1774 son of Stephen & Margaret (Miller) Libby (*Libby Family*, p. 65), d Limington 19 Feb 1847 ae 72y 10m (ibid., p. 116; Taylor, op. cit.)

ii Solomon, b 10 Oct 1777: d Sep 1815 ae 38y (Bible): m c1806 Jerusha Gowell (Althea M. Lewis, *Généalogie de la Famille Messervy*, p. 36, hereafter *Généalogie Messervy*)

iii Gideon, b 21 Nov 1779: d 1789 ae 10y (Bible)

iv Jane, b 10 Sep 1781: alive in 1846 (pension, op. cit.): m Scarborough 25 Jan 1806 Jacob Merrill, Jr. (MHGR, 3:238)

v David, b 24 Dec 1783: d Aug 1821 ae 38y (Bible): m Dresden 22 Nov 1812 Abigail Bickford (NEHGR, 66 [1912]:110), b Dresden 20 Apr 1789 dau of Paul & Elizabeth (Kendall) Bickford [see PAUL BICKFORD family]

vi Daniel, b 7 Dec 1785 [Bible gives 7 Nov 1785]: d Aug 1842 ae 57y (Bible): m Mary J. Sproul (*Généalogie Messervy*)

vii Eunice, b 28 Mar 1788: alive in 1846 (pension, op. cit.): m Dresden 9 Nov 1812 Harrison Blenn (NEHGR, 66 [1912]:109)

viii Elisha, b 8 Jul 1790: alive in 1846 (pension, op. cit.): m Sarah Leeman (*Généalogie Messervy*)

ix Reuben, b 8 Jul 1792: d Dresden 1868 (g.s., Herriman cem, Blinn Hill Rd.): m Dresden 6 Mar 1817 Elethere/Illathera Barker (NEHGR, 66 [1912]:110), b 1792, d Dresden 1856 (g.s., Herriman cem, Blinn Hill Rd.)

x William, b 23 Aug 1794: d in Army service Sep 1815 ae 21y (Bible)

xi Elizabeth/Betty Fogg, b 21 Jul 1797 [Bible gives 25 July 1796], bp Scarborough 1st Church 10 Jun 1798 (MHGR, 2:234): alive in 1846 (pension, op. cit.): m _____ Carlton (ibid.)

Janet S. Seitz, 11521 Upper Sunny Circle, Eagle River, AK 99577-7414

Meldrom, Sam[l] 71a   1 - 2 - 2 - 0 - 0
Wells Town, York County

SAMUEL MILDRAM, b Wells 2 Aug 1761 (g.s.; family bible record, probably written by Samuel Mildram Jr., in Mildram Collection at MHS [currently uncatalogued]) and bp Kennebunk 1st Parish 9 Aug 1761 son of Thomas & Mary/Molly (Annis) Mildram (records of First Parish of Kennebunk, on microfilm at MHS): d Wells 2 Aug 1827 (bible; g.s., Clark-Mildram cem transcribed in "Incriptions from Gravestones at Wells, Maine," NEHGR, 94 [1940]:38): m Kennebunk 7 Dec 1784 ABIGAIL DENNETT (Kennebunk First Parish records, at MHS) [m int Wells dated 4 Sep 1784 (VR)], b 31 Jul 1764 (bible) dau of John & Dorothy (Furbish) Dennett (Everett S. Stackpole, *Old Kittery and Her Families* [1903], p. 352), d Wells 30 Mar 1840 (bible; g.s., Clark-

Mildram cem, NEHGR, 94 [1940]:37). At ae 16y, Samuel enlisted for Rev War service in Capt. Samuel Waterhouse's company, Col. Jacob Gerrish's regiment, marching from home on 30 Mar 1778 (MS&S, 10:610). He saw service at Winter Hill from 2 Apr to 3 Jul 1778 (ibid.). In his father's will dated 7 Jul 1789 and probated 9 Oct 1790, Samuel was named executor and was left Thomas's homestead farm of 100 acres in Wells including a house and a barn (York Co. Probate #12982). Samuel was clerk and later moderator of the Independent Christian Baptist Society of Wells which became the Free Will Baptist Church, Wells Branch (E. G. Perkins, *Wells the Frontier Town of Maine* [1971], 2:42–43). He was chosen a tythingman for the Town of Wells in 1817 (ibid., 2:96).

Children: bible
- i John, b 6 May 1785: d 21 Dec 1785 (bible)
- ii Esther, b 26 Mar 1787: d Wells 10 Dec 1879 ae 92y 8m 14d (g.s., Clark-Mildram cem, NEHGR, 94 [1940]:37): m Wells 26 Dec 1814 Henry Clark of Waterborough (Wells VR), b c Jan 1785, d Wells 27 Mar 1861 ae 76y 2m 3d (g.s., Clark-Mildram cem, NEHGR, 94 [1940]:37)
- iii Clement, b 20 Aug 1789: d 19 Jan 1795 (bible)
- iv Permelia/Pamela F., b 9 Mar 1792: d Wells 15 Oct 1846 (g.s., Pine Hill cem, NEHGR, 94 [1940]:34; bible): m at Kennebunk 11 Jun 1815 David Chick (Kennebunk 1st Parish records, at MHS), b 23 Aug 1792 son of Thomas & Polly (Grant) Chick (Thompson Collection at MHS, Coll. 111, Box 6, Folder 19), d Wells 1861 (g.s., Pine Hill cem, NEHGR, 94 [1940]:34). David Chick was a clerk of the Wells Free Will Baptist Church (Perkins, op. cit., p. 43)
- v Susan, b 8 Jun 1794: d 4 Dec 1845 ae 51y 5m 26d (bible; g.s., Merriland cem, NEHGR, 94 [1940]:29): m Wells 20 Mar 1817 Henry Littlefield of Wells (VR), b c1791, d 17 Mar 1863 ae 72y (g.s., Merriland cem, NEHGR, 94 [1940]:30)
- vi Dorothy, b 31 Aug 1796: d Wells 1885 (g.s., Pine Hill cem, NEHGR, 94 [1940]:35): m Wells 5 Sep 1816 Eleazer Clark 4th (VR), b Wells 4 Oct 1793 son of Eleazer 3rd & Olive (Hobbs) Clark [see ELEAZER CLARK 3rd family, *Maine Families*, 3:48], d Wells 1864 (g.s., Pine Hill cem, NEHGR, 94 [1940]:35)
- vii Nancy, b 6 Mar 1799: d Wells 4 Apr 1880 ae 81y (g.s., Oceanview cem, NEHGR, 92 [1938]:326): m Wells 20 Jan 1825 John Gowen of Wells (VR), b c1800, d 28 Jun 1858 ae 57y 10m (g.s., Oceanview cem, NEHGR, 92 [1938]:326)
- viii Samuel Jr., b 14 Apr 1801: d Wells 7 Nov 1861 (bible; g.s., Clark-Mildram cem, NEHGR, 94 [1940]:38): m Wells 26 Jul 1827 Olive Hobbs (VR), b 3 Jan 1807 (g.s.) dau of Joseph Jr. & Abigail (Storer) Hobbs (Thompson Collection, op. cit., Box 7, Folder 21), d Wells 20 Jul 1848 (g.s., Clark-Mildram cem, NEHGR, 94 [1940]:37). Samuel served in the Maine House

of Representatives from Wells in 1834–36, 1839, 1843–45, and as York County Commissioner 1856–58 (*History of York Co, Maine* [1880], pp. 107, 109, 110)

ix Charles Augustus, b 15 Sep 1803: d Wells 18 Jan 1860 (bible; g.s., Clark-Mildram cem): m Wells 7 Feb 1830 Mary Anne Littlefield (VR), b Wells 19 Jul 1810 dau of Joseph & Mary/Polly (Clark) Littlefield (Thompson Collection, op. cit., Box 8, Folder 19) [see ELEAZER CLARK 3rd family, *Maine Families*, 3:48], d 23 Sep 1880 (g.s., Clark-Mildram cem). Charles Augustus served in the Maine House of Representatives from Wells in 1838 (*History of York Co*, p. 109)

x Abigail, b 24 Aug 1805: d Wells 27 Mar 1806 (bible)

xi Abigail, b 27 Mar 1807: d Wells 21 Oct 1892 ae 85y 6m (g.s., Pine Hill cem, NEGHR, 94 [1940]:35): m Wells 2 Dec 1827 Daniel Littlefield of Wells (VR), b 7 Mar 1803 brother of Mary Ann above (Thompson Collection, op. cit., Box 8, Folder 19), d Wells 14 Aug 1860 ae 57y 5m (g.s., Pine Hill cem, NEHGR, 94 [1940]:35)

xii Clement, b 25 Jul 1809: d Wells 20 Apr 1835 ae 25y (bible; g.s., Clark-Mildram cem, NEHGR, 94 [1940]:37)

Barbara Mildram, OceanView #109, 52 Falmouth Rd., Falmouth, ME 04105

Millbank, Phillip   40a   1 - 0 - 4 - 0 - 0
Lewistown Town and the Gore Adjoining, Lincoln County

PHILIP MILLBANKS, b c1739 (ae 39y in 1778, MS&S 10:729): d Lewiston 23 Feb 1811 ("Androscoggin History," Newsletter of the Androscoggin Historical Society, 5 [1992]): m Falmouth 15 Jan 1767 LUCY DYER (MHGR, 3:103 in which he was called Philip Mill Banks). Philip was listed as being of No. Yarmouth when he mustered at Falmouth to serve in the Continental Army for 9 months (MS&S 10:729). At the time, he was described as being 5'7" tall and dark complexioned.

Children as found, prob b Lewiston
i Katherine, b c Nov 1767: d 8 Apr 1831 ae 63y 4m 24d (g.s., Garcelon cem, Lewiston): m Lewiston 2 Mar 1787 Peter Garcelon (Janus G. Elder, *A History of Lewiston, Maine*, edited by David C. & Elizabeth K. Young [1984], hereafter Elder, p. 163), b 8 Jul 1765 and bp Gloucester MA 14 Jul 1765 son of James & Deliverance (Annis) Garcelon (ibid.) [see JAMES GARCELON family, *Maine Families*, 1:167], d 19 Jun 1827 ae 61y (ibid.)

ii Thankful, b c Jan 1772: d Durham 7 Aug 1864 ae 92y 7m (Elder, p. 260; Everett S. Stackpole, *History of Durham, Maine* [1899], p. 275): m 15 Jul 1790 Bela Vining (Elder, p. 260), b 12 Nov 1766 son of Benjamin & Mehitabel (Brooks) Vining (ibid., p. 273), d 17 Feb 1846 (ibid., p. 275)

iii Lisa, m Durham 19 Dec 1799 James Douglass (VR)

Constance Hanscom, 200 Orchard St., Belmont, MA 02178-2353

Moody, Jeremiah 42c 1 - 1 - 2 - 0 - 0
Pittston Town, Lincoln County

JEREMIAH/JEDIDIAH MOODY, b prob Hales Town [Weare] NH 18 Dec 1761 (Whitefield VR) son of Scribner & Sarah (Smith) Moody [see SCRIBNER MOODY family]: d Whitefield 1840–50 (USC): m c1785 RUTH CLOUGH (Joseph S. Bean, *Clan MacBean of North America*, Sixth edition [revised 1992], 1:550). [Note Bean identifies Jeremiah's mother as Sarah Bean, widow of William Smith, which is highly unlikely. Other items are also questionable.] Ruth was b 19 Nov 1766 parents unknown (Whitefield VR) and d Whitefield aft 1850 (USC, ae 85y). On 4 Nov 1788 Jeremiah's father conveyed to him 2 parcels of land in Pittston (Lin Co deeds at Ken Co Courthouse, 7:242–43). He purchased 250 acres, partly in Pittston and partly in Balltown, from Mark Pearson on 22 Mar 1788; and sold 200 acres of the same on 14 Jan 1793 (Lin Co deeds at Ken Co Courthouse, 3:490, 4:403). Jeremiah & Ruth res Whitefield [formerly Balltown].

Children: births VR Whitefield
 i John, b prob Pittston 3 Mar 1787 (Whitefield VR): d Whitefield 27 Sep 1809 (VR)
 ii Sarah, b prob Pittston 26 Feb 1789 (Whitefield VR): d Whitefield 12 Apr 1845 (VR): m Whitefield 10 Jan 1814 Samuel Palmer (VR), b Pittston 27 Jun 1790 son of Edward & Hannah Palmer (VR; date also given in Whitefield VR), d prob Whitefield aft 1850 (USC). He m (2) her sis Ruth
 iii Levi, b 10 May 1791: d Pittston 19 Oct 1858 ae 67y (VR; g.s., King's Mills cem, Whitefield): m Whitefield 23 Nov 1817 Mary/Polley Kincaid of Whitefield (VR), b prob Whitefield 7 Sep 1794 dau of Samuel & Sarah Kincaid (VR), res Pittston 1850 (USC Pittston Levi ae 56y, Polly ae 56y). There is no g.s. for her in King's Mill cem, Whitefield
 iv Nathaniel, b 25 Dec 1794: d Pittston 27 Jan 1886 ae 94y [sic] (VR; g.s., Maple Grove cem, East Pittston): m prob Alna aft Aug 1830 Mary Kimball of Alna (see below), b c1801, d Pittston c1885 (VR; g.s., Maple Grove cem, East Pittston). They res Whitefield & Pittston. On 14 Jun 1852 Nathaniel requested a guardian for his wife Mary (Ken Co Probate).

She owned land in Alna conveyed to her 31 Aug 1830 by Martha Kimball, wid of Ebenezer Kimball (ibid; Lin Co deeds 150:393)

v   Jeremiah/Jedediah, b 6 May 1796: d Pittston 8 Sep 1845 ae 49y 4m (g.s., King's Mills cem, Whitefield): m int Whitefield 27 Sep 1818 Annie McKnight (VR), b 19 Jul 1800 parents unknown (Whitefield VR), d prob Pittston 1888 (g.s., Kings Mills cem, Whitefield). She res Pittston 1850 (USC head of household, ae 50y)

vi Ruth, b 18 Nov 1801: d 1880 (g.s., Pine Grove cem, Dresden): m int Whitefield 27 Sep 1845 Samuel Palmer (VR) wid of her sis Sarah. They res Whitefield 1850 (USC, Samuel ae 60y, Ruth ae 52y)

vii Ruhama, b 15 Jan 1801: d Lee 2 Apr 1855 (*The Maine Seine*, 10 [1988]:4: 99): m Whitefield 18 Oct 1826 Purchase Lee (VR), b Dresden 2 Feb 1800 son of Nathan & Rebecca (Puffer) Lee (*The Maine Seine*, op. cit.), d Lee 19 Sep 1867 (ibid.). He m (2) her sis Eliza

viii Daniel, b 21 Mar 1805: d 11 Feb 1888 ae 83y "at Zina Blenn's in Dresden" (Pittston VR; g.s., Pine Grove cem, Dresden): m int Pittston 14 Mar 1829 Hannah Kincaid (VR), prob b Whitefield 19 Aug 1808 sis of Mary/Polley above, d Pittston 7 Jan 1863 ae 54y (VR; g.s., transcribed as 1886, Pine Grove cem, Dresden). They res 1850 Pittston next to Levi & Polly Moody

ix Hannah, b 9 Jul 1808: d Pittston 1 Feb 1891 ae 83y (VR): unm, res with her mother in 1850

x   Eliza C., b 26 Jan 1810: d Pittston Aug 1888 ae 74y [sic] (VR; g.s. gives 1809–1886, Maple grove cem, Dresden): m Whitefield 24 Jan 1856 Purchase Lee of Lee (VR) wid of her sis Ruhama. Eliza res with her mother in 1850

Sandra J. Ellis, 268 Prescott Hill Rd., Monmouth, ME 04259-7102

Moody, Scribner   42c   1 - 1 - 4 - 0 - 0
    Pittston Town, Lincoln County

SCRIBNER MOODY, b prob Exeter NH c1738 son of Clement & Elizabeth (Scribner) Moody (TAG, 61 [1986]:227): d Pittston bef 21 Feb 1812 (Ken Co Probate; David C. & Elizabeth K. Young, *Vital Records from Maine Newspapers, 1785–1820* [1993], p. 413, citing estate notice in *American Advocate*, issue of 17 Mar 1812): m prob Hales Town [now Weare] NH bef 9 Dec 1762 (when her father deeded them land) SARAH SMITH (TAG, op. cit.), bp Kingston NH 28 Jun 1744 dau of William & Sarah (Bean) Smith (NHGR 3:40, 5:111), d aft 1806 (named in Scribner's will). Scribner served in NH military in 1757–1758 (TAG, op. cit.). On 14 Oct 1786, Scribner, then of Poplin NH, bought 165 acres in

Pittston (Lin Co deeds at Ken Co Courthouse, 3:242). His will dated 27 Jan 1806 and filed 21 Feb 1812 named his wife Sarah and children Jeremiah, Sarah Batchlor, Scribner, Mary Moody, Loes [sic] Davis, Jonathan, William, Ruth Longfellow, Abigail Pratt, & John.

Children, all but John prob b NH
- i Jeremiah/Jedidiah, b 18 Dec 1761 (Whitefield VR): d Whitefield 1840–50 (USC): m c1785 Ruth Clough (Joseph S. Bean, *Clan MacBean of North America*, Sixth edition [revised 1992], 1:550) [see JEREMIAH/JEDEDIAH MOODY family]
- ii Sarah, m bef 1806 _____ Batchlor (father's will)
- iii Scribner Jr., b 26 Aug 1766 (Whitefield VR): d Whitefield 18 Jun 1845 ae 79y (g.s., Moody cem, Whitefield): m Pownalboro 25 Aug 1788 Martha Bayley (Wiscasset VR), b 21 Feb 1769 parents unknown (Whitefield VR), d Whitefield 6 Mar 1850 ae 81y (g.s., Moody cem, Whitefield)
- iv Jonathan, b 1 Feb 1771 (Whitefield VR): d Whitefield 31 Aug 1847 (g.s., Blackman cem, Whitefield): m (1) int Pittston 10 Nov 1794 Sarah Palmer (NEHGR, 46 [1892]:11), b 8 Oct 1771 parents unknown (Whitefield VR), d Whitefield 23 Aug 1828 (g.s., Blackman cem, Whitefield): of Windsor when he m (2) int Hallowell 10 Oct 1828 Margaret Clark (VR), b Whitefield c1802 dau of Thomas & Lois (Preble) Clark (Margaret's death rec in ME VR), d Randolph 28 Feb 1894 ae 92y (ibid.)
- v Mary, b Brentwood NH 10 Dec 1772 (Bean, op. cit.): d Whitefield 10 Dec 1856 ae 84y (g.s., Blackman cem, Whitefield): m int Nobleboro 4 Apr 1796 Clement Moody of Nobleboro (VR), b c1774 poss son of Richard Moody (George R. Moody & Robert E. Moody, "Descendants of Clement Moody of Exeter, N.H.," Moody papers, NEHGS), d Whitefield 5 May 1863 ae 88y 11m (g.s., Blackman cem, Whitefield)
- vi Lois, b c1774: d Machias 13 Dec 1866 ae 92y (g.s., West Kennebec cem, Machias): m Whitefield 20 Sep 1796 Samuel Davis (VR), b c1776, d Machias 7 Nov 1858 ae 84y (g.s., West Kennebec cem). They named a son Scribner Moody Davis
- vii William, b c1778: d Pittston 31 May 1824 ae 46y (VR; g.s., Old Moody cem, East Pittston): m Whitefield 26 Nov 1800 Mary/Polly Hunt (VR), b c1781, d Pittston 21 Jul 1865 ae 84y (VR; g.s., Old Moody cem, East Pittston)
- viii Ruth, b 3 Apr 1780 (Whitefield VR): d Windsor 17 Feb 1859 ae 79y (g.s., North Windsor cem): m int Whitefield 24 Apr 1802 Levi Longfellow (VR), b 12 Oct 1779 (Whitefield VR), d Windsor 21 Feb 1864 ae 84y (g.s., North Windsor cem)
- ix Abigail, b c1783: d 6 Sep 1871 ae 87y 10m (g.s., Weeks Mills cem, China): m Harlem 28 Aug 1805 Jones Pratt (China VR), b Abington MA 29 Mar 1785 son of Seth J. & Hannah (Hunt) Pratt (Windsor VR; Jayne Pratt

Lovelace, *The Pratt Directory* [1980], p. 344), d 9 Nov 1866 ae 81y 7m 11d (g.s., Weeks Mills cem, China). They res Windsor

x John, b Pittston 15 Feb 1791 (VR): d Pittston 20 Feb 1863 (VR; g.s., Old Moody cem, East Pittston): m (1) int Whitefield 20 Sep 1809 Eleanor/Elling Cressey (VR, note Pittston VR gives int 12 Dec 1811, but first child b 13 Mar 1811), b 1791–1794 (1820–1830 USC, Pittston), d prob bef 1840. [A transcript of her g.s. in Old Moody cem (g.s. no longer in existence) gives "Elling Crecy Moody, his wife, d. November 16, 1854." The Pittston VR give the same date for the death of one Elizabeth M. Moody, but there was no Elizabeth M. Moody nor Eleanor Moody enumerated in the 1850 USC of Pittston. Eleanor's last recorded child was Mary Ann, b 15 May 1838. Eleanor prob d bef 5 Nov 1840 when John had a dau Atree/Adra Ann by his second wife.] John m (2) int Pittston 3 Feb 1841 [sic] Mrs. Betsey (Nash?) Dudley prob wid of Jonathan Dudley (VR), b c1802 (ae 30–40y in 1840 USC, ae 48y in 1850 USC), d aft 12 Apr 1865 when she and dau Adra Ann conveyed the homestead property [which had been bequeathed to them through John's will] to Gilman Moody (Ken Co deeds 260:168). John was executor of his father's estate. John's will, dated 23 Jun 1862, named wife Betsey and his 11 surviving children (Ken Co Probate). [There is no evidence that Eleanor Cressey was an Indian princess of the Penobscot tribe as claimed by Joseph Bean, op. cit.]

Sandra J. Ellis, 268 Prescott Hill Rd., Monmouth, ME 04259-7102

Mosher, Elisha   50a   1 - 1 - 2 - 0 - 0
    Washington Town, Lincoln County
[and counted again as]
Mosier, Elisha   50a   1 - 1 - 2 - 0 - 0
    Washington Town, Lincoln County

ELISHA MOSHER [Jr.], b Dartmouth MA 19 Jun 1765 son of Elisha & Ann (Springer) Mosher (VR): d Belgrade 2 Jan 1847 ae 80y [sic] (VR; *Maine Farmer*, issue of 21 Jan 1847): m Vassalboro 13 Aug 1787 JUDITH CROWELL (VR), b Yarmouth MA 18 Aug 1767 dau of Lemuel & Elizabeth (Hawes) Crowell (VR) [see LEMUEL CROWELL family], d Belgrade 7 Nov 1832 ae 65y (VR; *Kennebec Journal*, issue of 23 Nov 1832). Elisha was doublecounted in the 1790 census as were several of the heads-of-household listed at the ends of Washington and Winslow towns in the published census on pp. 50a and 50c. His father of the same name is found in the published census on p. 50c under "Winslow Town, with its Adjacents," although he too was prob actually living in the Belgrade/Sidney area. Elisha Jr., with his parents and several siblings, came to the

Kennebec from Dartmouth MA prob bef 1785, the year his sister Lydia "of Vassalboro" filed marriage intentions with Jesse Page (Vassalboro VR). His father, Elisha Sr., lived in Augusta from 1795 to c1811 and was described on deeds as a miller and yeoman. His mother was a midwife and delivered babies in the Augusta area concurrently with Augusta's more famous midwife, Martha Ballard (Laurel Thatcher Ulrich, *A Midwife's Tale* [1990], p. 338). Elisha Jr. lived in Belgrade where he made his living as a farmer.

Children: births VR Belgrade
- i Hannah, b 28 Nov 1788: d Unity 15 Apr 1864 ae 77y (g.s., Farwell cem, Unity). While Hannah apparently never married, she did have a son Ira b Belgrade 26 May 1805 (VR). In 1850, Hannah, ae 63y, was living with her brother Elisha at Unity (USC)
- ii William, b 5 Aug 1790: d China 15 Apr 1854 (Ken Co Probate, M10): m Sidney 18 Jul 1813 Freelove Weeks (VR), b prob Sidney 1794 (g.s.) dau of Jethro & Penelope (Gorham) Weeks (Henry D. Kingsbury & Simeon L. Deyo, *Illustrated History of Kennebec County, Maine* [1892], p. 1063), d China 5 Mar 1881 (Ken Co Probate, M8; g.s., Weeks Mills cem)
- iii Anna, b 26 Jan 1792: d Augusta 6 Nov 1857 ae 65y (VR): m Augusta 1 May 1813 Parker Fletcher (VR), b 1781–1790 (USC 1830–40), d 1840–1850 (USC, Augusta)
- iv Elizabeth, b 31 Jan 1794: m int Belgrade Aug 1815 Joseph Rollins of Mercer (Belgrade VR) son of Jabez & Lydia (Haskell) Rollins (John R. Rollins, *Records of Families of the Name Rawlins or Rollins in the United States* [1874], p. 301). He m (2) int Sidney 15 Jun 1823 Thankful G. Scudder (VR), b Sidney 21 Dec 1795 dau of Jesse & Joanna (Robinson) Scudder (VR; Jesse and Joanna's 1787 marriage recorded Vassalboro)
- v Phebe, b 24 Feb 1796: d Augusta 10 Apr 1867 ae 71y (g.s., Brackett Corner cem, Augusta): m Belgrade 5 Jan 1817 Elias Taylor (VR), b Readfield 5 Jan 1792 son of Elias & Betsey (Knowlton) Taylor (VR) [see ELIAS TAYLOR family, *Maine Families*, 3:271], d Augusta 21 Mar 1842 ae 50y (g.s., Brackett Corner cem)
- vi Joseph, b 18 Jul 1798: d 12 Feb 1856 ae 57y (bur Farwell cem, Unity, stone now missing, inscription info from research recs of James B. Vickery, author of the *A History of the Town of Unity, Maine* [1954]): m China 2 Sep 1819 Nancy Hatch ("China Marriages 1792–1892," [TS, MSL, 1971], p. 28), b China c1796–97 dau of Sylvanus & Betty (Ballard) Hatch (*Genealogy and History of the Hatch Family. Descendants of Thomas & Grace Hatch of Dorchester, Yarmouth and Barnstable, Massachusetts* [1928], p. 237; ae 53y in 1850 USC, Unity; ae 64y in 1860 USC, Unity; parents' marriage in Vassalboro VR), d Unity 16 Aug 1864 (Vickery research recs)
- vii Elisha, b 21 Jul 1801: d Unity 15 Mar 1880 ae 79y 7m (g.s., Friends cem, Unity): m Unity 19 Jul 1837 Martha C. Stevens (Elizabeth M. Mosher &

Isabel Morse Maresh, *Marriage Records of Waldo County, Maine Prior to 1892* [1990], p. 23), b Unity 4 Feb 1813 dau of Benjamin R. & Sarah (Rich) Stevens (VR), d Unity 20 Jul 1891 ae 79y (g.s., Friends cem)

viii Clancey, b 16 Oct 1803: d 16 Oct 1803 (Belgrade VR)

ix Lemuel Crowell, b Jul 1805: d Norridgewock 12 Jan 1870 ae 65y 8m (Som Co Probate, 44:107; g.s., Riverview cem, Norridgewock): m Louisa Corson (letter dated 8 Apr 1994 from Stanton D. Colson, President, Corson Colson Family History Association, letter in possession of submitter), b Dearborn 8 Dec 1807 dau of Benjamin [and perhaps Lydia (Hussey)] Corson (Dearborn VR; *Downeast Ancestry*, 7 [1993]:1:28) [see MOSES CORSON family], d 12 Jul 1886 ae 78y 7m (g.s., Riverview cem)

x James Harvey, b 18 Jul 1807: d Belgrade 23 Feb 1878 ae 70y 7m 5d (Belgrade VR): m (1) Belgrade 20 Nov 1831 Judith Foss (VR), b c1808, d Belgrade 29 Oct 1832 ae 24y (VR; *Kennebec Journal*, issue of 23 Nov 1832): m (2) prob Belgrade c1836 Sarah T. Wellman (family Bible rec, transcribed in DAR Misc Rec [1940–41], p. 56; 1850 USC, Belgrade), b Belgrade 22 Jun 1815 dau of John & Lydia (Brayley) Wellman (VR), d Belgrade 29 Feb 1852 ae 36y 9m (VR, *Maine Farmer*, issue of 11 Mar 1852): m (3) Belgrade c1854 Mrs. Lucy Ann (____) Merchant wid of Edward Merchant (g.s. for Edward Merchant in same plot as James and Lucy Ann Mosher; 1850 USC, Belgrade, household of Edward Merchant and his wife Lucy A.; 1860 USC, Belgrade, household of James Mosher and Lucy A. which also contained 3 of Lucy's Merchant children). She was b 25 Oct 1822 (g.s.) and d 23 Sep 1889 (g.s., Old Yard cem, Belgrade)

Paul Mosher Aldrich, P.O. Box 217, Bristol, ME 04539
Elizabeth M. Mosher, RFD 1, Box 783, Belfast, ME 04915

Murch, Walter 18b 3 - 1 - 3 - 0 - 0
Gorham and Scarborough Towns, Cumberland County

WALTER MURCH, d aft 31 Jan 1804 (Cum Co deeds 44:517): m Gorham Nov 1758 JERUSHA BROWN (VR), b Eastham MA 29 May 1738 dau of Joseph & Susanna (Cole) Brown (VR), d aft 31 Jan 1804 (Cum Co deeds 44:517). Walter gave public service during the Rev War (TR Gorham).

Children: births VR Gorham

i James, b 29 Aug 1760: living Buxton 1832 ae 71y (Rev War pension #S29997): m int Gorham 5 Nov 1785 Jenny/Jane Bailey of Falmouth (VR) dau of John & Jane (Brady) Bailey (Leonard B. Chapman, "Early Settlers of Falmouth Neck" [TS, MHS, 1983], p. 123)

ii   Sarah, b 4 Dec 1762: m int Gorham 29 Sep 1781 William Irish (VR), b Gorham 12 Mar 1759 son of James & Mary Gorham (Phinney) Irish (VR), d Gorham 1815 ae 56y (Josiah Pierce, *History of the Town of Gorham, Maine* [1862], p. 178)
iii Benjamin, b Jan 1765 (g.s. gives b 10 Jan 1765): d 11 Jan 1849 (g.s., Locust Grove cem, Hampden): m Abigail Arey (g.s., Locust Grove cem, no dates) [see BENJAMIN MURCH family, *Maine Families*, 1:210]
iv   Susanna, b 12 Sep 1766: m Gorham 26 Mar 1789 Joshua Newcomb of Buxton as his 2nd wife (Gorham VR), b Wellfleet MA c1766 son of John & Abigail (Young) Newcomb (Bethuel M. Newcomb, *Andrew Newcomb 1618-1686 and His Descendants* [1923], p. 196), living Portland 1810 (USC) [see JOHN NEWCOMB family, *Maine Families*, 3:196]
v   Simeon, b 24 Feb 1769: d Unity c1833 ae 64y (Edmund Murch, *A Brief History of the Town of Unity* [1843], pp. 4, 5): m Gorham 27 Jan 1791 Rachel Paine (VR) who d prob Unity ae 86y (Murch, op. cit.). They moved from Gorham to Unity c1794
vi   Zebulon, b 19 Mar 1771: d Belfast bef 3 Aug 1833 when his 2nd wife filed intentions to remarry (VR): m (1) Buxton 23 Oct 1794 Molly/Polly Pennell (Cyrus Woodman, *Records of the Church of Christ in Buxton, Maine During the Pastorate of Rev. Paul Coffin*, [1989], p. 31), b Buxton 18 Nov 1771 dau of Thomas & Lydia (Sands) Pennell (VR) [see EPHRAIM SANDS family, *Maine Families*, 3:243], d prob Belfast bef Oct 1826 when Ephraim filed intentions to remarry: m (2) int Belfast 19 Oct 1826 Lydia (____) Smith (VR) prob wid of Caleb Smith who had d Belfast 23 May 1824 (VR). She m (3) cert Belfast 20 Aug 1833 Judah Caval (VR)
vii Affia, b 12 Apr 1773: m Unity 2 Dec 1802 William Hunt (VR), b Gorham 25 Mar 1781 son of Ichabod & Mary (Stone) Hunt (VR) [see ICHABOD HUNT family, *Maine Families*, 1:157]
viii Joanna, b 27 Sep 1775
ix   Ephraim, b 1 Feb 1778: d Castine 26 Nov 1848 (g.s., Castine cem): m 19 May 1799 Rebecca Cobb (*Boston Evening Transcript*, issue of 20 Mar 1929), b c1782, d Castine 14 Oct 1847 (g.s., Castine cem)
x   Edmund, b 27 Jan 1780: living Unity 1840 (USC)

Dana A. Batchelder, 258 South Sea Avenue, West Yarmouth, MA 02673

Nash, Jon[a]   11b   1 - 2 - 5 - 0 - 0
Bakerstown Plantation, Cumberland County

JONATHAN NASH, b Weymouth MA prob Oct 1752 or 1753 (Rev War pension #S31273) [note that his pension declaration, dated 14 Aug 1832, stated he was ae 79y and that he was b Weymouth MA in Oct 1775 (sic), an obviously wrong year of birth; his age at the time would calculate to a birth date circa 1752 or 1753]: d Auburn 23 Jan 1844 ae 92y (g.s., Mt. Auburn cem): m (1) Dorchester MA c1775 ANN BIRD (MOCA Rev Soldiers, #3599; date based on 1st child's birth in 1776), b Dorchester MA 5 Sep 1758 dau of Jacob & Elizabeth (Ward) Bird (William B. Trask, *The Bird Family: A Genealogy of Thomas Bird of Dorchester, Massachusetts* [1871], pp. 19–20), d Minot 15 Feb 1829 ae 70y (VR; g.s., Mt. Auburn cem): m (2) 24 Apr 1831 DEBORAH (CURTIS) CUTTER of Greene (Greene VR) wid of Dr. Ammi R. Cutter of Greene (as noted on her g.s.). She d Greene 12 Sep 1836 ae 64y (VR; g.s., Old Valley cem). Jonathan was a sergeant in the Rev War, first enlisting at Braintree MA in 1775 (MS&S 11:278–79; pension, op. cit.). He with his family settled in Bakerstown Plantation abt 1782 (ibid.). Jonathan was a captain in the militia when the Poland clerk recorded the births of his children and was a major when he died (g.s.). He was a representative to the MA General Court from the town of Minot in 1812 (Collections of the MHS, 2:121).

Children: dates and places of birth VR Poland, NEHGR, 88 [1934]:150

i Lemuel, b Dorchester MA 17 Oct 1776: d Auburn 19 Dec 1853 (VR) and bur Plains cem, Auburn with War of 1812 marker (no dates): m (1) 25 Feb 1799 Anna Mason of New Gloucester (Minot VR), b New Gloucester 7 Jun 1778 dau of Dr. Ebenezer & Anna (Cleavers) Mason (VR), d 13 Sep 1829 (Minot VR): m (2) Betsey Johnson (g.s., Plains cem, Auburn, no dates)

ii Sarah/Sally, b Worcester MA 2 Jul 1778: d Minot 11 Sep 1804 (VR): m Minot 26 Dec 1795 Philemon Harlow of Poland (Minot VR), b Plymouth MA 30 Dec 1774 son of Ebenezer & Lydia (Doten) Harlow (VR) [see EBENEZER HARLOW Jr. family, *Maine Families*, 3:120–21]. He was a Justice of the Peace

iii Susanna, b Worcester MA 2 Jun 1780: d 26 Sep 1855 (g.s., Tabor Farm cem, Auburn): m Minot 25 Dec 1800 James Harlow of Poland (Minot VR), b Plymouth MA 24 Aug 1781 brother of Philemon above (VR), d 19 Nov 1855 (g.s., Tabor Farm cem, Auburn). He was a soldier in the War of 1812

iv Martha, b Worcester MA 9 Jan 1783: m Minot 28 Aug 1800 Samuel Niles of Poland (Minot VR), b Poland 27 Nov 1777 son of Nathan & Jane (Gurney) Niles (NEHGR, 88 [1934]:56; Bridgewater MA VR)

v Nancy, b Worcester MA 9 Apr 1785: d 20 Oct 1845 (g.s., Briggs cem, Auburn): m Minot 15 Sep 1808 Jeremiah J. Merrill of Pejepscot (Minot VR), b Pejepscot [now Danville] 29 Mar 1782 son of John & Molly (Royal) Merrill (VR), d 12 Jul 1864 (g.s., Briggs cem, Auburn)

vi William, b Poland 23 Apr 1787: m int Minot 22 Jan 1813 Joanna Merrill (VR), b Pejepscot [now Danville] 7 Sep 1793 sister of Jeremiah above (VR)

vii Rachel, b Poland 11 Jul 1790: m Minot 5 Apr 1810 Salter Soper of Gray (Minot VR)
viii Mary/Polly, b Poland 23 Jul 1792: m int Minot 4 Jan 1812 Timothy Kyle of Minot (VR), b 10 Jan 1788 son of William & Zilpha (Merrill) Kyle (Charles Farnham Kyle, *Genealogy of the Kyle Family* [1938])
ix John B., b Poland 8 Jul 1794: d Poland 16 Apr 1883 (Janus G. Elder, *A History of Lewiston, Maine*, edited by David C. & Elizabeth K. Young [1984], p. 272): m int Minot 26 Jan 1816 Rachel C. Banks of Hartford (Minot VR), b No. Yarmouth 16 Jan 1797 (Elder, op. cit., p. 272) dau of William & Lydia (Woodbridge) Banks (Wilbur A. Libby, *Hartford, Maine History*, p. 58), d Rockford IL 2 May 1877 (Elder, op. cit., p. 272)
x Johannah/Joanna, b Poland 19 Oct 1795: d 2 Nov 1843 (g.s., Pearce cem, Hebron): m Minot 30 Nov 1815 Lebbeus Allen (VR), b Poland 4 Jul 1792 son of Abel & Mary (Dillingham) Allen (NEHGR, 88 [1934]:65), d 9 Sep 1872 (g.s., Pearce cem, Hebron)
xi Jacob, b Poland 13 Jul 1798

Gerald Linn Rawson, 190 Whitney Street, Auburn, ME 04210

Nason, Uriah   18c   2 - 3 - 3 - 0 - 0
Gorham and Scarborough Towns, Cumberland County

URIAH NASON, bp Berwick 1st Church 28 Jun 1744 son of John & Margaret (Lord) Nason (NEHGR, 82 [1928]:216; Everett S. Stackpole, *Old Kittery and Her Families* [1903], p. 629): d Gorham 13 May 1833 ae 91y (VR): m 20 Apr 1765 ABIGAIL KNIGHT of Windham (McLellan's *Gorham*, p. 695), b Windham 5 Dec 1744 dau of William & Mary (Haskell) Knight (Samuel T. Dole, *Windham in the Past* [1916], p. 41), d Gorham 5 Mar 1837 ae 98y (VR). Uriah was one of the first settlers in the northeast part of Gorham, arriving as early as 1764 (McLellan's *Gorham*, p. 695). He gave public service in the Rev War (TR Gorham).

Children: identified in VR Gorham [but the birthdates for some of the children are not given]; McLellan's *Gorham*, pp. 695–96
  i Abraham, b 22 Nov 1765: d 18 Sep 1848 ae 86y [sic] (Dr. Gertrude E. Hall, "Nason Data" in "State of Maine, Family Records, Miscellaneous Papers and Genealogies" [microfilm at MHS], 2:58): m Gorham 14 Feb 1793 Lydia Lombard (VR), b Gorham 25 Oct 1771 dau of Solomon & Lydia (Grant) Lombard (ibid.; McLellan's *Gorham*, 633), d 13 May 1833 ae 64y ("Nason Data" op. cit.)

ii William, b 1 Feb 1770: drowned Baldwin 1 Jan 1837, "killed by a mill wheel" ("Nason Data" op. cit.): m Gorham 8 Sep 1791 Elizabeth/Betsey Burnell (VR), b Gorham 21 Sep 1772 dau of John & Elizabeth (_____) Burnell (VR)

iii Samuel, b 1771: d Gorham (McLellan's *Gorham*, p. 696, no date given): m Windham 16 Jun 1793 Patty Mains ("Nason Data," op. cit.)

iv Lot, b c1775: d Gorham 7 Aug 1840 (McLellan's *Gorham*, p. 697): m 3 Jul 1797 Elizabeth/Betsey Lord of No. Yarmouth "at the home of Mr. J. Marsten of No. Yarmouth" (Gorham VR), b c1775, d 9 Sep 1859 ae 84y (McLellan's *Gorham*, p. 697)

v Margaret, b c Jul 1778: d Gorham 28 Dec 1855 ae 77y 5m (Albert J. Sears, *Early Families of Standish, Maine* [1991], p. 45): m Standish 8 Jul 1797 Thomas Cannell (VR), b Standish c1768 son of Philip & Jane (Sherlock) Cannell (Sears, op. cit., pp. 44–45) [see PHILLIP CANNELL family], d Gorham 12 Mar 1854 ae 86y (g.s., No. Gorham cem)

vi Abigail, m int Gorham 30 May 1799 Benjamin Mains of Windham (Gorham VR)

vii Joseph, b 30 Jan 1783: d 8 Apr 1860 (Sears, op. cit., p. 294): m Standish 10 Jun 1804 Elizabeth/Betsey Waterhouse (McLellan's *Gorham*, p. 696), b Scarborough 20 Nov 1781 dau of Joseph & Lydia (Harmon) Waterhouse (Sears, op. cit., p. 294), d Gorham 6 Aug 1863 (ibid.)

viii Uriah Jr., b c1785: d Gorham 6 Feb 1863 (McLellan's *Gorham*, p. 697): m Windham 5 Jun 1807 Jemima Snow (ibid.), b Gorham Jul 1785 dau of Thomas & Jane (Magne/Mague) Snow (ibid., p. 769) [see THOMAS SNOW family], d Gorham 6 Feb 1868 ae 82y (ibid., p. 697)

Dana A. Batchelder, 258 South Sea Avenue, West Yarmouth, MA 02673

Neal, Andrew   60b   1 - 3 - 2 - 0 - 0
Francisborough Plantation [now Cornish], York County

ANDREW NEAL, b Kittery 12 Mar 1742/3 son of John & Patience (Johnson) Neal (VR): poss d in Canada (Timothy W. Robinson & Theoda Mears Morse, *History of the Town of Morrill, Maine* [1944], hereafter *History of Morrill*, p. 273): m Wells 1 Oct 1778 JANE HUBBARD (VR) [he of Berwick on the m int], bp 1st Church Wells 20 Apr 1760 dau of John Heard & Hannah (Neal) Hubbard (NEHGR, 76 [1922]:179) [see JOHN HEARD HUBBARD family, *Maine Families*, 3:144–45]. Andrew was a Quaker and lived in Berwick when he married. Since he "married out" of the Quakers, he was disowned 18 Jun 1791 from the Dover NH Monthly Meeting (NHGR, 2:146). He removed to Francisborough

(Cornish) and moved from there with his family into the Kelsey house in Greene Plantation [Morrill] about 1799, but only lived there a short time. He later went to Canada (*History of Morrill*, p. 273). On 19 Jul 1802, Andrew Neal, blacksmith of Cornish, purchased land of Charles Kelsoe in Greene Plt (Wal Co deeds, 16:486). He and wife "Joan" sold part of this land to his son Johnson in 1805 (ibid., 16:488), and in the same year he and wife "Sally" sold another part to his son Isaac.

Children as found, b prob Berwick, perhaps others: *History of Morrill*, pp. 273–74 & cited sources
  i Johnson, b 4 Jul 1778 (Burlington VR; family records give 1779): d Burlington bet 1840–50 (USC): m (1) int Belfast 20 June 1807 _____ _____ (VR, the original record is torn and the name of his wife is illegible): m (2) int Belfast 29 Jun 1810 Betsy Boyington (VR), b 4 Jul 1788 (Burlington VR), d Burlington 25 Dec 1865 ae 79y [sic] (VR). [She was prob the Betsy Patterson of Saco, and poss Elizabeth dau of Robert & Elizabeth (Goodwin) Patterson who was b 18 Feb 1788, who m int Belfast 17 Jan 1808 Daniel Boyington of Greene Plt (VR; Gideon T. Ridlon, *Saco Valley Settlements and Families* [1895], p. 1100).] Johnson moved to Burlington in the late 1820s. He was a resident of Half Twp No. One East of Cold Stream Pond in 1830 census

  ii Isaac, b c1780: d Belmont 25 Jul 1840 (War of 1812 pension #12540): m Searsmont 1 Jun 1807 Hannah Hamilton (ibid.) [m int rec Belfast 12 May 1807 (VR)], b c1787, d Pittston 19 Jul 1865 ae 79y (VR). She lived in China and Pittston after her husband's death. He was a soldier in the War of 1812

  iii Olive, b 8 May 1784 (*History of Morrill*, p. 102): d 18 May 1853 (ibid.): "of Greene Plt" when she m Belfast Jan 1805 Robert Cross (VR) [*History of Morrill*, p. 102, says m 2 Apr 1803 citing family Bible rec], b Exeter NH 2 Sep 1784 son of Nathaniel & Martha (Woodman) Cross (*History of Morrill*, p. 101), d 22 Jan 1859 (ibid., p. 102). They moved to Jefferson Twp, Bellville, Richland Co, OH (ibid.)

  iv Silas, b 1788 [or 1783]: "of Morrill" when he d of dropsy 28 Dec 1858 ae 70y (Belfast VR) [*History of Morrill*, p. 192, states that Silas d Waldo 27 Dec 1858 ae 75y]: "of Belmont" when he m Belfast 13 Feb 1817 Elizabeth Annis of Unity (Belfast VR), b c1786, d Belmont Aug 1831 ae 45y (*History of Morrill*, p. 274)

  v Sarah

Alan H. Hawkins, 14 Adelbert Street, South Portland, ME 04106-6512

Noble, Christopher   16a   2 - 0 - 1 - 0 - 0
Flintstown Plantation [now Baldwin], Cumberland County

CHRISTOPHER NOBLE, bp Portsmouth NH 7 Apr 1723 son of Christopher & Lydia (Jackson) Noble ("Records of the South Church of Portsmouth, N.H.," NEHGR, 81 [1927]:431; GDMNH, p. 511): his death date has not been found, but he was not a head of household in 1800 (USC): m (1) Portsmouth NH 25 Dec 1744 MARTHA ROWE of Portsmouth NH (Albert J. Sears, *Early Families of Standish, Maine* [1991], hereafter Sears, p. 180), perhaps dau of Anthony & Joanna (Rouse) Rowe whose son Lazarus was the father-in-law of Christopher's twin sons: m prob (2) Standish 19 Jan 1794 ALICE LOWELL (Sears, p. 181) who was prob the Mrs. "Ellis" Noble who d Standish c Aug 1814 ae 90y (David C. & Elizabeth K. Young, *Vital Records from Maine Newspapers, 1785–1820* [1993], p. 432, citing Portland *Gazette*, issue of 22 Aug 1814). Christopher bought land at Allenstown NH in 1750 where he prob lived until 1763 when he moved to Barrington NH (Sears, p. 181). He settled in Pearsontown [Standish] about 1775 and was still of Pearsontown in 1783 when he sold a 30-acre lot there where he was living to his son-in-law, Charles Hall (ibid.). About that time, he took up residence in Flintstown on the 100-acre Lot #5 in the 2nd range west, bounded by the Saco River (ibid.). He mortgaged portions of this to Lazarus, Noah and Benjamin Rowe in 1794 and sold the remainder of the property in 1798 (ibid.).

Children: Sears, pp. 181–82
  i   Martha, bp Dover NH 22 May 1746 (*Collections of the Dover, New Hampshire Historical Society*, 1 [1894]:153): alive Nov 1814 but "probably d that year" (Robert Taylor, *Early Families of Limington, Maine* [1991], pp. 191): m Scarboro 6 Jun 1765 James McKenney (VR), b Scarboro 11 Mar 1742 son of John & Margaret (Wright) McKenney (Gideon T. Ridlon, *Saco Valley Settlements and Families* [1895], p. 914), bp 1st Church Scarboro 5 May 1742 (MHGR 1:168), d No. Limington 1813 (Taylor, op. cit., p. 191) [see JAMES McKENNEY family, *Maine Families*, 3:174]
  ii perhaps Anthony [and named for his grandfather Anthony Rowe], a Rev War pensioner living at Scarboro in 1820 and under the care of a guardian, Edmund Hagens ("Maine Estate Schedules from Rev War Pensions," NEHGR, 142 [1988]:208). At the time, he was dependent on the town for support, having no income nor family (ibid.). When he applied for his pension in 1818, he res Standish and stated he also lived there at his enlistment (Rev War pension #S36709). [Fisher's *Soldiers* states he was b Falmouth 1758, d 1826, and res Pearsontown/Standish]
  iii Christopher Jr., twin, reportedly b York 1760, bp Pearsontown 19 May 1776 (Sears, p. 181): drowned in the Saco River 9 May 1824 (Sears, p. 181): m Dec 1785 Joanna Rowe (ibid.) [m int Gorham 3 Sep 1785 (VR)],

b c1763 dau of Lazarus & Molly (Webber) Rowe (ibid.), d 20 Nov 1859 ae 96y 9m (ibid.). They lived at Baldwin
- iv John, twin, reportedly b York 1760, bp Pearsontown 19 May 1776 (Sears, p. 181): m 26 Dec 1791 Elizabeth Rowe (ibid., p. 182), b Portsmouth NH 1 Apr 1763 dau of Lazarus & Molly (Webber) Rowe and poss twin sister of Joanna above (ibid.). They live in Baldwin until about 1813 when they moved to Portland (ibid.)
- v Moses, bp Pearsontown 15 Feb 1776
- vi Lydia, bp Pearsontown 19 May 1776: m int Gorham 28 Jul 1781 Charles Hall (VR), b c1755 son of Charles & Jemima (Dolliver) Hall (Sears, pp. 94–96), d 1840 (Fisher's *Soldiers*, p. 326). He m (2) Sibel _____ (ibid.)

Helen Burnell Dotts, 7501 Palm Ave., #127, Yucca Valley, CA 92284

Nigh, Bartlett   37b   1 - 3 - 2 - 0 - 0
Fairfield Town, Lincoln County

BARTLETT NYE, b Sandwich MA 18 Aug 1759 son of Joseph & Elizabeth (Holmes) Nye (George H. Nye and Frank E. Best, *A Genealogy of the Nye Family* [1907], hereafter *Nye Family*, p. 98, 160–61): d 28 Feb 1822 ae 63y (g.s., Nye's Corner cem, Fairfield]: m DEBORAH ELLIS of Sandwich MA (*Nye Family*, p. 161), b c1764, d 26 Oct 1841 ae 77y (g.s., Nye's Corner cem, Fairfield). Bartlett was a Rev War soldier (Fisher's *Soldiers*, p. 585). He moved to Fairfield in 1788 and in 1812 was a representative to the General Court (*Nye Family*, p. 161).

Children: births VR Fairfield; *Nye Family*, p. 161
- i Thomas, b 21 Jul 1784: d Skowhegan 23 May 1868: m Clinton 31 Aug 1809 Sarah/Salley Burrell of Clinton (VR), b Clinton 11 Nov 1789 dau of John & Betsey (_____) Burrell (VR), d 27 Aug 1862 (*Nye Family*, p. 263). Thomas was deacon in the Christian Church for 60y (ibid.)
- ii Ellis, b 9 Dec 1785: d Fairfield 22 Aug 1848 ae 62y (VR; g.s., Nye's Corner cem): m Fairfield 3 May 1807 Martha/Patty Williams of Fairfield (VR) dau of Abraham & Abigail (Freeman) Williams (*Nye Family*, p. 263)
- iii Bartlett Jr., b 1 Feb 1788: d 13 Sep 1840 ae 52y (g.s., Maplewood cem, Fairfield): m Fairfield 13 Sep 1810 Mary Tobey (VR), perhaps the Mary Tobey b Fairfield 24 Oct 1790 dau of Samuel & Mary (_____) Tobey (VR), d Fairfield 8 Nov 1880 ae 90y (g.s., Maplewood cem)
- iv Jane, b 21 Jul 1790: m cert Fairfield 28 Jan 1813 John Atwood (VR)
- v Joshua, b 14 Oct 1792: d 31 Jan 1856 ae 63y 3m 17d (g.s., Maplewood cem, Fairfield): m Bucksport 22 Jan 1817 Mary Hincks (VR), b c1797, d 18 Dec 1873 ae 76y 2d (g.s., Maplewood cem, Fairfield). [Joshua and

Mary were enumerated in the 1850 USC at Fairfield. He should not be confused with 2 other Joshua Nyes at Fairfield in 1850, one with a wife Thankful and another with a wife Elizabeth]

 vi Franklin, b 14 Jun 1795: d Fairfield 19 Mar 1821 ae 26y (g.s., Nye's Corner cem)

 vii Sturgis, b 25 Apr 1797: d 20 Jan 1844 ae 51y [sic] (g.s., Nye's Corner cem, Fairfield): m int Fairfield 23 Sep 1820 Ruth Hincks of Bucksport (Fairfield VR), b Provincetown MA 17 Apr 1801 dau of Jesse Young Hincks (*Nye Family*, p. 264), d 21 Mar 1852 ae 51y (g.s., Nye's Corner cem)

 viii Stephen, b 29 May 1799: d Fairfield 21 May 1875 ae 76y (g.s., Nye's Corner cem): m int Fairfield 1 Oct 1820 Eleanor McKechnie (VR), b c1797, d 8 Apr 1876 ae 78y 8m 14d (g.s., Nye's Corner cem)

 ix Martha/Patty, b 21 Jul 1801: d 31 May 1870 (g.s., Nye's Corner cem): m Fairfield 7 Mar 1822 Nathan Fowler (VR), b 27 Dec 1795 (g.s.), d Fairfield 31 Jan 1870 (g.s., Nye's Corner cem). Nathan was a soldier in the War of 1812 (g.s.)

 x Heman, b 7 Jun 1803: d 16 Jun 1885 ae 82y (g.s., Nye's Corner cem, Fairfield): m int Fairfield 22 Jan 1826 Julia Wing (VR), b c1805, d 11 Jul 1871 ae 66y (g.s., Nye's Corner cem, Fairfield)

 xi Dolly, b 25 Aug 1805: d 13 Mar 1841 ae 35y 7m (g.s., Nye's Corner cem, Fairfield): m int Fairfield 19 Nov 1826 William Nowell (VR), b c1801, d 4 Dec 1880 ae 79y 5m (g.s., Nye's Corner cem, Fairfield). He prob m (2) 2 Jun 1842 Hannah Furbush of Clinton (VR Fairfield)

 xii Sarah/Sally, b 13 Oct 1810: d 18 Oct 1846 ae 36y (g.s., Nye's Corner cem): m Fairfield 23 Feb 1837 Benjamin Franklin Wing (VR), b c1806, d 23 Feb 1889 ae 82y (g.s, Nye's Corner cem). He prob m (2) Fairfield 12 May 1850 Lydia (Tobey) Hobbs wid of Sewall Hobbs (VR)

Carol F. Nye, RFD 1 Box 388, Belgrade, ME 04917-9722

Nigh, Elisha 37c 1 - 2 - 5 - 0 - 0
 Fairfield Town, Lincoln County

ELISHA NYE, b Sandwich MA 2 Nov 1757 son of Joseph & Elizabeth (Holmes) Nye (George H. Nye and Frank E. Best, *A Genealogy of the Nye Family* [1907], hereafter *Nye Family*, pp. 98, 160): d Fairfield 11 Mar 1846 ae 88y 4m (g.s., Fairfield Center cem): m 30 May 1779 SARAH MOREY of Plymouth MA (*Nye Family*, p. 160), b 1756 dau of Cornelius & Sarah (Johnson) Morey (William T. Davis, *Genealogical Register of Plymouth Families* [repr 1975], p. 186), d Fairfield

21 Jan 1835 ae 80y (VR; g.s., Fairfield Center cem). Elisha prob moved to Fairfield shortly after his marriage. He was a Rev War soldier (Fisher's *Soldiers*, p. 585).

Children, all b Fairfield, birth order uncertain: *Nye Family*, p. 160
   i Betsy, b 5 Oct 1784: m Fairfield 28 Jan 1802 Henry L. Rolfe (VR) who was b 13 Oct 1774 (Fairfield VR)
  ii Temperance, m int Fairfield 20 Jan 1808 Samuel Gilman of Waterville (Fairfield VR)
 iii Elisha, b 1788: d Grant Co, WI in 1855 (*Nye Family*, p. 260): m Fairfield 14 Mar 1805 Sabray Obryne [O'Brian] (VR). They moved to Grant Co WI abt 1840 (*Nye Family*, p. 260)
 iv Sally, b c1788: d 28 July 1845 ae 57y (g.s., Nye's Corner cem, Fairfield): m int Fairfield 20 Jan 1808 John W. Gifford (VR), b c1786, d 26 Jun 1865 ae 79y (g.s., Nye's Corner cem, Fairfield). He was a War of 1812 soldier (g.s.)
  v Joseph, b 31 May 1790: d 1865 (g.s., Nye's Corner cem, Fairfield): m int Fairfield 12 Nov 1820 Mary Freeman (VR), b Fairfield 25 Jul 1796 dau of Barnabas & Rhoda (____) Freeman (VR), d 1881 (Nye's Corner cem, Fairfield). He was a War of 1812 soldier (g.s.)
 vi Eunice, m Clinton 30 Aug 1809 James Burrell of Clinton (VR), prob b Clinton 28 Mar 1787 son of John & Betsey (____) Burrell (VR)
vii Alden, b 1794: d 25 Jan 1864 ae 69y (g.s., Nye's Corner cem, Fairfield): m Fairfield 2 Nov 1817 Eliza Freeman (VR), b Fairfield 27 Jan 1800 dau of Barnabas & Rhoda (____) Freeman (VR). He was a War of 1812 soldier (g.s.)
viii Cornelius, b 30 Apr 1796: d Lynn MA 11 Sept 1894 ae 98y 4m (g.s. Maplewood cem, Fairfield): m Fairfield 28 Sep 1820 Melinda Phillips (VR), b c Oct 1799, d 27 Jul 1861 ae 61y 9m (g.s., Maplewood cem, Fairfield). He was a soldier in the War of 1812 (g.s.; *Nye Family*, p. 261). They moved to Lynn MA in 1846 (ibid.)
 ix Sylvanus, b 26 Feb 1800: d Lewiston 12 Mar 1877 (*Nye Family*, p. 262): m Fairfield 9 Jan 1823 Mary Buck (VR), b Fairfield 9 Jul 1803 dau of Abner Buck (*Nye Family*, p. 262), d 30 Apr 1875 (ibid.). They moved from Fairfield to Clinton and then to Lewiston. Three of his eight children moved to Wisconsin
  x Abigail, d unm (*Nye Family*, p. 160)
 xi Peleg, d unm (*Nye Family*, p. 160)

Carol F. Nye, RFD 1 Box 388, Belgrade, ME 04917-9722

Nye, Elisha   39b   3 - 2 - 6 - 0 - 0
Hallowell Town, Lincoln County

ELISHA NYE, b Sandwich MA 22 Apr 1745 son of Stephen & Maria (Bourne) Nye (Hallowell VR; George H. Nye and Frank E. Best, *A Genealogy of the Nye Family* [1907], hereafter *Nye Family*, pp. 98, 164): d Hallowell 11 May 1833 ae 88y (VR): m (1) 2 Apr 1767 LUCY TOBEY dau of Eliakim Tobey of Sandwich MA (*Nye Family*, p. 165) who d Hallowell 22 Sep 1775 (VR): m (2) MEHITABLE ROBINSON dau of William Robinson of Falmouth MA (*Nye Family*, p. 165). She d Hallowell 12 Aug 1836 (VR). Elisha served in the Rev War (Rev War pension #S30011). He moved to Hallowell in 1781 (*Nye Family*, p. 165).

Children by 1st wife Lucy Tobey, b Sandwich MA: births VR Hallowell; *Nye Family*, p. 165
  i   Alvin, b 22 May 1768. He moved to Bangor (*Nye Family*, p. 269)
  ii Capt. Ansel, b 17 Dec 1769: d Hallowell 2 July 1847 ae 77y (VR): m Hallowell 10 Sep 1795 Dolly Bachelder (VR), b c1774 dau of Ebenezer & Susanna Bachelder of Boston MA (*Nye Family*, p. 270), d Hallowell 18 May 1854 ae 80y (VR)
  iii Maria, b 25 Mar 1771
Children by 2nd wife Mehitable Robinson, b Hallowell except as noted: births VR Hallowell; *Nye Family*, pp. 165–67
  iv Elisha, b Chilmark MA 8 Jun 1776: d "on a passage to Boston" 3 Dec 1813 ae 37y 6m (Hallowell VR): m cert Hallowell 20 Jan 1797 Nancy Young (VR)
  v   Lucy, b Chilmark MA 1 Jan 1778: m Hallowell 5 Oct 1794 Stephen Hinckley (VR), b 27 Aug 1762 son of Shubael & Mary (Clew) Hinckley (Hallowell VR) [see SHUBAEL HINCKLEY Jr family, *Maine Families*, 3:137]
  vi Abigail, b Falmouth MA 25 Dec 1780: m Hallowell 28 Nov 1799 Philip Lord (Hallowell VR), b Ipswich MA 4 Dec 1774 son of Philip & Elizabeth (Kimball) Lord (Hallowell VR)
  vii Susanna/Sukey, b 5 Jan 1783: m (1) int Hallowell 11 Oct 1800 Nathaniel Kent (VR): m (2) Hallowell 7 Oct 1805 Cabel Heath both of Augusta (Hallowell VR)
  viii Eunice, b 26 Sep 1784: d 17 Jul 1877 (*Nye Family*, p. 165): m Hallowell 31 Aug 1804 John Charles Shuff/Schuff of Augusta (Hallowell VR) who d 17 Nov 1838 (*Nye Family*, p. 165)
  ix Mehitable, b 30 May 1786. She had a son John Nye b Hallowell 24 Dec 1809 (VR)
  x   Charles, b 4 Feb 1788: d Bermuda 29 Sep 1819 ae 34y [sic] (Hallowell VR): m int Hallowell 6 Nov 1811 Alice Pollard (VR)

xi   Stephen, b 25 Aug 1791: d at sea Feb 1817 ae 25y 6m (Hallowell VR; *Nye Family*, p. 167)
xii   William, b 3 Jul 1793
xiii Robinson, b 9 Mar 1796: d Martinique Feb 1818 ae 22y (Hallowell VR)

Carol F. Nye, RFD 1 Box 388, Belgrade, ME 04917-9722

Palmer, Rich^d   59a   3 - 4 - 6 - 0 - 0
Buxton Town, York County

RICHARD PALMER, b Bradford MA 11 Dec 1744 son of Andrew & Jemima (Hardy) Palmer (VR): d Hollis 26 May 1807 ae 63y (John E. Frost, "Hollis (Maine) Record Book" [TS, MHS, 1967], hereafter Frost, p. 110): m Buxton 29 May 1766 JANE HOPKINSON of Narragansett No. 1 [Buxton] (Cyrus Woodman, *Records of the Church of Christ in Buxton During the Pastorate of Rev. Paul Coffin* [1989], hereafter Woodman, p. 19), b Bradford MA 19 Oct 1746 dau of John & Sarah (Morse) Hopkinson (VR), d 9 Oct 1834 ae 88y (Frost, p. 110; Jewett & Hannaford, *A History of Hollis, Maine, 1660–1976* [1976], p. 181). Richard and his brothers, James and Steven, settled in Narragansett No. 1 [Buxton] in the 1760s (ibid.). He moved across the river to Little Falls [Hollis] in the early 1790s (ibid.).

Children: Jewett & Hannaford, op. cit., p. 181
   i   Andrew, b Buxton Feb 1767: d Hollis 18 Jul 1843 ae 76y 5m (Frost, p. 110): m Buxton 3 Dec 1801 Sarah Hearl both of Phillipsburg [Hollis] (Woodman, p. 36), b c1776 dau of Joshua & Hannah (Bradbury) Hearl (the only Hearl family in this era living in the Buxton/Hollis vicinity), d 13 Aug 1844 ae 68y (Frost, p. 110)
   ii John, b Buxton c1771: d Buxton 28 Apr 1853 ae 82y (Frost, p. 105): of Little Falls [Hollis] when he m Buxton 8 Jun 1796 Charlotte Lane (Woodman, p. 32), b c1773 dau of Capt. Daniel & Mary/Molly (Woodman) Lane of Buxton (Gideon T. Ridlon, *Saco Valley Settlements and Families* [1895], pp. 875, 877), d 29 Sep 1837 ae 64y (Frost, p. 105)
   iii Jane, m Buxton 10 Jan 1799 William Dyer (Woodman, p. 34)
   iv Joses, b Buxton 1776: m Buxton 19 Jun 1799 Mary/Polly Atkinson both of Phillipsborough (Woodman, p. 34) dau of Moses & Rebecca (Woodman) Atkinson (Ridlon, pp. 448–49)
   v   James, b Buxton 1778: d 10 Mar 1840 ae 62y (g.s., Tory Hill cem, Buxton): of Phillipsburg when he m Buxton 25 Jul 1802 Elizabeth Bradbury of Buxton (Woodman, p. 37), b Buxton 14 Sep 1780 dau of Elijah & Sarah

(Lane) Bradbury (VR) [see ELIJAH BRADBURY family], d 26 Mar 1837 ae 57y (g.s., Tory Hill cem, Buxton)
- vi Richard, m int Hollis 7 Feb 1805 Lydia Knight (VR)
- vii Mary, b Buxton 1783: d Hollis 9 May 1833 ae 50y (Frost, p. 110)
- viii Hannah, b Buxton 1785: d 1 Dec 1847 ae 62y (Frost, p. 110)
- ix Paul, b Buxton 1787: d Hollis 12 Aug 1864 ae 77y (Frost, p. 110): m int Hollis 29 Apr 1815 Susan Woodman (VR), b c1789, d 14 Mar 1865 ae 76y (Frost, p. 110)
- x   Martha, b Buxton 1789: d Hollis 1 Jun 1855 ae 66y (Frost, p. 110)

Phyllis S. Williams, 7468 McKinley St., Mentor, OH 44060

Parsons, Joseph   71b   3 - 4 - 4 - 0 - 0
York Town, York County

JOSEPH PARSONS, b York 2 Apr 1746 son of Joseph & Miriam (Preble) Parsons (Lester M. Bragdon & John E. Frost, *Vital Records of York, Maine* [1992], p. 63, hereafter VR): d York 18 May 1810 (ibid., p. 411): m (1) York 9 Nov 1769 JERUSHA SAYWARD (ibid., p. 357), b 9 Feb 1748/9 dau of James & Bethula (Bradbury) Sayward (ibid., pp. 68–69), bur at York 30 Jan 1805 (ibid., p. 449): m (2) Wells 21 Nov 1805 MARY (BROWN) (WAKEFIELD) WASHBURN of Wells (VR), b c1766 dau of John & Elizabeth (_____) Brown (letter written in 1931 by Mary's great grandson, J. William Gale of Amesbury MA, to his daughter Louise Gale Haines, in possession of submitter), d 28 Jun 1836 ae abt 70y ("Diary of Jeremiah Weare, Jr., of York, Maine," NEHGR, 66 [1912]:312). She had m (1) Kennebunk 2 Dec 1784 John Wakefield (VR) and m (2) cert Kennebunk 7 Aug 1798 Thomas Washburn of Arundel (Wells VR). After her marriage to Joseph Parsons, she m (4) cert York 27 Jun 1820 Daniel Crosby (VR, p. 212) and m (5) York 31 Dec 1827 Maj. Eliakim Seavey (VR, p. 229). In the records, Joseph was called Joseph Parsons III or Tertius. Joseph dated his will 2 Feb 1810 in which he named his wife Mary and all of his children (all were still alive in 1810) (York County Probate #14564). Because of a lack of 3 "credible" witnesses, the will was disallowed but still entered into the probate volumes. The inventory dated 14 Aug 1810 showed real estate at York bordering the sea worth $1458 and personal property worth $513.42. A map of Joseph's property at York is shown in the probate records, in Vol. 22, p. 457.

Children by 1st wife Jerusha Sayward
- i   Thomas, b York 14 Oct 1770 (VR, p. 88): d c1823 (J. E. Greenleaf, *The Greenleaf Genealogy*, p. 340): m int Edgecomb 25 Jan 1797 Mary K. (Patty) Greenleaf (VR), b Edgecomb 1 Mar 1774 dau of Stephen & Mary (Knight) Greenleaf (VR)

ii John, b York 24 Jan 1773 (Westport VR): m int York 9 May 1799 Jemima Phillips (VR, p. 183), b York 26 Jun 1778 (notes of Lester Bragdon, Old York Historical Society) and bp 1st Parish York 18 Oct 1778 dau of Norton Woodbridge & Mary (Parsons) Phillips (YCGSJ, 4 [1989]:4:17; York VR, p. 160 which gives her parents' marriage), d Westport 2 Jul 1841 (ibid.)

iii Joseph Jr., bp 1st Parish York 22 Jan 1775 (YCGSJ, 4 [1989]:4:16): m York 15 Oct 1797 Lydia Averill (VR, p. 365), b York 7 Jan 1777 dau of Job & Margaret (Simpson) Averill (VR, p. 94)

iv Jerusha, b 1776 (York VR, p. 645) and bp 1st Parish York 30 Mar 1777 (YCGSJ 4 [1989]:4:16): d 1867 (York VR, p. 645): m York 19 Nov 1795 Samuel Weare (VR, p. 364), b York 7 Jun 1768 son of Jeremiah & Sarah (Preble) Weare (York VR, p. 484) [see JEREMIAH WEARE family]

v James, b York 4 Jul 1779 (letter written in 1864 by James's son, Alonzo, in possession of submitter), bp 1st Parish York 11 Jul 1779 (YCGSJ 4 [1989]:4:17): d York 1 Jan 1822 (Alonzo Parsons letter, op. cit.): m York 11 Oct 1802 Martha/Polly Harvey of Portsmouth NH (Alonzo Parsons letter, op. cit.) [intentions dated York 24 May 1802, VR, p. 186]

vi Jotham, bp 1st Parish York 31 Mar 1782 (YCGSJ 4 [1989]:4:17): d Kennebunk 2 Jan 1819 ae 38y (VR): m Kennebunk 11 Apr 1805 his stepsister Mary Wakefield (VR) dau of John & Mary (Brown) Wakefield (J. William Gale letter, op. cit.). She m (2) Kennebunk 23 Oct 1820 John Brown Jr. (VR)

vii Theodore, bp 1st Parish York 7 Nov 1784 (YCGSJ 4 [1989]:4:18): d York 28 Sep 1860 ae 76y (VR, p. 637): m int York 6 July 1810 his step-sister Ruth Wakefield of York (ibid., p. 196), b Sep 1794 dau of John & Mary (Brown) Wakefield and sis of Mary above (J. William Gale letter, op. cit.), d York 7 Jun 1888 ae 94y 9m (VR, p. 637)

viii Susanna, bp 1st Parish York 27 Mar 1788 (YCGSJ 4 [1989]:4:18). Susanna was alive and apparently single in 1810 (father's will)

ix Rufus, bp 1st Parish York 26 Sep 1790 (ibid., 4 [1989]:4:18). One Rufus Parsons had a wife Mary M. and three children and d Gloucester MA

Children by 2nd wife Mary (Brown) (Wakefield) Washburn: J. William Gale letter, op. cit.

x Timothy, b York c1808: d Kittery 12 Feb 1853 ae 45y (John E. Frost, "Kittery, Maine Record Book" [TS, MHS, 1978], p. 126): m York 23 Dec 1830 Mariah Tripp of York (John E. Frost & Joseph C. Anderson II, *Marriage Returns of York County, Maine to the Year 1892* [1993], p. 23), b c Jul 1803, d Kittery 22 Apr 1890 ae 86y 9m (Frost, op. cit., p. 126)

Joan Parsons Wang, 2720 E. Mel Curry Road, Bloomington, IN 47408

parsins, William 67a 2 - 5 - 4 - 0 - 0
Sanford Town, York County

WILLIAM PARSONS, b Bradford MA 22 Oct 1743 son of Rev. Joseph & Frances (Usher) Parsons: d Alfred 4 Aug 1826 ae 82y (g.s., Cong Churchyard, Alfred which states that William settled in Alfred in 1775 and that he was a son of Rev. Joseph P. Parsons of Bradford and a grandson of Rev. Joseph P. Parsons of Salisbury MA): m South Berwick 23 Feb 1769 ABIGAIL FROST BLUNT (NEHGR, 83 [1929]:11), b Newcastle NH 21 Sep 1744 dau of Rev. Joseph & Sarah (Frost) Blunt, d Alfred 4 Jul 1818 ae 73y (g.s., Cong Churchyard, Alfred which states that she was a dau of Rev. John Blunt of Newcastle NH). Abigail was received in full communion at the Berwick 1st Church 26 Jun 1768 (NEHGR 82 [1928]:501); William was received there 12 Apr 1772 (ibid., p. 503). They were dismissed to the church in Sanford 25 Feb 1791 (NEHGR 83 [1929]:148). William settled in Alfred, then a part of Sanford, in 1775. He was a farmer and a manufacturer of lumber and potash. He was a magistrate for many years as well as Town Clerk and Selectman for Alfred. He was much employed as town and county surveyor (Henry Parsons, *The Parsons Family* [1912], 1:109).

Children: births VR Alfred; all other info from *Parsons Family*, op. cit., unless otherwise stated
  i   Joseph, b South Berwick 21 Nov 1769, bp Berwick 1st Church 26 Nov 1769 (NEHGR 82 [1928]:501): d Eastbrook 20 May 1854: m Alfred 28 Oct 1805 Charlotte Sanders Sargent, b Boston MA 24 Jul 1782 dau of Paul Dudley & Lucy (Sanders) Sargent [see PAUL DUDLEY SARGENT family, *Maine Families*, 3:246–47], d Franklin 20 Jun 1865
  ii Sarah, b South Berwick 6 Oct 1771, bp Berwick 1st Church 20 Oct 1771 (NEHGR 82 [1928]:502): d Lincoln 20 Dec 1855: m aft 1790 John Leighton, b Kittery 18 Oct 1768 son of Maj. Samuel & Abigail (Frost) Leighton of Eliot (Kittery VR), d 1854
  iii Abigail Frost, b South Berwick 19 Jul 1773, bp Berwick 1st Church 1 Aug 1773 (NEHGR 82 [1928]:503): d 24 May 1842 ae 68y (g.s., Cong Churchyard, Alfred): m Col Daniel Lewis, b 1772 son of Maj Morgan & Sarah (Tripe) Lewis (Daniel Lewis, a minor upwards of 14y of age, son of Morgan Lewis late of Sanford, chose William Parsons to be his guardian 19 Apr 1791, York Co Probate 15:476; Morgan Lewis family rec in Frost's York VR [1992], p. 82), d 10 Mar 1833 ae 61y (g.s., Cong Churchyard, Alfred)
  iv John, b South Berwick 8 Sep 1775: d 2 Feb 1858 ae 82y 4m 25d (g.s., Cong Churchyard, Alfred): m int Lyman 4 Oct 1800 Love Brock of Lyman (VR), b 1779 dau of Simeon & Judith (Bunker) Brock [see SIMEON BROCK family], d 22 Feb 1857 ae 77y 10m 25d (g.s., Cong Churchyard, Alfred)

v   Frances Usher, b Alfred 4 Jan 1778: d Pittsfield NH 8 Sep 1865 and bur Gilmanton NH: m 29 Dec 1799 Gen. Samuel Leighton [int Kittery 20 Sep 1799 betw Mr Samuel Leighton Jr of Kittery & Miss Francies Parsons of Alfred (VR)], b Kittery 25 May 1771 bro of John above (VR), d 1848
vi William, b Alfred 14 Jun 1780 (g.s. which gives place and date of birth): d Kennebunk 8 Oct 1864 ae 84y (g.s., Hope cem): m Parsonsfield 14 Jan 1814 Mary Parsons, b 2 Aug 1792 dau of Col. Joseph & Lydia (Lord) Parsons (g.s. which gives place of birth and father's name; *A History of the First Century of the Town of Parsonsfield, Maine* [1888], p. 392), d Kennebunk 17 Apr 1874 (g.s., Hope cem)
vii Thomas, b Alfred 21 Jan 1783. He lived in Buenos Aires, Argentina where he m and d
viii Samuel, b Alfred 16 Mar 1785: d 1818: unm
ix Usher, b Alfred 18 Aug 1788: d Providence RI 19 Dec 1868: m 23 Sep 1822 Mary Jackson Holmes dau of Rev. Abial Holmes, D.D. & sis of Oliver Wendall Holmes, d in childbirth 1823. He was a surgeon on the flagship LAWRENCE commanded by Commodore Oliver H. Perry in the Battle of Lake Erie against the British 22 Sep 1813. In Aug 1820 he was chosen Professor of Anatomy & Surgery at Dartmouth College and in 1822 he took a similar position at Brown University (W. W. Clayton, *History of York County, Maine* [1880], p. 270)

Mrs. Dorothy Moore Tower, 65 Matthew Drive, Brunswick, ME 04011

Pettey, Saml 38a   1 - 2 - 5 - 0 - 0
Georgetown Town, Lincoln County

SAMUEL PATTEE, b Georgetown 10 May 1756 son of Jeremiah & Jane (Stuard) Pattee (VR) [see JEREMIAH PATTEE family, *Maine Families*, 3:210]: d Georgetown 31 Jul 1825 (VR): m Georgetown 3 Dec 1782 SARAH (SEWALL) McPHETTRAGE (VR), b Georgetown 6 Oct 1756 dau of William & Sarah (Chisam) Sewall (VR), d Georgetown 9 Oct 1836 (VR). Sarah was the wid of John McPhettrage whom she had m Georgetown 23 Jan 1777 (VR).

Children: births VR Georgetown
  i   Jeremiah, b 27 Mar 1783: m Bath 26 Dec 1819 Azubah Low (VR)
  ii Susannah, b 28 May 1785
  iii Samuel, b 16 Jun 1786: d Arrowsic 26 Oct 1849 (VR): m int Georgetown 20 Feb 1819 Mary Potter (VR)
  iv Sally, b 2 Jul 1788: d Arrowsic 17 Mar 1871 (VR)

> v William Sewall, b 5 Nov 1790: m bef 1826 Mary N. _____. They res Bath 1850 (USC)
> vi Benjamin, b 1 Aug 1792: m Georgetown 31 Dec 1822 Mary Low (VR Bath)
> vii Nancy, b 1 Jul 1794: d young
> viii Rachel McCobb, b 20 Aug 1795: d Arrowsic 23 Aug 1873 (VR)
> ix Elizabeth, b 25 May 1797: m int Georgetown 1 Apr 1827 John Powers (VR)

[See Marie Lollo Scalisi and Virginia M. Ryan, "Peter Pattee of Haverhill, Massachusetts: A 'Journeyman Shoemaker' and His Descendants," NEHGR 146 (1992):315–36, 147 (1993):73–86, 174–87.]

Marie Scalisi, 23 Valleywood Drive, Huntington Station, NY 11746

Peabody, Sam¹ 18c 2 - 0 - 1 - 0 - 0
Gorham and Scarborough Towns, Cumberland County

SAMUEL PEABODY, b Middleton MA 30 Jan 1721 son of Francis & Dorothy (Perkins) Peabody (VR; Cyrus Eaton, *Annals of the Town of Warren* [1877], p. 600; Selim Hobart Peabody, *Peabody Genealogy* [1909], hereafter Peabody, p. 39): d 1804 (ibid.): m Beverly MA 13 Apr 1749 RUTH TRASK (VR), bp Beverly MA 9 Jun 1728 dau of Josiah & Mary (_____) Trask of Beverly MA (VR; obit in *Eastern Argus* dated 18 Jan 1820 names her father as Josiah Trask, cited in David C. & Elizabeth K. Young, *Vital Records from Maine Newspapers, 1785–1820* [1993], p. 458), d Union 10 Jan 1820 ae 93y (obit, op. cit.). They lived in Gorham, New Marblehead (now Windham) and Cumberland. In 1792, he sold his estate in Gorham to Stephen Longfellow and removed to Union (Peabody; McLellan's *Gorham*, p. 709).

Children: all but Mary named in McLellan's *Gorham*, p. 709; all named in Peabody, p. 39
> i Mary, b Windham 29 Nov 1750
> ii Josiah, b Windham 9 Aug 1752: d Newburyport MA (Peabody, p. 74): m Mary Norton (ibid.) who d Newbury MA 24 May 1831 (VR; g.s., Byfield cem). He paid a poll tax in Gorham in 1773 (McLellan's *Gorham*, p. 709). He was a Rev War soldier (Peabody, p. 74)
> iii Ruth, d Portland 1795 (Peabody, p. 39): unm
> iv Mehitable, d Cumberland c1831 (Peabody, p. 39): m 27 Nov 1786 Alexander Barr (ibid.)

v Sarah
vi Betsey, m c1797 John Kieff of Union (Peabody, p. 39)
vii Anna, b 1767 (McLellan's *Gorham*, p. 709): d Portland 1 Feb 1860 (Peabody, p. 39)
viii Lucy, m Gorham 28 Jan 1791 Varnum Beverly (VR; McLellan's *Gorham*, p. 709)
ix Samuel, b Windham 1773: d Sep 1854 (Peabody, p. 74): m int Union 7 May 1794 Elizabeth Martin (VR), b 1774 dau of William Martin of Dixmont (Peabody, p. 74; g.s.), d 1848 (g.s., Simpson cem, Dixmont). He lived in Dixmont (McLellan's *Gorham*, p. 709)
x William, b 1775: m c1794–95 Melinda/Lynday Woodcock (Peabody, p. 74; John L. Sibley, *A History of the Town of Union, Maine* [repr 1987], p. 517), b 27 Jan 1777 dau of David & Abigail (Holmes) Woodcock of Medway MA and Union (ibid.). He paid a poll tax in Gorham 1790–92 (McLellan's *Gorham*, p. 709). He moved to Pen Co and d there (Sibley, op. cit.)
xi Stephen, d at ae 17y (Peabody, p. 39)
xii Apphia, m in the winter of 1794–95 David Woodcock (Sibley, op. cit., p. 517), b 23 Oct 1771 bro of Lynday above (ibid.)

Henry Tinkham, 1955 Congress St., Portland, ME 04102
Ervin Roberts, 66 Hillcrest Ave., So. Portland, ME 04106

Pease, James 26a 3 - 0 - 2 - 0 - 0
Barrettstown, Hancock County

JAMES PEASE, b Edgartown, Martha's Vineyard MA c1725 (Fisher's *Soldiers*, p. 609) and bp Edgartown MA 10 Jul 1726 son of Nathan & Sarah (Vincent) Pease (VR; Charles Edward Banks, *The History of Martha's Vineyard, Dukes County, Massachusetts* [repr 1966], hereafter Banks, 3:390, 395): d prob Appleton 6 Oct 1798 ae 73y (Hope VR; g.s., Pine Grove cem, Appleton): m Edgartown MA 29 Apr 1762 MARY MARCHANT (VR), b Edgartown MA c1725–30 dau of John & Miriam (Cleveland) Marchant (Banks, 3:292), d 12 Mar 1805 ae over 75y (Hope VR). After his marriage, James and Mary lived at Edgartown MA where all of their children were born. During the Rev War, he served on the ship GENERAL PUTNAM in the Penobscot Expedition (MS&S, 12:37; Anna Simpson Hardy, *History of Hope, Maine* [1990], p. 10). Probably near the time of the 1790 census, he moved to the part of Barrettstown that later became Appleton (death notice for son James).

Children, b Edgartown MA: baptisms VR Edgartown MA
i Aaron, b 26 Mar 1762 (Hope VR) and bp 6 May 1764: d Appleton (*History of Hope*, p. 361): m Edgartown MA 24 Sep 1786 Sarah/Sally

Norton (VR), b 22 Mar 1762 dau of Ansel & Deborah (Vinson) (Marchant) Norton (*History of Hope*, p. 330; Banks, 3:353)
ii   Miriam/Meriam, bp 13 Oct 1765
iii James, bp 5 Jul 1767: d Hope 3 Aug 1847 ae 82y 3m (David C. Young & Robert L. Taylor, *Death Notices from Freewill Baptist Publications 1811–1851* [1985], pp. 254-55; g.s., Pine Grove cem, Appleton): m Appleton 13 Jun 1796 Abigail Dunham (John L. Sibley, *History of Union, Maine* [1851], p. 448), b Edgartown MA c Nov 1777 prob dau of Samuel Dunham of Warren (*History of Hope*, p. 330), d 9 May 1863 ae 89y 5m 19d (g.s., Pine Grove cem, Appleton). James's obituary notice stated that he removed with his parents to Appleton when he was ae 24 or 25y
iv   Nathan, b c Jun 1770 and bp 16 Aug 1772: d 15 Mar 1854 ae 83y 9m 1d (g.s., Hart cem, Appleton Ridge): m c1795 Hannah _____ (Appleton VR), b c Apr 1775, d 7 Jan 1855 ae 79y 9m 1d (g.s., Hart cem, Appleton Ridge)

Elvera Stevens Pardi, 65 Clifton Street, Portland, ME 04101
Carolyn Morgan Bailey Lynch, 85 Land of Nod Road, Windham, ME 04062-4032

Pendelton, Nat^l 29b   1 - 1 - 10 - 0 - 0
   Isleborough Town, Hancock County

NATHANIEL PENDLETON, b Westerly RI or Stonington CT 22 Jan 1747 son of Thomas & Dorcas (Dodge) Pendleton (Everett Hall Pendleton, *Brian Pendleton and His Descendants* [1910], hereafter *Brian Pendleton*, p. 116) [Nathaniel Pendleton Family Bible, printed 1805, copy at Stephen Phillips Memorial Library, Searsport, states b 22 Jan 1749] [see THOMAS PENDLETON family]: drowned 28 May 1833 "by the upsetting of a boat, while crossing the river from Duck Trap to Islesboro" ae 84y (Family Bible; *Republican Journal*, issue of 6 Jun 1833): m (1) prob Westerly RI abt 1767 CYNTHIA WEST, b Westerly RI 12 Dec 1749 (Family Bible) prob dau of James & Zerviah (_____) West of Westerly RI (*Brian Pendleton*, p. 193, citing will of her mother "Survior" West), d 13 Apr 1810 ae 61y (Family Bible, op. cit.): m (2) Northport 29 Jul 1810 SALLY (SWEETLAND?) BRADFORD (VR) wid of William Bradford of Northport (*Brian Pendleton*, p. 193, citing Han Co Probate 4:314). According to Nathaniel's grandson, Sally was a Sweetland by birth (ibid., p. 194). During the Rev War, Nathaniel was an ensign in Col. Parson's 10th Continental Regiment of CT in 1776 (*Record of Service of Connecticut Men, War of the Revolution*, 1:99). This regiment was at the siege of Boston and took part in the battles of Long Island and White Plains (*Brian Pendleton*, p. 192). He came to Islesboro, as did his parents and brothers, and by 1800 moved to Northport (USC).

Children by 1st wife, Cynthia West: births in Family Bible, op. cit.
- i Abigail Gardner/Nabby, b Westerly RI 31 Aug 1768: d Islesboro 17 Jan 1867 (Family Bible) [*Brian Pendleton*, p. 347, states d 9 Nov 1867 ae 99y): m abt 1785 Dea. David Thomas Jr. of Marshfield MA (*Brian Pendleton*, p. 347)
- ii Nathaniel, b Westerly RI 22 Aug 1770: d young
- iii Cynthia A., b Westerly RI 28 Apr 1771 [sic, 8 months after the reported birth of her older brother]: d Bangor 28 Apr 1857 (g.s., Mt. Hope cem): m Islesboro 16 Nov 1789 Zenas Drinkwater (Alice MacDonald Long, *Marriage Records of Hancock County, Maine Prior to 1892* [1992], p. 11), b No. Yarmouth 9 Nov 1768 son of Micajah & Elizabeth (Bradford) Drinkwater (*Brian Pendleton*, p. 347), d Bangor 25 Jan 1853 ae 85y (g.s., Mt. Hope cem) [see ZENAS DRINKWATER family, *Maine Families*, 3:69]
- iv Sally, b Islesboro 25 Mar 1773: prob d young
- v Peggy, b Islesboro 5 Apr 1774: m abt 1791 Josiah Drinkwater (*Brian Pendleton*, p. 348), b 18 Nov 1770 bro of Zenas above (ibid.), d 3 Jul 1858 (ibid.). He m (2) abt 1799 Eunice Wyman (John S. Fernald, *The Drinkwater Family* [1904], p. 9) and m (3) aft 1834 Rachel Parker (ibid.)
- vi Elizabeth/Betsey, b Islesboro 2 Sep 1776: d bef 1802 (*Brian Pendleton*, p. 348): m Thomas Brazier of Northport (ibid.)
- vii Mary, b Lincolnville 16 Jan 1778
- viii Lucinda, b Islesboro 23 Feb 1779: d 2 Aug 1860 ae 81y (*Brian Pendleton*, p. 349): m (1) William Drinkwater (ibid.), b 16 Oct 1775 bro of Zenas & Josiah above (ibid.), d 27 Nov 1819 (ibid.): m (2) Northport 18 Jul 1824 William Philbrook 3rd (VR) son of William Jr & Diodama (Lassell) Philbrook (*Brian Pendleton*, p. 349): m (3) Northport 13 Dec 1831 Samuel Bullock (Elizabeth M. Mosher & Isabel Morse Maresh, *Marriage Records of Waldo County, Maine Prior to 1892* [1990], p. 11)
- ix Wealthy, b Islesboro 22 Jan 1781: m abt 1798 Mark Dodge of Islesboro (*Brian Pendleton*, p. 349), b c1774 (1850 USC). In 1850, Mark, ae 76y, and Wealthy, ae 70y, were enumerated at Northport
- x Nathaniel, b Islesboro 7 Sep 1784: lost at sea bef 1811 when his younger bro Nathaniel was born (*Brian Pendleton*, p. 194)
- xi Christiana, b Islesboro 22 Jun 1786: d East Corinth 13 Aug 1873 ae 87y (g.s., Corinthian cem) [*Brian Pendleton*, p. 350, states d 17 Aug 1874]: m (1) Islesboro abt 1804 Nathaniel Thomas of Portland (Family Bible, op. cit., 1st child b 1805), b Portland 14 Aug [prob 1782 or 1783] (ibid.), d at sea Sep 1810 ae 27y (*Brian Pendleton*, p. 350; Family Bible): m (2) Northport 9 Jan 1812 Dea. John Dunham Jr. (VR), b 10 Jun 1789 (Family Bible), d Northport 2 Jan 1849 ae 60y (*Republican Journal*, issue of 26 Jan 1849): m (3) Northport 4 Jul 1852 William Maddox of Lincolnville (Northport VR)

xii   Charlotte, b Islesboro 28 Jan 1787 [sic, 6 months after the reported birth of her sister]: m Boston MA 5 Jul 1819 William Atwood (VR)

xiii   Mercy Thomas, b Islesboro 20 Jun 1789 or 1790: m (1) Joseph Brown of Exeter NH (*Brian Pendleton*, p. 348): m (2) 1825 Jonas Stone Barrett (ibid.), b Concord MA 7 Nov 1801 son of Timothy & Sarah (Dudley) Barrett (ibid.), d Auburn CA 11 Sep 1864 (ibid.)

Children by 2nd wife, Sally (Sweetland?) Bradford: *Brian Pendleton*, p. 194

xiv   Nathaniel, b Northport 10 Aug 1811: d Deer Island, New Brunswick May 1871 (*Brian Pendleton*, p. 350): m Eastport 3 Nov 1834 Elizabeth (Stuart) Pendleton (ibid.) wid of his cousin Stephen Pendleton and dau of Sargent I. & Dorcas (Pendleton) Stuart (ibid.). She d Newburyport MA 1882 (ibid.)

xv   James, b c1812: d Bristol (*Brian Pendleton*, p. 194): m Bristol 31 Dec 1869 Jane (Meserve) McClain (ibid.; Dodge's *Bristol*, 2:226) wid of Leander McClain (*Brian Pendleton*, p. 194). James was raised at Bristol by his cousin, Mrs. Lois (Pendleton) Burns, and went by the name of James Burns (ibid.)

xvi   Sally, d young (*Brian Pendleton*, p. 194)

Mrs. Joyce E. Huntley, 1701 Algonquin Dr., Clearwater, FL 34615

Pendelton, Thomas   29b   1 - 2 - 4 - 0 - 0
Isleborough Town, Hancock County

THOMAS PENDLETON, b Westerly RI 3 Jan 1718/19 son of James & his 2nd wife Elizabeth (Brown) Pendleton (James N. Arnold, *Vital Records of Rhode Island 1636–1850*, 5 [1894]:4:122, hereafter Arnold, which mistakenly calls him "James"—that he was Thomas is confirmed in his father's will; Everett Hall Pendleton, *Brian Pendleton and His Descendants* [1910], hereafter *Brian Pendleton*, pp. 65–66): d Deer Island, New Brunswick 23 Mar 1806 (David C. & Elizabeth K. Young, *Vital Records From Maine Newspapers, 1785–1820* [1993], p. 460, citing *Eastern Argus*, issue of 25 Apr 1806): m Block Island [Shoreham] RI 21 Oct 1743 DORCAS DODGE (Arnold, 4 [1893]:4:17), b Block Island [Shoreham] RI 11 Feb 1722 dau of Nathaniel & Margaret (Pullin/Pulling) Dodge (ibid., 4 [1893]:4:9; *Brian Pendleton*, pp. 115–16), d 1796 (John Pendleton Farrow, *History of Islesborough, Maine* [1893], p. 249). [Note that *History of Islesborough*, p. 249, incorrectly gives Dorcas's father as Tristram Dodge.] Tradition states that Thomas Pendleton was a whalerman, and that on one of his voyages to Greenland, he stopped at Castine, where, captured by the beauty of the area, he determined to settle (*Brian Pendleton*, p. 115). He moved to what is now

Islesboro a few years before the Revolution (ibid.). At the first town meeting at Islesboro, on 6 Apr 1789, he was elected surveyor of highways and was afterwards active in town affairs (ibid.).

Children, b Westerly RI or Stonington CT: *Brian Pendleton*, p. 116
- i Samuel, b c1745: d bef 2 Apr 1828 when his will was probated (Han Co Probate, 13:78): m Block Island RI 1766 his first cousin Bathsheba Dodge (*History of Islesborough*, p. 250), b Block Island RI 13 May 1750 dau of Mark & Lydia (Rathbone) Dodge (Arnold, 4 [1893]:4:25), d 1828 (*Brian Pendleton*, p. 191) [see SAMUEL PENDLETON family, *Maine Families*, 3:215–16]
- ii Nathaniel, b 22 Jan 1747 [Nathaniel Pendleton Family Bible, printed 1805, copy at Stephen Phillips Memorial Library, Searsport, states b 22 Jan 1749]: d 28 May 1833 (Family Bible; *Republican Journal*, issue of 6 Jun 1833): m (1) prob Westerly RI abt 1767 Cynthia West: m (2) Northport 29 Jul 1810 Sally (Sweetland?) Bradford (VR) [see NATHANIEL PENDLETON family]
- iii Margaret, b c1749: d 20 Oct 1833 ae 84y (BHM, 9:38): m 1st Church of Stonington CT 7 Jun 1767 Sylvester Cottrell (*Brian Pendleton*, p. 194), b c1742, d St. John or St. Stephens, New Brunswick 20 Mar 1830 ae 88y (BHM, 9:38). They moved in their old age to New Brunswick where they died (*History of Islesborough*, p. 190)
- iv Thomas Jr., b c1750 [*History of Islesborough*, p. 250, states b 1749]: d New Brunswick (*Brian Pendleton*, p. 195): m abt 1776 Sarah Tewksbury (ibid., p. 195; first child b 1777). They moved to New Brunswick c1796, settling on an island in Passamaquoddy Bay later known as Pendelton Island
- v Gideon, b 11 Dec 1751: d Deer Island, New Brunswick Apr 1847 (*Brian Pendleton*, p. 196): m (1) abt 1778 Eunice Getchell (ibid.): m (2) Matilda Gilkey (ibid.) dau of John & Sylvina (Thomas) Gilkey (ibid., citing will of John Gilkey in Han Co Probate 6:430), d Feb 1855 (ibid.)
- vi Stephen, b c1753: d young (*Brian Pendleton*, p. 116)
- vii Joshua, b 2 Jun 1755: d Northport abt 18 Feb 1844 ae 94y [sic] (*Republican Journal*, issue of 1 Mar 1844): m (1) Nancy Nutter (*Brian Pendleton*, p. 197): m (2) Sally Ames who d bef 1820 USC (ibid.): m (3) int Lincolnville 7 Nov 1824 Katherine Patten of Lincolnville (VR) who survived him (ibid.). He lived at Islesboro until about 1810 when he moved to Northport (ibid.)
- viii Mary, b c1758: d Islesboro 25 Jul 1847 ae abt 90y (*Republican Journal*, issue of 30 Jul 1847): m Islesboro 2 Oct 1774 Joseph Boardman (*Brian Pendleton*, p. 198), b Boston MA 12 Aug 1753 (ibid.), d Islesboro 28 Nov 1831 (ibid.)
- ix Mark, d at ae 19y (*Brian Pendleton*, p. 116)

x Stephen, b 9 Feb 1763: d Lubec 29 May 1845 ae 82y (*Republican Journal*, issue of 2 May 1845 [sic]): m (1) Islesboro 25 Sep 1786 Prudence Dodge (*Brian Pendleton*, p. 199), b Block Island RI 23 May 1769 dau of Simon & Prudence (Rose) Dodge (ibid.), d Northport abt 1820 (ibid.) [*History of Islesborough*, p. 253, states d Northport 1827]: m (2) Eastport 16 Apr 1827 Martha Sherwood (*Brian Pendleton*, p. 200).

Mrs. Joyce E. Huntley, 1701 Algonquin Dr., Clearwater, FL 34615

---

peterson, abraham   51a   2 - 3 - 6 - 0 - 0
Winthrop Town, Lincoln County

ABRAHAM PETERSON, b Duxbury MA 6 Sep 1745 son of Joseph & Lydia (Howell) Peterson (*Mayflower Families Through Five Generations*, 3 [1980]:101, 308): d prob Jay bef 16 Nov 1818 when his heirs were named in the division of his mother's dower (Plymouth Co MA Probate #5787): of Duxbury MA when he m Marshfield MA 3 Mar 1768 PATIENCE BAKER (*Mayflower Families*, op. cit.), b Marshfield MA 14 Nov 1749 dau of John & Ruth (Barker) Baker of Pembroke MA (ibid.), alive 20 Aug 1818 (Oxf Co deeds, 15:409). Abraham was a Rev soldier from Duxbury (MS&S 12:246). In 1785, he sold his Duxbury farm and removed to Winthrop (William B. Browne, "The Peterson Family of Duxbury, MA," reprinted in *Genealogies of Mayflower Families from the NEHGR*, 3 [1985]:108). By 1815, he resided at Jay when he deeded his homestead farm, "it being lot number 4 in the eleventh range on the easterly side of the Androscoggin River in the said town of Jay containing 100 acres," to his son Charles (Oxf Co deeds, 15:204). A Patience Peterson was a head of household at Jay in 1820 and at Canton in 1830. Abraham was a descendant of George Soule and Richard Warren of the MAYFLOWER; his wife Patience was descended from Richard Warren, William Bradford and Edward Doty (*Mayflower Families*, op. cit.; Browne, op. cit.).

Children: first 3 recorded in *Mayflower Families*, op. cit. and Browne, op. cit., p. 108, last 6 births VR Jay
   i   Abraham, b say 1769
  ii   Carnalas/Cornelius, b say 1770: m c1791–92 wid Patience (____) Johnson (IGI LDS) who had a dau by her 1st marriage named Betsey Johnson b 18 Jul 1785 (Jay VR). Cornelius is not found in the 1800 census in Maine although a Patience Peterson was enumerated with a girl 10–16 (Betsey?) and 4 children ae under 10y
 iii   Sarah, b 1777 (Browne, op. cit., p. 108): d 7 Jun 1867 (ibid.): m Duxbury MA 12 May 1802 Sylvanus Weston (ibid.), b c1770 son of Zabdiel &

Hannah (Curtis) Weston (ibid.), d Duxbury MA 28 May 1830 ae 60y (ibid.)
- iv Lucy, b 30 Oct 1780
- v Joseph, b 17 Nov 1782: m Jay Jun 1805 [Lucy?] Thomas (VR)
- vi John, b 6 Dec 1784
- vii Lydia, b 17 Aug 1789: m Jay 2 Apr 1818 Moses Coolidge Jr. of Dixfield (Jay VR), b Jay 3 Mar 1792 son of Moses & Sarah (____) Coolidge (VR)
- viii Charles, b 28 May 1792: m Hannah ____ (Oxf Co deeds, 15:409). He purchased his father's homestead farm in Jay on 27 Oct 1815 in return for life support (Oxf Co deeds, 15:204). Hannah received a pension for Charles's service as a private in the War of 1812 in Capt. Peter Chadwick's Co., 34th U.S. Infantry (Virgil White, *Index to War of 1812 Pension Files* [1989], p. 1415)
- ix Ruth, b 13 Feb 1796

James H. Wick, RD #1 North Road, Wappingers Falls, NY 12590

Petty, Oliver   29a   1 - 2 - 1 - 0 - 0
Gouldsborough Town, Hancock County

OLIVER PETTY, b Walpole MA 31 May 1760 son of Ebenezer & Hannah (Farrington) Petty (VR; Rev War pension #W21953): d Gouldsboro 1831 (Muriel Sampson Johnson's *Early Families of Gouldsboro, Maine* [1990], hereafter *Gouldsboro*, p. 211 gives d 23 Aug 1831 citing Gouldsboro VR; pension, op. cit., gives d 3 Aug 1831 ae 72y): m Steuben Nov 1787 ABIGAIL YOUNG (pension, op. cit.), b c1771 (ibid.) perhaps dau of Noah Young of Gouldsboro, d Gouldsboro 27 Jan 1854 ae 82y 9m 19d (*Ellsworth American*, issue of 10 Feb 1854). Oliver was a Rev War soldier, a member of Capt. Hobby's Co (Fisher's *Soldiers*, p. 618).

Children: births VR Gouldsboro; births also given in pension, op. cit.
- i Timothy, b 9 Mar 1788: d 12 Jul 1841 ae 54y (*Gouldsboro*, p. 211 citing g.s.): m Gouldsboro 6 May 1816 Rachel Tracy (VR), b c1795 dau of Asa & Dorcas (Leighton) Tracy (*Gouldsboro*, p. 280), d Gouldsboro 2 Aug 1877 ae 82y (ibid. citing g.s.)
- ii Joseph, b 9 Apr 1790: d 4 Mar 1800 (*Gouldsboro*, p. 211)
- iii Alexander, b 19 Oct 1792: m Gouldsboro 20 Dec 1821 Sarah Johnson of Sullivan (VR) dau of Stephen & Hannah (Bickford) Johnson (L. A. Clark Johnson, *Sullivan and Sorrento Since 1760*; *Gouldsboro*, p. 147)

iv   Noah, b 16 Jul 1795: m Gouldsboro 11 Jan 1821 Elizabeth Johnson (VR) sis of Sarah above (*Gouldsboro*, p. 147)
v   Eunice, b 19 Jul 1797: d Gouldsboro 16 Jun 1865 (*Gouldsboro*, p. 211 citing g.s. Birch Harbor cem): m Gouldsboro 6 May 1816 Joshua A. Bickford (VR), b c1791 son of Joseph & Loisa (Rhodes) Bickford (*Gouldsboro*, pp. 27, 28), d Gouldsboro 12 Apr 1862 ae 71y (*Gouldsboro*, p. 28 citing g.s., Birch Harbor cem)
vi   Hannah, b 29 Oct 1799: d Gouldsboro 6 Sep 1893 (VR): m Gouldsboro 28 Dec 1829 Samuel Gouldsboro (VR), "Samuel Gouldsborough, son of Sally Waterman, born within this Town the 21 day of October 1805" (*Gouldsboro*, p. 109), d 1 Feb 1889 ae 84y (ibid. citing g.s.). The Gouldsboro town records indicate there was another Samuel Gouldsborough of Gouldsboro, b in 1785, d 1850, who could have been the father of Sally Waterman's child (ibid.)
vii Abial, b 29 Nov 1801: m Gouldsboro 22 Dec 1827 Elizabeth D. Ashe dau of Nathaniel & Lucy (Johnson) Ashe (*Gouldsboro*, p. 20)
viii Ebenezer, b 9 Jun 1804: m Gouldsboro 1 Aug 1828 Lucinda Hancock (VR), b c1816 dau of Samuel & Dorcas (Tracy) Hancock (*Gouldsboro*, p. 126)
ix   Barnabas, b 12 May 1807 [pension, op. cit., gives b 19 Jun 1807]: m Gouldsboro 9 May 1841 Rachel P. Stevens (VR), b Gouldsboro 22 Dec 1824 (VR)
x   Samuel, b 1 Dec 1811: d 26 Jun 1829 (*Gouldsboro*, p. 211)
xi   Abigail, b 15 Apr 1813: d bef 28 Dec 1857 when her husband remarried: m Gouldsboro 25 Jan 1835 Capt. Nahum Stevens (VR), b 14 Nov 1818 son of Jonathan & Abigail (Perry) Stevens (*Gouldsboro*, pp. 264–65). He m (2) Gouldsboro 28 Dec 1857 Pauline Clark of Steuben (VR)
xii Oliver, b 27 May 1817: d Aug 1858 (*Gouldsboro*, p. 212 citing g.s.): m Gouldsboro 2 Jul 1839 Mary Elizabeth Joy (VR), b c1820 (1850 USC)

Rev. Charles Austin Joy, The Church of Saint Andrew, 1004 Graydon Ave., Norfolk, VA 23507

Philbrooks, Ebenezor   33a   1 - 1 - 5 - 0 - 0
   Balltown Town, Lincoln County

EBENEZER PHILBRICK, b prob Rye NH 30 Aug 1755 (Whitefield VR) son of Ebenezer & Hannah (Moulton) Philbrick (Dr. Robert E. Philbrick, "Philbrick-Philbrook Families, Sheepscot, Maine to California" [TS, MSL, 1985], hereafter Philbrick, p. 3): d Whitefield 27 Sep 1822 (VR): m MEHITABLE BARTLETT (Philbrick, op. cit.), b Plaistow NH 24 Jan 1764 (Whitefield VR) dau of Jonathan & Lydia (Chase) Bartlett (VR) [see JONATHAN BARTLETT family, *Maine*

Families, 2:15], d Whitefield Sep 1835 (VR). Ebenezer came with his parents to Sheepscot about 1765 (Philbrook, p. 2). Over the years, he executed numerous land transactions in the Balltown area.

Children: births VR Whitefield except Bethiah
- i Bethiah, b 30 Jul 1781 (Philbrick, p. 6): d Bradford 28 Sep 1853 (g.s., Bradford cem): m Whitefield 25 Jun 1803 Elijah King (VR), b Balltown 28 Nov 1775 son of Benjamin & Ruth (Bartlett) King (Whitefield VR) [see BENJAMIN KING family], d Bradford 11 Mar 1845 (Harry H. Cochrane, *History of Monmouth and Wales* [1894], hereafter Cochrane, 2:96)
- ii Rachel, b Whitefield 7 Nov 1783
- iii Jonathan, b Whitefield 17 Mar 1788
- iv Samuel, b Whitefield 24 Aug 1790
- v Salley, b Whitefield 4 Aug 1792
- vi Abigail/Nabby, b Whitefield 15 Apr 1794: d 1885 (g.s., Shepherd cem, Jefferson): m int Whitefield 1 Sep 1819 Solomon Plummer (VR), b 1797, d 1877 (g.s., Shepherd cem, Jefferson)
- vii Ebenezer Jr., b Whitefield 24 Jan 1796
- viii Peter, b Whitefield 26 Mar 1798: d 9 May 1871 (g.s., Highland cem, Jefferson): m Jefferson 5 Apr 1823 Frances/Fanny Noyes (VR), b Whitefield 28 Jul 1802 dau of Moses & Sarah (Currier) Noyes (VR), d 15 Feb 1884 (g.s., Highland cem, Jefferson)
- ix Hubbard, b Whitefield 19 Oct 1800: d 3 Sep 1883 (g.s., Kings Mills cem, Whitefield): m Whitefield 1 May 1828 Mary/Polly Potter (VR), b Whitefield 16 Jul 1790 dau of Solomon & Jane (Leighton) Potter (VR) [see SOLOMON POTTER family], d 31 Oct 1873 ae 83y (g.s., Kings Mills cem)
- x Hiram, b Whitefield 15 Sep 1802
- xi Mara Ann, b Whitefield 4 Aug 1803

Thelma Eye Brooks, P.O. Box 136, Waterville, ME 04903

Tinney, Seth   20b   2 - 0 - 1 - 0 - 0
Harpswell Town, Cumberland County

SETH PHINNEY, prob b Barnstable MA 27 Jun 1723 son of Benjamin & Martha (Crocker) Phinney (MD, 11:132): m Barnstable MA 26 Oct 1748 BETHIAH BUMP/BUMPAS (MD, 33:165), prob b Barnstable MA 23 Aug 1729 dau of Samuel & Joanna (Warren) Bump/Bumpas (MD, 32:58). Joanna (Warren) Bumpas was a descendant of Pilgrim Richard Warren (MD, 14:227, 256; 21:78;

Mayflower Families Through Five Generations, Volume Two, Thomas Rogers Family, p. 244; *Mayflower Families In Progress Richard Warren of the Mayflower*, Fourth Edition [1991], pp. 129-30). Seth was named executor of his father's will dated 24 Mar 1758 (MD, 2:244). He was of Harpswell by Dec 1763 when his son Benjamin was born and was chosen tythingman at Harpswell 25 Mar 1766 (TR). Seth, his wife, and son Benjamin Finney were warned out of Brunswick 31 Jun 1791 (TR). His son Benjamin is the other male ae over 16y in the 1790 census. The given name of Seth's wife is not found after the birth of the twin sons. Bethiah is the presumed mother of all of the children. No land records or probate were found for Seth.

Children: first 3 b Barnstable MA (MD, 31:7); Martha and Relief identified as daus of Seth (Harpswell VR); Seth called "Jr." in his marriage intentions (Harpswell VR); Benjamin b Harpswell (Weld VR); remainder probable children based on the absence of any other Finney family in Harpswell

 i Zilpah/Zelpha, b Barnstable MA 30 Nov 1749 (MD, 31:7) [ae 70y in 1820 when her husband applied for a pension (see below)]: d Trenton 12 May 1820 ae 75y [sic] (g.s., Haynes cem): m Harpswell 10 Nov 1769 Ephraim Haynes ("Rev. Elisha Eaton and Rev. Samuel Eaton, Records of Harpswell Congregational Church," [TS, MHS], hereafter Harpswell CR), b Sudbury MA 15 May 1741 son of John & Mary (Taylor) Haynes (Haynes and Haynes, *Walter Haynes...and His Descendants*, p. 76) [ae 79y in 1820 (Rev War pension #S35383)], d Eden 24 Dec 1837 ae 102y [sic] (g.s., Haynes cem, Trenton). Ephraim m perhaps (2) Mary _____ (Fisher's *Soldiers*). He was a Rev War soldier (ibid.)

 ii son, twin, b Barnstable MA 10 Mar 1753: d "In about two hours after" (MD, 31:7)

 iii son, twin, b Barnstable MA 10 Mar 1753: d "In about two hours after" (MD, 31:7)

 iv Martha, b prob Barnstable MA c1755 (ae 85y, pensioner, 1840 USC, Brunswick): d Brunswick Nov 1842 (g.s., Growstown cem): m (1) Harpswell 29 Jan 1771 Abraham Barns (Harpswell CR), prob bp Harpswell 15 Mar 1760 son of Benjamin Barns "and wife" (ibid.), d bef Dec 1774 when Martha remarried: m (2) Harpswell 30 Dec 1774 William McGill (ibid.), b c1747 (ae 73y in 1820, NEHGR, 142 [1988]:304), d 19 Sep 1828 ae 81y (Rev War pension #W23952; g.s., Growstown cem states d 28 Sep). Martha received a pension for William's Rev War service (pension, op. cit.). They were members of the Growstown Freewill Baptist Church in Brunswick, Martha bp there as an adult in 1816 ("Records of the Growstown Freewill Baptist Church, Brunswick, Maine" [TS, MSL], hereafter Growstown CR)

 v prob Sarah, d Harpswell 24 Nov 1844 (Rev War pension #W21610): m (1) Harpswell 16 Dec 1779 John Cummings (Harpswell CR): m (2)

Harpswell 26 Oct 1786 William Alexander Jr. (Cum Co Marriage Returns) who d 11 Oct 1833 (pension, op. cit.). Sarah named a dau Bethiah (ibid.)

vi Seth Jr., bp as an adult in the Growstown Freewill Baptist Church in Brunswick 8 Mar 1828 (CR): d Feb 1834 (Growstown CR): m int Harpswell 1 Dec 1787 Sarah Cotton of Brunswick (Harpswell VR), her parentage uncertain as there were two Sarah Cottons b in Brunswick, one in 1764 and one in 1768 (VR). Seth was enumerated at Harpswell as a head-of-household in 1790 USC

vii Benjamin, b Harpswell 15 Dec 1763 (Weld VR): d Weld 4 Mar 1839 (VR): m (1) Brunswick 24 Jun 1793 Mary/Polly Wheeler (VR), b Bowdoin 15 Dec 1774 dau of Simon & Hannah (Reed) Wheeler (Weld VR; Ada Wheeler Miller, "History of the Joseph Wheeler Family," [TS, 1954], p. 26, copy in possession of submitter), d Weld c1825: m (2) int Weld 27 Dec 1825 Mrs. Martha White (VR), b c1787 (ae 63y 1850 USC Carthage with Samuel & Lavinia White), d aft 1860 (ae 73y 1860 USC Weld with Loren Phinney). Res Brunswick, Greene, Weld

viii Relief, m Harpswell 8 Jan 1784 Samuel Browning (Harpswell CR): poss res Greene 1810 (USC)

ix prob Hannah, d 1847 (Growstown CR): m 5 Nov 1789 Joseph Ward (Harpswell CR), prob b Harpswell 9 Apr 1768 son of Nehemiah & Hannah (_____) Ward (VR). Joseph and Hannah were bp as adults in the Growstown Freewill Baptist Church in 1800. The church records indicate Joseph was "excluded" from the church in 1831 (Growstown CR)

x prob Joanna, b aft 1770 (ae 50–60y, 1830 USC Harpswell): d aft 1830 (USC): m Harpswell 14 Feb 1790 Alexander Wilson (Harpswell CR), b 3 Jul 1759 and bp Harpswell 7 Oct 1759 son of Alexander and Catherine (Swanzey) Wilson (Charles Sinnett, "Ancestor James Wilson and his Descendants" [TS, n.d.], p. 10; Harpswell CR), d Harpswell 5 Nov 1828 (VR). Joanna named children Seth and Benjamin (Harpswell VR). She was prob named for her grandmother Joanna (Warren) Bumpas

Dorothy O. Crane, 31 Holly Hill Road, Wilmington, DE 19809

Phips, (Widdow)   61c   0 - 2 - 3 - 0 - 0
Kittery Town, York County

MIRIAM (FERNALD) PHIPPS (widow of George Phipps), b Kittery 12 Jul 1762 [sic] (Everett S. Stackpole, *Old Kittery and Her Families* [1903], p. 385) and bp Kittery 1st Church 19 Jul 1761 dau of Benjamin & Sarah (Fernald) Fernald (National Society of the DAR, "Records from the First Church in Kittery, Maine 1715–1797" [TS, MHS, 1979], hereafter "Kittery 1st Church," p. 72) [see

BENJAMIN FERNALD family]: m Kittery 20 Dec 1781 GEORGE PHIPPS (Joseph C. Anderson II & Lois W. Thurston, *Vital Records of Kittery, Maine to the Year 1892* [1991], p. 171) whose parentage has not been found. Miriam was named in her father's will dated 4 Mar 1798 and in the subsequent division of the estate (York Co Probate #5682). George Phipps was a soldier in the Rev War and served on the AURORA and MORRIS (Fisher's *Soldiers*, p. 621).

Children: bp First Church of Kittery ("Kittery 1st Church," pp. 90, 91)
  i   Capt. Robert F., bp 8 Jul 1785: d Portsmouth NH 1 Jan 1820 ae 36y (g.s., Union cem given in John E. Frost, "Portsmouth Record Book" [TS, MHS, 1955], 2:41): m Portsmouth NH 1807 Sally Bickford (David C. & Elizabeth K. Young, *Vital Records from Maine Newspapers, 1785–1820* [1993], p. 468, citing the Saco *Freeman's Friend*, issue of 2 May 1807), b c1784, d Portsmouth NH 22 Feb 1848 ae 64y (g.s., Union cem, "Portsmouth Record Book," op. cit., p. 41). Her obit in the *Exeter News-Letter*, issue of 28 Feb 1848, called her the wid of "Capt. Robert F. Phipps" (Scott Lee Chipman, *New England Vital Records from the* Exeter News-Letter, *1847–1852* [1994], p. 40)
  ii George, bp 8 Jul 1785
  iii Sarah, bp 27 Aug 1786
  iv Elizabeth, bp 26 Oct 1788

Judith H. Kelley, 96 Florence St., So. Portland, ME 04106

Pike, John   24b   1 - 1 - 2 - 0 - 0
    Rusfield Gore [now Norway], Cumberland County

JOHN PIKE, b Middleton NH 11 Jun 1763 son of Jacob & Joanna (Marshall) Pike (William B. Lapham, *Centennial History of Norway, Maine* [1886], hereafter Lapham, pp. 576–77; Dr. Osgood N. Bradbury, *Norway in the Forties* [1986], hereafter Bradbury, p. 312ff): d 27 Oct 1841 (ibid.; g.s., Pike's Hill cem, Norway): m (1) 1785 New Gloucester MARY TARBOX (Lapham, p. 577), b New Gloucester 2 May 1766 (ibid.), d 19 Jan 1813 (g.s., Pike's Hill cem, Norway; Lapham, p. 577): m (2) Otisfield SARAH PERRY (ibid.), b Otisfield 29 Oct 1776 (ibid.), d Aug 1861 ae 85y (ibid.). John came from Middleton NH to New Gloucester where he married. After the births of several children, he came to Norway following his bro Dudley who had moved there earlier [see DUDLEY PIKE family, *Maine Families*, 3:221–22]. There he put up a small one-story house (ibid.). In 1796, he built a larger house in which the family lived about 40 years. He moved to a farm in Oxford about 1835 where he died (Bradbury, pp. 312–14).

Children: Lapham, p. 577; Bradbury, p. 314ff
By 1st wife Mary Tarbox
- i Mary, b New Gloucester 15 Jun 1786: d New Gloucester 5 Oct 1859 at the "home of her dau Rosilla C. (Tucker) Morgan" (Bradbury, p. 314): m Norway 2 Oct 1802 Benjamin Tucker (ibid., p. 611), b Canton MA 20 Sep 1776 son of Benjamin & Jane (Babcock) Tucker of Milton, Stoughton, & Canton MA (ibid.), d 27 Oct 1857 (ibid.). Both Mary and Benjamin are bur Rustfield cem, Norway (Bradbury, p. 314–15)
- ii Samuel, b New Gloucester 11 Dec 1788: d Oxford 20 Dec 1871 ae 83y (ibid., p. 577; Bradbury, p. 315): m Waterford 1814 or 1815 (aft he returned from the War of 1812) Susan Wood of Waterford who d Sep 1856 (ibid.)
- iii Dolly, b New Gloucester 3 Jul 1790: d 15 Jul 1790 (ibid.)
- iv Robert, b prob Norway 28 Jul 1791: d Welchville 20 Jan 1868 (Bradbury, p. 316): m Norway 1812 Susanna Bickford (ibid.), b 7 Jul 1794 (ibid.), d 7 Feb 1858 (ibid.). Both are bur in Old Webber cem, Oxford Plains (ibid.)
- v Martha, b Norway 12 Jun 1793: d 3 Aug 1850 (Lapham, p. 377): m 4 Sep 1812 James Crockett (Bradbury, p. 317), b Gorham 24 Apr 1789 son of Joshua 3rd & Sarah (Hamblen) Crockett (VR)
- vi Jacob, b Norway 30 Mar 1795: d Strong 15 Mar 1847 (Bradbury, p. 318): m Urania Cummings dau of Elisha & Mary (Dolly) Cummings who came from Gray to Paris and from Paris to Norway as early as 1791 (A. O. Cummins, *Cummings Genealogy* [1904], pp. 210–11)
- vii Charles, b Norway 24 Mar 1797: d Argyle WI 5 Oct 1886 ae 89y (Bradbury, p. 319): m (1) 6 Jul 1819 Mary Wood of Hebron (ibid.), b Middleboro MA 6 Jul 1795 (ibid.), d aft 7 Apr 1837 when their last child was born (ibid.): m (2) Fidelia Way who res Monroe WI (ibid.)
- viii Hannah, b 18 Jan 1799: d 5 Jun 1802 (ibid.)
- ix Israel, b 20 Jun 1801: d New Gloucester 6 Jan 1859 (Lapham, p. 577): m (1) 18 Mar 1824 Rosella Cleveland (Bradbury, p. 320), b Medfield MA 18 Jun 1807 (ibid.), d 28 Dec 1827 (g.s., Pike's Hill cem): m (2) 9 Dec 1828 Lydia Morgan (Bradbury, p. 320), b New Gloucester 15 Dec 1798 (ibid.), d 7 Dec 1843 (g.s., Pike's Hill cem): m (3) 1 Oct 1844 Martha Morgan (Bradbury, p. 320), b New Gloucester 22 Jun 1805 (ibid.), d Mechanic Falls 18 Dec 1870 (ibid.)
- x Clarissa, b 22 Apr 1803: d 27 Jan 1804 (Lapham, p. 577)
- xi Luther Farrar, b Norway 22 Nov 1804: d 27 Nov 1896 (g.s., Pine Grove cem, Norway): m Norway 27 May 1834 Adaline Augusta Millett (Lapham, p. 578), b Norway 26 Feb 1807 dau of Nathaniel & Martha (Merrill) Millett (ibid., p. 554), d 21 May 1886 (Bradbury, p. 322; g.s., Pine Grove cem)
- xii Almira, b Norway 5 May 1807: d Norway 12 Nov 1838 (Lapham, p. 577): m William Hall of Norway (ibid., p. 517), b 4 Oct 1802 son of Elijah &

Lois (Thompson) Hall (ibid., pp. 516–17). They settled at Steep Falls, Norway. He m (2) 1 May 1839 Mary Farnum Town (ibid., p. 517)
xiii Joanna, b 30 Dec 1810: d 11 Aug 1811 (Lapham, p. 577)
By 2nd wife Sarah Perry
xiv Clarissa, b Norway 17 Feb 1814: d Norway 29 Aug 1887 (Bradbury, p. 329): m Jan 1833 Samuel Treat Beal son of William & Jerusha (Fluent) Beal (Lapham, p. 463; Bradbury, p. 329). They res Mechanic Falls
xv Calvin Farrar, b Norway 23 Sep 1816: d Oxford 3 Dec 1851 ae 35y (Lapham, p. 577; Bradbury, p. 329): m 13 Oct 1841 Sophronia Pierce of Lowell MA (Bradbury, p. 329) who d 1 Dec 1886 (ibid.). They res Lowell MA, Portland and Oxford. She m (2) 25 Jul 1868 Josiah Gates of Lowell MA (ibid.)

Allen R. Pike, P.O. Box 696, Carmel, NY 10512

Pits, John   68c   2 - 4 - 5 - 0 - 0
Waterborough Town, York County

JOHN PITTS, b poss Berwick 1736 poss son of Hannah (Goodridge) Pitts who later married ____ Glass (Merton T. Goodrich, "Errors Erased—The Family History of Josiah Goodridge of Berwick, Maine," TAG, 13 [1941]:214): d Harrison 1827 ae 91y (Gideon T. Ridlon, *Early Settlers of Harrison, Maine* [1877], p. 99): m Berwick 7 Feb 1765 JUDITH WOOD (John E. Frost & Joseph C. Anderson II, *Vital Records of Berwick, South Berwick & North Berwick, Maine to the Year 1892* [1993], p. 114), bp Berwick 1st Church 6 Sep 1744 dau of Stephen & Mary (____) Wood (NEHGR, 82 [1928]:216). John served in the Rev War (Fisher's *Soldiers*, p. 626). He moved from Berwick to Waterboro about 1769 (TAG, 13:214) and later relocated to Harrison, settling on the northwest side of Hobbs Hill (Ridlon, op. cit.)

Prob children, order uncertain
i Molly, m Waterboro 27 Apr 1788 John Smith (VR)
ii Thomas, b c1767 (1850 USC, Shapleigh): living Shapleigh 1850 (ibid.): m Shapleigh 19 Jun 1794 Hannah Low (VR), b c1777 (1850 USC, shapleigh) prob dau of Jedediah & Mary (Stewart) Low (Samuel D. Rumery, *Records of Kennebunk and Kennebunkport* [1928], 3:1214), living 1850 (USC)
iii Moses, d Waterboro 25 Jan 1853 (Samuel K. Hamilton, *The Hamiltons of Waterboro, Their Ancestors and Descendants* [1912], p. 87): m Waterboro 19 Jan 1797 Sarah/Sally Hamilton (VR), b Coxhall [now Lyman] dau of Benjamin & Judith (Ricker) Hamilton (Hamilton, op. cit.; York Co deeds, 100:51) [while her birthdate is unknown, her parents m in 1771 and her older sis was b Apr 1772], d Waterboro 15 Oct 1847 (Hamilton, op. cit.)

- iv Susanna, b Mar 1774 (g.s., Abbott cem, Ossipee NH): d Ossipee NH 1857 (ibid.): m Waterboro 18 Jan 1796 Nathan/Nathaniel Abbott, b c Apr 1773 son of Jonathan & Patience (Wood) Abbott (Ossipee NH VR), d Ossipee NH 31 Mar 1869 (VR)
- v Aaron, d Oxford MI bef Jun 1847 (Oakland Co MI Probate #504): m Waterboro 28 Mar 1799 Ruth Philpot (VR), b prob c1773 (Ronald Vern Jackson, *Mortality Schedule, Michigan, 1850* [1979], p. 42), d prob Montcalm Co MI Oct 1849 (ibid.)
- vi Samuel, b c1777 (g.s.): d Otisfield 19 Apr 1849 ae 72y (VR): m Otisfield 27 Apr 1800 Lydia Scribner (VR), b Otisfield c1780 dau of Daniel & Elizabeth (Taylor) Scribner (William S. Spurr, *A History of Otisfield* [1953], p. 531ff), d Otisfield 20 Dec 1866 ae 86y (VR)
- vii Sarah, b Waterboro 16 May 1782 (Shapleigh VR): d Berwick 28 Dec 1855 ae 73y 7m 9d (Wilbur D. Spencer, *Burial Inscriptions, Berwick, York County, Maine* [1922], p. 123): m Waterboro 29 Jul 1801 Moses Low (VR), b Sanford 24 Jul 1782 (Shapleigh VR) bro of Hannah above, living Berwick 1850 (USC)
- viii Edmund, m Waterboro 23 May 1805 Hannah Hamilton (VR) sister of Sarah/Sally above (York Co deeds, 100:52) [Note, although Hamilton's book, op. cit., indicates that Hannah, who married Edmund Pitts, was the dau of Richard & Experience (Hatch) Hamilton, the deeds associated with the settlement of Benjamin Hamilton's estate indicate that both Sarah/Sally and Hannah were his daughters]
- ix Benjamin, b c1787 (1860 USC, Waterboro): living Waterboro 1860 (ibid.): m int Waterboro 15 Apr 1809 Sarah Warren (VR), b Waterboro 21 Jun 1786 dau of Benjamin & Abigail (Philpot) Warren (NEHGR, 90 [1936]:240; York Co Probate 24:316ff), living Waterboro 1860 (USC)
- x Ruth, m Waterboro 4 Apr 1812 George Corson (VR), b Rochester NH 1790 son of Benjamin & Betsey (Smith) Corson (Clement F. Heverly, *Pioneer and Patriot Families of Bradford Co PA* [1913], 1:261)

Dana A. Batchelder, 258 South Sea Avenue, West Yarmouth, MA 02673

Potter, James   34c   4 - 0 - 4 - 0 - 0
Bowdoin Town, Lincoln County

Eld. **JAMES POTTER** [called "Jr" and "2nd"], b Brunswick 22 Feb 1733/4 son of William & Catherine (Mustard) Potter of Topsham (*Narration of the Experiences, Travels and Labours of Elder James Potter: Minister of the Gospel, and Pastor of the Baptized Church in Bowdoin, Commonwealth of Massachusetts* [1813], hereafter *Narration*, p. 5, copy at Colby College; Moses Woodman, "History of

Topsham, Begun in 1823 and Finished in 1840," published in *Bath Daily Times*, February–May 1924, at MSL): d Bowdoin 22 Mar 1815 ae 81y 1m (g.s., South cem): m int Brunswick 5 Dec 1759 MARY SPEAR of Brunswick (VR), b Brunswick 21 Apr 1739 dau of William & Elizabeth (____) Spear (VR), d Bowdoin 22 Jul 1822 ae 83y (g.s., South cem). James Potter's family moved to Topsham c1736 and on 26 Aug 1747 his father was killed by the Indians (*Narration*, p. 5; Topsham VR). On 16 Jan 1781 James with his "wife, four sons and five daughters" moved to the area in Bowdoin later called for him Pottertown (*Narration*, p. 7). He served in the Rev War on the Penobscot Expedition in Capt. Hinckley's Co. where James took command after Hinckley was killed (George A. Wheeler, M.D. and Henry W. Wheeler, *History of Brunswick, Topsham, and Harpswell Maine* [1878], p. 686). Raised in the Presbyterian faith, he later became a Baptist and was ordained in that faith on 5 Oct 1785 "with liberty to travel" (*Narration*, pp. 25–26). He was the minister of the First Baptist Church of Bowdoin for 23 years [now South Bowdoin Baptist Church] (Charlene B. Bartlett and Jayne E. Bickford, *Cemetery Inscriptions...of Bowdoin, Maine* [1993], p. 6). He was a founder of the Baptist society in Maine and traveled throughout the area preaching. In 1791 he stated he had "settled all my temporal concerns, distributing my property to my children hoping to have my mind unembarrassed with things of the world..." (*Narration*, p. 28).

Children, b Topsham: William, Matthew, John, Robert, Catherine, Martha (from Topsham VR, 2:25–26 citing Woodman's history); Mary (from obituary of daughter Lettice [Whitmore] Ball, in possession of submitter)

  i William, lost at sea bef Jan 1781 when his parents and 9 children moved to Bowdoin: unm (Topsham VR; *Narration*, p. 5). About 1791, James Potter stated "two of my children have been removed by death" (ibid., p. 28)

  ii Matthew, d Bowdoin ae 27y of bilious colic (Topsham VR citing Woodman's history): m Martha Spear (ibid.)

  iii Elizabeth, d Litchfield 24 Sep 1842 (notes of Oliver B. Clason in possession of Lois W. Thurston, Editor): m Topsham Apr 1784, as his 2nd wife, Daniel Cunningham both then of Pottertown (Topsham VR), b Harpswell 20 Sep 1757 son of Edward & Miriam (Webber) (MacGrah/McGray) Cunningham (VR; North Yarmouth VR), called "Deacon" when he d Litchfield 20 Dec 1846 (VR). He had m (1) cert Topsham 6 Nov 1780 Elizabeth Heddean/Hayden (VR)

  iv John, twin (Topsham VR), b Aug 1766 (based on g.s): d Bowdoin 10 Dec 1855 ae 89y 4m (g.s., South cem): m Topsham 18 Oct 1792 Abigail Farnham (VR), b Bowdoin 27 Sep 1769 dau of John & Abigail (Stover) Farnum (VR)

  v Robert, twin (Topsham VR), b Aug 1766 (see John above): d Ohio (Topsham VR citing Woodman's history): m Topsham 14 Jan 1794

Hannah Reed (ibid.) dau of "Old" John Reed of Topsham (ibid.). They moved to OH (ibid.)

vi Edward, d bef 1797 (wife's remarriage): m Bowdoin 1 Feb 1792 Martha Potter (Charles N. Sinnett, "The Potter Families in Maine and the West" [n.d.], p. 8), b Georgetown 1 Apr 1771 dau of John & Sarah (Snipe) Potter (VR; Bowdoin VR), d Bowdoin 24 Jun 1826 ae 52y (g.s., South cem). She m (2) Bowdoin 9 Sep 1797 as his 3rd wife Simon Conner (VR)

vii Catherine, b 11 Nov 1770 (Bowdoin VR) and bp Topsham 9 Jun 1771 ("Rev. John Murray's Book of Records: Baptisms and Marriages, Boothbay and Surrounding Towns" [TS, 1947, MSL], p. 10): d Bowdoin 17 Apr 1844 ae 74y (VR; g.s., South cem): m (1) Capt. Thomas Denham (Topsham VR, citing Woodman history), b c1765, d Bowdoin 19 Nov 1799 ae 34y (VR; g.s., South cem): m (2) cert Topsham 12 Mar 1817 William Graves (VR), b Topsham 4 Aug 1765 son of Johnson & Sarah (Staples) Graves (VR), d Topsham 12 Oct 1844 ae 79y (VR) [see JOHNSON GRAVES family, *Maine Families*, 2:115]

viii Martha, b c1772 (from g.s.): d Brunswick 14 Apr 1856 ae 83y 7m (g.s., Maquoit cem): m (1) 24 Feb 1791, as his 2nd wife, Josiah Simpson (Topsham VR), b c1749 (from g.s.) son of William & Agnes (Lewis) Simpson (Wheeler, *History of Brunswick*, p. 851), d Brunswick 25 Dec 1819 (g.s, Maquoit cem)

ix daughter, prob b c1774: prob the other child who d bef 1791 (*Narration*, p. 28)

x Mary, b 12 Oct 1776 (Family Ledger of Samuel Whitmore Sr. in possession of submitter): d Bowdoinham 2 Dec 1828 ae 52y (Doris M. Rowland, "Death Records of Bowdoinham, Maine" [TS, 1967], p. 135): m int Bowdoinham 7 Jan 1797 Samuel Whitmore (VR), b prob Medford MA 11 Jun 1768 son of Stephen & Mary (Whittemore) Whitmore (Family Ledger, op. cit.; Jessie W. P. Purdy, *Whitmore Genealogy* [1907], p. 46), d Bowdoinham 30 Oct 1818 ae 50y 4m 19d (Rowland, op. cit.)

Joyce E. Huntley, 1701 Algonquin Drive, Clearwater, FL 34615

Potter, Solomon 33a 1 - 3 - 4 - 0 - 0
Balltown Town, Lincoln County

SOLOMON POTTER, b Ipswich MA 29 Jul 1749 son of Samuel & Abigail (Cummings) Potter (Linwood Lowden, *Ballstown West* [1984], p. 23; Charles Edward Potter, *Genealogies of the Potter Families and Their Descendants in America* [1888], hereafter Potter, p. 11): d 25 May 1800 (family Bible rec) and his estate was in probate 1 Jul 1800 (Lin Co Probate, 9:58): m (1) 11 Jun 1776

JANE LEIGHTON (Lowden, op. cit.; Potter, p. 11), b Rowley MA 6 Dec 1755 (family Bible rec) dau of Jonathan & Mary (Boynton) Leighton of Rowley MA and Newcastle ME (George B. Blodgette & Amos E. Jewett, *Early Settlers of Rowley, Massachusetts* [repr 1981], p. 230, which gives b 1754), d 31 Aug 1794 (ibid.): m (2) 20 Sep 1795 RACHEL BARTLETT (Lowden, op. cit.; Potter, p. 11), b Plaistow NH 17 Apr 1757 dau of Jonathan & Lydia (Chase) Bartlett (VR) [see JONATHAN BARTLETT family, *Maine Families*, 2:15], d 23 Nov 1830 (g.s., Kings Mills cem, Whitefield).

Children by 1st wife, Jane Leighton: births from family Bible rec; Potter, p. 11
  i   Aaron, b Newcastle 1 Mar 1777: d Whitefield 19 Jun 1853 (VR): m 10 Nov 1800 Anna/Nancy McKinney (Potter, p. 11) [m int Whitefield 10 Oct 1800 (VR)], b 1774 (Potter, p. 11), d 1847
  ii Daniel, b Newcastle 16 Sep 1781: d 25 Jan 1870 (Potter, p. 11): m Whitefield 20 Oct 1805 Betsey Trask (VR), b 1787 dau of Jonathan & Betsey (Hodge) Trask (Potter, p. 11), d 1862 (ibid.)
  iii Solomon Jr., b Whitefield 25 Feb 1784 (Perry VR): d Perry 4 Jan 1864 (VR): m Jan 1812 Susan Hodge (Potter, p. 11), b Perry 29 Nov 1789 dau of Alexander Hodge (ibid., p. 12), d Perry 12 Jul 1861 (ibid.)
  iv Ezekiel, b Whitefield 26 Dec 1785 (VR): d Whitefield 13 Sep 1873 (VR): m Whitefield 2 Jan 1814 Mehitable Farr (Potter, p. 11), b Whitefield 2 Apr 1793 dau of Abraham Farr (VR), d Whitefield 17 Feb 1845 (VR)
  v   Hannah, b Whitefield 22 Apr 1788: d 26 Jun 1874 (Potter, p. 11): m Whitefield 14 Dec 1808 John Avery (VR), b 1782 son of Samuel & Lucy (____) Avery (Potter, p. 11), d 1848 (ibid.)
  vi Mary/Polly, b Whitefield 16 Jul 1790 (VR): d 31 Oct 1873 ae 83y (g.s., Kings Mills cem, Whitefield): m Whitefield 1 May 1828 Hubbard Philbrick (VR), b Whitefield 10 Oct 1800 son of Ebenezer & Mehitable (Bartlett) Philbrick (Dr. Robert E. Philbrick, "Philbrick-Philbrook Families, Sheepscot, Maine to California" [TS, MSL, 1985], p. 8) [see EBENEZER PHILBRICK family], d 3 Sep 1883 (g.s., Kings Mills cem, Whitefield)
  vii Jane, b Whitefield 11 Feb 1792 (VR): d 23 Feb 1872 (Potter, p. 11): m 9 Feb 1815 Levi Russell (ibid.), b 1784 son of Levi & Hannah (____) Russell (ibid.), d 1875 (ibid.)

Children by 2nd wife, Rachel Bartlett: births from family Bible rec
  viii John, b Whitefield 29 Sep 1797 (VR): d 25 May 1883 (g.s., Kings Mills cem, Whitefield): m (1) Jefferson 30 Jul 1816 Abigail Howard (Whitefield VR) [she was called Abigail Hayward on m int Whitefield dated 13 Jul 1816 (VR)], b 8 Sep 1797 dau of Daniel & Hannah (____) Howard (Whitefield VR), d Whitefield 16 Oct 1839 (VR; g.s., Kings Mills cem): m (2) int Whitefield 7 Jun 1840 Abigail (____) Welch wid of Benjamin Welch (VR), b c1797 (1850 USC, Whitefield), d 20 Dec 1884 (VR)

ix James, b Whitefield 1 Feb 1800 (VR): d 15 Mar 1875 (Potter, p. 11): m 23 Sep 1828 Mary Goulding (ibid.), b 1811 (ibid.), d 1876 (ibid.)

Thelma Eye Brooks, P.O. Box 136, Waterville, ME 04903

Priscott, Jediah   51c   1 - 0 - 1 - 0 - 0
Winthrop Town, Lincoln County

JEDEDIAH PRESCOTT, b Hampton NH 1 Jun 1719 and bp Hampton NH 18 Jun 1721 son of John & Abigail (Marston) Prescott (Everett S. Stackpole, *History of Winthrop, Maine* [1925], p. 553): d 24 Jul 1793 ae 74y (ibid.; William Prescott, M.D., *The Prescott Memorial* [1870], p. 237): m 12 May 1742 HANNAH BACHILER/BATCHELDER (ibid.), b Hampton NH 23 Oct 1720 dau of Samuel & Elizabeth (Davis) Batchelder (VR), d 11 Mar 1809 ae 89y (*Prescott Memorial*, p. 237). Jedediah Prescott lived in Exeter NH, now Brentwood NH, and in Deerfield NH before coming to Winthrop in 1780 where he settled on the school lot (*History of Winthrop*, pp. 208, 553). He operated a grist-mill on Snell Brook and also built a saw mill (ibid., p. 208). After his death, the property and mills were sold to Dea. Elijah Snell (ibid.).

Children: *Prescott Memorial*, pp. 250–52. [Note that *History of Winthrop*, p. 553, replaces the son Josiah below with a son named Odlin, b Brentwood NH 1743, d Winthrop 30 Sep 1825 ae 82y, m Elizabeth ___ who d 28 Mar 1830 ae 75y. This discrepancy between these two sources has not been resolved.]
  i Josiah, b 11 May 1743: d Deerfield NH 11 Oct 1781 of consumption (*Prescott Memorial*, p. 250): m c1760 Betsey Smith sis of Judge Ebenezer Smith of Meredith NH (ibid.) who d Grantham NH 1830 (ibid.). She m (2) Jeremiah Bean of Candia NH and m (3) Mar 1798 Dr. Jonathan Hill of the Gilmanton NH Ironworks (ibid.) widower of Josiah's sister Mercy below (ibid.)
  ii Elizabeth, b 5 Jan 1744/5: d 2 Apr 1814 (*History of Winthrop*, p. 672): m 1766 Nathaniel Whittier (ibid.), b Salisbury MA 23 Feb 1743 son of Nathaniel & Hannah (Clough) Whittier (ibid.), d Readfield 7 Apr 1798 (ibid.). In 1790, they were at Winthrop (USC)
  iii Jedediah Jr., b 20 Sep 1746: d Searsmont 31 Mar 1827 (*History of Winthrop*, p. 554): m 11 Sep 1772 Sarah Morrill of Salisbury MA (ibid.), b 28 Mar 1752 (ibid.) [perhaps she recorded as being b Salisbury 17 Mar 1752 and bp 22 Mar 1752 dau of John Jr. & Elizabeth (Clough) Morrill (David W. Hoyt, *The Old Families of Salisbury and Amesbury, Massachusetts* [1981], p. 775)], d Mt. Vernon 27 Oct 1802 (ibid.). In 1790, he was living at Winthrop (USC) where he was termed "one of the most

prominent men of the town" (*History of Winthrop*, p. 554). In 1792, with his bro-in-law Nathaniel Whittier, he bought that township of land called Goshen which was incorporated in 1802 as the town of Vienna (ibid.). In 1801, he moved to Mt. Vernon (ibid.)

iv   Abigail, b 11 May 1748: d Readfield c1808 (*Prescott Memorial*, p. 251): m Benjamin Carr (ibid.). In 1790, they were at Winthrop (USC)

v   Mercy, b 30 Oct 1751: d Gilmanton Ironworks Village NH 4 Oct 1797 (*Prescott Memorial*, p. 251): m 10 Mar 1778 Dr. Jonathan Hill (ibid.), b Stratham NH 11 Aug 1742 (ibid.), d 6 Jun 1818 (ibid.)

vi   John, b 29 Oct 1753: d Vienna 26 Jan 1831 ae 77y 3m (Prescott Memorial, p. 251): m c1775 Mehitable Morrill sis of Sarah Morrill who m John's brother Jedediah (ibid.). John was a Baptist minister (ibid.). In 1790, they were at Washington Town [Mt. Vernon] (USC)

vii Samuel, b Brentwood NH 5 Sep 1759 (Rev War pension #W2434 gives place of birth) [*History of Winthrop*, p. 555, gives b 5 Sep 1758]: d Hallowell 7 Nov 1841 ae 82y (VR) and bur New Sharon (*The Maine Seine*, 8:2:57; g.s., New Sharon cem): m (1) 8 Feb 1781 Betsey Whittier (*Prescott Memorial*, p. 251), b 24 Apr 1759 dau of Benjamin & Mary (Joy) Whittier [see BENJAMIN WHITTIER family], d New Sharon 12 Jul 1821 ae 62y (g.s., New Sharon cem): m (2) 2 Dec 1823 Martha (Clark) Molloy of Hallowell (pension, op. cit.; Hallowell VR) wid of John Molloy (ibid.), b Hallowell 19 Sep 1773 dau of Isaac & Alice/Else (Philbrook) Clark (VR). In 1790, Samuel was enumerated at Winthrop (USC)

viii Ruth, b 12 Mar 1761: d Rumney NH 15 Sep 1815 ae 54y 6m 3d (*Prescott Memorial*, p. 251): m 5 Jun 1783 Henry Hall of Deerfield ME (ibid.), b Chester NH 15 May 1762 (ibid.), d 1850 ae 88y (ibid.). He m (2) 29 Jul 1818 Ruth Fletcher of Hatley, Canada East (ibid.)

ix   Jesse, b 24 Sep 1763: d 15 Jan 1847 ae 83y 3m 22d (g.s., Bowley cem, New Sharon; *Prescott Memorial*, p. 252): m 1 Dec 1783 Mary/Polly Whittier [see JESSE PRESCOTT family]

x   James, b 23 Feb 1765 [*History of Winthrop*, p. 555, gives b 23 Feb 1767]: d Portland c1830 ae 65y (*Prescott Memorial*, p. 252): m int 27 Apr 1789 Mary/Polly Owen (*History of Winthrop*, p. 555) who was b 20 Dec 1767 (ibid.). In 1790, they were in Smithtown Plantation [Litchfield] (USC)

xi   Elijah, b 25 Jul 1766: d Vassalborough 28 Oct 1848 ae 82y 3m (*Prescott Memorial*, p. 252): m 24 June 1791 Hannah French of Dunstable NH (ibid.; *History of Winthrop*, p. 553). In 1790, he was enumerated at Winthrop (USC)

Eleanor W. Townsend, 71 Slab Meadow Rd., Morris CT 06763-1517

Priscott, Jesse   51c   1 - 0 - 4 - 0 - 0
Winthrop Town, Lincoln County

JESSE PRESCOTT, b Brentwood NH 24 Sep 1763 son of Jedediah & Hannah (Batchelder) Prescott (William Prescott, M.D., *The Prescott Memorial* [1870], p. 252; Everett S. Stackpole, *History of Winthrop, Maine* [1925], p. 553)) [see JEDEDIAH PRESCOTT family]: d 15 Jan 1846 ae 83y 3m (g.s., Bowley cem, New Sharon) [Charles C. Whittier's *The Descendants of Thomas Whittier and Ruth Green of Salisbury and Haverhill, Massachusetts* [1937] says Jesse d 15 Jan 1847]: m prob New Sharon 1 Dec 1783 MARY/POLLY WHITTIER (Prescott, op. cit.), b Salisbury MA 17 Jan 1763 dau of Benjamin & Mary (Joy) Whittier [see BENJAMIN WHITTIER family], d 7 Aug 1841 ae 78y 6m (g.s., Bowley cem, New Sharon). Jesse "left town about 1796" (*History of Winthrop*, op. cit., p. 553). He was enumerated at New Sharon in 1800 (USC) where he served as selectman in 1812.

Children: Prescott, op. cit.; Prescott Family Bible originally owned by Nancy (Prescott) Taylor, dau of Benjamin W. Prescott below, lately owned by Eileen Stocker of Wappingers Falls NY

    i   Hannah, b Winthrop 3 Apr 1785: d 6 Jul 1866 (Prescott Family Bible): m (1) New Sharon 17 Dec 1809 Nathaniel Small (Lora A. W. Underhill, *Genealogy of Edward Small of New England* [1934], p. 139), b Truro MA 6 Dec 1771 son of John & Sarah (Lewis) Small (ibid.), d 28 Oct 1830 ae 58y (g.s., Village cem, New Sharon): m (2) 31 Jul 1839 Daniel Follensbee (Prescott Family Bible)

   ii   Mary, b Winthrop 10 Oct 1786: d 30 Jul 1870 (Prescott Family Bible): m 8 Apr 1819 Briggs Howland (ibid.) who was b 25 Mar 1790 (ibid.), his parentage unknown

  iii   Ruth, b New Sharon 28 Oct 1791: d Parkman 25 Feb 1855 (Prescott Family Bible): m 11 Dec 1817 Winslow Harrington (ibid.)

   iv   Abel, b 22 Jun 1793: d Dunbarton NH 27 Jul 1875 (Prescott Family Bible): m 5 Apr 1819 Eleanor Harvey (ibid.)

   v   Olive, b 7 Apr 1795: d Chesterville 16 Aug 1880 (Prescott Family Bible): m Sep 1829 Eliphalet Wood (ibid.)

   vi   Benjamin Prescott, b 11 Apr 1797: d 21 Nov 1877 ae 80y 7m 10d (g.s., Bowley cem, New Sharon; Family Bible, op. cit.): m 24 Feb 1820 Hannah Howland (ibid.), b c1798, d 30 Jan 1869 ae 71y (g.s., Bowley cem, New Sharon)

  vii   Jesse L., b 21 Jun 1799: d Vienna 24 Aug 1871 (Prescott Family Bible): m 20 Nov 1823 Agnes M. Cass (ibid.)

 viii   Nathaniel, b 20 Sep 1801: d 18 Jan 1865 ae 63y 4m 16d (g.s., Bowley cem, New Sharon): m (1) 1825 Abigail B. Whittier (g.s.), b c1800, d 21 Oct

1843 ae 43y (g.s., Bowley cem, New Sharon): m (2) 1845 Emily H. Wood (g.s.), b c1825, d 30 Sep 1865 ae 40y 5m 18d (g.s., Bowley cem, New Sharon)
ix Elizabeth, b 10 Oct 1803: d 14 Sep 1804 (Prescott Family Bible)

Eleanor W. Townsend, 71 Slab Meadow Rd., Morris CT 06763-1517

Pulcifer, Joseph   42c   3 - 0 - 3 - 0 - 0
Pittston Town, Lincoln County

JOSEPH PULCIFER, b Gloucester MA 12 Jul 1740 son of Ebenezer & Huldah (Silley) Pulcifer (VR; parents' marriage recorded in James R. Pringle, *History of the Town and City of Gloucester, Cape Ann, Massachusetts* [1892], p. 130): d Pittston 29 Nov 1820 (VR; estate probated 10 Jul 1821, Ken Co Probate 1:9): m Gloucester MA 8 Oct 1767 ANNA HARRIS (VR) who d bef 1820 (pension, see below). [One Ann Harris was bp Gloucester MA 31 Oct 1742 dau of Samuel Harris (VR), although it has not been proven that this was the same who later m Joseph Pulcifer.] Joseph was a Rev War soldier and pensioner (Fisher's *Soldiers*, p. 642; Rev War pension #S37319). He is on a list of men who were at Valley Forge 1777–78 (Christine Huston Dodge, "Vital Records of Edgecomb and Newcastle to the Year 1892" [TS, Skidompha Library, Damariscotta]). At almost 80 years of age on 11 Jul 1820, he filed for a Rev War pension. He listed his assets as including "a small house on John Bailey's land worth about fifteen dollars, a small number of poor old articles of furniture" and stated that before receiving his pension he "was in part supported as a pauper." He also stated that he had lost his wife and had "no person who is a member of my family," that he was now feeble and unable to work (Rev War pension #S37319). When his estate was probated in 1821, Joseph Pulcifer, prob his son, was appointed administrator.

Children: births 1st three VR Gloucester MA
i Anna, b 21 Jun 1768: m int Pittston 8 Nov 1794 Samuel Davis of Hallowell (Pittston VR). Two of their children were delivered by Martha Ballard, Hallowell's noted midwife in 1795 and 1797 (Robert R. & Cynthia M. McCausland, *The Diary of Martha Ballard 1785–1812* [1992], pp. 355, 401). [One Samuel Davis of Hallowell m int Hallowell 4 Oct 1800 Deborah Ireland (VR) and on 2 Jul 1810, the *Portland Gazette* reported that the wife of Samuel Davis of Pittston, Deborah Nichols (sic), left with 3 children for Newbury (David C. & Elizabeth K. Young, *Vital Records From Maine Newspapers, 1785–1820* [1993], p. 154)]

ii Joseph, b 11 Jul 1770: m int Pittston 12 Sep 1794 Mercy/Marey Brown (VR). It was poss he who acted as administrator of his father's estate
iii Benjamin, b 12 Jan 1772: m Pittston 24 Apr 1800 Rachel Hunt (VR)
iv Elizabeth, b 17 Apr 1775 (Glidden/Hilton genealogical notes, Hilton vertical file, MHS): d 28 Sep 1817 ae 41y 5m (g.s., Alna Village cem, Alna): m Pittston 23 Oct 1800 Charles Glidden (VR), b Alna 21 Mar 1778 son of Benjamin & Eunice (Averill) Glidden of Newcastle (George W. Chamberlain, *The Descendants of Charles Glidden of Portsmouth and Exeter, New Hampshire* [1925], p. 172), d Alna 15 Apr 1830 (g.s., Alna Village cem). He m (2) int Alna 11 Mar 1819 Ruth Plummer (Chamberlain, op. cit., p. 172)

June Tracy MacNair, 119 Pine Street, Portland, ME 04102-3747

Rand, Jere^h 19a   2 - 1 - 3 - 0 - 0
Gorham and Scarborough Towns, Cumberland County

JEREMIAH RAND, bp 1st Cong Church Scarborough 25 Jul 1742 son of Nathaniel & Mary (Noble) Rand (MHGR, 1:168; Florence O. Rand, *A Genealogy of the Rand Family in the United States* [1898], p. 144): d Gorham 17 Oct 1818 ae 76y (McLellan's *Gorham*, p. 733): m Scarborough 31 Oct 1763 LYDIA BLAKE (MHGR, 3:87), her parentage uncertain [see below]. Jeremiah was living in Scarborough in 1771 (Bettye Hobbs Pruitt, *The Massachusetts Tax Valuation List of 1771* [1978], p. 718) and moved to Gorham by 1777 (McLellan's *Gorham*, p. 733). During the Rev War, he gave patriotic service as a resident of Gorham (Fisher's *Soldiers*, p. 647).

[Several published secondary sources disagree regarding Lydia Blake's parentage. McLellan thought she might have been a dau of Ithiel & Susannah (Martin) Blake who he believed came from Cape Cod MA (McLellan's *Gorham*, pp. 402 and 733), although no birth records for Ithiel's family was found in the VR of Cape Cod MA towns published in the *Mayflower Descendant*. Carlton E. Blake's *Descendants of Jasper Blake* [1980], p. 148, states more convincingly that Lydia was the Lydia Blake bp with siblings at Kensington NH in 1756, dau of Benjamin & Elizabeth (Boulter) Blake who emigrated from Nottingham NH to Scarborough and settled in Gorham.]

Children: McLellan's *Gorham*, p. 733 & cited sources
i Jeremiah Jr., b 19 Oct 1765 and bp Scarborough 5 Nov 1767 (MHGR, 2:80): d 8 Nov 1829 (Thorndike VR): m Gorham 14 Apr 1791 Lydia Jones

(VR), b Gorham 4 Feb 1772 dau of Henry & Lydia (____) Jones of Gorham (VR). They moved to Thorndike by 1820

ii Lydia, bp Scarborough 7 May 1769 (MHGR, 2:81): d Standish 13 Jan 1830 ae 61y (McLellan's *Gorham*, p. 635): m 12 Jul 1785 Jedediah Lombard Jr. (ibid., p. 733) [m int Gorham 23 Apr 1785 (VR)], b 1760 son of Jedidiah & Susan (Dorsett) Lombard (McLellan's *Gorham*, p. 633), d Standish 16 Mar 1842 ae 82y (ibid., p. 635). They lived in Gorham, but moved to Standish by 1790 (Albert J. Sears, *Early Families of Standish, Maine* [1991], p. 133)

iii Mary, b 23 May 1771 (Sears, op. cit., p. 113) and bp Scarborough 28 Nov 1771 (MHGR, 2:82): d 3 Aug 1832 (Sears, op. cit., p. 113): m Standish 26 Mar 1795 Knowles Higgins of Standish (ibid.) [m int Gorham 20 Dec 1794 (VR)], b 25 Sep 1773 son of Zacheus & Hannah (Knowles) (Warren) (Sparrow) Higgins (Sears, op. cit., p. 113), d 3 Jul 1831 (ibid.)

iv Elizabeth/Betsy, b c Nov 1774 (McLellan's *Gorham*, p. 733): d 4 Apr 1858 ae 83y 6m (Sears, op. cit., p. 195): m 20 Nov 1794 Eleazer Higgins Parker of Standish (ibid.), b c1770 son of Ebenezer & Esther (Higgins) Parker (ibid.), d Standish 29 Jan 1814 ae 43y from a bite from a wildcat which broke into his home and attacked his family (ibid.)

v John Blake, b Gorham 10 Oct 1781 (VR): d 18 Jun 1863 (McLellan's *Gorham*, p. 733): m 15 Jul 1799 his prob 1st cousin Ruth Blake (ibid.) [m int Gorham 22 Jun 1799 (VR)], b Gorham 2 Jun 1781 dau of Nathaniel & Mary (Fogg) Blake (VR)

David P. Rand, R2 Box 385E, Presque Isle, ME 04769

Rendal, Eliphelet   57a   1 - 1 - 2 - 0 - 0
    Berwick Town, York County

ELIPHALET RANDALL, bp Dover NH 7 Apr 1728 son of Samuel & Elizabeth (Macfield/Mayfield) Randall (*Collections of the Dover, N.H. Historical Society*, 1 [1894]:137): d prior to 15 Mar 1802 when his will was probated: m (1) LYDIA ROLLINS, b c1731 dau of Jeremiah & Elizabeth (Ham) Rollins (joint will dated 28 Apr 1797 of Eliphalet and Lydia, York Co Probate #15822, in which Lydia mentions homestead of "my Honord father Jeremiah Rollings of Sumersworth Deceased"). She d Berwick 20 Jul 1798 (John E. Frost & Joseph C. Anderson II, *Vital Records of Berwick, South Berwick and North Berwick, Maine to the Year 1892* [1993], hereafter VR, p. 295). Eliphalet m (2) Berwick 10 Sep 1801 ELEANOR (JOHNSON) LIBBY (VR, p. 200) wid of Nathaniel Libby of Berwick (Charles T. Libby, *The Libby Family in America* [1882], p. 93). She d Berwick 17 Apr 1826 ae 74y (VR, p. 298). Eliphalet was a Revolutionary soldier and served in Capt Ricker's Co. (Fisher's *Soldiers*, p. 648).

Children, as named in Eliphalet and Lydia's will; bp Berwick 2nd Church, NEHGR, 74 [1920]:215, 216, 218, 220, 224, 225, 226, 229
- i John Rollins, b c1749 (Randall Papers, a transcript of "two very much worn and old bits of paper found in a box formerly belonging to Almira Deering, widow of I. H. Deering of Waterboro, Me.," copy in possession of Joseph C. Anderson II, Dallas, TX) and bp 15 Apr 1756: d 25 Sep 1787 (ibid.): m cert Berwick 21 Sep 1773 Joanna Hanson (VR, p. 10) [see JOANNA (HANSON) RANDALL family]
- ii Lydia, bp 15 Apr 1756: d Berwick 11 Feb 1826 (VR, p. 263): m c1772 Joseph Chick (family rec in Berwick VR; first child b 1773), b c1744 son of Richard & Bethiah (Gould) Chick (will of Richard Chick, York Co Probate #2949), d Berwick 29 Dec 1819 ae 75y (VR, p. 263)
- iii Sarah, b c1754 and bp 15 Apr 1756: d Litchfield 24 Mar 1825 ae 71y (Oliver B. Clason, *History of Litchfield* [1897], p. 78; *Maine Inquirer*, issue of 7 Apr 1825): m Berwick 4 Nov 1773 John Chick of Kittery (VR, p. 119), b Kittery 1751 (*Index of Revolutionary Veterans Buried in Maine*, MOCA) bro of Joseph above, d Litchfield 23 Jun 1826 ae 75y (Rev War penson #S36871). John was a Rev War soldier in Capt Leighton's Co (ibid.). They moved to Litchfield in 1807
- iv Jeremiah, b c1754 and bp 15 Apr 1756: drowned at Wells 20 Sep 1821 (Berwick VR, p. 296): m int Berwick 31 Oct 1783 Hannah Gowel of Arundel (Berwick VR, p. 22) [see JEREMIAH RANDALL family]
- v Elizabeth, bp 15 Apr 1756: d York 1 Oct 1837 (VR): m William Frost, b 26 May 1747 son of John & Sarah (Gerrish) Frost (E. S. Stackpole, *Old Kittery and Her Families* [1903], p. 418), d York 2 Jun 1827. They had 16 children recorded at York including 4 sets of twins. He was a Revolutionary soldier (Rev War pension #W24250)
- vi James, prob twin, b Berwick 27 Oct 1758 (Robert L. Taylor, *Early Families of Limington, Maine* [1991], p. 270), bp with his bro Stephen 19 Jun 1761 (although on the baptismal record his name was left blank and NEHGR did not pick up this unnamed child in its transcription): d South Limington 16 May 1821 (ibid.): m Berwick 16 Dec 1779 Mary/Molly Shorey (VR, p. 122), b 17 Aug 1763 dau of Jacob & Hannah (Coss) Shorey (*Limington*, op. cit.), d South Limington 19 Sep 1850 ae 87y 10m (ibid.). He was a Rev soldier and a Quaker (ibid.; Rev War pension #W24720).
- vii Stephen, prob twin, b 1758 (Robert L. Taylor, *Early Families of Limerick, Maine* [1984], p. 115), bp 19 Jun 1761: d Limerick 18 Sep 1837 (ibid.): m (1) Berwick 13 Dec 1781 Anna Fogg (VR, p. 123), b Berwick 28 Jan 1761 and bp 26 Apr 1761 dau of James & Anna (____) Fogg (*Limerick*, op. cit., p. 115; NEHGR, 74 [1920]:225), d Berwick 1 Jun 1792 (*Limerick*, op. cit., p. 115): m (2) 6 Aug 1793 Lydia Abbott of Berwick (ibid.): m (3) Berwick 30 Dec 1814 Elizabeth McDonald (VR, p. 152). Stephen moved from Berwick to Limerick in his later years

viii Deborah/Debbey, b 28 May 1760 (*Limerick*, op. cit.), bp 13 Sep 1761: d Limerick 13 Jul 1818 ae 58y (*Limerick*, op. cit.): m Berwick 23 Oct 1787 Moses Philpot of Somersworth NH (Berwick VR, p. 129), b Somersworth NH 15 Jun 1759 son of Richard & "wid Mercy Philpot" (Robert S. Canney, *The Early Marriages of Strafford County, New Hampshire* [1991], p. 408; "Master Tate's Diary," NEHGR, 74 [1920]:35; *Limerick*, op. cit.), d Limerick 6 Dec 1847 ae 88y 6m 11d

ix Mary, bp 31 Mar 1764: not named in parents' will

x Martha, bp 31 Mar 1764: d Shapleigh 2 Mar 1846 ae 82y 10m (g.s., John E. Frost, "Shapleigh [Maine] Record Book," [TS, MHS], p. 13): m Berwick 19 Mar 1795 Edmund Coffin of Shapleigh (Berwick VR, p. 138), b c Jul 1769, d Shapleigh 3 Oct 1843 ae 82y 3m (g.s., bur with Martha)

xi Richard, bp 7 Jun 1767: d 19 May 1787 (Randall Papers, op. cit.)

xii Jotham, bp 11 Sep 1775: not named in parents' will

xiii Huldah, b c1770, bp 11 Sep 1775: d Limerick 1 Jan 1814 ae 44y (*Limerick*, op. cit., p. 68): m Berwick 10 Nov 1789 Reuben Hamilton (VR, p. 132), b Pownalborough 6 Sep 1769 son of Gabriel & Sarah (Metcalf) Hamilton (Wiscasset VR) [see GABRIEL HAMILTON family, *Maine Families*, 3:114–16], d Limerick 20 Dec 1854 ae 85y 4m (*Limerick*, op. cit., p. 68). He m (2) Limerick 1 Sep 1814 Mary (Hanscom) Ricker (ibid.).

Joseph C. Anderson II, 5337 Del Roy Drive, Dallas, TX 75229

Rendal, Jeremiah   57a   1 - 2 - 3 - 0 - 0
Berwick Town, York County

JEREMIAH RANDALL, b c1754 and bp Berwick 2nd Church 16 Apr 1756 son of Eliphalet & Lydia (Rollins) Randall [see ELIPHALET RANDALL family]: drowned at Wells 20 Sep 1821 ae 67y (John E. Frost & Joseph C. Anderson II, *Vital Records of Berwick, South Berwick and North Berwick, Maine to the Year 1892* [1993], hereafter VR, p. 296): m int Berwick 31 Oct 1783 HANNAH GOWEL of Arundel (Berwick VR, p. 22), prob the unnamed wid of Jeremiah Randall who d Berwick 16 Jul 1823 (VR, p. 296). Hannah was prob the Hannah Gowell b Kittery 19 October 1757 dau of Richard & Keziah (Fernald) Gowell (VR). Keziah, Hannah's prob mother, m (2) Timothy Hanscom and they settled at Arundel in 1774 (Stackpole, *Old Kittery and Her Families* [1903], p. 501). The only mention found of Jeremiah and Hannah's children is seen in the land records. On 7 Aug 1826, Keziah Rendall, Patty Rendall and Hannah Rendall, all of Berwick, singlewomen, sold for $1500 to Hiram Rendall of Berwick, yeoman, all their right "to the homestead farm of our father Jeremiah Rendall, deceased...meaning hereby to convey to said Hiram all the estate that descended to us from our father, and also all that has or may come to us from our brother Samuel Rendall" (York Co deeds 140:165).

Children, order uncertain: (York Co deeds 140:165)
- i Samuel, prob d by 7 Aug 1826 (York Co deeds 140:165)
- ii prob Hiram, b c1789 (1850 USC): d Berwick 30 Dec 1872 (VR, p. 279): m int Berwick 15 Jun 1827 Maria Coffin of Shapleigh (Berwick VR, p. 83), b c1810 (1850 USC Berwick), d Berwick 22 Jul 1882 (VR, p. 279)
- iii Keziah, b c1790: d 8 Mar 1877 ae 87y (John E. Frost, "South Berwick [Maine] Record Book" [TS, MHS], p. 142): m So. Berwick 30 Oct 1833 Ebenezer Goodwin (VR, p. 430), b c1780, d 12 Jan 1864 ae 84y (Frost, op. cit.)
- iv Martha/Patty, b c1793: d 9 Apr 1878 ae 84y 6m (John E. Frost, "North Berwick [Maine] Record Book" [TS, MHS])): m So. Berwick 5 Nov 1826 Dominicus Hubbard as his 2nd wife (VR, p. 424; YCGSJ, 2:49) son of Benjamin & Abigail (Hearl) Hubbard (ibid.). He d No. Berwick 16 Oct 1840 (VR, p. 653)
- v Hannah, b c1802: d Berwick 9 Jun 1872 ae 70y (Wilbur D. Spencer, *Burial Inscriptions, Berwick, York County, Maine to the Year 1922* [1922], p. 17): m int Berwick 3 Sep 1833 John Butler 2nd (VR, p. 90), poss son of Benjamin & Sarah (Gowell) Butler who are buried in the same plot as Hannah

Joseph C. Anderson II, 5337 Del Roy Drive, Dallas, TX 75229

Rendal, Joanna   57b   2 - 3 - 5 - 0 - 0
Berwick Town, York County

JOANNA (HANSON) RANDALL (widow of John Rollins Randall), b Dover NH 11 Feb 1752 dau of William & Bathsheba (____) Hanson (VR), d Berwick 2 Dec 1822 ae 69y (Randall Papers, a transcript of "two very much worn and old bits of paper found in a box formerly belonging to Almira Deering, widow of I. H. Deering of Waterboro, Me.," copy in possession of Joseph C. Anderson II, Dallas, TX): m cert Berwick 21 Sep 1773 JOHN ROLLINS RANDALL (John E. Frost & Joseph C. Anderson II, *Vital Records of Berwick, South Berwick and North Berwick, Maine to the Year 1892* [1993], hereafter VR, p. 10), b 1749 (Randall Papers, op. cit.), bp Berwick 2nd Church 15 Apr 1756 son of Eliphalet & Lydia (Rollins) Randall [see ELIPHALET RANDALL family], d 25 Sep 1787 (Randall Papers, op. cit.).

Children (surname RANDALL): guardianship papers, York Co Probate 16:332, 16:333; 1st four bp 2nd Church Berwick, NEHGR 74 [1920]:221, 230

  i Eliphalet, b c1774, bp 20 March 1781: d No. Berwick 8 Oct 1852 ae 78y (g.s., John E. Frost, "North Berwick [Maine] Record Book" [TS, MHS]): m Berwick 6 Dec 1801 Catherine Clark (VR, p. 145), b c1768, d 20 Nov 1837 ae 69y (g.s., Frost, op. cit.)

  ii Betty/Betsey, b c1777, bp 20 Mar 1781: d No. Berwick 1 Mar 1858 ae 81y (g.s., Frost, op. cit.): unm

  iii Lydia, b 1778 (John Wentworth, *The Wentworth Genealogy* [1878], 1:268–69), bp 20 Mar 1781: d 1860 (ibid.), prob the Mrs. Lydia Hall whose funeral was held at No. Berwick 7 Mar 1860 ("Journal of Eld. William Quint," YCGSJ, 2 [1987]:58): m Berwick 30 Nov 1797 John Hall (VR, p. 145), b 15 Oct 1774 son of Capt. William & Lydia (Wentwort) Hall of No. Berwick (*Wentworth Genealogy*, 1:268–69), d 1848 (ibid.)

  iv Mary/Molly, bp 20 Mar 1781: prob the Miss Molly Randall whose funeral was held at No. Berwick in 1849 (Quint Journal, op. cit.)

  v William, described as a minor under 14y of age on 7 May 1793 when his mother Joanna was appt his guardian. One William Randall m Lebanon 19 Feb 1818 Rebecca Hardison (VR) although no evidence has been found to affirm this was the same man

  vi Bathsheba, b c1784 (1850 USC): her funeral was held at No. Berwick 10 Apr 1862 (Quint Journal, op. cit.): m int Berwick 19 May 1805 Thomas Clark Jr (VR, p. 146), b c1785 (1850 USC), his funeral held 27 Dec 1856 (Quint Journal, op. cit.)

  vii John, b c1786: d No. Berwick 30 Apr 1811 ae 25y (g.s., Frost, op. cit.)

  viii Hanson, b c1788: d Lebanon 16 Apr 1859 ae 71y (VR): m (1) int Berwick 22 Jul 1811 Elizabeth/Betsey Chadbourne (VR, p. 63), b Berwick 18 Mar 1795 dau of Daniel & Mary (Twambley) Chadbourne (Chadbourne genealogy in progress by the Chadbourne Family Association, information courtesy of Elaine Bacon of San Jose CA), d 21 Feb 1815 ae 21y (g.s., Frost, op. cit.): m (2) Berwick 28 Nov 1822 Elizabeth/Betsey Smith (VR, p. 155), b Berwick 4 Nov 1792 dau of Moses & Susanna (Brackett) Smith (VR, p. 248), d 19 Jul 1878 ae 85y (g.s., Frost, op. cit.)

Joseph C. Anderson II, 5337 Del Roy Drive, Dallas, TX 75229

Renkins, Constant   46b   2 - 4 - 3 - 0 - 0
    Thomaston Town [later Rockland], Lincoln County

CONSTANT RANKINS, b York 17 Apr 1747 son of James & Priscilla (Shaw) Rankins (VR): d Thomaston 19 Dec 1831 (Eaton's *Thomaston*, 2:366): m (1) PATIENCE DINSLOW (ibid.), bp Harpswell 17 Aug 1756 dau of Benjamin

Dinslow ("Harpswell, Maine Vital Records...Recorded by Rev. Elisha Eaton 1754–1764 and by his son, Samuel Eaton, V.D.M., 1765–1843" [TS, MHS]): m (2) "at St. Georges now Thomaston" 22 Aug 1775 MARY TOLMAN (VR), b Stoughton MA 15 Feb 1748 dau of Isaiah & Hannah (Fuller) Tolman (VR; Thomaston VR). Constant served as a sergeant in the Revolution (MS&S 12:963). On 25 May 1768, he was one of the inhabitants of Sebascodogin in the District of Harpswell (alias Shapleigh Island) who signed his name to a petition requesting the General Court to form them into a separate precinct "that we may enjoy the privileges of the gospel in common with other Christians in a more decent and convenient manner" (BHM, 2:120). He moved to Thomaston in 1775 (Eaton's *Thomaston*).

Children by 1st wife Patience Dinslow
- i poss Hannah, d Augusta (Eaton's *Thomaston*, 2:366): m _____ Stone (ibid.). Res Augusta (ibid.)
- ii Priscilla, b Harpswell 18 Jul 1769 (VR): d Augusta 20 Mar 1817 ae 48y (VR): m c1792 Samuel Cummings (1st child b 1793; Albert O. Cummins, *Cummings Genealogy—Isaac Cummings 1601–1677 of Ispwich in 1638 and Some of his Descendants* [1904], p. 94; Philip A. Fisher, *The Fisher Genealogy* [1898], p. 53), b Stoughton MA 28 Nov 1761 son of Samuel & Elizabeth (Fisher) Cummings (ibid.), d Manchester 28 Jan 1853 ae 92y (g.s. Cummings cem)
- iii James, b Harpswell 5 Oct 1771 (VR): d Rockland (Eaton's *Thomaston*, 2:366). He was afflicted with epilepsy (ibid.)

Children by 2nd wife Mary Tolman, born Thomaston: births VR Thomaston; Eaton's *Thomaston*, 2:366
- iv Samuel, b 4 May 1776: d Thomaston 7 Apr 1842 (VR): m Thomaston 15 Nov 1802 Elizabeth Jameson (VR), b Thomaston 13 May 1776 dau of Robert & Deborah (Morton) Jameson (VR; Eaton's *Thomaston*, 2:281–82), d Rockland 4 Feb 1850 (VR)
- v Constant, b 4 Oct 1778: d Frankfort 1830 (DAR Lineage 151:194): m Thomaston 6 Aug 1802 Susannah Lindsey (VR), b Thomaston 25 May 1780 dau of John & Susannah (Robinson) Lindsey (VR; Eaton's *Thomaston*, 2:309), d 3 Mar 1871 (DAR Application #150 606)
- vi Mary, b 12 Oct 1781: d Albion 1 Jul 1860 ae 78y 9m (VR): m Thomaston 1 Feb 1810 Ellithan/Elathan/Elnathan Taylor (VR), b Sep 1783 (g.s.), d Albion 4 Mar 1857 ae 73y (VR)
- vii Joseph, b 14 Oct 1784: a mariner who d "abroad" (Eaton's *Thomaston*, 2:309)
- viii Hannah, b 21 Sep 1786: d Rockland 1 Aug 1862 (VR): m Thomaston 22 Apr 1806 Freeman Harden (VR), b Pembroke MA 4 Sep 1783 son of Perry & Mary (Swan) Harden (VR), d Rockland 23 Nov 1848 (VR)

ix Andrew, b 26 Dec 1788: living 1850 (USC): m (1) Thomaston 2 Jul 1812 Betsey Burns (VR): m (2) Rockland 13 Mar 1828 Mary (Havener) Holmes, b c1792 dau of Mathias & Eve Catherine (Ludwig) Havener (George A. Gray, *The Descendants of George Holmes of Roxbury 1596-1908* [1908], p. 200), d Rockland 29 Aug 1866 (VR)

x Esther, b 24 Apr 1791: m (1) Thomaston 7 Nov 1811 Israel Gardner (VR): m (2) Joseph Walker of Albion and res Aroostook Co (Eaton's *Thomaston*, 2:309)

Dana A. Batchelder, 258 South Sea Avenue, West Yarmouth, MA 02673

Rankin, Joseph   59b   1 - 2 - 5 - 0 - 0
Buxton Town, York County

JOSEPH RANKINS, b Lebanon 19 Aug 1756 (DAR Lineage 161:156): d Buxton 16 May 1831 (VR): m Buxton 12 Oct 1777 MEHITABLE DUNNELL (Cyrus Woodman, *The Records of the Church of Christ in Buxton, Maine During the Pastorate of Rev. Paul Coffin, D.D.* [repr 1989], p. 22), b c1754 dau of Joseph Dunnell (J. M. Marshall, *Celebration of the First Centennial Anniversary of the Incorporation of the Town of Buxton* [1874], p. 169), d Buxton 5 Mar 1846 (VR). Joseph served in the Revolution (MS&S 12:965; Rev War pension #W22022).

Children: births VR Buxton
  i Joseph Jr, b 7 Feb 1778: d Hiram 8 May 1851 (g.s. Village cem): m (1) Parsonsfield 1 Apr 1802 Jane Perry (VR), b Parsonsfield 10 May 1778 (Hubert Clemons, *Early Hiram Families* [1984], p. 25), d Hiram 13 Apr 1828 (g.s.): m (2) Betsey ____, b 1778 (Clemons, op. cit.), d Baldwin 10 Nov 1841 (*Downeast Ancestry*, 14:#5:159)
  ii Mehitable, b 12 Apr 1780: d Buxton 2 Mar 1852: m Buxton 3 Aug 1806 Samuel Edgerly, b Buxton 10 Aug 1783 son of John & Abigail (Brooks) Edgerly, d Buxton 12 May 1850
  iii Elizabeth, b 28 Feb 1782: d Buxton 21 Jan 1862 (VR): m (1) Buxton 19 Apr 1805 James L. Towle (VR), b Buxton 7 Dec 1781 son of Phineas & Sarah (Leavitt) Towle (VR), d Buxton 30 Sep 1807 (VR): m (2) Buxton 2 Jan 1815 Stephen Harmon (VR), b Buxton 23 Nov 1785 son of Joel & Pauline (Stimpson) Harmon (VR), d Buxton 28 Dec 1836 (VR)
  iv Mary, b 1 Jul 1784: d Buxton 5 Oct 1804 (VR)
  v Anna, b 17 Sep 1786: d Buxton 3 Jun 1820 (VR): m Buxton 13 May 1810 John Berry (VR), b Buxton 4 Apr 1786 son of Jonathan & Sarah Berry (VR), d Buxton 19 Jan 1832 (VR)

vi John, b 10 Aug 1789: d Buxton 19 Apr 1827 (VR): m Buxton 19 Sep 1813 Eleanor Hanscom (VR), b Buxton 16 Sep 1791 dau of William & Elizabeth (Sands) Hanscom (VR), d Buxton 10 Jan 1871 (VR)

vii Enoch, b 27 Oct 1792: d Buxton 28 Jul 1862 (VR): m Limington 3 Jul 1820 Eliza Abbott (Robert L. Taylor, *Families of Limington, Maine* [1984], p. 2), b Falmouth 14 Mar 1797 dau of Nathan & Mercy (Gowan) Abbott (ibid.), d Hiram 12 Dec 1839 (ibid.)

viii Ada/Eda, b 20 Apr 1796: d Buxton 18 Jan 1864 (VR): m Buxton 20 Sep 1818 Stephen S. Harmon (VR), b Buxton 3 Apr 1790 son of Nathaniel & Hannah (Starbird) Harmon (Artemas C. Harmon, *The Harmon Genealogy* [1920], pp. 29, 66)

Dana A. Batchelder, 258 South Sea Avenue, West Yarmouth, MA 02673

Richardson, Moses   25a   2 - 2 - 5 - 0 - 0
Standish Town, Cumberland County

MOSES RICHARDSON, b Newton MA 17 May 1738 son of David & Remember (Ward) Richardson (VR; Albert J. Sears, *Early Families of Standish, Maine* [1991], hereafter Sears, p. 216): d Standish 1794 (ibid.): m Newton MA 26 Apr 1763 LYDIA HALL (VR), b c1743 prob dau of Edward & Mary (Miller) Hall (Sears, pp. 212, 216), d 12 Nov 1823 ae 80y (ibid.). She m (2) Standish 13 or 28 May 1808 Ephraim Batchelder of Baldwin (ibid.). Moses lived in Brookline, Dorchester and Newton MA, and was of Pearsontown [now Standish] in Apr 1773.

Children: births VR Standish & cited sources
  i   Lydia, b Brookline MA 20 Jun 1763 (VR): d Baldwin 6 Nov 1827 (g.s., Peter Sanborn cem): m int Gorham 23 Oct 1781 Peter Sanborn (VR) [see PETER SANBORN family]
  ii Anna, b Brookline MA 5 Jun 1765 (VR): d New York State 22 Sep 1849 (Sears p. 216): m int Gorham 5 Nov 1783 her step-brother Samuel Batchelder (VR), b 21 Apr 1765 son of Ephraim & Apphia (Lowell) Batchelder (Sears, p. 216), d New York State 8 Oct 1819 (ibid.). They lived in Baldwin and Danville VT and migrated to New York State about 1810 (ibid.)
  iii Elizabeth, b Brookline MA 23 Aug 1767 (VR): m 1 Sep 1791 John Cummings Flint (Sears, p. 216)
  iv Moses Jr., b Dorchester MA 13 Mar 1770 (VR): living Standish in 1850 ae 80y (USC) but d in Baldwin (Sears, p. 216): m Standish 27 Nov 1806

  Jemima Eaton of Standish (MHGR, 5:236) dau of Israel & Sarah (Mackintyre) Eaton of Standish (Sears, p. 216). He was a one-legged man and a shoemaker (ibid.)

v Mehitabel, b Newton MA 22 May 1772 (VR): d 6 Apr 1821 ae 49y (Sears, p. 217): m 6 Nov 1792 Lemuel McCollistor (ibid., but incorrectly called "McCorrison" by Sears) [m int Gorham 17 Oct 1792 (VR)], b Gorham 28 Aug 1767 son of James & Deliverance (Rich) McCollistor (VR), d 19 Jan 1856 ae 86y [sic] (Sears, p. 217)

vi Mary/Molly, b Pearsontown [Standish] 20 Jun 1775 and bp 16 Jun 1776 (Sears, p. 217): m Standish 15 Dec 1796 Boaz Rich (MHGR, 5:233), b 23 Feb 1772 son of Lemuel & Mary (Colley) Rich of Standish (Sears, p. 217). They moved to Exeter about 1818 (ibid.)

vii Sarah, b Pearsontown 6 Dec 1776 and bp 8 Dec 1776 (Sears, p. 217): m Standish 11 Oct 1798 Joseph Butterfield Jr. of Standish (MHGR, 5:234), b 7 Dec 1775 son of Joseph & Mary (Harding) Butterfield (Sears, p. 41)

viii Aaron, b Pearsontown 1 Sep 1779 and bp 5 Sep 1779 (Sears, p. 217): m 13 Jan 1808 Mehitable Cummings of Standish (MHGR, 5:236) prob dau of Thomas & Rachel (Jackson) Cummings of Standish (Sears, p. 217)

ix Abigail, b Pearsontown 21 Jun 1782 (Sears, p. 217): d 11 May 1849 ae 67y (ibid.): m Standish 3 Mar 1803 her step-brother Sylvanus Batchelder of Baldwin (MHGR, 5:235), b 30 Oct 1777 son of Ephraim & Apphia (Lowell) Batchelder (Sears, p. 217), d 3 Feb 1868 ae 90y (ibid.)

x Edward, b Standish 14 Mar 1788 (Sears, p. 217). He lived in Lynn MA (ibid.)

Lois M. Griffiths, 338 Norris Hill Road, Monmouth, ME 04259-6925

Robins, Jonathan 36a 1 - 3 - 5 - 0 - 0
 Canaan Town, Lincoln County

JONATHAN ROBBINS, b Chelmsford MA 21 Jun 1750 son of John Jr. & Susannah (Harwood) Robbins (VR): d Norridgewock Dec 1825 ae 75y (VR) [his g.s. in Riverview Cem, Norridgewock, states he d 9 Dec 1824 ae 75y]: m Townsend MA 10 Jul 1771 ELIZABETH EMERY (Chelmsford MA VR), b Townsend MA 3 May 1750 dau of Zachariah & Esther (Stevens) Emery (VR; Rev. Rufus Emery, *Descendants of John and Anthony Emery* [1891], p. 323), d Norridgewock Jun 1826 ae 76y (VR) [her g.s. in Riverview cem, Norridgewock, states she d 8 Jun 1825 ae 75y]. Jonathan was a sergeant in Capt. Minott's company during the Rev War (Fisher's *Soldiers*, p. 665). In 1781, he sold his land at Carlisle MA to his brother John Robbins (Middlesex MA deeds, 82:397) and removed to Canaan and later to Norridgewock. In Oct 1793, Jonathan served on a committee at Norridgewock "to look up stones to underpin the meeting house and to notify the people to come and dig them and another day to haul them to the spot" (Norridgewock TR). In 1803, he and his sons Isaac and Luke were listed as taxpayers in Norridgewock (NEHGR, 97 [1943]:395).

Children
- i   Isaac, bp Chelmsford MA 2 Feb 1772 (VR): d Chelmsford MA 28 Aug 1775 (VR)
- ii Betty, bp Chelmsford MA 27 Feb 1774 (VR): d Chelmsford MA 1 Sep 1775 (VR)
- iii Isaac, b Chelmsford MA 4 Apr 1776 (VR): m int Norridgewock 19 Feb 1806 Nancy Ward of Madison (VR). On 31 Jul 1818, he sold land in Norridgewock to John Robbins (Som Co deeds, 3:512)
- iv Luke, b Chelmsford MA 17 Apr 1778 (Norridgewock VR), bp 17 May 1778 (Chelmsford MA VR): d 11 Apr 1854 (g.s., Pond Street cem, Bradford): m (1) Norridgewock 5 Mar 1801 Salome Brown both of Norridgewock (VR) who d Fairfield 6 Apr 1812 (Rome VR): m (2) Norridgewock as a resident of Mercer 25 May 1814 Mary Hibbard/Hebberd of Norridgewock (VR), b c1788–89, d 18 Jan 1870 ae 81y (g.s., Pond Street cem, Bradford)
- v   Levi, b Chelmsford MA 15 Jul 1780 (Norridgewock VR): d Norridgwock 6 Sep 1815 ae 30y [sic] (VR): m Norridgewock 6 Mar 1803 Jane Gilman "both of a place called Oak Hill" (Norridgewock VR)
- vi Betsey/Betcy, b Canaan 4 Aug 1782 (Norridgewock VR): m Norridgewock 18 Jun 1801 Joshua Goodridge Jr. "of Carrytonko" (Norridgewock VR)
- vii Lucy, b Canaan 13 May 1785 (Norridgewock VR): m Norridgewock 12 Mar 1807 Tillson Bozworth "of Carrytonk Plantation" (Norridgewock VR)
- viii Zilpah, b Canaan 15 Jul 1787 (Norridgewock VR): m Norridgewock 12 Jul 1814 Simeon Richardson Jr. of Madison (Norridgewock VR), b c Aug 1788, d Madison 13 May 1860 ae 71y 9m (g.s., Jewett cem)
- ix Persis, b Canaan 27 Apr 1790 (Norridgewock VR): m Norridgewock 3 Nov 1812 Edmund Parker Jr. both of Norridgewock (VR)
- x   John, b Norridgewock 1 May 1794 (VR): d Norridgewock 10 May 1880 ae 86y (VR): m Norridgewock 26 May 1816 Susannah M. Schofield (VR), b Topsham c1793, d of consumption Jul 1849 ae 56y (Norridgewock VR) [g.s., Riverview cem, gives d 31 Jul 1859 ae 55y]

Janet H. Riley, 161 Forest St., Sherborn, MA 01770
Eleanor Robbins Sprague, 7 Academy St. Apt. #1, Calais, ME 04619

Russel, Jason   42c   1 - 1 - 1 - 0 - 0
Norridgewock Town, Settlement East of, Lincoln County

JASON RUSSELL, b Mason NH 2 Jun 1763 son of Jason & Elizabeth (Locke) Russell (Opel Louise Currier, *William Russell Family of Menotomy (Now Arlington), Massachusetts* [1980], p. 15): d 8 Oct 1840 (g.s., York cem, Brighton): m Norridgewock 8 Nov 1787 REBECCA LAUGHTON (VR), b prob Pepperell MA c1768 dau of John & Jane (Adams) (Lamson) Laughton (Currier, op. cit., p. 20), d 20 Feb 1848 ae 79y (g.s., York cem, Brighton). Jason was a grandson of the Jason Russell who was killed 19 Apr 1775 by British soldiers in his house at Menotomy [now Arlington MA] (Abram English Brown, *Beneath Old Roof Trees*, pp. 247–58). He was enumerated at Madison in 1810 (USC) and was at Brighton (North Hill) when it was incorporated in 1816 where he held the offices of tithingman and surveyor of highways (TR).

Children: all info from Currier, op. cit., p. 20, unless otherwise cited
  i   Silas, b Madison 22 Jan 1791 (Cambridge VR): m North Hill 8 Apr 1812 Deborah Foss, b Barrington NH 28 Oct 1792 (Cambridge VR). They lived at Cambridge ME
  ii Asa, b Madison 4 Feb 1793: d 30 Nov 1881 ae 88y (g.s., York cem, Brighton): m Brighton 19 Apr 1819 Mary/Molly Loveland (VR), b Sidney 10 Oct 1801 dau of Capt. James & Mary (____) Loveland, d 7 Jan 1888 ae 87y (g.s., York cem, Brighton). They lived at Brighton where he was a farmer and blacksmith
  iii Josiah, b 1795: m Serena ____
  iv William, b Madison 6 Sep 1796: d Athens 13 May 1864 ae 67y 8m 7d (g.s., Lord's Hill cem, Athens): m Brighton Jan 1820 Achsah Kelley (VR), b 1804 dau of Sylvanus & Temperance (____) Kelley, d Athens 1 Oct 1864 ae 60y 2m 24d (g.s., Lord's Hill cem, Athens)
  v   Betsey, b 1798: d 1871: m Brighton 8 Oct 1817 John Wyman Jr. (VR), b Clinton 17 Apr 1799 son of John & Abiel (____) Wyman (VR), d 1895. Both are bur Waltham MA
  vi Stephen, b 1800: m (1) Norridgewock 17 Feb 1820 Fidelia Laughton of Norridgewock (VR), b Norridgewock 7 Feb 1803 dau of John & Lydia (____) Laughton (VR), d 29 May 1860 ae 57y (g.s., Southside cem, Skowhegan). He poss m (2) 31 May 1861 Joanna Woodbury of Canaan. He was a Baptist minister for 22y in Sidney
  vii Jesse, b Madison 1803: d 12 Feb 1879 (g.s., South Solon cem, Cornville): m (1) int Brighton 18 Oct 1820 Lovina Wyman (VR), b Brighton 26 Oct 1806 dau of John & Bier (____) Wyman (VR), d 26 Aug 1848: m (2) Brighton Eliza P. Whittier who d 29 May 1884 ae 76y (g.s., South Solon cem, Cornville). They lived in Brighton

viii Belinda, b Madison 1805: d 6 Mar 1879 ae 74y 6m (g.s., York cem, Brighton): m Brighton 30 Mar 1823 Hiram Spofford (VR), b 29 Feb 1800 son of Amherst & Hannah (Emerson) Spofford (Bingham VR), d 1 Aug 1875 ae 75y 6m (g.s., York cem, Brighton)

ix Jason, b Madison 1807: m (1) Brighton 6 Apr 1826 Charlotte Wyman (VR), b Brighton 18 Sep 1808 sis of Lovina above (VR): m (2) Julia ____: m (3) Rachel ____. He lived in Brighton and Bridgewater ME

Lois M. Griffiths, 338 Norris Hill Road, Monmouth, ME 04259-6925

Sabine, Lewis   16a   1 - 1 - 2 - 0 - 0
Flintstown Plantation [now Baldwin], Cumberland County

LEWIS SABINE, b prob c1760 (ae 70–80y on both the 1830 and 1840 USC, Palermo): d prob Palermo bef 21 Feb 1848 when his widow sold land to her son (Wal Co deeds 62:324): m (1) Standish 13 Apr 1788 HANNAH THORN (VR) [he of Flintstown Plt on m int rec Standish 27 Mar 1787 (VR)]: of Palermo when he m (2) Whitefield 15 Dec 1818 ABIGAIL DAVIS (VR). In 1800, Lewis was enumerated in the census at Danville, Caledonia Co VT. He was back in Maine by 1810 when he is found at Palermo and where he was also enumerated in 1820, 1830, and 1840. According to Millard A. Howard's *An Introduction to the Early History of Palermo, Maine* (n.d.), the "Saban" family came from Scituate MA.

Children, all reportedly b VT, perhaps others

i Lewis Jr., b c1791: d Palermo 9 Jan 1860 ae 69y (g.s., Greely Corner cem): m (1) c1820 Sarah E./Sally Dow (1st child b 1821), b Jefferson 28 Nov 1804 dau of Peter & Mary (Kennedy) Dow (VR) [see PETER DOW JR. family, *Maine Families*, 1:85–86], d Palermo 18 Dec 1835 ae 29y (g.s., Greely Corner cem): m (2) c1836 Louisa Davis (g.s.; 1st child b 1837), b 1803, d 1892 (g.s., Greely Corner cem, Palermo)

ii Curtis, b c1795 (1850 USC, 33rd Twp, Han Co): d "of exhaustion on the march" at or near New Orleans LA 12 Apr 1864 (Civil War pension #67,896): m Great Pond 21 Aug 1831 Charity Collar (Christine R. Brown, *Ancestors and Descendants of Joshua Williams and John Collar* [1984], p. 230), b Fairfax (Albion) c1805 (ibid.; 1850 USC), d Eddington 27 Aug 1894 (g.s., Mt. Hope cem). In the Civil War and at an advanced age, Curtis served with Co D, 30th ME Infantry. His widow received a pension for his service (pension, op. cit.)

iii Pierce, b c1802 (1850 USC, Eddington, Pen Co): d bef 1860 (USC): m Winthrop 7 Dec 1823 Melinda Woodcock (Everett S. Stackpole, *History*

of Winthrop, Maine [1925], p. 696), b Winthrop 9 Aug 1800 dau of William & Lucy (Buzzell) Woodcock (ibid.), d aft 1860 (USC)
   iv Hiram, b c1806 (1850 USC, Palermo, listed as Hiram "Laban"): d Island Falls, Aroostook Co c1890 (g.s., Greely Corner cem, Palermo): reportedly m c1830 Margery/Mary Warner dau of Phineas Warner [Margery's surname based on the fact that their son, George Sabine, ae 10y, was in the Phineas Warner family at Freedom in 1850, according to tradition sent to live with his grandparents after his mother died], b c1813, d 19 Nov 1846 ae 33y (g.s., Greely Corner cem, Palermo)

Gordon Alan Morris, 98-401 Kaonohi St. #3, Aiea, HI 96701

Sandbourn, Peter   * *   1 - 3 - 2 - 0 - 0
Standish Town, Cumberland County

[Note: Examination of the original 1790 census sheets on microfilm confirm that Peter Sanborn was a head-of-household at Standish. His entry was overlooked on the 1908 published census. His household should have been included on p. 25a between the entries for "Sandbourn, John" and "Sandbourn, John, Ju^r."]

PETER SANBORN, b Hampton Falls NH 9 Jul 1751 and bp 14 Jul 1751 son of John & Lucy (Sanborn) Sanborn (Albert J. Sears, *Early Families of Standish, Maine* [1991], p. 227): d Baldwin 4 or 6 Aug 1827 (death date discrepancy between g.s., Peter Sanborn cem, Baldwin, and Rev War pension #S37367): m int Gorham 23 Oct 1781 LYDIA RICHARDSON both of Pearsontown [Standish] (Gorham VR), b Brookline MA 20 Jun 1763 dau of Moses & Lydia (Hall) Richardson (VR; Sears, op. cit., p. 227) [see MOSES RICHARDSON family], d Baldwin 6 Nov 1827 (Sears, op. cit., p. 227; g.s., Peter Sanborn cem). Peter lived in Pearsontown [Standish]. He served in the Rev War in Tupper's regiment, MA line, at Fishkill and White Plains, and was discharged in Mar 1779 (MS&S 13:779; pension, op. cit.). He bought land in Baldwin and paid for part of it with his pension money of 1818; then was refused a pension in 1820 because he already owned land ("Estate Schedules from Revolutionary War Pensions," NEHGR, 142 [1988]:202–3). In 1820, Peter and Lydia were living with their son Enoch 20y, and a granddaughter Eliza ae 12y (ibid.). He described himself as unable to work due to lameness and old age and without any income (ibid.). His wife Lydia was also unable to work (ibid.).

Children: births last 6 VR Standish
   i Levi, b 18 Dec 1781 (V. C. Sanborn, *Genealogy of the Family of Samborne or Sanborn* [1899], hereafter *Samborne/Sanborn*, p. 152): d 1786 (ibid.).

ii Rufus, b 22 Dec 1785: d Baldwin 26 Sep 1859 ae 74y (g.s., Peter Sanborn cem): m Baldwin 13 Nov 1806 Sarah Cram (Robert L. Taylor, *Early Families of Cornish, Maine* [1985], p. 27), b 10 Aug 1787 dau of Joseph & Abigail (Pugsley) Cram (ibid.) [see JOSEPH CRAM family, *Maine Families*, 2:61], d Baldwin 5 Oct 1848 (g.s., Peter Sanborn cem)

iii Levi, b 9 Sep 1787: d 14 Apr 1814 (*Samborne/Sanborn*, p. 152): unm (ibid.)

iv Peter, b 20 May 1790: d 13 Jul 1861 ae 71y (g.s., William Binford cem, Baldwin): m Phebe Elizabeth Binford (g.s.), b c1792, d 20 Oct 1880 ae 88y (g.s., William Binford cem, Baldwin)

v Aaron, b 27 Dec 1792: d 1803 (*Samborne/Sanborn*, p. 152)

vi Benjamin, b 10 Mar 1795: d West Baldwin 8 Jan 1874 ae 78y (*Maine Families*, 2:61 citing g.s.): m 17 Apr 1817 Abigail Cram of Baldwin (Taylor, op. cit., p. 27), b 17 May 1799 sis of Sarah above (ibid.), d West Baldwin 14 Sep 1882 (*Maine Families*, 2:61 citing g.s.)

vii Enoch, b 17 May 1800. He resided with his parents in 1820 (NEHGR, 142 [1988]:203)

Lois M. Griffiths, 338 Norris Hill Road, Monmouth, ME 04259-6925

Sands, James   59c   2 - 3 - 2 - 0 - 0
Coxhall Town [now Lyman], York County

JAMES SANDS, bp Ipswich MA 27 Oct 1745 son of Thomas & Edith (Patch) Sands (VR): d Lyman 15 Mar 1819 ae 72y (g.s., Cong Church cem): m (1) int Ipswich MA 5 Dec 1767 MARY LOW (VR), b Ipswich MA 14 Oct 1747 dau of John & Elizabeth (Baker) Low (VR; Benjamin F. Tripp, *Low Genealogy* [1937], p. 9ff), d Lyman bef Jun 1807 ae 60y (Portland *Eastern Argus*, issue of 4 Jun 1807) [note g.s. Cong Church cem, Lyman gives d 23 May 1808 ae 61y]: m (2) cert Lyman 18 Jul 1808 MARTHA DEARING of Alfred (NEHGR, 96 [1942]: 146). James acquired land in Coxhall 23 May 1774 (York Co deeds, 44:49). He gave service in the Rev War (TR Lyman). In his will dated at Lyman 27 May 1815, James named his beloved wife Martha, his daus Elisabeth Gray and Mary Edwards, and his sons Thomas, John, James, Nathan and Isaac (York Co Probate, 28:233ff).

Children, all named in James's will
i Elizabeth/Betty, b c Aug 1770: d Waterborough 16 Oct 1849 ae 79y 2m (John E. Frost, "Waterboro (Maine) Record Book" [TS, MHS, 1965], p. 83; John E. Frost, "York County, Maine Mortality Schedules" [TS, 1987, MHS], p. 20): m Lyman 6 Jun 1790 Andrew Gray (NEHGR, 95 [1941]:

246   *MAINE FAMILIES IN 1790*

      191), b c1770, d Waterborough 11 Feb 1850 ae 80y ("Waterboro Record Book," op. cit., p. 83) [see ANDREW GRAY family]
- ii Mary, b c1773: d Lyman 20 Nov 1850 ae 77y (g.s., Cong Church cem): m Lyman 11 Feb 1793 John Edwards (NEHGR, 95 [1941]:191) who d Lyman 3 Dec 1843 (John E. Frost, "York Co Record Book—Addenda to Record Books of Towns," [TS, 1975, n.p.])
- iii Thomas, bp Ipswich 12 Feb 1775 (VR): d Lyman 10 Jul 1824 ae 49y 5m (g.s., Cong Church cem): m cert Lyman 12 Mar 1797 Eunice Goodridge (NEHGR, 95 [1941]:193), b c1777, d Lyman 4 Sep 1841 ae 64y 8m 18d (g.s., Cong Church cem)
- iv John, b c1778: d Lyman 15 Jun 1842 ae 64y (g.s., Cong Church cem): m (1) Lyman 7 Oct 1804 Ruth Waterhouse (NEHGR, 95 [1941]:201), b Lyman 29 Apr 1783 dau of Jacob & Elizabeth (Wakefield) Waterhouse (VR), d Lyman 25 Mar 1809 ae 49y (g.s., Cong Church cem): he m (2) cert Lyman 30 Mar 1811 Phebe Littlefield (NEHGR, 96 [1942]:147), b c1787, d Lyman 9 Apr 1852 ae 65y (g.s., Cong Church cem)
- v James Jr., b c1781: d Lyman 29 Mar 1854 ae 73y (Gideon T. Ridlon, *Saco Valley Settlements and Families* [1895], p. 1137): m int Lyman 23 Sep 1805 Charity Gould (NEHGR, 95 [1941]:199), b c1781, d Saco 27 Aug 1865 ae 84y (Ridlon, op. cit.)
- vi Nathan, b c1787: d Biddeford 27 Nov 1851 ae 64y (g.s., Woodlawn cem): he was of Alfred when he m cert Lyman 21 Oct 1809 Sally Murphy (NEHGR, 96 [1942]:146), b c1788, d Biddeford 24 Oct 1854 ae 66y (g.s., Woodlawn cem)
- vii Isaac, b 20 Jan 1793 (*First Book of Records of the Town of Pepperellborough Now the City of Saco* [1896], p. 88): d Saco 19 Jan 1865 (John E. Frost, "Saco (Maine) Record Book" [TS, 1970, MHS], p. 237): m cert Lyman 23 Jan 1822 Dorcas Chadbourne (NEHGR, 96 [1942]:341), b Waterborough 3 Aug 1798 dau of Paul & Joanna (Yeaton) Chadbourne (Elaine Chadbourne Bacon, "The Chadbourne Family" [1989 Draft Edition, The Chadbourne Family Assoc.], family #24), d Saco 8 Feb 1876 (ibid.)

      Dana A. Batchelder, 258 South Sea Avenue, West Yarmouth, MA 02673

Sands, John   58c   1 - 3 - 2 - 0 - 0
    Buxton Town, York County

JOHN SANDS, bp Biddeford 18 Apr 1744 son of James Jr. & Hannah (____) Sands (MHGR, 6:336): d poss Buxton (Fisher's *Soldiers*, p. 688) although he was last seen living at Brownfield in 1816 (Oxf Co deeds 9:303) where his children settled: m Buxton 12 Dec 1776 MARY McLUCAS (Cyrus Woodman, *Records of the Church of Christ in Buxton, Maine During the Pastorate of Rev. Paul Coffin*, [1989], hereafter *Church of Christ*, p. 21) whose parentage has not been ascertained (see discussion below). During the Rev War, John was a private in Capt. Elden's Company which marched to Biddeford in response to armed vessels appearing to be coming into Winter Harbor (MS&S, 13:801). He also served in Capt. Jeremiah Hill's Company in Col. James Scammon's 30th Regiment (ibid.).

[Mary McLucas was poss a descendant of John & Mary (Cole) McLucas of York and Biddeford, the only early McLucas family known to have lived in Maine. But where she would fit in has not been determined. John moved with his family to Biddeford after 1744. He d at Biddeford bef 20 May 1746 when his wid Mary was appt administratrix of his estate (York Co Probate #20706). His children, named in the division of his estate, were John, Sarah, Joshua, Hannah and Mary. The dau Mary, b in 1741, may have been she who m Pepperellborough 2 Oct 1766 William Boynton (*First Book of Records of the First Church in Pepperrellborough*, p. 109). The son Joshua d before 13 Jul 1772 leaving only one surviving child, a son Benjamin (York Co Probate #12944). The son John m Biddeford 1 Oct 1748 Lydia Webber of York and the baptisms of their children were recorded in the Biddeford church recs but included no dau named Mary.]

Children, prob others who have not been identified
i Thomas, b Buxton (Eli Bean, "Brownfield, Maine Families" [microfilm at MHS, n.d.], 2:61): d Brownfield 12 Aug 1822 (Gideon T. Ridlon, *Saco Valley Settlements and Families* [1895], p. 1136): m Buxton 18 Jan 1801 Mary Steele (VR), b Buxton 14 Aug 1782 dau of John & Elizabeth (____) Steele (VR), d Brownfield 28 Dec 1822 (Ridlon, op. cit.)
ii John Jr., b Buxton 24 Dec 1783 (Bean, op. cit., 2:60): living Brownfield 1850 (USC): "of Porterfield" when he m Buxton 27 Nov 1806 Charlotte Steele (*Church of Christ*, p. 41), b Buxton 13 Apr 1785 sis of Mary above (VR)

Dana A. Batchelder, 258 South Sea Avenue, West Yarmouth, MA 02673

Sands, Sam¹   59b   2 - 0 - 7 - 0 - 0
Buxton Town, York County

SAMUEL SANDS, bp Biddeford 16 Dec 1744 son of Ephraim & Elizabeth (Jones) Sands (MHGR, 6:337) [see EPHRAIM SANDS family, *Maine Families*, 3:243]: living Buxton 1810 (USC): m (1) Buxton 5 Nov 1767 MARY BRADBURY (Cyrus Woodman, *Records of the Church of Christ in Buxton, Maine*

During the Pastorate of Rev. Paul Coffin, [1989], hereafter *Church of Christ*, p. 19), bp Salisbury MA 19 May 1745 dau of Thomas & Sarah (Merrill) Bradbury (VR): m (2) LYDIA ____ (Gideon T. Ridlon, *Saco Valley Settlements and Families* [1895], pp. 1135–36). Samuel served in the Rev War (MS&S, 13:802).

Children: baptisms *Church of Christ*, pp. 55, 56, 58, 63
- i Ephraim 3rd, b 17 Dec 1767 (DAR Application #200078), bp 23 Nov 1779: d Buxton 30 Mar 1852 (ibid.): m Buxton 20 Oct 1791 Abigail Ayer (*Church of Christ*, p. 28), b Sep 1769 (DAR, op. cit.) dau of Timothy & Elizabeth (____) Ayer (division of Timothy Ayer's estate, York Co Probate 18:499–500), d Buxton 1834 (DAR, op. cit.)
- ii Mercy, bp 23 Nov 1779
- iii Lydia, bp 23 Nov 1779: m Buxton 10 May 1798 Thomas Snow (*Church of Christ*, p. 33), b Cape Cod MA c1773 son of Thomas & Jane (Magne/Mague) Snow (McLellan's *Gorham*, p. 769) [see THOMAS SNOW family]
- iv Sarah, bp 23 Nov 1779: living Sterling NY 1850 (USC): m Buxton 19 Feb 1801 James Libby (*Church of Christ*, p. 35), b Eliot c1782 son of Azariah & Elizabeth (Paul) Libby (Charles T. Libby, *The Libby Family in America* [1882], p. 86), living Sterling NY 1860 (USC)
- v Samuel, bp 23 Nov 1779
- vi Mary/Polly, bp 15 Jul 1781: m Buxton 24 Sep 1801 James Rounds Jr. (*Church of Christ*, p. 36), b Buxton 1783 son of James & Rachel (Clay) Rounds [see RICHARD CLAY family]
- vii Eunice, bp 15 Aug 1784: m Buxton 10 Sep 1802 John Davis Jr. (*Church of Christ*, p. 37)
- viii Elizabeth, bp 9 Aug 1789

Dana A. Batchelder, 258 South Sea Avenue, West Yarmouth, MA 02673

Seger, Nath[1]   68b   2 - 1 - 2 - 0 - 0
Sudbury-Canada Town [now Bethel], York County

NATHANIEL SEGAR, b Newton MA 28 Jan 1755 son of Josiah & Thankful (Allen) Segar (William B. Lapham, *History of Bethel, Maine* [repr 1981], hereafter Lapham's *Bethel*, p. 613): d Hanover 10 Sep 1847 ae 93y (g.s., Hanover cem): m MARY RUSSELL (g.s.), b Andover MA 15 Oct 1764 dau of Benjamin & Mary (Favor) Russell (Marjorie M. Russell, *Russell Roots & Branches* [n.d.], p. 50; Lapham's *Bethel*, p. 606), d 6 Jun 1837 ae 82y [sic] (g.s., Hanover cem). In 1774, Nathaniel purchased land in Sudbury-Canada north of the Androscoggin River in that portion of Bethel later set off in 1843 and combined with Howard's Gore to form Hanover (Alfred F. Howard, *A History of Hanover, Maine 1774–1980*

[1980], p. 503). He came in the spring of that year and built a home which in a remodeled state still exists (1994). He returned to MA for the winter and the next year enlisted in the Continental Army serving until 1 Jan 1779 when he was discharged as a lieutenant. He then returned to Sudbury-Canada. On 3 Aug 1781, an Indian raid occurred at which time Nathaniel Segar, Benjamin Clark and Jonathan Clark were taken prisoner. Jonathan was allowed to return home but the other two were taken to Canada. After much suffering and hardship, they were released in 1782 and made their way back to Newton MA. After a period of rest and recovery, they then returned to Sudbury-Canada (Lapham's *Bethel*, p. 41, 46–51; *History of Hanover*, pp. 503–4). Nathaniel was a Revolutionary War pensioner applying at Bethel on 17 Sep 1832 ae 77y (Rev War pension #S31356).

Children, b Sudbury-Canada: births VR Bethel; all other info *History of Hanover*, pp. 505–6, unless otherwise cited
- i Pamelia/Permeley, b 18 Apr 1789: m Samuel Lufkin, b 15 Aug 1788 son of Benjamin & Mehitable (Abbott) Lufkin of Rumford (William B. Lapham, *History of Rumford, Oxford County, Maine* [1890], p. 369). He was the first white child b in Rumford and res on the road from Rumford Center to Andover (ibid., p. 370)
- ii Edmund, b 1 Apr 1790: d 18 Sep 1797 ae 7y (Lapham's *Bethel*, p. 613)
- iii Abigail, b 16 Sep 1792 [*History of Hanover* gives b 16 Sep 1791 which would seem more likely based on the the birth of Nathaniel and Mary's next child in May 1793]: d Hanover 9 Apr 1888 ae 96y: m Capt. William Barker Sr., b 22 Nov 1788 son of Jonathan Barker of Newry, d 2 Feb 1881 ae 92y. They res on her father's homestead
- iv Allan, b 13 May 1793: m (1) c1817 Elizabeth Howard, b Howard's Gore 24 Jun 1800 dau of Asa & Lydia (Spofford) Howard: m (2) c1833–34 Achsa Howard
- v Apphia/Assa, b 8 Nov 1794: d Upton 19 Dec 1861 ae 67y: m 1814 James Godwin, b 1791 son of William & Rachel (Harper) Godwin of Rumford, d Upton 20 Feb 1860 ae 69y
- vi Lucy, b 21 Jan 1796: m Ichabod Norton of Norridgewock. [Howard's *History of Hanover* has her marrying (2) Eli Twitchell, but the Lucy Segar he married was prob an aunt since she had a child b in 1794 (Lapham's *Bethel*, p. 627)]
- vii Mary/Polly, b 1 Sep 1797: m Daniel Estes, b 27 Dec 1801 son of Richard & Betsey (Bartlett) Estes (Lapham's *Bethel*, p. 526)
- viii Edmund, b 21 Oct 1798: m Betsey Powers, b Bethel 3 Nov 1803 dau of Arnold & Abigail (Howe) Powers (Lapham's *Bethel*, p. 599). He was the only of Nathaniel's sons to remain Bethel (ibid., p. 613)
- ix Russell, b 21 Feb 1800. He moved to OH (Lapham's *Bethel*, p. 613)
- x Nathan, b 6 Oct 1801. He moved to OH (Lapham's *Bethel*, p. 613)

xi John, b 4 Mar 1803: d 30 Oct 1882 ae 79y (g.s., E. Ellis cem, Rumford): m c1832 Lydia Farnum, b 23 Dec 1803, d 5 Nov 1864 ae 60y (g.s., E. Ellis cem, Rumford)
xii Nathaniel, b 4 Sep 1804. He moved west (Lapham's *Bethel*, p. 613)
xiii Submit, b 28 Feb 1806: d 28 Nov 1824 ae 18y (Lapham's *Bethel*, p. 613)

Warren D. Stearns, P.O. Box 35, Hanover, ME 04237

Simpson, Josiah   31b   2 - 0 - 1 - 0 - 0
Sullivan Town, Hancock County

JOSIAH SIMPSON, b York 9 Feb 1728/9 son of Samuel & Joanna (Webster) Simpson (Lester M. Bragdon & John E. Frost, *Vital Records of York, Maine* [1992], hereafter VR, p. 39): d Sullivan 16 Aug 1800 [or 1802] (g.s., York Hill cem): m (1) York 12 Nov 1754 PRUDENCE BRAGDON (VR, p. 139), b York 30 Sep 1729 dau of Joseph & Sarah (Stickney) Bragdon (VR, p. 21; will of Joseph Bragdon, York Co Probate #1812, 11:241; GDMNH, p. 106), d Sullivan prior to 1790 (BHM, 6:189) and bur York Hill cem, Sullivan: m (2) York 2 Oct 1791 ESTHER SAYWARD (VR, p. 364), perhaps she b York 12 Jan 1756/7 dau of James & Bethula (Bradbury) Sayward (VR, p. 69). Josiah went to sea when young and was in the expedition as a sailor in some of the vessels at the seige of Louisbourg in 1745 (BHM, 6:189). In 1759, he was Master of a transport carrying troops to Quebec during the same expedition in which Wolfe and Montcalm were killed (ibid.). After the Canadian war, he continued going to sea as a master of different vessels (ibid.). He moved to New Bristol [Sullivan] about 1772 where he built a house and sawmill, engaging from that time in the business of trading and manufacturing lumber (ibid.). He wrote his will 25 Mar 1797, describing himself as a merchant of Sullivan (BHM, 6:228). In it, he named his wife Esther to whom he left his real and personal property including a house, barn, saw mill, farm and sloop POLLY of 96 tons burden. He also named his sons Josiah Jr., James and John and daughters Joanna Downing and Anna Beane. His wife Esther and brother Paul [see PAUL SIMPSON family] were named executors.

Children by 1st wife, Prudence Bragdon: all but John and the second Josiah bp York First Parish (YCGSJ, 5:1 [1990]:13, 14, 15, 16)
  i Prudence, bp 23 Nov 1755: prob d young bef her sister Prudence was born
  ii Josiah, bp 18 Sep 1757: prob d young bef his brother Josiah was born
  iii Joanna, bp 11 Nov 1759: d Sullivan Sep 1825 (BHM, 6:193): m Richard Downing of Sullivan (ibid.) who was reportedly formerly of York

[although he is not seen in either the vital or church records at York]. One Richard Downing d Sullivan 1820 ae 74y (obit in *Hancock Gazette*, issue of 30 Nov 1820, abstracted in David C. & Elizabeth K. Young, *Vital Records from Maine Newspapers, 1785-1820* [1993], hereafter *Maine Newspapers*, p. 169)

iv James, bp 30 Aug 1761: d 13 Aug 1836 (BHM, 6:193): m (1) 25 Aug 1785 Elizabeth Bragdon (ibid.), b 1766 dau of Joseph Bragdon (ibid.), d 1806 ae 39y (obit in *Gazette of Maine*, issue of 24 Apr 1806 abstracted in *Maine Newspapers*, p. 542): m (2) 7 Jan 1807 Mrs. Jane Bragdon (ibid.)

v John, b 7 Dec 1763 (BHM, 6:190): d 20 Nov 1798 (ibid., 6:193): m 12 Feb 1789 Rachel Sullivan (ibid.), b Sullivan 10 Dec 1766 dau of Capt. Daniel & Abigail (Bean) Sullivan (ibid., 6:281), d 10 Aug 1806 (ibid.). John was lost on Cape Cod, master of the schooner RACHEL with his entire crew (ibid.). Rachel's obit, in the *Gazette of Maine*, issue of 28 Aug 1806, indicated that she left 5 orphan daughters (*Maine Newspapers*, p. 542). Her estate was adm by her bro and bro-in-law, James Sullivan and Ebenezer Bean (ibid.)

vi Jabez, bp 15 Sep 1765. He was not named in his father's will

vii Prudence, bp 14 Feb 1768. She was not named in her father's will

viii Anna, b 21 Nov 1771 (BHM, 6:190) and bp 24 Nov 1771: d 15 Nov 1828 (ibid., p. 1417): m 6 Jun 1791 Ebenezer Bean (ibid.), b 1 Oct 1760 (ibid.), d 28 Sep 1825 (ibid.)

ix Josiah, b prob Sullivan c1773-74 (BHM, 6:190): d Apr 1833 (ibid.): m 1792 Mary Sullivan (ibid., 6:196), b 1773 sis of Rachel above (ibid., 6:281), d Belfast 28 Apr 1857 ae 85y (VR; BHM, 6:281). He was for many years a prominent ship master (ibid.). At the time of his death, he was the light keeper on Petit Manan Island (ibid.).

Betty Meynell Hills, Box 23, HCR 32, Sullivan, ME 04664
Peggy Taylor Simpson, Jordan Pond Rd., P.O. Box 176, Seal Harbor, ME 04675

Simpson, Paul   31b   1 - 2 - 4 - 0 - 0
Sullivan Town, Hancock County

PAUL SIMPSON, b York 11 Sep 1740 son of Samuel & Joanna (Webster) Simpson (Lester M. Bragdon & John E. Frost, *Vital Records of York, Maine* [1992], p. 39): d Sullivan after Mar 1797 when he was named executor of his brother's will (BHM, 6:190, 228) and perhaps betw the censuses of 1810 and 1820 (two Paul Simpsons in Han Co in 1810 USC, one in 1820 USC who was prob Paul Jr.): m SUSAN DONNELL (BHM, 6:191). In his father's will, dated at

York 21 Feb 1767 and proved 12 Apr 1768, Paul received a part of the family homestead (York Co Probate #21025). He moved to Sullivan, perhaps accompanying or following his brother Josiah who moved there about 1772 [see JOSIAH SIMPSON family]. During the Revolution, he was a private in Capt. Daniel Sullivan's Co., Col. Benjamin Foster's Regt. called upon to do duty at Machias during the summer of 1777 (BHM, 3:39). By trade he was a shipmaster (ibid., 6:190).

Children
- i Paul Jr., b 6 Jul 1776 (BHM, 6:191): d 5 Sep 1845 (ibid., 6:196): m int Sullivan 19 Feb 1803 Hannah Sullivan (ibid.), b 4 Mar 1770 dau of Daniel & Abigail (Bean) Sullivan (ibid., 6:280), d 24 Jul 1849 (ibid.)
- ii Marian/Miriam, b 29 Nov 1779 (BHM, 6:191, 196): d Sullivan 28 Jan 1832 (ibid., 6:191): m int Sullivan 12 Dec 1801 Robert Gordon of Sullivan (ibid., 6:196). He m (2) Nov 1832 Sarah Allen Sargent (ibid., 2:130) dau of Paul Dudley & Lucy (Sanders) Sargent (ibid.) [see PAUL DUDLEY SARGENT family, *Maine Families*, 3:246–47]
- iii John, d unm (BHM, 6:191)
- iv Susan, d unm (BHM, 6:191)
- v Joanna, d young (BHM, 6:191)

Betty Meynell Hills, Box 23, HCR 32, Sullivan, ME 04664
Peggy Taylor Simpson, Jordan Pond Rd., P.O. Box 176, Seal Harbor, ME 04675

Skinner, Daniel   30a   2 - 2 - 3 - 0 - 0
    Orrington Town, Hancock County

DANIEL SKINNER, b Norton MA 29 Jun 1743 son of John Jr. & Mary (_____) Skinner (VR): d Jun 1841 ae 97y 11m (g.s., West Corinth cem, Corinth): m (1) Mansfield MA 6 Dec 1770 ABIGAIL BRIGGS (VR), b Norton MA 4 Feb 1752 dau of Phineas & Esther (Finney) Briggs (VR), d Mansfield MA 2 Jul 1775 (VR): m (2) Mansfield MA 2 May 1776 MIRIAM (_____) GROVER (VR). Daniel was a Rev War soldier serving first under Capt. Samuel White as a corporal and sergeant and later with Col. John Daggett's regiment of MA militia (MS&S 14:277). He moved to Brewer in 1784 where he kept a tavern and moved to Skinner Settlement [Corinth] in 1793 where he is believed to be among the first permanent settlers and where he built a house now known as the Daniel Skinner house (BHM, 6:100; *History of Penobscot County, Maine* [1882], p. 307). After Corinth was formed on 21 Jun 1811, the first Town meeting was held in the house of his son, Elijah Skinner (ibid.).

Children: BHM, 6:100
By 1st wife Abigail Briggs
- i Asahel, b Mansfield MA 28 Aug 1771 (VR): d Meigs Co OH 29 Mar 1868 (g.s., Miles cem, Rutland Twsp): m (1) Orrington 22 Feb 1798 Phoebe Gould (VR), b 7 Oct 1774 dau of Nathaniel & Ruthanna [or Ruhama] (Bickford) Gould [see NATHANIEL GOULD family, *Maine Families*, 2:112–13], d Meigs Co OH 13 Aug 1817 (Stillman C. Larkin, *The Pioneer History of Meigs Co OH* [1908], p. 136): m (2) Rutland Twsp, Meigs Co OH 19 Mar 1818 Jane Everton (VR), b 31 Oct 1790 dau of Thomas & Relief (Howe) Everton (Larkin, op. cit.), d Des Moines IA 1861 (ibid.)
- ii Hepzebah, b Mansfield MA 22 Jun 1773 (VR): d Brewer 10 Oct 1861 ae 87y 4m (BHM, 6:98): m Orrington 1 Nov 1796 Dea. Lot Rider (ibid.), b Wellfleet MA 19 Jun 1773 son of John & Hannah (Atwood) Rider of Brewer (ibid.), d Brewer 21 Apr 1846 (ibid.)
- iii Abigail, b Mansfield MA 2 Jul 1775 (VR): d Mansfield MA 2 Jul 1775 (VR)

By 2nd wife Miriam (____) Grover
- iv Azubah, b Mansfield MA 22 Feb 1777 (VR): d Corinth 19 Dec 1819 (Dorothy B. West, *Thomas Skinner of Malden, Massachusetts: Descendants* [1982], hereafter West, p. 33): m bef 1799 (when 1st child was born) Jacob Wheeler (BHM, 6:100), b Petersham MA 29 Sep 1771 (West, p. 33), d Corinth 21 Apr 1842 (g.s., West Corinth cem). He m (2) Abigail ____ who is buried next to him (adm of Jacob Wheeler's estate, Pen Co Probate 13:127)
- v Elijah, b Mansfield MA 22 Sep 1779 (VR): d Corinth 18 Apr 1857 ae 77y 6m 26d (g.s., West Corinth cem): m (1) Corinth 7 Mar 1802 Sarah/Sally Fisher (West, p. 33–34) who d Corinth 24 Feb 1827 ae 44y (g.s., West Corinth cem): m (2) Corinth 11 Nov 1828 Nancy (Nicols) Bodge (West, p. 33–34) wid of James Bodge and who d Corinth 24 Feb 1834 ae 50y (g.s., West Corinth cem): m (3) Hampden Elizabeth Crosby (West, p. 33–34). Elijah was a Selectman and Highway Surveyor for the town of Corinth
- vi Alona, b c Feb 1783: d 22 Mar 1835 ae 52y 1m 8d (g.s., Corinthian cem, Corinth): m Corinth 20 Feb 1803 Richard Palmer (West, p. 34), b Parsonsfield 5 Nov 1777 son of William & Mehitable (Blazo) Palmer (VR; *A History of the First Century of the Town of Parsonsfield, Maine* [1888], p. 391), d 1 Jan 1864 ae 86y 1m 25d (g.s., Corinthian cem, Corinth)
- vii Mason, b Brewer 5 Jul 1786 (West, p. 34): d 29 Jan 1872 (ibid.): m Rebecca Batchelder (BHM, 6:100). 5 of their children are bur at Exeter

Virginia L. Kane, P.O. Box 380, Big Flats, NY 14814-0380

Scofield, Thomas   * *
Brunswick Town, Cumberland County

THOMAS SKOLFIELD, b Ireland 1707 son of Thomas Skolfield (George A. Wheeler & Henry W. Wheeler, *History of Brunswick, Topsham, & Harpswell, Maine* [1878], hereafter Wheeler, pp. 802, 852): d Brunswick 6 Jan 1796 ae 89y and bur Old Maquoit cem (ibid.; George T. Little, "Brunswick Epitaphs," *The Maine Genealogist and Biographer*, 2 [1876]:92–93, hereafter MG&B) [Brunswick 1st Parish Church rec states d 6 Jan 1797 "aged 90 and past"]: m (1) Boston MA 6 Apr 1734 MARY ORR (*A Report of the Record Commissioners of the City of Boston, Containing Boston Marriages from 1799 to 1751* [1898], p. 221), b Ireland c1714 sister of John Orr Jr. (Erminie S. Reynolds & Kenneth R. Martin, *A Singleness of Purpose, The Skolfields and Their Ships* [1987], hereafter *Singleness*), d Brunswick 1 Aug 1771 in her 57th y (g.s., Old Maquoit cem; Wheeler, p. 852; MG&B, 2 [1896]:92–93): m (2) Brunswick 19 Aug 1776 MARTHA McPATRICK (VR) [Brunswick m ints call her Martha "McPatridge"]. Thomas's father, originally from England, was an officer in King William's army in 1690 and received a tract of land in Ireland for his services (Wheeler, p. 852). Thomas emigrated to America with the Orr family and first settled in Boston MA (ibid., p. 802). They moved to Maine by 1737 settling in Brunswick (*Singleness*, p. 1). He with others protested against the proceedings in the town meeting on 5 May 1743 (Brunswick TR). He was a prominent man in town and, in addition to many other offices, served as Town Clerk from 1752–1761 and from 1763–1765 (ibid.).

Children: births VR Brunswick
   i   Rebecca, b 8 Jul 1737: d Brunswick 7 Oct 1753 in her 17th y (VR; g.s., Old Maquoit cem)
  ii   Richard, b 6 Sep 1738: d 20 Feb 1762 (Brunswick VR) reportedly at No. Yarmouth harbor from a fall aboard the sloop INDUSTRY (*Singleness*, p. 10): m int No. Yarmouth 13 Sep 1760 Elizabeth Anderson (VR). They had a son Richard b posthumously 25 Apr 1762 (Brunswick VR)
 iii   Clement, b 1 Jun 1740: d Harpswell 22 May 1796 (g.s., Centre cem): m (1) Harpswell 25 Jun 1767 Mary Adams ("Rev. Elisha Eaton and Rev. Samuel Eaton, Records of Harpswell Congregational Church" [TS, MHS], hereafter Eaton CR): m (2) int North Yarmouth 6 Nov 1773 Alice Means of North Yarmouth (VR), b No. Yarmouth [now Freeport] dau of Thomas & Alice (Finney) Means (Harpswell VR; Wheeler, p. 67), d Harpswell 17 Apr 1822 (VR)
  iv   Anne, b 18 May 1742: m int Brunswick 19 Dec 1759 Robert Spear Jr. (VR)
   v   Thomas Jr., b 8 Jun 1744: d Mere Point, Brunswick 21 Jan 1824 (VR): m int No. Yarmouth 30 Jan 1772 Anna Anderson [see THOMAS SKOLFIELD Jr. family]

vi   Mary, b 10 Feb 1748: m Brunswick 19 Mar 1776 Robert Given (VR)
vii   Stephen, b 8 Jul 1751: d 1800–1810: m Topsham 21 Apr 1778 Margaret Knowles
viii   Martha, b 19 Mar 1753: m Brunswick 23 Oct 1777 Lewis Simpson (VR) [but their m int dated 28 Feb 1778 (VR Brunswick)]
ix   John, b 13 Jun 1755: d 1778 ae 23y aboard privateer SEA FLOWER which disappeared with all hands (*Singleness*, p. 10)
x   Joseph, b 1 Mar 1757: d Brunswick 25 Sep 1815 (VR): m (1) int North Yarmouth 15 Jan 1780 Dinah Rogers of North Yarmouth (VR), b c1758, d Brunswick 20 Mar 1797 in her 40th y (g.s., Old Maquoit cem): m (2) Georgetown 15 Oct 1798 Margaret Hall (VR) who d aft 1815 (*Singleness*, p. 152)
xi   William, b 27 Aug 1760: drowned at Hussey's Sound, Casco Bay 13 Oct 1821 (*Singleness*, p. 228) [his Rev War pension file states d 13 Oct 1821 (Rev War pension #W22223)]: m Brunswick 28 Dec 1786 Sarah Rideout ("Early Marriages in Brunswick," MG&B, 2 [1876]:58), b c1768, d prob Bowdoin aft 8 Feb 1848 (pension, op. cit.)

Marjorie Wardwell Otten, 201 4th St., Del Mar, CA 92014-3249

Scofield, Thomas   12a   2 - 5 - 4 - 0 - 0
   Brunswick Town, Cumberland County

Capt. **THOMAS SKOLFIELD** Jr., b Brunswick 8 Jun 1744 son of Thomas & Mary (Orr) Skolfield (VR; George A. Wheeler & Henry W. Wheeler, *History of Brunswick, Topsham, & Harpswell, Maine* [1878], hereafter Wheeler, p. 852) [see THOMAS SKOLFIELD family]: d Mere Point, Brunswick 21 Jun 1824 (VR): m int North Yarmouth 30 Jan 1772 ANNA ANDERSON (VR), b North Yarmouth 15 Apr 1750 dau of Jacob & Agnes (Finney) Anderson (VR) [see JACOB ANDERSON family, *Maine Families*, 3:5–6]. Thomas gave patriotic service in the Rev War (Fisher's *Soldiers*, p. 697). He was a master mariner and shipbuilder and was "probably the first Skolfield to skipper a vessel and probably the first to actually build one" (Erminie S. Reynolds & Kenneth R. Martin, *A Singleness of Purpose, The Skolfields and Their Ships* [1987], hereafter *Singleness*, p. 11). He inherited in 1771 land on Mere Point in Brunswick from his uncle, John Orr (ibid., p. 223).

Children, all b Mere Point, Brunswick: *Singleness*, p. 36
   i   Thomas, b Dec 1772: lost at sea, date unknown (*Singleness*, p. 223)
   ii   Susanna, b 1775: m Brunswick 12 Jan 1796 John Minot Jr. (VR)

iii Mary/Molly, b 1777: m Brunswick 20 Oct 1797 John Merryman (VR), b c1771 son of Hugh & Delight (Bailey) Merryman (Charles W. Sinnett, *Walter Merryman of Harpswell, Maine and His Descendants* [1905], p. 60), d Bath 4 Nov 1827 (ibid.)
iv Jacob, b 23 Dec 1780: living Mere Point, Brunswick in the late 1840s (*Singleness*, p. 48): m int Brunswick 26 Nov 1806 Hannah Stanwood (VR). He was a master shipbuilder (*Singleness*, p. 223)
v Joseph, b 29 Nov 1784: d Baltimore MD 2 Feb 1835 (*Singleness*, p. 215): m by 1808 Susanna Sylvester (ibid.)
vi John Orr, b 5 Oct 1785 (Sinnett, op. cit., p. 65): d Great Chebeague Island 1 Jun 1845 (ibid.): m 29 Apr 1810 Bethia Sprague Merryman (ibid.), b 14 Aug 1782 (ibid.), d 22 Jun 1843 (ibid.). He was referred to as "2nd" to differentiate him from his cousin, the son of his uncle Clement Skolfield
vii Sally, b 30 Nov 1790: m Brunswick 20 Mar 1810 Benjamin Stanwood (VR)
viii Ebenezer, b 13 Apr 1792: d Weld 1874 (*Singleness*, p. 207): m Brunswick 1 May 1817 Lavina Stanwood (VR). He was a mariner, trader and farmer (*Singleness*, p. 207)
ix Nancy, b c1794

Marjorie Wardwell Otten, 201 4th St., Del Mar, CA 92014-3249

Small, John   21c   1 - 1 - 3 - 0 - 0
North Yarmouth Town, Cumberland County

JOHN SMALL, b Falmouth 20 Mar 1760 son of John & Bethia (Wyman) Small (L. A. W. Underhill, *Descendants of Edward Small of New England* [1934], p. 117): d Cumberland 5 Oct 1828 ae 68y (g.s., North Jay cem): m Falmouth 5 Jun 1783 ABIGAIL MORSE (Cum Co Commissioners recs, 2:257), b prob Falmouth 10 Jun 1766 dau of Eliphalet & Hannah (Mayo) Morse (J. Howard Morse & Emily Leavitt, *Morse Genealogy*, "Anthony Morse" [1903], p. 84), d 25 Nov 1855 ae 89y (g.s., North Jay cem). John was a Rev War soldier, serving in Col. Jonathan Mitchell's regiment during the Penobscot Expedition (MS&S 14:315).

Children: births of all except Martha in VR No. Yarmouth; Rev. Allen Greely of No. Yarmouth, "North Yarmouth Families" (TS, MHS), 3:429–30
  i John, b No. Yarmouth 16 Apr 1784: d No. Yarmouth 10 Jul 1786 (VR)
  ii Prudence, b No. Yarmouth 23 Feb 1786: m No. Yarmouth 31 Mar 1808 Lemuel Wyman (VR), b No. Yarmouth 6 Sep 1784 son of Josiah & Nancy (Bradford) Wyman (VR)

  iii Elizabeth, b No. Yarmouth 23 Nov 1788: m No. Yarmouth 6 Jan 1807 David Staples of Gray (VR)
  iv Lucy, b No. Yarmouth 4 Jul 1792, bp as Lucy Merrill Small No. Yarmouth 1st Church 12 July 1792 (Augustus W. Corliss, *Old Times of North Yarmouth, Maine* [1977], p. 942): m No. Yarmouth 21 Feb 1815 Robert Barr (VR)
  v Reuben, b No. Yarmouth 17 Feb 1795, bp No. Yarmouth 1st Church 12 Apr 1795 (Corliss, p. 945): m int No. Yarmouth 28 Aug 1819 Mary Butterfield of Falmouth (VR)
  vi William, b No. Yarmouth 7 Nov 1797: d at sea unm ("North Yarmouth Families," op. cit.)
  vii Charles, b No. Yarmouth 6 Aug 1800: d No. Yarmouth 13 Aug 1801 (VR)
  viii Edward, b No. Yarmouth 15 Aug 1802: m Betsy _____ who d 8 Jul 1891 (g.s., North Jay cem)
  ix Martha ("North Yarmouth Families," op. cit.) [she was not listed in John Small's family record in the No. Yarmouth VR]

Clayton R. Adams, 6 Laurel Road, Brunswick, ME 04011

Small, Zachariah   14c   1 - 0 - 3 - 0 - 0
Falmouth Town, Cumberland County

ZACHARIAH SMALL, b Falmouth 21 May 1763 son of John & Bethia (Wyman) (Merrill) Small (L. A. W. Underhill, *Descendants of Edward Small* [1934], p. 117) [see JOHN SMALL family, *Maine Families*, 2:256–57]: d prob Westbrook bet 1820 and 1824 (1820 USC; Cum Co deeds 101:238): m JEMIMA GILMAN dau of Edward & Agnes (Stevens) Gilman (Cum Co deeds 19:175; S. T. Dole, *Windham in the Past* [repr 1974], p. 537; Dorothy Quinby Davis, "The Edward Gilmans of Exeter, New Hampshire and Falmouth, Maine" [TS, MHS, 1970], p. 8). Zachariah lived near his bros, Daniel and Joseph Small, in the part of Falmouth which became Westbrook, near the intersection of Cumberland and Pierce Streets (Cum Co deeds 101:238). He was a Revolutionary War pensioner, applying at Westbrook in 1818 ae 54y (Rev War pension #S37424).

Children, as found, order unknown
  i Nancy, m Falmouth 12 Nov 1805 Samuel A. Proctor son of Nathaniel & Sally (_____) Proctor (MHGR 4:167)
  ii Bethia, b Falmouth 10 Jun 1796 (*Eastern Argus*, issue of 17 Feb 1912): m Westbrook 23 Sep 1819 Isaac Bailey son of Benjamin & Mary (Blake) Bailey (ibid.; MHGR 4:283)

iii prob Lydia, m Westbrook 26 Dec 1819 James Thoits [sic] (MHGR 4:283) [m int Westbrook dated 11 Dec 1819 call him James "Tharlo" (Thurlow) (VR)]
iv Sally, m Westbrook 8 Jun 1826 Solomon Babb Jr. (J. A. Sargent & I. B. Mansur, *Babb Families of New England* [1987], p. 272; MHGR 5:18)

Clayton R. Adams, 6 Laurel Road, Brunswick, ME 04011

Snow, Tho[s]   19a   2 - 2 - 2 - 0 - 0
Gorham and Scarborough Towns, Cumberland County

THOMAS SNOW, b Harwich MA 1734 (Fisher's *Soldiers*, p. 730) [one Thomas Snow was b Harwich MA 19 Nov 1735 son of Nathaniel & Thankful (____) Snow (VR)]: d Gorham c1825 (McLellan's *Gorham*, p. 769): m 1762 JANE MAGNE/MAGUE (McLellan's *Gorham*, p. 769), b c1735, d Gorham 5 Mar 1837 ae 102y (VR). Thomas was a Revolutionary War soldier (MS&S 14:627). He and his family came from Cape Cod MA to Gorham about 1778 and settled in the northern part of town (McLellan's *Gorham*, p. 769). They were reportedly accompanied by Jane's mother and sister (ibid., although their names have not been identified).

Children, first 4 b Cape Cod MA: McLellan's *Gorham*, p. 769
  i Mercy, m c1782–83 John Chase (McLellan's *Gorham*, p. 769)
  ii Aaron, b c1766: d Jackson 20 Jul 1850 ae 84y (VR): m Standish 18 Mar 1790 Eunice Philbrick (VR), b Pearsontown [Standish] 18 Mar 1768 dau of Michael & Mary (____) Philbrick/Philbrook (Albert J. Sears, *Early Families of Standish, Maine* [1991], pp. 198–99), d Jackson 10 Mar 1847 (VR)
  iii Gideon, m (1) Gorham 28 Dec 1788 Joanna Edwards (VR): m (2) Susan Parsons (McLellan's *Gorham*, p. 769)
  iv Thomas, b c1773 (McLellan's *Gorham*, p. 769): m Buxton 10 May 1798 Lydia Sands (Cyrus Woodman, *Records of the Church of Christ in Buxton, Maine During the Pastorate of Rev. Paul Coffin*, [repr 1989], p. 33), bp Buxton 23 Nov 1779 dau of Samuel & Mary (Bradbury) Sands (ibid.) [see SAMUEL SANDS family]
  v Lydia, b Feb 1776 (McLellan,'s *Gorham*, p. 769): d Gorham 9 Jul 1850 ae 74y (ibid., p. 843): m Gorham 7 Nov 1793 Joseph Young 3rd (VR) who d Gorham c1810 (McLellan's *Gorham*, p. 843)
  vi Jemima, b Gorham Jul 1785 (McLellan's *Gorham*, p. 769): d Gorham 6 Feb 1868 ae 82y (ibid., p. 697): m Windham 5 Jun 1807 Uriah Nason Jr

("Nason Data" in "State of Maine, Family Records, Miscellaneous Papers and Genealogies" [microfilm, MHS], 2:58), b Gorham c1785 son of Uriah & Abigail (Knight) Nason (ibid.), d Gorham 6 Feb 1863 (McLellan's *Gorham*, p. 697) [see URIAH NASON family]

Dana A. Batchelder, 258 South Sea Avenue, West Yarmouth, MA 02673

Snowman, John 30c 1 - 2 - 3 - 0 - 0
Penobscot Town, Hancock County

JOHN SNOWMAN, Jr., b York 6 Aug 1755 son of John & Sarah (Staples) Snowman (Penobscot VR): m York 21 Dec 1780 COMFORT HORNE (VR), b 4 Aug 1762 (Penobscot VR) and bp Gosport, Isles of Shoals 12 Sep 1762 dau of Elisha & Tamesin (Randall) Horne (NEHGR 66 [1912]:223), d Penobscot 22 Feb 1834 (VR). John was one of the signers of a petition dated 17 Feb 1785 to the General Court of MA requesting that they be quieted on their land and incorporated into the town of Penobscot (BHM, 3:77). In 1796, he was on a committee to divide the town into eight school districts (ibid., 5:99). He was later a deacon in the Baptist Church at Penobscot (ibid., 6:146).

Children, b Penobscot: births VR Penobscot
- i James, b 8 Nov 1785: d in infancy
- ii James, b 22 Dec 1787: d Penobscot 22 Apr 1837 (VR): m Penobscot 31 May 1809 Theodosia/Dosha Perkins (VR), b York 15 or 16 Aug 1784 dau of Sparks & Tabatha (Stover) Perkins (Penobscot VR)
- iii John, b 4 Feb 1790. [One John Snowman Jr. m Penobscot 6 Nov 1811 Esther Scott (VR)]
- iv Sarah, b 21 Mar 1792: d Penobscot 15 Nov 1881 ae 89y 7m 7d (g.s., Castine Village cem): m (1) Penobscot 15 Apr 1813 Pelatiah Wescott (VR), b Penobscot 12 Jan 1793 son of Andrew & Mercy (Perkins) Westcott (Penobscot VR), d Penobscot 30 May 1844 (VR): m (2) 20 Apr 1849 Capt. Edward Perkins (Thomas Allen Perkins, *Jacob Perkins of Wells, Maine and His Descendants* [1947]), b 25 Jun 1789 bro of Theodosia above (Penobscot VR)
- v Hannah, b 1 Jun 1794: d 14 Mar 1872 ae 77y 10m (g.s., Penobscot): m (1) Penobscot 6 Nov 1811 Samuel Perkins (VR), b 15 Jul 1788 son of Isaac & Olive (Webber) Perkins (Penobscot VR), d at sea Nov 1816 ae 27y 5m (g.s., Penobscot): m (2) int Penobscot 23 Apr 1821 Capt. Stephen Grindle (VR), b Sedgwick 26 Mar 1781 (Penobscot VR), d 19 Oct 1855 ae 79y [sic] 7m (g.s., Penobscot)

vi   Thomas, b 10 Feb 1797: m int Penobscot 23 Apr 1823 Sarah Wight (VR)
vii Alexander, b 24 Jan 1799: m int Penobscot 16 Mar 1823 Susan Billings (VR)

> Howard E. Wescott Jr., 3031 Fairfield St., Ontario, CA 91761-6513
> Elizabeth Wescott, RR 2, Box 920, Apt. 202, Bucksport, ME 04416-9502

Somer, David   41a   3 - 2 - 5 - 0 - 0
New Castle Town, Lincoln County

DAVID SOMES, b Gloucester MA 11 Feb 1743/4 son of Morris & Lucy (Day) Somes (VR): d prob Edgecomb aft 1820 (USC): m abt 1769 JANE/JENNETT HOPKINS (based on birth of first child, but m certainly bef 15 Oct 1771 when a partition of the real estate of her father was made) dau of William & Mary (____) Hopkins (William D. Patterson, *The Probate Records of Lincoln County, Maine 1760–1800* [1895], p. 2, citing Lin Co Probate 1:8, 2:68–70). David's father was killed in an action at Cape Breton when David was a small boy (David Q. Cushman, *The History of Ancient Sheepscot and Newcastle* [1882], hereafter *Ancient Sheepscot*, p. 419). He left Cape Ann MA and came to Newcastle when a young man and resided at Sheepscot 7 or 8 years (ibid.). Later he moved to Newcastle where he bought 200 acres of wild land and built a grist mill (ibid.). "He saw the roughest side of pioneer life, being several times carried prisoner to Canada by the Indians but each time escaping with his life, although the treatment received at their hands seriously injured his health" (Christine Huston Dodge, "Vital Records of Edgecomb and Newcastle in the County of Lincoln Maine to the Year 1892" [TS, Skidompha Library, Damariscotta, 1979], hereafter Dodge's "Newcastle," p. 757, citing private record of Elizabeth Freeman Reed). He is credited with performing patriotic service during the Rev War (Fisher's *Soldiers*, p. 730). Jenny's father, William Hopkins, reportedly came from Ireland and settled prior to 1735 in the Sheepscot region (*Ancient Sheepscot*, p. 391). He was captured by the Indians and taken to Canada where he died (ibid.).

Children: *Ancient Sheepscot*, p. 419, & cited sources
  i   William, b 5 May 1770: d 27 Feb 1867 (hereafter Dodge's "Newcastle," p. 759): m int Newcastle 20 Nov 1798 Martha Cothran/Cochern (Christine Huston Dodge, "Vital Records of Edgecomb and Newcastle to the Year 1892, Volume II Marriages and Marriage Intentions" [1979], hereafter Dodge's "Marriages," p. 154) b c1780 dau of Robert Cochern (ibid.), d 9 Sep 1849 ae 69y (Dodge's "Newcastle," p. 758 citing Old Sheepscot cem)
  ii David Jr., b Feb 1772: d Edgecomb 7 Feb 1848 ae 76y (Dodge's "Newcastle," p. 758, citing g.s., Highland cem): m Newcastle 13 Apr 1797 Abigail Trask (Mildred Wood Munsey, "A Munsey-Wood Genealogy" [TS,

Skidompha Library, Damariscotta], p. 87), b 1777, d Edgecomb 4 Jul 1848 ae 71y (Dodge's "Newcastle," p. 758, citing g.s., Highland cem)

iii Nancy, b Sheepscot 25 Jun 1774 (Dodge's "Newcastle"): d 28 Jul 1866 (*Ancient Sheepscot*, p. 420): m (1) 19 Feb 1795 William Dodge (Dodge's "Marriages," p. 50) who d bef 1 May 1798 when the adm of the estate of William Dodge of Newcastle was granted to his wid Nancy (Patterson, op. cit., p. 336, citing Lin Co Probate 9:4): m (2) int Newcastle 11 Sep 1798 Ezekiel Stearns (Dodge's "Marriages," p. 155), b 25 May 1744 (*Ancient Sheepscot*, p. 420), d 22 Apr 1848 (ibid.)

iv Solomon, b c1775: d 28 May 1823 ae 48y (Dodge's "Newcastle," p. 759, citing g.s., Carol Dodge Farm, Edgecomb): m 3 Apr 1806 Hannah Davidson/Davison (Dodge's "Marriages," p. 154; *Ancient Sheepscot*, p. 419)

v Mary/Polly, m 26 May 1807 John Cochran (Dodge's "Marriages," p. 154)

vi Jane/Jenney, b 10 Jul 1785 (Dodge's "Newcastle," p. 866): d 22 Nov 1887 ae 102y 4m 12d (ibid., citing g.s., New cem, North Edgecomb): m Moses Wilson (*Ancient Sheepscot*, p. 419), b c1771, d 7 Mar 1842 ae 71y (Dodge's "Newcastle," p. 866, citing New cem, North Edgecomb)

vii Sally, m Feb 1806 Robert Henderson or Anderson (Dodge's "Marriages," p. 154; *Ancient Sheepscot*, p. 419)

viii Elizabeth/Betsey, b 17 Mar 1791 (*Ancient Sheepscot*, p. 375): d 2 Dec 1891 ae 100y 8m 15d (Dodge's "Newcastle," p. 234): m 24 Dec 1812 Daniel Dodge (*Ancient Sheepscot*, p. 375), b Edgecomb 25 Nov 1793 (ibid.), d 24 Mar 1862 (ibid.)

ix Margaret/Peggy, b c Jul 1795: d 29 Apr 1883 ae 87y 9m (Dodge's "Newcastle," p. 213): m Newcastle 2 Apr 1817 James Davidson/Davison (Dodge's "Marriages," p. 43), b c1788, d 18 Jul 1866 ae 78y (ibid.)

x Patty

xi Joel, drowned c 16 Jan 1804 (Dodge's "Newcastle," p. 757): m 29 Dec 1803 Jane Kennedy (Dodge's "Marriages," p. 154), b 4 Apr 1783 dau of Samuel & Martha (Hopkins) Kennedy (*Ancient Sheepscot*, p. 397). She m (2) Edgecomb 18 Jun 1812 William Sherman of Edgecomb (VR)

Cynthia Corrow, 427 Main St., Waterville, ME 04901

Spurlin, Benj[a]   29b   1 - 4 - 2 - 0 - 0
Mount Desert Town, Hancock County

BENJAMIN SPURLING, b Madbury NH 19 Sep 1752 (Muriel Sampson Johnson, *Early Families of Gouldsboro, Maine* [1990], hereafter *Gouldsboro*, p. 259; Fisher's *Soldiers*, p. 738 gives b Portsmouth NH): d Great Cranberry Isle 30 Dec 1836 (*Gouldsboro*, p. 259): m bef 1780 when 1st child was born FANNY GUPTILL (ibid.), b Berwick 3 Jan 1760 dau of John & Abigail (Goodwin) Guptill (ibid., p.

111) and bp 2nd Church of Berwick 17 Jan 1762 (NEHGR, 74 [1920]:226), d Great Cranberry Isle 12 Feb 1824 (*Gouldsboro*, p. 111). Benjamin settled on Great Cranberry Island on Spurling's Point in 1768. He served as a corporal in the Rev War and saw action in the Bagaduce Expedition in 1779 (MS&S 14:781; BHM, 6:68). He was also in Daniel Sullivan's company enlisting 28 Jul 1779 (ibid.). During the War of 1812, he was captured by the British at Norwood's Cove, but later released (*Gouldsboro*, p. 259).

Children, all b Great Cranberry Isle: births listed *Gouldsboro*, p. 259

i Sarah/Sally, b 23 Dec 1782: m (1) int Mount Desert 25 Apr 1796 Welch Moore (VR), b No. Yarmouth, d at sea 1805 (*Gouldsboro*, p. 184): m (2) Gouldsboro 3 Aug 1807 Jonathan Newman of Gouldsboro (VR), b 1 Nov 1781 son of Joseph & Charity (Young) Newman (*Gouldsboro*, p. 189), d 5 Sep 1863 (ibid.). He m (2) Sally's sister Fanny (Spurling) Stanley (ibid.)

ii Robert, b 13 Sep 1782: d c1844 (ibid., p. 260): m (1) int Mount Desert 1 Dec 1804 Mary Stanley (VR), b 25 Dec 1786 (VR Mount Desert), d 21 Feb 1843 (*Gouldsboro*, p. 260): m (2) 22 Jun 1843 Abigail Yeaton (ibid.), b 16 Jul 1812 dau of Lemuel & Abigail (Dunbar) Yeaton (ibid., p. 320)

iii Esther, b c1784: d c1785 (ibid., p. 259)

iv Thomas, b 16 Feb 1786: m 29 Aug 1807 Hannah Stanley (ibid.), b 15 Apr 1785 (VR Mount Desert) dau of Thomas & Hannah (Manchester) Stanley (*Gouldsboro*, p. 259), d c1841 (ibid.)

v Benjamin Jr., b c1787: d c1809 (ibid.)

vi Enoch, b 9 Oct 1789: d 26 Oct 1839 (*Gouldsboro*, p. 259): m cert Gouldsboro 10 Mar 1815 Hannah Newman (VR), b 18 Jan 1790 sis of Jonathan above (*Gouldsboro*, p. 189), alive 1850 (ibid.)

vii Dolly, b 29 Apr 1791: m cert Mount Desert 19 Nov 1810 Thomas Newman (VR), b 1 Feb 1785 bro of Jonathan and Hannah above (*Gouldsboro*, p. 189)

viii William, b 10 Feb 1793: m 20 Jan 1820 Nancy Stanley (ibid., p. 259), b 1 Jul 1798 dau of John & Phebe (Rich) Stanley (ibid.), d 17 Sep 1837 (ibid.)

ix Samuel, b 4 Dec 1794: drowned 20 Oct 1837 (ibid.): m 14 Sep 1825 Abigail Hadlock (ibid.), b 3 Jul 1808 dau of Samuel & Sarah (Manchester) Hadlock (ibid.) [see SAMUEL HADLOCK family, *Maine Families*, 2:121], d 17 Jan 1874 (ibid.)

x Fanny, b 19 Oct 1797: m (1) 31 Jul 1818 Sans Stanley (ibid., p. 262), b c1797 son of Sans & Elizabeth (Mayo) Stanley (ibid.), d 26 Jul 1858 ae 61y (ibid. citing g.s.): m (2) Jonathan Newman (ibid., p. 189), widower of her sis Sally above

xi Abigail, b 2 Sep 1799

Joy and Leonard Mayo, RFD #1, Box 285, Ellsworth ME 04605

Stephens, Benjn 19a   1 - 0 - 1 - 0 - 0
Gorham and Scarborough Towns, Cumberland County

BENJAMIN STEVENS, b Stratham NH 19 May 1716 son of Nathaniel & Sarah (Folsom) Stevens (NHGR, 1:189; GDMNH, p. 659): d c1791 (McLellan's *Gorham*, p. 774): m 29 May 1741 SARAH PRIDE of Falmouth (ibid.) prob dau of Joseph & Sarah (____) Pride of Falmouth (GDMNH, p. 568). She m (2) Gorham 21 Nov 1796 Col. Edmund Phinney as his 2nd wife (Marquis F. King, *Early Records of Gorham, Maine* [2nd Ed., 1991, edited by Russell S. Bickford], hereafter Gorham VR, p. 96; McLellan's *Gorham*, p. 774). Benjamin came from Falmouth and settled in Gorham before the French and Indian Wars (ibid., p. 773). He was one of Gorham's first selectmen, chosen in 1764 (ibid.).

Children, all but Nathaniel b Gorham: births VR Gorham, p. 161
- i Nathaniel, b Falmouth 12 Dec 1741: m Gorham 9 Jan 1766 Elizabeth Sinklor [Sinclair] (VR, p. 96)
- ii Sarah, b 7 Jan 1744: m Gorham 21 Nov 1765 Ezekiel Rich (VR, p. 96), b Truro MA 25 Nov 1738 son of Lemuel & Elizabeth (Harding) Rich (Ezekiel Rich family record in Gorham VR, p. 157, which gives his birth and parentage; McLellan's *Gorham*, pp. 735–36). They moved to Oxf Co (ibid.)
- iii Mehitable, b 15 Jul 1750: d aft 23 Jun 1780 when her last child was born (Gorham VR, p. 171): m Gorham 13 Oct 1765 Joseph Whitney (VR, p. 96), b Wiscasset 1 Mar 1739/40 son of Abel & Mary (Cane) Whitney (McLellan's *Gorham*, pp. 828–29), d 13 Mar 1819 (ibid., p. 833). He m (2) int Gorham 22 Sep 1781 Betty Phinney (VR, p. 69)
- iv Abigail, b 27 Apr 1753: m int Gorham 3 May 1775 James Rich (VR, p. 62), bp 2 Apr 1749 bro of Ezekiel above (McLellan's *Gorham*, pp. 735–36). They moved to Thorndike (ibid.)
- v Catharine, b 5 Aug 1757: d bef 1 Nov 1789 when her husband remarried: m Gorham 20 Nov 1777 Barnabas Bangs Jr. (VR, p. 95), b Gorham 1 Dec 1754 son of Barnabas & Loruhama (Elwell) Bangs (VR, p. 105; McLellan's *Gorham*, p. 392), d 25 May 1838 (ibid., p. 393). He m (2) Gorham 1 Nov 1789 Betty Cloutman (VR, p. 74)
- vi Benjamin, b 8 May 1763 [sic, McLellan's *Gorham*, p. 774, gives 8 May 1760]: d 29 Nov 1843 ae 83y (McLellan's *Gorham*, p. 774): m int Gorham 6 May 1784 Amy Webb of Falmouth (Gorham VR, p. 63), b c1754 prob dau of John & Elizabeth (Larrabee) Webb (McLellan's *Gorham*, p. 774), d 25 Nov 1814 ae 60y (ibid.)
- vii Joseph, b 14 Mar 1764: m 2 Sep 1784 Joanna Rackley of Pearsontown [Standish] (McLellan's *Gorham*, p. 774) [m int Gorham 10 Jul 1784 (VR, p. 63)], b Scarboro 22 Dec 1763 dau of Benjamin & Sarah (Jordan)

Rackliff (Albert J. Sears, *Early Families of Standish, Maine* [1991], p. 208). They moved to Unity in 1794 (ibid.)
viii Samuel, b 14 Apr 1766: m int Gorham 12 Mar 1791 Alice Golt of Allenstown (VR, p. 63) [note McLellan's *Gorham*, p. 774, calls her Alice "Goff"; one son b at Gorham was named "Samuel Gott Stevens" (VR, p. 162)]

Madeline Stevens Dodge, P.O. Box 232, Brooks, ME 04921-0232

Stevens, Nathaniel   21a   4 - 0 - 3 - 0 - 0
New Gloucester Town, Cumberland County

NATHANIEL STEVENS, b Gloucester MA 5 Jan 1728/9 son of William & Anna (Lufkin) Stevens (VR): d Litchfield 7 May 1817 (Oliver B. Clason, *History of Litchfield, Maine* [1897], hereafter Clason, p. 340): m Gloucester MA 27 Nov 1750 JERUSHA BENNETT (ibid.), b Gloucester MA 3 Sep 1732 dau of Anthony Jr. & Susannah (Haskell) Bennett (VR). Nathaniel moved with his family to New Gloucester in 1775 and then to Litchfield in 1790 to a part of town that became known as Steventown, named for his family. He served in the Rev War (Fisher's *Soldiers*, p. 751). His sons settled on surrounding farms with their families. Some later resettled in Piscataquis County (Clason; VR Guilford and Sangerville).

Children: all but Nancy b Gloucester MA (VR) and bp 4th Parish Church of Gloucester MA (church recs at Gloucester MA Public Library)
  i Jerusha, b 6 May 1751: d Richmond 30 Jan 1849 (Clason, p. 340): m int Gloucester MA 19 Dec 1769 Josiah Lane (VR). [Clason states she m Edward Peacock who could have been a second husband]
  ii Nathaniel, b 5 Mar 1753: d Gloucester MA 7 Sep 1754 (VR)
  iii Nathaniel, b 22 Nov 1754: d OH 20 Nov 1837 (Rev War pension #W9313): m New Gloucester 3 May 1779 Mary Francis (ibid.), b Gloucester MA 17 Dec 1754 dau of George & Hepzibah (Varrel) Francis (VR), d OH Mar 1848 (pension, op. cit.). Nathaniel was a Rev soldier and pensioner from New Gloucester (Fisher's *Soldiers*, p. 751; pension, op. cit.). He lived at Gloucester MA, Minot, Danville, Litchfield, and Guilford before moving in his later years to Ohio (ibid.). In 1838, his widow was a resident of Rutland, Meigs Co OH (ibid.)
  iv Elizabeth, b 10 Jan 1757: d aft 4 Dec 1794 when her last child was born and bef 7 Nov 1796 when her husband remarried (Clason, p. 187): m Abraham Jaquith (ibid.), b Billerica MA 15 Jun 1760 son of Abraham &

Elizabeth (Hill) Jaquith (ibid.), d 26 Nov 1808 (ibid.). He m (2) 7 Nov 1796 Hannah Meader and (3) Aug 1800 Hannah Curtis (ibid.)

v Susannah, b 24 Sep 1758: d Gloucester MA 7 Mar 1824 (VR): m Gloucester MA 6 May 1779 George Clark (VR) who d Gloucester MA 15 Apr 1820 (VR). They adopted an illegitimate son of her bro, Nathaniel. The child was b New Gloucester 1778 (VR) and took on the name of George Clark (*History of Gloucester*, op. cit., p. 169 in footnote)

vi James, b 21 Sep 1761: d Litchfield 22 Oct 1836 ae 75y 1m (g.s., Harriman cem): m (1) Ipswich MA 13 Apr 1786 Ruth Andrews of Ipswich MA (VR), bp Ipswich MA 22 May 1757 dau of Caleb & Anna (_____) Andrews (VR), d Litchfield "in travail" 25 Feb 1798 (Ipswich MA VR): m (2) 23 Aug 1798 Susanna (Bennett) Wharff (Clason, p. 340), b Gloucester MA 12 Jul 1763 dau of Capt. Isaac & Dorcas (Wharff) Bennett (VR) and wid of Joseph Wharff (Clason, p. 341) [see JOSEPH WHARFF family], d Litchfield 7 May 1833 ae 69y (g.s., Harriman cem): m (3) Eunice Webber wid of John Webber (Clason, p. 340), b c1762, d Litchfield 13 Oct 1835 ae 73y 5m 4d (ibid., p. 341) and bur Harriman cem: m (4) Litchfield 22 Nov 1835 Mrs. Hannah Woodman (Rev War pension #W2265) who applied for bounty land in 1835 as his widow. He was a Rev War soldier (ibid.). James and his first wife were enumerated in the 1790 census at Gloucester MA. He moved to Litchfield prior to 1798 when Ruth died

vii Sarah, b 14 Sep 1764: d Gloucester MA 7 Nov 1764 (VR)

viii Sarah, b 12 Oct 1765: m _____ Cleaves (Clason, p. 340)

ix William, b 4 Jun 1767: d Rutland, Meigs Co OH 17 Sep 1845 (g.s., Miles cem): m New Gloucester 3 May 1791 Sarah/Sally Witham (VR) [note Clason's *History of Litchfield* incorrectly gives William's wife as Sally Bennet], b Gloucester MA 6 Apr 1769 dau of John & Lois (Bray) Witham (VR), d Rutland, Meigs Co OH 20 Sep 1838 (g.s., Miles cem). William removed to OH in 1818

x John, b 2 Mar 1769: d Gardiner 25 Sep 1827 ae 54y [sic] (g.s., Libby Hill cem): m 27 Apr 1794 Sally Huntington (Clason, p. 340), b c1778, d Gardiner 27 Aug 1870 ae 92y (g.s., Libby Hill cem) [Gardiner VR gives d 16 Aug 1870 ae 95y]

xi Moses, b 2 Dec 1771: d Guilford 9 Mar 1838 (VR): m bef 14 Aug 1798 (when their son Joseph Wharff was born) Susanna Wharff (Clason, p. 390), b 10 Aug 1780 dau of Joseph & Susannah (Bennett) Wharff (ibid.) [see JOSEPH WHARFF family], d Guilford 5 Nov 1850 (Stevens MS, Guilford Public Library)

xii Amos, b 11 Oct 1773: d Litchfield 1 Sep 1828 ae 55y (g.s., Harriman cem): m 26 Mar 1797 Sally Wharff (ibid., p. 340), b 27 Jan 1782 sis of Susanna above (Clason, p. 390), d Litchfield 1 Dec 1856 ae 75y (g.s., Harriman cem). They lived at Litchfield

xiii Nancy, b New Gloucester Oct 1776 (Clason, p. 340): d Litchfield 18 Sep 1847 (Clason, p. 36): m 23 Nov 1820 John Bailey as his 2nd wife (ibid.) son of Jacob & Mary (____) Bailey (ibid.), d 23 Dec 1842 (ibid.)

Leslie Dow Sanders, P.O. Box 13, Marblehead MA 01945

Stevens, Trustum   14c   4 - 4 - 5 - 0 - 0
Falmouth Town, Cumberland County

TRISTRAM STEVENS, b Plaistow NH 8 Oct 1751 son of Peter & Ruth (Roswell) Stevens (VR): d 21 Nov 1803 ae 52y (clipping from *The Deering News*, issue of 28 Dec 1895, copy in Leonard Bond Chapman, "Grandpa's Scrapbook" [MS, MHS], pp. 14–16, hereafter *Deering News*): m Falmouth 12 Dec 1776 MARGARET PATRICK (VR), b Falmouth 17 Oct 1754 dau of David & Mary (Hawkins) Patrick (*Deering News*; Stevens sampler, typed copy in MS collection, MHS, submitted by Arthur K. Hunt, Brookline MA [1949], a descendant), d Oct 1821 (ibid.). Tristram moved to the Stroudwater section of old Falmouth in 1775 (Deering High School class of 1838, *Stroudwater Sketches* [1938], n.p.). He was a joiner [carpenter] by occupation and became known as the master ship-builder of Stroudwater (ibid.).

Children: *Deering News*
- i Samuel, b 28 Aug 1777: m Westbrook 26 Nov 1809 Mary/Polly Herrick (VR) dau of Daniel & Mary (Fickett) Herrick (Myrtle Kittridge Lovejoy, *This Was Stroudwater* [1985], pp. 190–91; *Deering News*)
- ii Tristram Coffin, b 6 Nov 1779: d Westbrook 3 Sep 1870 (Jacob Chapman, *Edward Chapman of Ipswich, Massachusetts, 1642–1678 and His Descendants* [1893], p. 39): m Westbrook 25 Oct 1810 Nancy C. Chapman (ibid.), b 18 Nov 1791 dau of Shadrach & Lydia (Starbird) Chapman (ibid.), d 24 Sep 1874 (ibid.)
- iii Margaret, b 28 Jan 1781: d 14 Oct 1785 from a kick by a horse (*Deering News*) and bur Evergreen cem, Portland
- iv Nancy, b 30 Nov 1783: m Portland 11 Oct 1801 Abraham H. Leonard (VR). He was a blacksmith and res in the vicinity of Windham (*Deering News*)
- v Eleanor, b 20 Nov 1785: d 14 Jun 1867 (g.s., Evergreen cem, Portland): m Newburyport MA 30 Oct 1806 Paul Merrill (VR). He was a tobacco merchant (*Deering News*)
- vi Michael, b 30 Nov 1787: d 3 Oct 1855 (g.s., Evergreen cem, Portland) [*Deering News* states he d Mar 1856 ae 68y]: m Portland 30 Jun 1811 Lucy

(Webb) Cobb (VR), b c1793 dau of Henry & Ann (Riggs) Webb (*Deering News*), d Portland 14 Nov 1885 (g.s., Evergreen cem) [*Deering News* states she d 14 Nov 1888 ae 94y 11m]. She was the wid of Daniel Cobb Jr. whom she had m in 1809 (*Deering News*)
- vii David, b 11 Apr 1789: m Westbrook 9 Jan 1820 Sophia Peaks (VR) [*Deering News* states they were m 12 Mar 1819], b c1793 dau of Mary (Thomes) (Peaks) Webb (*Deering News*), d Stroudwater 3 Apr 1878 ae 85y (ibid.)
- viii Charles, b 1791: m Portland 27 Nov 1825 Eunice Marriner (VR), b c1806, d 1849 ae 43y (g.s., Western cem, Portland)

Elvera Stevens Pardi, 65 Clifton St., Portland, ME 04101
Carolyn Morgan Bailey Lynch, 85 Land of Nod Road, Windham, ME 04062

Stillman, George   53a   2 - 2 - 4 - 0 - 0
Machias Town, Washington County

GEORGE STILLMAN, b Hartford CT 7 Mar 1751 (BHM, 5:27; g.s., Court St. cem, Machias) son of Nathaniel & Sarah (Allyn) Stillman (Margaret Kelley Nash, *Ancestral Lines of Fifty-Four Families, Wash Co, Machias* [1935–40], #50): d Machias 4 Nov 1804 (g.s., Court St. cem; obit in *Eastern Repository* given in David C. & Elizabeth K. Young, *Vital Records from Maine Newspapers, 1785–1820* [1993], p. 574): m Hartford CT (BHM, 5:27) c1781 REBECCA CROCKER (Nash, op. cit.), b Taunton MA 13 Mar 1752 dau of Rev. Josiah & Rebecca (Allen) Crocker (ibid.), d Machias 5 Feb 1799 (ibid.; g.s., Court St. cem). He came from Hartford CT to Machias in 1769 and became a mill owner and merchant in partnership with Stephen Smith (see George Stillman's will, dated 13 Sep 1804, Wash Co Probate 3:222). He was a Justice of the Peace, first Treasurer of the Town of Machias after its incorporation in 1784, and the first Treasurer and first Register of Deeds in Wash Co after its establishment in 1789. He was a charter member in 1778 of the Warren Lodge of Masons in (East) Machias. He was active, with the title of Major, in the defense of Machias during the Rev War (MS&S 15:26), and is referred to as "Lt. Col." in some official records. The title of "General" (as used on his memorial marker) was a state militia appointment. The "Papers (1775–1803) of Lt. Col. George Stillman" are in the New York Public Library.

Children, b Machias:
- i Rebecca Allyn, b 15 Mar 1783 (Beulah G. Jackman, *Earliest Records of Machias, Maine (1767–1827)* [n.d.], p. 2): d prob NY (living there in 1863 per *Memorial of the Centennial Anniversary of the Settlement of Machias*

[1863], p. 150): m Machias 10 Aug 1811 John Babcock Hillard (Jackman, op. cit., p. 40) widower of her sister Sarah below, b Bridgeport CT 1784 son of William Hillard (BHM, 5:27), d Brooklyn NY 1869 (ibid.). He was a schoolteacher and commanded a company of cavalry at Richmond VA during the War of 1812 (Machias Masonic records)

ii   Sarah/Sally, b 2 Feb 1785 (Jackman, op. cit., p. 2) [her g.s. states b 2 Jul 1785]: d Machias 25 Feb 1810 (g.s., Court St. cem): m 1807 John Babcock Hillard as his 1st wife (BHM, 5:27). Their son, George Stillman Hillard (1808–1879), was a noted man of letters and lawyer in Boston (*Dictionary of American Biography* [1930], IX:49)

iii George, b 12 Nov 1787 (Jackman, op. cit., p. 3) [his g.s. states b 13 Nov 1788]: d Rivannah Hall, Fluvanna Co VA 28 Jun 1868 (g.s., copied in Bulletin of the Fluvanna Co Historical Society, #10 & 11:29–32): unm. On his g.s. is inscribed "Moved to Richmond, Virginia, in 1810, served in the War of 1812, settled in Fluvanna Cnty in 1815, was a magistrate 30 years, and a member of the Legislature 13 years"

iv   Allen Crocker, b 5 Apr 1790 (Nash, op. cit.): moved to Alabama (ibid.)

v   Elizabeth Otis, b 22 May 1792 (NEHGR, 68 [1914]:23): d Boston MA 30 Jan 1850 (NEHGR, 4 [1850]:199): m (1) Machias 15 Oct 1814 James Otis Lincoln of Dennysville (Jackman, op. cit., p. 42), b Hingham MA c1789 son of Benjamin & Mary (Otis) Lincoln (NEHGR, 2 [1848]:296), d Hingham 1818 (ibid.): m (2) Apr 1823 Hon. James Savage, the famous antiquary and genealogist and author of *A Genealogical Dictionary of the First Settlers of New England*, b Boston 13 Jul 1784 son of Habijah & Elizabeth (Tudor) Savage, d Boston 8 Mar 1873 (*Dictionary of American Biography* [1930], 16:387)

vi   Samuel, b 4 Dec 1795 (g.s.): d Fluvanna Co VA 7 Aug 1874 (g.s., copied in Fluvanna Co Hist Soc Bulletin, op. cit.): unm. On his g.s. is engraved, "In connection with his brother George and Col. Robt. W. Ashlin, he conducted a mercantile business for more than 45 years at Rivanna Mills..." He and his brother, being stauch supporters of the Confederacy, were long estranged from their Yankee relatives and they left their fortunes to their southern friends

Zane A. Thompson, Rte. 1 Box 235A, Roque Bluffs, ME 04654

Stone, Josiah   71c   2 - 0 - 2 - 0 - 0
    York Town, York County

JOSIAH STONE, b York 27 Mar 1732 son of Benjamin & Abigail (Swett) Stone (Lester M. Bragdon & John E. Frost, *Vital Records of York, Maine* [1992], hereafter VR, p. 15): d York 23 Oct [or Aug] 1804 (VR, p. 404): m York 8 Dec

1757 HANNAH MILBURY (VR, p. 142), b York 13 Dec 1733 dau of Samuel & Elizabeth (Kingsbury) Milbury (VR, pp. 16, 82), d York 27 Oct 1797 (VR, p. 404). Josiah was on a 1757 list of York militia called the "train band"; in 1775, he was one of those elected to be town fence viewers, field drivers and hog reeves (Charles Edward Banks, *History of York, Maine* [repr 1990], 1:378, 2:214).

Children, b York: births VR York, p. 82; baptisms YCGSJ, 5:1 [1990]:14, 16
- i Samuel, b 15 Sep 1758, bp 1st Parish York 24 Sep 1758: d York 1844 (VR, p. 533): m York 10 Feb 1790 Mary Raynes [see SAMUEL STONE family]
- ii Sarah/Sally, b 4 Jan 1761, bp 1st Parish York 11 Dec 1760 [sic]: d York 25 Aug 1807 ae 47y (VR, p. 451)
- iii Josiah Jr., b 22 May 1771, bp 1st Parish York 2 Jun 1771: d 28 Apr 1852 (g.s., Laurel Hill cem, Saco): m (1) int York 30 Aug 1794 Dorcas Milbury Bickford of Biddeford (VR, p. 178), bp 1st Church of Biddeford 26 Jun 1776 dau of Pierce & Olive (Milbury) Bickford (MHGR, 7:184, 6:333), d 23 May 1825 ae 50y (family recs in possession of Janet H. Riley): m (2) 16 Sep 1826 Sophia Jacobs (ibid.; YCGSJ, 6 [1991]:59) [m int Lyman 28 Aug 1826 both of Lyman (NEHGR, 96 [1942]:344)], b Wells 28 Apr 1797 dau of Jonathan & Rebekah Scammon (Emery) Jacobs (VR), d 10 Sep 1883 (g.s., Laurel Hill cem, Saco)

Janet H. Riley, 161 Forest St., Sherborn, MA 01770

Stone, Sam¹   71c   1 - 0 - 1 - 0 - 0
York Town, York County

SAMUEL STONE, b York 15 Sep 1758 son of Josiah & Hannah (Milbury) Stone (Lester M. Bragdon & John E. Frost, *Vital Records of York, Maine* [1992], hereafter York VR, p. 82) and bp 1st Parish York 24 Sep 1758 (YCGSJ, 5:1 [1990]:14) [see JOSIAH STONE family]: d 1844 (York VR, p. 533): m York 10 Feb 1790 MARY RAYNES (VR, p. 172), b York 3 Nov 1759 dau of Daniel & Jane (Frost) Raynes (VR, p. 73) [see DANIEL RAYNES family, *Maine Families*, 3:233–34], d 1856 (York VR, p. 533).

Children as found, b York: births first 3 VR York, p. 86; baptisms first 3 YCGSJ, 5:1 [1990]:19–20
- i Daniel, b 7 Jun 1792, bp 1st Parish York 24 Sep 1792: m So. Berwick 31 Aug 1817 Harriet Goodwin of So. Berwick (VR), b 12 Apr 1800 dau of Maj. Jedediah & Hannah (Emery) Goodwin of Berwick (John Hayes Goodwin, *Daniel Goodwin of Ancient Kittery, Maine and His Descendants* [1985], p. 31)

ii Samuel Jr., b 27 Oct 1793, bp 1st Parish York 15 Jan 1794: m So. Berwick 16 Mar 1820 Kezia Emery of So. Berwick (VR)
iii Hannah, b 24 Sep 1796, bp 1st Parish York 30 Oct 1796
iv John, b c1799: d York 8 Nov 1817 ae 18y, listed on the death rec as a son of Samuel Stone (York VR, p. 414)
v perhaps Sarah A., b York 1802 ("Descendants of Nicholas Stone 1613–1689," YCGSJ, 7 [1992]:1:12; VR, p. 533): d 20 Jan 1885 (York VR, pp. 226, 533): m York 24 May 1827 Rosewell Webber (VR, p. 229), b York 18 Feb 1803 son of David & Jenny (Grant) Webber (VR, p. 109), d 2 Jul 1889 ae 86y 5m (York VR, p. 226)

Janet H. Riley, 161 Forest St., Sherborn, MA 01770

Sturdevant, abisha   45c   1 - 0 - 2 - 0 - 0
Starling Plantation [now Fayette], Lincoln County

ABISHA STURTEVANT, b Wareham MA 2 Sep 1769 son of Joseph & Mary (Gibbs) Sturtevant (Wayne VR; Robert H. Sturtevant, *Descendants of Samuel Sturtevant* [1986], families #5-142, 4-41, which gives b 12 Sep 1768), bp Wareham with siblings 7 Feb 1782 (Leonard H. Smith, *Records of the First Church of Wareham, Massachusetts, 1739–1891* [1974], p. 66): m 10 Sep 1789 MARY BILLINGTON (Wayne VR), b 19 Oct 1772 (Wayne VR). Abisha signed a petition submitted 20 Dec 1794 to the MA Senate and House of Representatives for incorporation of Sterling Plantation as a new town to be called New Sterling; the petition was approved 28 Feb 1795 (Joseph H. Underwood, *History of Fayette* [1956], p. 62). He settled in Wayne "at an early date" taking up a farm which he sold in 1840 (George W. Walton, *History of the Town of Wayne, Kennebec County, Maine* [1898], p. 185). At Wayne, he served as a clerk in the Baptist Church (ibid., p. 61) and was a town surveyor in the early 1800s (Wayne TR). Seven of his children attended the 5th District School in Wayne Village in 1809 (ibid., p. 95).

Children: births VR Wayne
i Sarah/Sally, b 30 May 1790
ii John, b 26 Feb 1792: m 13 Feb 1816 Jerusha House (Leeds VR), b Littleborough Plt (now Leeds) 20 Feb 1785 dau of Nathaniel & Lillis (Palmer) House (Leeds VR)
iii Mary/Polly, b 21 May 1794: m int Wayne 4 Dec 1819 David Lufkins (VR)
iv Rhoda, b Fayette 9 Apr 1796: d Forest City MN 3 Jan 1879 (Sturtevant, op. cit., #6-185): m c1816 David Judkins (ibid.)
v Martha/Patty, b 17 Feb 1798: m Wayne 6 Jun 1820 John Richards (VR)

vi Warren, b 11 Mar 1800: d 1 Dec 1877 ae 77y 8m 20d (g.s., Riverside cem, Willimantic): m Leeds 1 May 1823 Charlotte Manes (VR) dau of John & Olive (Day) Manes (Leeds VR). He was one of the early settlers of Willimantic (Conrad Van Hynig, *Willimantic, Maine, Past and Present* [1976], p. 10)

vii Abisha, b 20 Jun 1802: d Wayne (Sturtevant, op. cit., #6-404): m Wayne Apr 1823 Hannah Smith (VR)

viii Hannah, b 25 Oct 1804: m Wayne 4 Aug 1834 Richard Smith of Lynn MA (VR)

ix David, b 31 May 1807: d Leeds 21 Apr 1889 (Leeds VR): m (1) Betsey Burnham dau of Abner Burnham (Sturtevant, op. cit., #6-163), d Fayette 27 Sep 1835 (ibid.): m (2) Sophronia Richards dau of Samuel Richards (ibid.), b Parkman 21 Apr 1805 (ibid.; Wayne VR): m (3) int 11 Aug 1877 Almira (Day) Folsom (Sturtevant, op. cit.), b New Sharon dau of Samuel Day (ibid.; Elizabeth Knowles Folsom, *Genealogy of the Folsom Family 1638-1938* [1938], p. 23)

x Ichabod, b 15 Mar 1809: d Leeds 25 Sep 1886 (g.s., Evergreen cem, Wayne): m (1) Louisana (Brett?) (Stutevant, op. cit., #6-379) by whom he had 9 children: m (2) 27 Oct 1866 Mrs. Sarah J. Ames of N. Haven (Leeds VR). He was a Civil War soldier and enlisted from Ripley as a private in Infantry Co. D, 3rd ME Regiment; he was later discharged for disability (Report of Adjutant General's Office of the State of Maine for the years 1864 and 1865 [1866], 5:868, 1293)

xi Lot, b 20 Apr 1812

Maxine B. Hughes, 265 Main St., Dexter, ME 04930

Swan, James   68a   1 - 0 - 1 - 0 - 0
Sudbury-Canada Town, York County

JAMES SWAN, b Haverhill MA [the part set off as Methuen in 1725] 14 Mar 1721/2 [and bp Andover MA 1721/2 (VR)] son of Joshua & Sarah (Ingalls) Swan (VR Haverhill MA): prob he who d Bethel 12 Nov 1805 (VR): m Haverhill MA 10 Apr 1746 MARY SMITH of Haverhill MA (VR) who d Bethel 27 Oct 1801 (VR). James and Mary resided in Methuen MA where their first nine children were born. Before the Revolution, James was impressed into the English service, but with two others seized the ship and forced the captain to sail to Boston (William B. Lapham, *History of Bethel, Maine* [repr 1981], p. 40). Fearing prosecution, he came to Maine by 1769 where he was among the first settlers of Fryeburg and where his last 2 children were born. In 1779, he moved to Sudbury-Canada, now Bethel (ibid.). James was reportedly the man with whom Sabbatis, a well known Pequaket Indian, lived for many years in Fryeburg (ibid., p. 302).

Children: births first 9 VR Methuen MA, last 2 VR Fryeburg
  i Elizabeth, b Methuen MA 13 Jan 1746[/7] and bp Haverhill MA 18 Jan 1747 (VR): m Haverhill MA 12 Apr 1768 Jesse Dustin (VR), b Haverhill MA 20 Sep 1747 son of Jonathan & Susanna (Farnham) Dustin (VR) [see JESSE DUSTIN family, *Maine Families*, 3:74–75]
  ii Joseph Greeley, b Methuen MA 4 Oct 1748: d Bethel 10 Dec 1816 (VR): m Elizabeth Evans of Fryeburg (*History of Bethel*, p. 620) [see JOSEPH GREELEY SWAN family]
  iii Molley, b Methuen MA 8 Aug 1751: d young (*History of Bethel*, p. 620)
  iv Sarah, b Methuen MA 10 Apr 1754: d Methuen MA 6 Jan 1754[/5] (VR)
  v Sarah, b Methuen MA 9 Feb 1756: d Bethel 13 Jan 1802 (MGS "Gold Sheets," Vol. 6): m Fryeburg Abraham Russell (*History of Bethel*, p. 610), b Andover MA 1748 son of John Jr. & Hannah (Foster) Russell (ibid., pp. 606, 610), d Bethel 9 Dec 1839 (ibid.)
  vi Abigail, b Methuen MA 25 Aug 1758: m Jeremiah Farrington of Fryeburg (*History of Bethel*, p. 620)
  vii James, b Methuen MA 2 Dec 1760 and bp Haverhill MA 7 Dec 1760 (VR): res Bethel 1840 (Fisher's *Soldiers*, p. 766): m Andover MA 17 May 1787 Hannah Shattuck (VR) [he of Sudbury-Canada on m ints filed at Andover MA (VR)]. He was a Rev War soldier and pensioner (Rev War pension #S30142) and a head-of-household at Sudbury-Canada in 1790
  viii Elijah, b Methuen MA 5 Jul 1763: m Eunice Barton dau of Asa & Mercy (Bartlett) Barton (William B. Lapham & Silas P. Maxim, *History of Paris, Maine* [1884], p. 744), b c1772, d Paris 1839 ae 67y (obit in *Morning Star*, issue of 5 Jun 1839, in David C. Young and Robert L. Taylor, *Death Notices From Freewill Baptist Publications 1811–1851* [1985], p. 325). They moved to West Paris about 1822 (ibid.)
  ix Anne/Nancy, b Methuen MA 22 Sep 1765: m Jonathan Barker of Newry (*History of Bethel*, p. 620), perhaps he b Methuen MA 26 May 1754 son of Jonathan & Abigail (Mitchell) Barker and bro of Jesse who m Anne's sister Naomi (Martha Fifield Williams, *Sunday River Sketches* [1977], pp. 160–62)
  x Nathaniel, b Fryeburg 9 Jan 1769: m Mehitable Colby of Sutton MA (*History of Bethel*, p. 620)
  xi Naamah/Naomi, b Fryeburg 22 May 1771: d Newry 30 Jun 1850 ae 79y (*Sunday River Sketches*, op. cit., p. 162): m Jesse Barker (ibid.), b Methuen MA 30 Apr 1762 son of Jonathan & Abigail (Mitchell) Barker (ibid.), d Newry 16 Nov 1854 ae 92y (ibid.). They settled in Newry (*History of Bethel*, p. 620)

Gerald F. Gower, 453 Rt. 85, Raymond, ME 04071

Swan, Joseph G   68a   4 - 3 - 4 - 0 - 0
Sudbury-Canada Town, York County

JOSEPH GREELEY SWAN, b Methuen MA 4 Oct 1748 son of James & Mary (Smith) Swan (VR) [see JAMES SWAN family]: d Bethel 10 Dec 1816 (VR): m Fryeburg by 1772 (when 1st child was born) ELIZABETH EVANS (William B. Lapham, *History of Bethel, Maine* [repr 1981], hereafter Lapham's *Bethel*, p. 620), b Penacook [Concord] NH 12 Jun 1753 dau of Capt. John & Elizabeth (Stickney) Evans (Frank H. Swan, *Richard Swan and Some of His Descendants* [1927], p. 52). She m (2) 16 May 1827 Elisha Hammond of Denmark (ibid.). Joseph moved from Methuen MA to Fryeburg prob with his parents in the mid-1760s. He later moved to Bethel, perhaps about 1778 when his father moved to Bethel, and in 1790 lived next door to his parents.

Children: births VR Bethel
- i   John, b Fryeburg 13 Jul 1772: m (1) Elizabeth/Betsy Chapman (Lapham's *Bethel*, p. 503), b 27 May 1777 dau of Rev. Eliphaz & Hannah (Jackman) Chapman (ibid.), d Gilead 28 Aug 1801 (ibid.; VR Bethel): m (2) Bethel 30 Nov 1803 Elizabeth/Polly Eames (VR), b 1 Aug 1782 dau of Ebenezer & Elizabeth (_____) Eames (Lapham's *Bethel*, p. 521), d Bethel 7 Oct 1811 (VR)
- ii   Dudley, b Fryeburg 30 Sep 1774: m (1) Sarah/Sally Greene (S. A. Evans, *The Descendants of David Evans of Charlestown, Massachusetts* [1893], p. 18) [note that Lapham's *Bethel*, p. 620, states Dudley m "Mary" Green; Swan, op. cit., Evans, op. cit., and her obit all indicate she was Sarah/Sally], b Rowley MA c1777 dau of Thomas & Lydia (Kilborn) Green (Rev. William Warren, *History of Waterford, Maine* [1879], p. 295), d Waterford 8 Oct 1819 ae 43y (David C. and Elizabeth Keene Young, *Vital Records from Maine Newspapers, 1785–1820*, p. 583): m (2) Mrs. Sarah Lang (ibid.). He lived in Waterford
- iii James, b Fryeburg 17 Sep 1777: m Bethel 1 Sep 1803 Persis Eames (VR), b 29 May 1786 dau of James & Ruth (Field) Eames (Lapham's *Bethel*, p. 522). They settled in Newry
- iv   Caleb, b Bethel 20 Mar 1780: d in West Indies (Lapham's *Bethel*, p. 620)
- v   Elizabeth/Betty, b Bethel 15 Oct 1782: m David Coffin (Lapham's *Bethel*, p. 620)
- vi   William, b Bethel 28 Apr 1784: d Bethel 4 Jun 1785 (VR)
- vii Abigail, b Bethel 15 Dec 1787: d Concord NH 26 Jan 1861 (Swan, op. cit., p. 52): m 3 Jan 1808 Peter Walker (Bethel VR; Lapham's *Bethel*, p. 636, states they were m in Fryeburg), b 6 Jul 1780 son of James & Ruth (Abbot) Walker (Lapham's *Bethel*, p. 636), d Concord NH 2 Jun 1857 (Swan, op. cit., p. 52)

viii William, b Bethel 4 Nov 1790: m Bethel 9 May 1811 Betsey Howe (VR)
ix Hannah, b Bethel 17 Apr 1793: d 21 Apr 1881 (Swan, op. cit., p. 53): m John Warren (ibid.). They settled in Denmark (Lapham's *Bethel*, p. 620)
x Greeley, b Bethel 11 Nov 1795: d Bethel 27 Jan 1797 (VR)

Gerald F. Gower, 453 Rt. 85, Raymond, ME 04071
Warren D. Stearns, P.O. Box 35, Hanover, ME 04237

Tolpy, Henry   71b   3 - 4 - 7 - 0 - 0
    York Town, York County

HENRY TALPEY, bp Isles of Shoals NH 18 Dec 1746 son of Richard & Elizabeth (Carter) Talpey ("Church Membership, Marriages, and Baptisms on the Isles of Shoals in the Eighteenth Century," NEHGR, 66 [1912]:214; parents' marriage dated 7 Jan 1733/4 in NEHGR, 66 [1912]:144; will of Richard Talpey of York, York Co Probate #18414): prob he who d York 4 Oct 1815 (Lester M. Bragdon & John E. Frost, *Vital Records of York, Maine* [1992], hereafter VR, p. 456): m York 15 Dec 1772 MARY BERRY (York VR, p. 358), perhaps she bp York 22 Sep 1753 dau of Joseph Berry (YCGSJ, 4 [1989]:1:8), d 18 Feb 1837 ae abt 85y ("Diary of Jeremiah Weare, Jr., of York, Maine," [NEHGR, 66 [1912]:264, hereafter "Jeremiah Weare Diary"). Henry was a Rev War soldier and was commissioned at Wells 12 Jun 1776 as a 1st Lieut (MS&S, 15:831). In his father's will dated 2 Apr 1793, he received all the land that Richard Talpey bought of Joseph Stover and others where Henry then lived; all of Richard's interest in the mills at or near the lands at Cape Neddick [York]; the land Richard bought of Capt. John Stone; and his pew in the meeting house (York Co Probate #18414). Henry lived on his father's "upper farm" at Cape Neddick.

Children: Talpey Family Papers, compiled by Florence M. Talpey (1889–1974), at Old York Historical Society, York; & cited sources
i Elizabeth, b 14 Jul 1774 and bp 1st Parish York 17 Jul 1774 (YCGSJ, 5 [1990]:2:13): listed as a widow when she d York 27 Dec 1810 (VR, p. 452): m York 20 Dec 1792 Nathaniel Freeman Jr. (VR, p. 175). It was prob he who d York 20 Jun 1810 (VR, p. 451)
ii Mary/Polly, b 28 Aug 1777: d Wells 25 Feb 1859 ae 82y ("Incriptions from Gravestones at Wells, Maine," NEHGR, 93 [1939]:56): m int York 16 Dec 1799 Daniel Wheelwright Esq. of Wells (VR, p. 184), b c1764, d Wells 11 Apr 1847 ae 83y (NEHGR, 93 [1939]:56)
iii Sarah, b 18 Sep 1779: prob the "Widow E. [sic] Moulton" who d 25 Jul 1858 the cause of death listed as insanity (York VR, p. 436): m int York 10 Jan 1801 Daniel Moulton of Biddeford (VR, p. 185), a mariner and

son of Daniel & Eleanor (Raynes) Moulton (Moulton MS at Old York Historical Society, York, p. 32, citing York Co deed 68:209). He was prob the "son of Daniel Moulton" who d "abroad" 14 Nov 1801 (York VR, p. 446). Just one year later, a child of Daniel Moulton d 14 Dec 1802 (York VR, p. 447). The adm of the estate of Daniel Moulton, late of Pepperellborough [Saco], was granted to widow Sarah Moulton on 18 Apr 1803 and Henry Talpey acted as a surety (York Co Probate 19:201). On 15 Apr 1805, Sarah Moulton was declared incompetent to adm her late husband Daniel's estate (York Co Probate 20:33). Subsequent censuses found her in the household of her brother, Jonathan, and in 1850, Sarah, ae 70y, is listed as insane (USC York, Jonathan Talpey family)

iv Henry Jr., b 24 Apr 1782 and bp 1st Parish York 18 Sep 1782 (YCGSJ, 5 [1990]:2:14): d by suicide York 27 Feb 1853 ae 71y (VR, p. 433; g.s. Clark Rd. cem, transcribed in York VR, p. 639): m (1) int York 6 Nov 1804 Abigail Trafton (VR, p. 189), bp 1st Parish York 23 Sep 1782 dau of Tobias & Tabitha (____) Trafton (YCGSJ, 5 [1990]:2:14), d York 12 Oct 1820 ae 38y (VR, p. 417): m (2) York 6 Jan 1824 Abigail (Varrell) Gerry (VR, p. 220), b c1789 dau of Solomon & Mary (Moore) Varrell and wid of James Gerry/Garey (will of Solomon Varrell, York Co Probate 28:238–39; George Ernst file at Old York Historical Society, York, p. 11), d York 13 Sep 1862 ae 73y (g.s., Clark Rd. cem)

v Capt. James, b 14 Apr 1784 and bp 1st Parish York 8 Sep [prob 1784] (YCGSJ, 5 [1990]:2:14): d York 28 Dec 1872 ae 88y 8m (g.s., Clark Rd. cem, transcribed in York VR, p. 639): m (1) int York 21 Oct 1809 Paulina Swett (VR, p. 195), bp 1st Parish York 25 May 1786 dau of Capt. Nathaniel Jr. & Sarah (Carlisle) Swett of York (YCGSJ, 5 [1990]:1:18; parents' marriage in York VR, p. 358), d York 17 Jul 1836 ae 51y ("Jeremiah Weare Diary," NEHGR, 66 [1912]:264; g.s., Clark Rd. cem). According to Jeremiah Weare's diary, she "was found in the pig sty with a string wrapt around her neck," apparently distraught over the death of a daughter one month previously which "it is said she set her heart upon that child [whose death] drove her beyound her reason." James m (2) int York 11 Jun 1838 Eliza (Norton) Freeman (VR, p. 250), b c1800 dau of William & Olive (Young) Norton (Norton MS by Lillian Norton Horn, p. 8, and George Ernst workpapers on Norton family, both sources at Old York Historical Society, York), d York 17 Feb 1870 ae 69y 11m (buried with her parents, g.s., Norton Lot, transcribed in York VR, p. 657). She had m (1) York 15 Jul 1825 Theodore Freeman (VR, p. 223)

vi William, b 28 Jun 1786 and bp 1st Parish York 9 Nov 1786 (YCGSJ, 5 [1990]:2:14): d Aug 1809 (Talpey Family Papers. op. cit.)

vii Capt. Jonathan, b 5 Oct 1788 [his g.s. says b 7 Oct 1788] and bp 1st Parish York 8 Jul 1789 (YCGSJ, 5 [1990]:2:14): d 11 Sep 1863 (g.s., Clark Rd. cem, transcribed in York VR, p. 639): m York 25 Nov 1817 Elisabeth

Carlisle (VR, p. 208), b York 16 Feb 1796 (g.s.) and bp 1st Parish York 12 Jan 1797 dau of Daniel & Lydia (Wilson) Carlisle (YCGSJ, 4 [1989]:2:12; parents' marriage in York VR, p. 168), d York 8 Jan 1891 (g.s., Clark Rd. cem). Capt. Jonathan was a prisoner at Dartmoor Prison in England 1812–1815 for being a privateer during the War of 1812. An account of his experiences and several letters he wrote during his captivity were published in YCGSJ, 5 (1990):4:9–16

viii Nancy, b 22 Apr 1790 and bp 1st Parish York 23 May 1792 (YCGSJ, 5 [1990]:2:14): d Jan 1793 (Talpey Family Papers, op. cit.)

ix Lucy, b 27 Jul 1792 and bp 1st Parish York 17 Sep 1794 (YCGSJ, 5 [1990]:2:14): d aft 22 Jun 1883 when she was a patient at a hospital at Concord NH (Talpey Family Papers, op. cit.): m York 12 Aug 1818 Lieut. Samuel S. Stacey (VR, p. 210)

Dexter Talpey Spiller, 71 York Street, York, ME 03909

Tolpy, Thos 71c   1 - 3 - 4 - 0 - 0
York Town, York County

THOMAS TALPEY, bp Isles of Shoals NH 21 Apr 1754 son of Richard & Elizabeth (Carter) Talpey ("Church Membership, Marriages, and Baptisms on the Isles of Shoals in the Eighteenth Century," NEHGR, 66 [1912]:218; parents' marriage dated 7 Jan 1733/4 in NEHGR, 66 [1912]:144; will of Richard Talpey of York, York Co Probate #18414): m York 19 Jan 1775 MIRIAM ADAMS WHITNEY (Lester M. Bragdon & John E. Frost, *Vital Records of York, Maine* [1992], hereafter VR, p. 359), b York 6 May 1757 dau of Dr. John & his 2nd wife Hezekiah (Adams) Whitney (VR, pp. 75, 91). On 21 Apr 1775, Thomas was a member of a company of minutemen raised by the town of York under the command of Capt. Johnson Moulton, Esq. (Charles E. Banks, *History of York, Maine* [repr 1990], 1:404). In Richard Talpey's will dated 2 Apr 1793, he gave his son Thomas only 6 shillings; however he left to his grandsons John and Richard Talpey, sons of his son Thomas, his lower farm of 300 acres purchased from William Pepperrell with the buildings thereon, the appurtenances and stock of cattle (York Co Probate #18414). Should either John or Richard die before reaching age 21, then the share would fall to the "other sons of Thomas" (ibid.).

Children
  i John, b York 12 Aug 1775 (VR, p. 91) and bp 1st Parish York 9 Jun 1776 (YCGSJ, 5 [1990]:2:13): d bef Mar 1810 (estate of John Talpey, York Co Probate, 22:381): m int York 12 Nov 1803 Mary Clarke of York (VR, p. 188), poss she bp 1st Parish York 19 Jun 1785 dau of Daniel & Hannah

(Berry) Clarke (YCGSJ, 4 [1989]:2:11; Daniel & Hannah's marriage in York VR, p. 165). She was prob the "Mrs. Mary Talpey" who m (2) int York 17 Oct 1812 John Norton (VR, p. 199)

ii Mary, bp 1st Parish York 5 Jul 1778 (YCGSJ, 5 [1990]:2:13) [her birth was not recorded on the Thomas Talpey family record in the York VR, p. 91, which listed only the sons John and Richard]

iii Richard, b York 7 Sep 1778 (VR, p. 91) and bp 1st Parish York 9 May 1779 (YCGSJ, 5 [1990]:2:13): d York 15 Mar 1865 ae 85y 6m (g.s., Talpey Lot, transcribed in York VR, p. 639): m int York 13 Nov 1802 Sukey Kerswell [also written Susan Caswell] of York (VR, p. 186), b c Dec 1781 (g.s.) [prob Susanna the dau of Pelatiah "Casuel" bp 1st Parish York 9 Dec 1781 (YCGSJ, 4 [1989]:2:11)], d York 11 Jul 1876 ae 94y 7m (g.s., Talpey Lot)

iv Hannah, bp 1st Parish York 19 Jul 1781 (YCGSJ, 5 [1990]:2:13)

v Hepzebeth, bp 1st Parish York 8 Sep [prob 1784] (YCGSJ, 5 [1990]:2:14): d York 11 Mar 1869 ae 83y [sic] (g.s., Freeman Lot, transcribed in York VR, p. 642): m int York 3 Oct 1802 Jeremiah Freeman (VR, p. 186), b c1774, d York 19 Sep 1857 ae 83y (g.s., Freeman Lot)

vi Rufus, bp 1st Parish York 9 Nov 1786 (YCGSJ, 5 [1990]:2:14): d by Feb 1846 when the estate of Rufus "Tapley" of Bangor was probated (Ruth Gray, *Abstracts of Penobscot County, Maine Probate Records, 1816–1866* [1990], p. 217): m int Hallowell 2 Feb 1810 Sally Norcross (VR). [One Sally Hussey Norcross was b Hallowell 9 Apr 1791 dau of Philip 2d & Nancy (Hussey) Norcross (VR)]

vii Oliver, b York 28 Nov 1789 (VR Hallowell) and bp 1st Parish York 25 Aug 1790 (YCGSJ, 5 [1990]:2:14): d Hallowell 7 Nov 1874 ae 85y (VR): m (1) Hallowell 26 Dec 1813 Sally Matthews (VR), b Hallowell 15 Jan 1796 dau of William & Betsey (Groves) Matthews (VR), d Hallowell 9 Oct 1867 ae 71y 9m (VR): m (2) Hallowell 21 Sep 1868 Mrs. Julia (Emerson) Lincoln (VR) wid of Laban Lincoln [Laban Lincoln m int Hallowell 29 Oct 1842 Julia Emerson of Norridgewock (Hallowell VR)]. She d Hallowell 5 Mar 1880 ae 79y (VR)

viii Pollina, bp 1st Parish York 21 Aug 1792 (YCGSJ, 5 [1990]:2:14)

Dexter Talpey Spiller, 71 York Street, York, ME 03909

Thomas, Jesse   40c   4 - 0 - 1 - 0 - 0
Meduncook Town, Lincoln County

JESSE THOMAS, b Middleboro MA 26 Oct 1728 son of Edward & Abigail (Parlour) Thomas (MD 4:72, 7:242): d betw 20 Oct 1795 when he sold 140 acres of land on Hatchet Cove in Meduncook to his son Melzar (Lin Co deeds 37:40) and 1800 when he does not appear on the census: m SUSANNA ____ who d 28 Mar 1816 (Thomas Family notes, Priscilla Jones Collection, Stephen Phillips Memorial Library, Searsport). Jesse was of Pembroke MA 7 Sep 1757 when he was granted adm of his father's estate; he was of Meduncook Plt 26 Sep 1757 when he sold his share of his father's estate to his brother Hushai (Plymouth Co MA deeds 46:124, 50:90). He was one of several petitioners to the General Court in 1767 requesting that the courts be moved to the center of the county (BHM, 2:158). He was a member of the party which on 8 Dec 1768 discovered the wreck of the sloop KENNEBEC on False Franklin Island off Meduncook (Charles E. Allen, *History of Dresden, Maine* [1931], pp. 450–51). Jesse purchased 100 acres of land on Hatchet Cove, Lot #3, from Thomas Flucker on 30 Mar 1774 (Lin Co deeds 14:149). He served as 1st Lieut. in Col Wheaton's 4th Lin Co Regiment of MA Militia during the Rev War (MS&S 15:597). He was Treasurer of Meduncook Plt in 1783 and 1787–1793 (Melville Cook, *Records of Meduncook Plantation* [1985], p. 29). He was an appraiser of the estate of Jonah Gay, late of Meduncook, 24 Jun 1778, and of the estate of Jacob Davis, late of Meduncook, 14 Aug 1784 (William D. Patterson, *The Probate Records of Lincoln County, Maine 1760–1800* [1991], pp. 88, 130).

Children, prob all b Meduncook Plt: all information from Priscilla Jones Coll., op. cit., unless otherwise cited

  i   James, b 1758: d Harpswell 5 Apr 1829 ae 71y: m Harpswell 23 Feb 1786 Eleanor Randall ("Harpswell VR Recorded by Rev. Elisha Eaton, 1754–64, and by his son Samuel Eaton, V.D.M. 1765–1843" [TS, MHS], p. 33), b Harpswell Sep 1768 dau of Paul & Mary (McFarlin) Randall (VR), d Harpswell 3 Jul 1851 ae 82y 9m (g.s., Harpswell Centre cem, MHGR 9:328)
 ii   Azubah, b 1759: m Wellington Gay
iii   Mary, b 1762: d Waldo 13 Mar 1843 ae 81y: m Jonah Gay
 iv   Jesse, b 1764: d Camden 14 Jan 1853 ae 88y: m Sarah/Sally Bradford. He purchased land in Camden 30 May 1801 from Jeremiah Farnham (Lin Co deeds 52:44)
  v   Hushai, b 1769: d Lincolnville 8 Aug 1841 (*Republican Journal*, issue of 20 Aug 1841): m Camden 10 Sep 1797 Abigail Higgins (VR) dau of Benjamin & Sarah (Mathews) Higgins [see PHILIP HIGGINS family]. He left a will which was probated in Jan 1842 (Wal Co Probate #976)
 vi   Melzar, b 1769: d Friendship 1 Aug 1855 ae 85y 10m: m Lydia Morse. He res Friendship where he was Treasurer and Clerk several years (*Records of Meduncook*, op. cit., p. 29)

Ralph E. Hillman, 4302 James Dr., Midland, MI 48642

Thompson, Theodore   59a   2 - 2 - 1 - 0 - 0
Buxton Town, York County

THEODORE THOMPSON, b 1760–1765 son of Samuel & Sarah (Rounds) Thompson of Buxton (YCGSJ, 3 [1988]:53): d Standish 17 May 1833 (Rev War Bounty Land Warrant #49028-160-55) [note that his g.s. at Littlefield cem, Standish, as transcribed by MOCA, gives his age at death as 30y (sic) 4m 14d, perhaps a misreading for 60y 4m 14d]: m Buxton 19 Feb 1786 ELIZABETH SANDS both of Buxton (VR), b Buxton 7 May 1769 dau of James & Lydia (Fall) Sands (VR) [see JAMES SANDS family, *Maine Families*, 3:244], d Standish 11 Apr 1866 (g.s., Littlefield cem). Theodore was a Revolutionary War soldier (MS&S, 15:660).

Children: births VR Buxton

  i James Sands, b 6 Oct 1786: d Athens 17 Apr 1865 ae 73y [or 78y] (g.s., Athens cem): m int Buxton 2 Oct 1810 Sarah Bacon (Charles A. Meserve, "Records of Births and Deaths in the Town of Buxton" [TS, MHS, 1891], p. 235), b Gorham 12 Jan 1791 dau of Timothy & Mary (Irish) Bacon (VR)

  ii Samuel, b 20 Aug 1789: living Jackson 1860 ae 71y (USC): m int Buxton 26 Jul 1814 Hannah White (Meserve, op. cit., p. 235), b Buxton 8 Nov 1793 dau of John & Sarah (____) White (VR), living Jackson 1860 ae 65y (USC)

  iii Lydia Sands, b 1 Nov 1791: d Gorham 22 Jan 1884 ae 92y (McLellan's *Gorham*, p. 813): m Buxton 1 Jul 1812 Greenleaf Clark Watson (Meserve, op. cit., p. 235), b Gorham 14 Mar 1786 son of John & Tabitha (Whitney) Watson (McLellan's *Gorham*, p. 810) [see JOHN WATSON family], d Gorham 18 Dec 1863 (ibid., p. 813)

  iv Elizabeth, b 13 Jul 1794: d Buxton 31 Jul 1794 (VR)

  v Abigail, b 4 Apr 1798: living Standish 1870 (USC): m Buxton 21 Feb 1825 William Manchester (Meserve, op. cit., p. 235), b Windham c1802, living Standish 1870 ae 68y (USC)

  vi Thomas, b 1 Nov 1800: he was probably the Thomas Thompson who d 24 Apr 1837 ae 37y 5m 24d and bur in Littlefield cem, Standish): m 5 Sep 1821 Rachel Steele (YCGSJ, 3 [1988]:73). He perhaps had a second wife named Rebecca, as Rebecca Thompson wife of Thomas Thompson, who d 19 Apr 1881 ae 84y 8m 2d, is bur next to him at Standish (g.s., Littlefield cem)

Dana A. Batchelder, 258 South Sea Avenue, West Yarmouth, MA 02673

Thorn, Lucy   * *
    Topsham, Lincoln County

LUCY (FREEMAN) THORN (widow of William Thorn), b Falmouth abt 1753 dau of Joshua & Patience (Rogers) Freeman (Albert J. Sears, *Early Families of Standish, Maine* [1991], p. 88, which gives prob incorrect date of birth of 1743, see discussion below): d Canton 21 Mar 1833 ae abt 90y [sic] (ibid.; g.s., Pine Grove cem): m Falmouth 19 Dec 1771 WILLIAM THORN (*Journals of Rev. Thomas Smith and the Rev. Samuel Deane* [1849], p. 331), b Topsham 18 Aug 1749 son of William & Martha (____) Thorn (VR), d Topsham 6 Jul 1777 ae 28y (VR). The inventory of William's estate was taken 30 Sep 1777 by James Hunter, William Malcom and Joseph Malcom of Topsham and included 85 acres of land and one-eighth part of a sloop (Lin Co Probate 2:61). In order to sell William's real estate, Lucy Thorn of Topsham, widow, on 29 Jan 1792 was appt guardian of Sarah Thorn, Thomas Thorn, Elizabeth Thorn and Martha Thorn, the children of William Thorn Jr., deceased (Lin Co Probate, 5:48–49). She took oath to the sale of the real estate on 15 Mar 1792 (Lin Co Probate, 5:49). After her husband's death, Lucy supported herself and her children "by selling timber off the farm to the ship builders in Bath" (1896 letter written by Orrin Thorn, grandson, in possession of submitter). In her later years, she lived with her son Thomas in Canton.

[Although Lucy's age at death, as given on her gravestone, would indicate a birth year of c1743, this would appear to be in error. Her brothers Reuben and William were baptized at Harwich MA in 1741 and 1743, respectively (Sears, op. cit., pp. 87–88), followed by the baptisms of other siblings at Falmouth: Hannah in 1745, Mary in 1746 and Elizabeth in 1752 (Marquis F. King, *Baptisms and Admission from the Records of the First Church in Falmouth* [1898], p. 69). Had Lucy been b bef 1753, her name should have been included in these baptismal records. A 1753 birth date would indicate she was ae 18y at the time of her marriage and that she was 4y younger than her husband. Additionally, Lucy related to her family that she was a "young girl" when the British burned Falmouth in Nov 1775 (Orrin Thorn letter, op. cit.).]

Children, b Topsham: births VR Topsham
   i   Sarah, b 8 Nov 1772: no information after guardianship in 1792
  ii   Thomas, b 17 Jan 1773 [sic, prob s/b 1774]: d Canton 7 May 1852 ae 78y (g.s., Pine Grove cem): of Bowdoinham when he m (1) cert Topsham 27 Jan 1800 Jane/Jenny Owen of Topsham (VR) [but she was called Jenny Foster on the m int Topsham dated 10 Jan 1800 (VR)]: of Lisbon when he m (2) cert Topsham 14 Feb 1812 Mary Jack (VR), b c Feb 1780, d Canton 5 Apr 1859 ae 79y 1m 16d (g.s., Pine Grove cem). That Thomas's 1st wife was an Owen would seem to be confirmed by the fact that they

named one child John Owen Thorn (Rev. Charles N. Sinnett, "Ancestor Thomas Thorne and Descendants" [TS, 1928, MSL], p. 10)
iii Elizabeth, b 4 Sep 1774 [sic, prob s/b 1775]: d Bowdoinham 2 Aug 1841 ae 65y (VR; g.s., Ridge Rd. cem): m Bowdoinham 23 Dec 1799 John White (Jessie Whitmore Patten Purdy, *A Memorial to My Grandmother Sarah Thorne White* [1908], p. 8), b Topsham 15 Feb 1776 son of John & Mary (Malcom) White (VR), d Bowdoinham 9 Aug 1862 ae 86y (VR; g.s., Ridge Rd. cem)
iv Martha, b 26 Jan 1778: d Richmond 12 Jul 1861 (Sinnett, op. cit., p. 8): m 24 Apr 1800 Dea. Joseph Ring (Oliver B. Clason, *History of Litchfield, Maine* [1897], p. 285)), b 12 Apr 1776 son of Daniel & Lydia (Savage) Ring (ibid.), d 27 Oct 1869 (Sinnett, op. cit., p. 8)

Mrs. Joyce E. Huntley, 1701 Algonquin Dr., Clearwater, FL 34615

Tibbits, Edward   44c   1 - 0 - 4 - 0 - 0
Sandy River, First Township, Lincoln County

EDWARD TIBBETTS, b Plaisted Hill, Gardiner 17 Jun 1762 son of Solomon & Elizabeth (Spearing) Tibbetts (May T. Jarvis, *Henry Tibbets of Dover, New Hampshire and Some of His Descendants*, [1940], 1:226) and bro of Abigail Tibbetts [see PELTON WARREN family]: d Litchfield Mar 1846 (Oliver B. Clason, *History of Litchfield, Maine* [1897], hereafter Clason, p. 353): m (1) Topsham 6 Jul 1784 SARAH DOUGLAS (VR), b Topsham 19 Feb 1763 dau of Andrew & Jane (Alexander) Douglas (VR; Clason, p. 104), d 10 Apr 1814 ae 32y [sic] (ibid., p. 353): m (2) 21 Aug 1814 ANNIE (TAYLOR) JOHNSON (ibid., pp. 349, 353), b 16 Mar 1770 dau of James & Sarah (White) Taylor and wid of John Johnson (ibid.), d 15 Oct 1865 ae 95y 7m (ibid., p. 353). Edward went to Litchfield with his father in 1774 settling on the shore of Cobbossee pond (ibid.).

Children by 1st wife Sarah Douglas: births VR Litchfield except as noted
i Sarah, b 2 Jun 1785: d Gardiner 3 Dec 1846 ae 61y 5m 10d (VR): m 20 Apr 1807 James Peacock (Clason, p. 353), b 14 Dec 1782 (Gardiner VR).
ii Mary, b 30 Mar 1787: d Plymouth 6 Dec 1864 (Clason, p. 353): m (1) 12 Apr 1809 Samuel Gatchell as his 2nd wife (ibid., p. 123), b Brunswick 15 Aug 1745 son of Capt. John Gatchell (ibid.), d Litchfield 1822 (ibid.): m (2) James Johnson (ibid., p. 353), b 5 Jun 1796 son of John & Annie (Taylor) Johnson (ibid., p. 193)
iii Charity, b 2 Apr 1789: m 19 Oct 1807 John Britt son of John Britt Sr (ibid., p. 61). They lived at Litchfield until 1836 and then moved to Plymouth ME (ibid.)

iv   Solomon, b 2 May 1791: killed by "the cars" at Augusta 22 Apr 1856 ae 64y (Augusta VR; Clason, p. 354): m 23 Sept 1816 Elizabeth Butler (ibid.), b 12 Feb 1798 dau of John & Margaret (Goodwin) Butler (ibid., p. 75), d 1845 (ibid., p. 354)

v   James, b 7 May 1793: d Augusta 28 Jun 1869 ae 79y 3m [sic] (VR): m 22 Dec 1814 Sarah Gatchell (Clason, p. 354), b 22 Nov 1794 dau of John Simmons & Hannah (Tibbetts) Gatchell (ibid., p. 124), d Augusta 13 Dec 1870 ae 77y (VR). James lived at Litchfield several years, then moved to Piscataquis County and later to Gardiner (Clason, p. 354)

vi   Edward Jr., b c1795: m 13 Oct 1832 Judith Judkins (Clason, p. 354), b 27 Mar 1811 dau of Samuel & Zilpha (Hall) (Babb) Judkins (ibid., p. 194). They lived at Shirley and later moved out west (ibid.). [Note that the Litchfield VR gives Edward's birth as 30 Apr 1800, however in the 1850 USC at Monson he was listed as ae 55y]

vii   William, b 4 Feb 1796: d at sea (Clason, p. 354): m int Augusta 14 Jun 1817 Nancy Britt (VR)

viii   Charlotte, b 19 May 1798: d 1869 (Augusta VR): m Abner Towns (Clason, p. 354), b c1795, d Augusta 17 May 1873 ae 78y (VR)

ix   John, b c1800 [note that the Litchfield VR state he was b in Jul 1804, but census records and his g.s. indicate an 1800 birth date]: d Shirley 7 Aug 1886 ae 86y (g.s., Shirley cem): m int Augusta 17 Sep 1825 Asenath/Asenith Britt (VR), b c1796, d Shirley 13 Jan 1872 ae 76y (g.s., Shirley cem)

x   Andrew, b 8 Apr 1803: m 14 Mar 1824 Judith Stevens (Clason, p. 354), b 15 Feb 1805 dau of John & Sally (Huntington) Stevens (ibid., p. 343), d Gardiner 27 Aug 1849 ae 43y (VR). They lived in West Gardiner

xi   Robert, b 18 Oct 1808: m 4 Apr 1831 Nancy Gray (Clason, p. 354)

Child by 2nd wife Annie (Taylor) Johnson: birth VR Litchfield

xii   Eliza, b 2 Jun 1815: d 2 Sep 1887 ae 72y (Clason, p. 146): m Dec 1838 Levi C. Gray (ibid.), b 6 Dec 1819 son of Stephen & Catherine (Cooper) Gray (ibid.)

Maxine B. Hughes, 265 Main St., Dexter, ME 04930

Tilton, Cornelias   50a   1 - 3 - 4 - 0 - 0
    Washington Town, Lincoln County
[and prob counted again as]
Titton, Cornelius   50c   1 - 3 - 3 - 0 - 0
    Winslow Town, with its Adjacents, Lincoln County

CORNELIUS TILTON, b Chilmark, Martha's Vineyard MA 1738 son of John & Sarah (Gibbs) Tilton (Charles E. Banks, *The History of Martha's Vineyard, Dukes County, Massachusetts* [1925], 3:473): d Winslow 1839 ae 101y (ibid., 3:476) [note that Malcolm Tilton, *Ancestry and Descendants of Alfred Tilton* (1986) gives his death date as 3 Oct 1835]: m 16 Feb 1780 JEDIDAH PEASE (Banks, op. cit., 3:476), b 1759 dau of Fortunatus & Elizabeth (____) Pease (ibid., 3:397), d Oakland 3 Oct 1835 (ibid., 3:476). Cornelius was apparently doublecounted in the 1790 census as were several of the heads-of-household listed at the ends of Washington and Winslow towns in the published census on pp. 50a and 50c.

Children, first 5 b Martha's Vineyard: births VR Belgrade
- i Cornelius, b 27 Jan 1781: m 17 Dec 1801 Temperance Merchant of Sidney (Belgrade VR), b Yarmouth MA 6 Sep 1785 dau of Edward & Data (____) Merchant (Tilton, op. cit.), d May 1853 (ibid.; Belgrade VR)
- ii Jedida/Judith, b 4 Oct 1782: d Mercer 4 Apr 1862 (g.s., Mercer Corner cem): m Belgrade 26 Mar 1801 Otis Richardson (VR), b Attleborough MA 6 Dec 1780 son of Henry & Olive (Blackinton) Richardson (John A. Vinton, *The Richardson Memorial...* [1876]), d Mercer 15 Jan 1878 (g.s., Mercer Corner cem). They res Mercer in 1806
- iii Persis, b 8 May 1784: m Sidney 15 Jul 1802 William Stedman (VR), b Sidney 27 Feb 1781 son of James & Polly (____) Stedman (VR; see *History of Sidney, Maine 1792–1992* [Bicentennial Committee, 1992], p. 18)
- iv John, b 20 Dec 1785: d Orangeville NH 3 Nov 1863 (Tilton, op. cit.): m (1) Elizabeth Butter (ibid.): m (2) Amarilla Doty (ibid.). He lived at Wyoming NY
- v Elizabeth, b 30 Aug 1787: m Sidney 28 Sep 1808 James Weeks of Sidney (VR) [m int Belgrade 26 Aug 1808 (VR)]
- vi Sidney, b 15 Jan 1789: m int Belgrade 15 Sep 1811 Charles Bliss of Mercer (Belgrade VR)
- vii William, b 14 Jul 1790: d Olive Twsp, Noble Co OH 7 Feb 1892 ae 101½y (recs of Patricia Smith, Ada, OK): m Belgrade 1820 Zeporah Clark (VR), b Belgrade 12 Aug 1793 dau of Judge Sherebiah & Asenath (Linnell) Clark (VR)
- viii Nathaniel, b 20 Oct 1792: d Belgrade 18 Apr 1793 (VR)
- ix Sarah, b 20 Jun 1794: d in Illinois
- x Jeremiah, b 20 Jun 1796: m Belgrade 15 Aug 1819 Hannah Morrill (VR), b Dearborn 9 Sep 1799 dau of Peaslee Jr. & Nancy (Macomber) Morrill (VR)
- xi Love, b 29 Mar 1798: m int Belgrade 29 Oct 1818 David Taylor (VR), b 16 Apr 1794 son of Samuel & Elizabeth (Crowell) Taylor (Belgrade VR)
- xii Rhoda, b 28 Aug 1801
- xiii Clarissa, b 20 Jul 1804: m ____ Holmes (Tilton, op. cit.)

Carol F. Nye, RFD 1, Box 388, Belgrade, ME 04917

Thompson, Rev. John   55c   2 - 3 - 5 - 0 - 0
Berwick Town, York County

Rev. **JOHN TOMPSON**, b Scarboro 3 Oct 1740 and bp Scarboro 1st Church 12 Oct 1740 son of Rev. William & Anna (Hubbard) Tompson (*Sibley's Harvard Graduates*, hereafter *Sibley*, 16:247; MHGR, 1:166): d So. Berwick 21 Dec 1828 ae 88y "in the 61st year of his ministry" (John E. Frost & Joseph C. Anderson II, *Vital Records of Berwick, South Berwick and North Berwick, Maine to the Year 1892* [1993], hereafter VR, p. 545; g.s., Old Fields cem): m (1) Pearsontown [Standish] 22 Nov 1768 SARAH SMALL (*Sibley*, 16:248; Albert J. Sears, *Early Families of Standish, Maine* [1991], hereafter Sears, p. 286), b Somersworth NH 14 Apr 1748 dau of Joshua & Susannah (Kennard) Small of Kittery, Scarboro and Limington (Robert L. Taylor, *Early Families of Limington, Maine* [1991], p. 298), d Berwick 30 Aug 1783 (*Sibley*, 16:249): m (2) 9 Feb 1784 SARAH (ALLEN) MORRILL of Biddeford wid of Capt. Samuel Morrill (*Sibley*, 16:248) [m cert Berwick 9 Feb 1784 (VR, p. 22)], b Salisbury MA 14 Feb 1743 and bp 2nd Church of Salisbury MA 27 Mar 1743 dau of Elisha Allen of Salisbury MA and Biddeford (Sears, p. 287; David W. Hoyt, *The Old Families of Salisbury and Amesbury, Massachusetts* [1981], p. 438), d So. Berwick 24 Aug 1825 ae 83y (g.s., Old Fields cem). Rev. Tompson graduated from Harvard College in 1765 and afterwards studied theology with the Rev. Dr. Edward Wigglesworth of Cambridge MA (Sears, p. 286; *Sibley*, 16:248). On 26 Oct 1768, he was ordained as the first pastor of the Congregational church at Pearsontown where he remained until 1783 (Sears, p. 286). On 7 May 1783, he was installed as pastor of the First Church of Berwick, taking the place of Rev. Jacob Foster who had resigned 6 years earlier (Berwick 1st Church recs, on microfilm at MHS). He was pastor at Berwick [later South Berwick] for more than 40 years until he died. In his will dated 7 Mar 1826 and probated 2 Feb 1829, he named his sons William, Edward, Samuel, John S., William Allen, and Joseph, his dau Sarah Hayman, and 3 daus of his deceased dau Anna Goodwin (York Co Probate, 39:313).

Children by 1st wife, Sarah Small, first 7 b Pearsontown: Sears, pp. 287–88
  i   William, b 17 October 1769: d Standish 8 Jan 1859 ae 89y (Sears, p. 287): of Standish when he m Berwick 31 Mar 1793 Hannah Goodwin (VR, p. 135), bp Berwick 1st Church 23 Jul 1775 dau of Dea. Dominicus & Elizabeth (Littlefield) (Perkins) Goodwin (NEHGR, 82 [1928]:504; John Hayes Goodwin, "Daniel Goodwin of Ancient Kittery, Maine and His Descendants" [TS, Goodwin Family Assoc., 1985], hereafter "Daniel Goodwin," p. 29), d Standish 19 Oct 1831 (Sears, p. 287)
  ii Edward, b 18 Dec 1771: d Standish 29 Jan 1834 ae 64y (Sears, p. 288) [an account of the Sewall family in the York VR gives his death date as 19 Jan 1834 (Lester M. Bragdon & John E. Frost, *Vital Records of York,*

Maine [1992], hereafter York VR, p. 107)]: m Sarah Sewall (York VR, p. 107), b York 8 Jun 1776 dau of Capt. Joseph & Mercy (Sewall) Sewall (ibid., p. 106), d 6 Oct 1843 (ibid., p. 107) [Sears, p. 288, gives d 5 Oct 1843]

iii Samuel, b 10 Oct 1773: m Scarboro 1st Church 18 Jun 1795 Mary Lancaster (MHGR, 3:147). He went to live with his uncle, Justice William Tompson, in Scarboro and continued to live there (Sears, p. 288). Samuel had received from his father "a deed of moiety of my deceased brother's [i.e. William's] estate" and this constituted Samuel's full share of his father's estate (will, op. cit.)

iv Sarah, b 14 Jul 1775: d So. Berwick 18 Mar 1836 ae 61y (g.s., Old Fields cem): m Berwick 20 Aug 1809 Edward Payne Hayman (VR, p. 146), b c1770, d So. Berwick 25 Dec 1831 ae 61y (g.s., Old Fields cem)

v Anna, b 15 Mar 1777: d So. Berwick 23 May 1818 ae 41y (g.s., Old Fields cem): m Berwick 21 Mar 1802 Maj. Ichabod Goodwin (VR, p. 141), b Berwick 10 Jun 1770 son of Gen. Ichabod & Mary (Wallingford) Goodwin (VR, p. 283), d So. Berwick 23 Jun 1814 ae 44y (g.s., Old Fields cem)

vi Joseph, b 21 Jul 1778: d Mar 1859 ae 81y (Sears, p. 288): m (1) cert Berwick 3 Nov 1800 Betsey Clements of Somersworth NH (Berwick VR, p. 46) dau of Capt. Elisha & Mary (Waldron) Clements (Gideon T. Ridlon, *Saco Valley Settlements and Families* [1895], p. 1176), d 4 May 1819 (Sears, p. 288): he was of Frankfort when he m (2) Belfast 17 Feb 1820 Mary Durham of Belfast (VR) who d Mar 1864 (Sears, p. 288). Joseph, accompanied by his first wife, Betsey, and her parents, emigrated to Frankfort where he lived as a farmer (Ridlon, op. cit., p. 1177)

vii Mary, b 13 Aug 1781: d So. Berwick 28 Mar 1808 ae 27y (g.s., Old Fields cem) ["of tuberculosis" (Sears, p. 288)]

viii John Storer, b Berwick 5 Aug 1783 and bp Berwick 1st Church 5 Aug 1783 (NEHGR, 82 [1928]:505): d York 6 Nov 1863 ae 80y 3m (York VR, p. 512): m cert Berwick 8 Apr 1809 Susan Sewall of York (Berwick VR, p. 59), bp York 1st Church 8 Oct 1786 dau of Samuel & Hannah (Moulton) Sewall (YCGSJ, 5 [1990]:1:18; parents' marr in York VR, p. 156), d York 26 Apr 1864 ae 77y 6m (York VR, p. 512)

Children by 2nd wife, Sarah (Allen) Morrill: Sears, p. 288

ix Betsey, b Berwick 19 May 1785 and bp Berwick 1st Church 22 May 1785 (NEHGR, 82 [1928]:505): d So. Berwick 10 Jun 1817 ae 32y (g.s., Old Fields cem, buried alongside her parents): m So. Berwick 18 Dec 1814 Andrew Goodwin (VR, p. 419), b Berwick 7 May 1784 son of Gen. Ichabod & Mary (Wallingford) Goodwin and bro of Ichabod above ("Daniel Goodwin," pp. 29a, 30, 66, 66a), d So. Berwick 14 Nov 1843 ae 60y (g.s., Old Fields cem). He m (2) Berwick 4 Oct 1818 Betsey Wallingford (VR, p. 154) x William Allen, b Berwick 18 Apr 1787 and bp Berwick 1st Church 22 Apr 1787 (NEHGR, 82 [1928]:505): d So. Berwick 3 Oct 1835 ae 49y (g.s., Old Fields cem): m Portsmouth NH South Church 22 Nov 1813 Anna Maria Adams of Portsmouth NH (NEHGR, 83 [1929]:21)

Joseph C. Anderson II, 5337 Del Roy Drive, Dallas, TX 75229

Wardwell, Daniel, jun   30c   1 - 0 - 2 - 0 - 0
Penobscot Town, Hancock County

DANIEL WARDWELL Jr., b York 11 Jan 1760 [sic] (VR Penobscot) and bp 1st Parish York 11 Mar 1767 son of Daniel & Mercy (_____) Wardwell ("First Parish, York: Baptisms 1750–1800," YCGSJ 6 [1990]:1:16) [see DANIEL WARDWELL family, *Maine Families*, 1:280 and 3:316 in Addendum—note that Daniel Sr. married (1) 6 Jan 1755 Sarah Staples, for whom a death record has not been found; neither has a marriage record been found for him and Mercy]: d Penobscot 21 Jul 1844 (VR; Minnie H. Wardwell, "The Genealogical Record of Thomas Wardell and his Descendants in America since 1633" [TS, MHS, 1956], p. 12): m c1788 (based on birth of 1st child) MARY HUTCHINS, b Penobscot 14 Oct 1770 dau of Charles & Mary (Perkins) Hutchins (VR; Thomas Allen Perkins, *Jacob Perkins of Wells, Maine and His Descendants* [1947], p. 11), d Penobscot 25 Jan 1835 (VR; "Thomas Wardell," op. cit.). Daniel prob moved with his parents to the Penobscot area c1774. He was a shipmaster and privateer on the ship TRYPHENA in the Rev War (Fisher's *Soldiers*, p. 825).

Children, all b Penobscot: births VR Penobscot
i   Abigail, b 24 Dec 1789: d Penobscot 16 Dec 1855 (VR): m int Penobscot 8 Nov 1806 Benjamin Varnum (VR), b Penobscot 3 Feb 1792 son of Gershom & Dolley (Moore) Varnum (VR)
ii   Joel, b 20 Jul 1791: d Plattsburg NY 1814 as a soldier in the War of 1812 ("Thomas Wardell," p. 12)
iii   Sarah, b 4 Jun 1793: d 4 Jun 1794 (VR)
iv   Stephen, b 3 Jun 1795: d aft 1850 (USC): m Penobscot 4 Dec 1817 his cousin Mercy Hutchins (VR), b 27 Feb 1800 dau of William & Mercy (Wardwell) Hutchins [see WILLIAM HUTCHINS family, *Maine Families*, 1:158]. Stephen was an ordained minister of the Methodist Church, as were also 3 of his sons
v   Daniel, b 6 Jun 1797: d Penobscot 5 Sep 1798 (VR)
vi   Sylvia, b 14 May 1799: d Penobscot 1888 (g.s., Jeremiah Wardwell cem): m Penobscot 2 Jun 1817 her cousin Robert Wardwell (VR), b Penobscot 7 Dec 1796 son of Jeremiah & Elizabeth (Banks) Wardwell (VR) [see

JEREMIAH WARDWELL family], d Penobscot 1877 (g.s., Jeremiah Wardwell cem)
- vii Taylor, b 18 Apr 1801: d 19 Jun 1860 ae 59y (VR): m 26 Jan 1824 [int Penobscot 16 Nov 1823 (VR)] Sarah Dunbar
- viii Mary, b 7 Aug 1803: m Penobscot 30 Aug 1828 Rev. Joseph Smith of Wayne (Alice MacDonald Long, *Marriage Records of Hancock County, Maine Prior to 1892* [1992], p. 17)
- ix Irene, b 20 Mar 1806: d Penobscot 14 Jun 1826 (VR)
- x Daniel, b Aug 1808: d Penobscot 18 May 1818 after a fall from a horse (VR)
- xi Sally, b Dec 1810: d Penobscot Jan 1813 (VR)
- xii Loraine, b Dec 1813: d Penobscot 18 Oct 1813 [sic] (VR)
- xiii Joel, b 26 Apr 1817: d off Cape Cod MA Apr 1838 ae 22y after a fall from the bowsprit of the ROBERT MORRIS (Rev. Charles N. Sinnett, "The Wardwell Family of Mass. and Maine" [MS, Ft. Wayne IN Library, c1910])

Marjorie Wardwell Otten, 201 4th St. #222, Del Mar, CA 92014

Wardwell, Jeremiah 30c 1 - 3 - 4 - 1 - 0
Penobscot Town, Hancock County

JEREMIAH WARDWELL, b York 19 Dec 1756 (VR Penobscot) and bp 1st Parish York 8 May 1757 son of Daniel & Sarah (Staples) Wardwell ("First Parish, York: Baptisms 1750–1800," YCGSJ 6 [1990]:1:15) [see DANIEL WARDWELL family, *Maine Families*, 1:280 and 3:316 in Addendum]: d Penobscot 25 Oct 1825 (VR) ae 68y 2m (g.s., Jeremiah Wardwell cem): m Penobscot 14 Sep 1779 ELIZABETH/BETSY BANKS (VR), b Castine 5 Jun 1764 dau of Aaron Jr. & Mary (Perkins) Banks (VR Penobscot; Thomas Allen Perkins, *Jacob Perkins of Wells, Maine and His Descendants* [1947], p. 11) [see AARON BANKS Jr. family]. Jeremiah prob moved to the Penobscot area with his parents c1774. He was a privateer with his half-brother Daniel on the ship TRYPHENA in the Rev War (Fisher's *Soldiers*, p. 825). He engaged in real estate, lumbering and trading. He built the first Methodist Church east of the Penobscot in 1801. In 1797 he was appointed Colonel by Gov. Samuel Adams (Rev. Charles N. Sinnett, "The Wardwell Family of Mass. and Maine" [TS, Fort Wayne IN Library, c1910]).

Children, all b Penobscot: births VR Penobscot
- i William, b 23 Aug 1780: d 26 Aug 1830 (VR; Minnie H. Wardwell, "The Genealogical Record of Thomas Wardell and his Descendants in America

since 1633" [TS, MHS, 1956]): m Penobscot June 1798 [int Penobscot 28 Apr 1798 (VR)] his cousin Deborah Littlefield (VR), bp Wells 13 Apr 1777 dau of Stephen & Deborah (Perkins) Littlefield ("Records of the First Church of Wells, Maine," NEHGR 76 [1922]:185; *Jacob Perkins of Wells,* op. cit., p. 11)

ii Eliakim, b 29 Jun 1782: d Penobscot 18 Aug 1840 (VR): m Penobscot 23 Jun 1804 his cousin Catherine Reidhead (VR), b Castine 23 Feb 1784 dau of William & Olive (Banks) Reidhead ("Descent Chart of Robert Wardwell Moodie," *Orange County [CA] Genealogical Society Quarterly,* 7:101) [see AARON BANKS Jr. family], d Feb 1782 (ibid.)

iii Ruth, b 15 Jun 1785: d 18 Aug 1840 ("Thomas Wardwell," op. cit.): m int Penobscot 29 Nov 1807 Amos Perkins (VR)

iv Ebenezer, b 22 Apr 1787: m (1) int Penobscot 4 May 1811 Elizabeth Newbury (VR) who d Penobscot 19 Aug 1815 (VR): m (2) bef 10 Jul 1824 (when their 1st child was born) Joanna Robbins (Ebenezer Wardwell family rec in Penobscot VR), b Vinalhaven 19 Nov 1802 (ibid.). Ebenezer was a War of 1812 soldier (pension #SO-26184)

v Anna, b 7 Apr 1790: d Penobscot 16 Sep 1876 ae 80y [sic] 5m 7d (g.s., Capt. Daniel Wardwell cem): m Penobscot 31 Oct 1813 Daniel Wardwell (VR), b Penobscot 1 Dec 1786 son of Josiah & Hannah (Westcott) Wardwell (VR) [see JOSIAH WARDWELL family], d Penobscot 30 Nov 1851 ae 64y 11m 15d (g.s., Capt. Daniel Wardwell cem)

vi Elizabeth, b 7 Sep 1792: d Penobscot 5 Apr 1826 (VR): m Penobscot 25 Dec 1816 Cyrus Buker (VR)

vii Joseph, b 10 Oct 1794: d 10 May 1819 when lost at sea aboard the schooner ADEBARRAH of Penobscot (VR; "Thomas Wardwell," op. cit.): m Penobscot 6 Apr 1819 Hannah Atkins (VR)

viii Robert, b 7 Dec 1796: d Penobscot 1877 (g.s., Jeremiah Wardwell cem): m Penobscot 2 Jun 1817 Sylvia Wardwell (VR), b 14 May 1799 dau of Daniel & Mary (Hutchins) Wardwell [see DANIEL WARDWELL Jr. family]. Robert was a soldier in the War of 1812 (pension #WO-18314)

ix Lewis, b 1 Feb 1799: d Penobscot 4 Jan 1845 (VR): m (1) Penobscot 15 Aug 1819 Olive Wardwell (VR), b Penobscot 11 Dec 1790 dau of Josiah & Hannah (Westcott) Wardwell (VR) [see JOSIAH WARDWELL family], d bef 1830: m (2) int Penobscot 6 Mar 1830 Abigail Wardwell (VR), b Penobscot 9 May 1797 sis of his 1st wife Olive (VR)

x Seneca, b 29 Jan 1802: m 2 Dec 1824 Hannah Snow [m int Penobscot 21 Nov 1824 (VR)]

xi Vespasian, b 3 Apr 1804: d Penobscot 23 Jan 1876 ae 71y 9m (g.s., Leroy Wardwell cem): m (1) int Penobscot Aug 1828 Lucy Dunbar (VR) who d Penobscot 25 Aug 1868 ae 59y 11m 9d (g.s., Leroy Wardwell cem): m (2) Penobscot 13 Dec 1868 Joanna (Grindle) Wardwell (VR), b 21 Jan

1812 dau of John & Joanna (Hutchins) Grindle (Penobscot VR) and wid of Capt. Elizakim Wardwell (ibid.)
xii Mercy, b 4 Dec 1806: d Penobscot 30 Oct 1838 (VR): m 22 Oct 1827 Uriel H. Macomber [m int Penobscot 15 Sep 1827 (VR)]

Marjorie Wardwell Otten, 201 4th St. #222, Del Mar, CA 92014

Wardwell, Josiah   30c   1 - 1 - 4 - 0 - 0
Penobscot Town, Hancock County

JOSIAH WARDWELL, b York 26 Jan 1755 (Penobscot VR): m Penobscot c1786 HANNAH WESTCOTT (VR; Minnie H. Wardwell, "The Genealogical Record of Thomas Wardell and his Descendants in America since 1633" [TS, MHS, 1956], p. 7), b Penobscot 9 Oct 1766 (VR) dau of Samuel & Olive (Perkins) Westcott (Thomas A. Perkins, *Jacob Perkins of Wells, Maine and His Descendants* [1947], p. 9). During the Rev War, Josiah was impressed on board an English man-of-war and was kept there for 2 years. He escaped by swimming to the shore (Rev. Charles N. Sinnett, "The Wardwell Family of Mass. and Maine" [TS, Fort Wayne IN Library, c1910]).

[Several published sources have claimed that Josiah was a son of Daniel Wardwell of York by his first wife, Sarah Staples. This was probably based on the fact that Josiah named his first son and daughter Daniel and Sally (supposedly for his parents) and his second son and daughter Samuel and Olive (for his parents-in-law). Daniel Wardwell filed intentions at York on 24 Jan 1755 to marry Sarah Staples, only 2 days before the recorded birth of Josiah (Lester M. Bragdon & John E. Frost, *Vital Records of York, Maine* [1992], p. 140). Nine months later, on 26 Oct 1755, Daniel and Sarah brought their son Eliakim in for baptism at the York 1st Parish Church following Sarah's own baptism ("First Parish, York: Baptisms 1750–1800," YCGSJ, 6 [1990]:1:15). All of Daniel's later children, except the last, were also baptized at this church, but they included no son named Josiah. The only other adult Wardwell males living in York at the time of Josiah's birth were Daniel's older brothers Joseph (1718–1782) and Jeremiah (see JEREMIAH WARDWELL family). Little is known of Joseph other than that he had a wife Mary, but he would seem to be the best candidate to be Josiah's father.]

Children: births for all except Charles in VR Penobscot
    i   Daniel, b 1 Dec 1786: d Penobscot 30 Nov 1851 ae 64y 11m 15d (g.s., Capt. Daniel Wardwell cem): m Penobscot 31 Oct 1813 Anna Wardwell

(VR), b Penobscot 7 Apr 1790 dau of Jeremiah & Elizabeth (Banks) Wardwell [see JEREMIAH WARDWELL family], d Penobscot 16 Sep 1876 ae 80y 5m 7d (g.s., Capt. Daniel Wardwell cem)
ii Sally, b 22 Feb 1788: d Penobscot 28 Sep 1866 ae 78y 9m (g.s., Capt. Daniel Wardwell cem): m Penobscot 20 Oct 1806 her cousin Charles Hutchins (VR), b Penobscot 3 Oct 1786 son of William & Mercy (Wardwell) Hutchins (VR), d 17 Aug 1845 ae 59y (g.s., Capt. Daniel Wardwell cem) [see WILLIAM HUTCHINS family, *Maine Families*, 1:158; see also Addendum]
iii Olive, b 11 Dec 1790: d bef 1830 when her husband remarried: m Penobscot 15 Aug 1819 Lewis Wardwell (VR), b Penobscot 1 Feb 1799 bro of Anna above. He m (2) her sis Abigail below
iv Hannah, b 10 May 1792: d Penobscot 22 Nov 1858 (Jonathan Varnum family rec in Penobscot VR): m int Penobscot 21 Mar 1809 William Wescott Jr. (VR) whom she may not have actually married and who d shortly thereafter [see WILLIAM WESTCOTT Jr. family, *Maine Families*, 3:298]: m Penobscot as Hannah "Wardwell" 28 Dec 1811 Jonathan Varnum (VR), b Penobscot 30 Apr 1788 son of Gershom & Dolley (Moore) Varnum, d Penobscot 11 May 1860 (VR)
v Samuel, b 12 Dec 1795: d Penobscot 1 May 1867 (VR; "Thomas Wardell," op. cit.): m (1) Penobscot 6 Sep 1819 Abigail Wight (VR), b 27 Jun 1799 dau of Edward & Hannah (Perkins) Wight (Penobscot VR), d 12 Jun 1854 (Perkins, op. cit., p. 25): m (2) 1 Apr 1860 Alice Beal (War of 1812 pension #WC-30171)
vi Abigail, b 9 May 1797: m (1) int Penobscot 6 Mar 1830 her cousin Lewis Wardwell (VR) bro of Anna above and widower of Abigail's sis Olive: m (2) Penobscot 5 May 1853 Stephen Perkins as his 3rd wife (VR)
vii Charles, b 1799 (Ralph S. Wardwell, "Genealogy of the Wardwell Family" [TS, 1943]: m 8 Jul 1833 Mary Leach (ibid.)

Marjorie Wardwell Otten, 201 4th St. #222, Del Mar, CA 92014

Warren, Petten   43a   1 - 2 - 4 - 0 - 0
Pittston Town, Lincoln County

PELTON WARREN, m Hallowell 25 Dec 1769 [as "Patta" Warren] ABIGAIL TIBBETTS (VR) dau of Solomon & Elizabeth (Spearing) Tibbetts (J. W. Hanson, *History of Gardiner, Pittston and West Gardiner, Maine* [1852]; May Tibbetts Jarvis, *Henry Tibbetts of Dover, New Hampshire and Some of His Descendants* [1940], 1:226) and sister of Edward Tibbetts [see EDWARD

TIBBETTS family]. The first name of this man has caused confusion. Hanson, in his *History of Gardiner*, called him Pelatiah whereas primary records render his name Pelton, Petton, Petten or Patta. It is believed that Pelton is correct. Pelton and Abigail have the distinction of being the first family in the area to utilize the services of Martha Ballard, Hallowell's famous midwife. Writing in her diary on 15 January 1796 following one of her deliveries, Martha noted: "This is the 612th Birth I have attended at Since ye year 1777. The first I assisted was the wife of Petton [sic] Warrin in July 1778" (Robert R. & Cynthia M. McCausland, Editors, *The Diary of Martha Ballard 1785–1812* [1992], p. 360). Pelton's wife, Abigail, was murdered 18 Oct 1794 by Henry McCausland who "suddenly attacked her with a knife while in attendance at the bed of her sick mother" (James W. North, *The History of Augusta, Maine* [repr 1981], p. 494; *Diary of Martha Ballard*, op. cit., p. 314). [For a detailed account of the murder, see North's *History of Augusta*, pp. 337–38.] After his wife's murder, Pelton is not seen again in Maine census records although many of his children remained in the Kennebec region.

[One Pelton Warren was born at Stoughton MA 10 Feb 1740 son of Jonathan & Christian (Pelton) Warren (VR; J. M. Pelton, *Genealogy of the Pelton Family in America* [1892], p. 30–31). While there was no marriage nor death recorded for this Pelton in the Stoughton MA vital records, neither has any evidence been found indicating he was the same man who later lived in Pittston.]

Children: all but Sarah given in *History of Gardiner*, op. cit.
  i   Abigail, m William Sloman (*History of Gardiner*, op. cit.)
  ii   Hannah, prob bp 16 Aug 1772 ("Journal of Jacob Bailey," [TS, Wiscasset Public Library]): m _____ Pratt (*History of Gardiner*, op. cit.)
  iii poss Sarah, bp 13 Jun 1773 ("Journal of Jacob Bailey")
  iv   William Gardiner, b Hallowell 14 Dec 1774 (VR) [a William Gardiner Warren was bp 1 Feb 1774 ("Journal of Jacob Bailey"), the same if either birth or baptismal date is wrong]: d Gardiner betw 20 Dec 1838 and 15 Jan 1839, the dates when his will was written and probated (Ken Co Probate W-5): m Pittston 30 Nov 1797 Margaret/Peggy Marson (VR), b Pittston 12 May 1769 dau of Abner Marson of Pittston (Hallowell VR), d Gardiner 21 Apr 1845 ae 75y 4m (VR)
  v   Elizabeth/Betsey, b Pittston 29 Aug 1778 (VR), possibly the first child delivered in the Kennebec region by Martha Ballard, the diarist, although Martha remembered the date of birth as July 1778: d Pittston 26 Feb 1849 (VR): m Pittston 17 Nov 1795 Dennis Gould (VR), bp Kittery 21 Feb 1770 son of Joseph & Ruth (Remick) Gould (Joseph P. Thompson, "Kittery, Maine Second Church Records" [TS, MHS], p. 87; Everett S. Stackpole, *Old Kittery and Her Families* [1903], p. 463) [see JOSEPH GOOLD family, *Maine Families*, 3:90–91], d Pittston 4 Feb 1852 (VR)

- vi John, b c1787: d Turner 25 Nov 1846 (*History of Gardiner*, op. cit.): m c1805 Mary Chase who d 18 Jan 1830 (ibid.)
- vii James, b 1789: d 1829 (*History of Gardiner*, op. cit.)
- viii Cynthia, b c1790: m int Gardiner 24 May 1807 Enoch Tibbetts (VR)
- ix Fanny, b c1792: m (1) John Coombs (*History of Gardiner*, op. cit.): m (2) ____ Bartol (ibid.)
- x Charlotte, b c1794: m (1) James Smith (*History of Gardiner*, op. cit.): m (2) ____ Brown (ibid.)

Janet S. Seitz, 11521 Upper Sunny Circle, Eagle River, AK 99577-7414

Watson, John   19b   2 - 3 - 7 - 0 - 0
Gorham and Scarborough Towns, Cumberland County

JOHN WATSON, b Gorham 23 Sep 1741 son of Eliphalet & Elizabeth (Phinney) Watson (VR; McLellan's *Gorham*, pp. 807–9): d Gorham 26 Oct 1834 ae 93y (VR): m Gorham 5 Dec 1765 TABITHA WHITNEY (VR), b Kittery 16 Mar 1745/6 dau of Nathaniel & Hannah (Day) Whitney (VR) [see NATHANIEL WHITNEY family, *Maine Families*, 3:306], d Gorham 13 Sep 1831 ae 86y (VR). John was a Rev War soldier (MS&S, 16:711). When he filed for a pension at Gorham 31 Jul 1832, he stated he was ae 91y and had lived at Gorham when he enlisted (Rev War pension #S17186).

Children: births VR Gorham
- i Mercy, b 15 Oct 1766: d Gorham 18 Oct 1769 (VR)
- ii Martha, b 22 Apr 1769: d Buxton (McLellan's *Gorham*, p. 464): m Gorham 12 Jun 1788 David Davis (VR), b Gorham 20 Oct 1764 son of Prince & Sarah (Colman) Davis (VR; McLellan's *Gorham*, p. 463), d Buxton 29 Mar 1847 ae 82y 6m (John E. Frost, "Buxton (Maine) Record Book" [TS, MHS, 1968], p. 69)
- iii Edmund, b 17 Jan 1772: d Gorham 13 Dec 1847 ae 76y (McLellan's *Gorham*, p. 813): m Buxton 26 Jun 1797 Betsey Cressey of Gorham (Charles A. Meserve, "Records of Births and Deaths in the Town of Buxton" [TS, MHS, 1891], p. 69), b Gorham 31 Jan 1775 dau of John & Susanna (MacDonald) Cressey (VR; McLellan's *Gorham*, p. 449), d Gorham 1 Jan 1838 (ibid., p. 813)
- iv Colman Phinney, b 23 Feb 1774: d Harrison 2 Apr 1849 (Moulton, Sampson & Fernald, *Centennial History of Harrison, Maine* [1909], p. 690): m (1) Gorham 25 Jul 1802 Elizabeth Frost (VR), b Gorham 28 Feb 1782 dau of Nathaniel & Mary (Berry) Frost (VR; McLellan's *Gorham*, p. 505),

d Gorham Jul 1808 ae 26y (ibid., p. 813): m (2) 13 Jun 1847 Paulina Tuttle (Moulton et al., op. cit., p. 690), b ME c1799, living Harrison 1850 ae 51y (USC)
- v   Miriam, b 24 Dec 1776: d 1795 ae 19y after the birth of her dau Betsey (Albert Sears, *Early Families of Standish, Maine* [1991], p. 133): m Buxton 19 Sep 1793 Stephen Murch (Meserve, op. cit., p. 80), b Buxton 12 Apr 1770 son of Daniel & Mary (Simpson) Murch (ibid.; Sears, op. cit., p. 177), d 15 Aug 1867 (McLellan's *Gorham*, p. 695)
- vi   Tabitha, b 16 May 1779: d Waterville 27 Mar 1868 in her 92nd y (McLellan's *Gorham*, p. 759): m Gorham 5 Jan 1797 Josiah Shaw (VR), bp 31 Jul 1774 son of Josiah & Rebecca (Cox) Shaw (DAR Application #53202; McLellan's *Gorham*, p. 758), d Gorham 7 Nov 1852 ae 78y (ibid., p. 759)
- vii   Molly, b 9 Apr 1781
- viii   Sally, b 19 Mar 1784: d 7 Oct 1749 ae 65y (McLellan's *Gorham*, p. 442): m Gorham 9 Dec 1802 David Cobb (VR), b Barnstable MA 17 Jun 1778 son of David & Lucy (Bickford) Cobb (Isaac Cobb, "Early History and Genealogy of the Cobb Family in New England" [TS, MHS, n.d.]; McLellan's *Gorham*, p. 442), d Gorham 27 Sep 1837 ae 59y (ibid., p. 442)
- ix   Greenleaf Clark, b 14 Mar 1786: d Gorham 18 Dec 1863 (McLellan's *Gorham*, p. 813): m Buxton 1 Jul 1812 Lydia Sands Thompson (Meserve, op. cit., p. 235), b Buxton 1 Nov 1791 dau of Theodore & Elizabeth (Sands) Thompson (ibid.) [see THEODORE THOMPSON family], d Gorham 22 Jan 1884 ae 92y (McLellan's *Gorham*, p. 813)
- x   Desire, b 5 Dec 1788: d 11 Aug 1858 ae 69y (McLellan's *Gorham*, p. 427): m 30 May 1806 Nahum Chadbourne (ibid., p. 810), b Gorham 5 Apr 1784 son of Silas & Abigail (Crockett) Chadbourne (VR), d Gorham 6 Aug 1857 (McLellan's *Gorham*, p. 427)

Dana A. Batchelder, 258 South Sea Avenue, West Yarmouth, MA 02673

Weare, Jer[e]   71b   3 - 1 - 5 - 3 - 0
York Town, York County

JEREMIAH WEARE, b York 17 Mar 1728/9 eldest child of Joseph & Mary (Webber) Weare (Lester M. Bragdon & John E. Frost, *Vital Records of York, Maine* [1992], hereafter VR, p. 44) [see JOSEPH WEARE family]: d York 4 May 1821 ae 92y (VR, p. 418) [note that "Diary of Jeremiah Weare, Jr. of York, Me.," hereafter JW Diary, gives d 28 Mar 1821 (NEHGR, 55 [1901]:57)]: m York 30 Jan 1755 SARAH PREBLE (VR, p. 139), b York 17 Mar 1730/1 ("28th of march new style") (JW Diary, NEHGR, 66 [1912]:78) dau of Samuel & Sarah

(____) (Muchemore) Preble ("The Parentage of Sarah[4] Preble, Wife of Jeremiah[4] Weare of York, Maine," *Maine Genealogist*, 15 [1993]:3–6), d "after a long sickness" York 14 May 1801 ae abt 70y (ibid.; she was called an "innkeeper" on her obituary published in the *Portland Gazette*, issue of 25 May 1801 as cited in David C. & Elizabeth K. Young, *Vital Records from Maine Newspapers, 1785– 1820* [1993], p. 635). The 1790 census indicates that Jeremiah had three non-white free persons living in his household, probably helping to run the inn. Jeremiah's father, Joseph Weare, had servants named Hagor, Boston, Fanny, Jeffery, Jack and Rose, all of whom received baptism from the 1st Church of York between 1760 and 1771 (YCGSJ, 4 [1989]:4:13). Some of these may have later worked for Jeremiah. A probable member of Jeremiah's household in 1790 was Sherman, "an Ethiopen" who d 7 May 1825 ae abt 80y (JW Diary, NEHGR, 66 [1912]:262) and who was bp at the 1st Church of York 20 Jan 1771 as a "servant of M[r] Jeremiah Weare" (YCGSJ, 4 [1989]:4:13).

Children, all b York: births VR, p. 483–84; baptisms YCGSJ, 5 [1990]:2:15–17
  i son, d at birth
 ii Jeremiah Jr., b 3 Jun 1757 and bp 7 Aug 1757: d York 26 Jul 1842 (Rev War pension #W25949): m Lucy Webber [see JEREMIAH WEARE Jr. family]
iii Theodore, b 7 Sep 1759 and bp 16 Sep 1759: d York 16 May 1830 ae 70y (VR, pp. 463, 645): m (1) York 11 Sep 1786 Anna Perkins (VR, p. 363) who d 15 Sep 1786 ae 20y just 4 days after the marriage (ibid.; JW Diary, NEHGR, 66 [1912]:79): m (2) York 11 Jun 1795 Hannah Woodbridge of Vassalborough (York VR, p. 179) who d York 19 Jul 1814 (JW Diary, NEHGR, 64 [1910]:181) [note that g.s. states Hannah, wife of Capt. Theodore Weare, d 8 Nov 1818 ae 49y (York VR, p. 645)]. Theodore left a will naming his sons Theodore, Charles and Edward and his daus Sally Weare wife of William Weare [see JEREMIAH WEARE Jr. family] and Narcissa Weare, singlewoman (York Co Probate #19780, 41:172)
 iv Mary, b 20 May 1762 and bp 5 Sep 1762: d York c1765 ae abt 3y (VR, p. 484)
  v Timothy, b 4 Aug 1764 and bp 29 Sep 1765: d York 6 Sep 1791 ae 27y 1m 2d (JW Diary, NEHGR, 66 [1912]:79). He lived with John Weare [prob his uncle, see JOSEPH WEARE family] for 20 years and supposedly died of a cold contracted while loading a sloop "in the flats at the northern bay penobscot" (ibid.)
 vi John, b 29 Jun 1766 and bp 14 Sep 1766: d York Oct 1776 (VR, p. 484)
vii Samuel, b 7 Jun 1768 and bp 4 Sep 1768: d York 13 Nov 1856 ae 88y 5m 6d (VR, pp. 435, 645): m York 19 Nov 1795 Jerusha Parsons (VR, p. 364), b 1776 (York VR, p. 645) and bp 1st Church of York 30 Mar 1777 dau of Joseph & Jerusha (Sayward) Parsons (YCGSJ, 4 [1989]:4:16) [see

JOSEPH PARSONS family], d 1867 (York VR, p. 645). Samuel's will, dated 9 Jan 1856, gives a wealth of info abt his children and grandchildren (York Co Probate #19779, 77:377)

viii Sarah, b 28 Sep 1770 and bp 25 Nov 1770: d Wells 19 Oct 1849 ae 79y (g.s., Littlefield-Weare burial lot, "Incriptions from Gravestones at Wells, Maine," NEHGR, 93 [1939]:332): m York 14 Apr 1793 Amos Littlefield of Wells (York VR, p. 176), bp 1st Church of Wells 22 May 1763 son of Jeremiah & Sarah (Hatch) Littlefield (NEHGR, 76 [1922]:104; "Littlefield Family Newsletter," 3 [1993]:1:20), d Wells 28 Dec 1843 ae 81y (g.s., Littlefield-Weare burial lot, op. cit.)

ix Mary, b 26 Sep 1773 and bp 31 Jul 1774: d York 7 Mar 1859 ae 85y 5m 9d (VR, p. 383): m int York 27 Jan 1813 Samuel Norton (VR, p. 199), b c1775, d York 20 Nov 1820 ae 47y 10m (VR, p. 658)

Marjorie Wardwell Otten, 201 4th St. #222, Del Mar, CA 92014

Weare, Jer^e, J^r 71b   1 - 3 - 4 - 1 - 0
York Town, York County

JEREMIAH WEARE Jr., b York Friday 3 Jun 1757 and bp 1st Church of York 7 Aug 1757 eldest child of Jeremiah & Sarah (Preble) Weare ("Diary of Jeremiah Weare, Jr., of York, Me.," hereafter JW Diary, NEHGR, 55 [1901]:58; Lester M. Bragdon & John E. Frost, *Vital Records of York, Maine* [1992], hereafter VR, p. 97; "First Parish, York: Baptisms 1750–1800," YCGSJ, 5 [1990]:2:15) [see JEREMIAH WEARE family]: d York 26 Jul 1842 ae 85y (Rev War pension #W25949): m York Tuesday 18 May 1779 LUCY WEBBER (JW Diary, NEHGR, 55 [1901]:58), b York 10 Apr 1754 dau of Nathaniel & Lucy (Bradbury) Webber (VR, pp. 87, 97), d York 13 Sep 1846 (JW Diary, NEHGR, 66 [1912]:312). During the Rev War, Jeremiah served in the siege of Boston (ibid., 55 [1901]:56). He applied for a pension at York 3 Jun 1818 (pension, op. cit.). His family in 1820 included his wife Lucy ae 66y, dau Betsey Weare ae 32y, son Rufus Weare ae 36y, dau Lucy Weare ae 40y and grandson Ebenezer Littlefield Jr. ae 16y (ibid.). His widow Lucy applied for her pension 9 Sep 1843, with son Timothy deposing 27 Mar 1844 ae 52y (ibid.). Jeremiah was the diarist whose account of his family and local events spanned more than 50 years. He "was a farmer, mariner; built a vessel and commanded it, being shipwrecked. He was one of the crew of a privateer...He did not accumulate wealth, for he evidently was very glad to receive the pension in his later years. He had decidedly religious convictions, and evidently was an earnest member of his church" (introduction to JW Diary, NEHGR, 55 [1901]:55–56). Jeremiah received from his grandfather, Joseph Weare [see JOSEPH WEARE family], "a negrow boy named Pomp" who lived with him, later lived with his bro Samuel, then went to Arundel, then went to sea, and was later sold in the West Indies by the master of the vessel about 1801-2 (ibid.; NEHGR, 66 [1912]:79).

Children, b York: births VR York, p. 97; baptisms YCGSJ, 5 [1990]:2:15-17
 i son, b 26 Oct 1779: "did not breathe life" (York VR, p. 97)
 ii Lucy, b 25 Oct 1780 and bp 8 Jul 1784: d aft 1820 (pension, op. cit.): she had a relationship with but did not marry Ebenezer Littlefield, as he d at sea 24 Mar 1803, master of the brig FIDELITY which was "buried in the ocean four Days out," according to JW Diary, which also noted that Ebenezer Sr. "Left one son...named Ebenezer, Lucy Weare being the mother" (NEHGR, 66 [1912]:78). Ebenezer Littlefield Sr., a mariner, was b Apr 1775 son of Stephen and Deborah (Perkins) Littlefield (ibid.; York VR, p. 147). The adm of Littlefield's estate was granted to "Lucy Weare of York singlewoman" 10 Oct 1803 (York Co Probate #11741, 19:321). Their son, Ebenezer Littlefield Jr., was living with his mother and grandfather, Jeremiah Weare Jr., in 1820 (pension, op. cit.)
 iii William, b 29 Aug 1782 and bp 8 Jul 1784: d York 16 Jan 1848 ae 65y 4m 18d (VR, p. 485): m int York 28 Mar 1816 his cousin Sarah Weare (VR, p. 203), b York 13 Dec 1795 (VR, p. 485) dau of Theodore & Hannah (Woodbridge) Weare [see discussion below; see also JEREMIAH WEARE family], d York 20 Nov 1876 ae 80y (VR, p. 485). [In his will, Theodore Weare named his dau Sally Weare, wife of William Weare (York Co Probate #19780, 41:172). One Sally, dau of Theodore and "Sally" Weare, was bp at the 1st Church of York 21 Jun 1796 (YCGSJ, 5 [1990]:2:18). Theodore Weare and Hannah Woodbridge of Vassalboro m York 11 Jun 1795 (VR, p. 179). Hannah, wife of Capt. Theodore Weare d York 8 Nov 1818 ae 49y (VR, p. 645). No wife named Sarah or Sally has been found for any Theodore Weare of York other than the baptismal record shown above which must be in error]
 iv Rufus, b 2 Apr 1784 and bp 8 Jul 1784: d York 2 Jun 1853 (JW Diary, NEHGR, 66 [1912]:315)
 v Theodosia, b 26 Mar 1786 and bp 25 Sep 1786: d York 4 Mar 1858 ae 72y (VR, p. 436): m York 2 Aug 1813 Theodore Wilson (VR, p. 200), b c1787 son of Jonathan Wilson (JW Diary, NEHGR, 64 [1910]:180), d York 22 Aug 1850 ae 63y 2m (VR, p. 647)
 vi Betsey, b 10 Mar 1788 and bp 8 Jul 1789: d aft 1820 (pension, op. cit.)
 vii Moses, b 10 Mar 1790 and bp 26 Oct 1791: d Boston MA 7 Nov 1827 ae 37y leaving "a wife and two children gorge and Coorline in Boston the place of his residence" (JW Diary, NEHGR, 66 [1912]:312)
 viii Timothy, b 5 Mar 1792 and bp 23 May 1792: d aft 27 Mar 1844 when he deposed for his mother (pension, op. cit.)

ix Jeremiah, b 3 Jul 1794 and bp 16 Dec 1794: d York 4 Jul 1858 ae 63y (VR, p. 519) [JW Diary gives d 5 Jul 1858 (NEHGR, 66 [1912]:312)]: m York 26 Dec 1822 Mary Knight (VR, p. 218), b c1798, d York 30 Apr 1873 ae 75y (VR, p. 218). [One Mary dau of ____ & Dorcas Knight was bp York 4 July 1798 (YCGSJ, 4 [1989]:3:17). One William Knight m York 9 Feb 1797 Dorcas Lunt (VR, p. 181)]
x Mary, b 2 Sep 1796 and bp 21 Sep 1796: d York 27 Jul 1811 ae 14y (JW Diary, 63 [1909]:297)
xi Olive, b 19 Sep 1798: d York of "cough and fever" 16 Feb 1806 ae 7y (JW Diary, NEHGR, 63 [1909]:297)

Marjorie Wardwell Otten, 201 4th St. #222, Del Mar, CA 92014

Weare, Joseph   71b   1 - 0 - 0 - 0 - 0
York Town, York County

JOSEPH WEARE, b York 17 Mar 1704/5 son of Elias & Magdalene (Hilton) (Adams) Weare (Lester M. Bragdon & John E. Frost, *Vital Records of York, Maine* [1992], hereafter VR, p. 14; "Diary of Jeremiah Weare, Jr. of York, Me.," hereafter JW Diary, NEHGR, 55 [1901]:56): d York 18 Oct 1791 ae 86y (ibid.; VR, p. 404): m York estimated 28 Aug 1728 MARY WEBBER [no marriage record found although JW Diary, states that Mary had been married "fifty years save seven days" when she died (NEHGR, 63 [1909]:297)], b York 15 Apr 1710 dau of Dea. Samuel & Elizabeth (Young) Webber (ibid; VR, p. 18), d of small pox York 21 Aug 1778 in her 69th year (JW Diary, NEHGR, 63 [1909]:297). Joseph left a will dated 7 Jan 1779 and probated 19 Dec 1791 (York Co Probate #19769, 16:97–98). In it, he named his sons Jeremiah, Elias, John, Joseph, and Daniel and daughters Bathsheba Paul, Mercy Wardwell, Sarah Bragdon, and Phebe Perkins.

Children, all b York: births VR York, p. 44
  i Jeremiah, b 17 Mar 1728/9: d York 4 May 1821 (VR, p. 418): m Sarah Preble [see JEREMIAH WEARE family]
  ii Elias, b 6 Mar 1730/1: m York Apr 1760 his 1st cousin Ruth Banks (VR, p. 143), b York 18 Jan 1736/7 dau of Moses & Ruth (Weare) Banks (VR, p. 14; JW Diary, NEHGR, 55 [1901]:57)
  iii John, b 29 Nov 1732: d York 24 Aug 1812 ae 79y (JW Diary, NEHGR, 66 [1912]:156): m York 4 Feb 1764 Mary Goodwin (VR, p. 144), b York 23 May 1737 dau of Abiel & Sarah (Milberry) Goodwin (VR, p. 22), d York 9 Nov 1820 ae 83y (JW Diary, NEHGR, 66 [1912]: 265). In his will dated 27 Jul 1812, John gave all of his property to "my kinsman [nephew]

James Weare the son of my brother Daniel" in exchange for life support for both him and his wife (York Co Probate #19763, 23:460)

iv Joseph Jr., b 21 Oct 1734: d aft 1790 (USC): m int York 26 Nov 1763 Elizabeth Stone (VR, p. 146), b York 12 Jun 1735 dau of Benjamin & Abigail (Swett) Stone (ibid., pp. 15, 91), d York 20 Dec 1804 ae 71y (obituary in *Portland Gazette*, issue of 7 Jan 1805 as cited in David C. & Elizabeth K. Young, *Vital Records from Maine Newspapers, 1785–1820* [1993], p. 629)

v Mary, b 22 Nov 1736: d by 1778 when Jeremiah Weare Jr., in his diary, stated that her mother Mary (Webber) Weare was survived by 4 of her 5 daughters (JW Diary, NEHGR, 63 [1909]:297). She was the only child not mentioned in her father's will in early 1779

vi Bathsheba, b 31 Oct 1738: m York 23 Jun 1768 Stephen Paul of Kittery (VR, p. 150), bp 5 Dec 1742 son of Stephen & Mary (_____) Paul of Kittery (Everett S. Stackpole, *Old Kittery and Her Families* [1906], p. 645)

vii Mercy, b 6 Dec 1740: d at "majabigwaduce [Penobscot] with the fever" (JW Diary, NEHGR, 66 [1912]:78) aft 1791 when her father's estate was probated: m York Oct 1757 Jeremiah Wardwell (VR, p. 142), b York 19 Feb 1731/32 son of Eliakim & Ruth (Bragdon) Wardwell (VR, p. 33), d York aft 18 Apr 1764 when their son Joel was bp (YCGSJ, 5:2 [1990]:16) and bef 30 Jun 1765 when Jeremiah son of Mercy the widow of Jeremiah Wardwell was bp (YCGSJ, 5:2 [1990]:16). Mercy moved to Penobscot "in fall of the year 1778" (JW Diary, NEHGR, 66 [1912]:78)

viii Sarah, b 6 Jun 1743: d York 22 Mar 1787 leaving 8 sons & 2 daus, "one at the Brest" (JW Diary, NEHGR, 66 [1912]:78; VR, p. 397): m York 13 Sep 1764 Thomas Bragdon Jr. (VR, p. 147), b York 8 Apr 1738 son of Ens. Thomas & Mary (Came) Bragdon (VR, p. 43)

ix Daniel, b 24 Jan 1746/7: d of "gravil Disorder" York 10 Oct 1813 in the 69th y of his age [sic] (JW Diary, NEHGR, 64 [1910]:182): m Wells 25 Feb 1778 Abigail Littlefield of Wells (VR), b c1755 [perhaps the Abigail Littlefield bp at the 1st Church of Wells 20 Apr 1755 dau of Jonathan & Hannah (Sayward) Littlefield (NEHGR, 75 [1921]:314)], d York 5 Nov 1836 ae 81y (VR, p. 428; JW Diary, NEHGR, 66 [1912]:264). Daniel left a will dated 9 Jul 1813 naming his wife Abigail and six children (York Co Probate #19753, 24:393)

x Phebe, b 5 Dec 1748: d 2 Aug 1815 ae 67y (JW Diary, NEHGR, 66 [1912]: 156): m 29 Apr 1770 Joseph Perkins Jr. (ibid.; VR, p. 357), b York 11 Nov 1746 son of Joseph & Abigail (Wardwell) Perkins (VR, p. 70), d 20 Aug 1818 (JW Diary, NEHGR, 66 [1912]:156)

Marjorie Wardwell Otten, 201 4th St. #222, Del Mar, CA 92014

Whorfe, Joseph   21a   1 - 3 - 4 - 0 - 0
New Gloucester Town, Cumberland County

JOSEPH WHARFF, b Gloucester MA 21 Nov 1762 son of Arthur Jr. & Lydia (Cunningham) Wharff (VR) [for his ancestry, see *The Essex Genealogist* (Aug 1994), pp. 150–54]: d at sea 2 Jan 1795 (Oliver B. Clason, *History of Litchfield, Maine* [1897], hereafter Clason, p. 390): m Gloucester MA 11 Jun 1780 SUSANNA BENNETT (VR), b Gloucester MA 12 July 1763 dau of Capt. Isaac & Dorcas (Wharff) Bennett (VR), d Litchfield 7 May 1833 ae 69y (g.s., Harriman cem). She m (2) Litchfield 23 Aug 1798 James Stevens as his second wife (Clason, p. 340) [m int Litchfield 4 Aug 1798 (VR)] [see NATHANIEL STEVENS family]. Immediately after their marriage, Joseph and Susannah removed to New Gloucester (ibid., p. 390). He was a sea captain (ibid.). After Joseph's death, Susannah moved to the Stevenstown part of Litchfield where she married her second husband (ibid.).

Children, b New Gloucester: Clason, p. 390
- i   Susanna, b 10 Aug 1780: d Guilford 5 Nov 1850 (Stevens MS believed to be written by Menaids Fessenden Herring, Guilford Public Library): m bef 14 Aug 1798 (when their son Joseph Wharff Stevens was b) Moses Stevens (Clason, p. 390), b Gloucester MA 2 Dec 1771 son of Nathaniel & Jerusha (Bennett) Stevens [see NATHANIEL STEVENS family], d Guilford 9 Mar 1838 (VR)
- ii   Sally, b 27 Jan 1782: d Litchfield 1 Dec 1856 (g.s., Harriman cem): m 26 Mar 1797 Amos Stevens (Clason, p. 340), b Gloucester MA 11 Oct 1773 bro of Moses above (VR), d Litchfield 1 Sep 1828 ae 55y (g.s., Harriman cem)
- iii Lydia, b 10 Nov 1783: d Litchfield 27 Aug 1869 (Clason, p. 390): m Litchfield 27 Nov 1800 Joseph Lunt (VR), b Bath 3 Aug 1780 son of Joseph & Priscilla (Crocker) Lunt (Clason, p. 210), d Litchfield 1 Oct 1826 (ibid.)
- iv   Joseph, b 11 Nov 1785: d Litchfield 1 May 1862 ae 76y 6m (VR) and bur Oak Grove cem, Gardiner (Gardiner VR): m Phoebe Webber (Clason, p. 391), b c1788, d Gardiner 4 Jan 1872 ae 85y (VR)
- v   William, b 12 Oct 1787: d at sea 1812 (Clason, p. 392): m int Litchfield 1 Apr 1809 Rachel Penney of New Gloucester (Litchfield VR), b New Gloucester 3 Feb 1786 (Guilford VR), d Guilford 23 Dec 1858 (VR). She m (2) Robert Low as his 3rd wife (Guilford VR). William and Rachel's 1st child, Thomas Penny Wharff, was b Litchfield 5 Oct 1809 (VR). Robert Low, b New Boston NH 1 Mar 1781 (Guilford VR), was Piscataquis Co Treasurer 1839–40 (*Sprague's Journal of Maine History*) and one of the first two settlers of Guilford

- vi   Isaac B., b 23 Aug 1789: d Guilford 30 Jun 1878 (Clason, p. 390): m int Litchfield 9 Sep 1809 Sarah/Sally Penney of New Gloucester (Litchfield VR), b c1791, d Guilford 27 Feb 1869 ae 78y (VR). At the first town meeting of Guilford on 1 Mar 1816, Isaac was elected Surveyor of Highways (TR)
- vii Betsey, b 9 Mar 1792: d Litchfield 25 Jul 1861 ae 69y (Clason, p. 294): m Litchfield 19 Sep 1810 William Robinson Jr. (VR), b Litchfield 4 Mar 1787 son of William & Mary (Stinson) Robinson (VR), d 15 Aug 1835 (Clason, p. 294)
- viii Abigail, b 7 Nov 1793: d 3 Nov 1794 (Clason, p. 390)
- ix   Dorcas, b 18 Jul 1795: d Litchfield 12 Jun 1845 (Clason, p. 390): m (1) Litchfield 25 Dec 1815 David McIntyre (VR): m (2) Litchfield 1 May 1834 Wilkes Richardson as his 2nd wife (VR), b 2 Oct 1801 son of John & Bethiah (Herrick) Richardson (Clason, p. 281), d 24 Apr 1886 (ibid., p. 282). He m (3) Mary Arno (ibid., p. 281)

Leslie Dow Sanders, P.O. Box 13, Marblehead, MA 01945

Whitmore, Joseph   27c   1 - 3 - 3 - 0 - 0
Deer Isle Town, Hancock County

JOSEPH WHITMORE, b Dudley Centre MA 19 Jul 1755 (Family Bible in possession of Lucy Whitmore, Bucksport ME, 1930, copy printed in Benjamin L. Noyes, "Genealogical History of Deer Isle Families," FHL film #0896727) a proposed but unproven son of John Whitmore of Cambridge MA and Baldwin ME by his 2nd wife Mary (Burnell) Whitmore: d Deer Isle 14 Jun 1841 (Rev War pension #W22592) [g.s. at Colomy Point cem says d 1842]: m Castine 10 Nov 1780 ABIGAIL BABBIDGE (Family Bible, op. cit.) [pension, op. cit., says m 9 Nov 1781], b Harpswell 14 Sep 1764 dau of William & Rebecca (Bibber) Babbidge (VR; Noyes, op. cit.), d Deer Isle 21 May 1849 (g.s., Colomy Point cem). The 1800 USC states he was from Gorham from which place he went to Deer Isle as a young boy of ten with Seth Webb (George L. Hosmer, *An Historical Sketch of the Town of Deer Isle, Maine* [1905], p. 123). His pension record recites his one year six weeks service in Capt. Gideon Parker's Co., Col. Little's Regt. in 1776 serving at Cambridge, Long Island, White Plains, Trenton and Philadelphia. Webb sold him the north half of a 600 acre lot on Babbidge's Neck and half of Sheep Island in 1777 (Han Co deeds 1:316). As a proprietor of Deer Isle in 1808, he received a distribution which he sold in 1824 (Deer Isle Proprietors recs; Han Co deeds 45:503). Joseph's affidavit of 1820 for his pension relates his difficult situation with a wife described as sickly and infirm and his own debility and poor circumstances.

Children, all b Deer Isle: pension, op. cit.
- i John, b 14 Sep 1781: d Lincolnville 9 Dec 1851 (g.s., Fletcher cem): m int Deer Isle 7 May 1803 Deborah Trundy (VR), b c1785 dau of Samuel & Ann (Carey) Trundy (Noyes, op. cit.), d Lincolnville 13 Nov 1863
- ii Joseph, b 29 Jul 1783: drowned at sea 19 Sep 1813 going from Isle au Haut to Deer Isle (Vinalhaven VR; Noyes, op. cit. which gives 18 Sep 1813): m Deer Isle c1808 Susanna _____ (ibid.)
- iii William, b 19 Jul 1785: d at sea c1825 (Noyes, op. cit.; Grace Limeburner, "Folks of Orphan Isle" [TS, FHL film #859055]): m int Prospect 19 Jul 1809 Polly Abbott (Sedgwick VR), b 12 Aug 1793 dau of Peter & Sarah (_____) Abbott of Orphan Island [see PETER ABBOTT family], d Orphan Island 12 Mar 1851 ae 57y 7m (g.s., Whitmore cem)
- iv Mary, b 28 Oct 1787
- v Daniel, b 29 Feb 1790
- vi Rebecca, b 16 Mar 1792: d Swans Island 3 Apr 1873 (g.s., Atlantic cem): m Abel E. Staples of Swans Island (Noyes, op. cit.), b c1785 son of Moses & Judith (Eaton) Staples (Grace Bischoff, Genealogical Notes, Atlantic Cemetery, Swans Island, MOCA, Han Co, 2:420A), d Swans Island 20 Aug 1851 ae 66y (g.s., Atlantic cem). They res Swans Island
- vii Samuel, b 29 Apr 1794: d aft 1852 (Noyes, op. cit.): m Abigail M. Joyce of Swans Island (ibid.)
- viii James, b 10 Dec 1796. He res Mount Desert (Noyes, op. cit.)
- ix Lemuel, b 1 Apr 1798
- x Seth Webb, b 15 Oct 1800: m Lucy Stinson dau of William Stinson of Deer Isle (Noyes, op. cit.). They res Ellsworth (ibid.)
- xi Abigail, b 29 Nov 1802: m George York (Noyes, op. cit.)
- xii Sarah, twin, b 12 Nov 1806: d bef 1820 (pension, op. cit.)
- xiii Susan, twin, b 12 Nov 1806. In 1820, she was described as being ae 13y, "weakly and sickly" (pension, op. cit.)

Ralph E. Hillman, 4302 James Dr., Midland, MI 48642

Whiteher, Benjamin   44c   3 - 1 - 4 - 0 - 0
Sandy River, First Township [now Farmington], Lincoln County

BENJAMIN WHITTIER, b Salisbury MA 24 Oct 1736 or 1737 son of Nathaniel & Hannah (Clough) Whittier (year of birth given as "1737?" in Salisbury VR; Francis G. Butler's *A History of Farmington* [1885], p. 615, gives b 24 Oct 1736): d Chesterville 11 Nov 1822 from a fall from his carriage (ibid., p. 615): m int Salisbury MA 24 May 1755 MARY/MARCY JOY (VR), b Salisbury MA 17 Oct 1736 dau of Benjamin & Sarah (Sawyer) Joy (VR), d 5 Jul 1822 (*History of*

Farmington, p. 615). They lived many years at Salisbury MA, then moved about 1775 to Chester NH, then to Readfield ME and finally in 1783 to near Sandy River (ibid.). They lived on the west side of the river, on lot #22, where he was constable and tax collector and in 1801 Chairman of the Board of Selectmen (ibid.).

Children: births and other information from *History of Farmington*, pp. 615–16, unless otherwise cited [*History of Farmington* states that the first 9 were b Salisbury MA, last 3 b Chester NH; however Charles C. Collyer's *The Descendants of Thomas Whittier and Ruth Green of Salisbury and Haverhill, Massachusetts* [1937], p. 53, states the first 3 b Chester NH, others b Raymond NH; no children were recorded in the Salisbury MA VR; the other towns' records have not been verified]

i   Anna, b 3 Dec 1757: d NH 31 May 1759

ii   Betsey, b 24 Apr 1759: d New Sharon 12 Jul 1821 ae 62y (g.s., New Sharon cem): m 8 Feb 1781 Samuel Prescott of New Sharon (William Prescott, M.D., *The Prescott Memorial*, p. 251), b Brentwood NH 5 Sep 1759 son of Jedediah & Hannah (Bachiler) Prescott (ibid.; Rev War pension #W2434) [see JEDEDIAH PRESCOTT family], d Hallowell 7 Nov 1841 ae 82y (VR). He m (2) Hallowell 2 Dec 1823 Martha (Clark) Molloy of Hallowell (VR; pension, op. cit.)

iii   Benjamin, b 26 Apr 1760: d 29 Apr 1782

iv   Mary, b 17 Jan 1763: d 7 Aug 1841 (g.s. Bowley cem, New Sharon): m 1 Dec 1783 Jesse Prescott of New Sharon (Prescott, op. cit., p. 252) [see JESSE PRESCOTT family]

v   Moses, b 14 Sep 1764: d Farmington Aug 1833: m Betsey Flint, b Nobleboro 4 Sep 1771 dau of Thomas & Lydia (Pope) Flint [see THOMAS FLINT family, *Maine Families*, 2:95]

vi   Anna, b 2 Jul 1766: d 31 Jan 1819: m c1785 Joseph Hutchinson. They res Readfield

vii   Miriam, b 20 Jun 1768: d 9 Sep 1841: m 28 Dec 1790 Richard Maddocks of Chesterville who d 19 Jan 1839

viii   Sarah, b 20 Jul 1771: d Oct 1862: m c1795 Arnold Weathern who d 6 Mar 1853

ix   William, b 22 Feb 1774: d by "falling from a load of hay" 7 Aug 1806: m 2 Jun 1795 Nancy Butterfield (VR) [m int Farmington May 1795 calls them "both of a plantation called Chester" (VR)]. She d 1 May 1830

x   Ruth, b 18 Sep 1775: d 3 Feb 1866: m 22 Feb 1795 her cousin Jedediah Whittier [m int Farmington Feb 1796 (sic) calls him "of a plantation called Wyman"], b 2 Aug 1771 son of Nathaniel & Elizabeth (Prescott) Whittier, d 29 Oct 1841. They res Vienna

xi   Hannah, b 26 Apr 1777: d Nov 1865: m 24 Mar 1800 Simeon Norris [m int Farmington 8 Feb 1800 Simeon Norrice of Hallowell (VR)] xii Nathaniel, b 14 Jul 1779: d 30 May 1837: m 7 Nov 1813 Alice Sears (Everett S. Stackpole, *History of Winthrop, Maine* [1925], p. 579) [m int Farmington 24 Oct 1813, she "of Winthrop" (VR)], b Winthrop 22 Oct 1785 dau of Paul & Mercy (Stevens) Sears (*History of Winthrop*, pp. 578–79), d Farmington 12 Aug 1873 [see PAUL SEARS family, *Maine Families*, 2:250]

Eleanor W. Townsend, 71 Slab Meadow Road, Morris, CT 06763

Williams, Asa   39a   1 - 1 - 4 - 0 - 0
Hallowell Town, Lincoln County

ASA WILLIAMS, b Easton MA 8 Jun 1758 son of Seth & Susannah (Fobes) Williams (James W. North, *The History of Augusta, Maine* [repr 1981], hereafter North, p. 958): d Augusta 20 Jul 1820 ae 62y (VR; g.s., West River Rd. cem): m 16 Sep 1784 EUNICE FISHER of Stoughton MA (North, p. 959), b c1764, d 7 Jun 1832 ae 68y (Augusta VR; g.s., West River Rd. cem, Augusta, which gives her death date as 6 Jun 1832). Asa was a Rev War soldier (Fisher's *Soldiers*, p. 863). He lived at Easton MA until 1779 when he and his brother Seth went to Fort Western Settlement, now Augusta (North, p. 959). He settled on a farm on the river road to Sidney where he lived until his death (ibid., pp. 958–59).

Children: births first 6 VR Augusta, last 3 in North, p. 959
i Lusannah, b 31 May 1785 (Robert R. & Cynthia A. McCausland, *The Diary of Martha Ballard 1785–1812* [1992], p. 10) [VR Augusta gives b 30 May 1785]: d Augusta 27 Jun 1864 ae 79y (VR): m int Augusta 12 Nov 1809 Jonathan Hedge of Vassalboro (Augusta VR), b c1785 prob son of Barnabas & Thankful (Hallett) Hedge of Vassalboro, d Augusta 19 Oct 1868 ae 83y (VR). They lived in Augusta
ii Eunice, b 1 Mar 1787: d Augusta 20 Feb 1829 ae 41y (VR): unm
iii Sarah/Sally, b 27 Nov 1788: m Augusta 26 Nov 1816 Scotto Hedge of Vassalboro (Augusta VR) prob bro of Jonathan above. He was of Vassalboro when he m (2) Augusta 2 Mar 1842 Martha (Kimball) Partridge of Gardiner (Augusta VR)
iv Ruth, b 3 Dec 1790: d Augusta 17 Jan 1814 ae 23y (VR): unm
v Avice, b 15 Jul 1792: d Augusta 22 Jan 1814 ae 21y (VR): unm
vi Asa, b 27 Oct 1795: d Augusta 7 Jun 1857 ae 61y (VR): m Augusta 11 Sep 1833 Ruth Hovey (VR), b c1813, d Augusta 17 Jul 1860 ae 47y (VR)
vii Elizabeth, b 19 Dec 1798: d Augusta 3 Sep 1859 ae 60y (VR): m Augusta 25 Dec 1823 Charles Hamlen (VR), b Augusta 9 Dec 1799 son of Perez & Anna (Prescott) Hamlen (VR), d Augusta 25 Jan 1883 ae 83y (VR). He

m (2) int Augusta 22 Oct 1860 Roxanna (Laughton) Mayo (VR) wid of Stephen Mayo (Augusta VR; Hallowell VR). He was a trademan in Augusta and active in town affairs

viii Susan, b 9 Oct 1801: d Augusta 1 Jun 1857 ae 55y (VR): m Augusta 18 Jan 1826 Lewis Baker Hamlen (VR), b Augusta 30 Jun 1800 son of Lewis & Eleanor (Craig) Hamlen (VR). He m (2) Augusta 25 Nov 1858 Sarah A. Robinson (VR). He was a farmer and tradesman in Augusta

ix Vesta Gould, b 26 Aug 1804: d Augusta 28 Aug 1849 (VR): m Augusta 18 Jan 1826 Nehemiah Flagg (VR), b Augusta 31 Dec 1801 son of James & Fanny (Getchell) Flagg (VR; North, p. 863), d Augusta 12 May 1875 (VR). He m (2) 7 Dec 1865 Sylvia E. A. Flagg (North, p. 864). After Vesta's death, Nehemiah moved to CA where he lived 13y (ibid.). He later returned and settled in Boston MA (ibid.)

Elaine Bush Prince, 74 Dennison Ave., Framingham, MA 01701-6419

Williams, Samuel   45b   1 - 4 - 4 - 0 - 0
Seven Mile Brook Town [now North Anson], Lincoln County

Maj. **LEMUEL WILLIAMS**, b Easton MA 2 May 1751 son of Timothy & Elizabeth (Brittun) Williams (VR, recorded as "Elemuel"): d Woolwich while on a visit to his brother 23 Sep 1820 (VR; Ernest George Walker, *Embden Town of Yore* [1929], p. 113): m Pownalboro 28 Apr 1777 ANNA HILTON of Pownalboro (BHM, 7:85; Rev War pension #W22673), b Pownalboro 1758 dau of Lt. Moses & Rachel (_____) Hilton (*Embden Town of Yore*, op. cit., p. 114), d No. Anson 1850 (ibid.). [Anna poss d on or about 4 Sep 1850 as the account of Thomas Gray, guardian of Anna Williams, an "insane" (prob meant senile) person, late of No. Anson, included charges for "6 mos pension to Sep 4/50" (Som Co Probate records).] Lemuel, often called Elemuel, left Easton MA c1764 at about ae 13y with his family and settled in Woolwich. He was a Rev War soldier and pensioner (Rev War pension #W22673). When he applied for his pension in 1820, he had living with him his dau Melinda, 25, his son Joseph, 23, his son Morrell, 21, and his dau Anna, 16. In her pension declaration dated 1836, Anna said that she "has borne and raised...nineteen children, ten sons and nine daughters, besides one that died at its birth." Anna also stated that Lemuel moved with his family to Anson in 1791 [although *Embden Town of Yore* stated they moved there in 1781, p. 114, which would appear to be supported by the 1790 USC]. There, he served as Town Clerk and was the first selectman (ibid.). In his will dated 22 Sep 1820, Lemuel named his wife Anna, his oldest son Moses, his second son William, his son Lemuel, his dau Betsy Sawyer, his son

John, his dau Zerviah Rogers, his dau Rachel Withey, his dau Melinda, singlewoman, his dau Anna, singlewoman, his son Simeon, his son Joseph and his son Morrill (Som Co Probate, 2:461–62).

Children, b Woolwich and No. Anson, order uncertain: as named in Lemuel's will except as noted
- i Moses, b c1778–79: d Embden 26 Feb 1858 ae 79y (g.s., East New Portland cem): m int Anson 25 Sep 1805 Martha Butler of New Vineyard (Anson VR), b c Feb 1779 dau of Henry & Mehitable (Norton) Butler (Williams C. Hatch, *A History of the Town of Industry* [1893], p. 527; g.s.), d Embden 17 Sep 1858 ae 79y 7m (g.s., East New Portland cem). He was a shoemaker and farmer and res No. Anson, New Portland, and Industry before moving to Embden
- ii William, b 1781 (*Embden Town of Yore*, p. 115) [genealogical papers of Dr. Charles Crosby Williams on the Williams family, located at Bowdoin College Library, hereafter Williams Papers, gives b 16 Jun 1781]: d 5 Nov 1839 ae 58y 5m (g.s., Sunset cem, Anson): m Woolwich 22 Dec 1807 Amy Gray ("Records of the Rev. Josiah Winship, Woolwich Church," DAR Misc Rec, 13:2:32), b poss York 25 Nov 1788 (Williams Papers), d 20 Mar 1868 ae 79y 4m (g.s., Sunset cem, Anson)
- iii Lemuel, b 1783 (*Embden Town of Yore*, p. 115): d Athens 7 May 1846 ae 62y (g.s., Mt. Rest cem transcribed in Elaine Bush Prince, "Cemeteries in Athens, Somerset County, Maine" [1987], p. 27): m int Anson 14 Mar 1809 Dolly Dinsmore of Anson (VR), b Augusta 11 Apr 1793 dau of Thomas & Anna (True) Dinsmore (Robert R. & Cynthia A. McCausland, *The Diary of Martha Ballard 1785–1812* [1992], p. 262; "Historical Sketch of Early Masons," article in *Independent Reporter*, issue of 14 Aug 1919, p. 4, giving parentage of Dolly Dinsmore), d Athens 11 Jan 1875 ae 82y (g.s., Mt. Rest cem, transcribed in Prince, op. cit.). Lemuel moved to Athens about 1828 where he was the proprietor of the Somerset Tavern in the days of stage coach travel to Moosehead Lake
- iv Elizabeth B., b 1784 (*Embden Town of Yore*, p. 115) [Williams Papers gives b 25 Mar 1784]: d 19 Dec 1871 (Williams Papers): m Norridgewock 3 Jun 1800 Ephraim Sawyer of Anson (Norridgewock VR), b Madison 18 Dec 1772 (Williams Papers), d 9 May 1848 (Williams Papers)
- v Zerviah/Zeruiah, b 1786 (*Embden Town of Yore*, p. 115): d 20 Jun 1839 ae 53y (g.s., Fish cem, Anson): m Anson 1 Nov 1804 William Rogers of No. Anson (Anson VR), b c1785–86, d 10 Feb 1853 ae 67y (g.s., Fish cem)
- vi John, b 1787 (*Embden Town of Yore*, p. 115): d 1820 (ibid.): m int Anson 5 Jan 1808 Betsey Savage of Augusta (Anson VR), b Augusta 15 Aug 1783 dau of Edward & Mary (Heal) Savage (VR), d 1838 (Williams Papers). He lived near Anson on Seven Mile Brook (*Embden Town of Yore*, p. 112)

vii Lucinda, b 17 Apr 1789 (Williams Papers): d Farmer's Grove WI 17 Jul 1886 (ibid.): m Embden 28 Feb 1813 John Hilton of Embden (VR). Lucinda was not named in her father's will in 1820
viii Elihu, b 1791 (Williams Papers): d Anson 7 Jul 1818 ae 26y (David C. & Elizabeth K. Young, *Vital Records from Maine Newspapers, 1785–1820* [1993], p. 659): unm
ix Simeon, b 1793 (*Embden Town of Yore*, p. 115): d 14 May 1873 ae 78y 9m (g.s., Litchfield Plains cem, Litchfield): m Embden 16 Feb 1831 Mary Ann (Hilton) Tibbetts of Embden (VR), b Wiscasset cMar 1809 dau of Daniel & Mary/Polly (Brewer) Hilton (from death rec), d Litchfield 15 Nov 1895 ae 86y 8m 15d (Maine VR). They resided Anson in 1841 (Franklin Co deeds, 5:386), Winthrop in 1850 (USC) and Litchfield in 1860 (USC)
x Melinda, b 1795 (pension, op. cit.): d aft 1850 (USC): unm (Williams Papers)
xi Joseph, b 1797 (*Embden Town of Yore*, p. 115): d 9 Oct 1843 ae 46y (g.s., Sunset cem, Anson): m int Anson 5 Mar 1821 Abigail Spooner of New Portland (Anson VR), b c1800, d 5 Nov 1858 ae 58y (g.s., Sunset cem, Anson)
xii Morrill, b 1799 (*Embden Town of Yore*, p. 115) [Williams Papers gives b 24 Jul 1799]: d 29 Dec 1879 (Williams Papers; g.s., Bridge cem, Madison): m Anson 5 Dec 1822 Fatima Albee of No. Anson (VR), b Anson 29 Dec 1806 (Williams Papers), d 9 Oct 1885 (Hilton Papers at MHS; g.s., Bridge cem, Madison)
xiii Nathaniel, b 1801 (Williams Papers): unm (ibid.). He was not named in his father's will in 1820
xiv Rachel, b 1802 (*Embden Town of Yore*, p. 115): m bef 1820 (when her father wrote his will) _____ Withy
xv Anna, b c1804 (pension, op. cit.): living in 1820 (ibid.)

[Note there were 4 other children, 1 son and 3 daus, according to Anna's pension declaration, op. cit.]

Elaine Bush Prince, 74 Dennison Ave., Framingham, MA 01701-6419
Odile Williams, 4 Merrill St., Waterville, ME 04901

Williams, Nath[l]   52b   2 - 0 - 5 - 0 - 0
Woolwich Town, Lincoln County

NATHANIEL WILLIAMS, b Easton MA 20 Mar 1747 son of Timothy & Elizabeth (Brittun) Williams (VR; Georgetown VR): d Woolwich 23 Sep 1799 (VR; Dr. Buck, "Early Families of Woolwich, Maine," hereafter Woolwich

Families, DAR Misc Rec, 8:97); will probated 26 Nov 1799, William D. Patterson, *The Probate Records of Lincoln County, Maine 1760 to 1800* [repr 1991], pp. 354–56): m (1) 11 May 1773 SUSANNAH (WALKER) GRAY (Georgetown VR), b prob Woolwich 8 Sep 1752 dau of Capt. Solomon & Miriam (____) Walker (Ernest George Walker, *Embden Town of Yore* [1929], p. 113) and widow of James Gray (Georgetown VR) [see MOSES GRAY family, *Maine Families*, 1:129]. She d Woolwich 31 Jan 1792 (VR). He m (2) 11 Apr 1793 MEHITABLE PREBLE (Georgetown VR). Nathaniel was a Rev War soldier (Fisher's *Soldiers*, p. 864). He resided near the Walkers in Montsweag and worked as a tanner (Nathaniel's will; *Embden Town of Yore*, p. 113). In his will dated 13 May 1799, Nathaniel "of Woolwich" named his wife Mehetable, his son Timothy and his daus Abigail, Olive, Anne and Susanna.

Children by 1st wife, Susannah (Walker) Gray: births VR Woolwich
  i Timothy, b 27 Feb 1774: d Woolwich 2 Dec 1835 ae 62y (VR; g.s., Grover cem): m (1) Woolwich 25 Dec 1795 Abigail Blackman (VR) who d prob Woolwich 7 Jun 1820 ae 45y (VR; g.s., Grover cem): m (2) Woolwich 4 Jan 1821 Martha (Hilton) Collins (VR) who d by suicide Woolwich 27 Feb 1832 (VR)
  ii Betty, b 27 Jan 1777: d Woolwich 11 Jul 1778 (VR)
  iii Abigail, b 25 Apr 1779: m 1805 Joseph Cheney of Alna (Woolwich Families, op. cit.) son of Ralph & Lydia (Grover) Cheney of Wiscasset (Dr. Charles Crosby Williams, "Descendants of Richard Williams of Taunton MA through his son Nathaniel" [TS, Bowdoin College Library])
  iv Olive, b 30 May 1781: m 1804 Jesse White Jr. (Woolwich Families, op. cit.)
  v Anna, b 12 Jun 1783
  vi Susanna, b 4 Jun 1785

Child by 2nd wife, Mehitable Preble: birth VR Woolwich
  vii Betty, b 29 Apr 1794: d Woolwich 1 Dec 1794 (VR)

Elaine Bush Prince, 74 Dennison Ave., Framingham, MA 01701-6419
Odile Williams, 4 Merrill St., Waterville, ME 04901

Williams, Seth   39a   5 - 4 - 4 - 0 - 0
    Hallowell Town, Lincoln County

SETH WILLIAMS, b Easton MA 12 Dec 1756 son of Seth & Susannah (Fobes) Williams (Augusta VR): d Augusta 18 Mar 1817 (James W. North, *The History of Augusta, Maine* [repr 1981], hereafter North, p. 959): m Hallowell 1 Jan 1781

ZILPHA INGRAHAM (VR), b Stoughton MA 16 Apr 1761 dau of Jeremiah & Abigail (Hartwell) Ingraham (Augusta VR; North, p. 855), d Augusta 20 Sep 1845 ae 84y (VR). Seth was a Revolutionary War soldier and served in 1775 as a private in Capt. Macey's company from Easton MA. He moved with his brother Asa from Easton MA to Fort Western Settlement (later Augusta) in 1779 where he worked as a tanner (North, p. 959). He was a selectman in Augusta for sixteen years and represented Augusta in the General Court of MA in 1813 (North, p. 959).

Children: births VR Augusta except as noted
   i Hartwell, b 15 Nov 1781: d New Orleans LA 13 Oct 1818 (Augusta VR): m Augusta 25 May 1808 Sarah Bridge of Dresden (Augusta VR), b 19 May 1785 dau of Edmund & Phebe (Bowman) Bridge of Dresden (Augusta VR; North, p. 814), d Augusta 3 Sep 1834 (VR). Hartwell was a trader and a master mariner. He lived in Augusta
   ii Reuel, b 2 Jun 1783: d Augusta 25 Jul 1862 (VR): m Augusta 19 Nov 1807 Sarah Lowell Cony (VR), b 18 Jul 1784 dau of Daniel & Susanna (Curtis) Cony of Augusta (Augusta VR), d Augusta 17 Oct 1867 (VR). Reuel was a lawyer, representative, senator and elected to the U.S. Senate in 1837. He received a B.A. from Harvard in 1815 and an L.L.D. from Bowdoin College in 1855
   iii Moses, b 25 Jul 1785: d Augusta 3 Sep 1818 ae 33y (VR). He never married
   iv Seth, b 6 Nov 1787 (Robert R. & Cynthia A. McCausland, *The Diary of Martha Ballard 1785–1812* [1992], hereafter *Ballard Diary*, p. 78) [Augusta VR states he was b 5 Nov 1787]: d Augusta 11 Jan 1838 (VR): m Augusta 8 Aug 1816 Hannah Waters (VR) who d Augusta 16 Jul 1866 ae 71y (VR). He was a tanner and followed his father in business
   v Sarah/Sally, b 19 May 1789: d Augusta 28 Mar 1845 (VR): m Augusta 30 Nov 1815 her cousin Charles Williams (VR), b 14 Jun 1782 son of Edward & Sarah (Lothrop) Williams of Augusta (Augusta VR), d Augusta 13 Nov 1836 ae 54y (VR)
   vi Elizabeth, b 3 Feb 1792 (*Ballard Diary*, p. 221) [Augusta VR states she was b 2 Feb 1792]: d Augusta 2 Mar 1794 (VR)
   vii Abigail, b 31 Jan 1794 (*Ballard Diary*, p. 288) [Augusta VR states she was b 3 Feb 1794]: d Augusta 24 Sep 1848 ae 54y (VR): unm
   viii Daniel, b 12 Nov 1795: d Augusta 28 May 1877 ae 81y 6m (VR): m (1) Mary Sawtelle of Norridgewock (North, p. 962) who d Augusta 18 Jan 1827 ae 29y (VR): m (2) Augusta 2 Sep 1832 Hannah Bridge (VR), b 10 Sep 1810 dau of James & Hannah (North) Bridge (North, p. 814). Daniel was a lawyer, selectman, representative, Mayor, and Judge of Probate Court

ix   Edward, b 17 Nov 1797: d Augusta 10 Jul 1837 (VR): m (1) Louisa Lithgow (North, p. 962), b c1798 dau of James Noble Lithgow of Dresden (ibid.), d Augusta 1 Mar 1824 ae 26y (VR): m (2) Augusta 17 Nov 1832 Eliza Jane Perkins (VR). She m (2) Augusta 22 Dec 1840 William Bridge (VR; North, p. 962)
x   Eliza, b 30 Oct 1799: d Augusta 27 Aug 1883 ae 83y (VR): m Augusta 24 Dec 1821 Ebenezer Fuller (VR), b 25 Jan 1795 son of Francis Fuller of Readfield (Augusta VR; North, p. 873), d Augusta 7 Oct 1873 ae 78y (VR)
xi   Helen Marcia, b 3 Feb 1802: d Augusta 23 Mar 1873 ae 71y (VR): unm

Elaine Bush Prince, 74 Dennison Ave., Framingham, MA 01701-6419

Yeaton, Phillip   58a   2 - 1 - 3 - 0 - 0
Berwick Town, York County

PHILIP YEATON, b c1725 son of Philip Yeaton of Somersworth NH by a probable first wife whose name has not been found [he was b too early to have been a son of Philip Sr.'s 2nd wife, the wid Joanna (Pray) Roberts]: d Berwick 29 Mar 1817 ae 92y (John E. Frost & Joseph C. Anderson II, *Vital Records of Berwick, South Berwick and North Berwick* [1993], hereafter VR, p. 293): m Berwick 15 Feb 1749/50 DORCAS SMITH (VR, p. 193), b Berwick 15 Jul 1732 dau of John & Elizabeth (Heard) Smith (VR, p. 205; YCGSJ, 2 [1987]:70ff), prob the female ae over 45y in Philip's household in 1800 (USC). Philip was a soldier in the Louisbourg campaign in 1745. After his marriage, he settled in Berwick. He lived in the North Parish near the Blackberry Hill Meeting House (York Co deeds 98:74). On 8 Mar 1798, he deeded one-half of his homestead farm to his son, Richard (ibid.).

Children, all but Alice bp at the Berwick 2nd Church: NEHGR, 74 [1920]:216, 219, 220, 226, 227, 228, 229
   i   John, prob b in the early 1750s and bp with 4 siblings 3 Sep 1758: d bef 6 Apr 1780 when the adm of his estate was granted to his wid Molly (York Co Probate #20893): m Berwick 29 Sep 1774 Molly Jones (VR, p. 121) one of 7 children of John & Priscilla (Goodwin) Jones bp as a group at the Berwick 2nd Church 1 May 1761 (NEHGR, 74 [1920]:216, 225). She m (2) Berwick 27 Sep 1781 John Keay (VR, p. 123) son of Peter & Hannah (Roberts) Keay (YCGSJ, 7 [1992]:3ff). She m (3) Berwick 8 Dec 1814 Ichabod Tebbets (VR, p. 151) who was formerly married to Molly's sis, Catherine

ii   Joanna, b 17 May 1753 ("The Chadbourn(e) Family: 1989 Draft Edition" [TS, Chadbourne Family Assoc.]) and bp 3 Sep 1758: d Limerick 4 Mar 1826 ae 72y 9m and bur Waterboro (ibid.): m Berwick 26 Apr 1770 Paul Chadbourn (VR, p. 117), b Berwick 29 Mar 1748 son of Humphrey & Phebe (Hobbs) Chadbourn [see HUMPHREY CHADBOURNE family, *Maine Families*, 2:37–39], d No. Waterboro 31 Dec 1825 ("1989 Draft"). Paul moved to Coxhall [Lyman] in 1772 where he operated a mill, then moved to No. Waterboro in 1797 (ibid.)

iii Richard, bp 3 Sep 1758: d Berwick "by a fall from his house" 26 Nov 1811 (VR, p. 290): m Berwick 10 Nov 1774 Amey Brackett (VR, p. 121), bp Berwick 2nd Church 9 Nov 1755 dau of Isaac & Mary (Hamilton) Brackett (NEHGR, 74 [1920]:224; will of Isaac Brackett, York Co Probate #1588; Herbert I. Brackett, *Brackett Genealogy* [1907], pp. 285–86), d Berwick 14 Jan 1827 ae 72y (VR, p. 298). Richard was enumerated at Coxhall [Lyman] in 1790 (USC) where 2 of his sisters had settled, but was back in Berwick by 1800 (USC)

iv   Philip, bp 3 Sep 1758: either deceased or living away from Berwick on 3 Jan 1807 when his younger cousin was called Philip Yeaton "Jr." (York Co deeds 82:211)

v   poss Alice, b c1760 but not recorded in the Berwick baptismal records: d No. Berwick 29 Apr 1843 ae 82y (VR): m Berwick 9 Jan 1781 as his 2nd wife Eliphalet Pray (VR, p. 122), bp Berwick 1st Church 25 May 1749 son of Samuel & Dorothy (Cromwell) Pray (NEHGR, 82 [1928]:317), d No. Berwick 5 Feb 1837 ae 88y (VR, p. 651). Eliphalet had m (1) Berwick 23 Dec 1773 Mary Guptill (VR, p. 119)

vi   Elizabeth, b 28 Jan 1762 (*Maine Families*, 2:38) and bp 14 Feb 1762: d Lyman 20 Jun 1855 ae 93y (g.s., Chadbourne cem): m as his 2nd wife Berwick 18 Apr 1780 Simeon Chadbourn (VR, p. 123), b Berwick 16 Apr 1750 son of Humphrey & Phebe (Hobbs) Chadbourn and bro of Paul who m Elizabeth's sis Joanna ("1989 Draft," op. cit.) [see HUMPHREY CHADBOURNE family, *Maine Families*, 3:38], d Lyman 29 Oct 1846 ae 96y 6m (g.s., Chadbourne cem). He had m (1) Catherine Hanscom who d Lyman 21 Sep 1778 ae 26y (g.s., Chadbourne cem)

vii Experience, bp 16 Sep 1764: d Knox 4 Oct 1828 ae 64y (g.s., Knox Ridge cem): m Berwick 25 Mar 1782 Jeremiah Clements of Sanford (VR, p. 126), poss the Jeremiah Clements b Somersworth NH 30 Nov 1759 son of Job & Betty (Rollins) Clements of Somersworth NH ("Master Tate's Diary," NEHGR 74 [1920]:197), d Knox 13 May 1841 ae 83y (g.s., Knox Ridge cem)

viii Mary/Molley, bp 22 Jun 1766: d 11 Apr 1853 ae 86y 10m (g.s., Evergreen cem, Berwick): m Berwick 27 Nov 1786 Nehemiah Butler (VR, p. 129), b Berwick 29 Jul 1762 son of Samuel & Lydia (Kimball) Butler (VR, p.

220), d 28 Dec 1851 ae 89y 4m (g.s., Evergreen cem, Berwick) [see NEHEMIAH BUTLER family, *Maine Families*, 2:34]

ix Dorcas, b 3 Jul 1768 (Lebanon VR) and bp 10 Jul 1768: d Lebanon 5 Nov 1826 (VR): m Berwick 31 Oct 1786 Joseph Pray 3rd (VR, p. 129), b Berwick 17 Dec 1766 son of Capt. Joseph & Mary (Libbey) Pray (VR, p. 246), d Lebanon 25 Mar 1840 (VR)

x Phineas, b 10 Aug 1770 (Hallowell VR) and bp 23 Sep 1770: m Berwick 28 Sep 1794 Phebe Wentworth (VR, p. 138), b 9 Dec 1771 dau of Timothy & Amy (Hodgdon) Wentworth (John Wentworth, *The Wentworth Genealogy* [1878], 1:420; marriage rec in Hallowell VR gives her parents), d Hallowell 20 Apr 1864 ae 92y 4m (VR). They moved in 1798 to the part of Hallowell which later became Chelsea (Kingsbury & Deyo, *Illustrated History of Kennebec County, Maine* [1892], p. 763)

xi Sarah, b 25 Jun 1773 (*Wentworth Genealogy*, 2:146) and bp 1 Aug 1773: d 19 Sep 1847 (ibid., 2:146): m Berwick 18 Jan 1796 Samuel Wentworth (VR, p. 199), b 24 May 1773 son of Timothy & Amy (Hodgdon) Wentworth and sis of Phebe above, d 6 Nov 1849 (*Wentworth Genealogy*, 2:146). They res So. Berwick

xii Jacob, bp 23 Jun 1776

Joseph C. Anderson II, 5337 Del Roy Drive, Dallas, TX 75229

Young, Ezra   29c   2 - 0 - 2 - 0 - 0
Mount Desert Town, Hancock County

EZRA YOUNG, b Eastham MA 28 Nov 1735 son of David Jr. & Hannah (Twining) Young (MD, 17 [1915]:33): d Eden 12 Jun 1812 (George E. Street, *Mount Desert A History* [1926], p. 157): m Eastham MA 7 Aug 1760 CONSTANT MAYO of Eastham MA (MD, 31 [1933]:172), b Eastham MA 8 Apr 1737 dau of Jonathan & Thankful (Twining) Mayo (MD, 15 [1913]:140), d Eden 8 Apr 1816 (Street, op. cit., p. 157). Ezra and Constant settled at Duck Brook before 1774 when their son Ezra Jr. was born. His cattle mark was recorded at Mount Desert 18 Feb 1777 (VR). He was amoung the foremost citizens of Mount Desert holding many important offices in the towns of Mount Desert and Eden including committeeman, captain and major of the militia, selectman and Justice of the Peace (*Town Register of the Island of Mount Desert* [1909–10], pp. 59–60). Capt. Ezra Young was taken prisoner at Duck's Brook 24 Feb 1781 by the British on the war sloop ALLEGIANCE under the command of Capt. Mowatt. He was later released (Public Record Office, London, England, Masters Logs, Ad. 52, Vol. 2127, No. 4).

Children
- i Jonathan, b Eastham MA 26 Aug 1762 (MD, 31 [1933]:172): d Eastham MA 14 Aug 1767 (ibid.)
- ii Jonathan: b Eastham MA 23 Jul 1768 (MD, 31 [1933]:172): d Eastham MA 23 Nov 1769 (ibid.)
- iii Ezra, b Mount Desert Island 20 Jun 1774 (VR): m Sarah Hoges (Street, op. cit., p. 157)
- iv Rosanna, b Mount Desert Island 28 Nov 1782 (VR): d 15 Oct 1865 (g.s., Evergreen cem, Carrol's Hill, Southwest Harbor): m by her father 9 Dec 1804 Isaac Pepper Mayo (Street, op. cit., p. 156), b 17 May 1774 (g.s.) prob son of Joshua & Lydia (Pepper) Mayo of Eastham MA and Mount Desert Island, d 12 Jun 1866 (g.s., Evergreen cem, Southwest Harbor)

Joy and Leonard Mayo, RFD #1, Box 285, Ellsworth ME 04605

Please send new submissions of families and corrections for the *Maine Families in 1790* project to:

Maine Genealogical Society
P.O. Box 221
Farmington, ME 04938

ADDENDUM

MAINE FAMILIES IN 1790, Volume 1

The following corrections were received since the publication of *Maine Families*, Volume 3. See also the ADDENDUM items in *Maine Families*, Volume 2, pp. 325–26, and in *Maine Families*, Volume 3, pp. 315–22.

PAGE	FAMILY	CHANGES ARE UNDERLINED
1	Alden, Elizabeth	David Alden son of Benjamin & Hannah (<u>Brewster</u>) Alden
3	Allen, Joseph	[The following list of children for Joseph Allen is found in the Gray VR. Note revised order, some additional children, and revised birthdates] i Dorcas, b 18 Mar <u>1782</u> <u>ii</u> Statira, <u>b 20 Apr 1785</u> iii Andrew, <u>b 19 Jan 1787</u> iv Lucy, <u>b 14 May 1789</u> <u>v</u> Hannah, <u>b 20 Apr 1791</u> vi Daniel, b 10 Apr 1793 <u>vii</u> Otis, <u>b 20 Jul 1795</u> viii Joseph, b 24 Feb 1798 <u>ix</u> <u>Lydia, b 16 Apr 1800: d 9 Oct 1801</u> <u>x</u> Josiah, twin, b 9 Apr <u>1802</u> <u>xi</u> Susanna, twin, b 9 Apr <u>1802: d 9 Oct 1802</u> <u>xii</u> Elvira, <u>b 23 Aug 1804</u> <u>xiii</u> William, <u>b 8 May 1808</u>
4		<u>xiv</u> Emery, b 1 <u>May</u> 1812
26	Budge, James	He m Margaret Smart dau of <u>Robert</u> & Catherine (Percy) Smart of Brunswick (<u>BHM, 9:2; History of Penobscot County, Maine, p. 529</u>)
32	Burton, Nathan	v Mary, d 1854 enroute to MN (<u>Stephen Lee Robbins, Gray Family of Somerset & Washington Counties, Maine, pp. 35, 53, 55–56</u>). Her husband, John Gray, d Wesley <u>17 May 1832 ae 60y (g.s., Wesley Ridge cem)</u>

ADDENDUM

35	Card, Thomas	His wife, Elizabeth, m (1) Thomas Smart, b Brunswick 2 Aug 1739 son of <u>Robert</u> & Catherine (Percy) Smart (VR)
46	Clark, Ephraim	v Amos, *delete* d 8 Aug 1738, *add* <u>d Calais 1 May 1879 (g.s., Calais cem)</u>
73	Dennett, Jacob	Jacob m Elizabeth Smart, <u>b Brunswick 11 Jun 1741</u> dau of <u>Robert</u> & Elizabeth (Percy) Smart <u>(VR)</u>
158	Hutchins, William	He m (1) <u>Penobscot c1786 Mercy</u> Wardwell, b York <u>15</u> Oct 177<u>0</u> (VR Penobscot)<u>, bp York 6 Feb 1771 (YCGSJ, 5:2 [1990]:16)</u>, dau of Daniel & <u>Mary/Mercy</u> Wardwell iv Eliakim, m <u>int Penobscot</u> 31 Aug 1817 Sally Palmer <u>(VR)</u> vii Jesse, m <u>int Penobscot</u> 18 Mar 1821 Peggy Grindle of Sedgwick <u>(Penobscot VR)</u> x *delete* Alford, *add* Alfred
252	Smart, John	John, b Brunswick 17 Jul 1743 son of <u>Robert</u> & Catherine (Percy) Smart <u>(VR)</u>
253		iii Sarah, c <u>Sep 1777 (g.s.)</u> v John, <u>twin</u>, b 1 Jun 17<u>83</u>: d <u>Seboeis</u> 5 Aug 1853 ae 70y 2m (g.s.) vi <u>Olive Abigail</u>
264	Stubbs, Jeremiah	Jeremiah, b No. Yarmouth 24 Apr 1754 son of <u>Richard</u> & Mercy (Brown) Stubbs (VR). His wife, Jane Bradbury True, b No. Yarmouth <u>14 Mar</u> 1760 (VR) iii Sarah M., m <u>(1)</u> No. Yarmouth <u>8</u> Aug 1802 John Russell (VR): <u>m (2) No. Yarmouth 12 Feb 1806 Robert McGregor Moore (VR)</u>
280	Wardwell, Daniel	<u>Daniel prob m (2) bef Jul 1763 (when dau Temperance was bp) Mary/Mercy _____ (YCGSJ, 5:2 [1990]:16)</u> [Note additional children and revised birth order] *Delete 1st son Josiah, add:* <u>i</u> <u>Eliakim, bp York 26 Oct 1755 (YCGSJ, 5:2 [1990]:15)</u>

ii Jeremiah, *eliminate birth date for Elizabeth Banks*
iii Abigail, bp York 13 May 1759 (YCGSJ, 5:2 [1990]:15): d aft 30 Oct 1784 when her husband wrote a letter to her bro Jeremiah ("Penobscot Loyalists," *Downeast Ancestry*, 7:135, 149): m c1778 Daniel Brown of Bagaduce, a Loyalist who removed in 1784 to St. Andrews, New Brunswick (ibid.)
iv Tryphena, bp York 1 Aug 1761 (YCGSJ, 5:2 [1990]:16): d Scotland, Brant Co, Ontario, Canada 16 Jan 1813 (Norman Malcolm, "Malcolm-Wardwell Family Charts" [1934, NY City Public Library]): m 1776 Finlay Malcolm of Bagaduce ("Penobscot Loyalists," *Downeast Ancestry*, 7:149)
v Temperance, bp York 24 Jul 1763 (YCGSJ, 5:2 [1990]:16, mother's name of "Mercy" given on the record): d Frankfort 14 Aug 1838 [see DANIEL LOWE family, *Maine Families*, 3:170–71]: m 23 Jun 1801 widower Daniel Lowe of Frankfort (ibid.)
vi Sarah, bp 30 Jun 1765 (YCGSJ, 5:2 [1990]:16, mother's name of "Mercy" given on the record): m St. Andrews, New Brunswick 28 Oct 1784 Neal Brown of the 74th Regiment of Foot which had been stationed in Penobscot during the Rev War ("Penobscot Loyalists," *Downeast Ancestry*, 7:149)
vii Daniel
viii Mercy/Mary, b York 15 Oct 1770 (VR Penobscot)
Delete son Charles
ix Samuel

287	Whitmore, Francis	i	Stephen, d Bowdoinham 15 Apr 1816 (VR)
288		vi	Mary, b Medford MA 25 Dec 1750 (VR)
288	Whitmore, Stephen	i	Elizabeth Cutter, b 19 May 1764
			Insert following child:
		iii	Lydia, bp Medford MA 10 May 1767 (VR)
		iv	Samuel, d Bowdoinham 30 Oct 1818 (Doris M. Rowland, *Bowdoinham Deaths*, p. 135)

ADDENDUM

300	Ireland, Abraham	xiv Silas, b <u>1786</u>
305	Every-Name Index	*Delete:* Bailey, Olive (Landers), 300
		Delete: Bailey, Pegge, 300
		Delete: Bailey, Samuel, 300
		Delete: Bailey, Silas, 300
336		*Add:* <u>Ireland, Olive (Landers), 300</u>
		Add: <u>Ireland, Pegge, 300</u>
		Add: <u>Ireland, Samuel, 300</u>
		Add: <u>Ireland, Silas, 300</u>
358		*Delete:* Smart, Thomas, 26, 35(2), 252(2)
		Add: <u>Smart, Robert, 26, 35, 73, 252</u>
		Add: <u>Smart, Thomas, 35, 252</u>

ADDENDUM

MAINE FAMILIES IN 1790, Volume 2

PAGE	FAMILY	CHANGES ARE UNDERLINED
15	Bartlett, Jonathan	*insert after child Lydia:* vi Stephen, bp 5 May 1754 (North Parish Church, Plaistow NH [TS, Haverhill MA Public Library])
27	Brock, Francis	ix Betsey, m (1) int Lebanon 13 Nov 1820 John Woodsum (VR): m (2) Lebanon 4 Mar 1840 Levi Estus (VR)
72	Davis, Thomas	Hannah Bates was not a dau of Elijah Bates. Elijah's dau, Hannah, m John Woodman as proven by deeds disposing of Elijah's estate.
72	Dickey, Eleazer B.	Eleazer m 17 Aug 1784 Mary Hamlin (H. Franklin Andrews, *The Hamlin Family* [1902], p. 214, b Barnstable MA 17 Nov 1767 dau of Timothy & Mary (Hallett) Hamblin of Barnstable MA (ibid., p. 128), d Monroe 9 May 1852 (ibid., p. 214) v Pauline, b 7 Dec 1794 viii "Herbert" poss should be "Hallett" xiii Priscilla, b 19 Feb 1813
87	Fall, Ebenezer	i Tristram, b 1 Oct 1775
102	Francis, John	John was in Weld in 1810 census ix David Neal, m Marindy Whitney (VR Carthage)
108	Gordon, Ithiel	*Delete top two lines. Add:* Goadon, Thial 49b 1 - 1 - 2 - 0 - 0 Wales Plantation, Lincoln County
123	Hamlin, Timothy	v Nicholas, m (1) 25 Jul 1800 Deborah Cates (VR), b Gorham 10 Mar 1781 dau of Benjamin & Amy/Ann (Skillings) Cates (family Bible in DAR Misc Recs., 59A:21) [see BENJAMIN CATES family, *Maine Families*, 2:37], d 19 Jul 1815 (family Bible): m (2) Jun 1817 Hannah Rich (family Bible)

130	Haskell, John	vi	Betsey: *delete* "[see SMITH CRAM family]"
143	Hodgkins, Philip		Philip son of Philip <u>& Sarah (Griffin)</u> Hodgkins <u>who were m Newbury MA 13 Apr 1724 (VR)</u> vii James, b <u>c1775 (USC 1790–1820, m int Eden 20 Aug 1807</u> Mrs. <u>Tabitha D.</u> Smallidge <u>(VR)</u>
152	Jackson, Isaac	xii	Esther: *delete* "m Orchard Crommett." *Add* <u>m Washington ME 24 Jan 1835 Nathan G. Crummett, both of Patricktown Plt (Washington VR)</u>. [Orchard Crommett was the son of Nathan & Esther]
162	Joy, Samuel		Joy, Samuel 73c 2-2-5-0-0 <u>York</u> Town [not Berwick], York County
163	Joy, William		Joy, W^m <u>56b</u> 2-2-6-0-0 William m (2) 27 Dec 1808 Hannah <u>(Thurrell)</u> Hamilton <u>wid of John Hamilton [see JOHN HAMILTON family, *Maine Families*, 3:116]</u>, she d 21 Jan 1828
168	Knowlton, John		*After* [4th line] "d Kittery 18 Oct 1798 ae 34y (pension appl):" *Insert* <u>m int Kittery 14 Nov 1789 Dorcas Shapleigh (Joseph C. Anderson II & Lois Ware Thurston, *Vital Records of Kittery, Maine to the Year 1892* [1991], p. 246)</u>, bp 2nd Parish Kittery 4 Nov 1770 dau of Lt. James & Hannah (Bartlett) Shapleigh of Kittery
264	Smith, Ithiel		*Add following children by 2nd wife:* <u>vi</u> <u>Catherine, m Stephen Bowers and moved to NY (Albert J. Sears, *Early Families of Standish, Maine* [1991], hereafter Sears, p. 246)</u> <u>vii</u> Jonathan <u>viii</u> <u>Jesse, b c1788 (Sears, p. 246): d Grafton NH 15 Jun 1871 ae 83y 4m (ibid.)</u> <u>ix</u> David <u>x</u> <u>Josiah, b c1791 (Sears, p. 246): d 19 Jan 1880 ae 88y 10m (ibid.): m int 3 Nov 1812 Lucy Bean of Bethel (ibid.)</u>
268	Sprague, Capt. Eli	xvii	Mary Jane, *delete* "m Isaac Edgerly"

ADDENDUM

287	Tolman, Isaiah	Isaiah d Matinicus Island 15 Nov 1825 <u>ae 104y</u> (Charles A. E. Long, *Matinicus Isle, Maine, Its Story & Its People* [1926])
293	Warren, Walter	*After* [6th line] "dau of John & Elizabeth (Davis) Cotton (NEHGR 63:297/8)" *delete* "d Scarborough 7 Feb 1819 (NEHGR 130:190, Walter Warren Paper)." [This death refers to Walter's 2nd wife, not his 1st.] Walter m (2) widow Mary <u>(Randall)</u> Atwood (<u>NEHGR, 14:223;</u> Cum Co Deed 11:582)
294	Webb, Samuel	ii *Delete sentence* "[Georgetown VR mentions...]" *Insert following child betw Anna and John* ix <u>Bathsheba, b c1758, m John Gahan [see JOHN GAHAN family, in this volume]</u>
323	Young, George	[The family described in this sketch is not the one enumerated in 1790 at Cushing. That family was the family of George & Hannah Young, parents of the George Young who m Anne Johnston.] ii Margaret, b 8 Apr <u>1796</u>: m <u>19 Dec 1816 Capt. John</u> McIntyre <u>(Family Bible, copy in possession of Diana Overlock Sewell, Warren ME</u>)
324		iv Jane, d 17 <u>Oct</u> 1872 (g.s., Norton cem, Cushing): *delete her marriage date* viii Eliza, d <u>1895</u> x William James, *delete* "ae 80y in 1850 USC Waldoboro"
338	Every-name Index	*Add:* <u>Cobb, Elijah, 47</u> *Add:* <u>Cobb, Rachel, 47</u> *Add:* <u>Cobb, Sarah Jane (Bailey), 47</u>
339		*Delete:* Cole, Elijah, 47 *Delete:* Cole, Rachel, 47 *Delete:* Cole, Sarah Jane (Bailey), 47
378	Every-name Index	*Delete:* Nye, Carl F, 267 *Add:* <u>Nye, Carol F, 267</u>

ADDENDUM

MAINE FAMILIES IN 1790, Volume 3

PAGE	FAMILY		CHANGES ARE UNDERLINED
2	Additon, Thomas	v	Thomas, m Anna dau of Isaiah Beals, *not* "Buck"
26	Blodgett, Seth Jr.	iii	John, *delete birth info for his wife Lucy Perkins.* John m int Penobscot 5 Oct 1806 Lucy Perkins, b Penobscot 22 Mar 1788 dau of Daniel & Amy (Penny) Perkins [see *Maine Families*, 2:216]
38	Carll, Nathaniel		The sketch confuses Nathaniel Carll of Waterborough with Nathaniel Carle of Falmouth. See NATHANIEL CARLE family in this volume.
40	Cates, Joseph	ii	Abigail, d Readfield 27 Jun 1829 ae 80y 11m (g.s., Readfield Corner cem): m Gorham 6 Oct 1769 Ephraim Hunt (VR), b Falmouth 4 Jan 1743/4 son of Ichabod & Susanna (Frink) Hunt (*Index of Rev War Pensions in the National Archives* [NGS, 1976]; "Some Revolutionary War Soldiers Buried in Maine," *Downeast Ancestry*, [Oct 1982], p. 97), d 29 Mary 1831 ae 87y 11m (g.s., Readfield Corner cem)
45	Charles/Charls, John	ix	Elizabeth Farrington, b 2 May 1786 (g.s.; Thomas Page family Bible rec owned by Alan H. Hawkins, 14 Adelbert St., South Portland, ME 04106-6512)
56	Cutt/Cutts, Thomas	viii	Samuel, m Berwick 15 Oct 1767 Sarah Hill he of Pepperrellborough (Berwick VR), b Saco 14 Dec 1746 (VR), d Buxton 20 Jun 1832
63	Doane, Seath		*Add one child*
		vi	Abraham, b Eden 19 Dec 1781 (VR which does not name his parents; but he is named as a son of Seth in Han Co deed 21:222 dated 29 Oct 1802)

ADDENDUM

65	Dorman, Israel	*Insert one child:* i prob Temperance, b c1787 ii Israel iii Joseph iv Mary v Charlotte, unm in her bro Israel's will of 1850
90	Goodwin, Stephen	Stephen Goodwin m Olive Wyman dau of James & Bethiah (Millett) Wyman
111	Hall, Hatevil	ii Daniel, m Lorana Winslow, b 1 Jul 1737 dau of Job & Margaret (Barber) Winslow
121	Harmon, Benjamin	iii Nathaniel, *delete:* "They moved to Washington Territory"
150	Ireland, Abraham	Abraham...counterfeit bills (Ken Co Superior Judicial Court records, MSA)
157	Judkins, Benjamin	Delete Sarah Nealey as Mary Philbrook's mother. Sarah was Mary's step-mother. As proved in her father's will, Mary was a dau of his first wife whose name was Mary (Rockingham Co NH Probate #4593; Rockingham Co NH deeds 177:245).
162	Knight, Jeremiah	Children by 1st wife Mary Butler, b Pownal: births VR Freeport [Note additional children and revised order of births] i Hannah, b 2 Jan 1789: m Pownal 2 Apr 1812 William Sawyer ii Abigail/Nabby, b 4 Jan 1791 iii Aseneth, b 11 Feb 1793: m Pownal 22 Aug 1825 John Newbegin iv Reuben, b 29 Aug 1795 v Edward, b 25 Jul 1797 vi Jeremiah, b 10 Nov 1801 vii Mary, b 31 Jan 1804
163		Children by 2nd wife Susan Frost, b Pownal: births VR Freeport viii Sarah, b 24 Nov 1812 ix Olive, b 18 Jul 1823 *Delete:* "vi dau, m ____ Pierce (letter of Mrs. Florence Nason at MHS)"

ADDENDUM

192 Moulton, William
    i *Delete for William* d Pittston 15 Jul 1836 (VR). *Delete for William's wife Jane* d Pittston 18 Nov 1876 (VR). [These are the death dates of William's half-brother Oliver and his wife Salome.]

224 Pote, Increase
    i William, *delete all after* "Cum Co deeds 65: 366." *Add:* m c1800 Lucretia Kilpatrick, dau of Floyd & Mary (Carle) Kilpatrick [see FLOYD KILPATRICK family]. [Lucretia Kilpatrick was the aunt of Lucretia Locke. Lucretia Locke d 14 Dec 1807 (C. S. Tibbetts, "Falmouth, Maine Marriages and Deaths" [TS, MHS])]
    ii Elisha, m Lucy Kilpatrick, prob dau of Floyd & Mary (Carle) Kilpatrick [see FLOYD KILPATRICK family]

235 Reed, Bartholomew
    v Naomi, m 22 Nov 1795 Thomas Jepson as his 2nd wife (Janus G. Elder, *A History of Lewiston, Maine* [repr 1989], p. 227) [see THOMAS JEPSON family, *Maine Families*, 1:116]

246 Sargent, Paul D.
Delete "2nd wife Catherine _____." [Paul predeceased his 1st and only wife Lucy Sanders]
    x *Delete data given, replace with* Harriet Elizabeth, b Sullivan 2 Apr 1791: d Sullivan May 1833: unm (*Epes Sargent*, op. cit., p. 217)
    xi FitzHenry

248 Schoppe, Anthony
Anthony, d Jonesboro 17 Oct 1817 (personal affidavit in pension file, National Archives): m Boston MA 21 Nov 1784 Phebe Speare (*A Report of the Record Commissioners of the City of Boston, Containing Boston Marriages from 1752 to 1809* [1883], p. 103), b prob Braintree MA c1766 dau of William & Anna (Brackett) Speare, d Jonesboro 9 Sep 1839 (pension file, op. cit.).

271 Taylor, Elias
    v Elias, his wife Phebe Mosher was the dau of Elisha and Judith (Crowell) Mosher [see ELISHA MOSHER family in this volume]

ADDENDUM

272 Taylor, Elias   vi   John d Belgrade <u>6 Feb</u> 1881 <u>ae 86y</u> (g.s.): m Belgrade 22 Feb 1816 Ellice/Alice <u>Braley</u> (his father officiated) <u>(VR)</u>

277 Thompson, Cornelius   *Delete* [3rd line]: "prob dau of Nicholas & Hannah (Hadden) Smith (Rev. C. N. Sinnett, *Our Thompson Family* [1907])." [Research of Daniel H. Burrows (RD 1, Box 211A, Otisville, NY 10963) indicates that Nicholas and Hannah were not Hannah (Smith) Thompson's parents.]
Add after "Children b Brunswick:" <u>VR;</u> Sinnett, op. cit., & cited sources
Add following two children:
<u>viii</u>   <u>Robert, b 11 Sep 1757: d 1808 ae 51y: m 23 May 1783 his cousin Ruth Thompson, b New Meadows 29 Dec 1763 dau of James & Lydia (Brown) (Harris) Thompson</u>
<u>ix</u>   <u>Phineas, b 21 Jul 1760: went to sea in 1780 and vanished</u>

286 Turner, Benjamin   *Delete* "i   Mier [sic]"
[Note revised order and addition children]
<u>i</u>   David, <u>m (2) Nancy Boynton, b c1804 (1850 USC)</u>
<u>ii</u>   Nehemiah/<u>Mier</u>, m (1) Susan <u>Greenleaf</u>: m (2) Elizabeth <u>Williams</u>
iii   Benjamin
Delete child Sarah
<u>iv</u>   <u>Mary/Mollie, b 1788: d1836:</u> m James Boynton
<u>v</u>   Hollis
<u>vi</u>   James, m Lois <u>Gilpatrick</u>
<u>vii</u>   Lois, <u>m James Boynton</u>
Delete all info on son Daniel. Add following:
<u>viii</u>   <u>Daniel, b c1790: m Sadine Jackson dau of Levi Jackson</u>
<u>ix</u>   Joseph, m <u>Pamelia Day</u>
<u>x</u>   <u>Eunice, m Eben Whitten and res Montville</u>
<u>xi</u>   <u>Fanny, d soon aft her father</u>

287 Turner, David   *Add:*
<u>ix</u>   <u>John, b c1819, d 11 Feb 1850 (g.s., Old Greely's Corner cem, Palermo)</u>

ADDENDUM

304	Whitney, Daniel		Daniel m Louise <u>Stubbs [see SAMUEL STUBBS family, *Maine Families, 1:263*</u>]
310	Woodward, Samuel	xi	Mary, m Caleb <u>Barker (NEHGR, 66 [1912]: 109)</u>
		xii	Michael, <u>m (2) Gardiner 7 Jun 1849 Joanna (Godfrey) Stevens (VR)</u>
377	Every-name Index		NYE, Carol F., *add:* <u>169, 259</u>

SUBMITTER LIST

MAINE FAMILIES VOLUME 4

Abendroth, Kathi J.
Adams, Clayton R.
Aldrich, Paul M.
Anderson, Joseph C. II
Bailey, Leroy M.
Batchelder, Dana A.
Beardsley, Marjorie G.
Blaney, Chuckie
Bond, Theodore S.
Brooks, Thelma Eye
Brownell, Richard J.
Calvert, Eunice
Chadbourne, Earlene/ Kitty A.
Clark, Kenneth Alton
Conley, Deborah
Corrow, Cynthia
Crane, Dorothy O.
Davis, Joyce P.
Dodge, Madeline Stevens
Doherty, Thomas P.
Dorman, Frank
Dotts, Helen Burnell
Ellis, Sandra J.
Farnham, Russell C.
Flamion, Rosemary
Gower, Gerald F.
Griffin, Robert D.
Griffiths, Lois M.

Hanscom, Constance
Hanscom, Robert
Hawkins, Alan H.
Henley, Berkeley
Hillman, Ralph E.
Hills, Betty Meynell
Holmes, Mary Direxa (Haynes)
Hughes, Maxine B.
Huntley, Joyce E.
Joy, Charles Austin
Kane, Paula & Franklin
Kane, Virginia L
Lynch, Carolyn Morgan Bailey
Lynds, Ardell J. Parkman
Mackesy, Vincent A.
Mayo, Joy & Leonard
McKay, T. A.
MacNair, June Tracy
Mildram, Barbara
Morris, Gordon Alan
Nye, Carol F.
Otten, Marjorie Wardwell
Pardi, Elvera Stevens
Parkhurst, Peter G.
Pike, Allen R.

Prince, Elaine Bush
Rand, David P.
Rawson, Gerald L.
Riley, Janet H.
Roberts, Ervin
Sabin, Alice L.
Sanders, Leslie Dow
Sanderson, Mabel McAllister
Scalisi, Marie
Seitz, Janet S.
Simpson, Peggy Taylor
Smith, Danial R.
Smith, Myron C.
Spiller, Dexter T.
Stearns, Warren D.
Taverner, Elizabeth B.
Thompson, Zane A.
Thurston, Lois W.
Tinkham, Henry
Tower, Dorothy Moore
Townsend, Eleanor W.
Vickery, James E.
Wang, Joan Parsons
Weaver, Lois
Wescott, Howard E. Jr.
Wick, James H.
Wieser, Robert
Williams, Phyllis S.

EVERY NAME INDEX

The following Every Name Index compiled by Picton Press contains a total of 12,115 entries and includes all names found anywhere in this book. Women are indexed whenever possible under both their maiden and married name(s). Maiden names are given in parentheses, thus Mary (Smith) Jones. When the maiden name is unknown, it is given thus: Mary (--) Jones. As always with genealogical records, readers are cautioned to check under all conceivable spellings. We have grouped some similar spellings together and in such cases have added a cross-reference to other spellings, as an aid to your search.

Picton Press   September 14, 1994

[INDIANS]
  Sabbatis, 271
[ROYALTY]
  King William, 254
[SERVANTS]
  Boston, 294
  Fanny, 294
  Hagor, 294
  Jack, 294
  Jeffery, 294
  Rose, 294
  Sherman, 294
[UNKNOWN]
  Bethiah, 219
  Hannah (Farnham), 87
ABBOTT/ ABBOT
  --, 1
  Aaron, 2
  Abigail (Lord), 2
  Abigail (Nason), 4
  Abigail (Stover), 8
  Abigail Lord, 3
  Ammey (Pumroye), 7
  Amos, 6
  Amy, 5
  Anna (--), 2
  Anney, 3
  Benjamin, 1
  Betsey, 4-6
  Betsey (Herbert) Banks, 3
  Betty, 6
  Christian (--), 5
  Christian (Stimpson), 5

D, 1
Daniel, 2-3
Dorcas, 151
Dorcas (Spencer), 2
Ebenezer, 1-2
Edmund, 1, 3
Eliza, 239
Elizabeth, 4, 6
Elizabeth (Brackett), 6
Elizabeth (Frye), 4
Elizabeth (Herbert) Banks
  Wartman, 3
Esther, 1
Fanny (Clark), 7
Hannah, 7
Hannah (Chubb), 3
Hannah (Farnum), 4
Hannah (Hubbard)
  Hodsdon, 2
Hitty, 6
Ichabod, 2
Isaac, 6
James, 6
Jane (Fullerton), 8
Jeremiah, 6
John, 3-4
John Jr, 4
Jonathan, 4, 223
Joshua, 4, 6-8
Joshua Jr, 5
Keziah (Bragdon), 6
Legro, 2
Louise, 7

Lovisa, 7
Luvice, 7
Lydia, 233
Mary, 5-6, 102
Mary (--), 5
Mary (Legro), 1
Mary (Wood), 6
Mehetable, 6
Mehitable, 5-6, 21, 151
  249
Mercy (Gowan), 239
Molly, 5-6
Moses, 5-8
Nathan, 223, 239
Nathaniel, 223
Olive (Hearl), 1
Patience, 171
Patience (Wood), 223
Peter, 6-7, 301
Phebe, 5-6
Phebe (Abbott), 6
Phillip, 4
Polly, 8, 301
Rachel (Bickford), 8
Ruth, 273
Ruth (Bragg), 4
Ruth (Lovejoy), 4
Sally, 8
Samuel, 6-7
Sarah, 1-2, 5-6
Sarah (--), 7, 301
Sarah (Chadwick), 1
Sarah (Hussey), 9

327

ABBOTT/ ABBOT
(continued)
Sarah (Merrill), 7
Stephen, 1
Susana (Pitts), 223
Susannah, 4
Theophilus, 5-6
Thomas, 1
Thomas Jr, 1
ABENDROTH
Kathi Judkins, 146
148-149
ADAMS
Anna Maria, 286
Benjamin, 9
Clayton R, 49, 80, 153
257-258
Hezekiah, 276
Jane, 242
Magdalene (Hilton), 297
Mary, 254
Mary (Allen), 9
Mary (Field), 9
Mary (Johnson), 35
Miriam (Watson), 9
Richard, 35
Samuel, 9, 287
Sarah (Staples) Smith, 9
ADDITON
Anna (Beals), 320
Anna (Buck), 320
Bethia (Richmond), 149
Nancy (Keen), 149
Otis, 149
Thomas, 149, 320
ADLE
Catherine, 149
AHLQUIST
Earlene, 135
Earlene/ Kitty, 59
ALBEE
Fatima, 306
ALDEN
Benjamin, 313
David, 313
Elizabeth, 313
Hannah (Brewster), 313
ALDRICH
Gilbert, 137
Paul M, 63
Paul Mosher, 192
Syrena B (Ricker) Jepson
137
ALEXANDER
Hannah, 154
Jane, 281
Sarah (Phinney) Cummings
219

William Jr, 219
ALLEN/ ALLAN/ ALLYN
Abel, 195
Abigail (Hall), 8
Ama, 111
Amiable, 111
Andrew, 313
Catherine, 9
Catherine (Furbish), 8
Daniel, 313
David, 9
Deborah (Hawkes), 9
Dorcas, 9, 156, 313
Ebenezer, 9
Elisha, 284
Elizabeth, 103
Elvira, 313
Emery, 313
Hannah, 313
Isaac, 8-9
Isabella, 14-15
Jane (Hall), 9
Joanna (Nash), 195
Johannah (Nash), 195
John, 12
Joseph, 313
Josiah, 313
Lebbeus, 195
Lucy, 313
Lydia, 313
Mary, 9
Mary (Dillingham), 195
Otis, 313
Patience (Carle), 49
Rebecca, 267
Robert, 8-9
Samuel, vi
Sarah, 9, 267, 284-285
Sarah (Hussey), 9
Statira, 313
Susanna, 313
Thankful, 19, 248
William, 313
Zaccheus, 49
ALLEY
--, 126
Hannah (Brown), 126
John, 126
Joshua, 126
Tryphena (Heath), 126
ALMARY/ ALMONY
Hannah, 112
AMES [SEE ALSO EAMES]
Amos, 33-34
Mary (Bragdon), 33-34
Polly (Bragdon), 34
Sally, 213
Sarah J (--), 271

ANDERSON (SEE ALSO HENDERSON]
Agnes (Finney), 255
Anna, 254-255
Edward, 71
Elizabeth, 254
Jacob, 255
Joseph C II, iii, 2-3, 6, 38
40-41, 45, 95, 101, 114
116-118, 125, 176, 182
234-236, 286, 311
Mary Camilla, 122
Nancy, 177
ANDRE
Maj --, 145
ANDREWS
Amos, 11
Anna (--), 265
Anna (Hodsdon), 10
Betsey, 53
Betsey (Estes), 10
Caleb, 265
Elisha, 103
Eliza, 11
Elizabeth, 10, 103
Elizabeth (Sawtelle), 10
Elsie, 11
Hannah, 11
Hannah (Bean), 11
Hezekiah, 10
Huldah, 11
Jeremiah, 10
Jeremiah Jr, 10
Joanna (Pray), 103
John, 155
John Jr, 155
Julia, 11
Lucy (Rust), 10
Mary, 11
Olive, 103
Patty (Knight), 155
Phebe (Kimball), 10
Ruth, 265
Salome, 10
Sarah, 11
Sarah (Kinsman), 155
Stephen, 11
William, 10
ANICE/ ANNIS
Deliverance, 186
Elizabeth, 197
Lydia, 163
Mary, 184
Molly, 184
Pomp, 296
ARCHER
Allen, 13
Anna, 13

EVERY NAME INDEX

ARCHER (continued)
Ansel, 13
Anselm, 13
David Cobb, 13
Dorcas (Nickerson), 12
Eleanor (Durkee), 12
Eliakim S, 13
Eliza (Small), 13
Elizabeth, 13
Elizabeth (Tupper), 11
Esther (Ingalls), 13
George, 13
Hannah (Tupper), 13
Henry, 11
Henry G, 13
James, 12
Jane (Barfield), 13
John, 11-12
John Jr, 12
Joseph, 12
Lucy W (Colson), 12
Lydia Gates, 12
Mary, 12
Mary (--), 11
Mary (Seaton), 13
Mary (Smith), 12
Phoebe (Floyd), 13
Polly (Seaton), 13
Ruth, 13
Sally (Foster), 13
Sarah (Newcomb), 13
Susan (Giles), 13
Thomas, 13
William Gates, 12
AREY
Abigail, 193
ARNO
Mary, 300
ARNOLD
--, 56
Col --, 111
ASH/ ASHE
Elizabeth D, 216
Lucy (Johnson), 216
Nathaniel, 216
ASHLIN
Robert W, 268
ATHEARN
Rebecca, 63, 66
Sarah (Skiff), 66
Solomon, 66
ATKINS
Hannah, 288
ATKINSON
Abby (Plummer), 167
Ann (Lane), 157
Joseph, 157
Mary, 203

Moses, 157, 203
Nancy (Lane), 157
Oswell, 167
Polly, 203
Rebecca (Woodman), 157 203
Rosanna, 167
Sally (McAllister), 167
ATWOOD
Anna, 23
Charlotte (Pendleton), 212
Hannah, 253
Jane (Nye), 199
John, 199
Mary, 41-42
Mary (Randall), 319
Richard, 41
William, 212
AULD
Frances (McCobb) 155-156
James, 155-156
John, 155
Mary (McCobb), 155
Rachel, 155
Sally, 155
Sally (Knight), 156
Sarah, 155
Sarah (Knight), 156
AUSTIN
Andrew, 139
Benjamin, 51-52
Catherine, 82, 87
Eliza, 133
Elizabeth, 89
Elizabeth (Billings), 170
Hannah, 107-108
Ichabod, 170
Joseph, 52, 107
Judith (Jepson), 137
Mary (Hanson), 137
Mary (Hoag), 139
Mary T, 146
Miriam (Hussey), 137
Nathaniel, 137
Sarah, 51-52, 105
Sarah (Jepson), 139
Sarah (Pinkham), 51
Susannah, 170
AVERILL
Eunice, 154, 231
Job, 205
Lydia, 205
Margaret (Simpson), 205
AVERY
David, 103
Elizabeth (Allen), 103
Hannah (Potter), 226

John, 226
Lucy, 102-103
Lucy (--), 226
Lydia, 126
Samuel, 226
AYER
Abigail, 248
Elizabeth (--), 248
Jonathan, 121
Polly, 162-163
Timothy, 248
BABB
Sally (Small), 258
Sara, 35
Solomon, 258
Zilpha (Hall), 282
BABBIDGE
Abigail, 8, 300
Rebecca (Bibber), 300
William, 300
BABCOCK
Anna (Pettingill), 14
Henry, 14
Jane, 221
Jemima (Gould), 14
Jeremiah, 14
John, 14
Martha, 14
Martha (Healey), 13
Mary (Savage), 14
Mary (Tolman), 14
Mercy, 15
Mercy (--) Bickford, 14
Polly (Hinkley), 14
Samuel, 13-14
Sarah (Fish), 14
Sarah (Fisk), 14
Sybil, 14-15
Sybil (Pratt), 14
Tabitha (Savage), 14
Tilley (Ingraham) Perkins 15
Tily (Ingraham) Perkins, 15
BACHELDER [SEE BATCHELDER],
BACHILER [SEE BATCHELDER],
BACON
Apphia (Cole), 15
Elaine, 236
Hannah (--) Simons, 15
Mary, 15
Mary (--), 15
Mary (Irish), 279
Nathaniel, 15
Sarah, 279
Thomas, 15
Timothy, 279

EVERY NAME INDEX

BAGLEY
Dorothy, 73
Mary, 87, 89
BAILEY/ BAYLEY
Benjamin, 257
Bethia (Small), 257
Boston, 294
Carolyn Morgan, 210
Delight, 256
Elizabeth, 176, 179
Isaac, 257
Jacob, 266
Jane, 192
Jane (Brady), 192
Jenny, 192
John, 192, 230, 266
Leroy M, 9, 141
Martha, 189
Mary (--), 266
Mary (Blake), 257
Nancy (Stevens), 266
Olive (Landers), 316
Pegge, 316
Samuel, 316
Sarah, 177
Sarah Jane, 319
Silas, 316
BAKER
Abigail, 137
Elizabeth, 245
John, 161, 214
Nancy, 161
Patience, 214
Ruth (Barker), 214
Salome (Drury), 161
BALLARD
Betty, 191
Ebenezer, 121
Irena (Leeman), 160
Martha, 146, 191, 230, 291
Martha (Hanscom), 121
Telemecus, 160
BALLESTER
Sarah, 174
BANGS
Barnabas, 263
Barnabas Jr, 263
Betty (Cloutman), 263
Catharine (Stevens), 263
D, 110
Loruhama (Elwell), 263
BANKS
-- (--), 16
Aaron, 16
Aaron Jr, 16, 287-288
Avis (Lowder), 16
Betsey (Herbert), 3
Betsy, 16, 287

David, 3
Ebenezer, 17
Eliza Ann, 3
Elizabeth, 16, 286-287
   290, 315
Elizabeth (Herbert), 3
Esther, 17
James, 17
Josiah, 16
Lucy, 16
Lydia (Woodbridge), 195
Mary, 16
Mary (Leach), 16
Mary (Perkins), 16, 287
Moses, 297
Olive, 16, 288
Polly, 16
Rachel C, 195
Ruth, 297
Ruth (Weare), 297
William, 195
BARBER
Elizabeth, 155
Margaret, 321
BARFIELD
Jane, 13
BARKER
--, 21
Abby, 19
Abiah P (--) Kenniston, 17
Abigail, 19
Abigail (Gorham), 18
Abigail (Mitchell), 272
Abigail (Segar), 249
Abigail Gorham, 18
Anna (Hill), 17
Anne (Swan), 272
Caleb, 324
Daniel, 17
David, 19
Deborah (Gorham), 19
Deborah (Josslyn), 19
Elethere, 184
Elizabeth, 4, 18-19
Eunice (Riggs), 18
Hannah, 4
Hannah (Cowin), 17-18
Illathera, 184
Jeremiah, 18
Jesse, 272
Jonathan, 17, 249, 272
Josiah, 17
Julia, 18
Lewis, 17
Mary, 18
Mary (Heard), 17
Mary (Woodward), 324
Mary G, 19

Nancy, 18
Nancy (Pease), 17
Nancy (Swan), 272
Naomi (Swan), 272
Nathaniel, 17
Patience (Howland), 18
Phebe (--), 18
Ruth, 214
Sally (Pease), 17
Samuel, 18
Sarah, 18, 21
Sarah (Pease), 17
Susanna (Garrett), 18-19
Tamson, 18
Temperance (Garrett)
   Gorham, 18
William Sr, 249
BARNES/ BARNS
-- (--), 218
Abraham, 218
Benjamin, 218
Martha (Phinney), 218
Mary, 138
BARR
Alexander, 208
Lucy (Small), 257
Mehitable (Peabody), 208
Robert, 257
BARRETT/ BARRET
Jonas Stone, 212
L, 110
Mercy Thomas (Pendleton)
   Brown, 212
Sarah (Dudley), 212
Timothy, 212
BARTLETT
-- (Barker), 21
Ann (Clark), 19
Anna, 20
Anne (Hall), 19
Apphia, 21
Bethiah (--) Evans Merriam
   181
Betsey, 20, 249
Burry, 20
David, 167
Ebenezer, 19
Eleanor (Martin) Kimball
   174
Elisha, 21
Elizabeth (Segar), 19
Elizbeth Taylor, 43
Enoch, 19-20
Enoch Jr, 21
Hannah, 318
Joanna (Taylor), 43
John Heard, 181
Jonathan, 21, 153-154, 216

EVERY NAME INDEX

BARTLETT (continued)
Jonathan (continued)
226, 317
Lorana, 21
Lucy, 11, 21
Lydia, 21, 154
Lydia (Chase), 153, 216
226
Lydia (Frost), 20
Margaret (McAllister), 167
Mehitable, 154, 216, 226
Mercy, 272
Nancy, 20
Naomi, 21
Olive, 21
Patty, 21
Polly, 21
Priscilla, 65
Rachel, 226
Relief, 10-11, 20
Reuben, 20
Ruth, 153, 217
Samuel, 43, 174
Sarah, 144
Sarah (Barker), 21
Sarah G (Hinkson), 21
Stephen, 317
Submit, 20
Thankful, 11, 21
Triphena (Horr), 21

BARTOL
--, 292
Fanny (Warren) Coombs
292

BARTON
Asa, 272
Eunice, 272
Mercy (Bartlett), 272

BASTON
Seba, 75

BATCHELDER/ BACHELDER,ETC
--, 189
Abigail (Richardson), 240
Anna (Richardson), 239
Apphia (Lowell), 239-240
Dana A, 130, 223
Dana A, 51, 107, 121, 142
193, 196, 238-239
246-248, 259, 279, 293
Dolly, 202
Ebenezer, 202
Elizabeth (Davis), 227
Ephraim, 239-240
Hannah, 227(2), 302
Jonathan, 189
Lydia (Hall) Richardson
239

Margaret (Clark), 189
Martha (Bayley), 189
Rebecca, 253
Samuel, 227, 239
Sarah, 168
Sarah (Moody), 189
Sarah (Palmer), 189
Scribner Jr, 189
Susanna (--), 202
Sylvanus, 240

BATES
Hannah, 317
Joseph, 132
Susannah (Howard), 132

BAYLEY [SEE BAILEY],

BEAL/ BEALE
-- (Alley), 126
Alice, 290
Clarissa (Pike), 222
Jeremiah, 126
Jerusha (Fluent), 222
Mary (Archer), 12
Samuel, 12
Samuel Treat, 222
William, 222

BEALS
Anna, 320

BEAN/ BEANE
Abigail, 150, 251-252
Anna (Simpson), 250-251
Benjamin, 91
Betsey (Smith) Prescott
227
Charity (Tebbetts), 135
Ebenezer, 251
Elizabeth, 136
Hannah, 11, 156-157
Hannah (Smith), 91
Jeremiah, 227
Joseph, 135
Levi, 60
Lucy, 318
Luther, 11
Lydia (Kimball), 11
Mary, 135
Mehitable, 90-91
Polly, 135
Roxanna (Carpenter)
Corson, 60
Sarah, 187-188

BEEDLE/ BEETLE
Elizabeth, 36
Jedidah, 64

BELCHER
Margaret (More), 134
Martha Stoyell, 134
Supply, 134

BENNETT/ BENNIT
Abigail, 22
Andrew, 21-22, 97
Andrew H, 75
Anthony Jr, 264
Bethania (Brann), 22
Caroline (Page), 22
Clarissa (Dennison), 75
Deborah, 22
Dorcas (Wharff), 265, 299
Fanny, 294
Isaac, 22, 265, 299
Jael, 160
Jerusha, 264, 299
John, 22
Lydia (Brann), 21
Lydia (Brawn), 21
Margaret, 22
Margaret (Gilley), 21, 97
Mary, 22
Moses, 22
Peggy (Gilley), 97
Peter, 21-22
Samantha (Brawn), 22
Susanna, 265, 299
Susannah (Haskell), 264
William, 161

BERRY
Anna (Rankins), 238
Hannah, 276-277
John, 158, 238
Jonathan, 238
Joseph, 274
Mary, 274, 292
Mary (Lane), 158
Olive, 175
Polly (Lane), 158
Sarah, 120
Sarah (--), 238

BESSEY
Polly, 88

BEVERLY
Lucy (Peabody), 209
Varnum, 209

BIBBER
Rebecca, 300

BICKFORD
-- (--), 23
Abigail, 23, 184
Abigail (Tibbetts), 23
Daniel, 8
Dorcas Milbury, 269
Elizabeth (Fogg), 23
Elizabeth (Kendall), 23
184
Eunice (Petty), 216
George, 23
Gideon, 23

BICKFORD (continued)
  Hannah, 215
  Hannah (--), 8
  Henry, 23
  Hulda, 23
  Jemima, 42
  Joanna, 23
  John, 23
  Joseph, 216
  Joshua A, 216
  Loisa (Rhodes), 216
  Lucy, 293
  Martha (Mansfield), 23
  Mary, 125
  Mehitable (Hathorn), 23
  Mercy (--), 14
  Nathaniel Hathorne, 23
  Olive (Milbury), 269
  Paul, 23, 184
  Pierce, 269
  Rachel, 8
  Ruhama, 253
  Ruthanna, 253
  Sally, 220
  Sarah (Goubert), 23
  Susanna, 221
  William, 23
  William Kendall, 23
BICKMORE
  John, 22
  John Jr, 22
  Margaret (Bennett), 22
  Margaret (Meserve), 22
BILLINGS
  Abigail (Kilgore) Russell 151
  John, 151
  Nabby (Kilgore) Russell 151
  Phebe (Cole), 151
  Silas, 151
  Susan, 260
BILLINGTON
  Mary, 270
BINFORD
  Phebe Elizabeth, 245
BIRD
  Ann, 194
  Elizabeth (Ward), 194
  Jacob, 194
BISHOP
  Mary (Kane), 143
BLACK
  Hanah (Hamblin), 113
  Joab, 113
  Josiah, 113
  Marcy (Cookson), 113
  Sally, 80

  Sarah, 80
BLACKINTON
  Olive, 283
BLACKMAN
  Abigail, 307
BLACKSTONE
  Caroline, 75
BLAIR
  Mary, 96
  Rebecca (Knowles), 96
  William, 96
BLAISDELL
  Enoch, 83
  Ephraim, 82
  Ivory, 86
  John, 83
  Salley (Farnham), 86
  Sarah, 82-83, 86
  Sarah (Blaisdell) Farnham Horn, 83
  Sarah (McIntire), 83
  Thankful (Webber), 82
BLAKE
  Abigail (--) Girdy, 24
  Abigail (Giles), 25, 28
  Abigail (Norcross), 26
  Abigail (Richard), 24, 28
  Abigail (Thomas), 28
  Anna (Taylor), 24
  Annie (Taylor), 24
  Avadana, 25
  Benjamin, 231
  Betsey (Phillips), 24
  Betsy (Briggs), 24, 28
  Blake, 28
  Bradbury, 26
  Caleb, 24, 28
  Calvin, 24
  Clymena, 27
  Daniel Briggs, 24
  David, 25
  Dearborn, 25
  Dorinda, 27
  Dudley, 27
  Edward, 28
  Elizabeth (Boulter), 231
  Eunice (Carey), 29
  Eunice (Cary), 29
  Gilman, 27-28
  Grinfill, 29
  Hannah (Knight) Higgins 27
  Hannah (Page), 27
  Ithiel, 231
  Jairus, 24
  Joanna (Brackett), 26
  John, 24-27, 29
  Jonathan, 25

  Joseph, 29
  Louisa (Haskell), 24
  Lovina, 26-27
  Lovina (Blake), 26-27
  Lucinda (Smith), 25
  Lydia, 29, 231
  Martha (Dudley), 26
  Martha (Nelson), 25
  Mary, 25, 257
  Mary (Fogg), 232
  Mary (Patterson), 25
  Mary J (--), 25
  Mehitable (Lyford), 27
  Melentha, 27
  Melinda, 27
  Miranda, 27
  Nabby (Bonney), 28
  Nancy, 25-26
  Nancy (Libby), 24
  Nathaniel, 24-25, 232
  Paul, 25
  Paul Dearborn, 25, 28
  Permela, 27
  Phillip, 26
  Priscilla, 25
  Rachel (Emerson), 27
  Robert, 26-27
  Ruth, 232
  Ruth (Dearborn), 25
  Sally (Harwood), 28
  Samuel, 25, 28
  Samuel Jr, 28
  Samuel Ordway, 27
  Samuel Sargeant, 24, 28
  Sarah, 25
  Sarah (Evans), 28
  Silas, 29
  Sophia (Carey), 29
  Sophia (Cary), 29
  Susannah (Martin), 231
  Thatcher, 28
  William, 24-25
BLANCHARD
  Martha, 57
BLANEY
  Chuckie, 134, 169
BLAZO
  Mehitable, 253
BLENN
  Eunice (Meserve), 184
  Harrison, 184
BLETHEN/ BLITHEN/ BLITFIN
  Hannah, 131-132
  Phebe, 105
BLISS
  Charles, 283
  Sidney (Tilton), 283

EVERY NAME INDEX

BLODGETT
John, 320
Lucy (Perkins), 320
Seth Jr, 320
BLUNT
Abigail Frost, 39, 206
Anna, 145
John, 145, 206
Joseph, 206
Rebecca (Streeter), 145
Sarah (Frost), 206
BOARDMAN
Joseph, 213
Mary (Pendleton), 213
BODGE
James, 253
Nancy (Nicols), 253
BODWELL
Betsey, 119
BOISE
Mary Anne, 165-166
BOLTHOOD/ BOLTWOOD
Abigail (Hamilton), 114
Ebenezer, 114
Joanna, 114
John Turner, 114
Mary (Turner), 114
BOND
Hannah (Cranch), 29
Hannah Cranch, 30
Mary Roop (Cranch), 30
Miranda (Towns), 30
Phebe (Guptil), 30
Selina (Cranch), 30
Theodore S, 30
Thomas, 30
Thomazine Elizabeth Fielder, 30
William, 29-30
William Cranch, 30
BONNEY
Ichabod, 28
Mary (Turner), 28
Nabby, 28
BOODEN
Bashaba, 136
William, 136
BOODY
Sarah, 106
BOOTHBY
Elizabeth, 138
Molly (Deering), 81
Samuel, 81
Susanna, 81
BOSTON
Seba, 75
Susanna, 58

BOULTER
Elizabeth, 231
BOURNE
Charlotte, 116, 118
Maria, 202
Sarah (--), 116
William, 116
BOWDEN
--, 125
Ebenezer, 126
John, 126
Lydia, 125
Molly (Heath), 126
Paul, 125
Polly (Heath), 126
Prudence (Provinder), 125
Susanna (Heath), 126
BOWERS
Catherine (Smith), 318
Stephen, 318
BOWES
Lucy, 116
BOWKER
Eleanor Lee, 96
Elizabeth (Williams), 96
Jacob, 96
Lincoln, 96
Samuel L, 96
Samuel Lincoln, 96
BOWMAN
Phebe, 308
BOYINGTON
Betsy, 197
Daniel, 197
Elizabeth (Patterson), 197
BOYNTON
Hannah, 156
James, 323
John, 156
Lois (Turner), 323
Mary, 226
Mary (Hancock), 156
Mary (McLucas), 247
Mary (Turner), 323
Mollie (Turner), 323
Nancy, 323
William, 247
BOZWORTH
Lucy (Robbins), 241
Tillson, 241
BRACKETT
Amey, 310
Anna, 322
David, 32
Elizabeth, 6, 150
Hannah, 31
Isaac, 310
Jacob, 31

Jane (Fernald), 31
Joanna, 26
Joanna (Hall), 31
John, 31(2)
Kerenhappuck (--) Hicks 80
Keziah, 61
Lucy, 13
Lydia (Keay), 31
Mary, 115
Mary (Hamilton), 310
Mehitable, 115
Mehitable (Ricker), 115
Miles, 31
Miles Jr, 31
Miriam, 31
Miriam (Thompson), 31
Nancy (Fernald), 32
Sally (Heard), 31
Samuel, 31, 115
Susan (Brown), 31
Susanna, 236
Susannah, 31
Susannah (Heard), 31
BRADBURY
Abigail, 33, 70
Abigail Small (Lane), 33
Ann Pray (Hunt), 32
Anna, 33
Anna Maria (Knight), 33
Bethula, 204, 250
Cotton, 81
Elijah, 32, 156, 203-204
Elizabeth, 32, 203
Hannah, 203
Isaac, 33
Jabez, 33
Jane, 72
Joanna Lane, 33
Lucy, 159, 295
Mary, 247, 258
Olive, 81
Ruth (Weare), 81
Sallie Gleason (Howard) 32
Sarah, 32
Sarah (Lane), 32, 156 203-204
Sarah (Merrill), 248
Thomas, 248
BRADFORD
Abigail (Starling), 46
Elisha, 46
Elizabeth, 211
Hulda, 46
Joseph, 46
Mary (Butler), 46
Nancy, 256

BRADFORD (continued)
Polly (Butler), 46
Sally, 278
Sally (Sweetland), 210
212-213
Sarah, 278
William, 210, 214
BRADSTREET
Mary, 121
BRADY
Jane, 192
BRAGDEN/ BRAGDON
Anna, 37
Anne, 36
Arlotty, 35
Arthur, 182
Bethiah, 70
Betsey, 35
Betsey (Stevens), 36
Dominicus, 36
Dorcas (Woodbridge), 34
Ebenezer, 33, 36
Ebenezer Jr, 33-34
Elizabeth, 251
Elizabeth (Beedle), 36
Elizabeth (Wilson), 34
Elizabeth (Wooster), 34
Emma, 35
Hannah, 36, 87
Hannah (--), 36
Hannah (Bussell), 35
Hannah (Donnell), 34
Hannah (Judkins), 147
Hepzibah, 36
Isabella, 93
James, 33-34
Jane, 33-34
Jane (--), 251
Jane (Wilson), 33
Jemima, 36
Jeremiah, 34, 36, 147
Jeremiah 3rd, 35
Jeremiah Jr, 34
Jeremy, 36
Jethro, 35-36
Joanna (--), 35
Joanna (Wooster), 34-35
Joseph, 250-251
Julia, 35
Keziah, 6
Loiza, 35
Lydia, 33-34, 36
Martha, 36
Mary, 33-34, 94, 115
Mary (Came), 298
Mary (Johnson) Adams
35-36
Mary B (Dyer), 35

Mehetable, 182
Mehitabel (Joy), 37
Mehitabel (Marston), 182
Mehitable, 183
Mehitable (Hanscom), 36
Mercy, 36
Nahum, 35-37
Nancy (Hooper), 35
Oliver Wooster, 34-35
Phebe (Gray), 36
Polly, 34
Polly B (Dyer), 35
Prudence, 250
Ruth, 298
Samuel, 35-36
Sarah, 36
Sarah (Howard), 34
Sarah (Stickney), 250
Sarah (Weare), 297-298
Sarah H (Bragdon), 35
Theodore, 35
Thomas, 35, 298
Thomas Jr, 298
BRAGG
Dorothy (Ingalls), 4
Ruth, 4
Thomas, 4
BRAINERD
Abigail (Hall), 112, 160
Charlotte (Leeman), 160
Church, 112, 160
Josiah, 160
Mary (Chapman), 112
BRALEY/ BRAYLEY
Alice, 323
Ellice, 323
Lydia, 192
BRASBRIDGE
Sally, 101
BRAWN/ BRANN [SEE ALSO BROWN]
Abigail, 98(2)
Abigail (Gilley), 22
Abigail (Gray), 108
Alice (--), 22
Bethania, 22
Catherine, 98
Charles, 22
Dorcas, 21, 97(2)
Elizabeth (Musset), 97
Elsie (--), 22
George, 22, 108
Hagor, 294
Joseph, 22
Lydia, 21(2)
Mary (Bennett), 22
Peter, 97
Samantha, 22

BRAY
Lois, 265
BRAZIER
Betsey (Pendleton), 211
Elizabeth (Pendleton), 211
Thomas, 211
BRETT
Louisana, 271
BREWER
Ann (Ginn), 99
Capt --, 98
John, 99
Josiah, 99
Martha (Graves), 99
Mary, 306
Polly, 306
BREWSTER
--, 115
Hannah, 313
John, 115
Olive (Prime), 115
Sally (Hamilton), 115
BRIDGE
Eliza Jane (Perkins)
Williams, 309
Hannah, 308
Hannah (North), 308
James, 308
Phebe (Bowman), 308
Sarah, 308
William, 309
BRIGGS
Abigail, 252-253
Betsy, 24, 28
Eben, 27
Esther (Finney), 252
Melentha (Blake), 27
Phineas, 252
Silence (Hart), 24
BRITT
Asenath, 282
Asenith, 282
Charity (Tibbetts), 281
John, 281
John Sr, 281
Nancy, 282
BRITTUN
Elizabeth, 304, 306
BROCK
--, 37, 39-40
-- (--), 38
Abigail, 39
Abigail (Critchett), 38
Abraham, 38
Betsey, 39, 317
Betsey (Wallingford), 38
Betsy, 37
Betty, 39

EVERY NAME INDEX

BROCK (continued)
Damaris (Wentworth), 37 39-40
Deborah, 39
Dorcas (Taylor), 41
Elijah, 39
Elizabeth, 38-39
Elizabeth (Bunker), 40
Elizabeth (Bunker) Mason 40
Elizabeth (Libby), 38
Eunice (Hodsdon), 38
Experience, 38
Francis, 317
Hannah (Furbush), 37
Huldah (Winn), 37
Jane, 37-38
Jane (Pray), 37
Jane (Taylor), 41
John, 37, 39-41
Joshua, 37
Judith, 39-40
Judith (Brown), 39
Judith (Bunker), 39-41 206
Judith (Roberts), 39
Love, 39, 206
Lucy (Roberts), 41
Luke W, 40
Luke Wentworth, 41
Margaret, 103
Martha, 41
Mary, 40-41
Mary (Brock), 40-41
Mary (Shapleigh), 38
Molly, 38
Nabby, 39
Nancy (Kelley), 38
Nathaniel, 37-38
Patty, 39, 41
Polly, 39
Polly (Brock), 39
Sally, 39, 41
Samuel, 37-38
Sarah, 41
Simeon, 37-41, 206
Sophia, 38
Sophy, 39
Wentworth, 37-38
William, 38-41
BROOKS
Abigail, 43, 238
Betsey, 42
Deborah Atwood, 43
Elizabeth, 42
Elizbeth Taylor (Bartlett) 43
George, 41, 55

James, 43
Joanna, 43
John Thompson, 42
Lucy, 43
Martha, 43
Mary (Atwood) Thompson 41-42
Mehitabel, 187
Sally (Dean), 42
Thelma Eye, 154, 217, 227
Thomas, 43
BROWN
Ann Rebecca, 135
BROWN [SEE ALSO BRANN]
--, 292
Abigail (Brann), 98
Abigail (Wardwell), 315
Ann Rebecca, 135
Charlotte (Warren), 292
Daniel, 315
Elizabeth, 212
Elizabeth (--), 204
Hannah, 126, 182
Jack, 294
Jeremiah, 315
Jerusha, 192
John, 204
John Jr, 205
Joseph, 98, 192, 212
Judith, 39, 81
Lydia, 323
Marey, 231
Mary, 27, 58, 204-205
Mary (Wakefield) Parsons 205
Mercy, 231, 314
Mercy Thomas (Pendleton) 212
Neal, 315
Penny, iii
Sarah (Wardwell), 315
Susan, 31
Susanna (Cole), 192
BROWNELL
Richard J, 132
BROWNING
Relief (Phinney), 219
Samuel, 219
BUCK
Abner, 201
Anna, 320
Jonathan, 162
Mary, 201
Nancy, 130
BUCKLEY
John, 131
Lydia (Hopkins), 131

BUCKNAM
Anna, 153
Dolly (Pote), 180
Dorothy (Pote), 180
Jeremiah, 180
Phebe, 180
BUDGE
James, 313
Margaret (Smart), 313
BUFFUM
Caleb, 43-44
Dorcas (Hubbard), 44
Elizabeth, 44
Elizabeth (Estes) Osborn 43
Hannah, 45
Hannah (Rogers), 44
Hannah (Varney), 44-45
John, 44
Joshua, 43-44
Lydia, 45
Mary, 44
Mary (Dow), 44
Mary (Gaskill), 43
Patience (Rogers), 44
Samuel, 45
Sarah (Hanson) Estes, 44
BUKER
Cyrus, 288
Elizabeth (Wardwell), 288
BULLOCK
Lucinda (Pendleton) Drinkwater Philbrook, 211
Samuel, 211
BUMP/ BUMPAS
Bethiah, 217-218
Joanna (Warren), 217, 219
Samuel, 217
BUNKER
Betsey, 170
Elijah, 39-40
Elizabeth, 40
Esther (Ives), 15
Isaac, 15
John L, 15
Judith, 39-41, 206
Judith (--), 39-40
Mary (Bacon), 15
BURBANK
Elizabeth, 121
Priscilla, 80
BURGESS
Anna Maria (Judkins), 145
Benjamin, 63
David, 63
Desire (Taylor), 63
Experience (Crowell), 63
Experneice (Crowell), 62

BURGESS (continued)
  Hannah, 64
  Rebecca (Parker), 63
  William, 145
BURNAM
  Susanna, 74
BURNELL
  Betsey, 196
  Elizabeth, 196
  Elizabeth (--), 196
  John, 196
  Mary, 300
BURNHAM/ BURNAM
  Abner, 271
  Betsey, 271
  Eunice, 67
  Maria, 58
  Martha, 155
  Sarah, 69
  Temperance, 36
BURNS
  Betsey, 238
  Francis, 56
  James, 56, 212
  Joseph, 56
  Lois (Pendleton), 212
  Margaret, 56
  Margaret (--), 56
  Mercy, 138
  Robert, 56
BURRELL/ BURRILL
  Betsey (--), 199, 201
  Eunice (Nye), 201
  Grace (Gardner), 109
  Grace (Garnett), 109
  Hannah, 109
  James, 201
  Jeffery, 294
  John, 199, 201
  Salley, 199
  Sarah, 199
  Thomas, 109
BURROWS
  Elizabeth, 85
  Elizabeth (Witherell), 85
  Jonathan, 85
BURTON
  Mary, 313
  Nathan, 313
BUSSELL
  Hannah, 35
  Hannah (Eldridge), 35
  Isaac, 35
BUTLAND
  George, 138
  Mercy, 138
BUTLER
  Amy, 45

  Amy (Daggett), 45
  Bathsheba (Graves), 173
  Benjamin, 45-46, 235
  Betsey (Davis), 46
  Betsey (Johnson), 46
  Christopher, 164
  Ebenezer, 45
  Ebenezer Chancey, 46
  Ebenezer Cheney, 46
  Elizabeth, 282
  Gorham, 164
  Hannah (Grant), 105
  Hannah (Randall), 235
  Henry, 305
  Hulda (Bradford), 46
  James, 105
  Jedidah, 64, 66
  Jedidah (Beetle), 64
  John, 64, 282
  John 2nd, 235
  Joseph, 173
  Katherine (Luce) Johnson 46
  Keziah (Mason), 105
  Lovey, 46
  Lovina, 46
  Lydia (Kimball), 310
  Lydia (Luce), 164
  Margaret (Goodwin), 282
  Margaret (Martin), 173
  Martha, 305
  Martha (Gray), 108
  Mary, 46, 130, 321
  Mary (Stevens), 46
  Mary (Yeaton), 310
  Mehitable (Norton), 45 305
  Melinda, 46
  Moses, 105
  Nancy, 45
  Nehemiah, 310-311
  Phinehas, 173
  Polly, 46
  Ralph, 46
  Sally (Luce), 164
  Samuel, 310
  Sarah (Gowell), 235
  Sarah (Luce), 164
  Stephen, 108
  Thankful (Daggett), 66
  William, 46
  Zimri, 46
BUTMAN
  Deborah, 77
BUTTER
  Elizabeth, 283
BUTTERFIELD
  Joseph, 240

  Joseph Jr, 240
  Mary, 257
  Mary (Harding), 240
  Nancy, 302
  Sarah (Richardson), 240
BUXTON
  Mary, 152
BUZZELL
  Lucy, 244
CAIN/ CANE/ KANE
  Abigail, 47
  Abigail (--), 46
  Franklin, 47
  Joanna (Wilson), 47
  Joseph, 47
  Lydia, 47
  Margaret (Yeates), 47
  Mary, 47, 143, 263
  Mercy, 47
  Paula, 47
  Samuel, 46-47
  Virginia L, 253
CALHOUN/ COLQUEHOUN
  Elizabeth (Dennison), 77
  John, 77
CALVERT
  Eunice, 69, 150, 156, 172
CAME
  Mary, 298
CAMPBELL
  Abigail (Collins), 59
  Alexander, 59
  Elizabeth (Nickels), 59
  Nabby (Collins), 59
  Sally, 64
  Sarah, 64
CANDAGE
  Betsey, 54
CANNELL/ CAMEL
  Ann, 48
  Clark, 47
  Eleanor, 48
  Ellen, 48
  Jane, 48
  Jane (Sherlock), 47, 196
  Joseph, 48
  Margaret (Nason), 48, 196
  Nancy, 48
  Philip, 196
  Phillip, 47
  Phillip Jr, 48
  Rebecca (Green), 48
  Thomas, 48, 196
CANNEY
  Judith, 102
CANWELL
  Nabby, 69

CARD
  Elizabeth (--) Smart, 314
  Thomas, 314
CAREY/ CARY
  Ann, 301
  Eunice, 29
  Sophia, 29
CARLE/ CARLL
  Anna, 119
  Benjamin, 120
  Elizabeth (Doughty), 48, 152
  Hitty, 148
  Jonathan, 49
  Mary, 49, 152, 322
  Mehitable, 148
  Nathaniel, 48-49, 152, 320
  Patience, 49
  Rose, 294
  Samuel, 49
  Sarah, 49
  Sarah (Berry), 120
CARLETON/ CARLTON
  --, 184
  Betty Fogg (Meserve), 184
  Elizabeth (--), 4
  Elizabeth Fogg (Meserve), 184
  Jane, 87-88
  Jane (--), 88
  John, 88
  Mary, 54
  Peter, 4
  Peter Jr, 4
CARLISLE/ CARLILE
  Daniel, 276
  Elisabeth, 275
  Elizabeth, 276
  Lydia (Wilson), 276
  Sarah, 176, 275
CARLL [SEE CARLE],
CARMAN
  mary M, 54
CARPENTER
  Abigail, 134
  Benjamin, 134
  Dorcas (Chadbourne), 107
  Hannah (--), 134
  James, 106
  Olive (Gray), 106
  Roxanna, 60
  Sally (Wentworth), 106
  Simon, 107
  Susan (Gray), 107
  Thomas, 106
CARR
  Abigail (Prescott), 228
  Benjamin, 228

CARTER
  Abigail (Cain), 47
  Austin C, iii
  David, 47
  Elizabeth, 274, 276
  James, 47
  James Jr, 47
  Lydia (Day), 47
  Mary, 63
  Mercy (Cain), 47
CARY [SEE CAREY],
CASS
  Agnes M, 229
CASTIN
  Esther (Banks) Reidhead, 17
  Joseph, 17
CASWELL/ KERSWELL/ CASUEL
  Job, 137
  John, 137
  Mary (--), 137
  Mary (Jepson), 137
  Pelatiah, 277
  Sukey, 277
  Susan, 277
CATES
  Abigail, 320
  Amy (Skillings), 317
  Ann (Skillings), 317
  Benjamin, 317
  Deborah, 317
  Joseph, 320
CAVAL
  Judah, 193
  Lydia (--) Smith Murch, 193
CHADBOURN/ CHADBOURNE
  Abigail (Crockett), 293
  Benjamin, 160-161
  Betsey, 236
  Catherine (Hanscom), 310
  Daniel, 236
  Desire (Watson), 293
  Dorcas, 107, 246
  Earlene/ Kitty (Ahlquist), 59, 135
  Elizabeth, 104, 181, 236
  Elizabeth (Yeaton), 310
  Francis, 31
  Humphrey, 310
  Joanna (Yeaton), 246, 310
  Martha, 160-161
  Mary (Twambley), 236
  Nahum, 293
  Olive (Neal), 31
  Paul, 246, 310

  Phebe (Hobbs), 310
  Sarah (Heard), 160
  Silas, 293
  Simeon, 310
  Susannah (Brackett), 31
  William, 31
CHADWICK
  Abra (Wentworth), 1
  Emily, 64
  Peter, 215
  Sarah, 1
  William, 1
CHAFFIN
  Mary, 164
  Mercy, 164
  Mercy (Sanderson), 164
  Simon, 164
CHALMERS
  Esther (Farnham), 87-88
  William, 87-88
CHAMBERLAIN
  Abigail B (Jones), 142
  Capt --, 136
  Eleanor, 142
  Eliza (Austin), 133
  Nabby B (Jones), 142
  Nathaniel, 142
  Sarah (Furbush), 142
  Sarah (Hunter), 133
  Thomas Hunter, 134
  William, 133
  Wilson, 133
CHANDLER
  Abigail (Dennison), 73
  Hannah, 171
  John, 171-172
  Jonathan, 73
  Lydia (Taylor), 171
  Rachel (Mitchell), 73
  Rufus, 73
  Susannah (--), 34
CHAPMAN
  -- (Lambert), 160
  Anthony, 67
  Betsy, 273
  Eliphaz, 151, 273
  Elizabeth, 65, 165, 273
  Elizabeth (Lambert), 159
  Hannah (Jackman), 273
  John, 159-160
  Keziah, 159
  Lydia (Starbird), 266
  Mary, 112
  Nancy C, 266
  Nathaniel, 68
  Ruth, 68
  Sarah (Lincoln), 68
  Shadrach, 266

CHAPMAN (continued)
  Stephen J, 111
CHARLES/ CHARLS
  Elizabeth Farrington, 320
  John, 320
CHASE
  Apphia (Bartlett), 21
  Edmund, 61
  Hannah (Jordan), 145
  Jedidah, 67
  John, 258
  Jonathan, 145
  Joseph, 21
  Love (Corson), 61
  Lydia, 153, 216, 226
  Lydia Ann, 145
  Mary, 152, 292
  Mary (Buxton), 152
  Mercy (Snow), 258
  William, 152
CHENEY
  Abigail (Williams), 307
  Joseph, 307
CHESLEY
  Anna, 147
CHICK
  Bethiah (Gould), 233
  David, 185
  John, 233
  Joseph, 115, 233
  Lydia (Randall), 233
  Pamela F (Mildram), 185
  Permelia (Mildram), 185
  Polly (Grant), 185
  Richard, 233
  Sarah (Randall), 233
  Thomas, 185
CHIPMAN
  Mary, 112
CHISAM
  Sarah, 207
CHUBB
  Hannah, 3
CHURCHILL
  Lydia (Maxim), 69
  Mary, 69
  Polly, 69
  William, 69
CILLEY
  Joseph, 145
CLAFLIN
  Hannah, 143
CLAGHORN
  Jedidah, 65
CLARK/ CLARKE
  --, 117, 146
  Abigail, 34
  Abigail (Dennett), 71

Abigail (Hamilton), 118
Alice (Philbrook), 228
Amos, 314
Ann, 19
Ann (Harris), 117
Anna, 133
Anna (Hanscom), 113
Annar, 133
Asenath (Linnell), 283
Bathsheba (Randall), 236
Benjamin, 249
Betsey (Hamilton)
  116-117
Catherine, 236
Charles, 146
Chloe, 25
Daniel, 276-277
David, 71
Dorothy (Mildram), 185
Ebenezer, 113
Eleazer 3rd, 185-186
Eleazer 4th, 185
Elinor, 47
Eliza, 164
Elizabeth, 104
Elizabeth (Barker), 19
Else (Philbrook), 228
Ephraim, 314
Esther (Mildram), 185
Fanny, 7
George, 265
Hannah, 10
Hannah (Berry), 276-277
Henry, 185
Isaac, 228
James, 118
Jonas, 116
Jonathan, 249
Kenneth Alton, 173, 175
Lois (Preble), 189
Lucy (Bowes), 116
Lydia (Dennett), 70-71
Marcy (Higgins), 127
Margaret, 189
Martha, 228, 302
Mary, 105, 113, 186, 276
Mary D, 145
Nathan, 127
Nathaniel, 71
Olive (Hobbs), 185
Pauline, 216
Peter, 116-117
Polly, 17, 105, 186
Samuel, 19
Sarah, 43
Sherebiah, 283
Susannah (Stevens), 265
Thomas, 189

Thomas Jr, 236
Zeporah, 283
CLAY
  Abigail, 51
  Benjamin, 50, 54
  Daniel, 50
  Elizabeth, 51
  Esther (Flood), 50
  Hannah (Presson) Marriner
    Dunn Sawyer, 50
  Hepsibah (Hale), 50
  Jane (Hunnewell), 50
  Jemima, 51
  Jerusha (Elwell), 50
  Jonathan, 50, 54
  Mary, 51
  Mary (--), 49
  Mary (Roundy), 54
  Molly, 51
  Rachel, 50-51, 248
  Rachel (Pennell), 49-50
  Richard, 49-50, 248
  Richard Jr, 50
  Ruth (Gammon), 50
  Ruth (Whitten), 50
  Sally (Clough), 54
  Sarah, 50
  Thomas, 50
CLEAVERS
  Anna, 194
CLEAVES
  Sarah (Stevens), 265
CLEMENTS/ CLEMONS
  -- (Hamilton), 53
  Abigail, 53
  Abigail (Southwick), 157
  Abigail (Sudrick), 157
  Abner, 163
  Adaline (Frost), 53
  Benjamin, 52
  Betsey, 285
  Betsey (Conant), 52
  Betsey (Hanson), 52
  Betty (Rollins), 310
  Ebenezer, 52-53
  Elisha, 285
  Elizabeth (Conant), 52
  Emma (Lowell), 163
  Experience (Yeaton), 310
  Hannah (Lane), 157
  James, 53
  Jeremiah, 52, 310
  Joanna (Goodwin), 53
  Job, 310
  John, 53, 157
  Jonathan, 157
  Judith (Knox), 51
  Judith (Nock), 51

EVERY NAME INDEX

CLEMENTS/ CLEMONS
(continued)
Lewis, 53
Lucinda (White), 53
Lydia, 52-53
Margaret (Lord), 53
Mary, 53
Mary (Fernald), 52
Mary (Hayes), 53
Mary (Waldron), 285
Moses, 52
Olive (Hamilton), 53
Peggy (Lord), 53
Phebe, 52
Polly, 53
Polly (Fernald), 52
Rebecca, 170
Sally, 52, 105
Samuel, 51, 53, 105
Sarah, 52, 105
Sarah (Austin), 51-52, 105
Sarah (Knox), 53
Sarah (Nock), 53
Sarah (Rollins), 51
CLEVELAND
Miriam, 209
Rosella, 221
CLEW
Mary, 202
CLIFFORD
Mary (Brown), 27
CLOUGH
Abigail (Pecker), 54
Abigail (Sinclair), 54
Asa, 54
Asa Jr, 54
Benjamin, 54
Cheever Russell, 54
Daniel, 54
Daniel Jr, 54
Elizabeth, 227
Hannah, 227, 301
James, 54
Jane (Grover), 54
Jane (Lymburner), 54
Joanna S (Hinckley), 54
John, 54
Leonard, 54
Louisa, 54
Louisa (Ray), 54
Lydia, 54
Mary Jane (Wood), 54
Mary M (Carman), 54
Nabby (Pecker), 54
Nabby (Sinclair), 54
Polly (Tenney), 54
Ruth, 187, 189
Sally, 54

Zelotes, 54
CLOUTMAN
Betty, 263
COBB
Bethiah (Harding), 176
Betsey (Hatch), 55
Betty, 128
Daniel Jr, 267
David, 293
Ebenezer, 56
Elijah, 319
Elisha, 42, 55
Elisha Jr, 55
Elizabeth, 56, 62
Elizabeth (Murch), 42, 55
Ezekiel, 42, 55
Lucy (Bickford), 293
Lucy (Webb), 266
Mary, 176, 178
Mary A, 55
Molly (Murch), 55
Nancy (Poak), 55
Nancy (Poke), 55
Nancy (Thompson), 42, 55
Nathaniel, 176
Phebe, 55(2)
Rachel, 319
Rebecca, 193
Reuben, 55
Sally (Watson), 293
Samuel C, 55
Sarah Jane (Bailey), 319
Tabitha (Elwell), 55
William, 55
COBURN [SEE COLBURN],
COCHERN [SEE COTHRAN],
COCHRAN
John, 261
Mary (Somes), 261
Polly (Somes), 261
COFFIN
Betty (Swan), 273
David, 273
Edmund, 234
Elizabeth (Swan), 273
Maria, 235
Martha (Randall), 234
Mary (Warren), 106
COGGAN
Priscilla, 64
COGGINS
Anna, 127
COLBURN/ COBURN
Elizabeth (Lewis), 57
Fanny, 54
Hannah, 56
Hannah (Smith), 57

Jeremiah, 56
John, 57
Margaret (Burns), 56
Martha (Blanchard), 57
Mary, 57
Olive, 57
Olive (Colburn), 57
Oliver, 56-57
Rachel, 56
Rebecca, 57
Sally, 57
Sarah, 57
Sarah (Jewell), 56
William, 57
COLBY
Burry (Bartlett), 20
Ephraim, 20
Joseph, 20
Mehitable, 272
Molly (--), 20
COLE
-- (--), 58
Abigail, 58
Apphia, 15
Benjamin Wilson, 58
Charity, 58
Charles, 58
Eli, 57-58
Elijah, 319
Elizabeth (Buffum), 44
Elizabeth (Clay), 51
Elizabeth (Hill), 44
Eunice, 58
Ezra, 58
George Jr, 58
George M, 58
John, 44
Lydia, 59
Maria (Burnam), 58
Mary, 247
Mary (Brown), 58
Nancy (Buck), 130
Nathaniel, 51
Olive, 58
Olive (Wilson), 57-58
Peter, 130
Phebe, 151
Rachel, 319
Sally, 58-59
Sarah Jane (Bailey), 319
Sophia, 58
Sukey, 58
Susanna, 58, 192
COLLAR
Charity, 243
COLLEY
Mary, 240

COLLINS
Abigail, 59
Bethia, 59
Dolly (Ray), 59
Martha (Hilton), 307
Mary (Fickett), 59
Nabby, 59
Richard, 59
Richard Jr, 59
Sophia, 59
COLMAN
Sarah, 292-293
COLSON
Abigail (Archer), 13
Elizabeth (--), 126, 163
Elmina, 126
James, 163
Jeremiah, 163
Josiah, 126, 163
Lois, 163
Louisa, 163
Lucy W, 12
Moses, 13
Phoebe (Lowell), 163
Prudence (Heath), 126
Samuel Jr, 12
Sarah (Lowell), 163
Stanton D, 192
Susannah (Willey), 12
COMINGS
Amelia, 149
CONANT
Anne (Haskell), 52
Betsey, 52
Daniel, 52
Elizabeth, 52
Eunice, 139
CONNER
Martha (Potter) Potter, 225
Simon, 225
CONY
Daniel, 308
Judge --, 97
Sarah Lowell, 308
Susanna (Curtis), 308
COOK
Anna (Farnham), 87, 89
Jerusha (--), 89
John, 87, 89
John Jr, 89
COOKSON
Marcy, 113
COOLIDGE
Lydia (Peterson), 215
Moses, 215
Moses Jr, 215
Sarah (--), 215

COOMBS
Abner, 178
Anstress (Melcher), 178
Fanny (Warren), 292
Hannah (--), 178
John, 178, 292
Mehitable, 79
COOPER
Catherine, 282
Lydia, 129
Sally, 129
CORSON
Aaron, 61
Alanson, 60
Bathsheba (Hussey), 61
Bathsheba (Thayer), 61
Benjamin, 61, 192, 223
Betsey (Smith), 223
Betsy, 61
Betsy (Hatch), 61
Betsy (Perkins), 60
Elizabeth (Hatch), 61
Elizabeth (Perkins), 60
Esther (Nason), 60
Esther H, 142
Fanny, 60-61
George, 223
Huldah (--), 61
Isaac, 60
James, 61
John, 61, 142
Keziah (--), 61
Louisa, 192
Love, 61
Lydia (Hussey), 61, 192
Moses, 60-61, 192
Nancy (Tuttle), 60
Priscilla, 61
Ruth (Pitts), 223
Sally (Evans) Otis, 61
Sarah (Evans) Otis, 61
Seward, 61
Tamson, 60-61
Tamson (Hodgdon), 142
Theodate (Page), 61
COSS
Hannah, 233
COTHRAN/ COCHERN
Martha, 260
COTTON
Elizabeth (Davis), 319
Joanna, 140
John, 319
Sarah, 219
COTTRELL
Margaret (Pendleton), 213
Sylvester, 213

COUILLARD
Adam, 163
Betsey (Lowell), 163
Charles, 89
Elizabeth, 87-88
Margaret (Hood), 89
COVANT
Eunice, 139
COVELL
Sarah, 130
COWEN/ COWIN
Ephraim, 147
Hannah, 17-18
Mary, 147
Polly, 147
Sherman, 294
Susannah (Kilbourne), 147
COX
Rebecca, 293
CRABTREE
Elezaer, 170
CRAFT
Sarah, 53
CRAIG
Eleanor, 304
Esther (Lowell), 163
Samuel Jr, 163
CRAM
Abigail, 245
Abigail (Pugsley), 245
Joseph, 245
Smith, 318
CRANCH
Elizabeth (Lidstone), 29
Hannah, 29
Joseph, 29
Mary Roop, 30
Selina, 30
CRANE
Dorothy O, 219
CRAWFORD
James Jr, 179
Mary (Melcher), 179
CRESSEY/ CRECY
Betsey, 292
Eleanor, 190
Elling, 190
John, 292
Susanna (MacDonald), 292
CRITCHETT/ CRITCHET
Abigail, 38
Caleb, 38
John, 38
Lydia (--), 38
CROCKER
Josiah, 267
Martha, 120, 217
Priscilla, 299

CROCKER (continued)
  Rebecca, 267
  Rebecca (Allen), 267
CROCKETT
  Abigail, 293
  Deborah, 79
  Elizabeth (Roberts), 79
  Hannah (Thresher), 79
  James, 221
  Joshua 3rd, 221
  Martha (Pike), 221
  Richard, 79
  Sarah (Hamblen), 221
CROMMETT
  Esther (Jackson), 318
  Nathan, 318
  Orchard, 318
CROMWELL
  Dorothy, 310
CROSBY
  Daniel, 204
  Elizabeth, 253
  Mary (Brown) Wakefield Washburn Parsons, 204
CROSS
  Martha (Woodman), 197
  Nathaniel, 197
  Olive (Neal), 197
  Robert, 197
CROWELL
  --, 62
  Baxter, 60
  Deborah, 62-63
  Deborah (Webb), 62
  Deliverance, 62-63
  Elizabeth, 62-63, 283
  Elizabeth (Hawes), 62, 190
  Experience, 62-63
  Experience (Crowell), 62
  Isaiah, 63
  Judith, 62, 190, 322
  Lemuel, 62, 190
  Lucy, 62
  Moody, 62
  Nancy (Tuttle) Corson, 60
  Olive (Greene), 63
  Samuel, 62
  Thomas 2nd, 62
CUDWORTH
  Hannah, 173
  Joseph, 173
  Lydia (Tower), 173
CUMMINGS
  Abigail, 225
  Albert O, 237
  Elisha, 221
  Elizabeth (Fisher), 237
  John, 218

  Mary (Dolly), 221
  Mehitable, 240
  Priscilla (Rankins), 237
  Rachel (Jackson), 240
  Samuel, 237
  Sarah (Phinney), 218
  Thomas, 240
  Urania, 221
CUNNINGHAM
  Daniel, 224
  Edward, 224
  Elizabeth (Hayden), 224
  Elizabeth (Heddean), 224
  Elizabeth (Potter), 224
  Margaret, 167
  Mary, 117
  Miriam (Webber), 224
  Peggy, 165-166
  Robert, 57
  Ruth, 166
CURRIER
  Nathaniel, 8
  Sally (Abbott), 8
  Sarah, 217
CURTIS
  Adeline, 75
  Charity (Goodwin), 102
  Charles Jr, 7
  Deborah, 194
  Hannah, 215
  Isaac, 102
  Joan, 174
  John, 87
  John Jr, 88
  Joseph, 102
  Louise (Abbott), 7
  Lovisa (Abbott), 7
  Luvice (Abbott), 7
  Martha, 75
  Mary (Farnham), 87-88
  Mary (Goodrich), 102
  Mary (Goodridge), 102
  Rebecca, 77-78
  Ruth, 76
  Sarah, 177
  Simeon, 102
  Susanna, 308
CUSHING
  Dorothy (Bagley), 73
  Jane, 78
  John, 73
  John Jr, 78
  Jonathan, 72-73
  Loammi Betsey (Soule), 78
  Lucretia (Dennison), 72-73
  Mary (Sawyer), 73
CUTLER
  Mary, 171

CUTT/ CUTTS
  Sally (Colburn), 57
  Samuel, 57, 161, 320
  Sarah (Colburn), 57
  Sarah (Hill), 57, 320
  Thomas, 57, 320
CUTTER
  Ammi R, 194
  Deborah (Curtis), 194
  Elizabeth, 315
DAGGETT/ DAGGET
  Aaron, 67
  Amy, 45
  Andrew, 66
  Berintha, 65
  Betsey (Martin), 64
  Brotherton, 64, 66
  Daniel Weston, 65
  Deborah (Keene), 66
  Deborah (Upham), 64
  Edmund, 66
  Elijah, 67, 160
  Elizabeth (Martin), 64
  Emily (Chadwick) Marshall 64
  Hannah, 65-66
  Henry, 66
  James, 64
  Jedidah (Butler), 64, 66
  Jedidah (Chase), 67
  John, 252
  Jonathan, 64, 67
  Love, 160
  Lydia (Jameson), 65
  Margaret (Miller), 64
  Margaret (Smith), 160
  Martha (Maidman), 65
  Mary (Robinson), 64
  Matthew, 66-67
  Meribah (Jackson), 66
  Polly, 64
  Prince, 45
  Priscilla (Coggan), 64
  Rebecca, 67
  Rebecca (Athearn), 63 65-66
  Rebecca (Daggett), 67
  Rebecca (Luce), 65-66
  Rebecca (Peabody), 67
  Sally, 65
  Sally (Campbell), 64
  Samuel, 63-64, 66
  Sarah (Campbell), 64
  Sarah (Norton), 45
  Sarah (Wade) Stetson, 64
  Silvia Church (Weston), 64
  Thankful, 66
  Thankful (Daggett) Butler

DAGGETT/ DAGGET
(continued)
  Thankful (Daggett) Butler
  (continued)
    66
  Thomas, 63, 66
  Thomas Jr, 65-66
  Thomas Sr, 64-66
  William, 64

DAILEY
  Nathaniel, 146
  Rebecca (Judkins), 146

DANA
  Elizabeth (--), 116, 118

DAVIDSON/ DAVISON
  Hannah, 261
  James, 261
  Margaret (Somes), 261
  Peggy (Somes), 261

DAVIS/ DAVICE
  Abigail, 243
  Anna (Pulcifer), 230
  Betsey, 46
  David, 46, 292
  Deborah (Ireland), 230
  Deborah (Nichols), 230
  Dorcas (Goddard), 80
  Elizabeth, 227, 319
  Eunice (Sands), 248
  Gardner, 80
  Hannah, 81, 317
  Happy M (Dole), 80
  Jacob, 278
  Joanna, 148
  John, 80
  John Jr, 248
  Joyce P, 59
  Lois (Moody), 189
  Louisa, 243
  Martha (Watson), 292
  Olive (Mayhew), 46
  Prince, 292
  Samuel, 189, 230
  Sarah (Colman), 292
  Scribner Moody, 189
  Thomas, 317

DAY
  Abigail, 69, 170
  Almira, 271
  Benjamin, 67, 170
  Benjamin Jr, 68
  Betsey (Candage), 54
  Daniel, 68
  Elizabeth, 68
  Eunice, 68
  Eunice (Burnham), 67
  Hannah, 292
  Jane (Perham), 68

  Jane (Sproul), 68
  John, 67
  Lucy, 260
  Lydia, 47
  Lydia (Flint), 67
  Martha, 67
  Martha (Hatch), 68
  Martha (Knight), 67
  Mary, 68
  Mary (Sproul), 68
  Mary (Taylor), 170
  Mary (Young), 68
  Nancy (Milton), 68
  Nathaniel, 68
  Olive, 271
  Pamelia, 323
  Patty K, 67
  Polly (Sproul), 68
  Robert, 68
  Ruth (Chapman), 68
  Samuel, 271
  Sarah, 68
  Susanna, 68
  William, 68

DEAN/ DEANE
  Abigail (Baker), 137
  Anna, 42
  Archeleus, 42
  Cyrus, 137
  John, 137
  Margaret (Jepson), 137
  Mary (Higgins), 42
  Mary (Winslow), 137
  Sally, 42

DEARBORN
  Abijah, 124
  Fanny (Earl), 124
  Fanny (Hearl), 124
  Frances (Earl), 124
  Frances (Hearl), 124
  Mary (Whitten), 125
  Richard, 125
  Ruth, 25

DEARING
  Martha, 245

DECKER/ DICKER
  Ann (--), 69
  Charles, 69
  Hannah, 69
  James M, 69
  Joshua, 58
  Mary (Churchill), 69
  Nabby (Canwell), 69
  Nancy (Sweetser), 58
  Polly (Churchill), 69
  Sally (Cole), 58
  Sarah (Burnham), 69
  Susanna (Boston), 58

  Thomas, 58
  William, 69
  William Jr, 69

DELANO
  Betsey, 109
  Betty, 109
  David, 109
  Deborah (Holmes), 109

DENHAM
  Catherine (Potter), 225
  Thomas, 225

DENNETT/ DENNET
  --, 70
  Abigail, 70-71, 184
  Abigail (Carlile), 71
  Abigail (Hill), 69
  Betsey, 122
  Dorothy (Furbish), 184
  Ebenezer, 69-70
  Elizabeth (Smart), 314
  Hannah, 70
  Jacob, 314
  Joanna (Dennison), 71
  John, 184
  Lydia, 70-71
  Nicholas, 70
  Phebe (--), 70
  Sally, 58
  Samuel, 69-71
  Sarah, 70
  Sarah (Frost), 70

DENNISON
  Abigail, 72-73, 76-77
  Abigail (Haraden), 76
  Abner, 71, 75-76
  Adeline (Curtis), 75
  Alice (Hill), 78
  Ame (Lane), 76
  Amme, 76
  Amme (Sylvester), 77
  Andrew, 74
  Benjamin, 76
  Benjamin Griffin, 76
  Betsey, 78
  Betsey (Staples), 72
  Bradbury, 78
  Caroline (Blackstone), 75
  Clarissa, 75
  Cornelius, 74
  David, 72-74, 76, 78
  David Jr, 72-73
  Desire (Stetson), 71
  Dorcas, 78-79
  Dorcas (Lufkin), 73
  Dorcas (Soule), 71, 78
  Elizabeth, 77
  Elizabeth (Staples), 72
  Emerson, 78

EVERY NAME INDEX

DENNISON (continued)
 Emma, 76
 Emma (Lane), 76
 Esther, 72, 78
 George, 76, 78
 Gideon, 76
 Hannah (Moxey), 73
 Jane, 72
 Jane (Cushing), 78
 Jane (Haraden), 71
 Jenny, 72
 Jenny (Haraden), 71, 73
 Joanna, 72, 76
 Joanna (Emerson), 71
 John, 72-73, 75
 Jonathan, 73, 77, 79
 Joseph, 71-72, 75
 Joseph Haraden, 75
 Lillis, 75
 Lillis (Dennison), 75
 Lillis Turner (Sylvester) 75-76
 Louisa (Sylvester), 73
 Lucinda (Townsend), 73
 Lucretia, 72-73
 Lucy Jane, 75-76
 Lydia (Lufkin), 74
 Margaret (Hannaford), 78
 Martha, 77
 Martha (Doty), 71
 Martha Ann (Soule), 76
 Mary (Eaton), 75
 Mary (Griffin), 74
 Mary (Warren), 77
 Mary S (--), 74
 Mehetable (Soule), 72, 74
 Mehitable, 75
 Mehitable (Coombs), 79
 Mehitable (Soule), 72
 Patty, 77
 Penthea Stetson (Soule), 74
 Polly (Hodgskins), 76
 Priscilla, 73
 Rebecca (Curtis), 77
 Rufus, 75
 Ruth (Curtis), 76
 Sally, 77
 Sarah, 77
 Seba (Baston), 75
 Seba (Boston), 75
 Solomon, 77
 Sophronia, 75
 Susan, 75
 Susanna, 77
 Susanna (Haraden) Griffin 72, 74-75
 Timothy, 72, 78
 Washington, 78

DEXTER
 Jedida, 131
 Timothy, 23
DICKER [SEE DECKER],
DICKEY
 Eleazer B, 317
 Hallett, 317
 Herbert, 317
 Mary (Hamlin), 317
 Pauline, 317
 Priscilla, 317
DIEGO
 Jean, 158
 May, 158
DILLINGHAM
 Henry, 43
 Martha (Brooks), 43
 Mary, 195
 Melatiah, 71
DINSLOW
 Benjamin, 236-237
 Patience, 236-237
DINSMORE
 Anna (True), 305
 Dolly, 305
 Thomas, 305
DOANE
 Abraham, 320
 Dorcas (Eldridge), 130
 Ephraim, 130
 Experience (Hopkins), 130
 Joseph, 130
 Nancy (Buck) Cole, 130
 Seth, 320
DODGE
 Bathsheba, 213
 Benjamin, 133
 Betsey, 180
 Betsey (Somes), 261
 Daniel, 261
 Dorcas, 210, 212
 Elizabeth (Somes), 261
 Lydia (Rathbone), 213
 Madeline Stevens, 264
 Margaret (Pullin), 212
 Margaret (Pulling), 212
 Mark, 211, 213
 Mary (Merrow), 133
 Nancy (Somes), 261
 Nathaniel, 212
 Polly (Merrow), 133
 Prudence, 214
 Prudence (Rose), 214
 Rachel, 133
 Simon, 214
 Wealthy (Pendleton), 211
 William, 261

DOHERTY
 Thomas P, 178-180
DOLE
 Deborah, 79-80
 Deborah (Crockett), 79
 Eliza, 80
 Hannah, 80
 Happy M, 80
 John, 79-80
 Mary, 80
 Polly, 80
 Samuel, 80
 Sarah, 79
 Sarah (Plumer), 79
 Sarah E (Smellage), 80
DOLLIVER
 Jemima, 199
DOLLY
 Mary, 221
DONNELL
 Abigail, 84
 Benjamin, 84
 Hannah, 34
 Jonathan S, 180
 Rebecca (Melcher), 180
 Sally H (Bragdon), 35
 Samuel P, 35
 Sarah (Kingsbury), 84
 Susan, 251
DOOR/ DORE
 Elizabeth, 89-90
 Lydia, 63
 Lydia (Mason), 89
 Molly, 142
 Nancy Ann, 109
 Philip, 89, 91
DORCAS
 Tristram, 212
DORMAN
 Abigail (Libby), 81
 Benjamin, 81
 Charles, 81
 Charlotte, 321
 Frank, 81
 Hannah, 81
 Hannah (Davis), 81
 Hannah (Huff), 80
 Hannah (Look), 80
 Huldah, 81
 Israel, 321
 Jabez, 80
 John, 80-81
 Joseph, 321
 Judith (Brown), 81
 Lucy, 81
 Mary, 81, 321
 Nathaniel, 81
 Olive (Bradbury), 81

EVERY NAME INDEX

DORMAN (continued)
  Priscilla, 81
  Susanna (Boothby), 81
  Temperance, 321
DORSETT
  Susan, 232
DOTEN
  Lydia, 194
DOTTS
  Helen Burnell, 199
DOTY
  Amarilla, 283
  Edward, 214
  Martha, 72
DOUGHTY
  Elizabeth, 48, 152
  James, 48
  Mary (Robinson), 48
DOUGLAS/ DOUGLASS
  Andrew, 281
  Ann (Estes), 45
  Cornelius, 45
  Elijah, 45
  James, 126, 187
  Jane (Alexander), 281
  John, 45
  Lisa (Millbanks), 187
  Lucy, 126
  Lydia, 126
  Lydia (Avery), 126
  Lydia (Buffum), 45
  Phebe (Taylor), 45
  Sarah, 281
DOW
  Dorcas (Allen), 9
  Dorcas (Neal), 9
  Hannah, 79
  Hannah (Gove), 44
  Jedidiah, 9
  Josiah, 9
  Lydia, 138
  Mary, 44
  Mary (Kennedy), 243
  Moses, 44
  Neal, 9
  Peter, 243
  Peter Jr, 243
  Sally, 97, 243
  Sarah E, 243
DOWNING
  Joanna (Simpson), 250
  Mary, 63
  Richard, 250-251
DOWNS/ DOWNES
  --, 1
  Daniel, 102
  Hannah, 99
  John, 85

Joseph, 102
Judith (Canney), 102
Mary, 102
Phebe, 102
Susan, 85
DRESSER
  Lydia, 92
DREW
  Hannah Blunt (Judkins) 146
  John, 146
  Mary T (Austin), 146
DRINKWATER
  Cynthia (Pendleton), vi
  Cynthia A (Pendleton), 211
  Elizabeth (Bradford), 211
  Eunice (Wyman), 211
  Josiah, 211
  Lucinda (Pendleton), 211
  Micajah, 211
  Peggy (Pendleton), 211
  Rachel (Parker), 211
  William, 211
  Zenas, vi, 211
DRURY
  Salome, 161
DUDLEY
  Betsey (Nash), 190
  Hannah (Leavitt), 26
  Jonathan, 190
  Joseph, 26
  Martha, 26
  Sarah, 27, 212
DUNBAR
  Abigail, 262
  Lucy, 288
  Sarah, 287
DUNHAM
  Abigail, 210
  Christiana (Pendleton) Thomas, 211
  John Jr, 211
  Samuel, 210
DUNLAP
  Andrew, 179
  Richard, 178
DUNN
  Hannah (Presson) Marriner 50
DUNNEL/ DUNNELL
  Abigail, 83, 85
  Betsey (Lane) Moulton 158
  Elizabeth (Lane) Moulton 158
  John, 83, 158
  Joseph, 238
  Love, 157

Mehitable, 238
Polly (Farnham), 83
DUNNING
  Elizabeth, 180
  Elizabeth (Dunlap), 179
  Lois, 180
  Margaret, 177
  Peggey, 177
DUNTON
  Daniel, 88
  Elizabeth (--), 88
  Hannah (Farnham), 88
  Timothy, 88
DUREN
  Sarah, 49
DURHAM
  Mary, 285
DURKEE
  Eleanor, 12
DURRELL
  Sarah, 49
DUSTIN
  Elizabeth (Swan), 272
  Jesse, 272
  Jonathan, 272
  Susanna (Farnham), 272
DYER
  Elizabeth, 157
  Isabel, 59
  Jane (Palmer), 203
  Lucy, 186
  Mary, 116, 169
  Mary B, 35
  Polly B, 35
  William, 203
EAMES [SEE ALSO AMES]
  Ebenezer, 273
  Elizabeth, 273
  Elizabeth (--), 273
  James, 273
  Persis, 273
  Polly, 273
  Ruth (Field), 273
EARL [SEE HEARL],
EARLY
  Elizabeth, 102
  Sarah, 102
EATON
  Bathsheba (--), 75
  Capt --, 95
  Israel, 240
  James, 75
  Jemima, 240
  Joseph, 121
  Judith, 131-132, 301
  Mary, 75
  Sarah (Mackintyre), 240

EDGECOMB
Abigail (Lane), 157
Gibbins, 157
Rhoda (Elwell), 157
EDGERLY
Abigail (Brooks), 238
Isaac, 318
John, 238
Mary Jane (Sprague), 318
Mehitable (Rankins), 238
Samuel, 238
EDWARDS
Hannah, 158
Joanna, 258
John, 246
Mary (Sands), 245-246
EGGLESTON
Hezekiah, 174
ELDEN
Capt --, 247
Martha, 157
ELDER
Margaret, 183
ELDREDGE/ ELDRIDGE
Aaron, 2
Daniel Jr, 55
Dorcas, 130
Hannah, 35
Jeremiah, 130
Lydia, 130
Lydia (Hamilton), 130
Phebe (Cobb), 55
ELLIS
Deborah, 199
Martha, 130
Sandra J, 188, 190
ELWELL
Jerusha, 50
Loruhama, 263
Rhoda, 157
Tabitha, 55
EMERSON
Elizabeth, 155
Hannah, 243
Joanna, 71
Julia, 277
Rachel, 27
EMERY
Adah, 115
Elizabeth, 240
Esther (Stevens), 240
Hannah, 269
John, 94, 115
Kezia, 270
Lydia, 94
Mary (Bragdon), 94, 115
Rebekah Scammon, 269
Zachariah, 240

EMMONS
Hannah (Farnham), 87
Patrick, 87
ERSKINE/ ERSKIN
Christopher, 167
John, 166
Margaret, 133
Rosannah (McAllister), 167
ESTES
Ann, 45
Anna, 10
Benjamin, 43
Betsey, 10, 105
Betsey (Bartlett), 20, 249
Daniel, 20, 249
Eliza (Andrews), 11
Elizabeth, 43
Elizabeth (--), 43
James, 11
Mary (--), 20
Mary (Segar), 249
Polly (Segar), 249
Relief (Bartlett), 10-11, 20
Richard, 20, 249
Robert, 44
Sarah (Andrews), 11
Sarah (Hanson), 44
Stephen, 10-11, 20
Wait, 9
ESTUS
Betsey (Brock), 317
Levi, 317
EVANS
Bethiah (--), 180
Elizabeth, 272-273
Elizabeth (Stickney), 273
John, 273
Sally, 61
Sarah, 28, 61
EVERTON
Jane, 253
Relief (Howe), 253
Thomas, 253
FALL
Abigail, 82
Ebenezer, 317
Elizabeth, 141
John, 104
Judith, 52, 104
Lydia, 120, 279
Lydia (Jones), 104
Mary (Jones), 104
Tristram, 317
FARL [SEE EARL],
FARNHAM/ FARNAM/ FARNUM
Abigail, 83, 85, 224
Abigail (Dunnell) Smith

83, 85
Abigail (Fall) Wentworth
82
Abigail (Stover), 224
Anna, 84, 87, 89
Anna (Wingate), 83-84
Barachias, 102-103
Benjamin, 82-86, 91
Benjamin Jr, 82-83, 85
Betsy, 86
Betsy (Stinson), 88
Betty, 90
Catherine (Austin), 82, 87
Catherine (Wentworth), 84
Daniel, 87-88, 92
David, 82-87
David Jr, 85
Dolly, 84-86
Dorcas (--), 83
Dorcas (Frost), 91
Dorothy, 85
Dorothy (Heard), 90
Dorothy (Webber), 82-83
Dummer, 90-91
Dummer Jr, 90
Eliza (Horton), 85
Eliza (Kelley), 86
Elizabeth, 86, 90
Elizabeth (--), 82
Elizabeth (Austin), 89
Elizabeth (Barker), 4
Elizabeth (Burrows), 85
Elizabeth (Couillard)
 87-88
Elizabeth (Door), 89-90
Elizabeth (Stinson), 87
Enoch, 84
Esther, 87-88
Eunice, 87
Eunice (--), 102
Fanny (Stacy), 84
Fanny (Wood) Merrill, 91
Gains, 83
Gaius, 83
Guss, 83
Hannah, 4, 87-88, 91
Hannah (Bragdon), 87
Hannah (Farnham), 87
Jane, 86
Jane (Carlton), 87-88
Jenney, 86
Jeremiah, 84, 278
Jeremy, 84
Joanna, 88-89, 91
John, 84-85, 87, 89, 91
 224
Jonathan, 4
Joseph, 85, 102

**FARNHAM/ FARNAM/
FARNUM** (continued)
Joshua, 87-88
Kate (Wentworth), 84
Lois (Lord), 82, 85
Lois (Rowell), 88
Louise, 87
Lucretia, 83
Lucy, 89
Lydia, 250
Martha (Perkins), 84
Martha (Rowell), 88
Mary, 83, 87-88, 90-91
Mary (--), 87-88
Mary (Bagley), 87, 89
Mary (Grow), 87
Matthew, 82-85, 87
Mehitable (Bean), 90-91
Mehitable (Keggan), 85
Meribah (Goodwin), 102
Meribah (Lord), 90
Nabby, 84-85
Nancy, 84
Olive, 87-88, 90
Olive (Lord), 90
Olley (Lord), 90
Paul, 89-91
Paul Jr, 89-91
Phineas, 87
Phineha, 88
Polly, 83
Polly (Bessey), 88
Ralf, 90
Ralph, 89-90
Ralph Jr, 92
Russell C, 83, 85, 87
  89-90, 92
Salley, 86
Sally, 83
Sally (Hill), 91
Sally (Worster), 84
Samuel, 8, 83
Samuel Wingate, 84
Sarah (Blaisdell), 82-83, 86
Sarah (Kelley), 87
Susan (Downs), 85
Susan (Giles), 85
Susanna, 272
Thomas, 87-88
William, 88
Zebediah, 87-88
FARR
Abraham, 226
Mehitable, 226
FARRINGTON
Abigail (Swan), 272
Hannah, 215
Jeremiah, 272

FARWELL
Anna (Pattee), 111
Ebenezer Pattee, 111
Henry, 111
Isaac, 145
Relief (Gullifer), 111
FASSETT [SEE FOSSETT],
FAVOR
Mary, 248
FELCH
Daniel, 176
Olive (Maxwell), 176
FELLOWS
Margaret, 118
FERNALD/ FURNALD
Alice, 93
Benjamin, 92-93, 219-220
Benjamin Jr, 92
Catherine, 93
Catherine (--), 92
Deborah, 40
Ebenezer, 92
Elizabeth, 93
Ellis, 93
Eunice (Place), 93
Jane, 31
Jonathan, 93
Joseph, 93
Joshua, 92
Josiah, 92
Judith (Brock), 40
Keziah, 234
Lucy, 92-93
Lucy (Fernald), 93
Martha, 40
Mary, 52
Mary (Gunnison), 52
Miriam, 92-93, 219
Nancy, 32
Nathaniel, 52
Noah, 93
Patience (Mendum), 92
Patty, 40
Polly, 52
Robert, 93
Sally, 40
Sarah, 92, 219
Sarah (Fernald), 92, 219
Sarah (Weeks), 93
Sophia, 40
Sophy, 40
Tristram, 40
William, 92-93
FICKETT
Isabel (Dyer), 59
John, 59
Lydia Webb, 113
Mary, 59, 266

FIELD
Ruth, 273
FIFIELD
Hannah Cranch (Bond), 30
Noah, 30
FINNEY
Agnes, 255
Alice, 254
Esther, 252
FINNEY [SEE PHINNEY],
FISH/ FISK/ FISKE
Asa, 14
Eunice (Nourse), 27
Ezra, 27
Melinda (Blake), 27
Sarah, 14
Susannah (--), 14
William, 27
FISHER
Abigail, 172
Elizabeth, 237
Eunice, 303
Sally, 253
Sarah, 253
William, 172
FLAGG
Fanny (Getchell), 304
James, 304
Nehemiah, 304
Sylvia E A, 304
Sylvia E A (Flagg), 304
Vesta Gould (Williams)
  304
FLAMION
Rosemary, 143
FLETCHER
Anna (Mosher), 191
Huldah (Dorman), 81
Jeremiah, 81
Parker, 191
Ruth, 228
FLING
Mary, 146
FLINT
Betsey, 302
Deborah, 9
Elizabeth (Richardson)
  239
John Cummings, 239
Lydia, 67
Lydia (Pope), 67, 302
Thomas, 67, 302
FLOOD
Esther, 50
FLOYD
Phoebe, 13
FLUCKER
Thomas, 278

EVERY NAME INDEX

FLUENT
 Jerusha, 222
FLYE
 Jonathan, 170
 Phebe (Tuttle), 170
FOBES
 Susannah, 303, 307
FOGG
 Abigail (Meserve), 183
 Anna, 233
 Anna (--), 233
 Betty, 183
 David, 183
 Elizabeth, 23, 183
 Hannah, 182
 James, 233
 Margaret (Elder), 183
 Mary, 232
 Mary (Pickernale), 182
 Reuben, 183
 Seth, 182
FOLLANSBEE/
FOLLENSBEE
 Benjamin, 148
 Daniel, 229
 Hannah (Prescott) Small
  229
 Mehitable (Carle) Judkins
  148
FOLLETT/ FOLLET
 Dorothy (Parsons), 94
 John, 94
 John Jr, 93
 Joshua W, 94
 Lydia (Emery), 94
 Mary, 94
 Mary (Tripe), 93
 Mercy, 94-95
 Mercy (Mitchell), 93
 Robert, 93-94
FOLSOM
 Almira (Day), 271
 Elizabeth (Laplain), 159
 Hannah (Lapham), 159
 Jane B, 159
 Mary, 137
 Sarah, 263
 Tristam Jr, 159
FOOT
 Mary, 174
FORD
 Esther, 135
FOSS
 Deborah, 242
 Judith, 192
FOSSETT/ FASSET
 Anna (Clark), 133
 Annar (Clark), 133

 Eleanor, 133
 Henry Jr, 133
FOSTER
 Abner, 20
 Anna (Bartlett), 20
 Asa, 20
 Asael, 13
 Benjamin, 252
 Betsey, 97
 Dolley (--), 97
 Elizabeth, 97
 Esther, 182
 Hannah, 272
 Jacob, 284
 Lucy (Brackett), 13
 Lydia (Nelson), 20
 Nathaniel, 97
 Sally, 13
 Waity P, 167
FOWLER
 Martha (Nye), 200
 Nathan, 200
 Patty (Nye), 200
FOY
 Eunice, 101, 103
FRANCIS
 Col --, 67
 David Neal, 317
 George, 264
 Hepzibah (Varrel), 264
 John, 317
 Marindy (Whitney), 317
 Mary, 264
FREEMAN
 Abigail, 199
 Barnabas, 201
 Eliza, 201
 Eliza (Norton), 275
 Elizabeth (Talpey), 274
 Hepzebeth (Talpey), 277
 Jeremiah, 277
 Joshua, 280
 Lucy, 280
 Mary, 201
 Nathaniel Jr, 274
 Patience (Rogers), 280
 Reuben, 280
 Rhoda (--), 201
 Theodore, 275
 William, 280
FRENCH
 Hannah, 228
FRINK
 Susanna, 320
FROST
 Abigail, 206
 Adaline, 53
 Almira, 151

 Bartholomew, 70
 Betsey (Brock), 39
 Betty (Brock), 39
 Dominicus, 151
 Dorcas, 91
 Dorcas (Abbott), 151
 Elizabeth, 143, 292
 Elizabeth (Brock), 39
 Elizabeth (Randall), 233
 Hannah (--), 70
 James, 39
 James Jr, 39
 Jane, 269
 John, 233
 Lydia, 20
 Mary (Berry), 292
 Moses, 21
 Nathaniel, 21, 292
 Olive (Bartlett), 21
 Sally Abbott, 151
 Sarah, 70, 206
 Sarah (--), 21
 Sarah (Gerrish), 233
 Sarah Abbott, 151
 Susan, 321
 William, 233
FRY/ FRYE
 Abigail (Varney), 44
 Comfort, 137
 Ebenezer, 44
 Elizabeth, 4
 Elizabeth (Holton), 4
 John, 140
 Joshua, 44
 Martha (--), 140
 Mary, 140
 Mary (Buffum), 44
 Mary (Folsom), 137
 Silas, 137
 Timothy, 4
 William, 44
FULLER
 Abigail (Day), 69
 Ebenezer, 309
 Edward, 69
 Eliza (Williams), 309
 Francis, 309
 Hannah, 237
 James, 174
 Mary (--), 69
 Mary (Martin), 174
 Rachel (Lowell), 164
 Richard B, 164
 Thomas, 69
FULLERTON
 Jane, 8
FURBISH/ FUBUSH
 Catherine, 8

EVERY NAME INDEX

FURBISH/ FUBUSH
(continued)
Dorothy, 184
Hannah, 37, 200
Sarah, 8, 142, 181
FURNESS
Abigail (--), 162
Martha (Leigh), 162
Patty (Leigh), 162
Robert, 162
William, 162
GAGE
Amos, 95
Anna B (Sargent), 95
Charles C, 123
Eliza (Harriman), 122-123
Frances C (Stockbridge) 95
Leander, 95
Lois (Hovey), 95
Mary (Warren), 95
Mehitable (Kimball), 95
Thomas Hovey, 95
William, 95
GAHAN
Annah (Savage), 96
Bathsheba (Webb), 96, 319
Eleanor Lee (Bowker), 96
James, 96
Jeremiah, 96
John, 96, 319
Mary (Blair), 96
Mary (Whaling), 96
Peggy, 96
Samuel Webb, 96
Sarah Webb, 96
William Butler, 96
GALE
J William, 204-205
Louise, 204
GAMMON
Joanna (--), 50
Philip, 50
Ruth, 50
GARCELON
Deliverance (Annis), 186
James, 186
Katherine (Millbanks), 186
Peter, 186
GARDNER
Esther (Rankins), 238
Grace, 109
Israel, 238
GARNETT
Grace, 109
GARRETT
Richard, 18
Susanna, 18-19

Temperance, 18
GASKILL
Mary, 43
GATCHELL
Hannah (Tibbetts), 282
John, 281
John Simmons, 282
Mary (Tibbettts), 281
Samuel, 281
Sarah, 282
GATES
Deborah (Giles), 13
Josiah, 222
Margaret, 12
Sophronia (Pierce) Pike 222
GAY
Anna, 148
Azubah (Thomas), 278
Jonah, 278
Mary (Thomas), 278
Wellington, 278
GERRISH/ GERISH
Anna (Thompson), 94
Dolly (Farnham), 84-85
Dorothy (Farnham), 85
Ivory, 85
Jacob, 185
Joseph, 94
Margaret, 105
Margery, 119
Mary (Follett), 94
Peggy, 105
Sarah, 233
William T, 94
GERRY/ GAREY
Abigail (Varrell), 275
James, 275
GETCHELL
Eunice, 213
Fanny, 304
GIBBS
Mary, 270
Sarah, 282
GIBSON [SEE JEPSON],
GIFFORD
John W, 201
Sally (Nye), 201
GILES
Abigail, 25, 28
Deborah, 13
Susan, 13, 85
GILKEY
John, 213
Matilda, 213
Sylvina (Thomas), 213
GILLET
Lury Ann, 179

GILLEY/ GILL
Abigail, 22
Alice, 97
Betsey (Foster), 97
Catherine (Bran), 98
Dermont, 97
Dorcas, 97
Dorcas (Brawn), 21, 97
Elizabeth (Foster), 97
Else, 97
Isaac F, 98
James, 97
John, 21, 96-97
Margaret, 21, 97
Naomi (Hawes), 97
Peggy, 97
Rebecca (Quin), 97
Robert, 97
Sally (Dow), 97
William, 97
GILMAN
Agnes (Stevens), 257
Charlotte (Bourne) Swett Hamilton, 116
Edward, 257
Elizabeth, 121
Jane, 241
Jemima, 257
John Taylor, 116
Samuel, 201
Temperance (Nye), 201
GILPATRICK [SEE KILPATRICK],
GINN
-- (--), 98
Abraham, 99
Ann, 99
Ann (Riggs), 98
Daniel, 99
Delia, 99
Hannah (Downes), 99
Hannah (Keyes), 99
James, 98
Joanna (Swett) Paine, 99
Joshua, 99
Kirty (Stewart), 99
Margaret, 99
Peley, 99
Polly, 99
Sally, 99
Sally (Odom), 99
Samuel, 99
Sukey, 99
Susan, 99
Susanna (Page), 99
Thomas, 98
William Riggs, 99

EVERY NAME INDEX

GIPSON [SEE JEPSON],
GIRDY
   Abigail (--), 24
GIVEN
   Mary (Skolfield), 255
   Robert, 255
GLASS
   --, 222
   Hannah (Goodridge) Pitts 222
GLEASON
   Jesse, 143
   Rebecca, 32
   Sophia (Jones), 143
GLIDDEN
   Abigail, 56
   Benjamin, 154, 231
   Charles, 231
   Elizabeth (Pulcifer), 231
   Eunice (Averill), 154, 231
   Jeremiah, 147
   Lydia, 147
   Mary, 154
   Mehitable (--), 147
   Ruth, 154
   Ruth (Plummer), 231
GLYE
   Sarah, 170
GODDARD
   Dorcas, 80
   Peace, 137
GODFREY
   George, 130
   Joanna, 324
   Martha, 130-131
   Mercy (Knowles), 130
GODWIN
   Apphia (Segar), 249
   Assa (Segar), 249
   James, 249
   Rachel (Harper), 249
   William, 249
GOLDTHWAITE
   Jane (Miller), 121
   Jane Miller, 121
   Joseph, 121
GOLT/ GOFF
   Alice, 264
GOODRICH
   Ivory, 100
   Mary, 102
   Sarah, 102
GOODRIDGE/ GOODRIGE
   Abigail, 100-101
   Abigail (Preble), 99
   Benjamin, 99-100
   Benjamin Jr, 100
   Betcy (Robbins), 241

Betsey, 100-101
Betsy (Robbins), 241
Daniel, 99
Doris (Guptail), 100
Elizabeth, 101
Eunice, 246
Hannah, 222
Hiram, 100-101
Ichabod, 100
James, 100-101
Joshua Jr, 241
Mary, 101-102
Mary (Gubtail), 100
Mary (Guptill), 100
Mary (Shorey), 100
Molley, 100-101
Paul, 99-101
Sally (Brasbridge), 101
Sally (Twambley), 101
Sarah, 102
Stephen, 101
GOODWIN
   Abiel, 297
   Abigail, 101, 261
   Abigail (Martin), 101
   Abigail (Stone), 101
   Adam, 102
   Andrew, 285
   Anna (Tompson), 284-285
   Betsey (Andrews), 53
   Betsey (Tompson), 285
   Charity, 102
   Charles, 103
   Daniel, 6, 102
   Dominicus, 284
   Ebenezer, 235
   Elijah, 101, 103, 115
   Elijah Jr, 102-103
   Elizabeth, 197
   Elizabeth (Andrews), 103
   Elizabeth (Littlefield) Perkins, 284
   Eunice (Foy) Hammond 101, 103
   Experience (Pray), 103
   Hannah, 284
   Hannah (Earl), 125
   Hannah (Emery), 269
   Hannah (Hearl), 125
   Harriet, 269
   Hitty (Abbott), 6
   Ichabod, 285
   Isaac, 104
   Ivory, 142
   Jacob, 103
   Jedediah, 269
   Joan (Curtis), 174
   Joanna, 53

Joanna (Stanton), 103
Jonathan, 53, 103, 125
Keziah (Randall), 235
Lemuel, 103
Lucy (Avery), 102-103
Lydia, 102, 115
Margaret, 282
Martha, 103, 107
Martha (Pierce), 6
Mary, 125, 297
Mary (Downs), 102
Mary (Moulton), 104
Mary (Wallingford), 285
Mehitable (Abbott), 6
Meribah, 102
Olive, 106
Olive (Wyman), 321
Phebe (Downs), 102
Priscilla, 309
Relief (Jones), 142
Reuben, 102
Sally (Daggett), 65
Samuel, 65, 142
Sarah, 174
Sarah (Goodrich), 102
Sarah (Goodridge), 102
Sarah (Hodgdon), 142
Sarah (Milberry), 297
Simeon, 103
Stephen, 321
Thomas, 6
William, 101, 174
GORDON/ GOURDON/ GOADON
   Betsy, 148
   Henry, 174
   Ithiel, 317
   Marian (Simpson), 252
   Mary, 173-174
   Mary (Payson), 148
   Miriam (Simpson), 252
   Peter, 148
   Polly, 26
   Robert, 252
   Sarah Allen (Sargent), 252
   Tabitha (--), 174
   Thial, 317
GORHAM
   Abigail, 18
   Abigail (Sturgis), 18
   David, 18
   Deborah, 19
   Penelope, 191
   William, 18-19
GOUBERT
   Dinah (--), 23
   Nicolas, 23
   Sarah, 23

EVERY NAME INDEX

GOULD/ GOOLD
Bethiah, 233
Betsey (Warren), 291
Charity, 246
Dennis, 291
Elizabeth (Warren), 291
Hannah, 127
Jemima, 14
Joseph, 127, 291
Lydia (Dow), 138
Mary, 135, 138-139
Mary Brewster, 169
Moses, 127
Nathaniel, 253
Phoebe, 253
Ruhama (Bickford), 253
Ruth (Remick), 291
Ruthanna (Bickford), 253
Samuel, 138
Vinson, 169
GOULDING
Mary, 227
GOULDSBORO
Hannah (Petty), 216
Samuel, 216
GOVE
Hannah, 44
GOWAN/ GOWEN
Gerald F, 272
John, 185
Mercy, 239
Nancy (Mildram), 185
GOWEL/ GOWELL
Hannah, 233-234
Keziah (Fernald), 234
Molly, 141
Richard, 234
Sarah, 53, 235
GOWEN
Molly (Roberts) Hamilton 119
Stephen, 119
GOWER
Gerald F, 274
GRAFFAM
Drusilla, 24
GRAND
Andrew, 136
Grizzel, 53
GRANDIN
Mary Jane, 115
GRANT
Betsey (Estes), 105
Charles, 105
David, 105
Dorothy, 140
Elijah, 105
Elizabeth (Clark), 104

Eunice (Lord), 105
Grizzel, 53
Hannah, 105
Hannah (--), 104
Humphrey, 105
Jenny, 270
John, 104
John 3rd, 104
Jonathan, 105
Joseph, 105
Joshua, 52-53, 104
Joshua Jr, 105
Judith (Fall), 52, 104
Lt Col --, 109
Lydia, 195
Margaret (Gerrish), 105
Mary, 53, 104
Mary (Clark), 105
Mary (Lord), 105
Peggy (Gerrish), 105
Peter, 104-105
Phebe (Blethen), 105
Polly, 104, 185
Polly (Clark), 105
Rachel, 104
Sally (Clements), 52, 105
Sarah (Clements), 52, 105
GRAVES
Bathsheba, 173
Catherine (Potter) Denham 225
Johnson, 225
Martha, 99
Sarah (Staples), 225
William, 225
GRAY
Abigail, 108
Amy, 305
Andrew, 105, 245-246
Betsey (Sands), 105
Betty, 106
Betty (Sands), 105, 245
Caleb, 108
Catherine (Cooper), 282
David, 106-107
Ebenezer, 106
Eliza (Tibbetts), 282
Elizabeth, 106
Elizabeth (Marr) Worcester 107
Elizabeth (Sands), 105, 245
Hannah (Austin) Murrey 107-108
Hannah (McKusick), 107
James, 107-108, 154, 307
Jane (Worcester), 108
John, 107, 313
Levi C, 282

Lydia, 106
Lydia B (McKusick), 107
Margaret, 108
Martha, 106, 108
Martha (Goodwin), 107
Mary, 106, 108
Mary (Burton), 313
Mary (Hamilton), 107
Moses, 307
Nancy, 282
Nehemiah, 106
Olive, 106
Olive (Goodwin), 106
Phebe, 36
Polly, 106
Rachel, 106
Ruth, iii
Ruth S, 106
Sally, 106
Samuel, 106
Sarah, 106
Sarah (King) Richards, 106
Stephen, 282
Susan, 107
Susannah (Walker), 307
Thomas, 304
GREEN/ GREENE
John, 48
Lydia (Kilborn), 273
Mary, 48, 273
Mary (Stuart), 48
Olive, 63
Polly, 95
Rebecca, 48
Sally, 273
Sarah, 273
Thomas, 273
GREENLEAF
Amy, 160
Mary (Knight), 204
Mary K, 204
Patty, 204
Stephen, 204
Susan, 323
GRIFFIN
Ambrose, 77
Benjamin, 74
Daniel Jr, 74
Deborah (Butman), 77
Dorcas (Dennison), 79
John, 77
Joseph, 74
Leonard, 79
Martha (Dennison), 77
Mary, 74
Patty (Dennison), 77
Robert D, 73, 76-77, 79
Sarah, 318

EVERY NAME INDEX 351

GRIFFIN (continued)
  Susanna (Haraden), 72
    74-75
GRIFFITHS
  Lois M, 61, 240, 243, 245
GRINDLE
  Hannah (Snowman)
    Perkins, 259
  Joanna, 288
  Joanna (Hutchins), 289
  John, 289
  Peggy, 314
  Stephen, 259
GROVER
  Jane, 54
  Miriam (--), 252
GROVES
  Betsey, 277
GROW
  Edward, 87
  Joanna (--), 87
  Mary, 87(2)
  Olive (Farnham), 87
  William, 87
GUBTAIL [SEE GUPTILL],
GULLIFER/ GULLIVER/
  GULLIFIN/ GULLISON
  Abigail, 109, 111
  Abigail (Oliver), 109
  Amos, 111
  Betsey (Delano), 109
  Betsey (Page), 109
  Betty, 109
  Betty (Delano), 109
  Catherine, 110
  Charlotte (--), 109
  David, 109
  Delitha (Noble), 111
  Elitha (Noble), 111
  Eunice (Basset), 111
  Fannie, 111
  Felitha (Noble), 111
  Hannah (Burrill), 109
  Henry, 109
  Herbert M, 111
  John, 108-110
  Joseph, 110
  Keturah (Samson), 108
    110
  Lemuel, 110
  Nancy (Rose) Thurston
    110
  Nancy Ann (Dore) Smith
    109
  Patience (Tozier), 110
  Peleg, 110
  Relief, 111
  Rhoda, 109

Samson, 109
Sarah, 110
Sarah (Stanley), 110
Sarah Ann (Otis), 110
Sophia, 111
Sophie, 111
Sukey (Southeard), 111
Sukey (Southerd), 111
Susan (Tripp), 109
Susanna (Southeard), 111
Susanna (Southerd), 111
Thankful (Tozier), 110
Thomas, 108-110
GUNNISON
  Mary, 52
GUPTILL/ GUPTIL/
  GUPTAIL/ GUBTAIL
  Abigail (Goodwin), 261
  Benjamin, 100
  Dorcas (Stone), 100
  Doris, 100
  Elizabeth (--), 100
  Fanny, 261
  John, 261
  Mary, 100, 310
  Mary (--), 100
  Moses, 6
  Nathaniel, 100
  Phebe, 30
  William, 100
GURNEY
  Jane, 194
GYPSON (SEE JEPSON),
HADDEN
  Hannah, 323
HADLOCK
  Abigail, 262
  Samuel, 262
  Sarah, 127
  Sarah (Manchester), 262
HAGENS/ HAGGENS
  Edmund, 119, 198
  Edmund Jr, 119
  Mary Ann (Hamilton), 119
  Sukey (Hamilton), 119
  Susannah (Hamilton), 119
HAGER
  Elizabeth (Melcher), 180
  William, 180
HAINES [SEE HAYNES],
HALE
  Hepsibah, 50
HALEY
  Margaret, 121
  Rebecca, 183
HALL
  Abigail, 8, 112, 160
  Abigail (Whitney), 111

Allen, 112
Almira (Pike), 221
Ama (Allen), 111
Amiable (Allen), 111
Andrew, 9
Anne, 19
Charles, 198-199
Daniel, 321
Edward, 239
Elijah, 221
Esther, 112
Hatevil, 8, 321
Henry, 228
Jane, 9
Jane (Merrill), 9
Jemima (Dolliver), 199
Joanna, 31
John, 19, 236
Josiah, 111
Levina (Lyon), 112
Lois (Thompson), 222
Lorana (Winslow), 321
Lydia, 239
Lydia (Noble), 199
Lydia (Randall), 236
Lydia (Wentwort), 236
Margaret, 255
Maria (Lyon), 112
Mary, 112
Mary (Miller), 239
Mary Farnum (Town), 222
Meriah (Lyon), 112
Naoma (York), 19
Nathan, 112
Preserved, 111
Ruth (Fletcher), 228
Ruth (Prescott), 228
Sarah (Furbish), 8
Sibel (--), 199
William, 221, 236
Zilpha, 282
HALLETT
  Mary, 317
  Thankful, 303
HAM
  Elizabeth, 232
HAMBLEN/ HAMBLIN
  Almery, 113
  Daniel, 113
  Deborah (Jenkins), 112
  Ebenezer, 113
  Elizabeth, 113
  Gershom, 112-113
  Hannah, 113
  Hannah (Almary), 112
  Hannah (Almony), 112
  Hannah (Whitmore), 113
  Ichabod, 113

HAMBLEN/ HAMBLIN
(continued)
Jacob, 113
Jane (Small), 113
Lydia Webb (Fickett), 113
Mary, 113
Mary (Clark), 113
Mary (Clay), 51
Molly (Clay), 51
Samuel, 51, 113
Samuel Jr, 51
Sarah, 221
Statira, 113
Susan (McDonald) Usher 113
Temperance (Lewis), 51
HAMILTON
--, 53, 115
Abel, 117
Abial, 114-115
Abial Emery, 115
Abigail, 114-115, 118
Abigail (Hodsden), 114
Adah (Emery), 115
Adrial, 53
Benjamin, 222
Betsey, 116-117
Betsey (Bodwell), 119
Bial, 114
Charity (Keay), 114
Charlotte (Bourne) Swett 116, 118
David, 114
Deborah, 118
Deborah (--), 117
Elizabeth, 118
Elizabeth (--) Dana, 116 118
Experience (Hatch), 223
Gabriel, 107, 234
George, 117
Hannah, 197, 223
Hannah (--) Wilkinson, 119
Hannah (Millet), 119
Hannah (Thurrell), 318
Huldah (Randall), 234
James, 115
Joanna (Bolthood), 114
Joanna (Boltwood), 114
Joanna (Keay), 116
John, 117, 318
Jonas, 102, 114-115
Jonathan, 116-119
Jonathan 3rd, 114
Jonathan Jr, 118
Joseph, 116-118
Judith (Lord) Meads, 107
Judith (Ricker), 222

Lovey (Walker), 53
Lydia, 37, 130
M (--), 117
Margery (Gerrish), 119
Martha, 117
Mary, 107, 117-118 310(2)
Mary (Hanscom) Ricker 234
Mary (Manning), 116, 118
Mary Ann, 119
Mary Jane (Grandin), 115
Mehitable (Brackett), 115
Millet, 119
Molly (Roberts), 119
Olive, 53, 117
Oliver, 117
Patience, 104
Patty, 117
Reuben, 116, 234
Richard, 223
Rufus, 119
Sally, 115, 222-223
Sarah, 118, 222-223
Sarah (Metcalf), 234
Silas, 115
Solomon, 114
Sukey, 119
Susanna, 102, 115
Susannah, 119
HAMLEN/ HAMLIN
Anna (Prescott), 303
Charles, 303
Deborah (Cates), 317
Eleanor (Craig), 304
Elizabeth (Williams), 303
Hannah (Rich), 317
Lewis, 304
Lewis Baker, 304
Mary, 317
Mary (Hallett), 317
Nicholas, 317
Perez, 303
Roxanna (Laughton), 304
Sarah A (Robinson), 304
Susan (Williams), 304
Timothy, 317
HAMMOND
Elisha, 273
Elizabeth (Evans) Swan 273
Eunice (Foy), 101, 103
HAMOR
Sally, 127
Sarah, 127
HANCOCK
Dorcas (Tracy), 216
Elizabeth, 32, 156

Lucinda, 216
Mary, 156
Samuel, 216
Sarah (--), 156
William, 156
HANEY
Sarah, 99
HANLEY/ HANLY
Elizabeth, 133
Margaret (Erskine) McMurphy, 133
Roger, 133
HANNAFORD
Margaret, 78
HANSCOM/ HUNSCOMB
Abigail, 121
Abigail (Sands), 120
Anna, 113, 120
Anna (Carle), 119
Benaiah, 119-120
Benjamin Carle, 121
Betsey (Smith), 121
Catherine, 310
Constance, 187
Eleanor, 239
Elizabeth (Sands), 157, 239
Elizabeth (Smith), 121
Ezra Davis, 120
Jane Miller (Goldthwaite) 121
John, 119-120
John Jr, 120
Keziah, 157
Keziah (Fernald) Gowell 234
Keziah (Rogers), 119
Martha, 121
Mary, 234
Mary (Hill), 120
Mehitable, 36
Polly (Hill), 120
Priscilla, 120-121
Robert, 120-121
Sally (Merrow), 121
Sarah, 120
Sarah (Merrow), 121
Temperance (Burnham), 36
Thomas, 36
Timothy, 234
William, 120-121, 157 239
HANSON
Bathsheba (--), 235
Betsey, 52
Caleb, 138
Hannah (Sawyer), 44
Joanna, 233, 235
Judith (Jepson), 138

EVERY NAME INDEX 353

HANSON (continued)
Martha (Brock), 41
Mary, 119, 137
Mercy, 137
Nathan, 40-41
Patty (Brock), 41
Sarah, 44
Thomas, 44
William, 235
HARADEN
Abigail, 76
Daniel, 74
Deborah, 76
Jane, 71
Jenny, 71, 73
Jonathan, 74
Susanna, 72, 74-75
Susanna (Burnam), 74
HARDEN
Freeman, 237
Hannah (Rankins), 237
Mary (Swan), 237
Perry, 237
HARDING
Bethiah, 176
Elizabeth, 149, 171, 263
Josiah, 55
Mary, 240
Mary (Cutler), 171
Mary (Thompson) Young 42
Molly (Thompson) Young 42
Nathaniel, 42
Priscilla, 177-178
Samuel, 171
HARDISON
Rebecca, 236
HARDY
Jemima, 203
HARLOW
Ebenezer, 194
Ebenezer Jr, 194
James, 194
Lydia (Doten), 194
Philemon, 194
Sally (Nash), 194
Sarah (Nash), 194
Susanna (Nash), 194
HARMON
Ada (Rankins), 239
Benjamin, 121, 321
Benjamin Carle, 121
Eda (Rankins), 239
Elizabeth (Burbank), 121
Elizabeth (Rankins) Towle 238
Hannah (Starbird), 239

Joel, 238
Lydia, 196
Nathaniel, 239, 321
Pauline (Stimpson), 238
Priscilla (Hanscom) 120-121
Stephen, 238
Stephen S, 239
HARPER
Deborah (Dole), 79-80
James, 80
Rachel, 249
Samuel, 79
Sarah (Dole), 79
William, 79
HARRIMAN/ HERRIMAN
--, 123
Abigail, 122
Abigail Hatch, 123
Caroline, 122-123
Charles Whiting, 122
Dillon, 123
Eliza, 122-123
Eliza Dennett (Ladd), 122
Elizabeth (Gilman), 121
George, 122
Gilman, 122
Harriet, 123
Harrison, 122-123
Henrietta B (--), 122
Henry Dearborn, 122-123
James T, 122
James Thomas, 122-123
Joel, 121
Mary, 122
Mary (Bradstreet), 121
Mary A (Williams), 122
Mary Camilla (Anderson) 122
Olive (Porter), 123
Sarah (Lovell), 123
Simon, 121
Simon Bradstreet, 122
True Worthy, 121
HARRINGTON
Martha, 21
Ruth (Prescott), 229
Winslow, 229
HARRIS
Ann, 117, 230
Anna, 230
Benjamin, 168
Harriet N (McAllister), 168
Joshua, 81
Lydia (Brown), 323
Samuel, 230
Sarah (Dorman), 81

HART
Betty (Gullifer), 109
John, 109
Silence, 24
HARTFORD
Charity, 60
HARTWELL
Abigail, 15, 308
HARVEY
Eleanor, 229
Martha, 205
Polly, 205
HARWOOD
Sally, 28
Susannah, 240
HASKELL
Anne, 52
Betsey, 318
Eliphalet, 24
John, 181, 318
Louisa, 24
Lydia, 191
Mary, 195
Mary (Woodman), 24
Sarah (Merriam), 181
Susannah, 264
HATCH
Betsey, 55
Betsy, 61
Elisha, 68
Elizabeth, 61
Experience, 223
Jeremiah, 36
Joseph, 55
Lydia (Bragdon), 36
Mark, 42
Martha, 68
Mary (Atwood) Thompson Brooks, 42
Rachel (Colburn), 56
Rebecca (Hilton), 68
Sarah, 295
Sarah (Sawyer), 55
William, 56
HATHORN/ HATHORNE
Mehitable, 23
Silas, 98
Susannah, 164
HAVEN
-- (--) Marshall, 117
Joshua, 117
Mary (Cunningham), 117
Olive (Hamilton), 117
Samuel, 117
HAVENER
Eve Catherine (Ludwig) 238
Mary, 238

EVERY NAME INDEX

HAVENER (continued)
Mathias, 238
HAVENS
Christopher, 127
Mary (Higgins), 127
HAWES
David, 62
Elizabeth, 62, 190
Elizabeth (Cobb), 62
Naomi, 97
HAWKES
Amos, 9
Deborah, 9
Deborah (Flint), 9
HAWKINS
Alan H, 136-138, 140, 197
Mary, 266
HAYDEN/ HEDDEAN
Aaron, 143
Elizabeth, 224
Hannah (Claflin), 143
John, 143
Ruth Richards (Jones), 143
HAYES
David, 156
Dorcas (Allen), 156
Elijah, 53, 104, 181
Elizabeth (Chadbourne) 104, 181
Joseph, 156
Mary, 53
Mary (Grant), 53, 104
Mary (Knight), 156
Mary (Twombly), 104
Mehitable, 181
Polly (Grant), 104
HAYMAN
Edward Payne, 285
Sarah (Tompson), 284-285
HAYNES/ HAINES
Alice, 33, 157
Ephraim, 218
John, 218
Louise (Gale), 204
Mary (--), 218
Mary (Taylor), 218
Mary Direxa, 13
Zilpah (Phinney), 218
HAYWARD
Abigail, 226
HAZELTINE
Hannah (Boynton), 156
HEAD
Abigail (Harriman), 122
Abigail Hatch (Harriman) 123
Henry, 121
Henry A, 123

John, 123
Margaret (--), 123
HEAL/ HEALD
Mary, 305
Rebecca, 21
HEALEY/ HEALY
Abigail (Gullifer), 109
Martha, 13
Moses, 109
HEARD/ HURD
Dorothy, 90-91
Elizabeth, 309
Hannah (Brackett), 31
Joseph, 31
Mary, 17
Sally, 31
Sarah (Wentworth), 31
Susannah, 31
HEARL/ EARL/ FARL,
Abigail, 235
Anna (Wilkinson), 123
Dorothy (--), 124
Fanny, 124
Frances, 124
Hannah, 125
Hannah (Bradbury), 203
Ivory, 124
James, 124-125
John, 1
Joshua, 203
Martha (Huntress), 1
Moses, 124
Nancy (Wentworth), 125
Olive, 1
Olive (Junkins), 124
Rachel (Nason), 124
Samuel, 123-125
Sarah, 203
Sarah (Rann), 125
Thomas, 124
HEATH
Caleb, 202
Eldad, 125
Elmina (Colson), 126
Hannah (--), 125
Isaac, 125
Josiah, 125-126
Lucy (Douglass), 126
Lydia (Bowden), 125
Lydia (Douglass), 126
Merrill, 125-126
Molly, 126
Polly, 126
Prudence, 126
Sukey (Nye) Kent, 202
Susanna, 126
Susanna (Nye) Kent, 202
Tryphena, 126

Zebediah, 125-126
HEDDEAN [SEE HAYDEN],
HEDGE
Barnabas, 303
Jonathan, 303
Lusannah (Williams), 303
Martha (Kimball) Partridge 303
Sally (Williams), 303
Sarah (Williams), 303
Scotto, 303
Thankful (Hallett), 303
HEMMINGWAY/ HEMMENWAY
Jonathan, 40-41
Sally (Brock), 41
Sarah (Brock), 41
HENDERSON [SEE ALSO ANDERSON]
Robert, 261
Sally (Somes), 261
HENLEY
Berkeley, 123
HERBERT
Betsey, 3
Catherine (Stevens), 3
Elizabeth, 3
Henry, 3
HERRICK
Bethiah, 300
Daniel, 266
Mary, 266
Mary (Fickett), 266
Polly, 266
HERRIMAN [SEE HARRIMAN],
HERSEY
Abigail (Lewis), 143
Mehitable Lewis, 143
Zadock, 143
HIBBARD/ HEBBERD
Mary, 241
HICKS
Kerenhappuck (--), 80
HIGGINS
Abigail, 128
Abigail, 278
Abigail (Paine), 127
Anna (Coggins), 127
Benjamin, 128, 278
Deborah (Wasgatt), 127
Elizabeth (Macontior), 128
Elizabeth (McIntire), 128
Esther, 232
Hannah (Knight), 27
Hannah (Knowles) Warren Sparrow, 232
Henry, 127

EVERY NAME INDEX

HIGGINS (continued)
Israel, 126-127
Jonathan, 127
Knowles, 232
Marcy, 127
Marcy (Hopkins), 128
Mary, 42, 127-129
Mary (Rand), 232
Mary (Snow), 126
Mary (Spaulding), 129
Mary (Wiley), 128
Mary Wiley), 127
Mercy (Hopkins), 128
Oliver, 127
Philip, 127-129, 278
Polly (Hull), 127
Rebecca (Young), 126
Reuben, 128
Rhoda (Leland), 127
Ruth, 128
Sarah, 128
Sarah (Hadlock), 127
Sarah (Leland), 127
Sarah (Mathews), 128, 278
Seth, 127
Simeon, 128
Stephen, 127
Susanna (Philbrook), 128
Thankful, 128-129
Thomas, 127
Zaccheus, 126-127
Zacheus, 232
Zena (Stanwood), 127

HILL
Abigail, 69, 135
Abigail (Stevens), 91
Alice, 78
Anna, 17
Betsey (Smith) Prescott Bean, 227
Edmund, 81
Elizabeth, 44
Hannah, 139
Jeremiah, 91, 247
John Burley, 135
Jonathan, 227-228
Joseph, 139
Lucy (Dorman), 81
Martha (Crocker), 120
Mary, 120
Mercy (Prescott), 228
Nathaniel, 120
Olive, 105
Polly, 120
Sally, 91
Sally (Sawyer), 135
Sarah, 57, 320
Susanna, 143

Susanna (Whitcher), 139
HILLARD
George Stillman, 268
John Babcock, 268
Rebecca Allyn (Stillman) 267
Sally (Stillman), 268
Sarah (Stillman), 268
William, 268
HILLMAN
Ralph, 126
Ralph E, 8, 99, 129, 164 278, 301
HILLS
Betty Meynell, 251-252
HILTON
Anna, 304
Catherine, 170
Daniel, 306
Elihu, 306
James, 173
John, 306
Lucinda (Williams), 306
Magdalene, 297
Martha, 307
Mary (Brewer), 306
Mary Ann, 306
Mary Ann (Hilton) Tibbetts 306
Moses, 304
Polly (Brewer), 306
Rachel (--), 304
Rebecca, 68
Simeon, 306
HINCKLEY/ HINKLEY
Aaron, 179
Capt --, 224
Isabella, 179
Joanna S, 54
Lucy (Nye), 202
Mary (Clew), 202
Mary (Larrabee), 179
Mehitable, 70
Polly, 14
Shubael, 202
Stephen, 202
HINCKS
Jesse Young, 200
Mary, 199-200
Ruth, 200
HINKSON
Robert, 21
Sally (Swain) Silver, 21
Sarah G, 21
HISCOCK
Daniel, 68
Elizabeth (Day), 68
Eunice (Day), 68

Jane (McFadden), 68
Richard, 68
William, 68
HOAG
Mary, 139
HOBBS
Abigail (Storer), 185
Jonathan, 153
Joseph Jr, 185
Josiah, 153
Lydia (Tobey), 200
Mary (Kilpatrick), 153
Olive, 185
Phebe, 310
Sewall, 200
HOBSON
Andrew, 113
Statira (Hamblin), 113
HODGDON
Amy, 311
Capt --, 51
Molly (Gowell), 141
Sarah, 142
Stephen, 67
Suky, 141
Susan, 141
Tamson, 142
Thomas, 141
HODGE
Alexander, 226
Betsey, 226
Susan, 226
HODGES/ HOGES
Abigail (Brooks), 43
Allen, 43
Naomi, 43
Naomi (Hodges), 43
Sarah, 312
Tisdale, 43
HODGKINS/ HODGSKINS
James, 318
Philip, 318
Polly, 76
Sarah (Griffin), 318
Tabitha D (--) Smallidge 318
HODSDON/ HODSDEN
Abigail, 114
Amy (Nason), 129
Anna, 10
Anna (Estes), 10
Anna (Nason), 129
Benjamin, 129
Daniel Jr, 2
Eunice, 38
Eunice (Lord), 129
Fanny (Wadleigh), 129
Fanny (Wadley), 129

HODSDON/ HODSDEN
(continued)
Hannah (Hubbard), 2
Judith, 130
Keziah, 130
Lydia (Cooper), 129
Richard, 129
Robert, 129
Sally (Cooper), 129
Stephen, 10
Thomas, 100
William, 129
HOFFS
Barbara, 64
HOLBROOK
Abiah, 92
Abizah, 129
Benjamin, 92
Elisha, 92
Lucy (Fernald), 92
Lydia (Dresser), 92
Sarah (Higgins), 128-129
William, 92
HOLMES
--, 5, 283
Abial, 207
Abigail, 209
Abigail (Goodwin), 101
Clarissa (Tilton), 283
Deborah, 109
Elizabeth, 199-200
John, 101
Joseph, 101
Mary (Abbott), 102
Mary Direxa (Haynes), 13
Mary Jackson, 207
Oliver Wendell, 207
Patience, 5
HOLTON
Elizabeth, 4
HOMER
Jane (Lowell), 163
William, 163
HOOD
Margaret, 89
HOOK
Benjamin Jr, 123
Caroline (Harriman) 122-123
HOOPER
Charity, 114
Nancy, 35
HOPKINS
Barzilla, 130
Barzillah, 131
Bazilah, 130
Betty (Cobb), 128
Elisha, 130-131

Experience, 130
Experience (Scudder), 130
Hannah (Alexander), 154
Jane, 260
Jedida (Dexter), 131
Jennett, 260
John, 131
Joshua, 131
Levina, 154
Lydia, 131
Lydia (Eldridge), 130
Marcy, 128
Martha, 261
Martha (Godfrey) Howes 130-131
Mary (--), 260
Mercy, 128
Peter, 154
Roxana, 130
Simeon, 128
William, 260
HOPKINSON
Caleb, 50
Jane, 32, 203
John, 50, 203
Sarah (Clay) Safford, 50
Sarah (Morse), 50, 203
HORN/ HORNE
Comfort, 259
Elisha, 259
Richard, 83
Sarah (Blaisdell) Farnham 83
Tamesin (Randall), 259
HORR
Isaac, 21
Rebecca (Heald), 21
Triphena, 21
HORTON
Eliza, 85
HOSMER
Ruth, 20-21
HOUSE
Jerusha, 270
Lillis (Palmer), 270
Nathaniel, 270
HOUSTON [SEE HUSTON],
HOVEY
Joseph, 95
Lois, 95
Rebecca (Stickney), 95
Ruth, 303
HOWARD
Abigail, 226
Achsa, 249
Asa, 249
Betsey (Luce), 165
Caleb, 165

Capt --, 97
Daniel, 226
Edward, 131-132
Elizabeth, 249
Hannah (--), 226
Hannah (Blitfin), 131-132
Hannah (Blithen), 131-132
Joseph, 32
Judith (Eaton), 131-132
Lydia (Spofford), 249
Rebecca (Gleason), 32
Sallie Gleason, 32
Sarah, 34
Susanna (Mitchell), 131
Susannah, 132
HOWE
Abigail, 249
Betsey, 274
Betsey (--) Prescott, 11
Elsie (Andrews), 11
John Sr, 10-11
Mary (Newton), 11
Otis, 11
Relief, 253
Salome (Andrews), 10
HOWELL
Lydia, 214
HOWES
Joshua, 130
Martha (Godfrey), 130-131
HOWLAND
Abigail Jr, 28-29
Briggs, 229
Hannah, 229
Mary (Prescott), 229
Michael, 28-29
Patience, 18
HUBBARD
Abigail (Hearl), 235
Anna, 284
Anne, 148
Benjamin, 235
Dominicus, 235
Dorcas, 44
Dudley, 2
Francis, 148
Hannah, 2
Hannah (Neal), 44, 196
Jane, 196
Joan, 197
Joanna (Davice), 148
John, 148
John Heard, 44, 196
Martha (Randall), 235
Nancy, 148
Patty (Randall), 235
Philip, 2, 60, 91
Sarah (Nason), 71

HUFF/ HUFFE
Charles, 80
Hannah, 80
Moses, 129
Priscilla (Burbank), 80
Thankful (Higgins) 128-129
HUGHES
Maxine B, 271, 282
HULL
Charlotte (Phelps), 127
Polly, 127
Samuel, 127
HUNNEWELL
Anna, 182
Hannah (Brown), 182
Jane, 50
Richard, 182
HUNSCOMB [SEE HANSCOM],
HUNT
Abigail (Cates), 320
Affia (Murch), 193
Ann Pray, 32
Arthur K, 266
Ephraim, 320
Hannah, 178, 189
Ichabod, 193, 320
Mary, 189
Mary (Stone), 193
Polly, 189
Rachel, 231
Susanna (Frink), 320
Thankful, 99
William, 193
HUNTER
David, 132-133
Eleanor (Fossett), 133
Elizabeth (Hanley), 133
Elizabeth (Hanly), 133
Esther (Huston), 133
Henry, 132-133, 168
Henry Jr, 132
James, 133, 280
John, 133
Martha Stoyell (Belcher) 134
Nancy, 133, 168
Rachel (Dodge), 133
Ruth (Robinson), 133
Sarah, 133
Sarah (Wier), 132-133
Sarah (Wyer), 168
Thomas, 133-134
William, 133
HUNTINGTON
Cynthia, 139
Sally, 265, 282

HUNTLEY
Joyce E, 225
Joyce E (--), 212, 214, 281
HUNTRESS
Hosea, 11
Martha, 1
Mary (Andrews), 11
HURD [SEE HEARD],
HUSSEY
Abigail, 45
Alice (Gilley), 97
Bathsheba, 61
Benjamin, 97
Bethia (Varney), 9
Daniel, 9
Else (Gilley), 97
Lydia, 61, 192
Miriam, 137
Nancy, 277
Robert, 61
Sarah, 9
HUSTON/ HOUSTON
Esther, 133
Jane, 133
Jane (Houston), 133
Margaret, 67
Robert, 133, 140
Sarah (Jones), 140
HUTCHINS
Alford, 314
Alfred, 314
Charles, 286, 290
Eliakim, 314
Jesse, 314
Joanna, 289
Mary, 286, 288
Mary (Perkins), 286
Mercy, 286
Mercy (Wardwell), 290 314
Peggy (Grindle), 314
Sally (Palmer), 314
Sally (Wardwell), 290
William, 290, 314
HUTCHINSON
Anna (Whittier), 302
Constance B, iii
Joseph, 302
ILSLEY
Apphia (Merrill), 152
Joshua, 152
INGALLS
Dorothy, 4
Esther, 13
Lydia (Clough), 54
Putnam, 54
Sarah, 271

INGRAHAM
Abigail (Hartwell), 15, 308
Jeremiah, 15, 308
Tilley, 15
Tily, 15
Zilpha, 308
IRELAND
Abraham, 316, 321
Deborah, 230
Olive (Landers), 316
Pegge, 316
Samuel, 316
Silas, 316
IRISH
James, 193
Mary, 279
Mary Gorham (Phinney) 193
Sarah (Murch), 193
William, 193
IVES
Esther, 15
JACK
Mary, 280
JACKMAN
Hannah, 273
JACKSON
Esther (--), 318
H, 144
Isaac, 66, 318
Levi, 323
Lydia, 198
Meribah, 66
Rachel, 240
Sadine, 323
JACOBS
Jonathan, 269
Rebekah Scammon (Emery), 269
Sophia, 269
JAMES
Eleanor, 84
John Jr, 62
Lydia, 62
Lydia (Door), 62
JAMESON
Brice, 65
Deborah (Morton), 237
Elizabeth, 237
Lydia, 65
Priscilla (Bartlett), 65
Robert, 237
JAQUES
Ruth (Archer), 13
William, 13
JAQUITH
Abraham, 264
Elizabeth (Hill), 265

EVERY NAME INDEX

JAQUITH (continued)
  Elizabeth (Stevens), 264
  Hannah (Meader), 265
JELLERSON/ JELESON/ JELLISON
  Abel, 135
  Abigail (Carpenter), 134
  Abigail (Hill), 135
  Abijah, 135
  Betsey, 135
  Betsey (Wadlin), 134
  Caleb, 134
  Elizabeth (Maddock), 170
  Elizabeth (Wadlin), 134
  George, 134
  James, 134
  Marrian, 80
  Mary (Bean), 135
  Moses, 134
  Nahum W, 134
  Nathaniel, 170
  Olive, 134
  Polly (Bean), 135
JENKINS
  Deborah, 112
  Elizabeth, 137
  Mary (Chipman), 112
  Priscilla (Dorman), 81
  Samuel, 112
  Thomas, 81
JEPSON/ JIPSON/ GIPSON/ GYPSON, ETC
  --, 135
  Abel, 137
  Abigail (Varney), 138-139
  Abner, 137
  Abraham, 139
  Ann Rebecca (Brown), 135
  Anna, 138
  Bashaba (Booden), 136
  Caleb, 137
  Comfort (Frye), 137
  Dorothy (Grant), 140
  Elijah, 139
  Elizabeth, 135, 137-138
  Elizabeth (Boothby), 138
  Elizabeth (Jepson), 135
    138
  Esther (Ford), 135
  Hannah (Hill), 139
  Hannah (Plaice), 140
  Hannah (Roberts), 139
  Henry, 135
  Huldah, 139
  James, 135, 138
  Jedediah, 136, 138
  John, 136
  Judith, 137-138

Lois, 137
Lydia, 137, 140
Lydia (Runnels), 136
Lydia (Winslow) Morrison
  139
Margaret, 137
Margaret (Robinson), 136
  138
Mary, 137
Mary (Fry), 140
Mary (Gould), 135
  138-139
Mercy (Butland) Rines
  138
Naomi (Reed), 322
Oliver, 137
Peace (Goddard), 137
Phebe C (Page), 140
Samuel, 139
Sarah, 139
Syrena B (Ricker), 137
Thomas, 322
Timothy, 139-140
William, 135-136, 138-139
William Jr, 139-140
Zedediah, 136
JEWELL
  Sarah, 56, 166
JEWETT
  Sarah Orne, 43
JIPSON [SEE JEPSON], JOHNSON
  --, 36
  Abby (Barker), 19
  Abigail (Barker), 19
  Abigail Gorham (Barker)
    18
  Annie (Taylor), 281-282
  Betsey, 46, 194, 214
  Daniel, 19
  Edward, 143
  Eleanor, 232
  Elizabeth, 216
  Hannah (Bickford), 215
  Henry, 27
  James, 160, 281
  John, 4, 19, 281
  John Jr, 4
  Jonathan, 35
  Katherine (Luce), 46
  Lucy, 216
  Lydia (Osgood), 4
  Mary, 24, 35-36, 63
  Mary (Jones), 143
  Mary (Tibbetts) Gatchell
    281
  Mary G (Barker), 19
  Mercy (Bragdon), 36

Millia (--) Sanford, 27
Miranda (Blake), 27
Patience, 196
Patience (--), 214
Sally (Leeman), 160
Samuel, 121
Sara (Babb), 35
Sarah, 200, 216
Stephen, 215
Thankful (Smith), 27, 160
Thomas, 27, 46, 160
JOHNSTON
  Anne, 319
JONES
  --, 141
  Abigail (--), 159
  Abigail B, 142
  Belinda, 159
  Benjamin Richards, 143
  Catherine, 309
  Catherine (Allen), 9
  Daniel, 142
  Eleanor (Chamberlain)
    142
  Elizabeth, 182, 247
  Elizabeth Bracket (Young)
    143
  Esther H (Corson), 142
  Henry, 232
  Joanna (Cotton), 140
  Joanna (Leshur), 143
  John, 140-141, 309
  John Paul, 162
  Jonathan R, 142
  Joseph, 67
  Lemuel, 9
  Lemuel Howe, 143
  Lydia, 104, 231
  Lydia (--), 232
  Margaret (Huston), 67
  Margaret (McNeill), 143
  Martha (Day), 67
  Mary, 104, 142-143
  Mary (--), 141
  Mary (Kane) Bishop, 143
  Mary (Richards), 142
  Mary (Roberts), 141
  Mary (Savage), 141
  Mary Chase (Tappan), 141
  Mehitable, 141
  Mehitable (Wakeham), 140
  Mehitable Lewis (Hersey)
    143
  Mercy (Trott), 142
  Molly, 309
  Molly (Roberts), 141
  Nabby B, 142
  Nat, 141

JONES (continued)
  Nathaniel, 141
  Patty K (Day), 67
  Polly, 142
  Priscilla (Goodwin), 309
  Rebecca (Knox), 142
  Rebecca (Nock), 142
  Relief, 142
  Robert, 67
  Ruth Richards, 143
  Sally, 151
  Samuel, 141-143
  Sarah, 140, 143
  Sophia, 143
  Stephen, 141, 143
  Suky (Hodgdon), 141
  Susan (Hodgdon), 141
  Susanna (Jepson), 137
  Wait (Estes), 9
  William, 67, 141, 159
JORDAN/ JORDON
  Abner, 143-144
  Anna, 144
  Anna (Jordan), 144
  Benning Wentworth, 145
  Clemina Augusta (Welch) 145
  Climena Augusta (Welch) 144
  Ebenezer, 144-145
  Hannah, 144-145
  Hannah (True), 144
  Hannah (Wentworth), 144
  Isabella, 182
  John W, 144
  John Wentworth, 144
  Lydia, 144
  Lydia Ann (Chase), 145
  Lydia H, 144-145
  Mehitable (Roach), 144
  Nathan Bartlett, 144
  Nathaniel, 143-144
  Samuel Dyer, 145
  Sarah, 144, 183, 264
  Sarah (Jordan), 264
  Sarah Bartlett, 145
  Sarah Bartlett (Jordan), 145
  Susanna (Hill), 143
  Timothy, 144-145
  Wentworth, 144
JOSS
  Nathaniel, 178
  Priscilla (Melcher), 178
JOSSLYN
  Deborah, 19
JOY
  Benjamin, 301
  Charles Austin, 15, 216

  Hannah (Thurrell)
    Hamilton, 318
  Lydia (Hamilton), 37
  Marcy, 301
  Mary, 228-229, 301
  Mary Elizabeth, 216
  Mehitabel, 37
  Moses, 147
  Samuel, 37, 318
  Sarah (Sawyer), 301
  William, 318
JOYCE
  Abigail M, 301
JUDKINS
  --, 148
  -- (--), 147
  Anna (Blunt), 145
  Anna (Chesley), 147
  Anna (Gay), 148
  Anna (Morse), 145
  Anna Maria, 145
  Anne (Hubbard), 148
  Benjamin, 147-148, 321
  Betsey (Palmer), 147
  Betsy (Gordon), 148
  Catherine (Adle), 149
  Clarrissa, 145
  David, 147-148, 270
  Elisha, 149
  Eliza, 145-146
  Elizabeth (Knowles), 147
  Esther (Sweat), 148
  Esther (Swett), 148
  Eunice, 145-146
  Hannah, 147
  Hannah (--), 146, 148
  Hannah Blunt, 146
  Hitty (Carle), 148
  Jacob, 145
  Jesse, 147-148
  Joel, 146-147
  John, 148
  John Blunt, 146
  Jonathan, 148
  Joseph, 147-148
  Judith, 282
  Lorain Moody, 145
  Lydia (Glidden), 147
  Mary (Cowen), 147
  Mary (Fling), 146
  Mary (Philbrook), 321
  Mary D (Clark), 145
  Mehitable (Carle), 148
  Nancy, 149
  Nancy (Hubbard), 148
  Polly (Cowen), 147
  Rebecca, 146
  Rebecca (--), 146

  Rhoda (Sturtevant), 270
  Richard, 149
  Sally (Whittier), 149
  Samuel, 146, 148, 282
  Samuel Jr, 146-147
  Zachariah, 147
  Zilpha (Hall) Babb, 282
JUNKINS
  Olive, 124
KANE [SEE CAIN],
KEAY
  Betsy (Wentworth), 116
  Charity, 114
  Charity (Hooper), 114
  Hannah (Roberts), 31, 309
  Joanna, 116
  John, 114, 116, 309
  Lydia, 31
  Molly (Jones) Yeaton, 309
  Peter, 31, 309
KEEN/ KEENE
  Angeline M, 150
  Christina, 150
  Deborah, 66
  Eleazer, 149, 172
  Eleazer Jr, 150
  Elezer, 149
  Lucy, 149
  Lydia, 150
  Malinda, 150
  Maria (--), 150
  Marinda, 149-150
  Mary, 107
  Nancy, 149
  Polly, 107, 149
  Reuben, 150
  Rhoda (Marrow), 149, 172
  Sally, 149
  Samuel, 150
  Sarah, 149-150
KEGGAN
  Mehitable, 85
KELLEY
  Achsah, 242
  Eliza, 86
  Eunice (Farnham), 87
  Judith H, iii, 93, 220
  Louise (Farnham), 87
  Nancy, 38
  Sarah, 87
  Sylvanus, 242
  Temperance (--), 242
  William, 87
  William H, 87
KELSOE
  Charles, 197
  Joan (Hubbard), 197

KENDALL
Elizabeth, 23, 184
Elizabeth (--), 23
Uzziah, 23
William, 110
KENNARD
Susannah, 284
KENNEDY
Jane, 261
Martha (Hopkins), 261
Mary, 243
Samuel, 261
KENNEY
Joshua, 142
Mary (Jones), 142
Molly (Door), 142
Polly (Jones), 142
Samuel, 142
KENNISTON
Abiah P (--), 17
KENT
Nathaniel, 202
Sarah, 180
Sukey (Nye), 202
Susanna (Nye), 202
KERSWELL [SEE CASWELL],
KEYES
Hannah, 99
Samuel, 99
Samuel Jr, 99
Sukey (Ginn), 99
Susan (Ginn), 99
Thankful (Hunt), 99
KIEFF
Betsey (Peabody), 209
KILBORN
Lydia, 273
KILGORE
Abigail, 150-151
Abigail (Soule) Shurtleff 150
Almira (Frost), 151
Alvah, 151
Anna (York), 150
Elihu, 151
Eliphaz Chapman, 151
Elizabeth (Brackett), 150
Ira, 150-151
Irene (Shurtleff), 151
Jane (Severance), 151
Joanna, 150-151
John, 150-151
John Jr, 150
Julia Ann, 151
Julia Anne, 150
Lydia (Russell), 151
Moses, 150

Moses Hadley, 151
Nabby, 150-151
Phineas, 150
Phineas F, 151
Polly (Powers), 151
Sally, 21, 151
Sally (York), 151
Sally Abbott (Frost), 151
Sarah Abbott (Frost), 151
Urban, 151
KILPATRICK/ GILPATRICK/ PATRICK
Apphia (Merrill) Ilsley, 152
Arethusa, 153
Daniel, 152-153
David, 266
Elathusa, 153
Elizabeth, 152
Floyd, 49, 152-153, 322
Iland, 152
Lois, 323
Lucretia, 153, 322
Lucy, 153, 322
Lydia, 152
Margaret, 266
Mary, 153
Mary (Carle), 49, 152, 322
Mary (Carll), 152
Mary (Chase), 152
Mary (Hawkins), 266
Nancy (Wormell), 153
Nathaniel, 49, 152-153
KIMBALL
Ebenezer, 188
Eleanor (Martin), 174
Elizabeth, 202
Emma, 157
Hannah (Clark), 10
Joshua, 157
Lydia, 11, 310
Martha, 303
Martha (--), 188
Martha (Elden), 157
Mary, 187
Mehitable, 95
Naomi, 157
Phebe, 10
Samuel, 10
Timothy, 174
KINCAID
Hannah, 188
Mary, 187-188
Polly, 187-188
Samuel, 187
Sarah (--), 187
KING
Benjamin, 153-154, 217
Bethiah (Philbrick), 154

217
Edwin, 106
Elijah, 154, 217
John, 154
Levina (Hopkins), 154
Lydia (Peaslee), 154
Mary (Glidden), 154
Moses, 154
Peter, 154
Rice, 154
Ruth (Bartlett), 153, 217
Ruth (Glidden), 154
Sarah, 106
Sarah (--), 106
Sarah (Laplain), 158
Sarah (Taylor), 153
William, 158
KINGMAN
Mary, 14
KINGSBURY
Elizabeth, 269
Sarah, 84
KINSMAN
Sarah, 155
KIRWAN
Deborah B, 24, 29
KNAPP
Joseph, 21
Lydia (Bartlett), 21
KNIGHT
--, 297, 321
Abigail, 48, 195, 259, 321
Ammi-Ruhamah, 113
Anna Maria, 33
Aseneth, 321
Betsey, 155
Daniel, 67, 80, 155
Daniel Jr, 155
Dorcas (--), 297
Dorcas (Lunt), 297
Edward, 321
Elizabeth (Barber), 155
Hannah, 27, 321
Jeremiah, 321
Job, 80
Lucy (Webster), 155
Lydia, 155, 204
Marrian (Jellison), 80
Martha, 67
Martha (Burnham), 155
Martha (Patishall), 67
Martha (Pattishall), 155
Mary, 156, 204, 297, 321
Mary (Butler), 321
Mary (Dole), 80
Mary (Haskell), 195
Mary (Winslow), 155
Nabby, 321

EVERY NAME INDEX

KNIGHT (continued)
Nathaniel, 155
Nicholas T, 155
Olive, 321
Patty, 155
Polly (Dole), 80
Rachel (Auld), 155
Reuben, 321
Sally, 156
Sally (Auld), 155
Sarah, 156, 321
sarah (Auld), 155
Susan (Frost), 321
William, 155, 195, 297

KNOWLES
Amos, 147
Elizabeth, 147
Elizabeth (Libby), 147
Hannah, 232
Margaret, 255
Mercy, 130
Rebecca, 96

KNOWLTON
Betsey, 191
Dorcas (Shapleigh), 318
John, 318

KNOX/ NOCK
Aaron, 3
Ebenezer, 51
Elizabeth (Ricker), 51
Judith, 51
Rebecca, 142
Sarah, 53

KRETSCHMAR
Ida Smith, 69

KYLE
Mary (Nash), 195
Polly (Nash), 195
Timothy, 195
William, 195
Zilpha (Merrill), 195

LABAN [SEE SABINE],

LACHANCE
Dorothy K, 48

LADD
Betsey (Dennett), 122
Daniel, 122
Dorcas (Lowell), 163
Eliza Dennett, 122
Thomas, 163

LAMBERT
--, 160
Elizabeth, 159
Rhoda (Gulliver), 109
Robert, 160

LAMSON
Jane (Adams), 242

LANCASTER
Mary, 285

LANDERS
Olive, 316

LANE
Abigail, 157
Abigail Small, 33
Alcestis, 157
Alcestis (Lane), 157
Alice (Haines), 33, 157
Amme (Lane), 76
Ann, 157
Betsey, 11, 157-158
Betsey (Woodsum), 157
Charlotte, 203
Daniel, 157, 203
Deborah (Haraden), 76
Elizabeth, 157-158
Elizabeth (Hancock), 32, 156
Elizabeth (Woodsum), 157
Emma (Kimball), 157
Hannah, 157
Hannah (Bean), 156-157
Hannah (Boynton) Hazeltine, 156
Hannah (Merrill), 158
Isaac, 157-158
Jabez, 157
Jerusha (Stevens), 264
Joanna, 156
John, 32, 156-157
John Jr, 157
Joseph, 76
Josiah, 264
Keziah (Hanscom), 157
Living, 157
Love (Dunnel), 157
Mary, 157-158
Mary (Nowell), 156
Mary (Woodman), 203
Molly (Woodman), 203
Nancy, 157
Nathan, 158
Polly, 158
Samuel, 157
Sarah, 32, 156, 203-204
Sarah (Woodman), 157
Stephen Woodman, 157
William, 33, 157

LANG
Sarah (--), 273

LANPHER
Anson, 163
Mary (Lowell), 163
Polly (Lowell), 163

LAPHAM
Hannah, 159

LAPLAIN
Armand, 158
Belinda (Jones), 159
Drucilla (Standley), 159
Drucilla (Standley) Laplain 159
Elizabeth, 159
Hannah, 158-159
Hannah (Edwards), 158
James, 158
James Jr, 159
Jane (--), 158
Joseph, 158-159
Ormon, 158
Robert, 159
Salome, 158-159
Sarah, 158
William, 158-159

LARRABEE
Elizabeth, 263
Mary, 179

LAUGHTON
Fidelia, 242
Jane (Adams) Lamson, 242
John, 242
Lydia (--), 242
Rebecca, 242
Roxanna, 304

LAWRENCE
John L, 94
Lydia (Emery) Follett, 94
William, 7

LE BALLESTER
Sarah, 174

LEACH
James, 16
Mary, 16, 290

LEAVIT/ LEAVITT
Abigail, 70
Abigail (Bradbury), 70
Abigail (Dennett), 70
Bethiah (Bragdon), 70
Daniel, 70
Hannah, 26
Joseph, 70
Sarah, 238

LEEMAN/ LEMAN
Amy (--), 160
Amy (Greenleaf), 160
Betsey, 160
Charlotte, 160
Clarissa, 160
Elizabeth (--), 159
Irena, 160
Jacob, 159-160
Jacob Smith, 159
John, 159
Kesiah, 160

LEEMAN/ LEMAN
(continued)
Keziah (Chapman), 159
Levi, 160
Love (Daggett), 160
Mary (--), 160
Sally, 160
Samuel C, 160
Sarah, 184
Sophie, 160

LEGRO
Jane (Brock), 38
John, 38
Mary, 1
Sarah (Randall), 38
Thomas, 38

LEIGH/ LEE
Benjamin Chadbourne, 162
Martha, 162
Martha (Chadbourne) 160-161
Mary, 161
Nancy (Baker), 161
Nathan, 188
Patty, 162
Polly, 161
Purchase, 188
Rebecca (Puffer), 188
Ruhama (Moody), 188
Thomas, 161

LEIGHTON
Abigail (Frost), 206
Dorcas, 215
Elizabeth (Frost), 143
Jane, 217, 226
John, 143, 206
Jonathan, 226
Mary (Boynton), 226
Samuel, 143, 206-207
Samuel Jr, 207
Sarah (Jones), 143
Sarah (Parsons), 206

LELAND
Ezra, 127
Rhoda, 127
Sally (Hamor), 127
Sarah, 127
Sarah (Hamor), 127

LEONARD
Abraham H, 266
Nancy (Stevens), 266

LESHUR
Joanna, 143

LEWIS
Abigail, 143
Abigail Frost (Parsons) 206
Agnes, 225

Daniel, 206
Elizabeth, 57
Morgan, 206
Sarah, 229
Sarah (Tripe), 206
Temperance, 51

LIBBY/ LIBBEY
Abigail, 81
Andrew, 182
Anna (Farnham), 84
Azariah, 248
Charles, 38, 84
Drusilla (Graffam), 24
Eleanor (Johnson), 232
Elizabeth, 38, 147
Elizabeth (Paul), 248
Esther (Foster), 182
Henry, 183
James, 248
John, 24, 55, 84
Joseph, 182
Margaret (Meserve), 183
Margaret (Miller), 184
Mary, 311
Nancy, 24
Nancy (Farnham), 84
Nathaniel, 232
Sarah (Meserve), 182
Sarah (Milliken), 81
Sarah (Pray), 38, 84
Sarah (Sands), 248
Stephen, 184
Zebulon, 81

LIDSTONE
Elizabeth, 29

LINCOLN
Benjamin, 268
Elizabeth Otis (Stillman) 268
James Otis, 268
Julia (Emerson), 277
Laban, 277
Mary (Otis), 268
Sarah, 68, 96

LINDSEY
John, 237
Susannah, 237
Susannah (Robinson), 237

LINNELL
Asenath, 283

LITHGOW
James Noble, 309
Louisa, 309

LITTLEFIELD
--, 296
Abigail, 298
Abigail (Mildram), 186
Amos, 295

Daniel, 176, 186
Deborah, 288
Deborah (Perkins), 288 296
Dolly (Farnham), 86
Ebenezer, 296
Ebenezer Jr, 295
Ebenezer Sr, 296
Elizabeth, 284
Elizabeth (Maxwell), 176
Frost, 86
Hannah (Sayward), 298
Henry, 185
Jereiam, 295
Jonathan, 298
Joseph, 186
Mary (--), 176
Mary (Clark), 186
Mary Anne, 186
Nathaniel, 176
Phebe, 246
Polly (Clark), 186
Sally, 177
Samuel, 177
Sarah (Curtis), 177
Sarah (Hatch), 295
Sarah (Perkins), 176
Sarah (Weare), 295
Stephen, 288, 296
Susan (Mildram), 185
Tabitha, 175

LOCKE
Elizabeth, 242
Elizabeth (Kilpatrick), 152
Josiah, 152-153
Lucretia, 322
Mary (Stubbs), 152
Nathaniel, 152

LOMBARD
Abigail (Lumbert), 51
Butler, 51
Jedediah Jr, 232
Jedidiah, 232
Jemima (Clay), 51
Lydia, 195
Lydia (Grant), 195
Lydia (Rand), 232
Nathaniel, 51
Solomon, 195
Susan (Dorsett), 232

LONGFELLOW
Levi, 189
Ruth (Moody), 189

LOOK
Hannah, 80

LORD
Aaron, 2
Abigail, 2

LORD (continued)
- Abigail (Nye), 202
- Ammi Ruhamah, 70
- Andrew, 60-61
- Betsey, 196
- Elisha, 86
- Elizabeth, 196
- Elizabeth (Kimball), 202
- Eunice, 105, 129
- Experience (Brock), 38
- Grizzel (Grant), 53
- Hannah (Dennet), 70
- Hopey (--) Shackley, 61
- Humphrey, 105
- Ichabod, 2
- James, 37
- Jeremiah, 53
- John, 37-38, 117
- Judith, 107
- Judith (Meads), 108
- Keziah, 129
- Keziah (Brackett), 61
- Lois, 82, 85
- Lydia, 207
- Margaret, 53, 195
- Mary, 105
- Mary (Wise), 71
- Mehitable (Jones), 141
- Meribah, 90
- Nathan, 141
- Nathaniel, 37
- Noah, 61
- Olive, 90
- Olive (Hill), 105
- Olley, 90
- Peggy, 53
- Philip, 202
- Priscilla (Corson), 61
- Sarah (Nason) Hubbard, 71
- Sarah (Shackley), 86
- Thomas, 71
- Wentworth, 37

LOTHROP
- Sarah, 308

LOVEJOY
- Ruth, 4

LOVELAND
- James, 242
- Mary, 242
- Mary (--), 242
- Molly, 242

LOVELL
- Enoch, 123
- John, 122
- Priscilla, 122
- Prudence, 122-123
- Prudence (Whiting), 123
- Sarah, 122-123

LOW/ LOWE
- Azubah, 207
- Daniel, 315
- Elizabeth (Baker), 245
- Hannah, 222-223
- Jedediah, 222
- John, 245
- Mary, 106, 208, 245
- Mary (Stewart), 222
- Moses, 223
- Rachel (Penney) Wharff 299
- Robert, 299
- Sarah (Pitts), 223
- Temperance (Wardwell) 315

LOWDER
- Avis, 16

LOWELL
- Abner, 162-163
- Alice, 198
- Apphia, 239-240
- Benjamin, 163
- Betsey, 163
- Dorcas, 163
- Ellis, 198
- Emma, 163
- Esther, 163
- Jane, 163
- Lois (Colson), 163
- Louisa (Colson), 163
- Lucy, 164
- Lucy (Lowell), 164
- Lydia (Anice), 163
- Mary, 163
- Nathaniel, 163
- Phoebe, 163
- Polly, 163
- Polly (Ayer), 162-163
- Polly (Lowell), 163
- Rachel, 164
- Robert, 164
- Samuel, 162-163
- Sarah, 163
- Sarah (Webber), 162-163
- Stephen, 163-164

LUCE
- Betsey, 165
- Eliza (Clark), 164
- Freeman, 164
- George, 164
- Jedidah (Claghorn), 65
- Jeremiah, 164
- Joseph, 65
- Katherine, 46
- Lavina (Pease), 164
- Lydia, 164
- Maria, 165

- Mary (Chaffin), 164
- Mercy (Chaffin), 164
- Obadiah, 164
- Rebecca, 65-66
- Remember, 165
- Remember (Merry), 164
- Sally, 164
- Sarah, 164
- Sarah (Luce), 164
- Seth, 164
- Susannah (Hathorne), 164
- Thaddeus, 164
- Thankful, 165

LUDWIG
- Eve Catherine, 238

LUFKIN
- Aaron, 77
- Anna, 264
- Benjamin, 249
- Dorcas, 73
- Joseph, 73
- Lydia, 74
- Mehitable (Abbott), 249
- Pamelia (Segar), 249
- Permeley (Segar), 249
- Samuel, 249

LUFKINS
- David, 270
- Mary (Sturtevant), 270
- Polly (Sturtevant), 270

LUMBERT
- Abigail, 51

LUNT
- Bartholomew, 139
- Daniel, 139
- Dorcas, 297
- Eunice (Conant), 139
- Eunice (Covant), 139
- Hannah, 152
- Huldah (Jepson), 139
- Joseph, 299
- Lydia (Wharff), 299
- Priscilla (Crocker), 299

LYFORD
- Mehitable, 27

LYMBURNER
- Jane, 54

LYNCH
- Carolyn Morgan (Bailey) 210, 267

LYNDS
- Ardell J Parkman, 22, 98 110-111

LYON
- Eliab, 112
- Levina, 112
- Maria, 112
- Meriah, 112

EVERY NAME INDEX

LYON (continued)
  Meriah (Smith), 112
MACDONALD
  Susanna, 292
MACEWEN
  Andrew B W, iii
MACEY
  Capt --, 308
MACFIELD [SEE MAYFIELD],
MACKESEY
  Vincent A, 19
MACKINTYRE [SEE MCINTYRE],
MACNAIR
  June Tracy, 231
MACOMBER
  Mercy (Wardwell), 289
  Nancy, 283
  Uriel H, 289
MACONTIOR [SEE MCINTYRE],
MADDOCK/ MADDOCKS/ MADDOX
  Abigail (Day), 170
  Betsey (Bunker), 170
  Caleb, 170
  Catherine (Hilton), 170
  Christiana (Pendleton)
    Thomas Dunham, 211
  Dorcas (--), 170
  Elizabeth, 170
  Elizabeth (Smith), 170
  Ichabod Austin, 170
  John, 170
  Joshua, 170
  Mary (--), 170
  Miriam (Whittier), 302
  Oliver, 170
  Rebecca, 171
  Rebecca (Clements), 170
  Richard, 302
  Samuel, 170
  Sarah (Glye), 170
  Susanna, 171
  Susannah (Austin), 170
  William, 170, 211
MAGNE/ MAGUE
  Jane, 196, 248, 258
MAIDMAN
  Martha, 65
MAINS/ MANES
  Abigail (Nason), 196
  Benjamin, 196
  Charlotte, 271
  John, 271
  Olive (Day), 271
  Patty, 196

MALCOLM/ MALCOM
  Finlay, 315
  Joseph, 280
  Mary, 281
  Tryphena (Wardwell), 315
  William, 280
MANCHESTER
  Abigail (Thompson), 279
  Hannah, 262
  Sarah, 262
  William, 279
MANN
  Daniel, 113
  Elizabeth (Hamblin), 113
  Gershom, 76
  Hannah (Phinney), 113
  Lucy Jane (Dennison)
    75-76
  Lucy Lane (Dennison)
    75-76
MANNING
  Mary, 116, 118
  Mary (Dyer), 116
  Patrick, 116
MANSFIELD
  Anna (Atwood), 23
  John, 23
  Martha, 23
MANSON
  Robert Parker, 96
  Sarah Webb (Gahan), 96
MARCHANT
  Deborah (Vinson), 210
  John, 209
  Mary, 209
  Miriam (Cleveland), 209
MARR
  Elizabeth, 107-108
MARRINER
  Eunice, 267
  Hannah (Presson), 50
  John, 128
  Ruth (Higgins), 128
  Sarah (Roberts), 128
MARROW/ MERROW
  Abigail (Fisher), 172
  Catherine, 172
  Celia, 172
  Chloe (Titus), 172
  Daniel, 149, 171
  Eben, 172
  Elizabeth, 171
  Elizabeth (Harding), 149
    171
  Hannah, 171
  Hannah (Chandler), 171
  Katy, 172
  Margaret (Haley), 121

  Mary, 133
  Polly, 133
  Reuben, 172
  Rhoda, 149, 172
  Sally, 121
  Sally (Stevens), 172
  Samuel Harding, 172
  Sarah, 121, 172
  Timothy, 172
  William, 121
MARSH
  Angeline M (Keen), 150
MARSHALL
  -- (--), 117
  Emily (Chadwick), 64
  Joanna, 220
  Samuel, 117
  Thomas, 154
MARSON
  Abner, 291
  Margaret, 291
  Peggy, 291
MARSTON
  Hannah, 118
  Mehitabel, 182
MARTIN
  Abigail, 101
  Abigail (--), 173
  Ann, 174
  Betsey, 64, 175
  Charles, 173
  Charles Stuart, 173
  Eleanor, 174
  Elizabeth, 64, 173-175
    209
  Hannah, 174
  Hannah (Cudworth), 173
  John, 172-173
  John Jr, 172
  Lettice (Wilson), 172
  Lettice Wilson, 173
  Lucy, 173, 175
  Lucy (Martin), 173
  Lucy (Osier), 173
  Margaret, 173
  Margaret (--), 172
  Mary, 173-174
  Mary (Foot), 174
  Mary (Gordon), 173-174
  Mary (Gourdon), 173
  Mary (Stuard), 172-173
  Richard, 174
  Samuel, 174
  Sarah, 64, 173-174
  Sarah (Ballester), 174
  Sarah (Goodwin), 174
  Sarah (Le Ballester), 174
  Susannah, 231

MARTIN (continued)
  Thomas, 173
  William, 172-173, 209
MASON
  Abigail Lord (Abbott), 3
  Albert J, 3
  Anna, 194
  Anna (Cleavers), 194
  Ebenezer, 194
  Elizabeth (Bunker), 39-40
  Isaac, 40
  Keziah, 105
  Polly, 106
MATHER
  Elizabeth (Merriam), 181
  William, 181
MATTHEWS/ MATHEWS/ MATHES
  --, 129
  Betsey (Groves), 277
  Lucy, 177
  Mary (Higgins), 128
  Sally, 277
  Sarah, 278
  William, 277
MATTHEWS/MATHEWS/ MATHES
  Mary (Higgins), 129
  Sarah, 128
MAXIM
  Lydia, 69
MAXWELL
  Aaron, 175
  Abigail (Morrison), 175
  Alexander, 175
  Daniel, 175
  David, 175
  Elizabeth, 176
  Gershom, 175
  Lucy, 176
  Mary (Staples), 175
  Moses, 175
  Olive, 176
  Persis, 176
  Philadelphia, 175
  Philadelphia (Rankin), 175
  Sarah, 176
MAYFIELD/ MACFIELD
  Elizabeth, 232
MAYHEW
  Olive, 46
MAYO
  Anna, 42
  Constant, 311
  Elizabeth, 262
  Hannah, 256
  Isaac Pepper, 312
  Jonathan, 311
  Joshua, 312
  Joy, 262, 312
  Leonard, 262, 312
  Lydia (Pepper), 312
  Rosanna (Young), 312
  Roxanna (Laughton), 304
  Stephen, 304
  Thankful (Twining), 311
MCALLISTER/ MCCOLLISTER, ETC
  Abiel, 167
  Alfred, 167
  Ann (Miller), 165
  Archable, 165
  Archibald, 165-166
  Archibald Jr, 165-166
  Betsey (Stevens), 166
  Cushman, 167
  Deliverance (Rich), 240
  Enoch, 167
  Guy, 167
  Harriet N, 168
  Isaac Case, 167
  James, 240
  Jane (Trask), 167
  Job Cushman, 167
  Lemuel, 240
  Lucinda Atkinson (Nash) 167
  Lydia, 167
  Mabel, 168
  Margaret, 167
  Margaret (Cunningham) 167
  Martha (Poland), 167
  Mary, 166
  Mary Anne (Boise) 165-166
  Mehitable (Richardson) 240
  Peggy, 166
  Peggy (Cunningham) 165-166
  Polly, 167
  Richard, v, 165-166
  Richard Jr, 167
  Rosanna (Atkinson), 167
  Rosannah, 166-167
  Ruth (Cunningham), 166
  Sally, 167
  Sarah (Bachelder), 168
  Sarah (Jewell), 166
  Sarah (Thomas), 165-167
  Sarah F (Peaslee), 167
  Thomas, 168
  Waity P (Foster), 167
  William, 166
MCCAUSLAND
  Henry, 291
MCCLAIN
  Jane (Meserve), 212
  Leander, 212
MCCLUER/ MCCLURE
  Alexander, 168-169
  Alexander Wilson, 169
  Charles, 168-169
  Eliza, 168
  Lucretia, 168-169
  Margaret R (McKown) 169
  Mary (Wilson), 168-169
  Mary Ann, 169
  Mary Brewster (Gould) 169
  Nancy, 168-169
  Nancy (Hunter), 133, 168
  Ruth, 168
  Thomas, 133, 168-169
  Thomas Jr, 169
MCCOBB
  Frances, 155-156
  Mary, 155
MCCOLLISTER [SEE MCCALLISTER],
MCDONALD
  Susan, 113
MCFADDEN
  Jane, 68
MCFARLIN
  Mary, 278
MCGILL
  Martha (Phinney) Barns 218
  William, 218
MCINTYRE/ MCINTIRE/ MACKINTYRE, ETC
  Alexander, 82, 84
  David, 300
  Dorcas (Wharff), 300
  Elizabeth, 128
  John, 319
  Margaret (Young), 319
  Sarah, 83
MCINTYRE/ MCINTIRE/ MACKINTYRE, ETC
  Sarah, 240
MCKAY
  T A, 43, 56
MCKECHNIE
  Eleanor, 200
MCKENNEY/ MCKINNEY
  Anna, 226
  Henry P, 25
  James, 198
  John, 198

MCKENNEY/ MCKINNEY
(continued)
Margaret (Wright), 198
Martha (Noble), 198
Mary (Blake), 25
Nancy, 226
MCKNIGHT
Annie, 188
MCKOWN
Margaret R, 169
MCKUSICK
Ephraim, 151
Hannah, 107
Joanna (Kilgore) Searle 151
Lydia B, 107
Mary (Keen), 107
Polly (Keen), 107
William, 107
MCLELLAN
Elizabeth, 57, 121
MCLUCAS
Benjamin, 247
Hannah, 247
John, 247
Joshua, 247
Lydia (Webber), 247
Mary, 247
Mary (Cole), 247
Sarah, 247
MCMURPHY
Margaret (Erskine), 133
MCNEILL
Margaret, 143
MCPATRICK/ MCPATRIDGE
Martha, 254
MCPHETTRAGE
John, 207
Sarah (Sewall), 207
MEADER
Hannah (Curtis), 265
Sarah, 140
MEADS
Judith, 108
Judith (Lord), 107
MEANS
Alice, 254
Alice (Finney), 254
Thomas, 254
MEEK
Priscilla, 178
MELCHER
--, 177
Aaron, 179
Abner, 177-178
Andrew, 177
Anne (Morse), 177

Anne (Moss), 177
Anstress, 178
Betsey (Dodge), 180
Edward, 176, 179
Elizabeth, 177-178, 180
Elizabeth (Bailey), 176 179
Elizabeth (Dunning) 179-180
Elizabeth (Melcher), 177
Gladden, 179
Isabella (Hinckley), 179
Jane (Owen), 179
Janney (Owen), 179
John, 180
Joseph, 176, 178
Josiah, 177
Levinia, 178
Lois, 180
Lois (Dunning), 180
Lucy (Matthews) Spear 177
Lury Ann (Gillet), 179
Margaret (Dunning), 177
Margaret (Miller), 177
Margaret (Patten) Swett 178
Mary, 176-177, 179
Mary (Cobb), 176, 178
Myriam, 177
Nancy (Anderson), 177
Nancy (Morse), 177
Nancy (Moss), 177
Nancy (Soule), 179
Nathaniel, 177
Noah, 177-180
Peggey (Dunning), 177
Phebe (Bucknam), 180
Priscilla, 178
Priscilla (Meek), 178
Rachel, 180
Rebecca, 180
Rebecka, 178
Rebeckah (Purinton), 177
Reliance, 179
Sally (Littlefield), 177
Samuel, 177, 179-180
Samuel Jr, 180
Sarah (Morse), 177-178
Sarah (Moss), 177-178
Susan Melissa (Wells), 179
Susanna (Purinton) 177-178
Thankful, 179
Zoah, 179
MENDUM
Patience, 92

MERCER
Arlotty (Bragdon), 35
William, 35
MERCHANT
Data (--), 25, 283
Edward, 25, 192, 283
Joseph, 25
Lucy Ann (--), 192
Sarah (Blake), 25
Temperance, 283
MERRIAM
Abigail (Smith), 181
Bethiah (--) Evans 180-181
Elizabeth, 181
Elizabeth (Thatcher), 180
John, 181
Matthew, 180-181
Matthew Thatcher 181-182
Mehitable (Hayes), 181
Nathaniel, 181
Patience (Neal), 181
Persis, 181-182
Sarah, 181
MERRILL
Abel, 81
Abiel, 75
Apphia, 152
Asa, 91
Betsey (Candage) Day, 54
Betty, 49
Betty (Merrill), 49
Caleb, 54
Cutting, 152
Edmond, 152
Fanny (Wood), 91
Hannah, 158
Hannah (Lunt), 152
Huldah (Dorman) Fletcher 81
Humphrey, 49, 152
Isaac, 54
Jacob Jr, 184
Jane, 9
Jane (Meserve), 184
Jane (Noyes), 152
Jeremiah J, 194
Joanna, 194
John, 194
Louisa (Clough), 54
Lydia (Kilpatrick), 152
Martha, 221
May (Diego), 158
Mehitable (Dennison), 75
Molly (Royal), 194
Moses, 49
Nancy (Nash), 194

EVERY NAME INDEX

MERRILL (continued)
Ruth, 50
Sarah, 7, 248
Sarah (Carle), 49
Zilpha, 195
MERROW [SEE MARROW]
MERRY
David, 167
Jane (Trask) McAllister 167
Remember, 164
MERRYMAN
Bethia Sprague, 256
Delight (Bailey), 256
Hugh, 256
John, 256
Mary (Melcher), 177
Mary (Skolfield), 256
Molly (Skolfield), 256
Sarah (Bailey), 177
Thomas, 177
MESERVE
Abigail, 183
Abigail (Bickford), 23, 184
Anna (Hunnewell), 182
Betty (Fogg), 183
Betty Fogg, 184
Clement, 182
Daniel, 183-184
Daniel Sr, 182
David, 23, 184
Elethere (Barker), 184
Elisha, 182, 184
Elizabeth, 183
Elizabeth (Fogg), 183
Elizabeth (Jones), 182
Elizabeth Fogg, 184
Eunice, 184
Gideon, 183-184
Hannah (Fogg), 182
Illathera (Barker), 184
Isabella (Jordan), 182
Jane, 184, 212
Margaret, 22, 183
Mary J (Sproul), 184
Mehetable (Bragdon), 182
Mehitable (Bragdon), 183
Nathaniel, 182
Reuben, 184
Sarah, 182
Sarah (Jordan), 183
Sarah (Leeman), 184
Solomon, 182, 184
Susanna (Small), 182
William, 184
METCALF
Sarah, 234
Sarah (Day), 68

William, 68
MILBERRY/ MILBURY
Elizabeth (Kingsbury), 269
Hannah, 269
Olive, 269
Samuel, 269
Sarah, 297
MILDRAM/ MELDROM
Abigail, 186
Abigail (Dennett), 184
Barbara, 186
Charles Augustus, 186
Clement, 185-186
Dorothy, 185
Esther, 185
John, 185
Mary (Annis), 184
Mary Anne (Littlefield) 186
Molly (Annis), 184
Nancy, 185
Olive (Hobbs), 185
Pamela F, 185
Permelia, 185
Samuel, 184-185
Samuel Jr, 184-185
Susan, 185
Thomas, 184-185
MILLBANKS/ MILLBANK
Katherine, 186
Lisa, 187
Lucy (Dyer), 186
Philip, 186
Phillip, 186
Thankful, 187
MILLER
--, 178
Ann, 165
Barbara (Hoffs), 64
Elizabeth (Melcher), 178
George, 64
Jane, 121
John Jr, 178
Margaret, 64, 177, 184
Mary, 239
MILLETT/ MILLET
Adaline Augusta, 221
Bethiah, 321
Hannah, 119
Martha (Merrill), 221
Nathaniel, 221
MILLIKEN
Benjamin, 16
Lucy (Banks), 16
Sarah, 81
MILTON
Nancy, 68

MINOT
Capt --, 240
John, 30
John Jr, 255
Susanna (Skolfield), 255
Thomazine Elizabeth Fielder, 30
Thomazine Elizabeth Fielder (Bond), 30
MITCHELL
Abigail, 272
Betty, 74, 78
Dinah (--), 64
Isabella (Bragdon), 93
Joseph, 93
Mercy, 93
Nathan, 183
Polly (Daggett), 64
Rachel, 73
Susanna, 131
Thomas, 64
MOLLOY
Martha (Clark), 228, 302
MONTCALM
--, 250
MONTGOMERY
Betsey (Knight), 155
Elizabeth (Emerson), 155
John, 155
Lydia (Winslow), 155
Nathaniel, 155
MOODY
Abigail, 189
Adra Ann, 190
Annie (McKnight), 188
Atree, 190
Betsey (Nash) Dudley, 190
Clement, 188-189
Daniel, 188
Eleanor (Cressey), 190
Elizabeth (Scribner), 188
Elizabeth M, 190
Elling (Crecy), 190
Elling (Cressey), 190
Gilman, 190
Hannah (Kincaid), 188
Jedediah, 188
Jedidiah, 187, 189
Jeremiah, 187-189
John, 187, 190
Levi, 187-188
Lois, 189
Mary, 189
Mary (Hunt), 189
Mary (Kimball), 187
Mary (Kincaid), 187
Mary (Moody), 189
Mary Ann, 190

EVERY NAME INDEX

MOODY (continued)
Nathaniel, 187
Polly (Hunt), 189
Polly (Kincaid), 187-188
Richard, 189
Ruhama, 188
Ruth, 187-189
Ruth (Clough), 187, 189
Sarah, 187, 189
Sarah (Bean) Smith, 187
Sarah (Smith), 187-189
Scribner, 187-188
William, 189
MOORE/ MORE
Dolley, 286, 290
Dorothy, 171, 207
Margaret, 134
Mary, 275
Robert McGregor, 314
Sally (Spurling), 262
Sarah (Spurling), 262
Sarah M (Stubbs) Russell 314
Welch, 262
MOREY
Cornelius, 200
Sarah, 200
Sarah (Johnson), 200
MORGAN
Dorothea Morris, 79
Lydia, 221
Martha, 221
Rosilla C (Tucker), 221
MORRILL
Elizabeth (Clough), 227
Hannah, 283
John Jr, 227
Mehitable, 228
Nancy (Macomber), 283
Peaslee Jr, 283
Sarah, 227-228
Sarah (Allen), 284-285
MORRIS
Gordon Alan, 244
MORRISON
Abigail, 175
John, 139
Lydia (Winslow), 139
MORSE/ MOSS
-- (Melcher), 177
Abigail, 256
Anna, 145
Anne, 177
Benjamin, 177
Benjamin R, 178
Eliphalet, 256
Elizabeth, 79
Experience (Paine), 79

Hannah (Mayo), 256
John, 181
Jonathan, 79
Levinia (Melcher), 178
Lydia, 278
Nancy, 177
Sarah, 50, 177-178, 203
MORTON
Deborah, 237
MOSHER/ MOSIER
Ann (Springer), 62, 190
Anna, 191
Betty (Ballard), 191
Clancey, 192
Elisha, 62, 190-191, 322
Elisha Jr, 190-191
Elizabeth, 191
Elizabeth M, 192
Freelove (Weeks), 191
Hannah, 191
Ira, 191
James Harvey, 192
Joseph, 191
Judith (Crowell), 62, 190 322
Judith (Foss), 192
Lemuel Crowell, 192
Louisa (Corson), 192
Lucy Ann (--) Merchant 192
Lydia, 191
Martha C (Stevens), 191
Phebe, 191, 322
Sarah T (Wellman), 192
Sylvanus, 191
William, 191
MOSS
Hannah (--), 177
Hannah (Hunt), 178
Joseph, 177-178
MOULTON
Betsey (Lane), 158
Daniel, 274-275
Eleanor (Raynes), 275
Elizabeth (Lane), 158
Hannah, 216, 285
Jane (--), 322
Johnson, 276
Lucy (Bradbury), 159
Mary, 104
Oliver, 159, 322
Salome (--), 322
Salome (Laplain), 159
Sarah (Talpey), 275
Sararh (Talpey), 274
Thomas, 158
William, 159, 322

MOWATT
Capt --, 311
MOXEY
Hannah, 73
Henry, 73
Mercy (--), 73
MUCHEMORE
Sarah (--), 293-294
MURCH
Abigail (Arey), 193
Affia, 193
Anna (Dean), 42
Benjamin, 193
Betsey, 293
Daniel, 293
Edmund, 193
Elizabeth, 42, 55
Ephraim, 193
Hannah (Thompson), 42
James, 192
Jane (Bailey), 192
Jenny (Bailey), 192
Jerusha (Brown), 192
Joanna, 193
John, 42
Lydia (--) Smith, 193
Mary (Simpson), 293
Miriam (Watson), 293
Molly, 55
Molly (Pennell), 193
Polly (Pennell), 193
Rachel (Paine), 193
Rebecca (Cobb), 193
Sarah, 193
Simeon, 193
Stephen, 293
Susanna, 193
Walter, 192
William, 42
Zebulon, 193
MURDOCK
--, 168
-- (--), 169
George, 169
Nancy (McCluer), 168-169
MURPHY
Sally, 246
MURRAY/ MURREY
David, 57
Elizabeth (McLellan), 57
Hannah (Austin), 107-108
John, 107
Keziah (--) Corson, 61
Rebecca (Colburn), 57
Rebecca (Colburn) Murray 57
Robert, 57, 61

EVERY NAME INDEX 369

MUSSET/ MUSEET/ MUZEET
Elizabeth, 97
MYRICK
Betsey, 42
NASH
Ann (Bird), 194
Anna (Mason), 194
Betsey, 190
Betsey (Johnson), 194
Deborah (Curtis) Cutter 194
Jacob, 195
Joanna, 195
Joanna (Merrill), 194
Johannah, 195
John B, 195
Jonathan, 193-194
Lemuel, 194
Lucinda Atkinson, 167
Martha, 194
Mary, 195
Nancy, 194
Polly, 195
Rachel, 195
Rachel C (Banks), 195
Sally, 194
Sarah, 194
Susanna, 194
William, 194
NASON
Abigail, 4, 196
Abigail (Knight), 48, 195, 259
Abraham, 195
Amy, 129
Anna, 129
Betsey (Burnell), 196
Betsey (Lord), 196
Betsey (Waterhouse), 196
Caleb, 103
Dorcas, 119
Elizabeth (Burnell), 196
Elizabeth (Lord), 196
Elizabeth (Waterhouse) 196
Esther, 60
Jemima (Snow), 196, 258
John, 195
Joseph, 196
Keziah (Lord), 129
Lot, 196
Lydia (Lombard), 195
Margaret, 48, 196
Margaret (Lord), 195
Martha (Goodwin) Varney 103
Olive (Andrews), 103

Patty (Mains), 196
Philadelphia, 175
Rachel, 124
Robert, 103
Samuel, 196
Sarah, 71
Uriah, 48, 195, 259
Uriah Jr, 196, 258
William, 129, 196
NEAL
-- (--), 197
Andrew, 196-197
Betsy (Patterson) Boyington, 197
Dorcas, 9
Elizabeth (Annis), 197
Hannah, 44, 196
Hannah (Hamilton), 197
Isaac, 197
Jane (Hubbard), 196
John, 196
Johnson, 181, 197
Olive, 31, 197
Patience, 181
Patience (Johnson), 196
Sarah, 197
Sarah (Furbush), 181
Silas, 197
NEALEY/ NEALLY
Andrew, 17
Esther (Banks) Reidhead Castin, 17
J, 136
Sarah, 321
NELSON
James, 9
Jane (Hall) Allen, 9
Lydia, 20
Martha, 25
NEVERS
Phineas, 98
NEWBEGIN
Aseneth (Knight), 321
John, 321
NEWBIT
John, 67
Rebecca (Peabody) Daggett 67
NEWBURY
Elizabeth, 288
NEWCOMB
Abigail (Young), 193
John, 193
Joshua, 193
Sarah, 13
Susanna (Murch), 193
NEWHALL
Gustavus, 29

Lydia (Blake), 29
NEWMAN
Charity (Young), 262
Dolly (Spurling), 262
Fanny (Spurling) Stanley 262
Hannah, 262
Jonathan, 262
Joseph, 262
Sally (Spurling) Moore 262
Sarah (Spurling) Moore 262
Thomas, 262
NEWTON
Mary, 11
NICHOLS/ NICKELS/ NICOLS
Deborah, 230
Elizabeth, 59
Jane, 133
Jenny, 133
Nancy, 253
Sarah (Gullifer), 110
William, 110
NICKERSON
Bethiah (--), 27
Dorcas, 12
Dorinda (Blake), 27
Ephraim, 27
Joann, 42
Martha (Ellis), 130
Roxana (Hopkins), 130
Sarah (Covell), 130
Thomas, 27
William, 130
NIGH [SEE NYE],
NILES
Jane (Gurney), 194
Martha (Nash), 194
Nathan, 194
Samuel, 194
NOBLE
Alice (Lowell), 198
Anthony, 198
Christopher, 198
Christopher Jr, 198
Delitha, 111
Elitha, 111
Elizabeth (Rowe), 199
Ellis (Lowell), 198
Felitha, 111
Joanna (Rowe), 198-199
John, 199
Lydia, 199
Lydia (Jackson), 198
Martha, 198
Martha (Rowe), 198

NOBLE (continued)
Moses, 199
NOCK [SEE KNOX],
NORCROSS
Abigail, 26
Celia (Marrow), 172
Elijah, 172
Katy (Marrow), 172
Mary (Wiswall), 172
Nancy (Hussey), 277
Philip 2d, 277
Sally, 277
Sally Hussey, 277
Samuel, 172
NORRIS/ NORRICE
Hannah (Whittier), 302
Simeon, 302
NORTH
Hannah, 308
NORTON
Ansel, 210
Deborah (Vinson)
 Marchant, 210
Eliza, 275
Hannah (Daggett), 66
Ichabod, 249
Lucy (Segar), 249
Mary, 208
Mary (--) Talpey, 277
Mary (Weare), 295
Mehitable, 45, 305
Mercy (Osborn), 66
Mercy (Osborn) Norton, 66
Olive (Young), 275
Sally, 209-210
Samuel, 295
Sarah, 45, 209-210
William, 66, 275
NOURSE
Eunice, 27
NOWELL
Dolly (Nye), 200
Ebenezer, 104
Hannah (Furbush), 200
Mary, 156
Patience (Hamilton), 104
Rachel (Grant), 104
William, 200
NOYES
Fanny, 217
Frances, 217
Jane, 152
Moses, 217
Sarah (Currier), 217
NUTTER
Charity (Cole), 58
Jacob, 58
Lemuel, 58

Nancy, 213
Sally (Dennett), 58
NYE/ NIGH
Abigail, 201-202
Alden, 201
Alice (Pollard), 202
Alvin, 202
Ansel, 202
Bartlett, 199
Bartlett Jr, 199
Betsy, 201
Carl F, 319
Carol F, 25-26, 28, 46
 65-67, 165, 200-201
 203, 283, 319, 324
Charles, 202
Cornelius, 201
Deborah (Ellis), 199
Dolly, 200
Dolly (Bachelder), 202
Eleanor (McKechnie), 200
Elisha, 200-202
Eliza (Freeman), 201
Elizabeth (--), 200
Elizabeth (Holmes)
 199-200
Ellis, 199
Eunice, 201-202
Franklin, 200
Heman, 200
Jane, 199
John, 202
Joseph, 199-201
Joshua, 199-200
Julia (Wing), 200
Lucy, 202
Lucy (Tobey), 202
Maria, 202
Maria (Bourne), 202
Martha, 200
Martha (Williams), 199
Mary (Buck), 201
Mary (Freeman), 201
Mary (Hincks), 199-200
Mary (Tobey), 199
Mehitable, 202
Mehitable (Robinson), 202
Melinda (Phillips), 201
Nancy (Young), 202
Patty, 200
Patty (Williams), 199
Peleg, 201
Robinson, 203
Ruth (Hincks), 200
Sabrah (Obryne), 201
Sabray (O'Brian), 201
Salley (Burrell), 199
Sally, 200-201

Sarah, 200
Sarah (Burrell), 199
Sarah (Morey), 200
Stephen, 200, 202-203
Sturgis, 200
Sukey, 202
Susanna, 202
Sylvanus, 201
Temperance, 201
Thankful (--), 200
Thomas, 199
William, 203
O'BRIAN/ OBRYNE
Sabrah, 201
Sabray, 201
OBEAR
Joanna, 54
ODOM
John, 99
Sally, 99
Sarah (Haney), 99
OLIVER
Abigail, 109
ORR
John Jr, 254
Mary, 254-255
OSBORN
Elizabeth (Estes), 43
Isaac, 43
Mercy, 66
Samuel, 43
Sarah (Clark), 43
OSGOOD
Joanna (Obear), 54
John, 54
Lydia, 4
Sally (Clough) Clay, 54
OSIER
Lucy, 173
OTIS
Elwell, 61
Mary, 268
Sally (Evans), 61
Sarah (Evans), 61
Sarah Ann, 110
OTTEN
Marjorie Wardwell, 17
 255-256, 287, 289-290
 295, 297-298
OWEN
Jane, 179, 280
Janney, 179
Jenny, 280
Mary, 228
Mary (--), 180
Polly, 228
William, 180

PAGE
Betsey, 109
Betsy (Corson), 61
Caroline, 22
David, 27
Deborah (Bennett), 22
Elisha Sr, 191
Hannah, 27
Jesse, 191
John Wyman, 61
Lydia (Mosher), 191
Mary (Brown) Clifford, 27
Orrison, 22
Permela (Blake), 27
Phebe C, 140
Rachel (Emerson), 27
Samuel, 140
Sarah (Dudley), 27
Simon, 27
Susanna, 99
Theodate, 61
William, 27
Zeruiah (--), 140

PAINE
Abigail, 127
David, 45
Experience, 79
Hannah, 126
James, 46
Joanna (Swett), 99
John, 46
Lovey (Butler), 46
Melinda (Butler), 46
Nancy (Butler), 45
Rachel, 193

PALMER
Alona (Skinner), 253
Andrew, 203
Betsey, 147
Charlotte (Lane), 203
Edward, 187
Elizabeth (Bradbury), 32
 203
Hannah, 204
Hannah (--), 187
James, 32, 203
Jane, 203
Jane (Hopkinson), 32, 203
Jemima (Hardy), 203
John, 203
Joses, 203
Lillis, 270
Lydia (Knight), 204
Martha, 204
Mary, 204
Mary (Atkinson), 203
Mehitable (Blazo), 253
Paul, 204
Polly (Atkinson), 203
Richard, 32, 203-204, 253
Ruth (Moody), 187-188
Sally, 314
Samuel, 187-188
Sarah, 189
Sarah (Hearl), 203
Sarah (Moody), 187
Steven, 203
Susan (Woodman), 204
William, 253

PARDI
Elvera Stevens, 210, 267

PARIS
Susanna, 111

PARKER
Betsy (Rand), 232
Delia (Ginn), 99
Dudley, 99
Ebenezer, 232
Edmund Jr, 241
Eleazer Higgins, 232
Elizabeth (Rand), 232
Esther (Higgins), 232
Free, 99
Gideon, 300
Peley (Ginn), 99
Persis (Robbins), 241
Polly (Ginn), 99
Rachel, 211
Rebecca, 63

PARKHURST
Peter G, 162

PARLOUR
Abigail, 277

PARSON/ PARSONS/ PARSINS
--, 205
-- (--), 207
Abigail Frost, 206
Abigail Frost (Blunt), 39
 205
Alonzo, 205
Charlotte Sanders (Sargent)
 206
Col --, 210
Dorothy, 94
Frances (Usher), 206
James, 205
Jemima (Phillips), 205
Jerusha, 205, 294
Jerusha (Sayward), 204
 294
John, 39, 205-206
Joseph, 204, 206-207
 294-295
Joseph III, 204
Joseph Jr, 205
Jotham, 205
Love (Brock), 39, 206
Lydia (Averill), 205
Lydia (Lord), 207
Mariah (Tripp), 205
Martha (Harvey), 205
Mary, 205, 207
Mary (Brown) Wakefield
 Washburn, 204-205
Mary (Parsons), 207
Mary (Wakefield), 205
Mary Jackson (Holmes)
 207
Mary K (Greenleaf), 204
Mary M (--), 205
Miriam (Preble), 204
Patty (Greenleaf), 204
Polly (Harvey), 205
Rufus, 205
Ruth (Wakefield), 205
Samuel, 207
Sarah, 206
Susan, 258
Susanna, 205
Tertius, 204
Theodore, 205
Thomas, 204, 207
Timothy, 205
Usher, 207
William, 39, 206-207

PARTRIDGE
Joshua, 171
Martha (Kimball), 303

PATCH
Edith, 245

PATISHALL
Martha, 67

PATRICK [SEE KILPATRICK],

PATTEE
Anna, 111
Azubah (Low), 207
Benjamin, 208
Elizabeth, 208
Mary (Low), 208
Mary (Potter), 207
Mary N (--), 208
Nancy, 208
Rachel McCobb, 208
Sally, 207
Sarah, 110
Susannah, 207
William Sewall, 208

PATTEN
Abigail (Meserve) Fogg
 183
James, 183
Katherine, 213

EVERY NAME INDEX

PATTEN (continued)
Margaret, 178
PATTERSON
Elizabeth, 197
Elizabeth (Goodwin), 197
Mary, 25
Robert, 197
PATTISHALL
Martha, 155
PAUL
Bathsheba (Weare) 297-298
Elizabeth, 248
Mary (--), 298
Stephen, 298
PAYSON
Mary, 148
PEABODY
Anna, 209
Apphia, 209
Betsey, 209
Dorothy (Perkins), 208
Elizabeth (Martin), 173 209
Francis, 208
Josiah, 208
Lucy, 209
Lynday (Woodcock), 209
Mary, 208
Mary (Norton), 208
Mehitable, 208
Melinda (Woodcock), 209
Oliver, 117
Rebecca, 67
Ruth, 208
Ruth (Trask), 173, 208
Samuel, 173, 208-209
Sarah, 209
Stephen, 67, 209
William, 209
PEACOCK
Sarah (Tibbetts), 281
PEAKS
Mary (Thomes), 267
Sophia, 267
PEARCE [SEE PIERCE],
PEARSON
Gardner W, 109-110
Mark, 187
PEASE
Aaron, 209
Abigail (Dunham), 210
Albana, 18
Anna H (--), 18
Elizabeth (--), 283
Fortunatus, 283
Hannah (--), 210
James, 209-210

Jedidah, 283
Joseph, 17-18
Lavina, 164
Mary (Barker), 18
Mary (Marchant), 209
Meriam, 210
Miriam, 210
Nancy, 17
Nathan, 209-210
Polly (Clark), 17
Prince, 164
Sally, 17
Sally (Norton), 209-210
Sarah, 17
Sarah (Barker), 18
Sarah (Norton), 209-210
Sarah (Vincent), 209
PEASLEE/ PEASLEY
Anna (Jepson), 138
Enoch, 138
Joseph, 138
Lydia, 154
Lydia (Bartlett), 154
Martha (--), 138
Nathan, 154
Sarah F, 167
PECKER
Abigail, 54
Bartholomew, 54
Hannah (Russell), 54
Nabby, 54
PELTON
Christian, 291
PENDLETON
Abigail Gardner, 211
Bathsheba (Dodge), 213
Betsey, 211
Charlotte, 212
Christiana, 211
Cynthia (West), 210-211 213
Cynthia A, 211
Dorcas, 212
Dorcas (Dodge), 210, 212
Elizabeth, 211
Elizabeth (Brown), 212
Elizabeth (Stuart) Pendleton, 212
Eunice (Getchell), 213
Gideon, 213
James, 212
Jane (Meserve) McClain 212
Joshua, 213
Katherine (Patten), 213
Lois, 212
Lucinda, 211
Margaret, 213

Mark, 213
Martha (Sherwood), 214
Mary, 211, 213
Matilda (Gilkey), 213
Mercy Thomas, 212
Nabby, 211
Nancy (Nutter), 213
Nathaniel, 210-213
Peggy, 211
Prudence (Dodge), 214
Sally, 211-212
Sally (Ames), 213
Sally (Sweetland) Bradford 210, 212-213
Samuel, 213
Sarah (Tewksbury), 213
Stephen, 212-214
Thomas, 210, 212
Thomas Jr, 213
Wealthy, 211
PENNELL
Lydia (Sands), 193
Molly, 193
Polly, 193
Rachel, 49-50
Sarah (Duren), 49
Sarah (Durrell), 49
Thomas, 49, 193
PENNEY/ PENNY
Amy, 320
Rachel, 299
Sally, 300
Sarah, 300
PEPPER
Lydia, 312
PEPPERRELL
William, 276
PERCY
Catherine, 313-314
Elizabeth, 314
PERHAM
Jane, 68
PERKINS
Abigail (Wardwell), 298
Abigail (Wardwell) Wardwell, 290
Amos, 288
Amy (Penny), 320
Anna, 294
Betsy, 60
Charity (Hartford), 60
Daniel, 320
Daniel Jr, 81
Deborah, 288, 296
Dorothy, 208
Dosia, 259
Edward, 259
Eliab, 15

EVERY NAME INDEX 373

PERKINS (continued)
Eliza Jane, 309
Elizabeth, 60
Elizabeth (Littlefield), 284
Elizabeth (Pearce), 16
Gilbert, 60
Hannah, 290
Hannah (Snowman), 259
Isaac, 259
John, 16, 87-88
Joseph, 298
Joseph Jr, 298
Lucy, 320
Martha, 84
Mary, 16, 286-287
Mary (Dorman), 81
Mercy, 259
Olive, 289
Olive (Farnham), 87-88
Olive (Webber), 259
Phebe (Weare), 297-298
Ruth (Wardwell), 288
Samuel, 259
Sarah, 176
Sarah (Hamilton), 118
Sarah (Snowman) Wescott 259
Sparks, 259
Stephen, 118, 290
Tabatha (Stover), 259
Theodosia, 259
Tilley (Ingraham), 15
Tily (Ingraham), 15

PERRY
Abigail, 216
Jane, 134, 238
Oliver H, 207
Sarah, 220, 222

PETERS
Edward Dyer, 169
John, 169
Lucretia (McCluer) 168-169
Mary (Dyer), 169

PETERSON
Abraham, 214
Carnalas, 214
Charles, 214-215
Cornelius, 214
Hannah (--), 215
John, 215
Joseph, 214-215
Lucy, 215
Lucy (Thomas), 215
Lydia, 215
Lydia (Howell), 214
Patience (--) Johnson, 214
Patience (Baker), 214

Ruth, 215
Sarah, 214

PETTENGILL/ PETTINGILL
Anna, 14
Benjamin, 14
Edward, 33-34
Eliphalet, 33-34
Eliphalet Jr, 34
Jane (Bragdon), 33-34
Lydia (Bragdon), 33-34
Mary (Kingman), 14
Susannah (--) Chandler, 34

PETTY/ PETTEY/ PETTEE
Abial, 216
Abigail, 216
Abigail (Young), 215
Alexander, 215
Barnabas, 216
Ebenezer, 215-216
Elizabeth (Johnson), 216
Elizabeth D (Ashe), 216
Eunice, 216
Hannah, 216
Hannah (Farrington), 215
Jane (Stuard), 207
Jeremiah, 207
Joseph, 215
Lucinda (Hancock), 216
Mary Elizabeth (Joy), 216
Noah, 216
Oliver, 215-216
Rachel (Tracy), 215
Rachel P (Stevens), 216
Samuel, 207, 216
Sarah (Johnson), 215
Sarah (Sewall]
  McPhettrage, 207
Timothy, 215

PHELPS
Charlotte, 127

PHENIX
Richard, 58
Sophia (Cole), 58

PHILBRICK/ PHILBROOK/ PHILBROOKS
Abigail, 217
Alice, 228
Bethiah, 154, 217
Ebenezer, 154, 216-217 226
Ebenezer Jr, 217
Else, 228
Eunice, 258
Fanny (Noyes), 217
Frances (Noyes), 217
Hannah (Moulton), 216
Hiram, 217
Hubbard, 217, 226

John, 7
Jonathan, 217
Joshua, 128
Lucinda (Pendleton)
  Drinkwater, 211
Mara Ann, 217
Mary, 321
Mary (--), 258, 321
Mary (Potter), 217, 226
Mehitable (Bartlett), 154 216, 226
Michael, 258
Nabby, 217
Peter, 217
Polly (Potter), 217, 226
Rachel, 217
Salley, 217
Samuel, 217
Sarah (Nealey), 321
Susanna, 128
William 3rd, 211

PHILLIPS
Betsey, 24
Jemima, 205
Mary (Parsons), 205
Melinda, 201
Norton Woodbridge, 205

PHILPOT
Abigail, 223
Debbey (Randall), 234
Deborah (Randall), 234
Mercy (--), 234
Moses, 234
Richard, 234
Ruth, 223

PHINNEY/ FINNEY/ TINNEY
--, 218
Benjamin, 217-219
Bethiah (Bump), 217-218
Bethiah (Bumpas), 217
Betty, 263
Calvin Farrar, 222
Edmund, 263
Elizabeth, 292
Hannah, 113, 219
Joanna, 219, 222
Loren, 219
Martha, 218
Martha (--) White, 219
Martha (Crocker), 217
Mary (Wheeler), 219
Mary Gorham, 193
Polly (Wheeler), 219
Relief, 219
Sarah, 218
Sarah (Cotton), 219
Sarah (Perry), 222

PHINNEY/ FINNEY/ TINNEY (continued)
Sarah (Pride) Stevens, 263
Seth, 217
Seth Jr, 219
Sophronia (Pierce), 222
Zilpah, 218

PHIPPS/ PHIPS
Elizabeth, 220
George, 93, 220
Miriam (Fernald), 92-93, 219
Robert F, 220
Sally (Bickford), 220
Sarah, 220

PICKERNALE
Mary, 182

PIERCE/ PEARCE
--, 321
Elizabeth, 16
Sophronia, 222

PIKE
Adaline Augusta (Millett), 221
Allen R, 222
Almira, 221
Charles, 221
Clarissa, 221-222
Dolly, 221
Dudley, 220
Fidelia (Way), 221
Hannah, 221
Israel, 221
Jacob, 220-221
Joanna (Marshall), 220
John, 220
Luther Farrar, 221
Lydia (Morgan), 221
Martha, 221
Martha (Morgan), 221
Mary, 221
Mary (Tarbox), 220-221
Mary (Wood), 221
Robert, 221
Rosella (Cleveland), 221
Samuel, 221
Sarah (Perry), 220
Susan (Wood), 221
Susanna (Bickford), 221
Urania (Cummings), 221

PINKHAM
Abigail, 122
Sarah, 51

PITTS/ PITS
--, 222
Aaron, 223
Benjamin, 223
Edmund, 223

Hannah (Goodridge), 222
Hannah (Hamilton), 223
Hannah (Low), 222
John, 222
Judith (Wood), 222
Lydia (Scribner), 223
Molly, 222
Moses, 222
Ruth, 223
Ruth (Philpot), 223
Sally (Hamilton), 222
Samuel, 223
Sarah, 223
Sarah (Hamilton), 222
Sarah (Warren), 223
Susanna, 223
Thomas, 222

PLACE/ PLAICE
Elizabeth (--), 93
Eunice, 93
Hannah, 140
John, 93

PLUMMER/ PLUMER
Abby, 167
Abigail (Philbrick), 217
Nabby (Philbrick), 217
Ruth, 231
Sarah, 79
Solomon, 217

POAK/ POKE
Nancy, 55

POLAND
Martha, 167

POLLARD
Alice, 202

POPE
Lydia, 67, 302

PORTER
Mahala, 76
Olive, 123

POTE
--, 153
Anna, 153
Anna (Bucknam), 153
Dolly, 180
Dorothy, 180
Elathusa, 153
Elisha, 153, 322
Increase, 152-153, 322
Lucretia (Kilpatrick), 153, 322
Lucy (Kilpatrick), 153, 322
Mary Floyd, 153
William, 153, 322

POTTER
--, 225
Aaron, 226
Abigail (--) Welch, 226

Abigail (Cummings), 225
Abigail (Farnham), 224
Abigail (Hayward), 226
Abigail (Howard), 226
Anna (McKinney), 226
Betsey (Trask), 226
Catherine, 225
Daniel, 226
Edward, 225
Elizabeth, 224
Ezekiel, 226
Hannah, 226
Hannah (Reed), 225
James, 223-224, 227
Jane, 226
Jane (Leighton), 217, 226
John, 224-226
Martha, 225
Martha (Potter), 225
Martha (Spear), 224
Mary, 207, 217, 224-226
Mary (Goulding), 227
Mary (Spear), 224
Matthew, 224
Mehitable (Farr), 226
Nancy (McKinney), 226
Polly, 217, 226
Rachel (Bartlett), 226
Robert, 224
Samuel, 225
Sarah (Snipe), 225
Solomon, 217, 225
Solomon Jr, 226
Susan (Hodge), 226
William, 224

POWERS
Abigail (Howe), 249
Arnold, 11, 249
Betsey, 249
Betsey (Lane), 11
Eliphaz, 11
Elizabeth (Pattee), 208
Gideon, 20-21
Hannah (Andrews), 11
Huldah (Andrews), 11
Isaac, 151
John, 208
Jonathan, 11
Lucy (Bartlett), 11, 21
mary (Searle), 151
Polly, 151
Ruth (Hosmer), 20-21
Silas, 20
Submit (Bartlett), 20

PRATT
--, 291
Abigail (Moody), 189
Hannah (--), 14

EVERY NAME INDEX

PRATT (continued)
  Hannah (Hunt), 189
  Hannah (Warren), 291
  Henry, 14
  Jael (Bennett), 160
  Joanna (Dennison), 76
  Jones, 189
  Kesiah (Leeman), 160
  Paul, 160
  Seth J, 189
  Simeon, 76
  Sybil, 14
PRAY
  Alice (Yeaton), 310
  Amos, 130
  Capt --, 1
  Dorcas (Yeaton), 311
  Dorothy (Cromwell), 310
  Eliphalet, 310
  Experience (Smith), 37
  Jane, 37
  Joanna, 103, 309
  John, 37
  Joseph, 311
  Joseph 3rd, 311
  Judith (Hodsdon), 130
  Mary (Guptill), 310
  Mary (Libbey), 311
  Samuel, 310
  Sarah, 38, 84
PREBLE
  Abigail, 99
  Lois, 189
  Mehitable, 307
  Miriam, 204
  Samuel, 293
  Sarah, 205, 293, 295, 297
  Sarah (--) Muchemore, 293
PRESCOTT/ PRISCOTT
  Abel, 229
  Abigail, 228
  Abigail B (Whittier), 229
  Agnes M (Cass), 229
  Anna, 303
  Benjamin, 229
  Betsey (Smith), 227
  Betsey (Whittier), 228, 302
  Eleanor (Harvey), 229
  Elijah, 228
  Elizabeth, 26, 227, 230
    302
  Elizabeth (--), 227
  Emily H (Wood), 230
  Hannah, 229
  Hannah (Bachiler), 227
    302
  Hannah (Batchelder), 227
  Hannah (French), 228

  Hannah(Howland), 229
  James, 228
  Jedediah, 227-229, 302
  Jedediah Jr, 227
  Jediah, 227
  Jesse, 228-229, 302
  Jesse L, 229
  John, 228
  Josiah, 227
  Martha (Clark) Molloy
    228, 302
  Mary, 229
  Mary (Owen), 228
  Mary (Whittier), 228-229
    302
  Mehitable (Morrill), 228
  Mercy, 227-228
  Nancy, 229
  Nathaniel, 229
  Odlin, 227
  Olive, 229
  Polly (Owen), 228
  Polly (Whittier), 228-229
  Ruth, 228-229
  Samuel, 228, 302
  Sarah (Morrill), 227-228
PRESSON
  Hannah, 50
PRIDE
  Joseph, 263
  Sarah, 263
  Sarah (--), 263
PRIME
  Olive, 115
PRINCE
  Elaine Bush, 304, 306-307
    309
PROCTOR
  Nancy (Small), 257
  Nathaniel, 257
  Sally (--), 257
  Samuel A, 257
PROVINDER
  Prudence, 125
PUFFER
  Rebecca, 188
PUGSLEY
  Abigail, 245
PULCIFER
  Ann (Harris), 230
  Anna, 230
  Anna (Harris), 230
  Benjamin, 231
  Ebenezer, 230
  Elizabeth, 231
  Huldah (Silley), 230
  Joseph, 230-231
  Marey (Brown), 231

  Mercy (Brown), 231
  Rachel (Hunt), 231
PULLIN/ PULLING
  Margaret, 212
PUMROYE
  Ammey, 7
PURINTON/ PURRINGTON
  James, 177-178
  James Jr, 177
  Myriam (Melcher), 177
  Priscilla (Harding)
    177-178
  Rebeckah, 177
  Susanna, 177-178
QUIGGLE
  Elizabeth (Chapman), 65
    165
QUIMBY
  Benjamin, 150
  Fanny (Corson), 60-61
  John, 61
  Lydia (Keen), 150
  Mary (--), 150
  Moses Jr, 60
  Roxanna (Carpenter), 60
  Samuel, 150
  Tamson (Corson), 60-61
QUIN
  Rebecca, 97
RACKLIFF/ RACKLEY
  Benjamin, 263-264
  Joanna, 263
  Sarah (Jordan), 263
RAND
  Betsy, 232
  David P, 232
  Elizabeth, 232
  Jeremiah, 231
  Jeremiah Jr, 231
  John Blake, 232
  Lydia, 232
  Lydia (Blake), 231
  Lydia (Jones), 231
  Mary, 232
  Ruth (Blake), 232
RANDALL/ RENDALL/
  RENDAL
  Anna (Fogg), 233
  Bathsheba, 236
  Betsey, 236
  Betsey (Chadbourne), 236
  Betsey (Smith), 236
  Betty, 236
  Catherine (Clark), 236
  Debbey, 234
  Deborah, 234
  Deborah (Hamilton), 118
  Deborah Hamilton, 118

RANDALL/ RENDALL/ RENDAL (continued)
Eleanor, 278
Eleanor (Johnson) Libby 232
Eliphalet, 232-236
Eliphelet, 232
Elizabeth, 233
Elizabeth (Chadbourne) 236
Elizabeth (Macfield), 232
Elizabeth (Mayfield), 232
Elizabeth (McDonald, 233
Elizabeth (Smith), 236
Hannah, 234-235
Hannah (Gowel), 233-234
Hannah (Marston), 118
Hanson, 236
Hiram, 234-235
Huldah, 234
James, 233
James Marston, 118
Jeremiah, 233-234
Joanna (Hanson), 233, 235
John, 236
John Rollins, 233, 235
Jotham, 234
Keziah, 234-235
Lydia, 233, 236
Lydia (Abbott), 233
Lydia (Rollins), 232-235
Margaret (Fellows), 118
Maria (Coffin), 235
Martha, 234-235
Mary, 234, 236, 319
Mary (McFarlin), 278
Mary (Shorey), 233
Molly, 236
Molly (Shorey), 233
Patty, 234-235
Paul, 278
Rebecca (Hardison), 236
Richard, 234
Samuel, 232, 235
Sarah, 38, 233
Stephen, 233
Tamesin, 259
William, 118, 236

RANKIN/ RANKINS/ RENKINS
Ada, 239
Andrew, 238
Anna, 238
Betsey (--), 238
Betsey (Burns), 238
Constant, 236-237
Eda, 239
Eleanor (Hanscom), 239
Eliza (Abbott), 239
Elizabeth, 238
Elizabeth (Jameson), 237
Enoch, 239
Esther, 238
Hannah, 237
James, 175, 236-237
Jane (Perry), 238
John, 239
Joseph, 237-238
Joseph Jr, 238
Mary, 237-238
Mary (Havener) Holmes 238
Mary (Tolman), 237
Mehitable, 238
Mehitable (Dunnell), 238
Patience (Dinslow) 236-237
Philadelphia, 175
Philadelphia (Nason), 175
Priscilla, 237
Priscilla (Shaw), 236
Samuel, 237
Susannah (Lindsey), 237

RANN
Sarah, 125

RATHBONE
Lydia, 213

RAWSON
Gerald Linn, 195

RAY
Bethia (Collins), 59
Dolly, 59
Joseph, 59
Louisa, 54
Rachel (Strout), 59
William, 59

RAYNES
Daniel, 269
Eleanor, 275
Jane (Frost), 269
Mary, 269

REED
Bartholomew, 322
David, 158
Hannah, 219, 225
John, 225
Naomi, 322
Sarah (Laplain) King, 158

REEVES
Mary, 88

REIDHEAD/ REDHEAD
Catherine, 288
David, 17
Esther (Banks), 17
Olive (Banks), 16, 288
William, 16, 288

REMICK
Ruth, 291

RENDALL [SEE RANDALL]
RENKINS [SEE RANKIN],
REYNOLDS
Abigail (Pinkham), 122
John, 122
Joseph, 122
Mary (Harriman), 122
Samuel, 91

RHODES
Loisa, 216

RICH
Abigail (Stevens), 263
Boaz, 240
Deliverance, 240
Elizabeth (Harding), 263
Ezekiel, 263
Hannah, 317
James, 263
Lemuel, 240, 263
Mary (Colley), 240
Mary (Richardson), 240
Molly (Richardson), 240
Phebe, 262
Sarah, 192
Sarah (Stevens), 263

RICHARD/ RICHARDS
Abigail, 24, 28
Abigail (--), 28
Abigail (Thayer), 142
Benjamin, 142
John, 270
Joseph, 28
Martha (Sturtevant), 270
Mary, 142
Patty (Sturtevant), 270
Samuel, 271
Sarah (King), 106
Sophronia, 271

RICHARDSON
Aaron, 240
Abigail, 240
Anna, 239
Bethiah (Herrick), 300
David, 239
Dorcas (Wharff) McIntyre 300
Edward, 240
Elizabeth, 239
Henry, 283
Jedida (Tilton), 283
Jemima (Eaton), 240
John, 300
Judith (Tilton), 283
Lydia, 239, 244
Lydia (Hall), 239
Mary, 240

RICHARDSON (continued)
Mary (Arno), 300
Mehitable, 240
Mehitable (Cummings) 240
Molly, 240
Moses, 239, 244
Moses Jr, 239
Olive (Blackinton), 283
Otis, 283
Remember (Ward), 239
Sarah, 240
Simeon Jr, 241
Wilkes, 300
Zilpah (Robbins), 241
RICHMOND
Bethia, 149
RICKER
Avadana (Blake), 25
Capt --, 232
David, 25
Ebenezer, 130
Eliphalet, 137
Elizabeth, 51
Ezekiel, 52
Jedidiah, 52
Job, 91
Judith, 222
Keziah (Hodsdon), 130
Mary (Butler), 130
Mary (Farnham), 91
Mary (Hanscom), 234
Mehitable, 115
Mercy (Hanson), 137
Moses Jr, 130
Phebe (Clements), 52
Samuel, 52
Sarah (Bradbury), 32
Syrena B, 137
Timothy, 32
RIDEOUT
Sarah R, 255
RIDER
Hannah (Atwood), 253
Hepzebah (Skinner), 253
John, 253
Lot, 253
RIDLON
Daniel, 48
Eleanor (Cannell), 48
Ellen (Cannell), 48
RIGGS
Ann, 98, 267
Eunice, 18
Experience (Stanwood), 98
Jeremiah, 18
Joshua, 98

RILEY
Janet H, 241, 269-270
RINES
Mercy (Butland), 138
RING
Daniel, 281
Joseph, 281
Lydia (Savage), 281
Martha (Thorn), 281
ROACH
Mehitable, 144
ROBBINS/ ROBINS
Berintha (Daggett), 65
Betcy, 241
Betsy, 241
Betty, 241
David, 65, 165
Ebenezer, 165
Edward H, 142
Elizabeth (Chapman) Quiggle, 65, 165
Elizabeth (Emery), 240
eunice, 127
Isaac, 241
Jane (Gilman), 241
Joanna, 288
John, 240-241
John Chapman, 65
John Jr, 240
Jonathan, 240-241
Levi, 241
Lucy, 241
Luke, 241
Mary (Hebberd), 241
Mary (Hibbard), 241
Nancy (Ward), 241
Persis, 241
Salome (Brown), 241
Susannah (Harwood), 240
Susannah M (Schofield) 241
Thankful (Luce), 165
Zilpah, 241
ROBERTS
--, 153
Aaron, 119
Arethusa (Kilpatrick), 153
Catherine, 108
Elathusa (Kilpatrick), 153
Elizabeth, 79
Elizabeth (Fall), 141
Ervin, 209
Hannah, 31, 139, 309
Hannah (Small), 139
Joanna (Pray), 309
Judith, 39
Lucy, 41
Mary, 141

Mary (Hanson), 119
Molly, 119, 141
Samuel, 139
Sarah, 128
Thomas, 141
ROBINSON
Alexander, 133
Betsey (Wharff), 300
Daniel, 136
Elizabeth (Bean), 136
Jane (Nichols), 133
Jane (Nickels), 133
Jenny (Nichols), 133
Jenny (Nickels), 133
Joanna, 191
Margaret, 136, 138
Mary, 48, 64, 88, 139
Mary (Stinson), 300
Mehitable, 202
Ruth, 133
Sarah A, 304
Susannah, 237
William, 202, 300
William Jr, 300
ROGERS
Capt --, 76
Dinah, 255
Hannah, 44
Isac, 44
Jonathan, 44
Keziah, 119
Lydia (Varney), 44
Patience, 44, 280
Sarah (--), 44
Williams, 305
Zeruiah (Williams), 305
Zerviah (Williams), 305
ROLFE
Betsy (Nye), 201
Henry L, 201
ROLLINS/ ROLLINGS
--, 118
Abigail (Glidden), 56
Betty, 310
Deborah (Crowell), 62-63
Eliphalet, 56
Elizabeth (Ham), 232
Elizabeth (Mosher), 191
Hannah (Colburn), 56
Jabez, 191
Jeremiah, 232
John, 63
Joseph, 56, 191
Lydia, 232-235
Lydia (Haskell), 191
Mary (Downing), 63
Mary (Hamilton), 118
Sarah, 51

ROLLINS/ ROLLINGS
(continued)
Thankful G (Scudder), 191
Valentine, 63
ROSE
Mr --, 109
Nancy, 110
Prudence, 214
ROSWELL
Ruth, 266
ROUNDS
James, 51, 248
James Jr, 248
Mary (Sands), 248
Polly, 248
Polly (Rounds), 248
Rachel (Clay), 51, 248
Sarah, 279
ROUNDY
Mary, 54
ROUSE
Joanna, 198
ROWE
Anthony, 198
Benjamin, 198
Elizabeth, 199
Joanna, 198-199
Joanna (Rouse), 198
John Parker, 117
Lazarus, 198-199
Martha, 198
Mary (Hamilton), 117
Molly (Webber), 199
Noah, 198
ROWELL
John, 88
Lois, 88
Martha, 88
Mary (Reeves), 88
ROYAL
Molly, 194
ROYS
Mabel Foster, 151
RUNNELLS/ RUNNELS
Benjamin, 136
Hannah (Farnham), 91
Lydia, 136
Olive (Farnham), 90
Rebecca (Wentworth), 136
Samuel, 90-91
RUSS
Susan, 68
RUSSELL/ RUSSEL
Abigail (Kilgore), 151
Abraham, 272
Achsah (Kelley), 242
Asa, 242
Belinda, 243

Benjamin, 248
Benjamin Jr, 21, 151
Betsey, 242
Charlotte (Wyman), 243
Deborah (Foss), 242
Eliza P (Whittier), 242
Elizabeth (Locke), 242
Fidelia (Laughton), 242
Hannah, 54
Hannah (Foster), 272
Jane (Potter), 226
Jason, 242-243
Jesse, 242
Joanna (Woodbury), 242
John Jr, 272
Josiah, 242
Julia (--), 243
Levi, 226
Lovina (Wyman), 242
Luke Reilly, 151
Lydia, 151
Mary, 248
Mary (Favor), 248
Mary (Loveland), 242
Mehitable (Abbott), 21, 151
Molly (Loveland), 242
Nabby (Kilgore), 151
Polly (Bartlett), 21
Rachel (--), 243
Rebecca (Laughton), 242
Sarah (Swan), 272
Sarah M (Stubbs), 314
Serena (--), 242
Silas, 242
Stephen, 242
William, 242
Willoughby, 21
RUST
Lucy, 10
SABINE/ SABIN/ LABAN
Abigail (Davis), 243
Alice L, 53
Charity (Collar), 243
Curtis, 243
George, 244
Hannah (Thorn), 243
Hiram, 244
Lewis, 243
Lewis Jr, 243
Louisa (Davis), 243
Margery (Warner), 244
Mary (Warner), 244
Melinda (Woodcock), 243
Pierce, 243
Sally (Dow), 243
Sarah E (Dow), 243

SAFFORD
James, 50
Sarah (Clay), 50
Stephen, 50
SAMPSON
Louisa, 111
SAMSON
Keturah, 110
SANBORN/ SANDBOURN
Aaron, 245
Abigail (Cram), 245
Benjamin, 106, 245
Betty (Gray), 106
Elizabeth (Gray), 106
Enoch, 244-245
Joseph, 106
Levi, 244-245
Lydia (Richardson), 239, 244
Peter, 239, 244-245
Phebe Elizabeth (Binford), 245
Polly (Mason), 106
Rufus, 245
Sarah (Cram), 245
SANDERS
Leslie Dow, 266, 300
Lucy, 206, 252
SANDERSON
Mabel (McAllister), 166, 168
Mercy, 164
SANDS
Abigail, 120
Abigail (Ayer), 248
Abigail (Hanscom), 121
Anna (Hanscom), 120
Betsey, 105
Betty, 105, 245
Charity (Gould), 246
Charlotte (Steele), 247
Dorcas (Chadbourne), 246
Edith (Patch), 245
Elizabeth, 105, 157, 239, 245, 248, 279, 293
Elizabeth (Jones), 247
Ephraim, 193, 247
Ephraim 3rd, 248
Eunice, 248
Eunice (Goodridge), 246
Hannah (--), 246
Isaac, 245-246
James, 106, 120, 245, 279
James Jr, 246
John, 120, 245-246
John Jr, 247
Lydia, 193, 248, 258
Lydia (--), 248

SANDS (continued)
Lydia (Fall), 120, 279
Martha (Dearing), 245
Mary, 245-246, 248
Mary (Bradbury), 247, 258
Mary (Low), 106, 245
Mary (McLucas), 247
Mary (Steele), 247
Mercy, 248
Nathan, 245-246
Phebe (Littlefield), 246
Ruth (Waterhouse), 246
Sally (Murphy), 246
Samuel, 247-248, 258
Sarah, 248
Sarah (Hanscom), 120
Thomas, 120-121, 245-247

SANFORD
Millia (--), 27

SARGENT
Anna B, 95
Catherine (--), 322
Charlotte Sanders, 206
FiztHenry, 322
Harriet Elizabeth, 322
Jotham, 36
Lucy (Sanders), 206, 252
Paul D, 322
Paul Dudley, 206, 252
Sarah (Bragdon), 36
Sarah Allen, 252

SAVAGE
Annah, 96
Betsey, 305
Edward, 305
Elizabeth (Tudor), 268
Elizabeth Otis (Stillman) 268
Habijah, 268
Isaac, 14
Isabella (Allen), 14-15
James, 268
Jesse, 25
Lydia, 281
Mary, 14, 141
Mary (Heal), 305
Nancy (Blake), 25
Tabitha, 14-15

SAWTELLE
Elizabeth, 10, 171
Mary, 308

SAWYER
Betsy (Williams, 304
Elizabeth B (Williams) 305
Ephraim, 305
Hannah, 44
Hannah (Knight), 321

Hannah (Presson) Marriner Dunn, 50
Mary, 73
Phebe, 78
Sally, 135
Sarah, 55, 301
William, 50

SAYWARD
Bethula (Bradbury), 204 250
Esther, 250
Hannah, 298
James, 204, 250
Jerusha, 204, 294

SCALISI
Marie, 208

SCAMMON
Col --, 115
James, 84, 91
Mehitable (Hinkley), 70
Richard, 60
Samuel, 70
Sarah (Dennett), 70

SCHOPPE
Anthony, 322
Phebe (Speare), 322

SCOTT
Esther, 259

SCRIBNER
Benjamin, 44
Daniel, 223
Elizabeth, 188
Elizabeth (Taylor), 223
Lydia, 223
Mary (Dow) Buffum, 44

SCUDDER
Experience, 130
Jesse, 191
Joanna (Robinson), 191
Thankful G, 191

SEARLE
Elijah, 151
Joanna (Kilgore), 151
Mary, 151

SEARS
Alice, 303
Mercy (Stevens), 303
Paul, 303

SEATON
Mary, 13
Polly, 13

SEAVEY
Dorothy (Parsons) Follett 94
Eliakim, 204
Mary (Brown) Wakefield 204
Samuel W, 94

SEGAR/ SEGER
Abigail, 249
Achsa (Howard), 249
Allan, 249
Apphia, 249
Assa, 249
Betsey (Powers), 249
Edmund, 249
Elizabeth, 19
Elizabeth (Howard), 249
John, 250
Josiah, 19, 248
Lucy, 249
Lydia (Farnum), 250
Mary, 249
Mary (Russell), 248
Nathan, 249
Nathaniel, 248-250
Pamelia, 249
Permeley, 249
Polly, 249
Russell, 249
Submit, 250
Thankful (Allen), 19, 248

SEITZ
Janet S, 23, 57, 159 183-184, 292

SESSIONS
David, 21
Julia Ann (Kilgore), 151
Patty (Bartlett), 21
Peregrine, 151
Rachel (Stevens), 21

SEVERANCE
Jane, 151

SEWALL/ SEWELL [SEE ALSO SOULE]
--, 284
Gen --, 110
Hannah (Moulton), 285
Joseph, 285
Mercy, 285
Mercy (Sewall), 285
Samuel, 285
Sarah, 207, 285
Sarah (Chisam), 207
Susan, 285
William, 207

SHACKLEY
Hopey (--), 61
Sarah, 86

SHAPLEIGH
Dorcas, 318
Hannah (Bartlett), 318
Hannah (Furbush) Brock 37
James, 318
John, 37

SHAPLEIGH (continued)
  Mary, 38
SHATTUCK
  Hannah, 272
SHAW
  Josiah, 293
  Nathan, 15
  Priscilla, 236
  Rebecca (Cox), 293
  Tabitha (Watson), 293
SHERLOCK
  Elinor (Clark), 47
  Elinor (Tyldesley), 47
  Jane, 47, 196
  William, 47
SHERMAN
  Jane (Kennedy) Somes, 261
  William, 261
SHERWIN
  E, 110
SHERWOOD
  Martha, 214
SHOREY
  Hannah (Coss), 233
  Jacob, 233
  Mary, 100, 233
  Molly, 233
SHUFF/ SCHUFF
  Eunice (Nye), 202
  John Charles, 202
SHURTLEFF
  Abigail (Soule), 150
  Ephraim, 150
  Irene, 151
  Isaac, 150
  Rebecca (Whitmarsh), 150
SIBLEY
  T, 109
SILLEY
  Huldah, 230
SILVER
  Sally (Swain), 21
SIMMONDS
  William, 94
SIMONS
  Hannah (--), 15
SIMPSON
  Agnes (Lewis), 225
  Anna, 250-251
  Elizabeth (Bragdon), 251
  Esther (Sayward), 250
  Hannah (Sullivan), 252
  Jabez, 251
  James, 250-251
  Jane (--) Bragdon, 251
  Jeremiah, 43
  Joanna, 250, 252
  Joanna (Brooks), 43

  Joanna (Webster), 250-251
  John, 250-252
  Josiah, 225, 250-252
  Lewis, 255
  Margaret, 205
  Marian, 252
  Martha (Potter), 225
  Martha (Skolfield), 255
  Mary, 293
  Mary (Sullivan), 251
  Miriam, 252
  Paul, 251-252
  Paul Jr, 252
  Peggy Taylor, 251-252
  Prudence, 250-251
  Prudence (Bragdon), 250
  Rachel (Sullivan), 251
  Samuel, 250-251
  Susan, 252
  Susan (Donnell), 251
  William, 225
SINCLAIR/ SINKLOR
  Abigail, 54
  Edward, 54
  Elizabeth, 263
  Mary (Carleton), 54
  Nabby, 54
SKIFF
  Sarah, 66
SKILLINGS
  Amy, 317
  Ann, 317
SKINNER
  Abigail, 253
  Abigail (Briggs), 252-253
  Alona, 253
  Asahel, 253
  Azubah, 253
  Daniel, 252
  Elijah, 252-253
  Elizabeth (Crosby), 253
  Hepzebah, 253
  Jane (Everton), 253
  John Jr, 252
  Mary (--), 252
  Mason, 253
  Miriam (--) Grover 252-253
  Nancy (Nicols) Bodge, 253
  Phoebe (Gould), 253
  Rebecca (Batchelder), 253
  Sally (Fisher), 253
  Sarah (Fisher), 253
SKOLFIELD/ SCOFIELD/ SCHOFIELD, ETC
  Alice (Means), 254
  Anna (Anderson), 254-255
  Anne, 254

  Bethia Sprague
    (Merryman), 256
  Clement, 254, 256
  Dinah (Rogers), 255
  Ebenezer, 256
  Elizabeth (Anderson), 254
  Hannah (Stanwood), 256
  Jacob, 256
  John, 255
  John Orr, 256
  Joseph, 255-256
  Lavina (Stanwood), 256
  Margaret (Hall), 255
  Margaret (Knowles), 255
  Martha, 255
  Martha (McPatrick), 254
  Martha (McPatridge), 254
  Mary, 255-256
  Mary (Adams), 254
  Mary (Orr), 254-255
  Molly, 256
  Nancy, 256
  Rebecca, 254
  Richard, 254
  Sally, 256
  Sarah R(ideout), 255
  Stephen, 255
  Susanna, 255
  Susanna (Sylvester), 256
  Susannah M, 241
  Thomas, 254-255
  Thomas Jr, 254-255
  William, 255
SLOMAN
  Abigail (Warren), 291
  William, 291
SMALL
  Abigail (Morse), 256
  Bethia, 257
  Bethia (Wyman), 256-257
  Betsy (--), 257
  Charles, 257
  Daniel, 257
  Edward, 257
  Eliza, 13
  Elizabeth, 257
  Hannah, 139
  Hannah (Prescott), 229
  Jane, 113
  Jemima (Gilman), 257
  John, 229, 256-257
  Joseph, 257
  Joshua, 113, 284
  Lucy, 257
  Lydia, 258
  Martha, 257
  Mary (Butterfield), 257
  Mary (Clark), 113

EVERY NAME INDEX

SMALL (continued)
Nancy, 257
Nathaniel, 229
Prudence, 256
Reuben, 257
Sally, 258
Sarah, 284
Sarah (Lewis), 229
Susanna, 182
Susannah (Kennard), 284
William, 257
Zachariah, 257
SMART
Catherine (Percy), 313-314
Elizabeth, 314
Elizabeth (Percy), 314
John, 314
Margaret, 313
Olive Abigail, 314
Robert, 313-314, 316
Sarah, 314
Thomas, 314, 316
SMELLAGE
James, 80
Sally (Black), 80
Sarah (Black), 80
Sarah E, 80
SMITH
Abigail, 181
Abigail (Donnell), 84
Abigail (Dunnell), 83, 85
Benjamin Sr, 182
Betsey, 121, 223, 227, 236
Caleb, 193
Catherine, 318
Charles, 33, 183
Charlotte (Warren), 292
Chloe (Clark), 25
Danial R, 35
Daniel, 108
David, 318
Dorcas, 309
Ebenezer, 227
Elizabeth, 121, 170, 236
Elizabeth (Heard), 309
Elizabeth (McLellan), 121
Elizabeth (Meserve), 183
Elsie (Woodman), 182
Experience, 37
Hannah, 57, 91
Hannah (Hadden), 323
Hannah (Sturtevant), 271
Henry, 57
Ithiel, 318
James, 292
Jesse, 318
Joanna Lane (Bradbury) 33

John, 58, 121, 134, 222 309
Jonathan, 318
Joseph, 287
Joshua, 84
Joshua Jr, 84
Josiah, 318
Lucinda, 25
Lucy (Bean), 318
Lydia (--), 193
Margaret, 160
Margaret (Gray), 108
Mary, 12, 271, 273
Mary (Wardwell), 287
Meriah, 112
Molly (Pitts), 222
Moses, 236
Myron C, 108
Nancy Ann (Dore), 109
Nicholas, 323
Rebecca (Haley), 183
Richard, 271
Sally (Cole), 59
Samuel, 25, 183
Sarah, 187-189
Sarah (Bean), 188
Sarah (Colburn), 57
Sarah (Staples), 9
Stephen, 267
Sukey (Cole), 58
Susanna (Brackett), 236
Susanna (Cole), 58
Temperance, 44
Thankful, 27, 160
Thomas, 59
William, 187-188
SNIPE
Sarah, 225
SNOW
Aaron, 258
Betsey (Brooks), 42
Betsey (Myrick), 42
Daniel, 42
Deborah Atwood (Brooks) 43
Edward, 42
Elizabeth (Brooks), 42
Eunice (Philbrick), 258
Gideon, 258
Hannah, 288
Hannah (Paine), 126
Jane (Magne), 196, 248 258
Jane (Mague), 196, 248 258
Jemima, 196, 258
Joanna (Edwards), 258
Joshua, 126

Lydia, 258
Lydia (Sands), 248, 258
Mary, 126
Mercy, 258
Nathaniel, 258
Susan (Parsons), 258
Thankful (--), 258
Thomas, 43, 196, 248 258(2)
SNOWMAN
Alexander, 260
Comfort (Horne), 259
Dosia (Perkins), 259
Esther (Scott), 259
Hannah, 259
James, 259
John, 259
John Jr, 259
Sarah, 259
Sarah (Staples), 259
Sarah (Wight), 260
Susan (Billings), 260
Theodosia (Perkins), 259
Thomas, 260
SOMES/ SOMER
Abigail (Trask), 260
Betsey, 261
David, 260
David Jr, 260
Elizabeth, 261
Hannah (Davidson), 261
Hannah (Davison), 261
Jane, 261
Jane (Hopkins), 260
Jane (Kennedy), 261
Jennett (Hopkins), 260
Jenney, 261
Joel, 261
Lucy (Day), 260
Margaret, 261
Martha (Cochern), 260
Martha (Cothran), 260
Mary, 261
Morris, 260
Nancy, 261
Patty, 261
Peggy, 261
Polly, 261
Sally, 261
Solomon, 261
William, 260
SOPER
Rachel (Nash), 195
Salter, 195
SOULE
Mehetable, 74
SOULE [SEE ALSO

SOULE [SEE ALSO SEWALL] (continued)
SEWALL], Abigail, 150
Andrew, 76
Barnabas, 72
Betty (Mitchell), 74, 78
Charles, 75
Dorcas, 72, 78
George, 214
James, 75
Jane (Bradbury), 71
Jane (Dennison), 72
John, 74, 78
Loammi Betsey, 78
Mahala (Porter), 76
Martha (Curtis), 75
Martha Ann, 76
Mehetable, 72
Nancy, 179
Penthea Stetson, 74
Samuel, 75
Sophronia (Dennison), 75
Susan (Dennison), 75
SOUTHEARD/ SOUTHARD/ SOUTHERD
Abraham, 111
Amos P, 111
Fannie (Gullifer), 111
John, 111
Louisa (Sampson), 111
Sophia (Gullifer), 111
Sophie (Gullifer), 111
Sukey, 111
Susanna, 111
Susanna (Paris), 111
SOUTHWICK/ SUDRICK
Abigail, 157
SPARROW
Hannah (Knowles) Warren 232
SPAULDING
Mary, 129
SPEAR/ SPEARE
Anna (Brackett), 322
Anne (Skolfield), 254
Elizabeth (--), 224
Lucy (Matthews), 177
Martha, 224
Mary, 224
Phebe, 322
Robert Jr, 254
William, 224, 322
SPEARING
Elizabeth, 281, 290
SPENCER
Dorcas, 2
Elizabeth (Early), 102
Freethy, 6

Humphrey, 102, 115
Lydia (Goodwin), 102, 115
Sarah (Abbott), 6
Sarah (Early), 102
Simeon, 102, 115
Susanna (Hamilton), 102 115
SPILLER
Dexter Talpey, 276-277
SPOFFORD
Amherst, 243
Belinda (Russell), 243
Hannah (Emerson), 243
Hiram, 243
Lydia, 249
SPOONER
Abigail, 306
SPRAGUE
Eleanor Robbins, 241
Eli, 318
SPRINGER
Ann, 62, 190
Mercy (Babcock), 15
Studly, 15
SPROUL
Jane, 68
Mary, 68
Mary J, 184
Polly, 68
SPURLING/ SPURLIN
Abigail, 262
Abigail (Hadlock), 262
Abigail (Yeaton), 262
Benjamin, 261-262
Benjamin Jr, 262
Dolly, 262
Enoch, 262
Esther, 262
Fanny, 262
Fanny (Guptill), 261
Hannah (Newman), 262
Hannah (Stanley), 262
Mary (Stanley), 262
Nancy (Stanley), 262
Robert, 262
Sally, 262
Samuel, 262
Sarah, 262
Thomas, 262
William, 262
STACEY/ STACY
Fanny, 84
Ichabod, 84
Lucy (Talpey), 276
Samuel S, 276
STACKPOLE
Abigail (Brock), 39
James, 39

Nabby (Brock), 39
STANDLEY
Drucilla, 159
STANLEY
Elizabeth (Mayo), 262
Fanny (Spurling), 262
Hannah, 262
Hannah (Manchester), 262
John, 262
Mary, 262
Nancy, 262
Phebe (Rich), 262
Sans, 262
Sarah, 110
Thomas, 262
STANWOOD
Benjamin, 256
Experience, 98
Hannah, 256
Lavina, 256
Sally (Skolfield), 256
Zena, 127
STAPLES
Abel E, 301
Betsey, 72
Daniel, 73
David, 257
Elizabeth, 72
Elizabeth (Small), 257
John, 175
Judith (Eaton), 301
Lucy, 73
Lucy (Staples), 73
Mary, 175
Moses, 301
Rebecca (Whitmore), 301
Sarah, 9, 225, 259 286-287
Sarrah, 289
Susanna, 57
Tabitha (Littlefield), 175
STARBIRD
Hannah, 239
Lydia, 266
STARK
Col --, 95
STARLING
Abigail, 46
STEARNS
Benjamin Franklin, 11
Charles, 11, 21
Ezekiel, 261
John, 21
Julia (Andrews), 11
Martha (Harrington), 21
Nancy (Somes) Dodge, 261
Thankful (Bartlett), 11, 21
Warren D, 4, 11, 21, 95

STEARNS (continued)
  Warren D (continued)
    151, 274
STEDMAN
  James, 283
  Persis (Tilton), 283
  Polly (--), 283
  William, 283
STEELE
  Charlotte, 247
  Elizabeth (--), 247
  John, 247
  Mary, 247
  Rachel, 279
STETSON/ STYTSON
  Abigail (Dennison), 77
  Abner, 68
  Betsey (Dennison), 78
  Charles, 77
  Deborah, 68
  Deborah (Stetson), 68
  Desire, 72
  Elisha, 78
  Jacob, 64
  Rebecca (Curtis), 78
  Sarah (Wade), 64
  Stephen, 78
  Susan (Russ) Wiley, 68
  Susanna, 77
  Susanna (Day), 68
STEVENS/ STEPHENS
  --, 265
  Abigail, 91, 263
  Abigail (Perry), 216
  Abigail (Petty), 216
  Agnes, 257
  Alice (Goff), 264
  Alice (Golt), 264
  Amos, 265, 299
  Amy (Webb), 263
  Anna (Lufkin), 264
  Benjamin, 263
  Benjamin R, 192
  Betsey, 36, 166
  Catharine, 263
  Catherine, 3
  Charles, 267
  Chloe (Titus) Harding, 172
  Daniel Jr, 4
  David, 267
  Eleanor, 266
  Elizabeth, 264
  Elizabeth (Marrow), 171
  Elizabeth (Sawtelle), 171
  Elizabeth (Sinclair), 263
  Elizabeth (Sinklor), 263
  Esther, 240
  Eunice (--) Webber, 265

  Eunice (Marriner), 267
  Hannah (--) Woodman, 265
  Hannah (Barker), 4
  Henry, 90
  James, 172, 265, 299
  Jerusha, 264
  Jerusha (Bennett), 264, 299
  Joanna (Godfrey), 324
  Joanna (Rackley), 263
  John, 265, 282
  Jonas, 171
  Jonathan, 216
  Joseph, 171, 263
  Joseph Wharff, 299
  Judith, 282
  Lucy (Webb) Cobb, 266(2)
    267
  Margaret (Patrick), 266
  Martha C, 191
  Mary, 46
  Mary (Farnham), 90
  Mary (Francis), 264
  Mary (Herrick), 266
  Mehitable, 263
  Mercy, 303
  Michael, 266
  Moses, 265, 299
  Nahum, 216
  Nancy, 266
  Nancy C (Chapman), 266
  Nathaniel, 263-265, 299
  Oliver, 176
  Pauline (Clark), 216
  Persis (Maxwell), 176
  Peter, 266
  Polly (Herrick), 266
  Rachel, 21
  Rachel P, 216
  Ruth (Andrews), 265
  Ruth (Roswell), 266
  Sally, 172
  Sally (Huntington), 265
    282
  Sally (Wharff), 265, 299
  Sally (Witham), 265
  Samuel, 264, 266
  Samuel Gott, 264
  Sarah, 263, 265
  Sarah (Folsom), 263
  Sarah (Pride), 263
  Sarah (Rich), 192
  Sarah (Witham), 265
  Sophia (Peaks), 267
  Susanna (Bennett) Wharff
    265, 299
  Susanna (Wharff), 265
    299
  Susannah, 265

  Tristram, 266
  Tristram Coffin, 266
  Trustrum, 266
  William, 264-265
STEWART/ STUARD/
STUART
  Charles, 172
  Dorcas (Pendleton), 212
  Elizabeth, 212
  Jane, 207
  Kirty, 99
  Mary, 48, 172-173, 222
  Mary (--), 172
  Sargent I, 212
STICKNEY
  Elizabeth, 273
  Rebecca, 95
  Sarah, 250
STILLMAN
  Allen Crocker, 268
  Elizabeth Otis, 268
  George, 267-268
  Nathaniel, 267
  Rebecca (Crocker), 267
  Rebecca Allyn, 267
  Sally, 268
  Samuel, 268
  Sarah, 268
  Sarah (Allyn), 267
STIMPSON
  --, 5
  Abigail (--), 5
  Christian, 5
  Jonathan, 5
  Molly, 5
  Pauline, 238
STINCHFIELD
  John, 145
  Lydia H (Jordan), 145
  Sarah (Jordan), 144
  Sarah Bartlett (Jordan)
    Jordan, 145
  William, 145
STINSON
  Betsy, 88
  Elizabeth, 87
  James, 88
  Lucy, 301
  Mary, 300
  Mary (Robinson), 88
  William, 301
STOCKBRIDGE
  Frances C, 95
STONE
  --, 237
  Abigail, 101
  Abigail (Swett), 268, 298
  Benjamin, 268, 298

STONE (continued)
Daniel, 269
Dorcas, 100
Dorcas Milbury (Bickford) 269
Elizabeth, 298
Hannah, 270
Hannah (Milbury), 269
Hannah (Rankins), 237
Harriet (Goodwin), 269
John, 270, 274
Josiah, 268-269
Josiah Jr, 269
Judith (Meads) Lord, 108
Kezia (Emery), 270
Mary, 193
Mary (Gray), 108
Mary (Raynes), 269
Sally, 269
Samuel, 269-270
Samuel Jr, 270
Sarah, 269
Sarah A, 270
Skinner, 108
Sophia (Jacobs), 269
William, 108

STORER
Abigail, 185

STOVER
--, 125
Abigail, 8, 224
David, 106
Hannah, 126
Henry, 106
John, 106, 126
Joseph, 274
Mary (Warren) Coffin, 106
Patience (Young), 126
Rachel (Gray), 106
Sally (Gray), 106
Sarah (Boody), 106
Sarah (Gray), 106
Tabatha, 259

STREETER
Rebecca, 145

STROUT
Rachel, 59

STUARD [SEE STEWART],
STUART [SEE STEWART],
STUBBS
Jane Bradbury (True), 314
Jeremiah, 314
Louise, 324
Mary, 152
Mercy (Brown), 314
Richard, 314
Sarah M, 314

STURGIS
Abigail, 18

STURTEVANT/ STURDEVANT
Abisha, 270-271
Almira (Day) Folsom, 271
Betsey (Burnham), 271
Charlotte (Manes), 271
David, 271
Hannah, 271
Ichabod, 271
Jerusha (House), 270
John, 270
Joseph, 270
Lot, 271
Louisana (Brett), 271
Martha, 270
Mary, 270
Mary (Billington), 270
Mary (Gibbs), 270
Patty, 270
Polly, 270
Rhoda, 270
Sally, 270
Sarah, 270
Sarah J (--) Ames, 271
Sophronia (Richards), 271
Warren, 271

STYTSON [SEE STETSON],
SUDRICK [SEE SOUTHWICK],
SULLIVAN
Abigail (Bean), 251-252
Capt --, 115
Daniel, 33, 251-252, 262
Ebenezer, 84
Hannah, 252
James, 251
Mary, 251
Rachel, 251

SWAIN
Sally, 21

SWAN
Abigail, 272-273
Anne, 272
Betsey (Howe), 274
Betsy (Chapman), 273
Betty, 273
Caleb, 273
Dudley, 273
Elijah, 272
Elizabeth, 272-273
Elizabeth (Chapman), 273
Elizabeth (Eames), 273
Elizabeth (Evans), 272-273
Eunice (Barton), 272
Greeley, 274
Hannah, 274
Hannah (Shattuck), 272
James, 271-273
John, 273
Joseph G, 273
Joseph Greeley, 272-273
Joshua, 271
Mary, 237
Mary (Green), 273
Mary (Smith), 271, 273
Mehitable (Colby), 272
Molley, 272
Nancy, 272
Naomi, 272
Nathaniel, 272
Persis (Eames), 273
Polly (Eames), 273
Sally (Greene), 273
Sarah, 272
Sarah (--) Lang, 273
Sarah (Greene), 273
Sarah (Ingalls), 271
William, 273-274

SWANZEY
Catherine, 219

SWEETLAND
Sally, 210, 212-213

SWEETSER
Elizabeth (Morse), 79
Nancy, 58
William, 79

SWETT/ SWEAT
Abigail, 268, 298
Charlotte (Bourne), 116 118
Esther, 148
Jemima (Bickford), 42
Joann (Nickerson), 42
Joanna, 99
John, 176
John Barnard, 116
Joseph, 178
Margaret (Patten), 178
Nancy (Thompson) Cobb 42
Nathaniel, 176
Nathaniel Jr, 275
Paulina, 275
Sarah (Carlile), 176
Sarah (Carlisle), 275
Sarah (Maxwell), 176
Shebna, 42
Solomon, 42

SYLVESTER
Abner, 77
Abner Jr, 77
Amme, 77
Caleb, 71
Esther (Dennison), 72

SYLVESTER (continued)
  Henchman, 72
  Lillis Turner, 75-76
  Louisa, 73
  Sally (Dennison), 77
  Sarah (Dennison), 77
  Susanna, 256
  Susanna (Stetson), 77
TALPEY/ TOLPEY/ TAPLEY
  Abigail (Trafton), 275
  Abigail (Varrell) Gerry 275
  Elisabeth (Carlisle), 275
  Eliza (Norton) Freeman 275
  Elizabeth, 274
  Elizabeth (Carlisle), 276
  Elizabeth (Carter), 274 276
  Florence M, 274
  Hannah, 277
  Henry, 274
  Henry Jr, 275
  Hepzebeth, 277
  James, 275
  John, 276
  Jonathan, 275-276
  Julia (Emerson) Lincoln 277
  Lucy, 276
  Mary, 274, 277
  Mary (Berry), 274
  Mary (Clarke), 276
  Miriam Adams (Whitney) 276
  Nancy, 276
  Oliver, 277
  Paulina (Swett), 275
  Pollina, 277
  Polly, 274
  Richard, 274, 276-277
  Rufus, 277
  Sally (Matthews), 277
  Sally (Norcross), 277
  Sarah, 274-275
  Sukey (Kerswell), 277
  Susan (Caswell), 277
  Thomas, 276-277
  William, 275
TAPPAN
  Mary Chase, 141
TARBOX
  Abigail, 101
  Mary, 220-221
TAVERNER
  Bette Barker, 18, 113
  Elizabeth Barker, 18, 113

TAYLOR
  Alice (Braley), 323
  Anna, 24
  Annie, 24, 281-282
  Avis (Lowder) Banks, 16
  Betsey (Knowlton), 191
  David, 283
  Desire, 63
  Dorcas, 41
  Elathan, 237
  Elias, 24, 63, 191, 322-323
  Elizabeth, 223
  Elizabeth (Crowell), 62-63 283
  Ellice (Braley), 323
  Ellithan, 237
  Elnathan, 237
  James, 281
  Jane, 41
  Joanna, 43
  John, 323
  Love (Tilton), 283
  Lydia, 149, 171
  Mary, 170, 218
  Mary (Johnson), 24, 63
  Mary (Rankins), 237
  Nancy (Prescott), 229
  Phebe, 45
  Phebe (Mosher), 191, 322
  Samuel, 63, 283
  Sarah, 153
  Sarah (White), 281
  Wilder, 16
TEBBETTS [SEE TIBBETTS],
TENNEY
  George, 12
  Lydia Gates (Archer), 12
  Mary (Carleton), 54
  Nathan, 54
  Polly, 54
TEWKSBURY
  Sarah, 213
THARLO [SEE THURLOW]
THATCHER
  Oxenbridge, 180
  Sarah (Kent), 180
THAYER
  --, 168
  Abigail, 142
  Alvin, 61
  Bathsheba, 61
  Eliza (McCluer), 168
  Elizabeth, 168
  Elizabeth (Thayer), 168
  Jechonias, 168
  Solomon A, 168

THOITS
  James, 258
  Lydia (Small), 258
THOMAS
  Abigail, 28
  Abigail (Higgins), 278
  Abigail (Parlour), 277
  Abigail Gardner (Pendleton), 211
  Azubah, 278
  Christiana (Pendleton), 211
  David Jr, 211
  Edward, 277
  Eleanor (Randall), 278
  George, 28
  Hannah (Dorman), 81
  Hushai, 278
  James, 278
  Jesse, 277-278
  John H, 167
  Joseph, 81
  Lucy, 215
  Lydia (McAllister), 167
  Lydia (Morse), 278
  Mary, 278
  Melzar, 277-278
  Nabby (Pendleton), 211
  Nathaniel, 211
  Sally (Bradford), 278
  Sarah, 165-167
  Sarah (Bradford), 278
  Susanna (--), 28, 278
  Sylvina, 213
THOMES
  Mary, 267
THOMPSON/ TOMPSON
  Abigail, 279
  Anna, 94, 284-285
  Anna (Hubbard), 284
  Anna Maria (Adams), 286
  Betsey, 129, 285
  Betsey (Clements), 285
  Cornelius, 323
  Edward, 284
  Elizabeth, 129, 151, 279
  Elizabeth (Sands), 279, 293
  Hannah, 42
  Hannah (Goodwin), 284
  Hannah (White), 279
  James, 323
  James Sands, 279
  John, 42, 284
  John S, 284
  John Storer, 285
  Joseph, 284-285
  Lois, 222
  Lydia (Brown) Harris, 323
  Lydia Sands, 279, 293

EVERY NAME INDEX

THOMPSON/ TOMPSON
(continued)
Mary, 42, 285
Mary (Atwood), 42
Mary (Durham), 285
Mary (Lancaster), 285
Mary Atwood, 41
Miriam, 31
Molly, 42
Nancy, 42, 55
Phineas, 323
Rachel (Steele), 279
Rebecca (--), 279
Robert, 323
Ruth, 323
Ruth (Thompson), 323
Samuel, 279, 284-285
Sarah, 284-285
Sarah (Allen) Morrill 284-285
Sarah (Bacon), 279
Sarah (Rounds), 279
Sarah (Sewall), 285
Sarah (Small), 284
Susan (Sewall), 285
Theodore, 279, 293
Thomas, 279
William, 284-285
William Allen, 284, 286
Zane A, 268
THORN
Elizabeth, 280-281
Hannah, 243
Jane (Owen), 280
Jenny (Owen), 280
John Owen, 281
Lucy (Freeman), 280
Martha, 280-281
Martha (--), 280
Mary (Jack), 280
Orrin, 280
Sarah, 280
Thomas, 280
William, 280
William Jr, 280
THRESHER
Elizabeth (Morse) Sweetser 79
Hannah, 79
Hannah (Dow), 79
Jonathan, 79
THURLOW/ THARLO
James, 258
Lydia (Small), 258
THURRELL
Hannah, 318
THURSTON
Lois Ware, iii, 123

Nancy (Rose), 110
Nathaniel, 110
TIBBETTS/ TEBBETTS, ETC
--, 118
Abigail, 23, 281, 290-291
Andrew, 282
Annie (Taylor) Johnson 281-282
Asenath (Britt), 282
Asenith (Britt), 282
Catherine (Jones), 309
Charity, 135, 281
Charlotte, 282
Cynthia (Warren), 292
Edward, 281, 290-291
Edward Jr, 282
Eliza, 282
Elizabeth (Butler), 282
Elizabeth (Hamilton), 118
Elizabeth (Spearing), 281 290
Enoch, 292
Hannah, 282
Ichabod, 309
James, 281-282
John, 282
Judith (Judkins), 282
Judith (Stevens), 282
Mary, 281
Mary Ann (Hilton), 306
Molly (Jones) Yeaton Keay 309
Moses, 118
Nancy (Britt), 282
Nancy (Gray), 282
Robert, 282
Sarah (Douglas), 281
Sarah (Gatchell), 282
Solomon, 281-282, 290
William, 282
TILSON
George, 18
Nancy (Barker), 18
TILTON/ TITTON
Amarilla (Doty), 283
Clarissa, 283
Cornelias, 282
Cornelius, 282-283
Elizabeth, 283
Elizabeth (Butter), 283
Hannah (Morrill), 283
Jedida, 283
Jedidah (Pease), 283
Jeremiah, 283
John, 282-283
Judith, 283
Love, 283

Nathaniel, 283
Persis, 283
Rhoda, 283
Sarah, 283
Sarah (Gibbs), 282
Sidney, 283
Temperance (Merchant) 283
William, 283
Zeporah (Clark), 283
TINKHAM
Henry, 209
TINNEY [SEE PHINNEY],
TITTON [SEE TILTON],
TITUS
Chloe, 172
TOBEY
Eliakim, 202
Lucy, 202
Lydia, 200
Mary, 199
Mary (--), 199
Samuel, 199
TOLMAN
Hannah (Fuller), 237
Isaiah, 237, 319
Mary, 14, 237
TOLPEY [SEE TALPEY],
TOURTELOTTE
Abraham, 171
Abraham Jr, 171
Mallason (Walling), 171
Rebecca (Maddocks), 171
TOWER
Dorothy (Moore), 171, 207
Lydia, 173
TOWLE
Betsey, 83
Elizabeth (Rankins), 238
James L, 238
Phineas, 238
Sarah (Leavitt), 238
TOWN/ TOWNS
Abner, 282
Charlotte (Tibbetts), 282
Mary Farnum, 222
Miranda, 30
TOWNSEND
Eleanor W, 112, 160, 228 230, 303
Lucinda, 73
Robert, 77
Susanna (Dennison), 77
TOZIER
John, 110
Patience, 110
Sarah (Pattee), 110
Thankful, 110

EVERY NAME INDEX

TRACY
 Asa, 215
 Dorcas, 216
 Dorcas (Leighton), 215
 Lucretia (Farnham), 83
 Rachel, 215
 Thomas, 83
TRAFTON
 Abigail, 275
 John, 176
 Lucy (Maxwell), 176
 Tabitha (--), 275
 Tobias, 275
TRASK
 Betsey, 226
 Betsey (Hodge), 226
 Jane, 167(2)
 Jonathan, 226
 Josiah, 208
 Mary (--), 208
 Ruth, 173, 208
TREADWELL
 Huldah (Winn) Brock, 37
 James, 37
TREFETHEN
 --, 83
 Mary (Farnham), 83
TRICKEY
 Jenny (Dennison), 71
TRIPE
 Mary, 93
 Sarah, 206
TRIPP
 Mariah, 205
 Naomi (Bartlett), 21
 Rev --, 21
 Susan, 109
TROTT
 Mercy, 142
TRUE
 Anna, 305
 Hannah, 144
 Jane Bradbury, 314
TRUNDY
 Ann (Carey), 301
 Deborah, 301
 Samuel, 301
TUCKER
 Benjamin, 221
 Jane (Babcock), 221
 Mary (Pike), 221
 Rosilla C, 221
TUDOR
 Elizabeth, 268
TUPPER
 Col --, 10
 Elizabeth, 11
 Hannah, 13

 Margaret (Gates), 12
 William, 12
TURNER
 Asa, 86
 Benjamin, 323
 Betsy (Farnham), 86
 Daniel, 323
 David, 323
 Elizabeth (Farnham), 86
 Elizabeth (Williams), 323
 Eunice, 323
 Fanny, 323
 Hollis, 323
 James, 323
 John, 323
 Joseph, 323
 Lois, 323
 Lois (Gilpatrick), 323
 Mary, 28, 114, 323
 Mier, 323
 Mollie, 323
 Nancy (Boynton), 323
 Nehemiah, 323
 Pamelia (Day), 323
 Sadine (Jackson), 323
 Sarah, 323
 Susan (Greenleaf), 323
TUTTLE
 Nancy, 60
 Paulina, 293
 Phebe, 170
TWAMBLEY/ TWOMBLY
 Mary, 104, 236
 Sally, 101
TWINING
 Hannah, 311
 Thankful, 311
TWITCHELL
 Eli, 249
 Joseph, 10
 Lucy (Segar) Norton, 249
TYLDESLEY
 Elinor, 47
TYLER
 Rowland, 99
 Sally (Ginn), 99
ULMER
 Col --, 136
ULRICH
 Betsey (Leeman), 160
 Joseph, 160
UPHAM
 Deborah, 64
 Hannah (Burgess), 64
 Jabez, 64
URAN
 Anna (--), 124
 Anna (Wilkinson), 125

 Anna (Wilkinson) Earl, 124
 Anna (Wilkinson) Hearl 124
 James, 124-125
USHER
 Frances, 206-207
 Robert, 113
 Susan (McDonald), 113
VARNEY
 Abigail, 44, 138-139
 Abigail (Farnham), 83
 Abigail (Hussey), 45
 Bethia, 9
 Betsey (Towle), 83
 Davis, 103
 Ebenezer, 137
 Elijah, 9
 Elizabeth, 139
 Elizabeth (--), 9
 Elizabeth (Jenkins), 137
 Elizabeth (Varney), 139
 Hannah, 44-45, 119
 Hanson, 137
 John, 83
 Jonathan, 9, 139
 Joseph, 44
 Lois (Jepson), 137
 Lydia, 44
 Margaret (Brock), 103
 Martha (Goodwin), 103
 Samuel, 83
 Sarah (Allen), 9
 Temperance (Smith), 44
 Timothy, 45
 Zaccheus, 103
VARNUM
 --, 82
 Abigail (Wardwell), 286
 Benjamin, 286
 Dolley (Moore), 286, 290
 Gershom, 286, 290
 Hannah (Wardwell), 290
 Jonathan, 290
VARREL/ VARRELL
 Abigail, 275
 Hepzibah, 264
 Mary (Moore), 275
 Solomon, 275
VAUGHAN/ VAUGHN
 Charles, 62
 William, 161
VEAZIE
 Jeremiah, 131
VICKERY
 James B, 127
 John Jr, 175
 Lucy (Martin), 175

EVERY NAME INDEX

VINCENT
Sarah, 209
VINING
Bela, 187
Benjamin, 187
Mehitabel (Brooks), 187
Thankful (Millbanks), 187
VINSON
Deborah, 210
WADE
Jacob, 64
Lucy (Crowell), 62
Lydia (James), 62
Nathaniel, 121
Samuel, 62
Sarah, 64
WADLEIGH/ WADLEY
Betsey (Thompson), 129
Eliza Ann (Banks), 3
Elizabeth (Thompson), 129
Fanny, 129
John, 129-130
WADLIN
Betsey, 134
Elizabeth, 134
Jane (Perry), 134
Moses, 134
WADSWORTH
Alfred, 155
Lydia (Knight), 155
WAKEFIELD
Elizabeth, 246
John, 204-205
Mary, 205
Mary (Brown), 205
Ruth, 205
WAKEHAM
Edward, 140
Mehitable, 140
Sarah (Meader), 140
WALDO
Sally, 7
Samuel, 48
WALDRON
Mary, 285
WALKER
Abigail (Swan), 273
Esther (Rankins) Gardner 238
James, 273
Joseph, 238
Lovey, 53
Miriam (--), 307
Peter, 273
Ruth (Abbott), 273
Solomon, 307
Susannah, 307

WALLING
Mallason, 171
WALLINGFORD
Betsey, 38
Mary, 285
WANG
Joan Parsons, 205
WARD
Elizabeth, 194
Hannah (--), 219
Hannah (Phinney), 219
Joseph, 219
Nancy, 241
Nehemiah, 219
Remember, 239
WARDWELL
Abigail, 286, 288, 290, 298 315
Abigail (Wardwell), 288 290
Abigail (Wight), 290
Alice (Beal), 290
Anna, 288-289
Anna (Wardwell), 288-289
Betsy (Banks), 16, 287
Catherine (Reidhead), 288
Charles, 290, 315
Daniel, 16, 286-289 314-315
Daniel Jr, 286
Daniel Sr, 286
Deborah (Littlefield), 288
Ebenezer, 288
Eliakim, 288-289, 298 314
Elizabeth, 288
Elizabeth (Banks), 16 286-287, 290, 315
Elizabeth (Newbury), 288
Elizakim, 289
Hannah, 290
Hannah (Atkins), 288
Hannah (Snow), 288
Hannah (Westcott) 288-289
Irene, 287
Jeremiah, 16, 286, 289-290 298, 315
Joanna (Grindle), 288
Joanna (Grindle) Wardwell 288
Joanna (Robbins), 288
Joel, 286-287, 298
Joseph, 288-289
Josiah, 288-289, 314
Lewis, 288, 290
Loraine, 287
Lucy (Dunbar), 288

Mary, 287, 315
Mary (--), 314
Mary (Banks), 16
Mary (Hutchins), 286, 288
Mary (Leach), 290
Mercy, 289-290, 315
Mercy (--), 314-315
Mercy (Hutchins), 286
Mercy (Weare), 297-298
Olive, 288-290
Olive (Wardwell), 288, 290
Polly (Banks), 16
Robert, 286, 288
Ruth, 288
Ruth (Bragdon), 298
Sally, 287, 289-290
Samuel, 16, 290, 315
Sarah, 286, 315
Sarah (Dunbar), 287
Sarah (Staples), 286-287 289
Seneca, 288
Stephen, 286
Sylvia, 286, 288
Sylvia (Wardwell), 286 288
Taylor, 287
Temperance, 314-315
Tryphena, 315
Vespasian, 288
William, 287
WARNER
Margery, 244
Mary, 244
Phineas, 244
WARREN/ WAREN
Abigail, 291
Abigail (Philpot), 223
Abigail (Tibbetts), 290-291
Benjamin, 223
Betsey, 291
Charlotte, 292
Christian (Pelton), 291
Cynthia, 292
Elizabeth, 291
Fanny, 292
Hannah, 291
Hannah (Knowles), 232
Hannah (Swan), 274
James, 292
Joanna, 217, 219
John, 274, 292
Jonathan, 291
Margaret (Marson), 291
Mary, 77, 95, 106
Mary (Chase), 292
Mary (Randall) Atwood 319

EVERY NAME INDEX

WARREN/ WAREN (continued)
Patta, 290-291
Peggy (Marson), 291
Pelatiah, 291
Pelton, 281, 290-291
Petten, 290-291
Petton, 291
Polly (Green), 95
Richard, 214, 217
Samuel, 95
Sarah, 223, 291
Walter, 319
William Gardner, 291

WARTMAN
Betsey (Herbert) Banks, 3
Elizabeth (Herbert) Banks 3
Frederick, 3

WASGATT [SEE ALSO WESCOTT]
Deborah, 127
Eunice (Robbins), 127
Thomas Jr, 127

WASHBURN
Mary (Brown) Wakefield 204
Thomas, 204

WATERHOUSE
Betsey, 196
Capt --, 115
Elizabeth, 196
Elizabeth (Wakefield), 246
Jacob, 246
Joseph, 196
Lydia (Harmon), 196
Ruth, 246
Samuel, 185

WATERMAN
Sally, 216

WATERS
Hannah, 308

WATSON
Betsey (Cressey), 292
Colman Phinney, 292
Desire, 293
Edmund, 292
Eliphalet, 292
Elizabeth (Frost), 292
Elizabeth (Phinney), 292
Greenleaf Clark, 279, 293
John, 279, 292
Lydia Sands (Thompson) 279, 293
Martha, 292
Mercy, 292
Miriam, 9, 293
Molly, 293

Paulina (Tuttle), 293
Sally, 293
Tabitha, 293
Tabitha (Whitney), 279 292

WAY
Fidelia, 221

WEARE
--, 294, 296, 298
-- (--), 296
Abigail (Littlefield), 298
Anna (Perkins), 294
Bathsheba, 297-298
Betsey, 295-296
Charles, 294
Daniel, 297-298
Edward, 294
Elias, 297
Elizabeth (Stone), 298
Hannah (Woodbridge), 294 296
James, 298
Jeremiah, 205, 294-297
Jeremiah Jr, 294-296, 298
Jeremian, 293
Jerusha (Parsons), 205, 294
John, 294, 297
Joseph, 293-294, 296-297
Joseph Jr, 298
Lucy, 295-296
Lucy (Webber), 294-295
Magdalene (Hilton) Adams 297
Mary, 294-295, 297-298
Mary (Goodwin), 297
Mary (Knight), 297
Mary (Webber), 293 297-298
Mercy, 297-298
Moses, 296
Narcissa, 294
Olive, 297
Phebe, 297-298
Rufus, 295-296
Ruth, 81, 297
Ruth (Banks), 297
Sally, 294
Sally (--), 296
Sally (Weare), 294
Samuel, 205, 294-296
Sarah, 295-298
Sarah (Preble), 205, 293 295, 297
Sarah (Weare), 296
Theodore, 294, 296
Theodosia, 296
Timothy, 294, 296
William, 296

WEATHERN
Arnold, 302
Sarah (Whittier), 302

WEAVER
Lois, 34

WEBB
Amy, 263
Ann (Riggs), 267
Bathsheba, 96, 319
David, 63
David Jr, 63
Deborah, 62
Deliverance (Crowell) 62-63
Elizabeth (Larrabee), 263
Henry, 267
John, 263
Lucy, 266-267
Mary (Carter), 63
Mary (Thomes) Peaks, 267
Samuel, 96, 319
Sarah (Lincoln), 96
Seth, 300

WEBBER
Betsey (Martin), 175
David, 270
Dorothy, 82-83
Elizabeth (Martin), 175
Elizabeth (Young), 297
Jenny (Grant), 270
John, 265
Joshua, 174-175
Lucy, 294-295
Lucy (Bradbury), 295
Lydia, 247
Mary, 293, 297-298
Miriam, 224
Molly, 199
Nathaniel, 295
Olive, 259
Phoebe, 299
Rosewell, 270
Samuel, 297
Sarah, 162-163
Sarah A (Stone), 270
Thankful, 82

WEBSTER
Joanna, 250-251
Lucy, 155

WEEKS
Elizabeth (Tilton), 283
Freelove, 191
James, 283
Jethro, 191
Penelope (Gorham), 191
Rebecca, 92
Sarah, 93

EVERY NAME INDEX

WELCH
Abigail (--), 226
Benjamin, 226
Climena Augusta, 144-145
WELLMAN
John, 192
Lydia (Brayley), 192
Sarah T, 192
WELLS
Susan Melissa, 179
WENTWORTH
--, 36
Abigail (Fall), 82
Abra, 1
Amy (Hodgdon), 311
Andrew Pepperrell, 78
Benning, 78
Betsy, 116
Catherine, 84
Damaris, 37, 39-40
Eleanor (James), 84
Esther (Dennison), 78
Hannah, 144
John, 144
Kate, 84
Lydia, 236
Mark, 82-83
Martha (Bragdon), 36
Mary (Bickford), 125
Moses, 171
Nancy, 125
Nathaniel, 171
Patience (Abbot), 171
Phebe, 311
Phebe (Sawyer), 78
Rebecca, 136
Reuben, 84
Sally, 106
Samuel, 311
Sarah, 31
Sarah (Bartlett), 144
Sarah (Yeaton), 311
Silas, 125
Susanna (Maddocks), 171
Timothy, 311
WESCOTT/ WESTCOTT
[SEE ALSO WASGATT]
Elizabeth, 260
Hannah, 288-289
Hannah (Wardwell), 290
Howard E Jr, 260
Mercy (Perkins), 259
Olive (Perkins), 289
Pelatiah, 259
Samuel, 289
Sarah (Snowman), 259
William Jr, 290

WESCOTT/ WESTCOTT
[SEE ALSO WASGOTT]
Andrew, 259
WESSON
Col --, 135
WEST
Ann (Cannell), 48
Cynthia, 210-211, 213
Desper, 48
James, 210
Joseph, 48
Mary (Green), 48
Nancy (Cannell), 48
Zerviah (--), 210
WESTBROOK
Thomas, 48
WESTON
Arunah, 64, 174
Eliphas, 174
Hannah (Curtis), 215
Priscilla (--), 174
Rachel (Martin), 174
Sarah (Martin), 64, 174
Sarah (Peterson), 214
Silvia Church, 64
Sylvanus, 214
Timothy, 174
Zabdiel, 214
WETMORE [SEE WHITMORE],
WHALING
Mary, 96
WHALL
Lucy (Fernald) Fernald, 93
Robert, 93
WHARFF/ WHORFE
Abigail, 300
Arthur Jr, 299
Betsey, 300
Dorcas, 265, 299-299 300(2)
Isaac B, 300
Joseph, 265, 299
Lydia, 299
Lydia (Cunningham), 299
Phoebe (Webber), 299
Rachel (Penney), 299
Sally, 265, 299
Sally (Penney), 300
Sarah (Penney), 300
Susanna, 265, 299
Susanna (Bennett), 265 299
Thomas Penny, 299
William, 299
WHEATON
Col --, 278

WHEELER
Abigail (--), 253
Azubah (Skinner), 253
Hannah (Reed), 219
Jacob, 253
Mary, 219
Polly, 219
Simon, 219
WHEELWRIGHT
Daniel, 274
Mary (Talpey), 274
Polly (Talpey), 274
WHITCHER
Susanna, 139
WHITE
Amelia (Comings), 149
Elizabeth (Thorn), 281
George, 67, 176
Hannah, 279
Jesse Jr, 307
Joel, 149
Joel Jr, 149-150
John, 279, 281
Lavinia (--), 219
Lucinda, 53
Lucy (Keen), 149
Malinda (Keen), 150
Marinda (Keen), 149-150
Martha (--), 219
Mary (Malcom), 281
Olive (Williams), 307
Sally (Keen), 149
Samuel, 219, 252
Sarah, 281
Sarah (--), 279
Sarah (Keen), 149-150
WHITEHER [SEE WHITTIER],
WHITING
Prudence, 123
WHITMARSH
Rebecca, 150
WHITMORE/ WHITTEMORE, ETC
Abigail, 301
Abigail (Babbidge), 8, 300
Abigail M (Joyce), 301
Ammi-Ruhamah (Knight) 113
Daniel, 301
Deborah (Trundy), 301
Elizabeth (Cutter), 315
Francis, 315
Hannah, 113
James, 301
John, 300-301
Joseph, 8, 300-301
Lemuel, 301

EVERY NAME INDEX

**WHITMORE/
WHITTEMORE, ETC**
(continued)
Lucy, 300
Lucy (Stinson), 301
Lydia, 315
Mary, 225, 301, 315
Mary (Burnell), 300
Mary (Potter), 225
Mary (Whittemore), 225
Polly (Abbott), 301
Rebecca, 301
Sally (Waldo), 7
Samuel, 225, 301, 315
Sarah, 301
Seth Webb, 301
Stephen, 225, 315
Susan, 301
Susanna (--), 301
William, 7-8, 113, 301
WHITNEY
Abel, 263
Abigail, 111
Betty (Phinney), 263
Daniel, 324
Hannah (Day), 292
Hezekiah (Adams), 276
John, 276
Joseph, 263
Louise (Stubbs), 324
Marindy, 317
Mary (Cane), 263
Mehitable (Stevens), 263
Miriam Adams, 276
Nathaniel, 292
Tabitha, 279, 292
**WHITTEN/ WHIDDEN/
WITTEN**
Eben, 323
Eunice (Turner), 323
John, 50
Mary, 125
Ruth, 50
Ruth (Merrill), 50
WHITTIER/ WHITEHER
Abigail B, 229
Alice (Sears), 303
Anna, 302
Benjamin, 228-229
301-302
Betsey, 228, 302
Betsey (Flint), 302
Clymena (Blake), 27
Eliza P, 242
Elizabeth (--), 27
Elizabeth (Prescott), 26
227, 302
Hannah, 302

Hannah (Clough), 227, 301
Jedediah, 302
John, 27
Levi, 26
Lydia (Taylor), 149
Marcy (Joy), 301
Mary, 228-229, 302
Mary (Joy), 228-229, 301
Miriam, 302(2)
Moses, 149, 302
Nancy (Blake), 26
Nancy (Butterfield), 302
Nathaniel, 26, 227-228
301-303
Polly, 228-229
Polly (Gordon), 26
Ruth, 302
Ruth (Whittier), 302
Sally, 149
Sarah, 302
William, 27, 302
WICK
James H, 215
WIER/ WYER
Robert, 132
Sarah, 132, 168
WIER/WYER
Sarah, 133
WIESER
Robert Dean, 54
WIGGLESWORTH
Edward, 284
WIGHT
Abigail, 290
Edward, 290
Hannah (Perkins), 290
Sarah, 260
WILEY
Mary, 128
Susan (Russ), 68
WILKINS
John Hubbard, 30
Thomazine Elizabeth
Fielder, 30
Thomazine Elizabeth
Fielder (Bond) Minot, 324
WILKINSON
Anna, 123-125
Dorcas (Nason), 119
Hannah (Varney), 119
James, 123
John, 119
Joseph, 119
Mary (--), 123
WILLEY
Susannah, 12
WILLIAMS
--, 306

Abgail (Higgins), 128
Abigail, 307-308
Abigail (Blackman), 307
Abigail (Freman), 199
Abigail (Spooner), 306
Abraham, 199
Amy (Gray), 305
Anna, 304-307
Anna (Hilton), 304
Asa, 303, 308
Avice, 303
Betsey (Savage), 305
Betty, 307
Charles, 308
Daniel, 308
Dolly (Dinsmore), 305
Edward, 308-309
Elemuel, 304
Eliza, 309
Eliza Jane (Perkins), 309
Elizabeth, 96, 303, 308
323
Elizabeth (Brittun), 304
306
Elizabeth B, 305
Eunice, 303
Eunice (Fisher), 303
Fatima (Albee), 306
Hannah (Bridge), 308
Hannah (Waters), 308
Hartwell, 308
Helen Marcia, 309
John, 128, 305
Joseph, 304-306
Lemuel, 304-305
Louisa (Lithgow), 309
Lucinda, 306
Lusannah, 303
Martha, 199
Martha (Butler), 305
Martha (Hilton) Collins
307
Mary, 18
Mary (Sawtelle), 308
Mary A, 122
Mehitable (Preble), 307
Melinda, 304-306
Morrell, 304
Morrill, 305-306
Moses, 304-305, 308
Nathaniel, 306
Odile, 145, 306-307
Olive, 307
Patty, 199
Phyllis S, 33, 37, 158, 204
Rachel, 305(2), 306(2)
Reuel, 308
Ruth, 303

WILLIAMS (continued)
　Ruth (Hovey), 303
　Sally, 303, 308
　Sally (Williams), 308
　Samuel, 304
　Sarah, 303, 308
　Sarah (Bridge), 308
　Sarah (Lothrop), 308
　Sarah (Williams), 308
　Sarah Lowell (Cony), 308
　Seth, 303, 307-308
　Simeon, 305
　Susan, 304
　Susanna, 307
　Susannah (Fobes), 303, 307
　Susannah (Walker) Gray 307
　Timothy, 304, 306-307
　Vesta Gould, 304
　William, 304-305
　Zeruiah, 305
　Zerviah, 305
　Zilpha (Ingraham), 308
WILSON
　Alexander, 219
　Benjamin, 57, 219
　Catherine (Swanzey), 219
　Elizabeth, 34
　Jane, 33
　Jane (Somes), 261
　Jenney (Somes), 261
　Joanna, 47
　Joanna (Phinney), 219
　Jonathan, 296
　Lettice, 172
　Lydia, 276
　Mary, 168-169
　Moses, 261
　Olive, 57-58
　Priscilla (--), 47
　Samuel, 47
　Seth, 219
　Susanna (Staples), 57
　Theodore, 296
　Theodosia (Weare), 296
WING
　Alpheus, 145
　Benjamin Franklin, 200
　Clarrissa (Judkins), 145
　Julia, 200
　Lydia (Tobey) Hobbs, 200
　Sally (Nye), 200
　Sarah (Nye), 200
WINGATE
　Anna, 83-84
　Samuel, 83
WINN
　Daniel, 175

　Huldah, 37(2)
　James, 175
　Olive (Berry), 175
　Philadelphia (Maxwell) 175
WINSLOW
　Job, 139, 321
　Lorana, 321
　Lydia, 139, 155
　Margaret (Barber), 321
　Mary, 137
　Mary (Robinson), 139
WISE
　Mary, 71
WISWALL
　Abigail (Clements), 53
　Jeremiah Jr, 53
　Mary, 172
　Sarah (Craft), 53
　William, 53
WITHAM
　John, 265
　Lois (Bray), 265
　Sally, 265
　Sarah, 265
WITHERELL
　Elizabeth, 85
WITHEY/ WITHY
　--, 306
　Rachel (Williams) 305-306
WOLFE
　--, 250
WOOD
　Abiel, 159
　Dorothy (Hurd), 91
　Eliphalet, 229
　Emily H, 230
　Enoch, 91
　Fanny, 91
　Fanny (Colburn), 54
　Judith, 222
　Mary, 6, 221
　Mary (--), 222
　Mary Jane, 54
　Olive (Prescott), 229
　Patience, 223
　Samuel, 54
　Stephen, 222
　Susan, 221
WOODBRIDGE
　Dorcas, 34
　Hannah, 294, 296
　Lydia, 195
WOODBURY
　Joanna, 242
WOODCOCK
　Abigail (Holmes), 209

　Apphia (Peabody), 209
　David, 209
　Lucy (Buzzell), 244
　Lynday, 209
　Melinda, 209, 243
　William, 244
WOODMAN
　Elsie, 182
　Hannah (--), 265
　Hannah (Bates), 317
　John, 317
　Joshua, 125
　Martha, 197
　Mary, 24, 203
　Molly, 203
　Rebecca, 157, 203
　Sarah, 157
　Susan, 204
WOODSUM
　Abigail (Hamilton), 115
　Betsey, 157
　David, 115
　Elizabeth, 157
　Elizabeth (Dyer), 157
　John, 115
　Mary (Brackett), 115
　Michael, 157
WOODWARD
　Joanna (Godfrey) Stevens 324
　Mary, 324
　Michael, 324
　Samuel, 324
WOOSTER
　Abigail (Clark), 34
　Elizabeth, 34
　Joanna, 34-35
　Oliver, 34
WORCESTER/ WORSTER
　Catherine (Roberts), 108
　Elizabeth (Marr), 107-108
　Jane, 108
　Jonathan, 108
　Simeon, 107-108
　William, 108
WORMELL
　Nancy, 153
WORSTER
　Sally, 84
WRIGHT
　Abigail (Farnham), 85
　Margaret, 198
　Nabby (Farnham), 84-85
　Thomas, 85
WYMAN
　Abiel (--), 242
　Bethia, 256
　bethia, 257

WYMAN (continued)
Bethiah (Millett), 321
Betsey (Russell), 242
Bier (--), 242
Charlotte, 243
Eunice, 211
James, 321
John, 242
John Jr, 242
Josiah, 256
Lemuel, 256
Lovina, 242-243
Nancy (Bradford), 256
Olive, 321
Prudence (Small), 256
YEATES
Margaret, 47
YEATON
-- (--), 309
Abigail, 262
Abigail (Dunbar), 262
Alice, 310
Amey (Brackett), 310
Dorcas, 311
Dorcas (Smith), 309
Elizabeth, 310
Experience, 310
Jacob, 311
Joanna, 246, 310
Joanna (Pray) Roberts, 309
John, 309
Lemuel, 262
Mary, 310

Molly (Jones), 309
Phebe (Wentworth), 311
Philip, 309-310
Philip Jr, 310
Phillip, 309
Phineas, 311
Richard, 310
Sarah, 311
YORK
Abigail (Bean), 150
Abigail (Whitmore), 301
Anna, 150-151
Elizabeth (Thompson), 151
George, 301
Isaac I, 151
Job, 151
John, 21, 150-151
Naoma, 19
Polly (Bartlett) Russell, 21
Sally, 151
Sally (Jones), 151
Sally (Kilgore), 21, 151
Urban, 21
YOUNG
Aaron, 57
Abigail, 193, 215
Anna (Mayo), 42
Anne (Johnston), 319
Barnabas, 42
Charity, 262
Constant (Mayo), 311
David, 57
David C, 15

David Jr, 311
Eliza, 319
Elizabeth, 297
Elizabeth (--), 57
Elizabeth Bracket, 143
Ezra, 311-312
Ezra Jr, 311
George, 319
Hannah (--), 319
Hannah (Twining), 311
Jane, 319
Jonathan, 312
Joseph 3rd, 258
Lydia (Snow), 258
Margaret, 319
Martha (Brooks)
    Dillingham, 43
Mary, 68
Mary (Colburn), 57
Mary (Thompson), 42
Mary B, 32, 103-104
Molly (Thompson), 42
Nancy, 202
Noah, 215
Olive, 275
Patience, 126
Rebecca, 126
Rosanna, 312
Sarah (Hoges), 312
William James, 319
Zebulon, 43
ZIEGLER
Barbara, iii

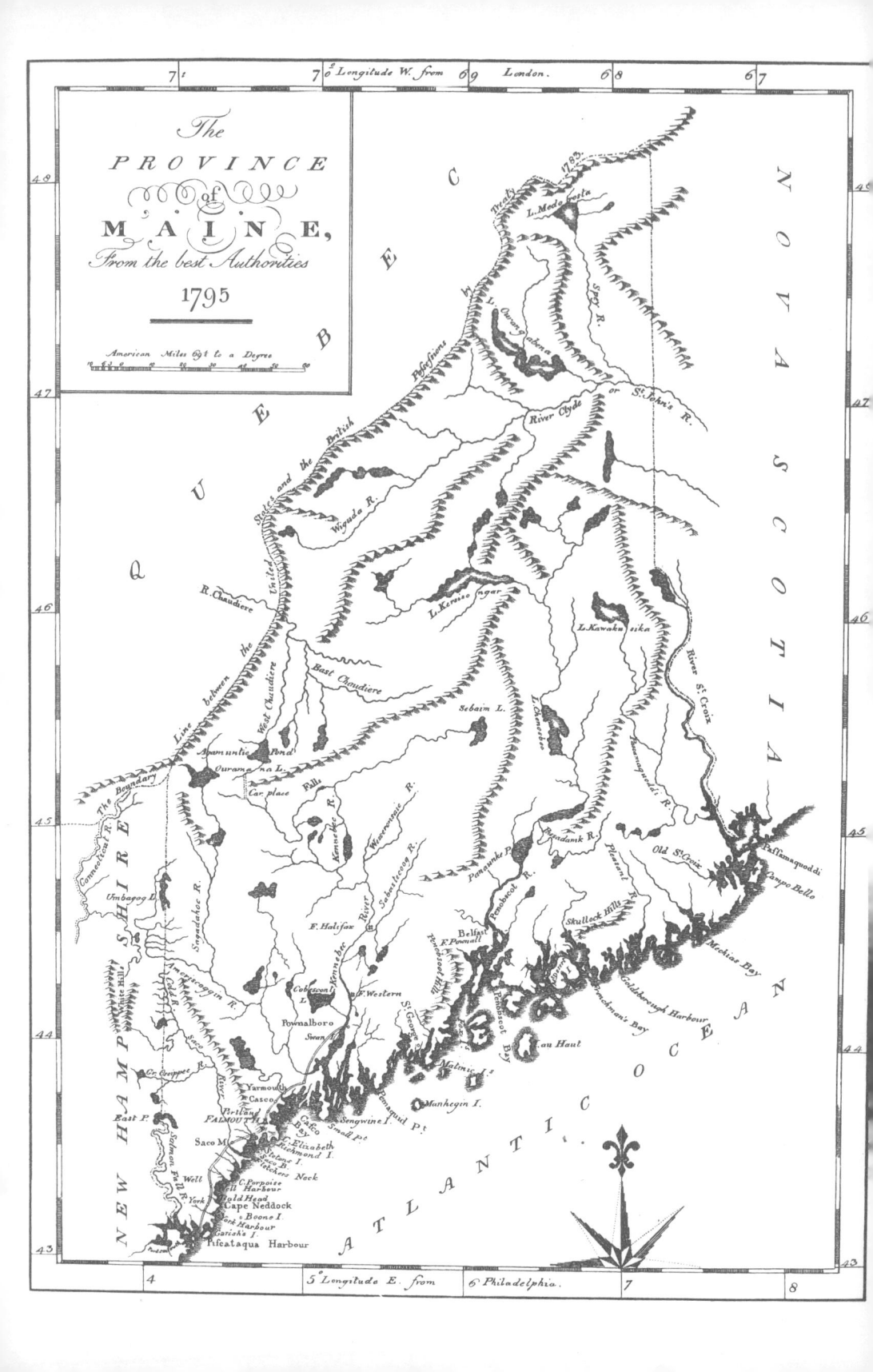

The
PROVINCE
of
MAINE,
From the best Authorities
1795